MW00679391

Corporate Social Responsibility and Corporate Governance

This is IEA conference volume no. 149

Corporate Social Responsibility and Corporate Governance

The Contribution of Economic Theory and Related Disciplines

Edited by

Lorenzo Sacconi
Margaret Blair
R. Edward Freeman

and

Alessandro Vercelli

First published 2011 by
PALGRAVE MACMILLAN

Palgrave Macmillan in the UK is an imprint of Macmillan Publishers Limited,
registered in England, company number 785998, of Houndmills, Basingstoke,
Hampshire RG21 6XS.

Palgrave Macmillan in the US is a division of St Martin's Press LLC,
175 Fifth Avenue, New York, NY 10010.

Palgrave Macmillan is the global academic imprint of the above companies and has
companies and representatives throughout the world.

Palgrave® and Macmillan® are registered trademarks in the United States, the United
Kingdom, Europe and other countries

ISBN 978–0–230–23654–7   hardback

This book is printed on paper suitable for recycling and made from fully managed and
sustained forest sources. Logging, pulping and manufacturing processes are expected
to conform to the environmental regulations of the country of origin.

A catalogue record for this book is available from the British Library.

A catalog record for this book is available from the Library of Congress.

10   9   8   7   6   5   4   3   2   1
20   19   18   17   16   15   14   13   12   11

Printed and bound in Great Britain by
CPI Antony Rowe, Chippenham and Eastbourne

Contents

Part III CSR, Social Standards and Multi-Stakeholder Organisations According to the Behavioral Economics Perspective

Acknowledgements

The contributions to this edited collection – even though in some case thoroughly re-elaborated – are the proceedings of the International Economics Association (IEA) international research workshop held in Trento (Italy) on 11–13 July 2006, under the title 'Corporate Social Responsibility and Corporate Governance: the Contribution of Economic Theory and Related Disciplines'.

The editors thank the IEA for its decision to promote the workshop and for helping to secure its success, reflected not only in the presentation of original papers that are published here, but also by the highly stimulating and enriching discussion that took place in those two days. Hence we thank all the papers' presenters, discussants and participants in IEA workshop that contributed substantially to the quality of the this book. In particular, in addition to the authors of papers that appear here as book chapters, the following: Kaushik Basu, Giuseppe Bellantuono, Carlo Borzaga, Francesco Denozza, Thomas Donaldson, Giulio Ecchia, Herbert Gintis, Michele Grillo, Benedetto Gui, Annalisa Luporini, Ignazio Musu, Ugo Pagano, Vittorio Pelligra, Edward Rock, Francesco Silva, Roberto Tamborni, Alessandro Vercelli, Josef Wieland, Stefano Zamagni, Enrico Zaninotto.

Organizational and financial support given to the IEA workshop and the subsequent work by the inter-university center of research EconomEtica (Milan) and the LaSER (Laboratory for Social Responsibility Ethics and Rationality) of the Trento University Department of Economics, is gratefully acknowledged. Moreover financial aid received after the workshop by the Italian Ministry for University and Research under the national research project PRIN n.2007B8SC7A, helped the re-elaboration of texts and preparation of this edited collection, and is also gratefully acknowledged.

Last but not least we thank Manuela Seppi for her invaluable help in the editing of the book.

List of Tables

List of Figures

Notes on the Contributors

Luciano Andreozzi is Assistant Professor, Department of Economics, University of Trento, Italy.

Masahiko Aoki is Henri and Tomoye Takahashi Professor Emeritus of Japanese Studies in the Economics Department, and a Senior Fellow of Stanford Institute of Economic Policy Research (SIEPR) and Freeman Spogli Institute for International Studies (FSI) at Stanford University, USA.

Leonardo Becchetti is Professor of Economics, University of Rome, 'Tor Vergata', Rome.

Avner Ben-Ner is Professor, Center for Human Resources and Labor Studies Carlson School of Management, University of Minnesota.

Margaret Blair is Milton R. Underwood Chair in Free Enterprise, Vanderbilt University Law School, USA.

Bruce Chapman is Professor of Law, Associate Dean of the Faculty of Law, University of Toronto, Canada.

Ernie Englander is Associate Professor of Strategic Management and Public Policy, George Washington University, School of Business, USA.

R. Edward Freeman is University Professor and Elis and Signe Olsson Professor of Business Administration, Academic director of Business Roundtable Institute for Corporate Ethics, and a senior fellow of Olsson Center for Applied Ethics, at Darden School of Business, University of Virginia, USA.

Bruno S. Frey is Distinguished Professor of Behavioural Science at Warwick Business School, University of Warwick, Professor of Economics at the University of Zurich, and Research Director at CREMA (Center for Research in Economics, Management and the Arts).

Allen Kaufman was Professor of Management, Whittemore School of Business, University of New Hampshire, USA.*

Li-Wen Lin is University of Illinois and Department of Sociology, Columbia University, USA.

* Allen Kaufman died in 2007, shortly after the submission of the chapter he co-authored with Ernie Englander.

Margit Osterloh is Professor of Management Science at Warwick Business School, University of Warwick, Professor of Management (em.) at the University of Zurich, and Research Director at CREMA (Center for Research in Economics, Management and the Arts).

Noemi Pace is Assistant Professor Department of Economics Cà Foscari University of Venice.

Bidhan Parmar is Assistant Professor, Darden School of Business, University of Virginia, USA.

Louis Putterman is Professor of Economics, Department of Economics, Brown University, Providence, USA.

Ting Ren is Assistant Professor, HSBC School of Business, Peking University, China.

Lorenzo Sacconi is Professor of Economics and Unicredit Chair in Economic Ethics and Corporate Social Responsibility at the University of Trento, and director of EconomEtica, Inter-university Research Center, University of Milan-Bicocca, Italy.

Lynn A. Stout is Paul Hastings Professor of Corporate and Securities Law at the University of California, Los Angeles School of Law, USA.

Viktor J. Vanberg is Professor of Economics, University of Freiburg, Germany.

Alessandro Vercelli is Professor of Economics, Department of Economic Policy, Finance and Development, University of Siena, Italy.

Andrew Wicks is Ruffin Professor of Business Administration, Director of the Olsson Center for Applied Ethics, Darden School of Business, University of Virginia, USA.

Cynthia A. Williams is Professor of Law, University of Illinois College of Law, USA.

Oliver E. Williamson is Edgar F. Kaiser Professor Emeritus of Business, Haas School of Business. Professor Emeritus of Economics and Law, University of California Berkeley. Nobel Laureate.

Hossam Zeitoun is a doctoral candidate at the University of Zurich.

Introduction
Lorenzo Sacconi

1 About the general subject of this book

As early as 2005, well before the eruption of the global financial crisis, the atten-tion of the international economic press was attracted by the corporate social responsibility (CSR) phenomenon. *The Economist,* in particular, acknowledged the spectacular growth of company CSR initiatives throughout the world, and through the relations between companies, business associations, stakeholders' representative groups, NGOs, universities, international organizations, and yet others. What struck *The Economist* as especially disturbing was that:

> Today all companies, but especially the big ones, are enjoined from every side to worry less about profits and to be socially responsible instead. Surprisingly, perhaps, these demands have elicited a willing, not to say avid, response in enlightened boardrooms everywhere: companies at every oppor-tunity now pay elaborate obeisance to the principle of CSR. They have CSR officers, CSR consultants, CSR Departments, and CSR initiatives coming out of their ears. (*The Economist,* 22 January 2005, p. 11)

The idea – along with a famous dictum by Milton Friedman of the 1970s – was that boards of directors, insufficiently committed to making profits for their shareholders, were instead engaging in 'pernicious benevolence' by being philanthropic with money taken not from their own pockets but from those of the corporate shareholders. What in fact this view entailed was that CSR (i) is not a business-related but a philanthropic activity that 'altruistic' manag-ers undertake by misusing corporate money, (ii) as such, it is in contrast with profit maximization and, lastly, (iii) it is a manifestation of managerial slack and (moral) self-dealing.

Barely three years later, however, *The Economist* viewed CSR very differently. It now stated that 'done badly, [it] is just a fig leaf and can be positive harm-ful. Done well, though, it is not some separate activity that companies do on the side, a corner of corporate life reserved for virtue. It is just good business' (*The Economist,* 19 January 2008, p. 3, *Special report*). And a little further on: 'The more this happens, ironically, the more the days of CSR may start to seem numbered. In time it will simply be the way business is done in the 21st century' (p. 22). To explore further what was understood by the term 'good business', we quote again from the same issue of *The Economist:* 'Some people complain that this sort of "good corporate citizenship" is merely another form of self-interest. Correct and good. They should be happy that this category has grown. The difficulty with CSR comes when companies get it out of proportion. For instance, there is a lot of guff about responsibility being at the core of a firm's strategy...' (leader, p. 13).

Thus, CSR was deemed no longer to be merely philanthropic, but rather an appendix of the core business strategy of any large company operating in the turmoil of the global economy. In fact, companies are involved in a series of challenges with their stakeholders that might essentially affect their business and economic functioning itself. Hence CSR may be understood as the appropriate method for addressing those challenges. Once it was recognized as no longer alien to the proper business and economic functioning of the corporation, however, the second tenet also had to be changed. Henceforth CSR could be reduced to a mere tool (according to an *instrumental* view) for the achievement of the traditional shareholder value maximization objective – the function of the corporation – namely as no more than a detail of the overall strategy of making as much profit as possible. It was something that no longer needed to be denoted by a distinct word or understood as a motivation distinct from the 'selfish' shareholder-value strategy. Of course, managerial slack was no longer involved, as long as this reduction of CSR to a tool for shareholder value maximization was granted.

This changed appraisal, which does not involve any real change of mind, quite clearly illustrates the typical dogmatic attitude of libertarian supporters of the 'free market economy' towards how capitalism 'should' work when they are faced by recalcitrant facts – such as the evidence that sometimes, albeit not systematically, corporations are not exclusively focused on shareholder value maximization, but pursue other objectives and take account of different and also, to some extent, conflicting interests. This evidence was initially dismissed as resulting from misguided decisions by self-serving ideologues entrenched within corporate boards or pressure groups and lobbies. Thereafter, once the anomaly had proved to be widespread in the real world of companies and business organisations, an attempt is made to reconcile recalcitrant facts with the doctrine's core dogmas.

In fact, neither view was satisfactory. The international movement of CSR, including initiatives at company level, and multi-stakeholder initiatives at national and international levels such as the ONU global compact and many others, allows a more ambitious interpretation. If facetious use may be made of the terminology of the philosophy of history, these facts can be understood as the epiphenomena of a deeper confrontation between two partly conflicting tendencies on the battleground of corporate governance models. On the one hand the tendency predominant in the past thirty years and which has consisted in the devolution of the most important economic decisions to private market agents – that is, corporations such as privately owned firms or public companies. On the other hand, the tendency to require these same private agents to account for more than just the efficiency of their results seen in terms of narrow profit maximization: they should also accept social responsibility for their conduct, understood as producing fair and mutual advantages for all the involved stakeholders, and the internalization of social costs engendered by the pursuit of mere profit maximization.

An unconventional reading of the Coase Theorem gives economic substance to this interpretation of the CSR movement: since neither the real world government nor real markets and firms can be considered as governance mechanisms with zero transaction costs, it is possible to experiment with alternative private governance forms aimed at internalizing part of the social and transaction costs of the traditional private governance forms through the emergence of social norms for corporate responsibility. On this view, CSR is defined as an 'extended model of corporate governance' in which those who run the firm (entrepreneurs, directors, top managers) have fiduciary duties (namely obligations and responsibilities) that range from owners and shareholders (in the case of ownership and control separation) to all of the other corporate stakeholders (individuals and social groups with essential interests involved in the company's management). And since these duties act as an internal constraint on the sphere of managerial/entrepreneurial autonomy not concretely regulated by the law, they assume the form of responsibility principles expressed by shared social norms, self-regulatory codes and standards, soft laws and so on (Sacconi 2006b, 2006a).

Thus understood, CSR is not an entirely new notion in the domain of corporate governance. Back in the 1930s the idea that public companies were fiduciaries of constituencies much broader than shareholders was put forward and widely discussed as one of the possible interpretations of the very reason for the large corporations' existence.

In his earlier writing Berle maintained that corporate powers were held in trust not only of the corporation per se but also for individual members of it (Berle 1931). Dodd (1932) challenged this view by arguing that the directors of a corporation must (if they had not already) become trustees not merely for shareholders but also for other constituents of corporations, such as employees, customers, and particularly the entire community. Later Berle conceded to Dodd, and admitted that modern directors act *de facto* and *de jure* as administrators of a community system, although he remained rather cautious about admitting this as the 'right disposition' (Berle 1959). (Aoki 2010, p. 15, n. 1)

A very similar idea was advanced in the 1980s in the much more precise formulation allowed by new developments in stakeholder theory mainly as a theory of strategic management but also as a view of corporate governance (Freeman 1984; Freeman and Evan 1990; Evan and Freeman 1993; Donaldson and Preston 1995; Freeman et al. 2010). According to stakeholder theory, descriptively a corporation is a constellation of interacting stakeholders (positively acting together or in any case abstaining from interfering with and obstructing the other stakeholder cooperations) coordinated through the firm's managerial and entrepreneurial strategy and the governance structure, so that they are induced to cooperate in order to create as much value as possible to their mutual advantage:

> The basic idea of creating value for stakeholders is quite simple. Business can be understood as a set of relationships among groups that have a stake in the activities that make up the business. Business is about how customers, suppliers, employees, financiers (stockholders, bondholders, banks etc. ...) communities and managers interact and create value. To understand a business is to know how these relationships work. And the executives' or entrepreneur's job is to manage and shape these relationships. (Freeman et al. 2010, p. 24)

The normative reading of stakeholder theory (see Donaldson and Preston 1995), however, adds an important element to that description: the recognition that all stakeholders are sources of ends for the corporation. That is to say, they all have legitimate interests that *must* be reflected in the corporate objective function. In other words – to rephrase Kant's second formulation of the categorical imperative – all of the stakeholders are not just *means* for the pursuit of the interests of one single patron of the firm (the owners of corporate physical assets), they also give rise to *purposes* to be pursued by the proper management of the company (which also entails that they are, to a certain extent, complementary). CSR can thus be straightforwardly understood as the formal recognition at corporate governance level of the obligations owed to all the stakeholders because they are legitimate *sources of ends* for corporations.

Nevertheless, most mainstream economists have ignored this perspective and continue to maintain that the multi-stakeholder corporation, even if imagined for a desirable purpose, does not have a uniquely defined objective function, so that a multi-stakeholder objective function would open the way to managerial slack and self-dealing. By contrast, shareholder maximization, albeit in the long run, would allow the internalization of those stakeholders' interests that are instrumental to shareholder value maximization (cf. Jensen 2001), leaving the remaining unaccounted interests to the protection provided by the law of contracts (see Tirole 2001): a rather paradoxical conclusion, considering that the theory of the firm sees contracts as typically incomplete and thus as not protective at all.

But, since the relevance of CSR as a global phenomenon cannot be ignored, economists to date have tended to deal with it by reducing CSR to 'corporate philanthropy' more or less in line with, and instrumental to, profitability. Drawing on recent developments in economic psychology, Benabou and Tirole (2010) observe that pro-social behaviors enable understanding of the increasing interest shown towards CSR in relation to: (1) firms' adoption of a more long-term perspective; (2) the delegated exercise of pro-social behavior on behalf of stakeholders; and (3) insider-initiated corporate philanthropy, even if their conclusions are skeptical about the efficiency of these corporate policies with respect to the economic function of the firm. By contrast, Heal (2008) considers a number of corporate cases that apparently show that pro-social and pro-environment corporate policies pay in terms of profitability.

There is no intrinsic need, however, to understand the economic theory of the modern corporation as entailing this reduction of corporate social responsibility to 'instrumental philanthropy'. Consider the following standard components of the contemporary new-institutional theory of the firm: (i) the idea that corporate authority is necessary for the coordinated use of information in joint production under incomplete knowledge and asymmetric information requiring flexibility of the collective decision process (Simon 1951; Arrow 1974); (ii) the 'efficient monitor' view of the entrepreneur as discouraging moral hazard in team production (Alchian and Demsetz 1972 – even if these authors dissimulate the existence of authority in the firm); (iii) the idea of hierarchy as a way to protect specific investments in incomplete contract contexts where the agents' motivations are opportunistic (Williamson 1975, see also Williamson *infra*). Consider, moreover, the view of the firm's governance as the result of a multi-party contract, as in GHM theory, where (iv) the optimal firm control structure results from an intertemporal bargaining decision model involving at least two parties, such that *ex ante* they choose an allocation of residual rights of control (authority) in order to prevent the inefficient *ex post* renegotiation of each party's essential decision that otherwise would affect the incentive to undertake specific investments at a *mid-way* decision step in the parties' diachronic strategic interaction (Grossman and Hart 1986; Hart and Moore 1990; Hart 1995). Or (v) the theory of enterprise ownership which predicts that alternative ownership forms will emerge as different cases from the very same basic decision exercise of transaction costs minimization, and ranging over different, case by case, configurations of all the stakeholders' contract costs and authority costs (Hansamann 1986, 1996).

All of these theories implicitly conceive the choice of a proper corporate governance form as the solution of a mixed-motives game among different players (Harsanyi 1977) – namely corporate stakeholders – with partially conflicting interests and incentives, who nevertheless also gain a mutual advantage from coordination and mutual cooperation. Put otherwise, a proper solution for the corporate governance problem is the solution of an (albeit implicit) bargaining problem; a situation whereby all the stakeholders can substantially and mutually profit if they are able to cooperate and carry out the joint plan of team production. But it is nevertheless also a situation such that their interests clash over the distribution of the surplus generated by their mutual cooperation. Choosing a governance structure and strategy means selecting a bundle of decision rights and obligations allowing for the selection of a joint plan of action (or abstention from acting) with an expected outcome which is efficient, in the sense that the value created (or surplus) is as large as possible, but also reasonably fair because it represents a distribution mutually acceptable to all the stakeholders involved, even though they all claim as much as possible of the surplus. In this situation – typical of any company – value creation and efficiency cannot be separated from fairness and distributive justice. Separation would entail the failure of the enterprise as a value creation endeavor (this is also a version of the 'separation thesis' rejected by stakeholder theorists; see Freeman et al. 2010). Moreover, because any governance structure allocates authority as long as it assigns decision rights and discretionary powers, under any second-best governance solution (among those conceivable in the real world economy) a risk of abuse of authority against the non-controlling parties is always lying in wait. Hence this problem must be faced by an appropriate balance not just in the *ex post* distribution of payoffs but also in the *ex ante* allocation of rights, powers and responsibilities that allow effective achievement of the proper distributive balance. Hence the choice of the best feasible corporate governance form appears to be a natural candidate as a solution in terms of the 'social contract' among all of the corporate stakeholders. It is an agreement reached in a pre-firm Hobbesian 'state of nature' in order to attain an acceptable consensus on the authority structure, the allocation of ownership and control, and the infrastructure of rights and obligations that allows all stakeholders to access fair shares of the surplus produced through their cooperation – what typically makes sense for the 'constitutional contract of the firm' (Sacconi 2000, see also for a previous view Vanberg 1993). According to this perspective, granted that ownership and control are allocated to a specific class of stakeholders – for example stockholders in the typical capitalist firm – CSR can be understood as the set of obligations owed to the non-controlling stakeholders that any complex structure of corporate governance would entail in order to satisfy the model of a fair 'social contract'.

To date, this has been obscured to a large part of the economic profession by the belief that efficient financial markets would be enabled to circumvent this collective choice problem by their impersonal ability to optimally select those parties that will undertake corporate control, while simultaneously setting the price at which they can buy this right and settling up with all the interests involved. In other words, the efficient financial market of ownership and control thus evades the imperfections of the real world markets and the concrete incompleteness and inefficiencies of contracts. This explains, for example, why the GHM model in fact comprises descriptions of alternative corporate governance and control structures, with associated different ways in which costly multi-party bargaining may occur *ex post*. But *ex ante*, the choice among these different alternatives is not explicitly modeled as a 'constitutive' collective decision concerning the best control structure of a voluntary association among the interested parties. This decision is left implicitly to the financial market of ownership and control. This is assumed firstly to be able to price all of the control structures by computing all the renegotiation effects due to contract incompleteness under each of them, and, secondly, to sell them to the potentially most efficient owners able to average all these costs out through proper pre-payments to the parties, who relinquish their control claims and are thus at risk of suffering authority abuse. A similar motivation seems to lie behind the statement that the 'shareholder-value' model would have said the last and final word about the evolution of corporate governance and control forms (Hansamann and Kraakman 2001).

Unexpectedly – save for those giving an unconventional interpretation to the CSR movement – the global financial crisis that began in the summer of 2007 gainsaid much of the confidence in the key assumptions of the prevailing model of corporate governance – the shareholder value doctrine: *first*, the belief that the real world financial markets are able to collect all the relevant knowledge required to fix the 'true' monetary value of any economic enterprise and firm; and *second*, the belief that in order to successfully align the principal's and the agent's interests, managerial incentives must be linked to stock prices, thereby turning the corporate manager from the old-fashioned figure of somebody else's 'fiduciary' – legally and morally required to be 'other regarding' – into that of a selfish share-value maximizer, whose interests are immediately identified with that of the company's owners. Thus, it can at least be hypothesized that a model of multi-stakeholder corporate governance, based on the idea of corporate social responsibility, could have performed better. That is it could have prevented hazardous behaviors that, claiming to maximize profits, have in effect damaged all of the firms' stakeholders, with catastrophic external effects on the world economy, without even benefitting shareholders in general.

Hence, the alternative view of corporate governance, which understands governance structures as institutions for achieving a fair balance among different stakeholders with different and complementary specific investments at stake and engaged with reciprocal cooperation and coordination problems, once again comes to the fore. Consider in this regard the cooperative bargaining game approach to the firm (Aoki 1984, see also Aoki 2010); the idea that governance structures are mediating hierarchies (Blair and Stout 1999, 2010 *infra*) in firms modeled as 'team production' (Rajan and Zingales, 2000); and the 'social contract theory of the firm' (Sacconi 1991, 2000). To be sure, these are not just rationalizations of the normative claims implicit in the CSR movement; they are also much wider and general ways to explain and interpret different forms of corporate governance empirically observed in the US – namely instances of the *business judgment* principle – and at the international level (Blair and Stout 1999; Elhauge 2005a,b; Aoki 2001). CSR can be comfortably accommodated within these perspectives.

From this point of view, different forms of corporate governance derive from various specifications of the agreement among the stakeholders – both those who own different but complementary investments and assets to be used in joint production (Aoki 2010) and those who are interested in minimizing bad external effects. Moreover, there is no reason to insist on the main objection against the multi-stakeholder corporation view traceable back to the tenet that multi-stakeholder corporate governance would leave the corporate objective function undetermined because of the multidimensionality of the objectives and, consequently, would increase the scope for managerial discretion and opportunism (Jensen, 2001). Actually, since its very beginnings (cf. Aoki, 1984), this view of the economics of the firm has shown that the objective function of a multi-stakeholder enterprise is not at all undetermined but, at least from the theoretical point of view, perfectly defined. It consists in maximizing the Nash product of the stakeholders' payoffs (net of the no-cooperation status quo) that they receive from the bargaining game played when making specific investments and participating in team production by employing interdependent assets (see also Sacconi 2006b, 2006a).

Once corporate governance is understood as an economic institution self-sustainable in a given interaction domain – i.e. once it is conceived as an equilibrium regularity of behaviors supported by mutually consistent expectations based on a mental model representation of the same ongoing equilibrium regularity (Aoki 2001) – the issues of the endogenous choice of the balancing criteria suitable for equilibrating different stakeholders' claims becomes obviously important. The question that then arises is how to identify the norm that will emerge from the process of collective choice among stakeholders as the bundle of rights and duties (or responsibilities) that they would accept. The social contract line of thought provides analytical answers to such a question. From the firm's constitutional contract perspective, stakeholders would agree on the Nash bargaining solution of the game wherein the allocation of rights over assets used to undertake joint production is at stake (which is the same as a distribution proportional to 'relative needs', see Brock 1979; Sacconi 1991, 2006a). Such solution reflects the relative urgency of the players' needs for these rights. Thereafter, in the distribution game played when productive efforts have already been carried out, they would agree to distribute the cooperative surplus according to the Shapley value for coalition games, and this distribution would reflect the relative importance of the stakeholders' contribution given to any possible formation of the productive team (Brock 1979; Sacconi 1991, 2000, 2006a). Finally, in analogy with Binmore's theory of the social contract (Binmore 2005), the constitutional choice on the governance structure of the firm (allocation of rights and of responsibilities which give access to the surplus) should satisfy the condition of an 'agreement under the veil of ignorance', as well as the condition of sustainability in a non-cooperative state of nature, namely the condition of being a Nash equilibrium. If these conditions hold, then the constitutional choice of the corporate governance structure must be compatible with the Rawlsian Maximin and the egalitarian Nash bargaining solution calculated within the symmetrical set of the equilibria that are equally possible under the symmetrical translation of the outcome space with respect to the players' (stakeholders) positions. In other words, in the presence of alternative possible allocations of ownership and control rights/responsibilities and compensation obligations, the Pareto-dominant egalitarian solution will be chosen instead of the allocation associated with the (utilitarian) maximum efficiency (see Sacconi Chapter 8, *infra*).

All of the foregoing models are convergent specifications of the multi-stakeholder objective function of the socially responsible corporation, and they are the basis for ascribing to it extended fiduciary duties owed to stakeholders. Thus, contemporary game theory helps us to specify both of these concepts in a way that should be quite natural to the modern economist.

Beyond the use of complex analytical models, however, the problem of how stakeholders' equilibration principles are agreed could (maybe should) be addressed by using experimental methodology. Such an analysis is particularly important because the convergence on principles of fair balancing – whose pursuit may be ascribed to the firm as a goal – would then be observed as emerging from (experimentally simulated) real life interactions amongst rationally bounded agents. In fact, the main objection against the multi-stakeholder governance model, whereby it would be impossible to maximize an objective function inclusive of many different objectives at the same time, owes its substance neither to a logical argument (which is obviously false), nor to an efficiency argument – for it is clear that protecting many specific investments in a balanced way rather than permitting just one of them at a time to overrule all the others, would work much better in terms of surplus creation. Its strength lies instead in the suggestion that a mono-stakeholder objective function would be a much simpler task requiring much less cognitive effort, being at the same time very simply accountable by boundedly rational managers unable to process a great deal of information and to control many different variables at the same time. Testing experimentally the convergence of many stakeholders and managers on fair balancing principles would signal that it is not beyond the cognitive capacity of managements to uncover the guiding principles for their own conduct also in the stakeholder corporation. The literature is sparse on the issue of experimental choice of equilibrating principles of fairness (see Yaari and Bar Hillel 1984). But recently some experimental studies have been conducted on agreement under the veil of ignorance over fair division principles involving strong and weak stakeholders of productive organizations (see Sacconi and Faillo 2010).

So far, we have introduced the idea of multi-stakeholder equilibration principles as the basis for endowing the company with social responsibilities – namely extended fiduciary duties owed to the non-controling stakeholders. But an additional problem is that of compliance with CSR norms or standards, and in particular the question of what exogenous or endogenous incentives may support the fulfillment of commitments and conformity with agreed CSR principles by those who control the company – owners or managers. Particularly relevant in this regard are the studies on the role and the explanation of social norms and soft law (Posner 2000; Sacconi 2000; Stout 2006; Blair et al. *infra*, 2006; Sacconi 2006). The theory of reputation has been seen traditionally as the natural candidate to answer this problem. But the limitations of reputation mechanisms (Kreps et al. 1983; Fudenberg and Levine, 1989) are also well known (Kreps, 1990) and have been considered in analyses devoted to determining the cognitive role played by explicit general ethical principles in circumventing the cognitive fragilities that characterize these mechanisms in the case of contractual incompleteness and unforeseen contingencies (Sacconi 2000, 2006, 2007; Sacconi and Moretti 2008). Moreover, there is the concrete risk that the long-run player (i.e. the firm) in a reputation game can adopt sophisticated strategies consisting in a mix of opportunistic and compliant behavior, and the adoption of these strategies will induce acquiescence by the short-run players (i.e. the stakeholders). In these cases, reputations would not only support compliance with CSR norms, but also a high level of deviation from them (see Andreozzi, Chapter 9 *infra*).

Nevertheless, the emergent model of corporate governance is supported not just by the new-institutional economics perspective and its game-theoretical formulations. It is also consistent with recent developments in behavioral economics which justify organizational forms based on motivational systems more complex than mere self-interest. To cite only a few of these results, in recent years, thanks to the use of experimental and behavioral economics methodologies, significant progress has been made in the analysis of the complexity of incentive mechanisms. Some authors have studied the relative effectiveness of explicit and implicit incentives in the presence of non-purely self-interested agents (Fehr, Gächter, Kirchsteiger, 1997; Fehr, Klein and Schmidt, 2007). Others have focused on analysis of the problems of the 'hidden cost of reward', 'motivational crowding out' and more in general on the perverse effects of monetary incentives, formal rules and exogenous sanctions when agents are intrinsically motivated (Frey, 1997; Gneezy and Rustichini, 2000; Fehr and Falk, 2002; Fehr and List, 2005). Despite the initial narrow focus of these studies on labor contracts, they can make a wider contribution to the economic analysis of organizations and their governance structures (by considering, for example, the managerial incentive problem within a new view of the principal–agent relationship) because they not only recognize the complexity of incentives, but also provide empirical proof of the relevance of reciprocity, social preferences and other complex motivations within organizations (see also Gintis and Kurama 2008).

According to the behavioral economics perspective, the self-sustainability of CSR norms can be explained by factors such as the existence of agents (stakeholders and firms) characterized by preferences that are much more complex than those traditionally assumed by game theorists, and the complexity of the networks of relations in which agents interact. With respect to the first point, the fiduciary relationship between firms (those who exercise authority in their governance) and stakeholders has been studied on the assumption that agents have conformist and reciprocity-based preferences with respect to compliance with *ex ante* impartially agreed principles of fairness (Sacconi 2007b, 2008, 2010). Thus the 'sense of justice' becomes an effective motivation in fostering compliance with CSR norms. The study of games, like the repeated trust game recast as a psychological game (Rabin 1993) under the assumption that agents (firms and stakeholders) are characterized by conformist preferences shows that equilibria of sophisticated abuse are destabilized – i.e. conformist preferences 'refine' the equilibrium set so that those conducts which would allow the firm to abuse stakeholders by inducing them to give in to sophistcated abuse are discarded from the equilibrium set of strategies. Subjects playing the stakeholder's role in the game punish the firm by not entering the relation with it even if this decision is costly in terms of sacrificing positive monetary payoffs. Such a sanctioning behavior can be explained with the stakeholders' intention of avoiding a wide deviation from conformity with CSR principles that would occur if they acquiesced to the firm's abusive conduct (again, see Sacconi 2010). With regard to the second aspect, Sacconi and Degli Antoni (2009, 2010) draw upon studies on the sustainability of long-run cooperation in networks of agents to elaborate on the relation among complex preferences, the adoption of CSR practices, and the development of social capital understood as a network of stable cooperative relations between the firm and its stakeholders.

2 An overview of the book's contents

This book includes some of the most important and original pieces of research conducted in recent years by outstanding scholars in the field of corporate governance and social reasonability in order to develop and discuss the line of inquiry outlined above. In truth, the book does not illustrate a unique point of view on the subject; rather, it reflects different views on the matters that I have outlined in the first part of this introduction.

2.1 Part I concerns the nature of the firm and its governance structure: human asset specificity, team production and the stakeholder approach. It explores different perspectives on the nature of the firm, such as transaction costs, team production and stakeholder theories. On this basis, consideration is made of the possibility of abuse of discretion by those who govern the productive organization, and hence the reason for extending responsibility to various categories of stakeholders.

In Chapter 1 the Nobel laureate Oliver Williamson states that, although the lens of contract/governance developed in the transaction costs perspective makes significant provision for organization theory, applications pose new challenges. A recurrent theme is that mutual gains will be realized by crafting governance structures that mitigate hazards, in particular by providing credible contracting safeguards for the equity investors by means of the creation of a board of directors that is awarded to the equity investors to serve as monitor. However, a comparison of this theory of the board as monitor with the board in practice – states Williamson – reveals serious disparities, one possible remedy for which is to use the contract with labor (which, like shareholders, also faces a collective action problem) as a template. But a board of directors so actively engaged in running the firm and interfering with the management – as would happen if it functioned as the 'Union of investors' – would undermine the imperatives of effective delegation to managers. In order to provide the shareholders with a monitoring capability without undue detriment to the integrity of delegation, Williamson suggests a modulated view of the board, such that it: (1) presumes that the normal relation between the leadership of the firm and the board is cooperative, yet (2) provides for periodic intervention by the board if and as the essential variables fall outside of control limits, (3) does not begrudge the information, expertise, and initiative asymmetries that the management enjoys over board members, yet (4) because these asymmetries pose foreseeable hazards, takes in advance measures to mitigate downside drift.

What is of greatest relevance to the main subject of this book is the overall picture of (second-best) effective corporate governance emerging from Williamson's chapter. On the one hand, the firm as a hierarchy is not only the tool designed to protect shareholders' investments because a degree of managerial autonomy is recognized as unavoidable. On the other hand, the role of the board as protective of equity holders is parallel to the employees' protection against opportunistic behavior exercised by those running the company in the case of a renegotiation of the labor contract that would expropriate the employees' specific investments in human assets. Such a guarantee should be provided by an institutional arrangement able to solve workers' collective action problems, such as an effective union. While this view bucks the trend at a time when unions have been losing much of their force in many capitalist economies, it also raises the question as to whether better protection could not be guaranteed by a board of directors committed to protecting not only equity holders' investments but also human asset-specific investments. Good corporate governance thus consists of a situation where different stakeholders, endowed with specific assets, are all guaranteed against different types of opportunistic behavior, while the managers are nevertheless granted limited but not renounceable discretion in running the firm.

In Chapter 2, Masahiko Aoki – the author to whom the multi-stakeholder perspective on corporate governance is most indebted within economic theory – returns to the never-ending debate on whether the corporation is the property of the stockholders, or whether the board should owe fiduciary duties to the stakeholders in general. He suggests that the current resumption of force by the stakeholder perspective is the result of two important factors that can be traced back to two concepts – *human asset essentiality* and *corporate social capital* – and he discusses their important implications for the stakeholder–society view of corporate governance. The former concept is extended to distinguish between discrete forms of organizational architecture and the corporate governance structures associated with each of them. Aoki views the firm-specificity of workers' human assets, as well as their complementarities with physical or managerial assets, as ubiquitous in modern corporations, especially in the emergent technological environment. They may not necessarily be incompatible with the stockholder-controlled corporate governance structure. The latter concept – corporate social capital – is then applied to interpret the roles of so-called corporate social responsibility (CSR) programs. Why, Aoki asks, do corporations engage in various non-economic activities to meet societal demands that are beyond their legal obligations? The chapter discusses this issue from the perspective that corporations (and their stockholders and other stakeholders) are players not only in economic games but also in the social-exchange game embedding the former. It analyzes how corporate social capital accumulated through CSR can compensate for the sacrifice of pecuniary economic assets, and how the former can nonetheless indirectly complement the accumulation of the latter.

In Chapter 3, R. Edward Freeman, Andrew Wicks and Bidhan Parmar undertake the ambitious project of showing that stakeholder theory (reinvented in its current form by Ed Freeman in the 1980s) is not only a useful way to understand capitalism, but also a theory capable of incorporating most arguments advanced by the alternative economic views of the firm, such as the arguments of Friedman, Jensen, and Williamson, often seen as opponents of stakeholder theory. Thus stakeholder theory can be conceived as the most general and encompassing view of capitalism, able to return to its very essence – that is, entrepreneurship. The proper understanding of the stakeholder approach conceives it as a theory on how business actually does and can work, answering the crucial question of 'How is value creation and trade sustainable over time?' Freeman, Wicks and Parmar view this question as also being the essential one to be asked in the realm of practical ethics. The answer, provided by the idea of 'stakeholder capitalism', is based – according to the authors – on three principles derived from the mechanics of stakeholder theory: value can be created, traded, and sustained because (i) stakeholders can jointly satisfy their needs and desires by entering into voluntary agreements which are for the most part kept; (ii) stakeholders party to agreements are willing to accept responsibility for the consequences of their actions, so that when third parties are harmed, they must be compensated, or a new agreement must be negotiated with all the parties affected; (iii) human beings are complex psychological creatures capable of acting in accordance with many different values and from many different points of view.

The view that it is the complexity of human motivations and cognition that makes voluntary cooperation in value creation among stakeholders possible, at the same time inducing them to act responsibly toward harmed third parties, is indubitably very attractive. It would also reconcile narrow shareholder maximization with the wider view of value creation for the mutual advantage of all stakeholders, which inevitably raises the issue of possibly conflicting claims over the surplus distribution. The idea is that when faced with possible trade-offs between opposing stakeholders' interests, a stakeholder-oriented management would reframe the situation with a new entrepreneurial idea that makes it possible to see the situation again in terms of a purely cooperative endeavor (see also Freeman et al. 2010).

A comment is in order here. Emphasizing 're-framing' as a cognitive solution for apparently unanswerable social dilemmas is a major step forward with respect the traditional view of individualist economic rationality (see, for example, Bacharach's 'team thinking'; Bacharach 2006). But it should not be confused with a way of brushing the dust of conflict under the carpet. Even if the corporation is seen as a mutually advantageous and basically cooperative enterprise potentially producing benefits for all its stakeholders, nevertheless typically latent will be distributive conflicts on the distribution of what is essentially a surplus generated by joint cooperation. This is true in so far as stakeholders have contrasting claims over the surplus shares. In order to cooperate they must also solve the distributive problem by agreeing on a principle of justice that prevents the outbreak of conflict. Cooperation and conflict are simultaneously present and they cannot be dissolved by reshaping the situation as one in which the parties will not be faced by the division problem – at least this would not be allowed within the non-holistic multi-stakeholder approach that views stakeholders as legitimate separate agents. The idea of a social contract may intervene at this point by providing a mental model or a re-framing of the situation whereby the parties, even if seen as separated agents, may avoid conflict by agreeing on a governance structure that allows them to select a joint plan of action corresponding to an efficient and fair distribution. The 'veil of ignorance' reframes the situation by changing the stakeholders' view: from that of each individual group engaged in a zero-sum distributive conflict to that of symmetrically situated individuals each confronted by essentially the same decision problem. The problem of how to reach an agreement on a productive/distributive solution that would permit their joint cooperation and prevent conflict among them by giving an acceptable answer to the claim of whichever stakeholder is involved. The veil of ignorance provides such a mental framing in that it induces each stakeholder to account for whatever stakeholder point of view and to identify terms of agreement that are invariant from the perspective of each of them.

In Chapter 4, Allen Kaufman and Ernie Englander go further in the attempt to integrate concepts from law and economics concerning corporate governance, and from stakeholder theory and behavioral economics. Team production and resource-based economics furnish the theoretical foundations: the team production model resides firmly within the behavioral law and economics literature; resource-based economics belongs to the strategic management literature and arguably extends team production into useful management tools. It is here that the *homo socius* of behavioral economics comes into the picture. The new 'rational actor' supplies team production with the psychological 'raw material' with which to describe the firm as a cooperation game in which corporate directors coordinate the surplus allocations and distributions that stakeholders consider fair. Mutual gain sets the baseline 'fairness' standard within the market. Fairness, however, is conceived here in a particularly 'soft' version. The choice of allocations does not obey any intrinsic or objective, impartial standard, in so far as what matters is only the parties' subjective estimate that cooperation (Pareto efficiency) beats non-cooperation. Thus mutual-gain 'fairness' (economic efficiency) has a minimal ethical content – does no harm – but its assessment depends wholly on each group's voluntary agreement to a deal. Consequently, Kaufmann and Englander dissent from the usual stakeholder theory interpretation whereby boards can select among the primary distributive policies of mutual gain and impartiality. Product and financial market competition constrain US boards from deviating far from a Pareto/Kaldor–Hicks standard, so that they concur with economists that directors cannot choose between an impartial standard and mutual gain (reciprocity/procedural justice) – see, for example, the chapter by Viktor Vanberg (chapter 6 below). Public policy, instead, is the proper domain for remedying 'unfair' market outcomes.

In this domain, correctives may rely on direct redistribution or they may take the form of regulatory initiatives to strengthen the least advantaged party's bargaining position. But managers, even when they participate in the polity, may also continue to hold the minimalist view of procedural justice, which, in effect, corroborates market outcomes. Historically, US corporate managers have demonstrated a preference for both of these two views.

Of indubitable interest is the opening of a new perspective on how corporate managers are not only active in the corporate governance domain but also players in the more general polity realm (a point also made in Aoki's contribution). However, a question can be raised about the adequacy of a view on the management of stakeholders' cooperation that seeks to evade the problem of distributive conflict, i.e. such that no attempt is made to go beyond the mere assertion of an efficient mutually advantageous result. To be sure, the most acute supporter of the agreement-for-mutual-advantage view of ethics also clearly saw that such a contractarian theory should at the same time select one among the many possible Pareto-efficient allocations, and a unique distributive principle for the univocal solution of a bargaining game (see Gauthier 1986). The question is not relevant solely to the theoretical question of the stability of a multi-stakeholder agreement, from which a social norm of corporate governance may emerge (see the translation of the social contract methodology into the corporate governance domain entailing an application of the Rawlsian maximin, cf. Sacconi *infra*). I is also relevant to the proper description of how boards of directors perform their mediating role amongst different stakeholders' claims and interests.

This last point has been made by the two main legal theorists of the corporate board as an impartial mediating hierarchy, and who have written Chapter 5 in this book. Margaret Blair and Lynn Stout start their chapter with the observation that for most of the last three decades, corporate governance scholarship has been dominated by the powerful paradigm termed the principal–agent model, and which holds that the corporation must be understood as a nexus of private contracts, of which the most important is the contract between the shareholders of the firm (the 'principals') and the directors and executive officers (the shareholders' 'agents'). According to this contract – the model says – the directors and executives will run the firm so that the shareholders' wealth is maximized. Even though an entire generation of experts has embraced the principal–agent model, it is impossible not to observe how many aspects of corporate law are inconsistent with the paradigm's tenets, giving rise to what can be termed – to use Thomas Kuhn's phraseology – the paradigm's anomalies. Blair and Stout list the following: (1) corporate law does not grant shareholders the legal rights of principals; nor do they burden directors with the legal obligations of agents; (2) corporate law does not treat shareholders of solvent firms as sole residual claimants; (3) far from being a vacuous fiction, legal personality is a key feature of the corporate form; and (4) corporate law does not impose any obligation on directors to maximize shareholder wealth.

As in the hard sciences, however, a paradigm cannot be rejected solely because of the accumulation of anomalies. What is needed for a significant conceptual shift to occur is the emergence of a new paradigm, and this may come about quite randomly. According to Blair and Stout, in the domain of corporate law and governance such a new paradigm seems to be arising because a number of theorists have recently begun to study the different problem of how to protect and encourage 'specific' investments – specialized resources that acquire their highest value only when used in a particular process or project. In fact, when corporate production requires more than one individual or group to make specific investments, problems of intra-firm opportunism arise if shareholders try to exploit each other's specific investments or the specific investments of creditors, employees, customers, and other groups. Board governance, while worsening agency costs, may then counteract these intra-firm types of opportunism. Focusing on the problem of specific investment – Blair and Stout continue – the new perspective suggests that the proper purpose of the public corporation is not to maximize shareholder wealth but to promote long-term, value-creating economic production under conditions of complexity and uncertainty, doing so in a manner that yields surplus benefits not only to shareholders but also to other groups that make specific investments in corporations.

2.2   Part II of the book considers alternative normative foundations of CSR based on new developments in the 'social contract' and other rational choice theories – expanding on issues such as distributive justice, constitutional choice, collective rational agency and commitment, and different kinds of reputation. Some of the questions left unanswered in the first part of the book are now tackled: for example, how to balance different stakeholders' claims and how far the choice of fair equilibrating principles may go within the domain of corporate governance. What results is the discussion of CSR as a normative model of the productive organization and its governance, the purpose being to ascertain whether corporate obligations can be extended to serve different stakeholders' interests; and then discussion of the role that the 'social contract over the constitutions of the firm' can play in providing a model foundation. Also discussed are the rational choice models required to cope with the problem of endogenous sustainability of such normative models, with particular regard to the question of whether self-interest is sufficiently strong in the long run to support some kind of CSR. This typical tenet of economists is scrutinized under the heading of 'reputation effects'. The result is a recognition of both equilibrium *existence* and *selection* problems that can only be solved by taking an explicit (not simply self-interested) ethical-impartial perspective. This also entails a change in the idea of rational agency and commitment.

In Chapter 6, Victor Vanberg challenges the idea of giving CSR a contractarian foundation by re-examining the project in light of his personal and competent account of constitutional political economy. His aim is to re-establish the role and goal of corporations operating in a market economy as near as possible to that envisaged by great libertarian (but not contractarian) economists like Friedman and Hayek. In his reply to Sacconi (2006b) he assumes not only that markets are effectively places where a Smithian 'invisible hand' is at work, but also that this model is reflected by the rules of the game for market economies with which we comply under our constitutional contracts. In order to avoid confusion in applying a contractarian-constitutionalist perspective to the issue of CSR, Vanberg recommends a clear distinction to be drawn between two levels of 'social contract': on the one hand, the social contract among all members of a polity that establishes the rules of the 'economic game'; on the other, the various social contracts into which persons, in the course of playing the 'economic game', enter, or which they establish, when participating in any joint enterprise. The social contract at the societal level defines the rules according to which the economic game is to be played in a jurisdiction, and it has systematic priority over social contracts of the second kind because it defines the constraints within which the latter may be concluded. The social responsibility for a well-functioning market game – Vanberg maintains – is 'divided': the social responsibility of the member of a polity *in playing the market game* is to pursue their ambitions in a fair, rule-abiding manner. Their social responsibility *for the market game* is the responsibility that they share as members of the respective political community and that they exercise through their government.

The main conclusion that Vanberg draws for the issue of CSR is that the very point of playing the market game under the current constitutional contract is to relieve the participants from the responsibility of considering, as they play the game, all the consequences that their actions may possibly have for the 'common good', and to allow them, instead, to concentrate their attention on playing the game successfully within the constraints defined by its legal and moral rules: in other words, the maximization of profits within the legal constraints. But what about cases in which – as Vanberg concedes – there are good reasons to consider CSR-demands as 'appropriate' moral demands, i.e. as demands that point to actual conflicts between profit interests and common interests? When the 'market game' produces patterns of outcomes that the participants consider undesirable, they have reason to seek a remedy in a suitable adjustment of the rules of the game at constitutional level. The remedy – Vanberg contends – cannot be found in calling upon the players to sacrifice their own ambitions to play the game successfully in order to compensate for deficiencies in its rules. The only viable option is to exercise political responsibility at the polity level where the rules are established. In fact – Vanberg says – serious problems of 'constitutional prudence' and democratic legitimacy arise when CSR-demands become a competing force with, and a substitute for, the formal legislative process by creating factual constraints that 'channel' corporate conduct in ways that only the CSR-advocates define as 'socially responsible'.

Vanberg's penetrating analysis warrants careful consideration, from both the methodological and factual points of view, but which cannot be satisfactorily provided in an introduction. Nevertheless, let us consider the latter viewpoint. Factually, Vanberg's argument seems to lose much of its force when the more realistic hypothesis is made that under most latitudes constitutional contracts do not prescribe such strict compliance with the improbable ideal of a perfect competitive market and its normative tenet of profit maximization as the sole legitimate goal for the firm's management. Consider, for instance, Blair and Stout's (*de jure condito*) interpretation of American corporate law, the co-determination tradition in German corporate governance (see Osterloh et al. Chapter 12 *infra*), and article 41 of the Italian Constitution. These are all examples of the many ways in which real world 'constitutional contracts' allow wide margins for the post-constitutional establishment of corporate governance norms providing for transaction spheres where – so to speak – the market ideal fails.

From the former viewpoint, these facts can be accommodated by a slightly different interpretation of the social contract methodology which gives more autonomy to small-scale, local social contracts with respect to the general social contract agreed at societal (maybe international) level (for an articulation of this idea see Donaldson and Dunfee 1999). Within the delimitation fixed by general and abstract principles ('meta-norms') agreed upon in the large-scale social contract, the social contract itself requires that room must be given to small-scale social contracts on lower level norms – these being understood not as simple post-constitutional laws but as norms generated according to the same social contract methodology, even if on a smaller scale and with a more concrete and reduced-range domain of application. Thus all of the stakeholders of a well-defined and nearly self-contained domain of social interaction are allowed to agree on a small-scale social contract in order to establish social norms regulating their interaction in the relevant domain. Before such agreement can be translated into mandatory laws by a political decision (which is not necessary in general), these norms must prove able to generate a social institution (Aoki 2001): that is, a regularity of behavior within a given domain of interaction which is reflected in the mental (normative and descriptive) model commonly shared by all the participants in the domain; Which in its turn induces a set of mutual beliefs on the behavior adopted by all of the participants so that they make decisions that replicate the same regularity of behavior. The small-scale social contract is the cognitive device whereby participants in the domain can *ex ante* reach a general agreement on the (normative) mental model of their repeated interaction. It in its turn induces them to behave according to the regularity in practice.

This two-tier articulation of the social contract methodology seems particularly appropriate in view of the impossibility of assuming that the parties negotiate a perfectly detailed constitution, which would require unbounded rationality of those who draw up and subscribe to it. On the contrary, the reason for adhering to the social contract methodology is exactly that it is a way to introduce, by a hypothetical agreement negotiated through counterfactual reasoning, a set of general and abstract principles providing guidance for behaviors to be maintained when the occurrence of unforeseen events renders incomplete and fruitless any attempt to write a detailed contract comprising every possible legal proviso. Moreover, such a wisely incomplete constitutional contract would be suited to managing states of the world wherein the perfect competitive market does not work, as is typically the case when the institutional design of large corporations is required. In fact, these are institutions intended to prevent opportunistic behaviors and transaction costs that would not materialize if real world market transactions adhered to the efficient 'invisible hand' model – whereas it is exactly the 'invisible hand' that justifies the profit maximization rule as the normative model valid for (null size) firms' behavior. In the real world states of the economy, the constitutional contract would establish only general principles of efficiency and fairness based on mutual impartial agreements, and it would enable the participants in the relevant economic domains to agree on a small-scale social contracts in order to develop the impartially acceptable governance rules. Moreover, before such norms can be adopted as new articles of the overall constitution, they will have to be tested in terms of self-sustainability as social institutions voluntarily adhered to in the relevant domains. So, why should the CSR movement not be considered as representing the emergence of such intermediate institutions of governance developed through the stakeholders' dialog and agreement in order to enable their cooperation and the prevention of negative externalities on them?

These remarks are the natural introduction to Lorenzo Sacconi's chapters 7 and 8, where two steps toward a comprehensive Rawlsian view of CSR, and the game theory of its implementation, are presented. Chapter 7 defines CSR as a multi-stakeholder model of corporate governance and objective function based on the extension of fiduciary duties toward all of the firm's stakeholders. In accordance with the prevailing opinion on its voluntariness, CSR is viewed as a normative model that companies may undertake on the basis of decisions autonomous in terms of the explicit adoption of expressed self-regulatory norms and standards. This is to be understood as an institution in Aoki's sense (see above); but added to Aoki's definition is an explicitly expressed norm including prescriptive principles and normative standards of behavior. The establishment of this norm is explained in terms of a Rawlsian *social contract*:

that is, a unanimous and impartial agreement among the corporate stakeholders that must be reached under a 'veil of ignorance' about the particular stakes that each of them holds (and with respect to any other personal traits). It takes place in the hypothetical bargaining that precedes the repeated non-cooperative game between the firm and each of its stakeholders. The Rawlsian social contract performs essential functions in solving the basic game-theoretical problems faced in the implementation of the very broad idea of multi-stakeholder corporate governance. These are: (i) *construing* commitments to allow definition of a game of reputation such that reputation effects can be attached to compliance with the CSR normative model; (ii) *selecting* just one of the many equilibria possible in such a game as the unique equilibrium *ex ante* acceptable by all under the condition of impartial and impersonal agreement; (iii) *refining* the set of possible equilibria so that only those reflecting conformist motivations deriving from the *ex ante* social contract are retained as true candidates for the *ex post* emergence of the equilibrium to which actual individual actions will converge (on this, however see part III of this essay, Sacconi 2010).

In Chapter 7 the social contract works as a gap-filling device with respect to the holes in the incomplete contracts linking stakeholders (or the most essential of them) with the firm. In a context of incomplete contracts and unforeseen contingencies, the repeated reputation game involving the firm (or those who control it) and each stakeholder would be badly specified because contingent strategies and commitment would be undefined with respect to unforeseen contingencies. Thus, at the outset of the stakeholders/firm interaction, a social contract must be established on a set of general and abstract principles of fair treatment, and precautionary (non-contingent) standards of behavior, which can be adapted to unforeseen contingencies. In the absence of such an explicit norm, no regularity of reputation-based behavior on the part of the firm could emerge through its interaction with stakeholders. Chapter 8 illustrates the main result of the theory, which concerns the second role of a Rawlsian social contract: that is, the *ex ante* impartial selection of a unique equilibrium amongst the many possible in the repeated trust game involving the firms and its stakeholders. Elaborating on Binmore's *Natural Justice* (2005) and its re-evaluation of John Rawls's egalitarian and maximin principle of justice within a game-theoretical perspective, this task is accomplished again from the *ex ante* (under the 'veil of ignorance') point of view, but in a way that makes it possible to find a unique course of action that satisfies the requirement of incentive compatibility (i.e. a Nash equilibrium). To see the relevance of this analytical construction to the main subject of the book, consider that many scholars of corporate governance – accustomed as they are to accepting second-best solutions – would be ready to relinquish any claim of fairness in order to achieve nothing more than the most efficient constitution of the firm. Remarkably enough, the original application of the Rawls–Binmore social contract to the choice of corporate governance structures yields quite the opposite suggestion. In order to be consistent with the requirement of self-sustainability, the agreement selects the constitution with the best *egalitarian* solution among all the alternative feasible constitutions. That is to say, a constitutional arrangement must be chosen such that, within its feasible outcome set, the solution that maximizes the position of the worst-off stakeholder is accepted by all because this is the *best* solution with respect to all the *egalitarian* solutions feasible under alternative constitutions.

Luciano Andreozzi in Chapter 9 reconsiders the question of whether self-interest in the long run may be sufficient to support CSR policies devoted to the fair treatment of stakeholders in terms that are not in the immediate self-interest of the owners or the shareholders of the company. He concludes, from specific economic analysis, that it is not enough. The proponents of CSR, according to Andreozzi, face a dilemma which is deeply rooted in all forms of moral reasoning: if a code of ethics only prescribes choices that are compatible with enlightened self-interest, it is at least hypocritical to mask it with anything different from normal decency and prudence. Standard results in the theory of repeated games, and in particular the so-called *folk theorem*, can be used to show that a rational firm has a reputational incentive to adopt (and respect) a code of ethics. At first sight, this approach can be criticized on the same grounds as before: the use of repeated game considerations introduces precisely the concern for one's future reputation that makes any appeal to ethics redundant. However, it is a consequence of the folk theorem that repetition of a game among the same players produces an enormous number of equilibria, some of which are efficient while others are not. Hence, while trust and trustworthiness are *possible* outcomes of reputation, they are by no means the only ones. An extremely simplified evolutionary model is proposed to make this point. It is based on the repetition of the so-called Trust Game involving a population of firms and a population of customers. It is shown that many stable states exist, some of which only contain fair and trustworthy firms, while others contain firms that are moderately dishonest but are still able to induce customers to trust them. This suggests that a code of ethics may be viewed as a signal emitted by firms in order to coordinate better with their customers on one of the many equilibria of the repeated game they play.

Bruce Chapman in Chapter 10 examines a basic aspect of the legal structure of modern corporations. To make sense of it, he suggests a change in the notion of rational agency which is conducive to the CSR view of corporate governance. It is widely believed that limited liability, where the personal assets of shareholders in a corporation are insulated against any claims made by creditors against the corporation, is a kind of special 'concession' granted to those investors. But asset partitioning – Chapman suggests – would be a quite natural consequence if we were prepared to think of the corporation as a rational agent distinct from its shareholders. Supporting this explanation, however, requires a richer and more developed conception of rational agency. According to Chapman, a rational actor is an agent that is responsive both to reasons *and* to the normative requirements of practical rationality. This requires an agent to respect its prior commitments in a way that merely acting for reasons does not. The notion of rational agency typically used in economics restricts it to conduct that is responsive solely to reasons. This explains why individuals, under the familiar backward induction arguments, have difficulty in abiding by their prior commitments (i.e. making credible promises or threats) unless there are ongoing (typically, 'long-run' or reputational) self-interested reasons to do so. By contrast, under the richer conception of rational agency, we can identify the actor with a 'rational association', which is exemplified by the corporation, where capital lock-in, and its kindred idea of (affirmative) asset partitioning, is the norm. Chapman then asks what advantage is to be gained from approaching the problem in this way, rather than on the basis of economic arguments emphasizing the benefits for shareholders. His reply is that the argument from rational association carries implications that go further than asset partitioning. Not only do shareholders enjoy the benefits that flow from limited liability and entity shielding, but under rational association they are also committed to other stakeholders in a way that limits what they can rationally do in order to maximize their profits. Thus the argument moves from asset partitioning to the broader obligations that a corporation as a rational association must discharge to non-shareholder stakeholders.

2.3   Part III concerns the design of norms and organizations according to the behavioral economics approach and its relation to CSR and the multi-stakeholder governance of organizations. It considers alternative approaches to the organizational and normative design of CSR, with a special emphasis on the self-regulation and 'assurance mechanisms' that may operate through endogenous market mechanisms. It also expands on the contributions that recent developments in behavioral economics may make to the design of the internal organization of the firm and to multi-stakeholder models of corporate governance, according to a perspective which does not assume that managers and members of the organization are simply self-interested maximizers.

In Chapter 11, Margaret M. Blair, Cynthia A. Williams and Li-Wen Lin point out that, even though reputational enforcement mechanisms can be quite powerful in getting large, highly visible organizations to fulfill contract requirements and social norms, the same communicative capabilities that can make reputation important can also be used to publish misleading information, distort perceptions, and generally introduce at least as much noise as useful information into the process of determining whether legitimate expectations have been met on all sides. Hence the authors of this chapter discuss the role of another enforcement mechanism that they claim is rapidly becoming extremely important in global business and trade. This is the use of third-party, non-governmental standard-setting, inspection, assurance and certification services based on quantifiable standards and metrics with which such services can measure and report on performance by parties to actual and potential contracts. Many of these performance metrics define standards for acceptable social and environmental behavior, as well as for such things as quality control and on-time delivery, so that third-party assurance services also appear to exercise a regulatory function, importing and enforcing norms of acceptable conduct throughout supply chains connecting firms located in faraway places. Blair, Williams and Lin's thesis is that a number of factors are coming together in the global business environment to cause the demand for management standards and third-party assurance services to explode. In fact, the role played by standardization and third-party assurance is rapidly becoming so important that, in some parts of the world where rule of law is weak, business norms unreliable, and regulation of business practices erratic or non-existent, private sector players may be turning to third-party assurance services as the dominant mechanism for regulating business and enforcing contracts.

Chapter 12, by Margit Osterloh, Bruno Frey and Hossam Zeitoun, focuses on the relation between co-determination models in corporate governance and some results in behavioral economics related to the analysis of human asset specificity. Considering empirical studies on co-determination laws that report mixed effects, the authors point out that *mandatory co-determination* imposes a too rigid framework upon companies, without making sure that enough knowledge investors (workers) are represented on the board. But at the same time they suggest that *voluntary co-determination rules* have a promising future. Osterloh, Frey and Zeitoum consider that a modern corporation's key task is to generate, accumulate and transfer firm-specific knowledge as these are the essential bases for a sustainable competitive advantage. Financial *and* knowledge investments must be combined to produce what are commonly called synergies or quasi-rents that need to be divided in a way perceived to be fair by the participants. In particular, knowledge investors should not feel exploited; otherwise they will refuse to make firm-specific investments and will prefer to make investments in outside options. Granted that labor contracts are necessarily incomplete, corporate governance rules and the board in particular must ensure that the *ex post* bargaining position of participants does not put their investments at risk. Given this perspective, similar to that adopted in other chapters in this book, the authors advance three novel reform proposals that would improve voluntary co-determination. *Firstly*, the board should rely more on *insiders*. The percentage of insiders relative to outsiders should be determined by the relationship of firm-specific knowledge capital with financial capital. *Secondly*, these insiders should be elected by, and responsible to, those *employees of the firm who make firm-specific knowledge investments*. *Thirdly*, a *neutral person* should chair the board. His or her main task is to enable the board members to engage in a productive discourse to the mutual benefit of all members of the firm. The chairperson should also make sure that the board members are prepared to contribute to the firm's common good and refrain from rent seeking. These proposals, according to the authors, have major advantages over the reforms suggested by the dominant corporate governance approach. They provide incentives for knowledge investors and countervail the dominance of executives; they strengthen intrinsic work motivation and loyalty to the firm through distributive as well as procedural justice; and they ensure diversity on the board while lowering transaction costs. Moreover, this approach overcomes the separation between theories focused on value generation and theories focused on value distribution by showing how value generation and value distribution interact.

Leonardo Becchetti and Noemi Pace's premise in Chapter 13 is that the debate on CSR generally presumes a trade-off between higher consideration for stakeholders other than shareholders and the economic performance of the firm. They show that this is not always the case by devising a possible virtuous circle between a specific kind of CSR (care for worker relationships in work organization) and performance. They take the point of view that one of the main features of modern corporations is that most productive activities take the form of trust games (i.e. complex activities requiring the sequential interaction of workers, with no overlapping skills, where one worker may trust the following worker, whereas the latter may or may not abuse the former), so that it can be shown that the quality of relationships among workers (trust and trustworthiness) may be crucial in preventing paradoxical inefficient outcomes. This entails that individual pay for performance schemes or tournament structures may have counter-intuitive effects because they are based on a presumption that workers are untrustworthy and worsen their relationships. Hence, if the costs of investing in the quality of worker relationships are lower than the output gains arising when passing from third-best to first-best productive solutions, a CSR policy supporting worker relationships may establish a virtuous circle with efficiency. The assumptions and conclusions of the chapter are grounded on the observed empirical reality. The existence of relational preferences for co-workers is demonstrated by empirical evidence, while a game-theoretical model helps explain puzzles such as the less frequent than expected recourse to pay-for-performance schemes and the recent propensity of modern corporations to hire teams and to invest in the improvement of the working environment. Since under the different versions of their model the authors quite naturally find that cooperative solutions supporting trust relations become slightly easier in the case of repeated games, corporate trust games also suggest a novel limitation on corporate turnover policies because frequent changes of the organization's members reduce opportunities to develop relational goods and foster trust among workers.

Who controls an organization makes a difference. It is for this reason that strategic control is contested and usually rests in the hands of owners or their agents, the board of directors and executives, who rarely share it with other stakeholders. Any influence that other stakeholders – consumers, employees, community – may have is typically exercised through markets or political channels. It is therefore interesting to investigate what happens if, for whatever reason, various stakeholder groups ordinarily excluded from control gain some measure of it. This is the research question that Avner Ben-Ner and Ting Ren raise in Chapter 14 of the book, where they examine the effect of participation in decision-making on strategic matters by different groups of stakeholders – employees, executives, community representatives, owners and customers – on organizational efficiency and the well-being of key stakeholder groups. In order to carry out a preliminary empirical study, Ben-Ner and Ren focus on a narrowly-defined industry (nursing homes for the elderly) in a single state in the US, Minnesota, in order to minimize unobserved heterogeneity in industry characteristics, legal, cultural and social influences and geographic conditions, and so that they can study for-profit, non-profit and government organizations that operate side by side in the same industry and market. According to the authors, the nursing homes industry is particularly interesting because its customers – elderly residents – are frail and vulnerable and therefore cannot thoroughly evaluate the care that they receive and lack the strongest elements required for market competition: 'voice' and 'exit'. Family and friends often have a fiduciary role (in the legal sense), but they are rarely present in a nursing home long enough to witness the nature and quality of care provided. In the economic jargon, contractual relationships are characterized by such strong information asymmetries to the disadvantage of customers that the typical market principle of 'customer sovereignty' would be impossible. In these circumstances – Ben-Ner and Ren contend – corporate social responsibility (CSR) is a particularly powerful concept. The dataset resulting from the empirical study provides rich information on organizational characteristics, decision-making participation by stakeholder groups, organizational outcomes, and residents' and employees' well-being, so that the authors are able to study the impact of strategic decision-making by one or more stakeholder groups on: (i) organizational efficiency; (ii) the well-being of employees; and (iii) residents. Ben-Ner and Ren find that the identity of stakeholders with strategic control powers matters for these outcomes. Different stakeholder groups have different effects on the three sets of outcomes considered in the chapter.

In the final chapter of the book, Avner Ben-Ner and Louis Putternam argue that in a world of social human beings who tend to relate to companies as if they were social and moral agents in their own right, there are pressures on even profit-maximizing companies to project favorable social personae. This is also instantiated by the example that those companies that pay their employees more than the opportunity cost of their labor are rewarded with higher effort due to normal human reciprocity. This chapter reports an experimental study of social preferences based on person-to-person, rather than person-to-company, interactions, and which shows that trusting and trustworthiness are supported by social motivations to reciprocate trust and to avoid harming by misleading. The fact that laboratory manipulations that make an interaction partner more real, and that allow him or her to project a favorable image, lead to a greater degree of trust and to the conduct of more business (sending, trusting) suggests that companies may also benefit from investing in benevolent personae (take this as an aspect of CSR). In the experiments reported, trusting and trustworthiness were increased significantly by opportunities to exchange proposals and counterproposals, and they further increased when verbal messages could also be sent. Most agreements reached by the simple exchange of proposals were adhered to, with a still higher rate of follow-through when the subjects had also 'chatted' and/or when the agreement had the characteristic of being efficient and 'fair'. The modal agreement was the most equitable of the efficient sets of actions, and such agreements were carried out by both parties significantly more often than were other agreements. That so many participants refrained from behaving opportunistically toward anonymous partners highlights the impact of social norms on interactions of the kind that make up so much of the everyday life of organizations. And the observed powerful effects of communication suggest that the more 'real' the persons with whom an individual interacts, the more likely it is that these norms will be triggered.

References

Alchian, A. and A. Demsetz (1972) 'Production, Information Costs and Economic Organization', *American Economic Review*, vol. 62(5), pp. 777–95.
Aoki, M. (1984) *The Cooperative Game Theory of the Firm*. Oxford: Oxford University Press.
Aoki, M. (2001) *Toward a Comparative Institutional Analysis*. Cambridge, MA: MIT Press.
Aoki, M. (2010) *Corporations in Evolving Diversity*. Oxford: Oxford University Press.
Arrow, K. (1974) *The Limits of Organizations*. New York: WW. Norton and Company.
Bacharach, M. (2006) *Beyond Individual Choice, Teams and Frames in Game Theory*, edited by N. Gold and R. Sugden. Princeton, NJ: Princeton University Press.
Benabou, R. and J. Tirole (2010) 'Individual and Corporate Social Responsibility', *Economica*, vol. 77(305), pp. 1–19.
Binmore, K. (2005) *Natural Justice*. London: Blackwell.
Blair, M. and L. Stout (1999) 'A Team Production Theory of Corporate Law', *Virginia Law Review*, vol. 85(2), p. 247.
Brock, H.W. (1979) 'A Game Theoretical Account of Social Justice', *Theory and Decision*, vol. 11, pp. 239–65.
Donaldson, T. and L.E. Preston (1995) 'Stakeholder Theory and the Corporation: Concepts, Evidence and Implication', *Academy of Management Review*, 20(1), pp. 65–91.

Donaldson, T. and T.W. Dunfee (1999) *Ties that Bind: A Social Contract Approach to Business Ethics*. Cambridge, MA: Harvard Business School Press.

Economist, 22 January 2005.

Economist, 19 January 2008.

Elhauge, E. (2005a) 'Sacrificing Corporate Profits in the Public Interest', *New York Law Review*, vol. 80(3), pp. 733–869.

Elhauge, E. (2005b) 'Corporate Managers' Operational Discretion to Sacrifice Corporate Profit in the Public Interest', in B.L. Hay, R. N. Stavinis and R. Vietor (eds), *Environmental Protection and the Social Responsibility of Firms*. Washington, DC: Resources for the Future.

Evan, W. and R.E. Freeman (1993) 'Stakeholder Management and the Modern Corporation: Kantian Capitalism', in T.L. Beauchamp and N. Bowie (eds), *Ethical Theory and Business*. Englewood Cliffs, NJ: Prentice-Hall.

Fehr, E. and J.A. List (2004) 'The Hidden Costs and Returns of Incentives – Trust and Trustworthiness Among CEOs', *Journal of European Economic Association*, vol. 2(5), pp. 741–71.

Fehr, E. and A. Falk (2002) 'Psychological Foundations of Incentives', *European Economic Review*, vol. 46, pp. 687–724.

Fehr, E., A. Klein and K.M. Schmidt (2007) 'Fairness and Contract Design', *Econometrica*, vol. 71(1), pp. 121–54.

Fehr, E., S. Gächter and G. Kirchsteiger (1997) 'Reciprocity as a Contract Enforcement Device', *Econometrica*, vol. 65, pp. 833–60.

Freeman, R.E. (1984) *Strategic Management: A Stakeholder Approach*. Boston, MA: Pitman.

Freeman, R.E. and W. Evan (1990) 'Corporate Governance: A Stakeholder Interpretation', *Journal of Behavioral Economics*, vol. 19(4), pp. 337–59.

Freeman, R.E., J. Harrison, A. Wicks, B. Parmar and S. De Colle (2010) *Stakeholder Theory: The State of the Art*. Cambridge: Cambridge University Press.

Frey, B. (1997) *Not Just for the Money: An Economic Theory of Personal Motivation*. London: Edward Elgar.

Fudenberg, D. and D.K. Levine (1989) 'Reputation and Equilibrium Selection in Games with a Patient Player', *Econometrica*, vol. 57(4), pp. 759–78.

Gauthier, D. (1969) *Morals by Agreement*. Oxford: Clarendon Press.

Gintis, H. and R. Kurama (2008) 'Corporate Honesty and Business Education: A Behavioral Model', in P.J. Zak (ed), *Moral Markets*. Princeton, NJ: Princeton University Press.

Gneezy, U. and I.A. Rustichini (2000) 'Pay Enough or Don't Pay at All', *Quarterly Journal of Economics*, vol. 115(2), pp. 791–810.

Grossman, S. and O. Hart (1986) 'The Costs and Benefits of Ownership: A Theory of Vertical and Lateral Integration', *Journal of Political Economy*, vol. 94, pp. 691–719.

Hansmann, H. (1996) *The Ownership of Enterprise*. London and Cambridge, MA: The Belknap Press of Harvard University Press.

Hansmann, H. and R. Kraakman (2001) 'The End of History in Corporate Law', 89, *Geo L. J.* pp. 439–41.

Hart, O. and J. Moore (1990) 'Property Rights and the Nature of the Firm', *Journal of Political Economy*, vol. 98, pp. 1119–58.

Heal, A.L.G. (2008) *When Principles Pay: Corporate Social Responsibility and the Bottom Line*. New York: Columbia Business School Publications.

Jensen, M.C. (2001) 'Value Maximization, Stakeholder Theory, and the Corporate Objective Function', *Journal of Applied Corporate Finance*, vol. 14(3), pp. 8–21.

Jones, T.M. (1980) 'Corporate Social responsibility Revisited, Redefined', *California Management Review*, vol. 22(2), pp. 59–64.

Kreps, D. (1990) 'Corporate Culture and Economic Theory', in J.E. Alt and K.A. Shepsle (eds), *Perspectives on Positive Political Economy*. Cambridge: Cambridge University Press.

Nash, J. (1950) 'The Bargaining Problem', *Econometrica*, vol. 18, pp. 155–62.

Posner, E.A. (2000) *Law and Social Norms*. Cambridge, MA: Harvard University Press.

Rabin M. (1993) 'Incorporating Fairness into Game Theory', *American Economic Review*, vol. 83(5), pp. 1281–302.

Sacconi, L. (1991), *Etica degli affari, individui, imprese e mercati nella prospettiva dell'etica razionale*. Milano: Il Saggiatore.

Sacconi, L. (2000) *The Social Contract of the Firm: Economics, Ethics and Organisation*. Berlin: Springer Verlag.

Sacconi, L. (2006a) 'A Social Contract Account For CSR as Extended Model of Corporate Governance (I): Rational Bargaining and Justification', *Journal of Business Ethics*, vol. 68(3), pp. 259–81.

Sacconi, L. (2006b) 'CSR as a Model of Extended Corporate Governance, an Explanation Based on the Economic Theories of Social Contract, Reputation and Reciprocal Conformism', in F. Cafaggi (ed.), *Reframing Self-regulation in European Private Law*. London: Kluwer Law International.

Sacconi, L (2007a) 'A Social Contract Account for CSR as Extended Model of Corporate Governance (II): Compliance, Reputation and Reciprocity', *Journal of Business Ethics*, no. 75, pp. 77–96.

Sacconi, L. (2007b) 'Incomplete Contracts and Corporate Ethics: A Game Theoretic Model Under Fuzzy Information', in F. Cafaggi, A. Nicita and U. Pagano (eds), *Legal Orderings and Economic Institutions*. London: Routledge.

Sacconi, L. (2008) 'CSR as Contractarian Model of Multi-Stakeholder Corporate Governance and the Game-Theory of its Implementation'. Discussion paper no. 18/2008 del Dipartimento di economia, Università di Trento.

Sacconi, L. (2010) 'A Rawlsian View of CSR and the Game Theory of its Implementation (Part III): Conformism and Equilibrium Selection', in L. Sacconi and G. Degli Antoni (eds), *Social Capital, Corporate Social Responsibility, Economic Behavior and Performance*. Basingstoke: Palgrave Macmillan (in print).

Sacconi, L. and G. Degli Antoni (2010) 'Modeling Cognitive Social Capital and CSR as Preconditions for Sustainable Networks of Cooperative Relations', in L. Sacconi and G. Degli Antoni (eds), *Social Capital, Corporate Social Responsibility, Economic Behaviour and Performance*. Basingstoke: Palgrave Macmillan.

Sacconi, L. and M. Faillo (2010) 'Conformity, Reciprocity and the Sense of Justice. How Social Contract-based Preferences and Beliefs Explain Norm Compliance: the Experimental Evidence', *Constitutional Political Economy*, vol. 21(1), pp. 171–201.

Simon, H. (1951) 'A Formal Theory of Employment Relationship', *Econometrica*, vol. 19, pp. 293–305.

Stout, L. (2006) 'Social Norms and Other-Regarding Preferences', in J.N. Drobak (ed.), *Norms and the Law* Cambridge: Cambridge University Press.

Tirole, J. (2001) 'Corporate Governance', *Econometrica*, vol. 69(1), pp. 1–35.

Vanberg, V.J. (1992) 'Organizations as Constitutional Order', *Constitutional Political Economy*, vol. 3(2), pp. 223–55.

Williamson, O. (1975) *Market and Hierarchies*. New York: The Free Press.

Yaary, IM.E. and M. Bar-Hillel (1984) 'On Dividing Justly', *Social Choice and Welfare*, vol. 1, 1–24.

Zingales, L. and R. Rajan (2000) 'The Governance of the New Enterprise', in X. Vives (ed.), *Corporate Governance: Theoretical and Empirical Perspectives*. Cambridge: Cambridge University Press.

Part I

Nature of the Firm and its Governance Structure: Human Asset Specificity, Team Production and the Stakeholder Approach

1
Corporate Governance: A Contractual and Organizational Perspective

*Oliver E. Williamson**

The much-heralded transformation of corporate governance by 'intellectual currents in finance and economics and new transactional developments' (Romano, 2005a, p. 359) notwithstanding, corporate governance controversies continue. This chapter uses the lens of contract/governance to examine the huge disparities between the theory of the board of directors as vigilant safeguard for the interests of the equity investors and the board of directors in practice.[1] What is responsible for these disparities? How should they be interpreted? What should be done?

I begin the chapter with a sketch of 'pragmatic methodology'. The lens of contract/governance is then described in section 2 and applied to the paradigm problem with which transaction costs economics has been concerned – namely, vertical integration. Applications to finance and labor are set out in section 3, where the theory of the board of directors as active monitor is set out. Boards in practice are then examined in section 4. Reasons for the disparities between theory and practice are examined in section 5 and a modulated theory is proposed. The hazards of downside drift and capture are discussed in section 6. Conclusions follow.

1 A framework

Corporate governance is a vast subject to which business and legal practitioners, policy wonks, and all of the social sciences have contributed. Out of this vast buzzing, blooming confusion, where does the essence reside? How do we sort the sheep from the goats?

* This chapter has benefited from the remarks of those who attended the presentation of the paper at the University of Paris X (May 2006) and the suggestions of Robert Seamans.

3

Because 'any direction you proceed in has a very high a priori probability of being wrong' when studying poorly understood and complex phenomena, of which corporate governance is one, 'it is good if other people are exploring in other directions' (Simon, 1992, p. 21). Such pluralism does not, however, imply that anything goes. Some good ideas turn out to be a dead end. Yet that too is instructive if 'science ... advances primarily by unsuccessful experiments that clear the ground' (Friedman, 1997, p. 196). But then how are we to judge experimental success?

Describing himself as a native informant rather than as a certified methodologist, Robert Solow's 'terse description of what one economist thinks he is doing' (2001, p. 111) takes the form of three precepts: keep it simple; get it right; make it plausible. Keeping it simple is accomplished by stripping away inessentials, thereby to focus on first order effects – the 'main case', as it were – after which qualifications, refinements and extensions can be introduced. Getting it right entails working out the logic. And making it plausible means to eschew fanciful constructions.

Solow observes with reference to the simplicity precept that 'the very complexity of real life ... [is what] makes simple models so necessary' (2001, p. 111). Inasmuch as 'the social sciences ... deal with phenomena of the greatest complexity' (Simon, 1957, p. 89), with which view E.O. Wilson concurs (1999, p. 183), there is no realistic prospect of explaining everything. But there is more to it than a concession to bounded rationality: 'Most phenomena are driven by a very few central forces. What a good theory does is to simplify, it pulls out the central forces and gets rid of the rest' (Friedman, 1997, p. 196). The object is to uncover central features and key regularities by the application of a *focused lens*.

Getting it right 'includes translating economic concepts into accurate mathematics (or diagrams, or words) and making sure that further logical operations are correctly performed and verified' (Solow, 2001, p. 112). Especially in the public policy arena (but also more generally), one of these further logical operations is to ascertain whether putative 'inefficiencies' survive comparative institutional scrutiny. Because any display of inefficiency simultaneously represents an opportunity for mutual gain, the parties to such transactions have an incentive to relieve inefficiencies (in cost-effective degree). What are the obstacles? What is the best feasible result?

Plausible simple models of complex phenomena ought 'to make sense for "reasonable" or "plausible" values of the important parameters' (Solow, 2001, p. 112). In addition, because 'not everything that is logically consistent is credulous' (Kreps, 1999, p. 125), fanciful constructions that lose contact with the phenomena are suspect – especially if alternative and more veridical models yield refutable implications that are congruent with the data.

This last brings me to a fourth precept: derive refutable implications to which the relevant (often microanalytic) data are brought to bear. Nicholas

Georgescu-Roegen had a felicitous way of putting it: 'The purpose of science in general is not prediction, but knowledge for its own sake', yet prediction is 'the touchstone of scientific knowledge' (1971, p. 37).

To be sure, new theories rarely appear full blown but evolve through a progression during which the theory and evidence are interactive (Newell, 1990, p. 14):

> Theories cumulate. They are refined and reformulated, corrected and expanded. Thus, we are not living in the world of Popper ... [Theories are not] shot down with a falsification bullet ... Theories are more like graduate students – once admitted you try hard to avoid flunking them out ... Theories are things to be nurtured and changed and built up.

Sooner or later, however, the time comes for the reckoning. All would-be theories need to stand up and be counted.

2 The lens of contract/governance[2]

2.1 Key concepts

Whereas most contractual theories of economic organization focus on *ex ante* incentive alignment, the lens of contract/governance focuses predominantly on the *ex post* governance of ongoing contractual relations. Three conceptual features are noteworthy in this connection.

First, the lens of contract approach to economic organization is congruent with James Buchanan's remark that 'mutuality of advantage from voluntary exchange ... is the most fundamental of all understanding in economics' (2001, p. 29). The lens of contract/governance attempts to implement this by joining it with a reformulation of the problem of economic organization that had earlier been advanced by John R. Commons: 'the ultimate unit of activity ... must contain in itself the three principles on conflict, mutuality and order. This unit is a transaction' (Commons, 1932, p. 4). Not only does the lens of contract/governance take the transaction to be the basic unit of analysis, but governance is viewed as the means by which to infuse *order*, thereby to mitigate *conflict* and realize *mutual gains*.

Second, and pertinent to this emphasis on governance, adaptation is taken to be the main problem of economic organization, of which two kinds are distinguished: autonomous adaptations in the market that are elicited by changes in relative prices (Hayek, 1945) and coordinated adaptations of a 'conscious, deliberate, purposeful kind' accomplished with the support of hierarchy (Barnard, 1938). Conditional on the attributes of transactions, adaptations of both kinds are important – which is to say that the combined study of both markets *and* hierarchies (rather than the old ideological divide between markets *or* hierarchies) results.

Third, as among the various purposes served by economic organization, the lens of contract/governance holds that that economizing on transaction costs is the main case, broadly in the spirit of Frank Knight's observation that (1941, p. 252; emphasis added):

> Men in general, and within limits, wish to behave economically, to make their activities *and their organization* 'efficient' rather than wasteful. This fact does deserve the utmost emphasis; and an adequate definition of the science of economics ... might well make it explicit that the main relevance of the discussion is found in its relation to social policy, assumed to be directed toward the end indicated, of increasing economic efficiency, of reducing waste.

The austere challenge of operationalizing these concepts is thereupon posed. Transaction cost economics responds by making explicit provision for the attributes of human actors that bear on contracting. Specifically, all complex contracts are incomplete (by reason of bounded rationality), some contracts are subject to defection hazards (by reason of opportunism), and parties are endowed with 'feasible foresight', thereby to look ahead and uncover possible hazards. In addition, whereas the details of firm and market organization are scanted under the lens of choice set-ups, the microanalytics of both governance structures and transactions come under scrutiny when examined through the lens of contract. Thus firm and market are described as alternative modes of governance that differ in discrete structural ways. Specifically, each generic mode of governance (market, hybrid, hierarchy) is defined as a syndrome of attributes (which differ in incentive intensity, administrative control, and contract law respects) that give rise to different adaptive strengths and weaknesses.

Of these attribute differences, I call attention here principally to the way in which contract law regimes vary across modes. By contrast with economic orthodoxy, which implicitly assumes that there is a single, all-purpose law of contract that is costlessly enforced by well-informed courts, the lens of contract treats court ordering as a special case and gives prominence to private ordering, the mechanisms of which vary among alternative modes of governance.

Specifically, whereas the contract law of markets is legalistic (and corresponds to the ideal transaction in both law and economics, in that both parties can readily turn to alternative suppliers and buyers should the transaction break down), hybrid transactions and, especially, hierarchical transactions are ones for which continuity is valued. Legal rules thus give way to the more elastic concept of 'contract as framework' for hybrid transactions, where the framework 'never accurately indicates real working relations, but ... affords a rough indication around which such relations vary, an occasional guide in cases of doubt, and a norm of ultimate appeal when the relations cease in fact to work' (Llewellyn, 1931, p. 736).[3]

The conscious, deliberate, purposeful adaptations to which Barnard referred are realized through administration. These entail taking transactions out of markets and organizing them internally – to which the contract law of internal organization applies. Except as 'fraud, illegality or conflict of interest' are shown, courts have the good sense to refuse to hear disputes that arise within firms – with respect, for example, to transfer pricing, overhead, accounting, the costs to be ascribed to intra-firm delays, failures of quality, and the like. In effect, the contract law of internal organization is that of *forbearance*, according to which the firm becomes its own court of ultimate appeal (Williamson, 1991). Firms for this reason are able to exercise fiat that markets cannot.[4]

Upon naming the transaction as the basic unit of analysis, the critical attributes of transactions (for governance structure purposes) are: (1) the condition of asset specificity, in that such assets cannot be redeployed to alternative uses and users without loss of productive value; (2) the disturbances (uncertainty) to which contracts are subject; and (3) the frequency with which transactions recur. Differential contractual hazards are traced principally to the value of continuity, which vary directly with asset specificity, in conjunction with disturbances to which cooperative adaptations are needed.

2.2 The simple contractual schema

The predicted relation between transactions and modes of governance is derived from application of the discriminating alignment hypothesis – to wit, transactions, which differ in their attributes, are aligned with governance structures, which differ in their cost and competence, so as to effect a transaction cost economizing alignment. The paradigm transaction is vertical integration (or, in more mundane terms, the make-or-buy decision). Not only is vertical integration the obvious candidate transaction (Coase, 1937), but it is a fortuitous choice because transactions in the intermediate product market *are less beset with asymmetries of information, budget, legal talent, risk aversion, and the like* than are many other transactions. It is nevertheless gratifying that the simple contractual schema applies both to intermediate product market transactions and (with variation) to the study of transactions more generally.

With reference to vertical integration, assume that a firm can make or buy a component and assume further that the component can be supplied by either a general purpose technology or a special purpose technology. Letting k be a measure of asset specificity, the transactions in Figure 1.1 that use the general purpose technology are ones for which $k = 0$. In this case, no specific assets are involved and the parties are essentially faceless. Transactions that use the special purpose technology are those for which $k > 0$. Such transactions give

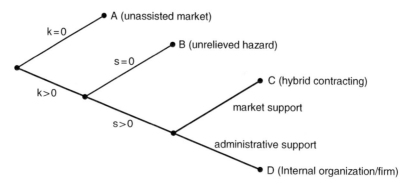

Figure 1.1 Private sector organization

rise to bilateral dependencies, in that the parties have incentives to promote continuity, thereby to safeguard specific investments. Let s denote the magnitude of any such safeguards, which include penalties, information disclosure and verification procedures, specialized dispute resolution (such as arbitration) and, at the limit, integration of the two stages under unified ownership. An s = 0 condition is one for which no safeguards are provided; a decision to provide safeguards is reflected by an s > 0 result.

Node A in Figure 1.1 corresponds to the ideal transaction in law and economics: there being an absence of dependency, governance is accomplished through competition and, in the event of disputes, by court awarded damages. Node B poses unrelieved contractual hazards, in that specialized investments are exposed (k > 0) for which no safeguards (s = 0) have been provided. Such hazards will be recognized by farsighted players, who will price out the implied risks.

Added contractual supports (s > 0) are provided at Nodes C and D. At Node C, these contractual supports take the form of inter-firm contractual safeguards. Should, however, costly breakdowns continue in the face of best bilateral efforts to craft safeguards at Node C, the transaction may be taken out of the market and organized under unified ownership (vertical integration) instead. Because added bureaucratic costs accrue upon taking a transaction out of the market and organizing it internally, internal organization is usefully thought of as the *organization form of last resort*: try markets, try hybrids, and have recourse to the firm only when all else fails. Node D, the unified firm, thus comes in only as higher degrees of asset specificity and added uncertainty pose greater needs for cooperative adaptation.

Note that the price that a supplier will bid to supply under Node C conditions will be less than the price that will be bid at Node B. That is, because the added security features at Node C serve to reduce the contractual hazard, as compared with Node B, so the contractual hazard premium will be reduced. One implication is that *suppliers do not need to petition buyers to provide safeguards*. Because buyers will receive goods and services on better terms (lower price) when added security is provided, buyers have the incentive to offer credible commitments.

Not only, moreover, does the simple contractual schema inform make-or-buy decisions, the repeated application of which permits the boundary of the firm to be derived, but any issue that arises as or can be construed as a contracting problem can be examined to advantage in very similar efficient governance terms – although additional complications sometimes accrue.

3 Applications to finance and labor

3.1 Debt and equity as governance structures

Debt and equity are normally thought of as modes of finance, but they are also usefully viewed as alternative modes of governance. Expressed in transaction cost economics terms, the basic regularity is this: debt is well-suited to finance generic assets that can be redeployed to alternative uses and users with little loss of productive value whereas equity is reserved for financing specific assets for which continuity (in the same uses and by the same users) is valued.[5]

Arrayed by increasing degree of asset specificity, suppose that a firm is seeking to finance the following: general-purpose, mobile equipment; a general-purpose office building located in a population center; a general-purpose plant located in a manufacturing center; distribution facilities located somewhat more remotely; special-purpose equipment; market and product development expenses; and the like. Also assume that the governance structure for debt requires the debtor to observe the following stylized rules: (1) stipulated interest payments will be made at regular intervals; (2) the business will continuously meet certain liquidity tests; (3) sinking funds will be set up and principal repaid at the loan-expiration date; and (4), in the event of default, the debt-holders will exercise pre-emptive claims against the assets in question. If everything goes well, interest and principal will be paid on schedule. But debt is unforgiving if things go poorly. Failure to make scheduled payments thus results in liquidation. The various debt-holders will then realize differential recovery in the degree to which the assets in question are redeployable.

Specifically, debt works well for projects for which k = 0 and rules-based governance applies. This corresponds to Node A in the simple contractual schema. As, however, the value of k increases, the value of liquidation claims declines and the terms of debt finance will be adjusted adversely (as at Node B). Confronted with the prospect that specialized investments will be financed on adverse terms, the firm might respond by sacrificing some of the specialized investment features in favor of greater redeployability. But this entails tradeoffs: production costs may increase or quality decrease as a result. Might it be possible to avoid these by inventing a new governance structure of a Node C kind to which mutual gains (added continuity and adaptability in exchange for added safeguards) can be projected? In the degree to which this is feasible, the value-enhancing benefits of investments in specific assets could thereby be preserved.

Suppose that a financial instrument called equity is invented and assume that equity has the following governance properties: (1) it bears a residual-claimant status to the firm in both earnings and asset-liquidation respects; (2) it contracts for the duration of the life of the firm; and (3) a board of directors is created and awarded to equity that (a) is elected by the pro rata votes of those who hold tradable shares, (b) has the power to replace the management, (c) decides on management compensation, (d) has access to internal performance measures on a timely basis, (e) can authorize audits in depth for special follow-up purposes, (f) is apprised of important investment and operating proposals before they are implemented, and (g) in other respects bears what Eugene Fama and Michael Jensen refer to as a decision-review and monitoring relation to the firm's management (1983).

The board of directors thus serves as a credible commitment, the effect of which is to reduce the cost of capital for projects that involve limited redeployability. Not only do the added controls to which equity has access have better assurance properties, but equity is more forgiving than debt. Efforts are therefore made to work things out and realize adaptive benefits that would otherwise be sacrificed when disturbances push the parties into a maladapted state of affairs.[6]

What, if anything, however, is to be made of Node D in the simple contractual schema, where Node D refers to taking transactions out of the market and organizing them internally? Albeit a bit of a stretch, Node D finance is akin to retained earnings. Because such finance is decided upon internally and is not subject to normal market tests, such finance should be reserved for projects that are especially difficult for outsiders to evaluate – of which research and development is an example. Retained earnings, like the decision to make rather than buy in the intermediate product market, should be thought of as the financial option of last resort.[7]

3.2 The board as monitor: double feedback

W. Ross Ashby's model of double feedback (1960) and Herbert Simon's examination of the architecture of complexity (1962, 1973) are broadly consonant with the proposition that adaptation is the central problem of economic organization. Ashby established that all adaptive systems that have a capacity to respond to a bimodal distribution of disturbances – some being disturbances in degree; others being disturbances in kind – will be characterized by double feedback. As shown in Figure 1.2, disturbances of both kinds originate in the environment (E). The feedback divide is this: operating decisions are made and implemented in the primary feedback loop by the reacting part (R) with the benefit of extant decision rules whereas strategic decisions of a more

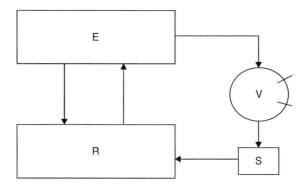

Figure 1.2 Double feedback

consequential and longer-run kind are processed through the essential vari-ables (V) and the step functions (S) in the secondary feedback loop.

In effect, the reacting part (R) works out of the presumption that successive state realizations are variations in degree to which the application of extant routines will yield an efficacious response. Indeed, the routines employed by the operating part remain unchanged so long as performance falls within the control limits on the essential variables (V) in the secondary feedback loop. If and as, however, performance falls outside of these control limits, the secondary feedback loop interprets this as a disturbance in kind for which new routines (changes in parameter values or new rules) are needed to restore performance to acceptable levels. These changes are introduced into the reacting part as step functions (S). So described, the primary feedback loop is implementing extant decision rules in real time in a mechanical way whereas the secondary feedback loop is activated episodically by changes in kind (and possibly with reference to longer-run (strategic) considerations). Evolutionary systems that are subject to such bimodal disturbances will, under natural selection, necessarily develop two readily distinguishable feedbacks (Ashby, 1960, p. 131).

Simon's discussion of the organizational division of decision-making labor in the firm is in the same spirit. From 'the information processing point of view, division of labor means factoring the total system of decisions that need to be made into relatively independent subsystems, each one of which can be designed with only minimal concern for its interaction with the others' (Simon, 1973, p. 270). That is accomplished by grouping the operating parts into separable enti-ties within which interactions are strong and between which they are weak and by making temporal distinctions of a strategic versus operating kind. Problems are thus factored in such a way that the higher-frequency (or short-run) dynamics are associated with the operating parts while the lower-frequency (or long-run) dynamics are associated with the strategic system (Simon, 1962, p. 477).

So where does the board of directors fit within this double-feedback scheme of organization?[8] A simple interpretation of the secondary feedback loop is to view the board as being located at the essential variables (V), where it performs decision-review and monitoring functions. If and as the essential variables are pushed outside of the control limits, the board signals the need for strategic adaptations to be made by the management, which is located at the step functions (S).

Thus whereas the reacting part (R) uses extant routines to respond to small and familiar disturbances in the environment (E) on a continuing basis, the secondary feedback loop deals with exceptions. Unless individual or successive disturbances push the essential variables (V) outside of their control limits, the board remains in a passive mode of nodding approval and the management advises the operating parts to continue business as usual. If and as disturbances push the essential variables outside their control limits, the board alerts the management to take corrective action.[9] Parameter changes or new routines are introduced into the reacting part with the purpose of restoring the essential variables to acceptable levels. The board then remains in a vigilant mode and monitors the efficacy of the management initiated changes. If and as the essential variables are brought back within the control limits, the board returns to its standby mode of nodding approval.

Albeit crude, this interpretation appears to *implement the conception of the board of directors as performance monitor.*

3.3   The contract with labor

Because the firm is unable to own its labor, Node D is irrelevant and the comparison comes down to Nodes A, B and C. Node A corresponds to the case where labor is easily redeployed to other uses or users without loss of product value (k = 0). Thus, although such labor may be highly skilled (as with many professionals), the lack of firm specificity means that, transition costs aside, neither worker nor firm has an interest in crafting penalties for unwanted quits/terminations or otherwise creating costly internal labor markets (ports of entry, promotion ladders), costly information disclosure and verification procedures, and costly firm-specific dispute settlement machinery. The mutual benefits do not warrant the costs.

Conditions change when k > 0, since workers who acquire firm-specific skills will lose value if prematurely terminated (and firms will incur added training costs if such employees quit). Here, as elsewhere, unrelieved hazards (as at Node B) will result in demands by workers for a hazards premium, and recurrent contractual impasses, by reason of conflict, will result in inefficiency. Because continuity has value to both firm and worker, governance features that deter termination (severance pay) and quits (nonvested benefits) and that address and settle disputes in an orderly way (grievance systems) to which the parties ascribe confidence have a lot to recommend them. These can, but need not, take the form of 'unions'. Whatever the name, the object is to craft a collective organizational structure (at Node C) in which the parties have mutual confidence and that enhances efficiency (Barron and Kreps, 1999, pp. 130–8; Williamson, 1975, pp. 27–80, 1985, pp. 250–62).

But so what? How does this inform our understanding of the finance transaction? As developed in section 5, comparing the governance of labor with the governance of equity provides useful perspective for interpreting the disparity between boards of directors in theory and boards in practice.

4   Boards in practice

Examining corporate finance through the lens of contract yields the result that the main purpose served by the board of directors is to safeguard equity investments, thereby to reduce the cost of capital, which function is discharged by the board serving as monitor. This benign interpretation is, I submit, an instructive place to begin. But how does this square with boards in practice? What are the disparities between the ideal board and actual boards? Not only do we need to know how things work in practice, but we need to understand the tradeoffs and obstacles, natural and contrived, if feasible and effective reforms are to be devised.[10]

4.1   Miles Mace (1971)

Mace's book, *Directors: Myth and Reality*, has the purpose of challenging the myths and telling the reality: 'As a participant on, and observer of, boards of directors for over 25 years, I have developed a healthy skepticism about the prevailing [mythical] concept of the board of directors. Specifically, it seemed important to ask what directors *actually do* in fulfillment of their responsibilities' (1971, p. 8; emphasis added).

His 'final summary' of directors in large and medium-sized firms where the CEO and board members own only a few shares of stock is this (Mace, 1971, pp. 205–6):

- [CEOs] with de facto powers of control select the members of the boards.
- [CEOs] determine what boards do and do not do.
- Directors selected are usually heads of equally prestigious organizations with primary responsibilities of their own.
- Heads of businesses and financial, legal, and educational organizations are extremely busy [people] with limited motivation and time to serve as directors of other organizations.
- Most boards of directors serve as advisors and counselors to the [CEOs].
- Most boards of directors serve as some sort of discipline for the organization – as a corporate conscience.

- Most boards of directors are available to and do make decisions in the event of a crisis.
- A few boards of directors establish company objectives, strategies, and broad policies. Most do not.
- A few boards of directors ask discerning questions. Most do not.
- A few boards evaluate and measure the performance of the president and select and de-select the president. Most do not.

Pertaining to item 3 on this list, Mace quotes from one executive as follows (1971, p. 90):

> The board is part of the image of the company. The caliber and stature of the outside board members, both just as names and as people circulating in the business community, contributes to the image of the company. When I look at a company, I look at who is on the board ... The type of people on a board does, in a series of informal and intangible ways, have a good deal to do with what the character of a company is. Is it a respectable and conservative company, or is it highly speculative? The investing public, you know, really care who is on the board.

In addition, Mace observes that one of the functions played by the board with respect to discipline and corporate conscience (item 6) is that the CEO and his subordinates 'know that periodically they must appear ... before a board of directors consisting of respected, able people of stature [who], no matter how friendly, cause the company organization to do a better job of thinking through their problems and of being prepared with solutions, explanations, or rationales' (1971, p. 180).

Such effects notwithstanding, Mace concludes that the role of the board as a corporate conscience is mixed (1971, p. 181):

> Usually the symbols of corporate conscience are more apparent than real, and [CEOs] with complete powers of control make the compensation policies and decisions. The compensation committee, and the board which approves the recommendations of the compensation committee, are not in most cases decision-making bodies. These decisions are made by the [CEO] and in most situations the committee and board approval is perfunctory. The [CEO] has de factor powers of control, and in most cases he is the decision maker. The board does, I believe, tend to temper the inclinations of [CEOs] with de facto control, and it does contribute to the avoidance of excesses. Thus it serves the important role of a corporate conscience.

With reference to item 10, Mace identifies two crisis situations where the role of the board of directors is more than advisory'. One is if the CEO were to die or become incapacitated; the second is if performance is 'so unsatisfactory that a change must be made' (1971, p. 182) – which recalls Oswald Knauth's view that 'the degree of success that management must produce to remain in office is surprisingly small. Indeed, management must fail obviously and even ignominiously before the dispersed forces of criticism become mobilized for action' (1948, p. 45).

4.2 Michael Jensen (1993)

Jensen opens his section on 'The Failure of Corporate Internal Control Systems' with the observation that 'By nature, organizations abhor control systems, and ineffective governance is a major part of the problem with internal control mechanisms. They seldom respond in the absence of a crisis' (1993, p. 852). He thereafter makes a series of observations about boards in practice and recommends how boards should be reformed. I take up the latter in section 6.

Jensen's main observations about boards in practice are these: (1) board culture typically emphasizes 'politeness and courtesy at the expense of truth and frankness' (p. 863); (2) the board has a serious information deficit and lacks financial expertise (p. 864); (3) legal liability encourages risk-averse behavior by boards (p. 864); (4) neither managers nor non-manager members of the board own substantial fractions of their firm's equity (p. 864); and (5) the board in a well-functioning organization will normally be inactive and exhibit little conflict. Jensen concludes that 'bad systems or rules, not bad people, underlie the general failings of boards of directors' (p. 863) and that the board 'becomes important primarily when the rest of the internal control system is failing' (p. 866).

Taken together, Mace and Jensen describe the board of directors in the large corporation as follows: (1) the CEO is in de facto control of the operation and composition of the board; (2) outside members of the board are at an enormous information and expertise disadvantage to the management; (3) most boards most of the time are responding with nodding approval; (4) boards can and often do move into a more active mode when the corporation experiences adversity; and (5) albeit unmentioned, the very existence of the board affords an opportunity for shareholders to 'vote the rascals out'.

4.3 Bengt Holmstrom and Steven Kaplan (2003)

Recent corporate governance scandals notwithstanding, Holmstrom and Kaplan contend that corporate governance underwent significant improvements during the 1980s and 1990s. Thus although they are dismayed that so many boards have approved anti-takeover measures, much as poison pills and staggered boards (2003, p. 15), and that some CEO compensation packages are outlandishly generous (p. 14), they have a generally favorable view of corporate governance changes that have taken place since the 1980s. Specifically, whereas it was common for corporate managements to 'think of themselves as representing not the shareholders, but rather ... [as] "balancing" the claims of all important corporate "stakeholders"' before 1980 when 'only 20% of the compensation of U.S. CEOs was tied to stock market performance' (p. 10), both have changed. Hostile takeovers and restructuring provided a wake-up call for complacent and inefficient firms in the 1980s, which restructuring has continued during the 1990s at the initiative of incumbent managements (p. 12). Contributing factors to the more recent restructurings have been the significant degree to which the equity based compensation of CEOs has increased (to almost 50 per cent of the total compensation of CEO by 1994) and the increase in share ownership of large institutional investors from under 30 per cent in 1980 to over 50 per cent in 1996 (pp. 12, 14). Indicative of these changes, the Business Roundtable in 1997 changed its position on business objectives to read 'the paramount duty of management and the board is to the shareholder and not to ... other stakeholders' (p. 13).[11] A downside of the increased executive stock and option ownership is that 'the incentive to manage and manipulate accounting numbers' has also increased (p. 13), to which the practice of post-dating options has recently been uncovered.

Overall, Holmstrom and Kaplan are of the view that corporate governance in the US not only compares favorably with other countries but that it has been getting better. They counsel that it should not be judged on the basis of worst excesses – as at Enron, WorldCom, Tyco, Adelphia, Global Crossing, and others (p. 8).

Even so, there is no denying that boards in practice do not closely track the boards in theory that are described in subsection 3.2. So what is responsible for the disparities? What changes in the contract between the firm and the equity investors would be needed in order to accomplish the putative purpose of having the board serve as vigilant monitor? Would other valued purposes be sacrificed? What are the ramifications for board design?

5   Theory and practice disparities examined

Confronted with the disparities between the theory of the board as credible commitment instrument for the shareholders and the practice of the board as being (normally) under the effective control of the CEO, what are we to conclude? Three possible explanations suggest themselves:

1. The theory is right but the implementation mechanisms are seriously defective, as a consequence of which the legitimate purposes of the board of directors have been seriously compromised.
2. The theory is right as far as it goes, but it does not go far enough.
3. The theory is wrong.

My discussion addresses the first two.

5.1 The mechanisms of implementation

The logics for governing contracts in the intermediate product market, finance and labor were set out in sections 2 and 3. The intermediate product market was included because this transaction was the obvious paradigm problem, both because it was simpler and because of the intellectual history of transaction cost economics. The finance transaction was examined because of its centrality to the study of corporate governance. But why examine the contract for labor?

The reason for including labor is that labor, like equity finance, is confronted with serious collective action problems. Interestingly, labor and finance have solved these collective action problems very differently. If the mechanisms for governance that have been set up in support of labor transactions work relatively well while those that support equity finance are weak, why not reshape that governance of equity finance along the lines of labor?

Table 1.1 sets out the key features of contract between the firm (the 'buyer') and suppliers of intermediate product, equity finance, and labor – all on the assumption that the suppliers make non-redeployable investments ($k > 0$) for which contractual hazards are posed. Each supplier is assumed to name the break even price at which trade will take place, given whatever security arrangements the parties have worked out.

Note that intermediate product market transactions are one-on-one contracts for which each party can be presumed to be well informed and in possession of the requisite expertise. Credible contracting can be presumed to work well for such transactions. By contrast, equity finance and labor are many-on-one transactions to which 'the many' need to develop a collective action machinery. The board of directors (elected by the pro rata votes of the shareholders) serves this role for equity finance. The labor union performs this function for the workers. But note the vast differences between these two instruments of collective action: the leadership of the union is elected by the workers, the union is funded by the workers, information and expertise asymmetries between firm and workers are greatly reduced as a consequence, specialized dispute settlement mechanisms are carefully crafted, and other graduated mechanisms are operative; by contrast, the leadership of the board and the leadership of the firm are usually one and the same (the CEO), the board has no independent source of funds, the board is at a disadvantage to the management in information and expertise respects, the board eschews conflict and has access to only drastic measures for relief.

In consideration of all of the disadvantages that the suppliers of equity finance have in comparison to labor, why not use the governance of labor as the template for equity finance? Since, after all, the suppliers of finance are the owners of the firm, surely the owners can direct the firm to provide the funds for the board to hire qualified staff for the board, thereby to rectify the conditions of information and expertise asymmetries. And surely the board can insist that the

Table 1.1 Governance comparisons among alternative types of transactions

	Suppliers of		
Bargaining Relation to the Buyer	Intermediate Product	Equity Finance	Labor
Numbers Collective Action Unit	one-on-one unneeded	many-on-one board of directors	many-on-one labor union
Leadership of Collection Action Decided by	unneeded	CEO	workers
Funding for Collective Action Provided by	unneeded	the firm	the workers (dues)
Information Asymmetry	parity	greatly disadvantaged	~ parity
Expertise Asymmetry	parity	greatly disadvantaged	~ parity
Dispute Resolution Mechanisms	information disclosure and verification; arbitration	board meetings; annual meetings	grievance machinery; arbitration
Other Protection For Suppliers	penalty payments	remove CEO; takeover	penalty payments (e.g., severance); collective bargaining; slowdown; strike

chair of the board be one of their own rather than the CEO. Once, moreover, the board has a backup staff to supply information and expertise, it can participate more knowledgeably in strategic decision-making. Indeed, powers could also be devolved upon the shareholders to propose and vote binding resolutions.[12] Inasmuch as such reforms would appear to entail modest costs and would go a long way toward redressing the separation of ownership from control that has beset corporate governance over the past century, what are the obstacles?

The obvious obstacle is that such reforms would be vigorously resisted by the management. But why should such resistance prevail? An enlightened ownership that now understands why it has been so ineffectual and what needs to be done can presumably make the case to roll over incumbent managements.

Indeed, if there are mutual gains to be made upon moving from what can be presumed to be a Node B outcome (current practice) to a Node C credible contracting outcome (proposed practice), why don't the incumbent managers pre-empt the prospective assault from equity by proposing the reform itself and realizing for itself much of the gain? An obvious obstacle here is that the management cannot propose such a reform without admitting to prior and ongoing abuse of its delegated responsibilities; and the board could not accept such a proposal without confessing to its complicity. Better to leave well enough alone – in which event the directors will continue, as Lucien Bebchuk and Jesse Fried (2004) contend, 'to collude with CEOs rather than accomplish their role of guardian of shareholders' interests' (Tirole, 2006, p. 32). Still, if the benefits are sufficiently great, the extant inefficiency cannot stand. New firms will appear that will adopt the superior mechanisms from the outset, which poses a competitive threat. Or reforms that the firm refuses to originate might be imposed by takeover or regulation.

5.2 Trade-offs

The puzzle of persistent inefficiency nevertheless raises the possibility that there are unexamined trade-offs. The one on which I will focus is that the mechanisms that I have ascribed to the 'activist board' are very intrusive and prospectively *compromise the integrity of delegation*. Andrei Shleifler and Robert Vishny raise some of the pertinent issues as follows (1997, p. 741):

> In principle, one could imagine a contract in which the financiers give funds to the manager on the condition that they retain all the residual control rights. Any time something unexpected happens, they get to decide what to do. But this does not quite work, for the simple reason that the financiers are not qualified or informed enough to decide what to do – the very reason they hired the manager in the first place.

To be sure, the reformed board that I describe does not contemplate that the board 'gets to decide what to do' when the unexpected occurs. The board that I describe is, however, informed by its own staff, rather than the management, when the essential variables are outside of their control limits; and the board evaluates the efficacy of management responses in an informed and nuanced way. Indeed, the board could engage the management in an extended discussion on the merits before some actions are taken – to include the possibility that some proposed actions are revised or rejected.

Thus although the board does not by itself 'decide what to do', the board is actively involved in a dialog with the management when the essential variables go outside of the control limits. LBOs and start-ups aside, this is a much more intrusive role for the board than is currently played by boards. Interestingly, however, Jensen takes the position that leveraged buyouts and venture capital funds presage the future for effectively redesigning the board in the modern corporation (1993, p. 869):

> LBO associations and venture capital funds provide a blueprint for managers and boards who wish to revamp their top-level control systems to make

them more efficient. LBOs and venture capital funds are, of course, the preeminent examples of active investors in recent U.S. history, and they serve as excellent models that can be emulated in part or in total by virtually any corporation. The two have similar governance structures, and have been successful in resolving the governance problems of both slow growth or declining firms (LBO associations) and high growth entrepreneurial firms (venture capital funds).

I contend instead that LBOs and venture capital firms are evanescent forms of organization that possess properties that are non-replicable in the ongoing modern corporation. Both feature concentrated ownership and high-powered incentives that cannot be sustained once the project succeeds (or fails, as the case may be). LBOs and start-ups are both variants upon Rudolf Spreckels' remark that 'When I see something badly done, or not done at all, I see an opportunity to make a fortune.'

The LBO sees something badly done, mobilizes financing, pays the requisite premium to gain control of the firm, replaces the incumbent management, and reshapes the firm and its financing. Thus debt is substituted for equity, thereby to restore a more efficient mix of debt and equity in relation to the firm's assets,[13] and unrelated or underperforming parts are sold or spun off. The big reward comes when the firm is taken public again.[14] In the interim, the new management and the banks, insurance companies, and investment bankers that package the deal are *actively involved* in the management and reshaping of the corporation. Once the firm goes public, the high-powered incentives and the premium upon real-time responsiveness give way to a steady-state modern corporation with managers (rather than financial entrepreneurs) at the helm, lower powered incentives, and diffuse ownership. (If, in the fullness of time, many of the benefits of LBOs are undone by backsliding, the LBO process could be repeated.)

Start-up firms, especially of those in the area of high technology, may also be aimed at improvements on something badly done but more often arise out of perceived opportunities to provide something altogether new (Shane, 2001). These latter are high-risk undertakings that combine venture capitalists with entrepreneurial, technical, and legal talent in a race to be first. High-powered incentives and real-time involvement by all of the critical actors (as managers or directors) are practiced.[15] If and as the start-up succeeds, the big rewards are realized when the firm goes public. Thereafter, the firm progressively takes on the characteristics of a business-as-usual enterprise, as more of the action devolves to the primary feedback loop as routines set in.[16]

Not only, therefore, is going public where the big rewards are realized, but once an LBO or start-up firm is taken public it thereafter undergoes a change in kind. (It is as if the crucial first leg of the race is assigned to athletes who run the 100 yard dash, who then pass the baton not to another sprinter but to a long distance runner instead.) Note, moreover, that this reflects the objective needs of the firm rather than the exhaustion of the transition team. Continued active involvement in the management of the firm by the transition team or their successors beyond the time at which the firm has crossed the threshold of competitive viability is not only unneeded but will be counterproductive if, as I contend, high-velocity and steady-state operations differ in kind. Figure 1.3 is illustrative.

Two stages are distinguished: the transition stage (where the outside owner-ship is concentrated, possesses specialized expertise, and is actively involved in helping to implement real time adaptations in a high-velocity, high-risk environment) and the mature stage (where diffuse ownership supplants concentrated ownership, professional managers move to the helm, risks are reduced, and the occasion for novel adaptations gives way to routines). The active involvement of the board in the mature stage can not only result in over-monitoring and induce management to focus on short-run performance (as discussed in agency-theoretic terms by Tirole (2006) and others)[17] but the dual-management capability that would attend the creation of an activist board (of the kind that I describe in section 5.1) could degrade the performance of the firm by inviting conflict with the professional management, as a result of which confusion, delay, and demoralization set in.

As interpreted with reference to delegation, whereas the optimal degree of outside ownership involvement peaks at r_1^* for the transition stage, the peak drops to r_2^* for the mature firm. Implicit to the argument is the assumption that organization, like the law, has a life of its own (which I discuss further in section 6) and that students of organization need to come to terms with this condition. An implication, with reference to the foregoing, is this: the time for

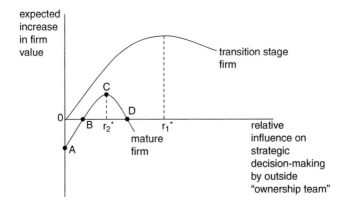

Figure 1.3 Stage-related benefits of outside 'control'

taking an LBO or start-up public cannot be pushed off into the distant future without sacrificing incentive intensity. To the contrary, as the restructuring and innovative purposes of these firms get resolved, the window of opportunity begins to close. LBO sponsors (such as KKR) thus cash out and look for other firms where restructuring benefits reside and successful entrepreneurs either take on managerial functions (in the now successful start-ups) or look to deploy their entrepreneurial talents elsewhere. To everything, as it were, there is a season.

More importantly, whereas it is common to condemn the 'structural weaknesses' that beset the contract between the suppliers of equity finance and the firm (as shown in Table 1.1), those weaknesses now take on a new meaning: they have the purpose in part of preserving the *integrity of delegation*. Lest the quasi-autonomy of delegates be compromised by delegants who (wittingly or unwittingly) slip into an activist mode, contractual safeguards for the delegates (managers) are needed as well as contractual safeguards for the delegants (stockholders). The vexing problem is how to do this without undue sacrifice to the *integrity of monitoring*. What are the properties of a modulated board? And what are the downside hazards?

6   The downside

I will take it that a modulated board has limited monitoring capabilities, is predisposed to work with the management in a supportive way, yet can exercise real power (to include replacing the CEO for unacceptable performance and acceding to takeover if the terms are judged to be favorable for the ownership if not the management). That sounds very much like many actual boards. End of story?

Not really. The problem is that boards which, by design, are structurally weak are also susceptible to capture. Indeed, the negative region (between points A and B) on the mature firm curve is one where the board has been seriously compromised. To be sure, that is not an inevitable result. There are nevertheless reasons to expect that the structural weaknesses in the contract between equity and the firm will frequently be resolved in favor of the full-time leadership of the firm as compared with the part-time board.

Robert Michels's famous Iron Law of Oligarchy is pertinent in this context: 'It is organization which gives birth to the dominion of the elected over the electors, of the mandatories over the mandators, of the delegates over the delegators. Who says organization, says oligarchy' (1915 [1962], p. 365). Philip Selznick subsequently elaborated (1966, pp. 9–10; emphasis added):

> … if we recognize that all administrative officials are bureaucrats, the bishop no less than the tax collector, then we may be able to understand the general nature of the problem, separating it from the personal qualities or motives of the individuals involve. Officials, like other individuals, must take heed of

the conditions of their existence. Those conditions are, for officials, *organizational*: in attempting to exercise some control over their own work and future they are offered the opportunity of manipulating personnel, funds, and symbols. Among the many varied consequences of this manipulation, the phenomena of inefficiency and arbitrariness are ultimately among the least significant. The difference between officials and ordinary members of an organized group is that the former have a special access to and power over the machinery of the organization; while those outside the bureaucratic ranks lack that access and power.

If we are to comprehend these bureaucratic machines ..., it is essential to think of an organization as a dynamic conditioning field which effectively shapes the behavior of those who are attempting to remain at the helm.

The basic regularity is this: 'in the exercise of discretion there is a tendency for decisions to be qualified by the special goals and problems of those to whom delegation is made' (Selznick, 1966, p. 258).

Specifically, if the original contract provided for participation by the board in degree r_2^* in Figure 1.3, there are natural and contrived forces that will tend to push the de facto degree of board involvement to the left. An example of a natural force is Karl Marx's description of the transformation of the handicraft mode of organization into hierarchy by reason of adapting to disturbances the 'accidental repetition [of which] gets repeated, develops advantages of its own, and gradually ossifies' (1967, p. 337). More often, I conjecture, and certainly more ominous are changes that are consciously introduced by CEOs in a strategic way, the cumulative effect of which is to transform the board into a compliant instrument of the management. Such boards not only do the bidding of the CEO but are reduced to apologists.

In consideration of the accidental or purposeful hazards of capture, what to do? Interestingly, Michels did not despair of democracy because the ideal would be compromised by oligarchy. Rather, he advised that 'nothing but a serene and frank examination of the oligarchical dangers of democracy will enable us to minimize these dangers' (Michels, 1962, p. 370). Similarly, I do not condemn boards because their structural weaknesses can lead to downside consequences. Rather, out of awareness that some of these structural weaknesses confer benefits on delegation,[18] I inquire into the possibility of avoiding the worst downside consequences. Problems of two kinds are posed. One is where a (possibly well-intentioned) board is misled by a management that massages and manipulates the data. The second goes to composition of the board effects.

Smoothing performance or, worse, 'hitting the numbers' (thereby to reap incentive compensation benefits) are examples of the first kind.[19] (The backdating of options is another more recent example of manipulation, although this is often done with the actual or tacit approval of the board.)

Examples of the second kind involve composition of the board effects. An obvious composition of the board concern is with the ratio of officers to independent board members, but the qualifications and predilections of independent board members are also pertinent. Those with and without business experience and expertise are usefully distinguished.

In principle, independent board members who possess financial or business expertise are better able to relate and have more to offer by way of sound judgment and informed critique than do those who are lacking in these respects. The objectivity of such independent board members can nevertheless be compromised if they are part of what Bang Nguyen-Dang refers to as 'corporate elite's small world ... [of] cross-directorships' (2005, p. 6), an illustration of which is executive compensation at Verizon, where 'Verizon's compensation committee ... consists of ... [four] chief executives or former chief executives', three of whom sit on other boards with the Verizon CEO (Morgenson, 2006, p. A16). This is by no means an isolated example (Bebchuk and Fried, 2004, chap. 2), moreover. Outside executives who possess the requisite expertise but lack objectivity – because of overlapping interests they are 'in this together' – compromise the board.[20]

A second class of problematic board members are those who, though lacking in expertise, possess 'gravitas'. Such board members can be expected to be more compliant: (1) as the ratio of board payments to their other income is higher; and (2) their susceptibility to indirect rewards – such as 'contributions' to the board member's place of employment (as with eleemosynary institutions), or to favored charities, or out of the prospect of reciprocity (e.g., procurement) from the board member's place of employment (Bebchuk and Fried, 2004, pp. 27–8) – is higher.[21]

To be sure, it is altogether understandable that a CEO would seek to appoint directors who are perceived to be 'compatible' (Barnard, 1938, p. 224). The possibility that insecure or grasping CEOs will cross the line from constructive support to using obeisance as a selection criterion is where the problem resides.

Downside drift, in either or both of these respects, is especially troublesome if boards that have once been compromised (have become the compliant instruments of the management) are unlikely to be restored to a principled status. In that event, added downside checks upon the modulated board warrant consideration. Without purporting to know that net benefits can reliably be projected,[22] the following list of possibilities is tentatively proposed:

1. Efforts should be undertaken to better assure the integrity of accounting procedures and reports;
2. Egregious lapses of integrity (back-dating of options; large undisclosed executive benefits) should become presumptive causes for termination;

3. The composition of the board should be scrutinized, with special attention to nominees of executives and professionals with close ties to the CEO and to independents who lack expertise and are susceptible to accepting, even seeking, membership in anticipation of favors;
4. As a matter of good public policy, state regulatory commissions should adopt default rules that remove poison pills, staggered boards, and other obstacles to takeover;[23]
5. The board should be co-chaired, one of the co-chairs being the CEO and the other an independent director.

Jensen takes a stronger position with respect to this last. He recommends that an independent member of the board rather than the CEO should be the chair (1993, p. 866). Plainly, removing the CEO from chair (or co-chair) status signals an intention to empower shareholders. And it might have precisely that effect – possibly with a confrontational result that compromises the efficacy of delegation.[24] Confrontational or not, most CEOs should not be expected to embrace such a change. One response would be to marginalize the board by reducing board meetings to a pro forma exercise. Discharging board recommendations in a minimally acceptable fashion is another. Inasmuch as Jensen's proposal can be implemented later if the co-chair 'teaming' of the CEO with an independent board member fails to have salutary effects, my suggestion is to try the co-chair option first.

Whatever, the list is merely suggestive and is by no means exhaustive. The basic points are these: downside drift is a serious concern if the integrity of the board is to be preserved; all reforms should be undertaken to the extent they are cost-effective; and all reforms should be mindful that the integrity of delegation needs to be factored into the calculus.[25]

7 Conclusions

The modern corporation is unquestionably a complex organization, a manifestation of which is the lack of agreement on the nature of and purposes served by the board of directors. The general strategy that I recommend for dealing with this (and other issues of complex economic organization) is to address the phenomena in a combined contractual and organizational way.

Inasmuch as the lens of contract/governance stands on the tripartite foundations of law, economics, and organization theory (Williamson, 1985, 1991, 2005), provision for organization is made at the outset.[26] But there is more: although the lens of contract/governance makes significant provision for organization theory, applications pose new challenges. Some of the general lessons need to be particularized; some additional regularities may have to be recognized; and the ramifications need to be worked out – often by appealing to efficiency considerations to push the logic to completion.

A recurrent theme of the governance of contractual relations is that mutual gains will be realized by crafting governance structures that mitigate hazards. In the context of corporate governance, the obvious lesson is that mutual gains will be realized by providing credible contracting safeguards for the equity investors (thereby to move the transaction from Node B to the more efficient Node C). The creation of a board of directors that is awarded to the equity investors to serve as monitor is responsive to that purpose.

A comparison of this theory of the board as monitor with the board in practice reveals serious disparities, one possible remedy for which is to use the contract with labor (which, like shareholders, also faces a collective action problem) as a template. This disclosed to me what may be obvious to others: a board of directors that is reshaped along these lines will create a dual-management capability, the effect of which will be to undermine the imperatives of effective delegation. The upshot is that the board of directors should be designed with reference to two purposes: provide the shareholders with a monitoring capability without undue sacrifice to the integrity of delegation.[27]

Two issues are thereby posed: how should such a board be described? And how can the properties of this board be preserved in the face of asymmetries of information, expertise, and initiative that favor the full-time management in relation to the part-time board members?

I describe the modulated board as one that (1) presumes that the normal relation between the leadership of the firm and the board is cooperative, yet (2) provides for periodic intervention by the board if and as the essential variables fall outside of control limits, (3) does not begrudge the information, expertise, and initiative asymmetries that the management enjoys over board members, yet (4) because these asymmetries pose foreseeable hazards, measures are taken in advance to mitigate downside drift (in self-aggrandizement, accounting deceit, and corporate charter protective respects). Albeit a different prescription from what I anticipated when this project was begun, this is my recommendation nevertheless.

Notes

1. As will become quickly apparent, I focus almost entirely upon corporate governance in the US. It is nevertheless noteworthy, as Bengt Holmstrom and Steven Kaplan observe, that 'other countries have begun to move toward the U.S. model' (2003, p. 16).
2. Readers who are familiar with the transaction cost approach to economic organization should move directly to section 3. This section is included for those who lack the background or could use a refresher. Much of this section draws upon my paper, 'The Theory of the Firm as Governance Structure: From Choice to Contract' (2002).

3. This last is important, in that recourse to the courts for purposes of ultimate appeal serves to delimit threat positions. As compared with contract as legal rules, the more elastic concept of contract as framework facilitates cooperative adaptations across a wider range of contractual disturbances, which is important as continuity takes on added importance.

4. Timely adaptation is facilitated by an understanding that orders that are ambiguous with respect to or even exceed the scope of authority are to be fulfilled first and disputed later (Summers, 1969, pp. 538, 573).

5. The remainder of this subsection is based on Williamson (1988, pp. 579–80). For a related paper that examines debt financing for different assets, see Shleifler and Vishny (1992). Note that a governance interpretation of corporate finance provides yet another challenge to the Modigliani–Miller theorem that the cost of capital in a firm is independent of the mode of finance.

6. Shleifler and Vishny (1992) also emphasize that maladaptation is the main disability of non-redeployable assets.

7. Note that Node D vanishes for some transactions, of which labor is an example, because it is not feasible or even illegal for the firm to own some inputs.

8. Jensen locates the board 'at the apex of the internal control system' (1992, p. 862), but where in the scheme of things is this?

9. Note that the board does not itself 'decide what to do' (Shleifler and Vishny, 1997, p. 741).

10. What I have referred to as the remediableness criterion is pertinent, which criterion eschews the usual comparison of an actual condition with a hypothetical ideal – it being elementary that all extant modes of organization are inferior to a hypothetical ideal. The remediableness criterion counsels that an extant mode of organization for which no superior feasible mode can be described and implemented with expected net gains is presumed to be efficient (Williamson, 1995, 1996). For earlier discussions that prefigure remediableness, see Coase (1964) and Demsetz (1967). Also see Dixit (1996) for related discussion.

    The remediableness criterion can be thought of as a response to the public policy proverb that 'the best is the enemy of the good'. Insistence upon feasibility eliminates hypothetical ideals from consideration. But what of the implementation? Feasible alternatives that cannot be implemented also fail the remediableness test.

    Thus although insistence on feasibility screens out digressions on hypothetical ideals, insistence on implementation will eliminate some superior feasible alternatives. This last is disconcerting, especially if the repeated display of superior feasible alternatives attracts cumulative support that wears down the obstacles to implementation. In that event, the insistent display of superior feasible alternatives (currently implementable or not) clearly serves a beneficial purpose.

11. Jean Tirole summarizes (but does not expressly subscribe to) the following objections that have been made of the 'stakeholder–society governance structure' (2006, pp. 59–60);

    (1) 'Giving control rights to non-investors may discourage financing in the first place,' since the safeguard for equity is compromised;
    (2) 'Deadlocks may result from the sharing of control ';
    (3) Managerial accountability is compromised: 'the socially responsible manager faces a wide variety of missions, most of which are by nature unmeasurable,' with the result that 'managers [are] less accountable; and

(4) 'It is not obvious that social goals are best achieved by directors and officers eager to pander to their own ... customers and policy makers.'

12. Lucian Bebchuk has recently recommended that shareholders should be given the power 'to initiate and *vote to adopt* changes in the company's basic corporate governance arrangements ... [to] include the power to adopt provisions that would allow shareholders, down the road, to initiate and vote on proposals regarding specific corporate decisions" (2005, p. 836; emphasis added). It is his view that increasing shareholder power to intervene in this way will "improve corporate governance and enhance shareholder value' (2005, p. 836).

13. Thus, suppose that over the course of time that the efficient debt to equity ratio undergoes a transformation. Specifically Williamson (1988, p. 585):

Suppose ... that a firm is originally financed along lines that are consistent with the debt and equity financing principles set out [in Section 3] above. Suppose further that the firm is successful and grows through retained earnings. The initial debt-equity ratio thus progressively falls. And suppose finally that many of the assets in this now-expanded enterprise are of a kind that could have been financed by debt.

Added value, in such a firm, can be realized by substituting debt for equity. This argument applies, however, selectively. It only applies to firms where the efficient mix of debt and equity has gotten seriously out of alignment. These will be firms that combine (1) a very high ratio of equity to debt with (2) a very high ratio of redeployable to nonredeployable assets.

Interestingly, many of the large leveraged buyouts in the 1980s displayed precisely these qualities.

14. Tirole also describes LBOs as a 'transitory form of organization. LBO sponsors and limited partners want to be able to cash out, in the form of a return to public corporation status or negotiated sales' (2006, p. 48). He furthermore observes that the LBO specialist 'KKR sticks to the companies for five to ten years before exiting' (2006, p. 48).

15. As Jensen observes, 'the close relationship between the LBO partners or venture fund partners and the operating companies facilitates the infusion of expertise from the board during times of crisis. It is not unusual for a partner to join the management team, even as CEO, to help an organization through such emergencies' (1993, p. 870).

16. Henry Hansmann contrasts the use of special charter provisions by venture capital start-up firms that have a relatively short expected life with publicly traded firms that consistently defer to the default terms provided by corporate law (2006, p. 9). The former are intended to elicit high-powered incentives. The later are more well-suited to business-as-usual.

17. The interesting paper by Marco Pagano and Ailisa Roell (1998) is especially noteworthy. An obvious difference between their paper and mine is that they work out of a variant of the formal agency theory setup while I work out of a less formal governance setup in which greater provision for organization theory is made. Other differences are these: they are concerned with corporate governance in continental Europe (where 'most companies are not listed on stock exchanges, and even when they are, a single large shareholder or a tightly knit group of shareholders retains a controlling stake' (1998, p. 188)) whereas I am concerned with corporate governance in the US; their perspective is that of an initial owner who retains a controlling stake and who may wish to preserve his discretion by limiting the 'over-monitoring' in relation to

that purpose (pp. 188–90); they focus principally on the non-cooperative case where 'each investor needs to verify some basic facts about the value of the company, existence of a sound business plan, adequacy of the asset base, competence of the management, etc.' (p. 201) rather than use collective organization for this purpose; the main trade-off faced by the entrepreneur in their model is 'between avoiding excessive monitoring [staying private with a few large shareholders] and containing the cost of the company's shareholder base [going public]' (pp. 203–5), which is not unrelated to but is different from the tradeoff in US <u>firms that have gone public</u> between the integrity of delegation and the integrity of monitoring.

18. Note that Michels and Selznick focus on the breakdown of organization ('organization says oligarchy') but do not discuss the constructive purposes served by delegation. Indeed, if optimal delegation varies among different types of organization and, within a given type, among organizational designs, then the susceptibility to oligarchy will presumably differ in intentional, systematic respects. Such considerations should be folded into the organizational calculus.

19. Measures of performance at the essential variables can be compromised by a failure to choose the relevant measures (by reason of omission of appropriate measures or inclusion of misleading measures) or a failure to report accurately and intelligibly on the readings that are taken. In principle, accountants and auditors who subscribe to and live up to high standards of professional ethics will relieve such concerns. But by the same token, the integrity of the performance measures will be compromised if these professionals toady to the management.

20. The compensation of Home Depot CEO Robert Nardelli has recently come under scrutiny in this connection. As Julie Creswell reports (2006, p. A1):

A growing source of resentment among some is Mr. Nardelli's pay package. The Home Depot board has awarded him $245 million in his five years there. Yet during that time, the company's stock has slid 12 percent.

Why would a company award a chief executive that much money at a time when the company's shareholders are arguably faring far less well? Some of the former Home Depot managers think they know the reason, and compensation experts and share holder advocates agree: the clubbiness of the six-member committee of the company's board that recommends Mr. Nardelli's pay.

Two of those members have ties to Mr. Nardelli's former employer, General Electric. One used Mr. Nardelli's lawyer in negotiating his own salary. And three either sat on other boards with Home Depot's influential lead director, Kenneth G. Langone, or were former executives at companies with significant business relationships with Mr. Langone.

In addition, five of the six members of the compensation committee are active or former chief executives ... [who] have a harder time saying no to the salary demands of fellow chief executives.

21. Tirole's succinct summary of the Bebchuk and Fried (2004) critique of the appointment of directors by the CEO is as follows (2006, p. 32):

Directors dislike haggling with or being 'disloyal' to the CEO, have little time to intervene, *and further receive a number of favors from the CEO*: the CEO can place them on the company's slate, increasing seriously their chance of reelection, give them perks, business deals (perhaps after they have been nominated on the board, so that they are formally 'independent'), extra compensation on top of the director fee, and charitable contributions to nonprofit organizations headed by directors, or reciprocate the lenient oversight in case of interlocking directorates ... Directors also happily acquiesce to takeover defenses.

22. The efficacy of some plausible reforms is not borne out by the data. For example, Roberta Romano's empirical examination (2005b) of the auditing recommendations of Sarbanes–Oxley shows that there is no empirical basis for introducing these rules; and the study by Guner, Malmendier, and Tate (2005) on the influence of financial experts finds that 'financial experts on boards do have a significant impact on board decisions, but not necessarily in the interest of shareholders'.

23. Hansmann's treatment of the efficacy of default provisions in state corporate law is pertinent.

24. Jensen is alert to these concerns and 'hasten[s] to add that I am not advocating continuous war in the boardroom. In fact, in well-functioning organizations the board will generally be relatively inactive and will exhibit little conflict" (1993, p. 866). In the degree to which a presumption of greater cooperation is favored by a co-chair arrangement, which I believe that it is, that should be factored in.

25. This last could be subsumed under cost effectiveness but is included separately because it is deserving of more attention.

26. As I have discussed elsewhere, organization theory informs the economics of contract in five respects: the description of human actors; the intertemporal responsiveness of organization; the proposition that alternative modes of governance differ in discrete structural ways; the notion that much of the action resides in the microanalytics; and the importance of cooperative adaptation (Williamson, 2002, pp. 173–6).

27. Asset specificity has a bearing on the trade-offs: greater monitoring capability is warranted as equity-financed investments in nonredeployable projects increase, *ceteris paribus*; and greater management autonomy is warranted as the nonredeployability of management assets increase, *ceteris paribus*.

References

Ashby, W.R. (1960) *Design for a Brain.* New York: John Wiley & Sons.

Barnard, C. (1938) *The Functions of the Executive.* Cambridge, MA: Harvard University Press.

Barron, J.N. and D.M. Kreps (1999) *Strategic Human Resources – Frameworks for General Managers.* New York: Wiley Press.

Bebchuk, L.A. and J. Fried (2004) *Pay without Performance: The Unfulfilled Promise of Executive Compensation.* Cambridge, MA: Harvard University Press.

Bebchuk, L.A. (2005) 'The Case for Increasing Shareholder Power', *Harvard Law Review*, vol. 118(3), pp. 833–917.

Buchanan, J. (2001) 'Game Theory, Mathematics, and Economics', *Journal of Economic Methodology*, vol. 8(1), pp. 27–32.

Coase, R. (1937) 'The Nature of the Firm', *Economica*, N.S.(4), 386–405.

Coase, R. (1964) 'The Regulated Industries: Discussion', *American Economic Review*, vol. 54 (May), 194–7.

Commons, J. (1932) 'The Problem of Correlating Law, Economics, and Ethics', *Wisconsin Law Review*, vol. 8, 3–26.

Creswell, J. (2006) 'With Links to Home Depot Board, Chief Saw Pay Soar as Stock Fell', *New York Times*, 24 May, p. A1.

Demsetz, H. (1967) 'Toward a Theory of Property Rights', *American Economic Review*, vol. 57 (May), pp. 347–59.

Dixit, A. (1996) *The Making of Economic Policy: A Transaction Cost Politics Perspective*. Cambridge, MA: MIT Press.

Fama, E. and M.C. Jensen (1983) 'Separation of Ownership and Control', *Journal of Law and Economics*, vol. 26 (June), pp. 301–26.

Friedman, M. (1997) in Brian Snowdon and Howard Vane, 'Modern Macroeconomics and its Evolution from a Monetarist Perspective', *Journal of Economic Studies*, vol. 24(4), pp. 192–222.

Georgescu-Roegen, N. (1971) *The Entropy Law and Economic Process*. Cambridge, MA: Harvard University Press.

Guner, A. B. and U. Malmendier and G. Tate (2005) 'Financial Expertise of Directors', *NBER Working Paper* 11914. Cambridge, MA.

Hansmann, H. (2006) 'Corporation and Contract', *ECGI Law Working Paper* No. 66/2006 Yale Law School, New Haven, CT.

Hayek, F. (1945) 'The Use of Knowledge in Society', *American Economic Review*, vol. 35 (September), 519–30.

Holmstrom, B. and S. Kaplan (2003) 'The State of U.S. Corporate Governance: What's Right and What's Wrong?', *Journal of Applied Corporate Finance*, vol 15, Spring, pp. 8–20.

Jensen, M. (1993) 'The Modern Industrial Revolution, Exit, and the Failure of Internal Control Systems', *The Journal of Finance*, July, pp. 831–80.

Knauth, O. (1948) *Managerial Enterprise: Its Growth and Methods of Operation*. New York: W.W. Norton.

Knight, F. (1941) 'Review of Melville J. Herskovits' "Economic Anthropology"', *Journal of Political Economy*, vol. 49, pp. 247–58.

Kreps, D. (1999) 'Markets and Hierarchies and (Mathematical) Economic Theory', in Glenn Carroll and David Teece (eds), *Firms, Markets, and Hierarchies*. New York: Oxford University Press.

Llewellyn, K. N. (1931) 'What Price Contract? An Essay in Perspective', *Yale Law Journal*, vol. 40, pp. 704–51.

Mace, M. (1971) *Directors: Myth and Reality*. Cambridge, MA: Harvard University Press.

Marx, K. (1967) *Capital*, vol. 1. New York: International Publishers.

Michels, R. (1915) *Political Parties: A Sociological Study of the Oligarchical Tendencies of Modern Democracy*. New York: Collier Books.

Morgenson, G. (2006) 'Advice on Boss's Pay May Not Be So Independent', *New York Times*, 10 April, p. A16.

Newell, A. (1990) *United Theories of Cognition*. Cambridge, MA: Harvard University Press.

Nguyen-Dang, B. (2005) 'Investor Recognition Hypothesis, Firm Value, and Corporate Governance: Evidence from Media Coverage of CEOs', Working paper, HEC Paris School of Management.

Pagano, M. and A. Roell (1998) 'The Choice of Stock Ownership Structure: Agency Costs, Monitoring and the Decision to Go Public', *Quarterly Journal of Economics*, vol. 113(1), February, pp. 187–225.

Romano, R. (2005a) 'After the Revolution in Corporate Law', *Journal of Legal Education*, vol. 55, September, 342–59.

Romano, R. (2005b) 'The Sarbanes–Oxley Act and the Making of Quack Corporate Governance', *Yale Law Journal*, June, pp. 1521–610.

Selznick, P. (1966) *TVA and the Grass Roots*. New York: Harper Torchbook.

Shane, S. (2001) 'Technological Regimes and New Firm Formation', *Management Science*, vol. 47, 1173–90.

Shleifer, A. and R. Vishny (1992) 'Liquidation Values and Debt Capacity: A Market Equilibrium Approach', *Journal of Finance*, September.

Shleifer, A. and R. Vishny (1997) 'A Survey of Corporate Governance', *Journal of Finance*, June, pp. 737–83.

Simon, H. (1957) *Models of Man*. New York: John Wiley & Sons.

Simon, H. (1962) 'The Architecture of Complexity', *Proceedings of the American Philosophical Society*, vol. 106 (December), 467–82.

Simon, H. (1973) 'Applying Information Technology to Organization Design', *Public Administrative Review*, vol. 33 (May-June), 268–78.

Simon, H. (1992) *Economics, Bounded Rationality, and the Cognitive Revolution*. Brookfield, CT: Edward Elgar.

Solow, R. (2001) 'A Native Informant Speaks', *Journal of Economic Methodology*, vol. 8 (March), 111–12.

Summers, C. (1969) 'Collective Agreements and the Law of Contracts', *Yale Law Journal*, vol. 78 (March), 537–75.

Tirole, J. (2006) *The Theory of Corporate Finance*. Princeton, NJ: Princeton University Press.

Williamson, O. (1975) *Markets and Hierarchies: Analysis and Antitrust Implications*. New York: Free Press.

Williamson, O. (1985) *The Economic Institutions of Capitalism*. New York: Free Press.

Williamson, O. (1988) 'Corporate Finance and Corporate Governance', *Journal of Finance*, vol. 43 (July), 567–91.

Williamson, O. (1991) 'Comparative Economic Organization: The Analysis of Discrete Structural Alternatives', *Administrative Science Quarterly*, vol. 36 (June), 269–96.

Williamson, O. (1995) 'The Politics and Economics of Redistribution and Inefficiency', *Greek Economic Review*, vol. 17(2), 115–36.

Williamson, O. (1996) *The Mechanisms of Governance*. New York: Oxford University Press.

Williamson, O. (2002) 'The Theory of the Firm as Governance Structure: From Choice to Contract', *Journal of Economic Perspectives*, vol. 16 (Summer), 171–95.

Williamson, O. (2005) 'The Economics of Governance', *American Economic Review*, vol. 95 (May), 1–18.

Wilson, E. (1999) *Consilience*. New York: Alfred Knopf.

2
Human-Asset Essentiality and Corporate Social Capital in a Stakeholders-Society Perspective

Masahiko Aoki

It is well known that an important conceptual issue was first raised in a seminal debate between Dodd and Bearle in the early 1930s regarding whether the corporation is the property of the stockholders, or if the board should owe fiduciary duties to the stakeholders in general. To date it does not seem that this issue has been resolved. One view became more powerful and prevalent at one time, but then its influence relatively declined in response to public opinion, emergent economic environments and business landscape, particular events (such as the Asian financial crisis and the Enron scandal) and so on. Recently the stakeholders–society view seems to be somewhat regaining its momentum. There seems to be two important factors for this. One is the rising importance of human knowledge assets for corporate competitiveness in spite of, or rather because of, the development of digital information technology. The other is the rising public awareness of the values of natural environments which corporate activities are embedded in, as well as exert significant impacts on.

In this essay I would like to introduce two relatively unutilized concepts that are of considerable relevance to these two phenomena and discuss their important implications to the stakeholders–society view of corporate governance. They are *human asset essentiality* and *corporate social capital*. The former concept is originally due to Hart (1995). But, whereas he used the concept primarily to rationalize the notion of the 'firm-as-property-of-physical-assets-owners' view, I extend it to distinguish different discreet forms of organizational architecture and fitting corporate governance structure associated with each of them. In particular, it can shed new light on the information roles of the stock market at the time when workers' human assets are indispensable for the management to exploit the value of non-human physical assets. It has been a customary thought that the firms-specificity of workers' human assets, as well as their complementarities with physical or managerial assets, would make the stakeholders–society view a warranted one. But those phenomena are considered to be rather ubiquitous in modern corporations and, as we will argue, they themselves may not necessarily be incompatible with the stockholder-controlled corporate governance structure. I posit that human assets essentiality as defined rigorously below is the concept which can shed new and discriminating light on the stakeholders–society view in emergent technological environment.[1]

I will then conceptualize the notion of corporate social capital and apply it to interpret the roles of the so-called corporate social responsibility (CSR) programs. Why are corporations engaged in various non-economic activities to meet societal demands (such as environmental protection) beyond their legal obligations? In other words why do corporations 'over-comply' (Heal, 2005) with the social demands? Does it benefit corporations (their stockholders and possibly others)? Common-sense-wise, an answer may appear obvious. However, it may not necessarily be so for the prevailing framework of economists' thinking: 'corporations do not need to do anything beyond legal obligations in order to serve stockholders interests'. The second part of the essay discusses this issue from the perspective that corporations (and their stockholders and other stakeholders) are players not only in economic games but also in the social-exchange game embedding the former. It analyzes how corporate social capital accumulated through CSR can compensate the sacrifice of pecuniary economic assets, how the former can nonetheless indirectly complement the accumulation of the latter, and how the former can be transformed into the latter against an institutional change in environmental rights arrangement. In this perspective not only the community in which the corporation is embedded in is, and ought to be, beneficiaries of the corporation, but also the corporation itself benefits from social exchanges with the community.[2]

1   Human assets essentiality and discreet forms of corporate governance

The standard view of the corporate firm in economics is that of a hierarchical series of principal–agency relationships. The architecture of the internal organization is viewed as a nested hierarchical structure composed of the principal-cum-supervisor and the agents-cum-subordinates, within which the authority of decision-making is delegated from the former to the latter only within a contractual limit. The top management of the internal organization is considered as the agent of the investors who exercise their control through the financial market (and the board of directors) within the orbit of the legal setting. In essence, corporate governance is simply viewed as dealing with 'the ways in which suppliers of finance to corporations assure themselves of getting a return on their investment' (Shleifer and Vishny, 1997). However, I posit that there are various patterns of linkage between corporate governance (CG) mechanisms (institutions) and organizational architecture (OA) as a non-market information system, the workings and implications of which cannot be adequately understood in terms of the standard framework. In this section, I propose a simple framework for classifying discreet patterns of the linkage between CG and OA by specifying basic conditions for each of them to be viable.

One possible conceptual and analytical approach to the linkage between CG and OA is to treat the corporate firm as the domain of a game between the manager, the workers and the investors (of various types) and regard a stable linkage between a particular type of CG and OA as an instance of equilibrium outcome of strategic interplay among those players. Multiple equilibria can result even from game with a simple structure, among which the selection may be conditioned by the values of institutional parameters surrounding the domain of the game (the exogenous rules of the game). The formal rules of law, institutional organization of market processes, business–government relationship and prevailing social norms may be reckoned as constituting such parameters. By incorporating workers as explicit players of the game alongside investors and managers, this approach may be regarded as an attempt to operationalize the so-called stakeholder–society view of CG within a limited framework (Aoki 1984, 2001). On the other hand, it also anticipates the conventional property-rights-based control of organizational hierarchies as one particular equilibrium out of the many that are possible under certain conditions. This particular equilibrium solution corresponds to the standard, 'corporations-as-property-of-stockholders' view. Thus, the game-theoretic view can be regarded as a more general approach that treats the traditional debate between the two views from a higher level and reconstructs the standard perspective as a special case.

I developed a fairly elaborated game-theoretic approach to the linkage between CG and OA in a previous writing (Aoki, 2001, particularly chapter 4 and Part III). There I identified four modes of stable equilibrium linkage between CG and OA: property-rights-based control of organizational hierarchy, co-determination and workers' participation in work-site control, relational contingent governance of the team-like OA, and the venture capitalist governance of tournament among entrepreneurial start-up firms. As easily inferred, these four modes of CG–OA linkages may be considered as representing embryonic models of the traditional Anglo-American, traditional German, traditional Japanese, and Silicon Valley institutions, respectively. Therefore I will hereafter refer to them as the AA, G, J and SV models respectively. This essay proposes a simple, alternative way of characterizing those four discreet forms of OA–CG linkage and a new one which may provide a new perspective for the stakeholders-society view in emergent technological environment.

Let us simply assume that the domain of the (corporate) firm comprises the manager, the workers and investors. To differentiate and identify the characteristics of the five equilibrium modes of CG–OA linkage in the simplest terms, let us envision that the building blocks of OA are simply composed of three elements: manager's human assets (MHA), workers' human assets (WHA), and investor-supplied non-human assets (NHA). In the literature, the firm-specificity of WHA is sometimes referred to as a key notion for specifying the nature of CG and/or OA. For example, the 'board-as-the-trustee-of-stakeholders' view by Blair and Stout (1999), as well as my previous work (Aoki 1984) high-lights such a notion. Some others refer to complementary relationships between MHA and WHA as an important defining factor of CG–OA linkage. For exam-ple, Rajan and Zingales (2000) points to the growing importance of MHA and WHA in rejecting the relevance of property rights in NHA for understanding the nature of an emergent CG mode. Although those views have substantial merits for understanding some aspects of diversity in CG–OA linkages, I argue that the firm-specificity of WHA, as well as complementarities between MHA and WHA as such, are rather ubiquitous phenomena of modern corporate firms and can-not constitute crucial factors for distinguishing one mode of CG–OA linkage from possible others. Firm-specificity of WHA or complementarities between MHA and WHA can make the internal relationships between WHA and MHA relational and subject their joint outcomes to individual or collective bargaining within the firm between the holders of these assets. But I argue that these aspects of human assets alone do not necessarily have a distinct impact on corporate governance. As we will see below, CG–OA linkages that are broadly similar to Anglo-American, German and Japanese models may well all involve firm-specificity of both human assets, as well as complementarities between them.

Instead, as classificatory tools, we adopt the following two related notions. First, we use the Edgeworth notion of complementarity between MHA/WHA on one hand and NHA on the other [not between MHA and NHA]. Second, we use the notion of 'essentiality' as first introduced by Hart (1995, p. 45) to under-stand the role of MHA/WHA within a particular OA: if the ownership control of NHA by the holder of either of the HAs will not increase the marginal product of this HA in the absence of cooperative association of the other HA, we say that the latter HA is essential for the OA. In other words, XHA (X = M or W) is essen-tial, if its organizational association is 'indispensable' in order for YHA (Y ≠ X) and NHA to be complementary.[3] Intuitively, a type of HA may be said essential if its absence cannot be compensated by the control over NHA by the holder of the other type of HA (e.g. whether managers substitute increased control over NHA in the absence of cooperation from workers). Essentiality is a condition that is concerned with complementary relationship between either of HA and NHA at a particular value of the other HA (i.e., at zero input). Thus complemen-tary relationship among two types of HAs is neither sufficient nor necessary for the essentiality of either of them. Even if MHA and WHA are mutually comple-mentary in cooperation, one or both of them may not be essential under the above definition. Within a particular OA, one or both of HAs can be essential, or neither of them may be essential. Depending on which combination of essentiality holds, we can distinguish different types of CG–OA linkage.

It is important to note at the outset that these relationships among the assets are not solely technologically predetermined. We posit that the uses of MHA, WHA, and NHA are controlled strategically by the respective stakeholders (owners). Thus a mode of strategic interactions and their stable outcome, on one hand, and a mode of relationships among various assets, on the other, are mutually conditional under possible impacts of institutional parameters (such as political, social, and market-related) outside the corporate domain possibly in a path-dependent manner.

A   Property-rights-based governance of unilateral essentiality (AA model)

Let us start out with the classical case of essentiality following the property rights approach formulated by Hart (1995) and his associates. Let us assume that

- MHA is *essential* in that the marginal product of WHA cannot be enhanced without the input of MHA, even if the ownership of NHA (i.e., the residual rights of control to decide on the use of NHA in contractually unspecified situations [Hart, 1985]) is endowed to the workers.
- Asymmetrically, WHA is *not essential* in that the ownership of NHA is *complementary* to MHA even without the cooperation of firm-specific WHA so that the marginal value of MHA can be increased with the ownership of NHA.

Note that these two conditions of *unilateral* essentiality do not preclude the complementarities stemming from cooperation between MHA and firm-specific WHA. They are specified under the default conditions of non-cooperation which defines the bargaining positions of the two stakeholders, MHA and WHA, in sharing firm-specific surplus. The first condition of MHA's essentiality may be interpreted as capturing the essence of hierarchical ordering of organizational activities in which WHA is accumulated and/or used within that context and limits specified by the manager. The second condition is prominent in the property rights approach of Hart. If these two conditions hold, they would imply that the integration of management and ownership of NHA is the second-best solution.[4] It enables the manager to improve on its bargaining position over the distribution of firm-specific surplus vis-à-vis the workers by means of investment in MHA and thus motivates him/her to invest more in MHA, resulting in higher overall efficiency.

If the manager is financially constrained and needs to rely on equity financing, then (s)he has to yield fundamental control rights to the stockholders and be subjected to an incentive contractual arrangement as an agent of the stockholders. The present value sum of expected streams of profit accruing to the stockholders is called the fundamental stock value. (Note the distinction between the (gross) value-added by the firm inclusive of contractual payments to the employees and the stock value of the firm as residual after them.) The fear of discharge from the job in the event of a financially depressed state (i.e., career concerns), as well as the prospect of incentive payments in the event of an excellent corporate-value state, motivates the manager to make the best effort. Under this scheme, an investor who conceives of a new business plan to enhance the stock value may take over the firm through open bids in the stock market and replace the management. This event can occur, even if the implementation of the plan induces the reduction of gross value-added of the firm and accordingly the breach/termination of (implicit) contracts with the employees. The role of the government in this model could be that of the liberal state which would not interfere with private employment contracting but only enforce private contracts as a third party.

This is the type of CG–OA linkage which is most familiar to economists and reminiscent of the essential feature of the so-called Anglo-American model, so that much does not need to be said about this here. But one question that is highly relevant to us is whether or not this is the only possible solution. If not, what situation warrants other solutions becoming strategically viable?

B   Co-determination based on bilaterally limited essentiality (G model)

As in the first case, let us start with a simple situation in which the manager is not constrained by financial resources to own NHA. Suppose that

- WHA and the (partial) residual rights of control over NHA are complementary in that workers' marginal satisfaction from investment in WHA can be enhanced if combined with the (partial) ownership of NHA even without relational association with MHA.
- MHA and the (partial) residual rights of control over NHA are complementary in a similar manner as above.

The first condition anticipates a situation, as in artisanship or craft production, where workers can increase their marginal satisfaction from investment in WHA if they can also control tools, work-site set-ups, use of equipment in response to emergent events, etc. Unlike the case of unilateral worker control, however, the second condition suggests that 'craft' production on the shopfloor may benefit from integration into a wider OA where MHA also plays a significant role. If the residual rights of control over NHA are complementary *both* to MHA and WHA, then according to the definition by Hart, *neither* MHA nor WHA are (unilaterally) essential. However, we may twist a rigorous definition a little and refer to this case intuitively in terms of MHA and WHA being *bilaterally essential* to OA to the extent that the other party's control over NHA is *limited*.

Generally speaking, the manager may prefer not to give workers a wage premium or partial residual rights of control, yet may need to grant workers one or the other in order to motivate the accumulation of WHA by the workers. Under this scenario, two institutional arrangements may be possible (as subgame perfect equilibria in the framework of repeated games between the manager and the worker), depending on the value of external institutional parameters that constrain the mechanism of wage determination (Aoki, 2001, pp. 287–91). If the standard wage rate is set external to the firm, such as through an industrial agreement between an industrial association and industrial union, and the state 'enables' the industrial agreement to be generally enforceable (as in the case of German corporatism), then cooperation between the holder of MHA and that of WHA may be sustainable on the basis of sharing residual-rights-of-control such as through workers' participation in formal governance structure, the works councils, workers' stockownership plans, etc. If the state is 'liberal' and does not intervene in private wage-contracting and wage determination remains decentralized, the classical Hartian solution may emerge on the basis of workers' sharing in firm-specific surplus in the form of wage premium while the residual rights of control exclusively accrues to the manager.

If the manager is constrained financially, outside investors need to be invited to provide financial resources and participate in CG structure. In the case that control rights are shared with employees, such as in the form of German co-determination, it can be shown that outside investors prefer long-term lending to equity participation, because in this way their preference in corporate control becomes congruent with those of the workers in restraining excessive risk-taking on the part of the manager (Aoki, 2001, pp. 287–91). In that sense, corporatism, co-determination and the *Hausbank* system in the traditional German model may be considered as constituting an institutionally complementary cluster, while another cluster may include stock market control, hierarchically ordered HA, and the liberal state.

C Relational contingent governance of symmetric essentiality (J model)

In the classical hierarchy, the essentiality of HA is exclusively and unilaterally attributed to the owner of MHA. Let us now adopt the following alternative hypotheses:

- The respective contributions of MHA and WHA in cooperation are *inseparable* in the sense that their marginal products are not individually distinguishable or observable.
- Both MHA and WHA are *symmetrically essential* to each other in that their (unobservable) marginal products cannot be enhanced only by individual control of NHA without mutual cooperation.

The first condition corresponds to the concept of 'team' property of OA originally conceptualized by Alchian and Demsetz (1950) and elaborated later by Holmstrom (1979). Such a property may be thought to hold if the design of OA involves information-sharing across the management and the workers, as well as among the workers, as an indispensable feature for its efficient operation. The second condition implies that even if the external supply of NHA is necessary for the operation of this type of OA, NHA and either of an individual HA in isolation cannot be in complementary relationships. Then, it can be shown that the following type of CG is the second-best (Aoki, 2001).

A relational monitor-cum-investor (alternatively a delegated monitor for the investors) sustains the ongoing relationships with the team composed of the holders of MHA and WHA. As far as she observes that the collective performance of the team exceeds a certain critical threshold point, she delegates the residual rights of control over NHA to the team and receives a constant contractual rate of returns to investment. Meanwhile, any surplus can be distributed among the holders of MHA and WHA according to organizational rules or conventions (such as seniority rules). When the collective performance falls below the critical point, she decides whether to bail out the team if preserving the continuation value of the team is judged to be worthwhile, or else withdraw the investment and punish the badly-performing team by its desolution. Since the control rights shift between the team of HA holders and the relational monitor contingent on the value state of the firm, this model may be called the relational contingent governance model.

The effectiveness of this type of CG for inducing the efficient cooperation of the HA holders is enhanced under a number of further conditions. First, HA holders may become more cooperative when the individual value of outside opportunities for each of them is lower. This would be the case when other organizations in the economy are likewise organized as teams of long-term associations so that the re-employment of individual HA holders disbanded from a failed team becomes harder without the substantial loss of essentiality. Thus the convention of long-term employment in the organization field is considered to be an institutional complement to the linkage between the relational contingent governance and the team-like OA. Second, speaking more concretely, the role of relational monitor may be considered to be approximated by the so-called main bank, who has relational associations with client firms. Thus, the institutionalization of the main bank system also constitutes an element of a complementary cluster surrounding this linkage. Where the demand for external capital declines or banks become less effective in monitoring, however, the incentives of HA holders may be lessened due to lack of external discipline and their moral hazard behavior may become less controllable. Thirdly, in the former two models, the role of the government may be characterized as 'neutral' in the sense of a third-party contract enforcer (the so-called liberal state as in the AA model) or that of enabling employees' and employers' organizations to jointly attain the status of quasi-state organs (the so-called 'enabling state' (Streeck, 1997) as in the G model). In this model, the role of the government may become relational vis-à-vis the monitoring agents (banks) in assuring rents for them to make credible commitment to costly bailout of moderately depressed firms.

D Venture capital governance of encapsulated essentialities (SV model)

Some aspects of relationships between venture capitalists (VC) and entrepreneurial start-up firms (ESFs) are known to be somewhat akin to the relational contingent governance (Aoki, 2001, chapter 14; Kaplan and Stromberg, 2003). VC initially provides only a limited amount of seed money for founding ESF and afterwards it decides whether to provide further funding to the latter, restructure their management and salvage potential values of their HA, or liquidate it, contingent on the progress of its development efforts. In successful cases, the relationships will be terminated by Initial Public Offering (IPO) of the ESF or its acquisition by an established firm within a niche market. As it is normally the case that the VC initially provides seed money to multiple ESFs proposing similar development projects and become increasingly selective in later-stage financing, the process may be thought of as a tournament game played among ESFs with the VC as a judge.

Within each ESF, a high degree of (symmetric) essentiality of HAs is incorporated. This may appear also somewhat similar to the previous case, but two differences are central. One is that the essentiality of HAs in EFSs is not so much due to the inseparability of the HAs within the team, but to the decisive mutual importance of HAs relative to NHA. Note that our notion of essentiality is based on a complementary relationship between NHA and HAs in the absence of mutual relational associations of HAs. In the current case, even if holders of HA are separated from particular ESFs, whether or not they will have access to the ownership of NHA will be irrelevant to their productivities (otherwise, the classical proprietor firms of Hartian type will result). Second, highly specialized HAs are encapsulated within individual ESFs in the context of a cluster of ESFs, but not integrated within a single Chandlerian type of firm that hierarchically coordinates a host of activities. Each ESF is specialized, and compete with others, in the development of a particular module of a potentially large innovative product system. The design of such a product system is not decomposed into modular designs by *ex ante* centralized planning as in the case of unilateral essentiality (e.g., the case of the development of IBM System/360), but it evolves through *ex post* combinations of successful modular designs. In order for such mechanisms to be workable, only simplified interface rules among modular products are publicly made open *ex ante* or interim through communications mediated by VCs and other means. It implies that technological and attribute complementarities among modular products are minimized so that their design efforts can be made separable without hierarchical ordering. Thus, when comparing ESF's activities to traditionally integrated Chandlerian firms, it is more appropriate comparing the cluster of ESFs and VCs combined, but not each ESF individually. If we look at VC-ESFs as a relational system, the basic nature of its OA may be summarized by the following dual characteristics:

- Essential HAs are *encapsulated* within each ESF in a context of clustered VC-ESFs.
- The VC governs this OA through tournament-like competitions among ESFs utilizing stage financing.

Under the condition of a high degree of uncertainty involved in the development of modular designs and their system integration, this linkage is known to have two distinct characteristics: (1) it can generate option values by running parallel development efforts (experiments) by multiple ESFs (Baldwin and Clark, 2001), and (2) it can generate externalities by attributing higher marginal probability of winning the tournament to the incremental accumulation of HAs that are encapsulated within each ESF (Aoki and Takizawa, 2002).

E   Governance of reciprocal essentiality by stakeholders–society (STK-S model)

In the J model, the roles of MHA and WHA are not clearly distinct because of the sharing of information as well as the sharing responsibilities for decision-making in the OA. The accumulation of MHA was geared more towards the ability to induce and support information sharing and consensus among organizational participants. However, suppose that in the wake of intensified global competition, the development of IT, diversifying social values and by other possible reasons, the MHA faces a set of new challenges to be more autonomous and innovative. Suppose that the use of MHA needs now to be directed more toward devising and implementing a distinctive business model comprised of such matters as: new organizational architectural design fitting new technology, long-term market strategy, devise of organization-specific reward-incentive system, cooperative relations with the labor union, corporate values to be shared with the workers, etc.

Recall that a crucial factor distinguishing the property rights-based control of hierarchal OA (the AA model) from the relational contingent governance of the team-like OA (the J model) was unilateral vs symmetric nature of essentiality among HAs involved. Thus, if the needs for more distinct and autonomous role of MHA can be coped with merely by distancing MHA from WHA and reducing the essential role of WHA, then the process may eventually transit to the model of managerial unilateral essentiality (the AA model). However, in order for such transition to be possible, the management needs to be able to implement its distinct business model by using NHA without the cooperation of specific

WHA (recall the conceptualization of essentiality). There may be cases, however, in which such processes may be problematic because of path-dependent characteristics of NHA essentiality even if it was ambiguously inseparable from that of MHA. Then a possible shift could be a decoupling of MHA and WHA from what used to be in an ambiguous, symmetric essentiality relationship and then re-couple them as mutually more distinct, but reciprocally indispensable partners.[5] On the other hand, suppose that in the traditional AA model the importance and specificity of WHA arises and MHA eventually cannot increase its productivity or effectiveness of its business model by the mere control of NHA without the cooperation of specific WHA. Such evolution would also lead to a fundamental change in the essentiality of NHA. These two different evolutionary paths may lead to the following same hypothetical possibility.

• Both MHA and WHA become complementary with NHA only through mutual cooperation. Thus MHA and WHA are *reciprocally essential*.

This condition of reciprocal essentiality may appear to be closely related to the usual condition of mutual specificity between MHA and WHA, but is actually more specific in that the complementary role of NHA ownership to MHA is at issue. From the purely theoretical point of view, reciprocal essentiality of HAs implies that 'the ownership structure [of NHA] does not matter since neither party's [HA] investment will not pay off in the absence of agreement with the other' (Hart, 1995, p. 48). How shall we interpret this claim in our context?

In contrast to the AA model, the role of NHA is reduced and the major function of the holder of MHA is considered as the creation and sustenance of productive internal linkage with WHA. To evaluate the value of the internal linkage, product market evaluations (thus current profits) are fundamental. However, the product market can evaluate only the present outcome of the internal linkage, not possible outcomes in the future. In addition, a valuable internal linkage takes time to build. The stock market may be potentially in a better position to predict future outcomes by aggregating dispersed information, expectations and values prevailing in the economy if they can filter noises to a reasonable degree. If the management lets it be known as part of its business model that a proportion of the value created by the complementary linkage accrues to the stockholders according to a certain rule and if the stock market is informative, the fundamental stock value may be constructed as a summary statistic correlated to future values of the linkage. If the board of directors is entrusted to effectively replace or appoint top management contingent on the (expected) stock value, the management can be disciplined to create and sustain a valuable internal linkage. On the other hand, the stockholders themselves may be motivated to do a better job of monitoring if they can benefit from making good evaluative judgments. Therefore, there are complementarities between the creation and sustenance of internal linkage on one hand and the stock market evaluation and monitoring on the other. However the primary function of the stock market is informational one and the controlling function is not inherent although not necessarily be excluded.

In sum, in this model, MHA and WHA are reciprocally essential, while their linkage and the monitoring by the holders of NHA are mutually complementary. In this sense, MHA, WHA and NHA are respectively playing constitutive roles in CG–OA structure. This structure may be said most appropriately to correspond to the stakeholders–society view. The question remains as regards how the signaling function of the stock market may be implemented as crucial corporate governance decision-making, such as on the replacement of MHA when it fails to create and sustain the productive internal linkage. There may be a variety of cases depending on corporate history, factor market environments, legal setting, political-economy institutions and others. Either bank, takeover bidder, private equity funds, the board of directors or possible others may play primary roles in this respect. No single solution seems to be dictated. But this may be expected because the reciprocal essentiality of HAs implies that ownership structure is theoretically 'irrelevant' in the Hartian sense (Hart 1995, p. 47), which ought to be now interpreted as that ownership structure can be 'diverse'. As WHA are essential in the implementation of business model, even the voice of their holders can be of relevant as important inputs into the CG process through their own organizations (unions) and/or their implicit influence on the board. Whichever the case may be, however, the purpose of restructuring ought not to be merely to increase the stock value at the sacrifice of the holders of WHA, if the internal linkage between MHA and WHA is still regarded as potentially valuable and they cannot be substituted by control of NHA.

We may now summarize the argument so far in Table 2.1.

Table 2.1 Comparison of hypothesized linkages between CG and OA

Model	Corporate governance	Organizational architecture	Finance market	Political state
AA	Property rights based	Unilateral essentiality of MHA	Stock market control	Liberal
G	Codetermination	Bilaterally limited Essentialities	Partial control by bank	Corporatism
J	Relational, contingent	Inseparable Essentialities	Relational, contingent control by bank	Relational
SV	VC-run tournament	Encapsulated essentiality	Staged control by VC	Liberal
STK-S	Stakeholders-society	Reciprocal essentialities	Summarized evaluation of internal linkage	

2 Corporate social responsibility and corporate social capital

This section proposes yet another concept useful for the stakeholders' view, corporate social capital, and applies it to interpret the role of CSR programs and its implications for corporate governance. I suggest that corporations should be viewed as not only the players of the game on the economic transaction domain, but also as the players of the game on the social exchange domain. I will present a basic idea about how the game on the domain of the social-exchange can be conceptualized and assume that one of objects of the players in that game is to accumulate capacity to derive social reputation as distinct from market-specific reputation capital. I call such capacity as corporate social capital (CSC) and regard the Corporate Social Responsibility programs (CSR) as one type of strategy for corporations to accumulate it at some economic costs. I will then discuss its implication to the corporate governance from the stakeholders-society perspective, as well as its complementarities to market-specific reputation capital and its transformation to the latter at the time of institutional change in environmental rights arrangements.

Let us start with a brief, general description of what I mean by the social-exchange domain. It is analogous to the economic transaction domain, but made distinct from the latter in terms of agent's intention, technical rules of the domain and possibly by instruments of play. Suppose there is *a community (group) of agents who interact with (relate to) each other using social symbols (such as words, gestures, gift-giving and the like) or actions (such as helping) with the intention of affecting emotional payoffs of targeted agents (as well as those of their own) and with unspecified obligations of reciprocity.* We call the set of such mutually interactive agents and the sets of their instruments as the domain of social-exchange and their interactions as play of the social-exchange game. A few words need to be said to distinguish it from other types of domains of game.[6]

Although exchanges of social symbols (speech action) may be involved in economic and other domains as well, those in the social-exchange domain are distinct by the nature of *unspecified reciprocity* and their intended purposes. In contrast, any economic transaction can be essentially a contract which cannot be implemented without specific mutually agreements, although they may be unilaterally or bilaterally defaulted. Second, the utterance of speech or dispatch of other social symbols in social exchanges may be generated by sender's own interests/emotions (e.g., appreciation, impression, anger, empathy, togetherness, jealousy, and so on), but their messages are intended to have impacts on receiver's emotional payoffs, either positive (e.g., pride, satisfaction, consolation, retribution, and so on) or negative (e.g., shame, regrets, feeling of excluded, and so on). In that sense, they are distinct from mere speech act or the so-called 'cheap talk' in the 'signaling game' in economic transaction domain. Social exchange can be symmetric in terms of mode of instruments (e.g., friendly conversations, disputes, gift-exchange, mutual help and so on) or asymmetric (e.g., exchange of gift-giving, help, provision of common goods, on one hand, and speech act such as appreciation, praise, etc., on the other).

If one develops capacity to derive more positive (alternatively negative) signals from others in the social-exchange domain, we say that his/her social capital accumulates (alt. depreciates), because they are considered as individually possessed assets generating emotional payoffs over time and/or deriving benefits in other domains (economic, political and organizational).[7] In order to accumulate social capital, however, one may need to reciprocate positive symbolic/substantive acts to others in the same domain or perform positive action in other domains. The basic features of social-exchanges thus indicate the strategic nature of social-exchanges, as well as their possible linkages to actions in other domains. Agents exchange social symbolic/substantive actions as they consider the most fit/desirable in order to increase, and to make the best use of, social capital in response to their imperfect knowledge and beliefs regarding the ways how the others would act and react.[8] In that sense, social-exchanges become the play of a game.[9] Thus we call the agents in this game as the players.

Now let us apply the idea of the social-exchange game to interpret the social meaning of the so-called CSR programs. Suppose that corporations adopt strategies regarding whether or not, as well as how, to make costly contributions to social agenda distinct from its normal profit-making economic activities in specific markets. Instead, agents in the community (who are not limited to customers or suppliers of corporations in relevant markets) may evaluate those strategies and express their opinions, positive or negative, which would be attributed to corporations as corporate social capital. Then we ask: why should corporate firms not be solely engaged in economic transactions in product, capital and labor markets? Is there any point for them to be engaged in social exchanges with the community of citizens at large beyond their own markets? By posing questions in this way I set aside from my immediate concern such matters as corporate brand names embodying accumulated reputations in relevant markets (in terms of product qualities, after-purchase services, delivery timing and the like). Costly signaling (such as advertisement) which would not directly affect utilities of buyers may also be left outside the scope of our discussion (although advertisement may promote the so-called conspicuous consumptions). I do not mean that brand names and advertisements are not important for understanding social implications of corporate behavior. Certainly they are. The point is that the nature and roles of corporate reputation, signaling and the like operating within specific markets of relevance have been extensively analyzed and fairly well understood in economics. I am concerned with whether or not corporate firms accumulate their own social capital, as distinct from market-specific reputation capital? The conceptual distinction between market-specific reputation capital and corporate social capital is sometimes subtle and ambiguous in practice but crucial.

An obvious starting point is that many corporate activities cause external diseconomies of various kinds beyond their own market relationships and reaching to wider communities and their commons. Remedies for them prescribed by economists, lawyers, governments and others include Pigouvian tax subsidies, Coasian direct bargaining between generators and recipients of externalities, quantity and other regulations, as well as market-regulation-hybrids such as the creation of emission-rights markets. However, it is increasingly recognized nowadays that these measures alone may not be perfect and incomplete by various reasons, e.g., capacity limits of the public authority in information processing, the lack of proper incentives for public administrators, difficulties of setting up direct and mediated bargaining and reaching formal agreements among various interest groups, increasing assertiveness of environmental movements and so on.[10] But corporate firms and citizens at large can be directly and informally engaged in social exchanges.

In other words, corporate firms may increasingly be recognized as players in the global commons game embedded in the society. If corporate firms pollute natural environments and/or generate health hazards through their economic activities, these firms may incite people to react adversely by criticisms, protests, etc., even if those economic activities are not immediately illegal within current legal framework. On the other hand, corporate firms can, if they wish, directly provide resources for social benefits such as environmental protection, poverty reduction, public health, educational and scientific progress, and so on through the so-called corporate social responsibility (CSR) programs. For a while let us assume that these programs do not immediately contribute to their profits nor are legally called for.[11] In response to social contributions which are costly, however, the citizens at large possibly ascribe social recognitions to provider corporations, which would constitute their corporate social capital. Corporate social capital may not be immediately cashed in; rather, it it may be enjoyed by various corporate stakeholders in non-pecuniary manner – for example, the pride of employees working for a socially reputable corporation, the satisfactions of environmentally conscious stockholders owning 'green' stocks, or the amenities of citizens living in a clean local community. These benefits may compensate the pecuniary costs of CSR programs. This much is common sense. But there can be more than just that.

If stockholders try to select their portfolios only from stocks of corporate firms engaged in CSR programs, theoretically they must perform worse in terms of financial performance, because they restrict the universe from which stocks can be picked. But, interestingly enough, empirical evidences seem to suggest a possibility, if not conclusively, that expenditures for CSR and stock price performance may be correlated, contrary to the theoretical prediction (e.g., Dowell, Hart and Yeung, 2000; King and Lennox, 2001).[12] Why? One simple, but plausible reason could be that profitable corporate firms may be more willing to contribute to a costly CSR program. But profitability can be statistically controlled and a more subtle possibility is that there may be complementarities between social capital investment and product-specific reputation capital. Let us consider the following possibility. The development and commercialization of environmentally friendly technology may be costly and its social value may not necessarily be fully appreciated by potential buyers of its products. For example, potential buyers of eco-cars may value the savings of gasoline costs but may not be willing to bear the full external costs in terms of higher car prices. Thus, managerial calculus of market-specific reputational capital alone may not immediately warrant a corporate firm to pursue the costly technological development and commercialization. However, the failure to do so may be damaging to the accumulation of corporate social capital ascribed by the society at large, while investment in environmentally-friendly technology may enhance the accumulation of corporate social capital. The attribution of such social standing may also amplify the value of market-specific reputation, because the former may enhance the beliefs of potential buyers of products regarding their user-cost-efficiency, durability, and the like, as well as its symbolic-values to them (e.g., environmental 'conspicuous' consumption). In other words, higher social corporate capital may serve as positive signal (analogous to advertisement) and contribute to prospects of long-term profits net of costs of CRS.[13]

Another possibility is that investment in corporate social capital is a way to insure the corporation against possible changes in property rights arrangements in the commons domain, which stock markets incorporate into their valuations. For example, corporate behavior exerting external effects on natural environments may not have been noticed and contested so far by the society, but the possibility of facing social criticism, product boycotts, litigations, and so on against the same behavior may rise in future, according as social consciousness and information dissemination regarding those effects rise. Such social challenges amount to an attempt for a realignment of de facto property rights in the global commons domain, i.e., shifts of environmental rights from the corporate sector to the community at large. The accumulation of social capital may guard corporate firms against possible damages that may be brought about by such institutional change, while corporate firms with thin social capital may be more vulnerable. In other words, corporate social capital facilitates the adaptability of corporate firms to such institutional change. Relative distribution of social capital accumulation across corporate firms then may be reflected in their valuations by stock markets.

Notes

1. This part of the current essay is drawn from the theoretical portion of Aoki and Jackson (2008). I am thankful to Oxford University Press and co-author Gregory Jackson for their permission to reproduce part of the chapter.
2. Concepts utilized in this part of the essay, such as social-exchange game, (corporate) social capital and so on, as well as their implications in broader contexts, are more fully discussed in Aoki (2007b).
3. Suppose the production function is represented by function of three differentiated inputs, F(MHA, WHA, NHA). If the cross-derivative of F with respect to MHA and WHA is positive, then MHA and WHA are said to be complementary. If its partial derivative with respect to XHA ($X = M$ or W) increases at $Y = 0$ ($Y \neq X$) when the ownership control of NHA is endowed to the holder of XHA, then we say XHA is essential. The latter is neither sufficient nor necessary for the former.
4. In the world of asymmetric information the first-best solution cannot be implemented. If there were a unique implementable first-best solution, then comparative institutional analysis would lose meaningful subject of study.
5. Aoki, Jackson and Miyajima (2007) and Aoki and Jackson (2008) report empirical results that the most competitive part of the Japanese corporate sector is indeed moving along this line.
6. For a more elaborated classification of domains of societal games, see Aoki (2001, 2007a,b,c).
7. Notions of social capital as individual assets are also found in rational-choice sociology of Coleman (1990) and reflexive sociology of Bourdieu (1986) and differ from collective notions as advanced by Putnam (1993) and Hayami (2006). Putnam's social capital comes into being not through individual intentional action, but is said to be 'inherited' with its origins hidden in the mist of the past. The existing stock cannot be thus individually owned. A collectivist notion of social capital along the customary usage of the word 'capital' in economics is articulated by Hayami as 'the structure of informal social relationships conducive to developing cooperation among economic actors with the effects of increasing social product'. However, he also develops a subtle argument to allude the dualistic, individualistic nature of social capital.
8. We only assume that agents have a consistent preference ordering over the internal states of game (profiles of action choices) imperfectly known to them, and that they are not necessarily exclusively self-interested. See Aoki (2007b).
9. Readers may recognize certain parallels between my concept of the domains of games and Bourdieu's concept of 'fields of social relations' (1981), as well as between our individualistic concepts of social capital (1986). Bourdieu even alluded to the game nature of the fields (Bourdieu and Wacquant 1992, pp. 98–101). However, Bourdieu's social capital is regarded as instruments of dominance over others, while mine is not necessarily limited as such.
10. See Ostrom (2005) for a decent discussion of the limits of centralized control of 'social dilemma'.
11. What is recognized as corporate social responsibility by different societies seems to hinge on ways how social-exchanges have been structured historically in each economy. For example, American corporate executives tend to think their ethical accountabilities as the most important corporate values while Japanese and European corporate executives tend to place higher values on environmental responsibility. See Study on Corporate Values by the Aspen Institute and Booz Allen and Hamilton: http://www.boozallen.com/publications/article/659548.

12. For a good survey on this and discussion of related subject see Heal (2005).
13. The reverse may not necessarily be the case. For example, tobacco companies may have less social capital, but some of them may have high reputations among smokers.

References

Alchian, A. and H. Demsetz (1950) 'Production, Information Costs, and Economic Organization', *American Economic Review*, vol. 62, pp. 777–95.

Aoki, M. (1984) *The Cooperative Game Theory of the Firm*. Oxford: Oxford University Press.

Aoki, M. (2001) *Toward a Comparative Institutional Analysis*. Cambridge, MA: MIT Press.

Aoki, M. (2007a) 'Endogenizing Institutions and Institutional Change', *Journal of Institutional Economics*, vol. 3, pp. 1–31.

Aoki, M. (2007b) 'Linking Economic and Social Exchange Games: From the Community Norm to CSR', http://ssrn.com/abstract=1031555.

Aoki, M. (2007c) 'Three-level Approach to the Rules of Societal Games', mimeo.

Aoki, M., G. Jackson and H. Miyajima (eds) (2007) *Corporate Governance in Japan: Organizational Diversity and Institutional Change*. Oxford: Oxford University Press.

Aoki, M., and G. Jackson (2008) 'Understanding an Emerging Diversity of Corporate Governance and Organizational Architecture: An Essentially-based Analysis', *Industrial and Corporate Change*, vol. 17(1), pp. 1–27.

Aoki, M. and H. Takizawa (2002) 'Information, Incentives, and Option Value: The Silicon-Valley Model', *Journal of Comparative Economics*, vol. 30, pp. 759–86.

Baldwin, C.Y. and K.B. Clark (2001) 'Capabilities and Capital Investment: New Perspectives on Capital Budgeting', in D.H. Chew (ed.), The New Corporate Finance: Where Theory Meets Practice. New York: McGraw Hill Irwin, pp. 117–31.

Blair, M., and L. Stout (1999) 'A Team Production Theory of Corporate Law', *Virginia Law Review*, vol. 85, pp. 247–328.

Bourdieu, P. (1981) 'Men and Machines', in K. Knorr-Cetina and A.V. Cicourel (eds), *Advances in Social Theory and Methodology: Toward an Integration of Micro and Macro Sociologies*. London: Routledge and Kegan Paul, pp. 304–17.

Bourdieu, P. (1986) 'The Forms of Capital', in J. Richarson (ed.), *Handbook of Theory and Research for the Sociology of Education*. New York: Greenwood Press, pp. 241–58.

Bourdieu, P. and L.J.D. Wacquant (1992) *An Invitation to Reflexive Sociology*. Chicago: University of Chicago Press.

Coleman, J. (1990) *Foundations of Social Theory*. Cambridge, MA: Harvard University Press.

Dowell, G., S. Hart and B. Yeung (2000) 'Do Corporate Global Enviromental Standards Create or Destroy Market Value?', *Management Science*, vol. 46, pp. 1059–74.

Hart, O. (1995) *Firms, Contracts, and Financial Structure*. Oxford: Clarendon Press.

Hayami, Y. (2006) 'Social Capital, Human Capital and Community Mechanism: Toward a Consensus among Economists', draft.

Heal, G. (2005) 'Corporate Social Responsibility: An Economic and Financial Framework', *The Geneva Papers on Risk and Insurance – Issues and Practice*, vol. 30(3), pages 387–409.

Holmstrom, B. (1979) 'Moral Hazard and Observability', *Bell Journal of Economics*, vol. 10, pp. 74–91.

Kaplan, S.N. and P. Stromberg (2003) 'Financial Contracting Theory Meets the Real World: An Empirical Analysis of Venture Capital Contracts', *Review of Economic Studies*, vol. 70, pp. 281–315.

King, A.A. and M.J. Lennox (2001) 'Does It Really Pay To Be Green? An Empirical Study of Firm Environmental and Financial Performance', *Journal of Industrial Ecology*, vol. 5(1), pp. 105–16.

Ostrom, E. (2005) *Understanding Institutional Diversity*. Princeton, NJ: Princeton University Press.

Putnam, R.D. (1993) *Making Democracy Work*. Princeton, NJ: Princeton University Press.

Rajan, R. G., and L. Zingales (2000) 'The Governance of the New Enterprises', in X. Vives (ed.), *Corporate Governance: Theoretical & Empirical Perspectives*. Cambridge, UK: Cambridge University Press, pp. 201–26.

Shleifer, A. and R.W. Vishny (1997) 'A Survey of Corporate Governance', *Journal of Finance*, vol. 52, pp. 737–87.

Streeck, W. (1997) 'German Capitalism: Does It Exist? Can It Survive?', in C. Crouch and W. Streeck (eds), *Political Economy of Modern Capitalism*. London: Sage, pp. 34–54.

3
Stakeholder Theory as a Basis for Capitalism[1]

R. Edward Freeman, Andrew C. Wicks and Bidhan Parmar

1 Introduction

For the past 25 years, a group of scholars has developed the idea that a business has stakeholders – that is, there are groups and individuals who have a stake in the success or failure of the business. There are many different ways to understand this concept, and there is a burgeoning area of academic research in both business and applied ethics on so-called 'stakeholder theory'. This literature seems to represent an abrupt departure from the usual understanding of business as a vehicle to maximize returns to the owners of capital. This more mainstream view, call it 'shareholder capitalism', or 'the standard account', has come under much recent criticism, and the 'stakeholder view' is often put forward as an alternative.

The purpose of this chapter is to examine these claims and to try and show that, in fact, stakeholder theory is a more useful way to understand the essence of capitalism. But adopting 'stakeholder capitalism' is fully compatible with most arguments for a more narrow 'shareholder capitalism'.

We begin by outlining the bare mechanics of stakeholder theory, as it has developed over the last 25 years. We then turn in the next sections to the arguments of Milton Friedman, Michael Jensen, and Oliver Williamson, often cited as opponents of stakeholder theory, and suggest that all are compatible with the main ideas of stakeholder theory. We highlight what we also take to be key differences with these largely economic approaches to business. We suggest that while these approaches are compatible with stakeholder theory, it makes more sense to return to the very roots of capitalism, the theory of entrepreneurship. We suggest how stakeholder theory needs to be seen as a theory about how business actually does and can work. We deduce several principles which form the basis for stakeholder capitalism.

2 The basic mechanics of stakeholder theory

There are a number of accounts of the history of stakeholder theory (Freeman, 1984; Donaldson and Preston, 1995; Phillips, 1997; Slinger, 1999; Freeman, 2005). However, there is little analysis of the underlying basis of the theory. Freeman (1994) suggests that most theories of business rely on separating 'business' decisions from 'ethical' decisions. This is seen most clearly in the popular joke about 'business ethics as an oxymoron'. More formally we might suggest that we define:

The Separation Fallacy

It is useful to believe that sentences like, 'x is a business decision' have no ethical content or any implicit ethical point of view. And, it is useful to believe that sentences like 'x is an ethical decision, the best thing to do all things considered' have no content or implicit view about value creation and trade (business).

Wicks (1996) and others have shown how deeply this fallacy runs in our understanding of business, as well as in other areas in society. There are two implications of rejecting the Separation Fallacy. The first is that almost any business decision has some ethical content. To see that this is true one need only ask whether the following questions make sense for virtually any business decision:

The Open Question Argument

(1) If this decision is made for whom is value created and destroyed?
(2) Who is harmed and/or benefited by this decision?
(3) Whose rights are enabled and whose values are realized by this decision (and whose are not)?

Since these questions are always open for most business decisions, it is reasonable to give up the Separation Fallacy. We need a theory about business that builds in answers to the 'Open Question Argument' above. One such answer would be 'Only value to shareholders counts', but such an answer would have to be enmeshed in the language of ethics as well as business. (We shall see later that Friedman, unlike most of his expositors, actually gives such a morally rich answer.) In short we need a theory that has as its basis what we might call:

The Integration Thesis I

Most business decisions, or sentences about business have some ethical content, or implicit ethical view. Most ethical decisions, or sentences about ethics have some business content or implicit view about business.

Yet another way to articulate this idea is:

The Integration Thesis II
(1) It makes no sense to talk about business without talking about ethics.
(2) It makes no sense to talk about ethics without talking about business.
(3) It makes no sense to talk about either business or ethics without talking about human beings.

One of the most pressing challenges facing business scholars is to tell compelling narratives that have the Integration Thesis at its heart. This is essentially the task that those scholars, called 'stakeholder theorists', have begun over the last 25 years: (1) challenges much work that is done in the name of 'value-free economics and science'; (2) challenges much work that is done by philosophers who have little knowledge of either economics or business; and (3) challenges much work done in all of the business disciplines which ignores 'the human sciences' or 'humanities' or, more concretely, the fact that most human beings are pretty complex. Stakeholder theory has developed primarily around (1). Its future development and usefulness depend largely on how it deals with (2) and (3).

To begin to address (1) we need to go to the very basics of ethics and we suggest that something like the following principle is implicit in most reasonably comprehensive moral views.

The Responsibility Principle
Most people, most of the time, want to and do accept responsibility for the effects of their actions on others.

Clearly the Responsibility Principle is incompatible with the Separation Fallacy. If business is separated from ethics, there is no question of moral responsibility for business decisions; hence, the joke is that business ethics is an oxymoron. More clearly still, without something like 'the Responsibility Principle,' it is difficult to see how ethics gets off the ground. 'Responsibility' may well be a difficult and multifaceted idea. There are surely many different ways to understand it. But if we are not willing to accept the responsibility for our own actions (as limited as that may be due to complicated issues of causality and the like), then ethics understood as how we reason together so we can all flourish is likely an exercise in bad faith.

One response to the Responsibility Principle is that some people in fact do not want to be responsible or ethical. They simply want to get away with as much as possible at the expense of others. People sometimes act 'opportunistically and with guile'. While there is some truth in this view the question is one of starting points. Start with the Responsibility Principle and you still have to deal with the problem of opportunism, but it does not become a fundamental consideration defining organizational design. Start with opportunism, and one is likely to leave out important ideas like human dignity, cooperative endeavors, the creative spirit, all of which we suggest are the cornerstones of capitalism. We need a more thorough understanding of the Responsibility Principle, its origins, and implications, on either account.

It is now easy to see that the genesis of 'stakeholder theory' is simply the Integration Thesis plus the Responsibility Principle. Give up the Separation Fallacy, in part because of the Open Question Argument, and there is little alternative. People engaged in value creation and trade are responsible precisely to 'those groups and individuals who can affect or be affected by their actions', i.e., stakeholders. For most businesses, as we currently understand it today, this means paying attention at least to customers, employees, suppliers, communities, and financiers.

'Stakeholder theory' does not mean that representatives of these groups must sit on governing boards of the firm, nor does it mean that shareholders (we prefer 'financiers' as a more inclusive term) have no rights. It does imply that the interests of these groups are joint, and that to create value, one must focus on how value gets created for each and all stakeholders. How value gets created for stakeholders is just how each is affected by the actions of others as well as managers.

'Stakeholder theory' is fundamentally a theory about how business works, at its best, and how it could work. It is descriptive, prescriptive, and instrumental at the same time and, as Donaldson and Preston (1995) have argued, it is managerial. Stakeholder theory is about business and how to effectively manage a business. 'Effective' can be seen as 'Create as much value as possible'.

For the most part writers on stakeholder theory have taken an approach that looks at reasonably large existing businesses. They have tried to use the idea to address issues such as 'corporate social responsibility', 'corporate legitimacy', 'theory of the firm' and even macro-societal issues such as 'building the good society'. With rare exceptions there has been little thought given to a host of important issues that have concrete practical significance: how are we to understand value creation and trade at the simplest level? How do entrepreneurs create and sustain value? How does value creation and trade take place within and among multiple state regimes? While at first glance these questions may seem intractable, we want to suggest that we can take a stakeholder approach to them to yield some interesting insights, and to highlight some assumptions about both business and political philosophy, which we may wish to make optional.

There are a number of competing 'standard accounts' of value creation and trade. They all revolve around the idea that shareholders or owners or investors are entitled to the residual gains that accrue from value creation and trade. Stakeholder theory suggests that matters are more complicated, – that is, that they involve stakeholder relationships – and that human beings are more complex than is assumed by the standard accounts. We shall look, in turn, at the views of three influential theorists, Milton Friedman, Michael Jensen and Oliver Williamson.

3   The Friedman problem: business as maximizing shareholder value

Since the first formal articulation of stakeholder theory more than twenty years ago, there has been a great deal of debate about the difference between the views of business that are centered on stockholders and those that are centered on stakeholders. Milton Friedman's *New York Times Magazine* article, 'The Social Responsibility of Business is to Increase its Profits,' has been long juxtaposed against stakeholder theory and the ensuing debates have revealed few new or useful insights. In an attempt to move beyond the narrow supposed stakeholder/stockholder dichotomy, we spell out our reading of Friedman's controversial article which we believe to be compatible with Stakeholder theory – in fact we see Friedman as an early stakeholder theorist.

Friedman writes, 'It may be in the long-run interest of a corporation that is a major employer in a small community to devote resources to providing amenities to that community or to improving its government'. He goes on to say that it is wrong to call this social responsibility because, 'they [the actions] are entirely justified in its [the corporation's] self-interest'.

For Friedman, supporting stakeholder interests is not about social responsibility; it's about capitalism. According to Friedman, the purpose of business is to 'use its resources and engage in activities designed to increase its profits so long as it stays within the rules of the game, which is to say, engages in open and free competition, without deception or fraud' (CF 133).

All this sounds well and good to us. A key difference between our view and that of Friedman is what makes business successful. Friedman believes that it is maximizing profits. We believe that in order to maximize profits, companies need great products and services that are wanted by customers, solid relations with suppliers that keep operations on the cutting edge, inspired employees who stand for the company mission and push the company to become better, supportive communities that allow businesses to flourish. So in our view Friedman could have written the above quotation as:

Business is about making sure that products and services actually do what you say they are going to do, doing business with suppliers who want to make you better, having employees who are engaged in their work, and being good citizens in the community, all of which may well be in the long-run (or even possibly the short run) interest of a corporation. Stakeholder management is just good management and will lead to maximizing profits.

Under this reading Friedman is at least an instrumental stakeholder theorist. He may also believe that individuals have a responsibility not to destroy the basis of capitalism – freedom in his view. In his book *Capitalism and Freedom* he spells out that one of the virtues of the market economy is that it protects individuals from conformity and the abuse of political power. For Friedman, power must be checked and used responsibly. Since in his view economic freedom is a large subset of political freedom, we may deduce that he would agree that economic power is also subject to responsible use. Friedman may come to something like stakeholder theory out of more than just instrumentalism; he could see it as we do, as the very basis of capitalism.

There may also be a difference in the theories about the way the world works. Friedman may actually believe that if you try to maximize profits you will. We believe that trying to maximize profits is counterproductive because it takes attention away from the fundamental drivers of value – stakeholder relationships. There has been considerable research that shows that profitable firms have a purpose and values beyond profit maximization (Collins and Porras, Waddock et al.).

Both we and Friedman agree that business and capitalism is not about social responsibility. We contend that stakeholder theory is about business and value creation – as we said above, it is managerial. Economics is not fundamentally about value creation – it's an idealized and abstracted view built around the goals of prediction, not around the way that actual business works.

Despite the differences we believe that Friedman's maximizing shareholder value view is compatible with stakeholder theory – after all the only way to maximize value sustainably is to satisfy stakeholder interests.

4   The Jensen move: business as agency

Michael Jensen, in a paper titled 'Maximization, Stakeholder Theory and the Corporate Objective', argues that stakeholder theory needs an objective function, namely value maximization. He says, 'value maximization states that managers should make all decisions so as to increase the total long-run market value of the firm. Total value is the sum of all financial claims on the firm – including equity, debt, preferred stock, and warrants.' Jensen argues that stakeholder theory is incomplete because it does not offer answers to the questions 'how do we keep score, & how do we want the firms in our economy to measure better versus worse?' His argument is built on two major premises.

First, Jensen states that purposeful corporate behavior requires a single value objective function. He gives the example of a manager who is forced to choose between maximizing profit or market share – given that every incremental increase in market share comes at higher cost. Here he believes that managers are forced to choose between the two goals and that value maximization offers them an objective principle for making the trade-off. He continues, 'A firm can resolve this ambiguity by specifying the trade-offs among the various dimensions, and doing so amounts to specifying an overall objective function such as $V = f(x,y,...)$ that explicitly incorporates the effects of decisions on all the goods or bads (denoted by $(x,y,...)$) affecting the firm (such as cash flow, risk, and so on).'

We do not believe that the complexity of management can be simplified to such an extent. Primarily the variety of metrics used in a firm cannot be folded so easily into one overall objective function. Firms and people do not simply arrange values and preferences in hierarchical and easily understandable decision trees. Jensen's view ignores lexicographical orderings, or dictionary orderings. Additionally to create a final score or objective measure of the kind that Jensen wants, different metrics must be weighted. The process of choosing weights for these metrics requires some other notion of purpose or mission – it requires firms to answer the question, 'Who are we and who do we want to be?' These questions go beyond objective value maximization.

Second, Jensen claims that total firm value maximization makes society better off. He also admits that for this to be true there must be some special conditions in place. He says, 'When monopolies or externalities exist, the value maximizing criterion does not maximize social welfare. By externalities I mean situations in which the decision-maker does not bear the full cost or benefit consequences of his or her choices; water and air pollution are classic examples.' For Jensen, Ronald Coase provides the solution to these issues by reassigning property rights to avoid a second best solution. But, of course, there are no arguments for Coase's blatantly utilitarian reasoning. Both Jensen and Coase simply ride roughshod over the idea of rights, assuming, as had been argued by Charles Fried, that everything is alienable, even our right to bargain at all. Fried suggests, and we agree, that such a view is at best incoherent. So, Jensen's faith that total firm value maximization makes society better off is dependant on a number of further arguments. While these arguments may be interesting to economists and philosophers, they don't serve much purpose to understand how value gets created.

Jensen as much as acknowledges this point as he comes to see stakeholder theory as the primary vehicle for understanding how value creation and trade takes place. He says,

> We can learn from the stakeholder theorists how to lead managers and participants in an organization to think more generally and creatively about how the organization's policies treat all important constituencies of the firm. This includes not just financial markets, but employees, customers, suppliers, the community in which the organization exists, and so on.

Jensen calls the coupling of the objective function and stakeholder theory Enlightened Value Maximization. Like Friedman, Jensen can be seen as an instrumental stakeholder theorist. He believes that managers need to make trade-offs and that they should be guided by the principle of enlightened value maximization. For a second time we see that if we interpret stakeholder theory as a theory about how value gets created, we have little difference with economists like Friedman and Jensen.

5 The Williamson result: business as transaction cost economizing

In a path-breaking paper Ronald Coase questioned the economic orthodoxy of the time, and wondered why some transactions seem to be organized by markets as economic theory demands, while others seem to be organized by hierarchical arrangements, such as firms. Coase's answer, that most of the time there is a cost to using the pricing mechanism, and that when these 'transaction costs' are sufficiently high, someone will organize the transaction via a hierarchy or firm, as opposed to a market. The literature on 'transaction costs' or 'markets and hierarchies' is now a well-established area of social science.

Indeed, Oliver Williamson, one of Coase's principal modern disciples, has suggested that we can understand transaction cost theory in terms of contracts and that the standard account of firms as a nexus of contracts follows. Shareholders still bear the residual risk, while other stakeholders have arranged bilateral contracts with built-in safeguards, so that shareholders are entitled to the returns. There is no need to give a 'stakeholder account' of transaction cost theory in this interpretation of Williamson's view.

The first point to make here is that, like the standard account, this view does not offer much practical insight into how to create value and trade. The best it can do is to exhort us to 'understand the structure of transaction costs'. While this may seem like little, recent work on e-business, supply chain management, and other issues resulting from the application of information technology offers much illumination of the actual practices of value creation and trade. However, on closer examination of these issues, all of them look like analyses of stakeholder relationships. After all, how can one see supply chain management as anything other than integrating the supplier–firm–customer chain of events? So, it may be that to turn transaction cost theory toward the practical understanding of value creation and trade, one needs to overlay a stakeholder network.

Second, Freeman and Evan (1990) have questioned Williamson's analysis here by introducing the idea that if contracts have safeguards, then the question of who pays the cost of the safeguards is relevant. For instance, if management and labor contract against a backdrop of the liberal state complete with safeguards for labor such as labor boards, processes that must be followed under penalty of law, etc., then both parties have successfully exported the costs of the safeguards of their contract to society as a whole. Indeed we suggest that a distinction between *exogenous safeguards* (where the costs are externalized to society or other stakeholders) and *endogenous safeguards* (where the parties to the contract pay the cost of contracting including safeguards) is crucial for seeing the necessity for a stakeholder approach to markets and hierarchies.

In a recent paper, Williamson and Bercovitz (1996) seem to accept this idea at least in part. They suggest that shareholder boards be seen as endogenous safeguards. They even suggest that stakeholder-oriented 'Boards of Overseers' may well be a good idea to get more stakeholder input into the value creation process, of which stakeholders are clearly a part. But, they fail to adequately deal with the criticism that safeguards have costs. The implication of such a view is that the contractual arrangements that we observe will be a function of how parties to the contract have been able to either accept or offload the costs of safeguards. This process is not necessarily a transaction cost economizing process, but rather a political one. If the parties to the contract can externalize the costs of safeguards to others, such as taxpayers, then we would expect to see them use their own power in the political process to realize such gains. In fact we are appealing to nothing more than the strict 'opportunism' assumption in transaction cost theory. (The only way to explain voluntary interactions with stakeholders or endogenous safeguards, would be to appeal to either a lack of political power, or something like the responsibility principle and subsequent stakeholder theory.) On Williamson's well-known diagram, slightly revised, it would be difficult to tell if a particular governance mechanism appeared at node B or at node D (see Figure 3.1).

In summary, the argument is this. Assume a version of the modern state, the rule of law, and a set of institutions that makes contracting viable. One can then understand the creation of value and trade against this backdrop of background institutions. In a world in which these institutions emerge so that financiers have the right to the residuals of the firm, something like the standard story emerges. Absent these institutions and we are left wondering who pays or should pay for whose safeguards. If this is in fact an open question, then a series of other questions is relevant. Could it be interesting to imagine a world where there are only endogenous safeguards? A world in which there are no background institutions, or where there is only the presumption that value creation and trade will continue over time? A world in which there are many conflicting and competing background institutions and there is the desire for value creation and trade to continue over time?

We want to suggest that these last questions must take us substantially beyond what has been done so far in the transaction cost literature, and must put us firmly in the middle of stakeholder theory. Transaction Costs Economics

Williamson's Original Diagram

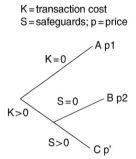

K = transaction cost
S = safeguards; p = price

Revised Diagram

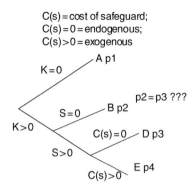

C(s) = cost of safeguard;
C(s) = 0 = endogenous;
C(s)>0 = exogenous

Figure 3.1 Transactions cost theory

(TCE) simply focuses too heavily on one sort of governance mechanism, traditional boards of directors. And TCE is too concerned with yielding the traditional view of economics. However, we have suggested that one can use TCE reasoning to see that if the costs of safeguards were assigned differently, then other arrangements may well be possible. We don't see those arrangements, because of the current way we think about safeguards as 'primarily, government's job'.

However, TCE's idea of stakeholder boards of overseers is actually quite an interesting one. Suppose such a board's task were to: (1) reduce information asymmetry among key stakeholders so that management could more easily create even more value; (2) view the interest of financiers, customers, suppliers, communities and employees as joint; and, (3) assume the continuation of the corporation through time. It may well turn out that such a board becomes a very effective 'governance mechanism' to help managers create as much value as possible for stakeholders.

6 Business activity as entrepreneurial opportunity

6.1 Entrepreneurship theory

In a path-breaking article that both summarizes and extends the entrepreneurship literature, S. Venkataraman has suggested that understanding entrepreneurship can fill the gap left by the standard accounts of business activity. He suggests that:

In most societies, most markets are inefficient most of the time, thus providing opportunities for enterprising individuals to enhance wealth by exploiting these inefficiencies. (The Weak Premise of Entrepreneurship)

And, alternatively:

> Even if some markets approach a state of equilibrium, the human condition of enterprise, combined with the lure of profits and advancing knowledge and technology, will destroy the equilibrium sooner or later. (The Strong Premise of Entrepreneurship)[2]

In a second paper, Venkataraman connects entrepreneurship with the stakeholder literature by claiming that:[3]

> The essence of the corporation is the competitive claims made of it by diverse stakeholders. It is a fact of business life that different stakeholders have different and often conflicting expectations of a corporation. Indeed, the firm itself can be said to be an invention to allow such conflict to be discovered, surfaced, and resolved, because conflicting claims have to be discovered and methods for resolution executed... This inherent conflict is a feature not only of the established giant corporation, but also of the very act of creation of the productive enterprise. Entrepreneurship involves joint production where several different stakeholders have to be brought together to create the new product or service.

According to this view, the existence of entrepreneurial activity in a society acts as an equilibrating force. It offers an alternative to stakeholders whose needs are not being met by the current arrangement.[4] There is both a weak and strong equilibrating process.

> The weak equilibrating process holds that whenever a stakeholder justifiable believes that the value supplied by him or her to a firm is more than the value received, the entrepreneurial process will redeploy the resources of the 'victimized' stakeholder to a use where value supplied and received will be equilibrated. The strong equilibrating process holds that if the redeployment of individual stakeholders does not work freely and efficiently and serious value anomalies accumulate within firms and societies, the entrepreneurial process will destroy the value anomalies by fundamental rearrangements in how resources and stakeholders are combined.[5]

The very processes of entrepreneurial activity whereby entrepreneurs find or create opportunities because they have knowledge or experience that others don't depends on understanding how stakeholder interests have been or cannot be satisfied.

In the following sections we want to unpack these processes in more practical terms to see how value creation and trade can actually come about.

6.2   The entrepreneur as deal maker

Suppose that Smith has a particularly good recipe for bread. He finds that friends and relatives are always taking second and third helpings of bread at dinner, asking for the recipe, and cornering Smith for tips on how to bake such good bread. Smith reasons that if the bread is so good, there must be people who are willing to pay for the bread, and after all who cannot use the extra cash? So, Smith starts to sell his bread to others. Perhaps he delivers it to steady customers or even 'contracts' with the local grocer to sell the bread in her store. Smith has become an entrepreneur. And, perhaps the standard account can explain Smith's success or failure.

On the standard account we would expect the growth and development of Smith Bread Company to be a function of the market for bread. We would try to understand the structure of that market focusing, for instance, on matters such as the number of buyers and sellers, the product ranges of each, and the price points of the offerings. If Smith Bread Company succeeds it would be because Smith is able to offer a similar product at perhaps a lower price, or perhaps with another feature that buyers of bread want. If Smith Bread Company fails it would be because others offered the same product at a lower price. In fact, the strict neoclassical view of the standard account would suggest that all of the information regarding features and product performance is reflected in the price of the product. A 'second-best' version of this view, akin to Michael Porter's view of strategy, argues that in most real markets it would be slightly more complex, and Smith could position the company to take advantage of those complexities or not. In short Smith's success or failure is a matter of the market for bread. Understand that market and you'll understand all you need to know about Smith Bread Company.

None of this gives much advice to Smith or explains how Smith Bread Company really came about. This view of markets as consisting of buyers and sellers is interesting only to the extent that the question 'How does this market work?' is an interesting one. Understanding the Dutch flower market, the Chicago futures market, the coffee exchange in Uganda, and others is a set of interesting questions but ultimately they are questions about the distribution of value in very specialized situations, rather than its creation in the first instance.

Let us go further and suppose that Smith's bread is a big hit with all who try it. Soon Smith must quit his full-time job (perhaps Smith is professor of economics and moral philosophy at Edinburgh) and devote all day to baking bread. He quickly realizes that the kitchen oven is being monopolized by the bread baking, so he invests money in another oven and fixes up the spare room to do nothing but bake bread. But, even this is not enough. The demand for Smith's bread is so great that he decides to invest his savings and perhaps talks to his local banker about a loan. Smith builds a bread factory, and hires workers to bake the bread in the ovens. Smith spends his time directing the baking and selling of bread.

The markets and hierarchies view is relevant here. It would suggest that Smith Bread Company is successful just if Smith is correct that he can organize some of the transactions internally via the authority relationship, such as hiring workers to bake the bread, rather than buying bread in the market for bread and reselling it. Indeed this view might tell us that if it could be done more cheaply, it may well be in Smith's interest to begin to grow his own wheat. The success of Smith's venture will not be solely a function of the market for bread, but also a function of the markets for the factors of production, e.g., the labor market and the market for ingredients such as wheat and yeast.

While this view is a more detailed analysis of what is happening to Smith Bread Company, it gives little practical advice, for how is Smith to know that the transaction costs of organizing transactions inside the firm is actually lower than using the market mechanism?

Now let's take a more fine-grained view of Smith's enterprise. What must Smith do to be successful? He must buy raw materials from suppliers that he can be assured are of good quality. He must have employees who will make the bread as Smith would, and this is easier when these employees come to want to make the bread as Smith would. He must find customers who want and who enjoy his bread so much that they buy it again and again.[6] To the extent that he has extended his financial resources to include the bank, relatives, or even shareholders, Smith must make a return for these other financiers, as well as profits (in some form) for himself. And, perhaps more subtly Smith must be a good citizen in the community. At a minimum Smith must not use his property to harm others. Suppose for instance that Smith's new bakery emitted noxious fumes, smelled by other members in the community. Smith would come under pressure to do something about it, and if Smith lived in a relatively free society, community members could claim that Smith has damaged them, and sue for relief, either through the courts, or via legislation.

In short when Smith successfully, over time, satisfies customers, financiers, suppliers, employees and the community, then Smith Bread Company prospers. Notice that the success of Smith Bread Company is still dependent on the market for bread, and the various factor markets, but Smith now has some tangible advice about how to create value and sustain it.

Venkataraman has suggested that the conflicts that exist between actors in the factor markets will ultimately be sorted out by the entrepreneurial process (the strong or weak force). But, alternatively, we can look at these conflicts from the standpoint of Smith and the stakeholders in Smith Bread Company. From Smith's point of view, his job is to try and solve these conflicts in a way that is good for the 'joint enterprise' that is Smith Bread Company. When customers have complaints, he wants to solve these complaints so that they do not stop buying bread. Now there will be limits to what Smith is able to do, and against these limits, the entrepreneurial forces will operate. When employees become disgruntled so that they do not put forth their best effort or even think about leaving, Smith wants to find a way to keep creating a sufficient level of value for them to stay. Again there will be limits, but practically speaking, Smith always seeks to test these limits: *To create as much value as possible for all stakeholders.*

As a practical solution to this problem, Smith needs to see the interests of stakeholders as moving in roughly the same direction. He also needs to see that the interests of one stakeholder may well be enhanced in the presence of others.[7] Many stakeholder theorists have focused on the inherent conflict between stakeholder interests, and in doing so, they have forgotten that stakeholder interests are also joint. Many other theorists have claimed that stakeholder theory claims that all stakeholders are equally important. Again, they have forgotten the real world beginnings of the theory. All are not equally important at all points of time, but all have the equal right to bargain about whatever their interests are. (We take this to be a simple statement of some notion of classical liberalism.) And, all interests have to roughly go together over time, or else in a relatively free society, stakeholders will turn to the state for restitution.

Now there seems to be no difference in understanding value creation in a stakeholder manner no matter if the setting is a large multinational or a small start-up. Perhaps three quick examples will be sufficient.

Patricia is a manager of ABC Pharma. She is responsible for a project that works on diabetes. She must deal simultaneously with employees who are doing the research, potential customers (including a chain of wholesalers, retailers, agents, agencies, and the medical community), suppliers of chemicals, testing agents, and the like. She has to be cognizant of the interests of financiers as well as the community, which is fairly well understood in this instance due to the intrusive nature of state intervention in the pharmaceutical industry. If she is successful, she will get all of these diverse interests going in roughly the same direction over time. Sometimes she will have to trade one off against the other, but she must discover a way to make them work together.

Jennifer had an idea to start a catalog company that offered automobile radio and stereo equipment. To do so she had to negotiate arrangements with a host of suppliers, find lists of potential customers, hire employees to design catalogs, fill orders, and deal with customer questions, and continually meet with the banks and family members that provided the original financing. As the business grew she had to negotiate a land deal to build a warehouse. This involved a number of permits from agencies, and visits to neighboring parcels of land to talk about water usage, potential environmental problems, and other 'social issues'. If Jennifer was successful, it was because she managed to put together a deal so that all of these stakeholders were winners over time. In the beginning suppliers and financiers may well have been most important, and it may be that communities became important only later. But, if Jennifer's company is to be sustainable, all stakeholder relationships have to push in roughly the same direction.

Rinaldo and his friends have an idea for a new computer game. One friend is a very good programmer. Rinaldo's expertise is in getting a team of people to work together. He gathers together a team with differing sources of expertise, puts together a business plan, and finds some funding from venture capitalists and another small computer game start-up. Initially Rinaldo will have to focus on keeping the team engaged in what they are doing and managing the expectations of the financiers. But, soon will come the time to beta test the product, and potential customers will be needed. Eventually, if successful, Rinaldo will have to worry about getting a supplier to manufacture the finished product. And, given the current arrangement of social institutions, Rinaldo will have to worry about how the game is viewed by the broader community. For instance, if the game is about how teenagers can commit more juvenile delinquency, there may well be a move to boycott the game, or label it as unsuited for minors.

In all three of these examples, entrepreneurs, both start-up and existing venture entrepreneurs, have to become enmeshed and engaged in stakeholder relationships. They have to solve conflicts while preserving the joint nature of these relationships. They have to be responsible for the effects of their actions, if they want their ventures to survive. They have to understand that employees, customers and other stakeholders are complex beings, and that they cannot manage with a 'one size fits all' point of view. It is important to understand competition, but only in so far as they are unable to continue to create maximum value for stakeholders. We want to suggest that these ideas, which spring from a groundfloor view of value creation and trade, can be generalized into a set of principles for rewriting our understanding of capitalism.

6.3 Stakeholder capitalism

The Separation Fallacy in part prevents us from having such a robust and morally rich conception of business. On the one hand the emergence of business ethics has meant trying to connect the existing business discourse with ethical theory. On the other hand, this view has a consequence, which many ethicists do not find quite so palatable. We believe that it equally makes no sense to have a discourse of ethics, which is absent some reasonably sophisticated ideas about the nature of value creation and trade. Here there is a bigger problem. Most of our ethical theory and conceptual apparatus has evolved from a political view that puts as the first question of political philosophy: How is the state to be justified? We challenge you find any modern book on political philosophy or ethical theory that includes an entry for 'business' in the index.

Rarely will you find an entry for 'economics' and there certainly is no other account than the standard one set out above.[8] Since John Rawls there has been increased interest in the intersection of economics and political theory, but that interest has stayed at the very highest levels of abstraction with game and decision theorists, and has as yet failed to yield much practical insight.

We want to suggest that we might alternatively ask, as the first question of political philosophy or practical ethics,[9] 'How is value creation and trade sustainable over time?' If we could answer that question we might then ask, 'What role is left for the state?' We believe that this approach to political philosophy and ethics may well yield some useful insights. We want to sketch out the answer to the first question, and in doing so suggest that the resulting 'stakeholder capitalism' can begin to address the second question.

Roughly the answer goes like this. Value creation and trade is sustainable over time if it is conducted in accordance with the following three principles which build on what we earlier called the 'bare mechanics' of stakeholder theory:

The Principle of Stakeholder Cooperation
Value can be created, traded, and sustained because stakeholders can jointly satisfy their needs and desires by making voluntary agreements with each other, that for the most part are kept.

The Principle of Stakeholder Responsibility
Value can be created, traded, and sustained because parties to an agreement are willing to accept responsibility for the consequences of their actions. When third parties are harmed, they must be compensated, or a new agreement must be negotiated with all of those parties that are affected.

The Principle of Complexity
Value can be created, traded, and sustained because human beings are complex psychological creatures capable of acting from many different values and points of view.

While we have articulated these principles elsewhere, we want to say a little about how each of them leads to the sustainability of value creation and trade. The first principle simply restates the argument of this chapter, that value creation is best understood as participating in a deal that satisfies multiple stakeholders over time. It is fundamentally about how value gets created. Now if this works, there can well be a presumption that the deal will continue: that the contract that stands for the multilateral arrangements of stakeholder interests over time, will continue. The possibility of this continuing arrangement yields sustainability. Of course, not all businesses are sustainable forever. Companies come and go. But, they emerge and disappear precisely because the managers or entrepreneurs have either continued to satisfy the interests of stakeholders or not.

The second principle may well turn out to be a sufficient condition for the emergence of the kind of stakeholder capitalism that we have in mind.[10] Imagine a world in which companies do not try to get away with meeting minimum standards set by the state, but in which companies understand that the interests of their customers correspond exactly to their own interests. If a product does harm in an unanticipated way, the company wants to stand behind the product. After all, if we are unwilling to be responsible for the effects of our action, then ethics simply can't get off the ground, except in a Hobbesian kind of brutish way. Imagine that same world, where stakeholders do not sue companies for effects where the stakeholders were the main protagonists. We have in mind some peculiarly American examples of suing a company because the coffee was hot and caused a burn. Where there is a strong sense of responsibility, where that is built into thinking about business, and where thinking about business is built into thinking about ethics, we would see a flourishing of entrepreneurship like never before.

The third principle simply says that the psychology of the standard accounts of business activity, that business people are greedy one-dimensional profit-maximizers, is disingenuous. The very idea that value creation and trade flourishes is built on a notion that we may well be different, have different needs and values, as well as share some needs and values. The entrepreneur that is successful must understand the nature of authority relationships, the social nature of human interaction, the complex nature of in-groups and out-groups, and other psychological issues. Milgram, Goffman, Freud, Jung, Zimbardo, Klein, and others are as relevant to our understanding of value creation and trade as are Samuelson, Arrow and Debreu.

6.4   Implications for practice

We believe that the implications for the practice of business are fairly straightforward. We want to make three suggestions for how we can more easily enact the story of stakeholder capitalism.

First, let's end all of this talk that the only responsibility of a business is to create shareholder value. The recent growth spurt of unethical activity has added fuel to the fires of business ethicists, but the real problem is not one of business ethics. Rather we have let our idea of 'good management' get hijacked by a narrow idea that is not about how value creation and trade works. Of course, shareholders have to win and win big. So do customers, suppliers, employees, and communities if we want to sustain value creation and trade. We must return our idea of 'good management' to something like the ideas suggested here – or another set where business and ethics are not separated.

We have tried to show that this is even implicit in the work of Friedman, Jensen, and Williamson.

Second, let's continue to develop a deep and sophisticated understanding of human behavior in all aspects of our lives. Let's not send business to the moral ghetto, so that in most of our lives we are complicated fathers and mothers, partners, lovers, and citizens, yet in business we are greedy little bastards trying to maximize self-interest and beat the other guy. The assumptions that we make daily about value creation and trade create a commons. We need to destroy most of the current commons and replace it with a more robust one that treats human beings with dignity as the complex creatures that we are.

Finally, let's apply the first principle of stakeholder capitalism to our enterprise of thinking about value creation and trade. We will find more robust accounts, more useful theories and ideas, if we work together across disciplines, schools, geographies, cultures and other boundaries. Value creation and trade is a vast human endeavor. We will create sustainable value if we work together, sorting out our very real conflicts as we go, rebuilding both ethics and business from the ground up.

Notes

1. We are grateful to S. Venkataraman, Gordon Sollars, Jeffrey Harrison, Rama Velamuri, Saras Sarasvathy, Susan Harmeling, Robert Phillips, Laura Dunham, and John McVea, as well as a number of other colleagues and seminar participants at a variety of universities, for many helpful comments on the ideas in this chapter.
2. S. Venkataraman, 'The Distinctive Domain of Entrepreneurship Research', *Advances in Entrepreneurship, Firm Emergence and Growth*, vol. 3, Greenwood, CT: JAI Press, 1997, pp. 119–38 at p. 121.
3. S. Venkataraman, 'Stakeholder Value Equilibration and the Entrepreneurial Process', in R. Edward Freeman and S. Venkataraman (eds), *Ethics and Entrepreneurship*, The Ruffin Series, Volume 3, pages 45–57, The Society for Business Ethics, at p. 46.
4. This is the reason behind the insight that 'behind every disgruntled stakeholder and critic of a company, lies a business opportunity'.
5. Venkataraman, 'The Distinctive Domain of Entrepreneurship', at 50.
6. Strictly speaking this premise is not necessary. There are some businesses that rely on one-time purchases. But, in the real world, managers and entrepreneurs think of customers as wanting to buy again and again. This is the whole reason for brands.
7. A simple example of what we have in mind here is the fact that our interests are better served when we are on the same faculty as Venkataraman where we can easily work together.
8. Of course, there are exceptions. Marx understood only too well that ethics makes no sense outside of value creation and trade. Unfortunately he did not have a sophisticated enough view of value creation and trade to make his ideas sustainable. And, earlier, people such as Adam Smith had no such separation. Amartya Sen's book, *Ethics and Economics*, is a brilliant analysis of how all of this started in economic theory.

9. As pragmatists, we are not putting much stock into differentiating between these questions, although we understand the arguments that they are different.
10. We are grateful to Professor Gordon Sollars for this insight.

References

Agle, B. R., Mitchell, Ronald K., and Jeffrey A. Sonnenfeld (1999) 'Who Matters to CEOs? An Investigation of Stakeholder Attributes and Salience, Corporate Performance, and CEO Values', *Academy of Management Journal*, vol. 42(5), 507–26.

Andriof, J., S. Waddock, B. Husted and S. Sutherland Rahman (eds) (2002) *Unfolding Stakeholder Thinking*. Sheffield, UK: Greenleaf Publishing Limited.

Berman, S., A. C. Wicks, S. Kotha and T. Jones (1999) 'Does Stakeholder Orientation Matter: An Empirical Examination of the Relationship Between Stakeholder Management Models and Firm Financial Performance', *Academy of Management Journal*, vol. 42, 488–506.

Blair, M. (1995) 'Whose Interests Should Be Served?', in Max Clarkson (ed.), *Ownership and Control: Rethinking Corporate Governance for the Twenty First Century*. Washington, DC: The Brookings Institution, pp. 202–34.

Boatright, J. (1994) 'Fiduciary Duties and the Shareholder-Management Relation: Or, What's So Special about Shareholders?', *Business Ethics Quarterly*, vol. 4, 393–407.

Clarkson, M. (1995) 'A Stakeholder Framework for Analyzing and Evaluating Corporate Social Performance', *Academy of Management Review*, vol. 20, 92–117.

Collins, J. and J. Porras (1994), *Built to Last*. New York: Harper.

Donaldson, T. and T. Dunfee (1999) *Ties That Bind: A Social Contracts Approach to Business Ethics*. Boston, MA: Harvard Business School Press.

Donaldson T. and Lee Preston (1995) 'The Stakeholder Theory of the Corporation: Concepts, Evidence, and Implications', *Academy of Management Review*, vol. 20, 65–91.

Dunham, L., J. Liedtka and R.E. Freeman (2004) 'Enhancing Stakeholder Practice: A Particularized Exploration of Community', Darden School Working Paper.

Emshoff, J. (1978) *Managerial Breakthroughs*. New York: AMACOM.

Evan, W. and R.E. Freeman (1993) 'A Stakeholder Theory of the Modern Corporation: Kantian Capitalism', in T. Beauchamp and Norman Bowie (eds), *Ethical Theory and Business*. Englewood Cliffs, NJ: Prentice Hall.

Freeman, R.E. (1984) *Strategic Management: A Stakeholder Approach*. Boston, MA: Pitman.

Freeman, R.E. (1994) 'The Politics of Stakeholder Theory', *Business Ethics Quarterly*, vol. 4(4).

Freeman, R.E. (2004) 'The Stakeholder Approach Revisited', *Zeitschrift für Wirtschafts – und Unternehmensethik*, vol. 5(3), pp. 228–41.

Freeman, R.E. and W. Evan (1990) 'Corporate Governance: A Stakeholder Interpretation', *The Journal of Behavioral Economics*, vol. 19(4), pp. 337–59.

Freeman, R.E. and D. Gilbert (1988) *Corporate Strategy and the Search for Ethics*. Englewood Cliffs, NJ: Prentice Hall Inc.

Freeman, R.E. and J. Emshoff (1981) 'Stakeholder Management: A Case Study of the U.S. Brewers and the Container Issue', in R. Schultz (ed.), *Applications of Management Science*. Greenwich: JAI Press, vol. 1.

Freeman, R.E. and James Emshoff (1979) 'Who's Butting Into Your Business', *The Wharton Magazine*, Fall, 44–8, 58–9.

Freeman, R.E. and J. McVea (2001) 'Stakeholder Theory: The State of the Art', in Michael A. Hitt, R.E. Freeman and Jeffery Harrison (eds), *The Blackwell Handbook of Strategic Management*. Oxford: Blackwell Publishing.

Freeman, R.E., J. McVea, A.C. Wicks and B. Parmar (2004) 'Stakeholder Theory: The State of the Art and Future Perspectives', *Politeia*, vol. 20(74).

Freeman, R.E., J. Harrison and A.C. Wicks (2007) *Managing for Stakeholders: Business in the 21st Century*. New Haven, CT: Yale University Press.

Freeman, R.E., J. Harrison, A.C. Wicks and Simone de Colle (2010) *Stakeholder Theory: The State of the Art*. Cambridge University Press.

Fried, C. (1981) *Contract as Promise: A Theory of Contractual Obligation* Cambridge, MA: Harvard University Press.

Friedman, M. (1962) *Capitalism and Freedom*. Chicago: University of Chicago Press.

Goodpaster, K. (1991) 'Business Ethics and Stakeholder Analysis', *Business Ethics Quarterly*, vol. 1, 53–73.

Goodpaster, K. and Tom Holloran (1994) 'In Defense of a Paradox', *Business Ethics Quarterly*, vol. 4, 423–30.

Graves, S. and S. Waddock (1990) 'Institutional Ownership and Control: Implications for Long-Term Corporate Performance', *Academy of Management Executive*, vol. 37, 1034–46.

Graves, S. (1994) 'Institutional Owners and Corporate Social Performance', *Academy of Management Journal*, vol. 37(4), 1034.

Harrison, J. and J.O. Fiet (1999) 'New CEOs Pursue Their Own Self-Interests by Sacrificing Stakeholder Values', *Journal of Business Ethics*, vol. 19, 301–8.

Harrison, J. and Caron St John (1994) *Strategic Management of Organizations and Stakeholders*. St Paul: West Publishing Company.

Jensen, M. (2002) 'Maximization, Stakeholder Theory and the Corporate Objective', *Business Ethics Quarterly*, vol. 12(2), 235–56.

Jones, T. (1995) 'Instrumental Stakeholder Theory: A Synthesis of Ethics and Economics' *Academy of Management Review*, vol. 20, 92–117.

Jones, T. and Andrew C. Wicks (1999) 'Convergent Stakeholder Theory', *Academy of Management Review*, vol. 24, 206–21.

Kochan, T. and S. Rubenstein (2000) 'Towards a Stakeholder Theory of the Firm: The Saturn Partnership', *Organizational Science*, vol. 11(4), 367–86.

Luoma, P. and J. Goodstein (1999) 'Stakeholders and Corporate Boards: Institutional Influences on Board Composition and Structure', *Academy of Management Journal*, vol. 42, 553–63.

Marens, R. and A.C. Wicks (1999) 'Getting Real: Stakeholder Theory, Managerial Practice, and the General Irrelevance of Fiduciary Duties Owed to Shareholders', *Business Ethics Quarterly*, vol. 9(2), 273–93.

Martin, K. and R.E. Freeman (2004) 'The Separation of Technology and Ethics in Business Ethics', *Journal of Business Ethics*, vol. 53(4), 353–64.

Mitchell, R.K., Bradley R. Agle and Donna J. Wood (1997) 'Toward a Theory of Stakeholder Identification and Salience: Defining the Principle of Who and What Really Counts', *Academy of Management Review*, vol. 22, 853–86.

Ogden, S. and R. Watson (1999) 'Corporate Performance and Stakeholder Management: Balancing Shareholder and Customer Interests in the UK Privatized Water Industry', *Academy of Management Journal*, vol. 42, 526–38.

Orts, E. (1997) 'A North American Legal Perspective on Stakeholder Management Theory', in F. Patfield (ed.), *Perspectives on Company Law* (London: Kluwer), vol. 2, pp. 165–79.

Phillips, R. (1997) 'Stakeholder Theory and a Principle of Fairness', *Business Ethics Quarterly*, vol. 7, vol. 51–66.

Phillips, R. and J. Reichart (1998) 'The Environment as a Stakeholder: A Fairness-Based Approach', *Journal of Business Ethics*, vol. 23(2), 185–97.

Phillips, R., R.E. Freeman and A.C. Wicks (2003) 'What Stakeholder Theory Is Not', *Business Ethics Quarterly*, vol. 13(4), 479–502.

Porter, M. (1998) *Competitive Advantage*. New York: The Free Press.

Preston, L. (1986) *Social Issues and Public Policy in Business and Management: Retrospect and Prospect*. College Park: University of Maryland College of Business and Management.

Venkataraman, S. (2002) 'Stakeholder Equilibration and the Entrepreneurial Process', in R.E. Freeman, and S. Venkataraman (eds), *The Ruffin Series #3, Ethics and Entrepreneurship*. Charlottesville, VA: Philosophy Documentation Center, pp. 45–57.

Waddock, S.A., C. Bodwell and S.B. Graves (2002) 'Responsibility: the New Imperative', *Academy of Management Executive*, vol. 16(2), pp. 132–48.

Wicks, A.C. (1996) 'Reflections on The Practical Relevance of Feminist Thought to Business', *Business Ethics Quarterly*, vol. 6(4), 523–32.

Wicks, A.C., R.E. Freeman and D. Gilbert (1994) 'A Feminist Reinterpretation of the Stakeholder Concept', *Business Ethics Quarterly*, vol. 4, 475–97.

Wicks, A.C. and R.E. Freeman (1998) 'Organization Studies and the New Pragmatism: Positivism, Anti-Positivism, and the Search for Ethics', *Organization Science*, vol. 9(2), pp. 123–40.

Wicks, A.C., R.E. Freeman and B. Parmar (2004) 'The Corporate Objective Revisited', *Organization Science*, vol. 15(3), pp. 364–9.

Wicks, A.C., R.E. Freeman and B. Parmar (forthcoming) 'Business Ethics in an Era of Corporate Crisis', Darden School Working Paper.

Williamson, O. (1984) *The Economic Institutions of Capitalism*. New York: Free Press.

Williamson, O. and J. Bercovitz (1996) 'The Modern Corporation as an Efficiency Instrument: The Comparative Contracting Perspective', in Carl Kaysen (ed.), *The American Corporation Today*. New York: Oxford University Press, pp. 327–59.

4
Behavioral Economics, Federalism and the Triumph of Stakeholder Theory

Allen Kaufman and Ernie Englander

1 Introduction

As in the Cold War's conclusion, when the Berlin Wall fell, stakeholder theory's victory over financial agency theory occurred with a tumultuous event – the 2001 stock market crash. Financial agency theorists were left to concede that financial markets were less than perfect (Jensen, Murphy and Ruck, 2004; Jensen, 2002). Even Michael Jensen, agency theory's most prominent apostle, proclaimed himself an 'enlightened' stakeholder advocate. This qualification permitted Jensen to distinguish himself from those managerial theorists who had for two decades resisted agency theory's advance. Yet, his distance seems rather odd, given the recent widespread acceptance of behavioral economics and law. For, when these are incorporated into stakeholder theory, the contentious descriptive disagreements find a satisfactory resolution, leaving discord on that enduring ethical issue – a fair surplus divide.

In their recent article, 'The Corporate Objective Revisited', Sundaram and Inkpen (2004a) hearken back to pre-enlightened agency theory by reciting the well-worn complaints against stakeholder theory. The authors summarize these in a series of questions posed to stakeholder advocates: (1) 'How should a manager identify the important stakeholders and on what basis should other stakeholders be classified as unimportant?'; (2) 'Who should determine the criteria that distinguish important and unimportant stakeholders?'; and (3) '[W]hose [core] values should be represented in such management decision making?' (Sundaram and Inkpen, 2004a, pp. 352–3). Answers to these questions, Sundaram and Inkpen insist, require a discriminating economic theory.

Unfortunately, the stakeholder response, offered by Freeman, Wicks and Parmar (2004), conforms to Sundaram and Inkpen's stereotype. For Freeman, Wicks and Parmar dismiss economic theory, insisting that it derives from self-contained academic discursive communities rather than from empirical explorations into 'how managers operate'. Once scholars embark on this inquiry, Freeman, Wicks, Parmar insist, values become the linguistic/behavioral medium by which managers consolidate corporate associations. And, once placed on this terrain, then, stakeholder theory provides the means for answering Sundaram and Inkpen's queries: stakeholder theorists distinguish between normative stakeholders, those who gain moral standing by making contributions to the firm and derivative stakeholders, those who can constrain the corporate association even though they make no contribution (Phillips, 2003; Mitchell, Agle, and Wood, 1997). The board of directors has the legal authority to distinguish among these stakeholder groups and to distribute rights and obligations among these stakeholder groups (Phillips, Freeman and Wicks, 2003).

To be sure, this stakeholder formulation appropriately seizes on the firm's voluntary, associative character. Yet, the firm's constituents contribute assets and incur risks to participate in market, economic activities. And, as such, the firm's 'stakeholders' must share an imperfect language to assist in making two key economic decisions: (1) who are the legitimate and who are the derivative stakeholders; and (2) who should sit on the board? Still, stakeholder theorists have good reason to be skeptical of neoclassical economics. Its assumptions that all act opportunistically and that all can calculate rationally and fully hardly correspond to studies on the managerial experience of corporate coordination. But, advances in behavioral law and economics now provide a cogent economic logic that readily fits into a stakeholder model (Jolls, Sunstein & Thaler, 1998; Blair & Stout, 1999; Kaufman & Englander, 2005). Once appropriated, stakeholder can readily offer answers to Sundaram and Inkpen's questions that stay within the queries' frame.

In brief, we argue that: (1) the firm's economic purpose designates legitimacy to *core* stakeholders, to those who add value, assume unique risk, and can incur harm; (2) the board serves as the principal who coordinates these core stakeholders to sustain competitive advantage and new wealth creation; and (3) state incorporation law, Delaware in particular, reinforces the board's function. These, in turn, supply selection criteria for board membership.

We aim to synchronize concepts from behavioral law and economics with stakeholder theory (Harrison and Freeman, 1999; Jones and Wick, 1999; Marens & Wicks, 1999). The first section elaborates the economic model. Team production and resource-based economics furnishes the foundation, the first layer (Blair and Stout, 1999; Barney, 1991; Grant, 1996; Conner and Prahalad, 1996). The team production model firmly resides within the behavioral law and economics literature; resource-based economics belongs to the strategic management literature. Arguably, resource-based economics extends team production's constructs into useful managerial tools. The section begins with behavioral economics' *homo socius*. The new 'rational actor' supplies team production with the 'raw material' for categorizing (describing) the firm as a cooperation game in which corporate directors broker (coordinate) the surplus divides (or allocations) that stakeholders consider fair (Aoki, 1984). Mutual gain sets the baseline 'fairness' standard within the market. The divide itself has no objective, impartial standard – only the parties' subjective estimate that cooperation (Pareto and Kaldor/Hicks efficiency) beats non-cooperation. Thus, mutual gain 'fairness' (economic efficiency) has an intrinsic ethical standard, do no harm. But, its assessment depends wholly on each group's voluntary agreement to a deal.

This formulation integrates ethical (distributive) norms and strategic action. Yet we dissent from the usual stakeholder rendition that enables boards to select among the primary distributive policies of mutual gain and impartiality (Freeman & Evan, 1990; Phillips, Freeman & Wicks, 2003; Donaldson & Dunfee, 1999). Product and financial market competition constrain US boards from deviating far from a Pareto/Kaldor/Hicks standard. Thus, we concur with economists that directors cannot choose between an impartial standard (Rawls' difference principle, utilitarianism) and mutual gain (reciprocity/procedural justice) (Barry, 1989; Fehr & Gaecheter, 2000; Bowles, 2004). Public policy, instead, becomes the site for remedying 'unfair' market outcomes. Here, we simply follow the customary distinction between local justice and public policy (global) justice (Elster, 1992; Rawls, 1999, Phillips, 1997; Phillips, 2003; and Child & Marcoux, 1999 critique of Freeman & Evan, 1990).

Unregulated markets reproduce bargaining advantages. Among them, liquidity confers to 'money market managers' substantial power. A focal firm corporate control group may fully structure divide/allocation rules to benefit the most powerful – that is, shareholders and managers; or the control group may strike deals that distribute benefits to coalesce stakeholders into a new wealth generating team. Moreover, team production generates (descriptive, instrumental) concepts – value creation, unique risk and strategic information – that corporate directors can deploy in constructing an economic strategy and in assembling a board demographically fitted to the firm's core competencies (Kaufman & Englander, 2005; Prahalad, 1993). These concepts coincide neatly with resource-based economics' powerful contributions to strategic practice (Barney, 1991; Grant, 1996). As conceived by these two theories, the board, rather than senior managers per se, acts as the team trust initiator (trustor) (Whitener et al., 1998; Kaufman & Englander, 2005; McKnight and Cummings, 1998; Bhattachraya, Devinney & Pillutla, 1998; Lewicki & Bunker, 1995; Gulati, 1995). And, because various constituents participate in the firm's surplus value (e.g., above spot-market wages) and because new wealth creation occurs over extended capital allocation periods, we use total value maximization as the corporate objective – a maxim on which agency and stakeholder theorists can now concur (Jensen, 2002; Post, Preston & Sachs, 2002).

Section 2 considers how corporate law defines the board as coordinator and team fiduciary. Our argument challenges the widely held academic belief that the state courts actually conceive of shareholders as the corporate principal and directors as their agent. To right this factual error, we review Delaware corporate law. This defines directors as the principal and encumbers them with fiduciary duties to the firm as a going concern. By defining directors as corporate trustees, Delaware demands that they behave in other-regarding ways – that they should be trustworthy (Bainbridge, 2002a; Hardin, 2002). On this matter, behavioral law and economics has remained silent while stakeholder theory has exhibited a bias towards fairness, towards impartiality. By including these behavioral law and economic analytics (along with a customary ethical norm) into stakeholder theory, we generate a variant that affords individually corporate boards a cogent competitive tool and collectively a persuasive 'technocratic' public policy language.

2   The managerial thesis and stakeholder theory

2.1   Managerial theory's enduring relevance

The theory of the firm (despite the definite article, 'the') has been contested among and between neoclassical economists and managerial theorists. Stakeholder theory belongs to the latter, even if it has not directly entered formal economic debates. In the immediate post-WWII years, neoclassical economics spent little time considering the firm. Instead, they pursued a general equilibrium model (Arrow & Debreu, 1954). Economists constructed this based on *homo economicus*, who had unlimited rational powers (unbounded rationality), full information and selfish motivation. These sufficed to demonstrate that perfectly competitive markets equilibrated efficiently.

Managerial theorists found the exercise useful but raised a simple objection: as a historical fact, firms existed and markets churned. The most influential managerial works came from Carnegie Mellon University (CMU). Unlike their neoclassical counterparts, the CMU group proceeded from behavioral assumptions that humans had limited mental abilities (bounded rationality), that they acted from imperfect information, and that they would engage in cooperative (other regarding) undertakings (Simon, 1955, 1959; Cyert & March, 1963). Firms, consequently, formed to augment bounded decision-making powers.

This formulation, however, lacked sufficient precision and pushed managerial theorists to consider alternatives. Initially, transaction cost economics appeared the most promising. Oliver Williamson (1970), himself a CMU product, combined the two traditions. He agreed with his CMU mentors that humans had unbounded rationality and imperfect information. But he dissented on rationality's collaborative nature. Accordingly, Williamson presumed an imperfect, opportunistic *homo economicus*. With these assumptions in hand, Williamson set about to offer a systematic answer to Coase's (1937) famous question – how do firms improve on market transactions (Williamson, 1985; Englander, 1986)? Managerial hierarchies appear, Williamson argued, when administrative rules are less costly to perform than contractual arrangements. Thus, in Williamson's rendering, firms are transaction-cost minimizing devices and managers sophisticated accountants.

2.2 Resource-based economics

At first, managerial economists found Williamson's formulation insightful but lamentably insufficient (Ghosal & Moran, 1996). They agreed that transaction costs rose as firms invested in specialized assets. But the firm's ability to assemble, coordinate and sustain specialized innovative assets seemed a better account of the firm's potential 'economizing' advantages than transaction cost reduction.

Resource-based managerial theorists have contributed the most in developing an alternative. These scholars, following the lead of Penrose (1959, 1995), and Nelson and Winter (1982), argued that the firm could improve on the market by combining complementary assets into unique competitive know-how relationships (Wernerfelt, 1984; Barney, 1991; Wernerfelt, 1995; Grant, 1996; Barney, 2001; Kay, 1997). So long as managers could preserve this know-how within the firm's singular social relationships, then, the firm's members would enjoy above-average returns, both on capital and labor. Thus, rather than conceiving the firm as a transaction cost minimizing organization, resource-based theorists depicted the firm as a rent-seeking collaborative project and managers as coordinators (Amit & Schoemaker, 1993).

Moreover, resource-based economics contested Williamson's opportunism premise. Conner and Prahalad (1996) develop the latter argument explicitly. They reason that cognitive limitations, even when all act non-opportunistically, establish sufficient motivation for individuals to collaborate in hierarchical arrangements. These command systems allow knowledgeable managers to direct uninformed and inexperienced workers, thereby economizing on learning costs and augmenting innovation opportunities.

2.3 *Homo socius* and team production

Most neoclassical economists remained outside these debates, pursuing instead a theory based on joint or team production. Like their transaction cost and resource-based counterpoints, neoclassical economists introduced bounded rationality and imperfect information. These two sufficed to account for the gains that occurred when individuals entered joint, team production relations (Alchian & Demsetz, 1972; Aoki, 1984). These economists, who chronologically preceded resource-based theorists, recognized that firms were able to generate innovations faster than solitary efforts by melding complementary assets into coordinated action. And, so long as firms sustained their joint production advantageous, they earned quasi-rents, which like resource-based theorists, defined the firm's primary aim.

Team production addresses this issue by introducing 'other regarding' behavior such as bounded self-interest. The concept comes from behavioral economics, which like managerial theory, has deep connections to the CMU managerial school (Bowles, 2004). Nevertheless, behavioral economics has not been adequately integrated into stakeholder theory.

Although cooperation brings gains, neoclassical economists have had great difficulty in explaining why individuals would cooperate. Economists encounter two hindrances. First, because the firm can temporarily escape the market's price setting mechanism, the team has no way of disaggregating marginal contributions (the non-separability problem). Hence, the team must devise a method for allocating the surplus that exceeds marginal returns. Second, individuals of the *homo economicus* variety find it difficult to agree on division and work rules or effort – the free-rider problem (Alchian and Demsetz, 1972; Holmstrom, 1982; Hart, 1990). As rational economic agents, each seeks to maximize utility, and each is indifferent to the other. Thus, each wishes to gain as much as possible while expending as little as possible. This 'preference' order can easily turn cooperative behavior into a prisoner's dilemma (PD), where all recognize cooperation to be the best choice but defection the rational (default) choice (Hardin, 1982).

One solution would have the individuals distribute control rights to a member who would act as coordinator and set surplus-division and work rules (Alchian and Demsetz, 1972, 1973). However, the solution comes with inherent problems: how would the individuals select the 'owner' endowed with control and residual rights (Grossman and Hart, 1986)? Even if the team members could resolve this issue, they would encounter another: the owner has the right to sell off the team's assets, discouraging team members from making firm specific human capital investments (Rajan and Zingales, 1998). Finally, how would the 'owner' set division and work rules, *ex ante* or *ex post*? If *ex ante*, then, members have incentives to shirk: if *ex post*, then each fights for the largest share, stalling or even preventing a final division and repeated play.

2.4   The behavioral foundation for team (joint) production

Recent advances in behavioral economics has provided an economic agent who does not have the same maximizing, non-other regarding attributes. *Neo-homo economicus'* 'other-regarding' behavior easily accommodates cooperation. Those engaged in this research enterprise have identified numerous behavioral and cognitive characteristics – e.g., aversion to loss, over-optimism, self-serving bias, other regarding preferences and spite – that are not found in neoclassical economics' rational actor model. We consider those – bounded self-interest (fairness, spite, endowment) and bounded rationality (rule of thumb) – that rewrite *homo economicus* into a cooperative species (Sen, 2002; Jolls, Sunstein and Thaler, 1998; Bowles, 2004).

The concept of bounded self-interest comes primarily from empirical studies. Behavioral psychologists have used an experiment, the ultimatum game, to assess whether actual (rather than theoretically constructed) individuals behave acquisitively (self-interestedly) or with regard to others (fairly) (Fehr and Gächter, 2000). Like the PD, the ultimate game is deceptively simple. The game has two players. One acts as the proposer, the other as the responder. Each can receive a sum of money if they strike a deal. The proposer sets the divide and offers it to the responder. If she rejects the offer, then, neither gets the proposed payoff. If she accepts then they each get the sum allocated by the proposer. Neither knows the other's identity. And, they play the game only once. This eliminates reputation effects, retaliation, and learning from the game (Kahneman, Knetsch and Thaler, 1986).

Unfortunately, the experiments do not follow the predicted pattern. Instead, they demonstrate that individuals act with regard to others. Individuals have bounded self-interest as well as bounded rationality. Thus, ultimatum game deals get struck within a well-defined range. It functions as a convention, a rule of thumb. It appears as a 50/50 split, adjusted for bargaining power. Common parlance would label such a deal fair. This rule of thumb has real clout. The responder's willingness to impose harm on both of the players illustrates fairness' power.

That each plays by a rule of thumb conforms neatly to cognitive psychologists' objections to *homo economicus*. They have long doubted the economist's construct of a rational actor who calculates alternative options with exacting scientific accuracy. Indeed, experimental research has demonstrated that individuals calculate probabilities by using rule of thumb (heuristic) devices (Tversky and Kahneman, 1974; Simon, 1955; Simon, 1959).

The ultimatum game provides another lesson: human behavior is malleable. When experimenters slightly alter the game's circumstances, alternative behavioral patterns arise. Still, they do not conform to rationality's predictions. Ultimate game outcomes also vary when rules or processes are changed. Even a change in the game's name, substituting 'exchange' for 'ultimate', has a significant effect. In the exchange game (played exactly as the ultimatum game), the proposers typically offered less and responders usually accepted. A simple name change permits previously unacceptable behavior. This is an important point to remember when we review fiduciary duty later in this chapter (Hoffman, McCabe, Shachat and Smith, 1994).

In all, the ultimatum game provides two generalizations about human nature. First, human behavior varies (Bowles, 2004). The empirical experiments uncovered distinctive response patterns – selfishness, mutualism, spite, and altruism. Of these, other-regarding behavior dominates. However, it typically does not arise from altruism. To the contrary, the ultimatum game suggests that the proposer acts fairly because, on average, it outperforms rational maximization. Thus, the ultimatum game reveals reciprocal rather than altruistic other regarding behavior (Greenfield and Kostant, 2003; Kahan, 2001). Individuals willingly reduce their immediate gain when they know others adhere to rules that all deem fair (Rabin, 1993). And, both adjust their expectations according to their bargaining power. Reciprocity reformulates self-interested behavior: individuals best promote their self-interest when they recognize that gains occur through cooperation and that cooperation bounds self-interest (Thaler, 2000; Bowles, 2004).

Second, process matters. One can accept an outcome that breaks the norm when the process denies the proposer free will. And, both can act like rational economic actors when the game signals acquisitive behavior to be the norm. For managerial theorists, this finding is hardly novel. It merely reinforces well established literatures about the managerial function and about setting rules for communication and negotiation (Barnard, 1938; Raiffa, 1982).

Bounded self-interest, loss aversion (endowment/entitlement), rule of thumb (fairness) and spite offer the material for a complex utility function, one that better explains experimental results than the utility function found in neoclassical economics (Fehr and Schmidt, 1999; Rabin, 1993; Bolton and Ockenfels, 1999; Bowles, 2004). Together they provide the basis for cooperation and for "rational" resistance. Each may refuse offers that, while giving them gains over the non-agreement point, challenge their sense of entitlement and fairness.

Of course, resistance comes with costs – with effort expended, harm imposed, and increased risk for disagreement. For an agreement to occur, one party must either concede to the other's best outcome or the two must make concessions. To strike a rational agreement, each must make concessions that are the other finds fair, i.e., that the other's bargaining power (endowment and entitlement) demands.

2.5   Team production and the coordination function

The coordination function emerges out of efforts to mitigate costly and contentious bargaining. This analysis relies heavily on Aoki's *Co-Operative Game Theory of the Firm* (1984) (see also Rajan & Zingales, 1998). The coordinator stands in for the price system that if it were operative, would indifferently set terms among all stakeholders, including third parties (Aoki, 1984). Background conditions – the distribution of rights (entitlements), income and wealth (endowments) – affect each party's bargaining power. These (or, their lack) contribute to each party's willingness to set reserve prices and to inflict injury when unfair deals provoke outrage, thereby, turning the best of intentions into disagreeable behavior (Luo, 2005; Morrison & Robinson, 1997). The coordinator must carefully explain the bargaining advantages and disadvantages that each bears, if each is to acknowledge the others actual circumstances.

Fairness itself serves as a rule of thumb that minimizes conflict (Rabin, 1993). Fairness functions by setting expectations that allow for long-term cooperative relationships in which both parties can gain (Phillips, 1997). And deviations from the rule can provoke 'irrational' behavior, refusal to close a mutual advantage deal. Yet fairness itself has no readily objective designation. Placed within an economic vernacular, a deal is either optimal or suboptimal (Hardin, 1995). It either allows for the largest surplus possible under given circumstances or it falls short. The optimal outcome, however, has no unique division or surplus allocation rule and requires that human agency reach an accord (Barry, 1989).

Consequently, the players may delve deeply into distributive justice and select a rule on which all can agree, e.g., Rawls' difference principle (Rawls, 1999). Or, they may accept mutual gain as the distributive norm and proceed formally by adopting a bargaining scenario. For example, the one with the most to lose concedes (Nash equilibrium). Or, the players might just adopt the simple 50/50 rule, disregarding bargaining differences among them (Barry, 1989).

To be an effective replacement, the coordinator develops informational and communication skills to accomplish the following: (1) for assessing each stakeholder's contributions, risks and bargaining power; (2) for facilitating agreement on the surplus division rule that each finds fair, i.e., one that recognizes each party's bargaining power and entitlements; (3) for defining the team's unique know-how and planning ways to augment it; (4) for monitoring and administratively enforcing division and work rules; and (5) for forecasting future market opportunities and threats (Phillips, 2003). All of this requires specialization – individuals schooled in the coordination functions abstract principles. However, proficiency in abstract reasoning does not suffice. A coordinator must be able to apply these principles in practice and to earn a reputation by her brokered deals.

This description suggests that coordinators have flexibility in selecting between a mutual gain procedure and an impartial standard (Phillips, 1997). But markets operate through mutual gain transactions (Barry, 1989, 1995; Nozick, 1974; Gauthier, 1986). And competition imposes a bargaining power band between capital and labor. Hence, coordinators typically must adhere to mutual gain's bargaining logic, though tempered by reciprocity (Bowles, 2004; Fehr and Gächter, 2000; Fehr and Schmidt, 1999; Phillips, 2003). Outcomes must reproduce bargaining differences among the contracting parties. Take disadvantaged labor and advantaged capital. Labor gains bargaining power from firm-specific human capital investments. On the other hand, capital's fungible nature advantages it over labor. Capital resides in financial portfolios that, with electronic speed, traverse financial instruments to obtain maximum risk adjusted returns. Nevertheless, reciprocity tempers capital. It must acknowledge labor's bargaining power (effort and shirking), forcing deals that beat the theoretic minimum above non-cooperation.

Because mutual gain (Pareto or Kaldor/Hicks efficient) 'naturally' belongs to market transactions, we label it *focal-firm* or *local* distributive justice, thereby recognizing that the state may readjust market outcomes based on an impartial (utilitarian or a Rawlsian minimax) standard (Barry, 1989; Elster, 1992; Rawls, 1999). This logic differs from that found in Phillips (1997, 2003). He claims that market-brokered deals are impartially fair. Those who engage in these negotiations may employ fairness when procedures permit full discussion. However, market outcomes hardly conform to a fairness standard whether in the Rawlsian or utilitarian sense. And, we speak of the coordinator as a neutral or technocratic broker (Phillips, 2003). A discussion of this distinction occurs in a later section.

2.6 Core competencies and team production

If coordinators are to be successful, they must gain each team member's trust. The team's constituents consider the coordinator trustworthy when individual self-interest encapsulates the team interest (Hardin, 2002; Whitener et al., 1998). Coordinators' self-interest derives from their privileged participation in a small, but powerful community.

As the teams grow in complexity, the coordination function cannot be performed by a single individual. The team's core competencies coalesce and evolve as members invest in team-specific skills which impose unique risk on each and collectively render market substitutability baseless (Blair and Stout, 1999; Bainbridge, 2002a). This complexity requires a set of coordinators – in corporate governance terms, a board of directors. Their combined know-how can apprehend the diverse human capital components that comprise the firm's innovative powers (Mohrman, Cohen, and Mohrman, Jr., 1995).

Value creation, unique risk and strategic information comprise the basic categories for selecting corporate directors (coordinators) who can reproduce, in effect, the firm's core competencies – the firm's core stakeholders (Kaufman and Englander, 2005). To illustrate, consider the US corporate setting in which control (board) and residual rights (shareholder/portfolio investor) are separated. Value creation refers to those stakeholders who have specialized skills to generate the firm's competitive advantage. Because these core stakeholders (employees, suppliers and customers) invest in specialized human capital and capital stock, they incur unique risk. Here, we consider the firm as a supply chain member. Hence, customers (e.g., original equipment manufacturers) cooperate with suppliers to augment productivity and product functionality (Kaufman, Wood & Theyel, 2000). Team members possess skills that do not easily transfer to other firms. The individual's skill has full value only within the team's social interactions.

Shareholders, too, create value even though they neither participate in the firm's core processes nor assume unique risk. Actually, the category shareholder has become an anachronism. Today, shareholders typically find themselves part of an investor's diversified portfolios. These investors allocate liquid capital as alternative investments (stocks, bonds, commercial loans, real estate, etc.) promise higher yields than current ones. And, money market managers (institutional investors) have aggregated investor capital into large funds that can augment and diminish a firm's value. Thus, investors, while they keep financial score, incur diversified risk, adjusted to their preferences. A corporate board (a team coordination committee) requires members who have expert knowledge on the capital markets, if the team is to compete effectively against other financial instruments.

Boards require strategic information beyond the financial markets – for example, on commodity markets and on technological possibilities. Such information is neither readily available nor easily decipherable. Hence, boards (coordination committees) must include outside coordinators with specialized knowledge, i.e., know-how in those domains critical to the firm's success.

Finally, the firm's practices may impose unique risk on non-contractual stakeholders who endure third-party harm (negative externalities). The chemical industry provides a salient example since its toxic substances can degrade a community's environmental well-being. A region dependent upon a single employer or industry supplies another example. Should technological improvements or outsourcing jobs dislocate workers, then, the community will confront economic hardships that are above the market average. When a cooperative team imposes unique risks on third-party stakeholders, the board must have directors familiar with this group's circumstances, if the firm is to avoid harm (unethical behavior) – by pushing costs onto others.

With such a diverse group won't coordination committees (boards) simply become an arena for distributive conflicts? Won't these squabbles merely undo the solution that a neutral technocrat provided? Or, perhaps, the board will work by compromise, 'satisficing' each stakeholder group instead of maximizing 'surplus value'. Behavioral research has shown that powerful incentives are available for consolidating groups – even those whose short-term interests may conflict. (Bainbridge, 2002a). Individuals bond well when they identify themselves as part of an 'in-group'. In fact, empirical research indicates that coordinators develop a social network that promotes trust and open dialogue (Westphal, 1999).

3   State incorporation acts and directors' fiduciary duties

All of these corporate coordination activities occur, in theory, without government assistance, without the law and police powers. Yet, as a historic fact, complex teams that amalgamate production factors take on a special legal status – the business corporation. Incorporation requires a coordination committee, the board of directors. The directors' public identity legally emerges from the law from incorporation and regulatory initiatives.

Consider the classical liberal account of the state that proceeds from Hobbes' brutish state of nature where all would gladly concede to a dictator if that would guarantee security (Olson, 2000). The state, by monopolizing military force, abates civil strife and patterns cooperative behavior. Yet, even the most authoritarian state cannot suppress crime nor fully enforce all contractual promises and fiduciary obligations. The state merely reduces the risks of contract and fiduciary breaches.

Risk reduction provides the central impetus for state incorporation laws. Within a secure property rights system, suppliers and customers develop ongoing, mass production relationships. Inter-firm supply chain dependencies increase business risk. Specialized assets and relational contracts put each firm at risk – the risk to be held up or to be gouged. Under these circumstances, the integrated firm betters the market in managing the asset and bearing the risk (Williamson, 1985). However, vertical integration requires large amounts of capital for the initial purchases and for daily cash flow requirements. These large capital sums typically exceed an investor's, a creditor's or a group of investor/creditors' risk limitations. Incorporation grants limited liability for an investor class, shareholders (Klein & Coffee, Jr., 2004). Reduced financial risk lessens equity capital's cost.

Limited liability forms the usual economic account for incorporation. But, team production offers another – a coordination committee. Incorporation acts establish the corporate board as coordinator and inscribe the board, corporate directors, with fiduciary duties (a duty of care and a duty of loyalty) to the corporation as a going concern (Stout, 2003). Thus, corporate law facilitates coordination by assuring stakeholders that the board is trustworthy (Rock & Wachter, 2002). The law imposes on directors a local obligation to assure the welfare of all corporate stakeholders.

3.1 US federalism and corporate law

In the United States, federalism stands among the most efficacious means for restraining governmental abuse (Hardin, 2003). The states' rivalries and their common competition against the federal government lessen the chance for government mischief whether by the states or the national government. Within these overlapping jurisdictions, incorporation and internal governance belong to the states and stakeholder regulation belongs to the federal government (Romano, 1993). In principle, state governments allow for a geographic pluralism that engenders competition for corporate franchise revenues although there is disagreement over whether this turns into a 'race to the bottom' or a 'race to the top' (Cary, 1974; Winter, 1977; Bebchuk, 1989; Romano, 1993). There is also a third account in which interest groups, investment bankers and lawyers benefit from Delaware's dominance and lobby to sustain it (Macey & Miller, 1987).

During the twentieth century, state competition for business incorporations has turned into an anachronism. Delaware has effectively 'won' the race, at least for large publicly traded firms as nearly half of the firms listed on the New York Stock Exchange and almost 60 per cent of the Fortune 500 firms are incorporated in Delaware. Data also clearly show that that nearly all corporations that leave their home state to incorporate in another end up in Delaware (Bebchuk and Cohen, 2003; Bratton and McCahery, 2004). Consequently, we follow convention and use Delaware as our standard for our discussion of state corporate law and regulation.

3.2 Contract vs trust

An incorporation charter instructs corporate directors to act on behalf of all of the firm's constituents and treat each of them equitably. The charter legally obliges directors to consider the corporate team's interests first. This legal restraint on *homo economicus* (i.e., board members acting in their own self-interest) does not arise from contract law but rather from trust law. Both trust and contract come into play in the legal definition of the firm. Yet they uneasily amalgamate into the business corporation (Kaufman & Zacharias, 1992).

This amalgam now divides legal scholars, with one group emphasizing contract and the other trust. Those who stress corporate law's contractarian language belong to the law and economics movement (Easterbrook and Fischel, 1991; Coase, 1937; Meckling and Jensen, 1976; Cheung, 1983). It speaks repeatedly of the firm as a spontaneous association of individuals choosing to organize themselves in order to produce and sell something, but having no public responsibilities. In contrast, team production (arising within the constructs of behavioral law and economics) considers the law to be an enabling device that binds the firm by encumbering directors with fiduciary duties (Eisenberg, 1989, 1999; Bebchuk, 1989). Where law and economics labels directors as private-sector rational actors, team production portrays directors' standing ambiguously: as the firm's principal and fiduciary, the directors coalesce private-contracting stakeholders into a publicly traded firm.

Trust and contract form the conceptual building blocks of US corporate law. Contract seems clear enough. But why trust? Why has it been an enduring tradition within US corporate law? Why hasn't contract law, on which the firm's activities depend solely, informed state incorporation statutes? The answer seems simple enough. Trust law predated contract law. And, trust's properties – enablement, elasticity and flexibility – have sustained its prominence in corporate law (Sitkoff, 2004; Maitland, 1981).

A trust is a state-enforceable bargain that was originally established between a donor and a trustee (Langbein, 1995). In the pure donative trust, the law regulates relationships in which a donor (settlor) employs another (trustee) who acts on a beneficiary's behalf. The trustee or fiduciary assumes responsibilities to preserve and augment the beneficiary's property without the donor's oversight. Even though the donor and the trustee enter into a contractual agreement, the beneficiary's dependency (vulnerability) binds the state to ensure the trustee's loyalty (Sitkoff, 2004). In its classical legal formulation, the fiduciary duty of loyalty forbids the trustee to engage in self-interested transactions, even when these can be profitable for the beneficiary. Corrective action requires the trustee to disgorge any profits (Langbein, 1995).

3.3 Law and economics

The law and economics movement does not deny that, historically, trust first facilitated the business corporation's formation. Yet, if history granted trust prominence in corporate law, then trust rested on a contingent privilege. Consequently, law and economics scholars have enjoined an abstract logic (like their classical legal predecessors) to bring corporate law under contract's dominion.

Their deductive argument begins with Frederic Maitland's original account of trust's historic contractual basis (Langbein, 1995; Maitland, 1981). Trusts work like contracts in two essential ways. First, trust arrangements involve autonomous individuals who enter into a voluntary, but legally binding agreement. Donor trusts are, in effect, contracts for a third-party beneficiary (Langbein, 1995; Atiyah, 1995). Second, the donor and the trustee, like the promisor and promisee in contract law, typically rely on default rules.

In recent years, the courts have distinguished between short-term and long-term contracts, rendering trust unnecessary to corporate law (MacNeil, 1980; Atiyah, 1995). When individuals enter discrete, short-term contracts, contingencies and their associated risks rarely matter. In contrast, long-term contracts inevitably encounter contractually unspecified events and outcomes. To enter a long-term contract, the parties must trust the other to act in good faith, to suppress opportunist impulses, and fulfill obligations (MacNeil, 1980).

When one party breaches the contract, the injured party seeks redress from the courts. The courts willingly order compensation when the plaintiff demonstrates that the defendant has acted unconscionably or in bad faith. To do this, the courts use *ex ante* reasoning. Thus, good faith has taken on a fiduciary-like quality. Each must strive, when the unexpected arises, to assure the contract remains mutually beneficial (Langbein, 1995).

Finally, law and economics advances only a superficially satisfying answer to the knotty question: to whom are directors accountable (Dodd, 1932)? Law and economics tries to banish ambiguity through the use of modern microeconomic theory, in particular, financial agency theory. The argument proceeds by analogy and transports agency law into corporate law. Financial agency theory declares that the shareholders are the principals and the boards are their agents (Easterbrook and Fischel, 1991).

This contractual logic does yield substantive insights. Law and economics scholars, for example, present a better account of the courts' permissiveness with fiduciary duties than trust doctrine. Under certain conditions, the courts find director self-dealing beneficial to the corporation. For example, the Delaware court permits directors and senior managers to dispose of corporate assets self-servingly as long as the corporation is treated fairly and outside or independent directors approve the transaction (Bainbridge, 2002b).

This contractual logic provides an equally satisfying explanation for the courts' long refusal to subordinate the business judgment rule to the duty of care. Until the 1980s, the courts routinely deferred to the lesser business judgment rule rather than the prudent person rule, unless unusual circumstances were proven (such as self-serving deals, fraud, or illegality) (Dent, 1981; Horsey, 1994). Where the prudent person rule asks the courts to consider whether directors acted reasonably, with the care of a prudent person, the business judgment rule simply acquiesces to the firm's internal hierarchy as a legitimate arbiter (Bainbridge, 2002b).

3.4 Behavioral law and economics

Trust law, by demanding that the fiduciary acts in another's interest, differs substantively from contracts (Marens & Wick, 1999). Yet contracts are the mediating mechanism that coalesce individuals and groups into corporate production teams. Why then does corporate law rely on a legal tradition outside contracts? Why trust? Why fiduciary duty? Since the 1960s, differences between trust and contract have narrowed. But, the two have not collapsed into one.

Delaware illustrates this argument. Corporate case law in Delaware defines the board as the corporation's authoritative body or as the corporation's principal (Springer, 1999; Bainbridge, 2002a). Shareholders elect directors, but Delaware instructs directors that their fiduciary obligation extends both to the shareholders and the corporation itself (Johnson and Millon, 2005). Delaware's incorporation charter is unequivocal on the corporate board's primacy and on its authority to oversee the firm (Bainbridge, 2002b; Rock, 2000; Clark, 1985). The charter plainly states that the corporation shall be under the direction of a board of directors who are encumbered with fiduciary duties.

The board assembles a management team or delegates this responsibility to senior executives. The board has the authority to specify administrative work rules, to draw and redraw the firm's boundaries, and to provide incentives for recruiting, retaining, and motivating employees. In all, the board animates the firm's physical assets (capital stock) by allowing or disallowing human capital access to these resources (Rajan and Zingales, 1998). Once hired, corporate officers conduct business as the directors' agents. They, not directors, come under agency law – contrary to financial agency theory (Langevoort,

2003; Rock, 2000; Johnson and Millon, 2005; Marens & Wick, 1999). Still, directors remain accountable to shareholders who are endowed with specific rights: (1) the right to vote on directors, bylaw amendments, mergers, sales of corporate assets and dissolution; and (2) the right to initiate derivative suits. More important, shareholders, as institutional investors, hold boards accountable by reallocating funds among financial portfolios, and augmenting the value of some instruments and diminishing the value of others.

3.5   Team production and trust

The team production model uses these legal facts to counter claims that fiduciary status is a mere default rule and that the duty of care is subordinate to the business judgement rule (Blair and Stout, 1999, 2003). The counterpoint begins with corporate law's specific adaptation of trust. How does the fiduciary relationship between directors and the corporation differ from the donative trust law? From agency law? How has the concept of trust been adapted within corporate law?

Each fiduciary relationship involves trustworthiness and trust; all make demands that exceed spot market contract relations; and all rely on the courts as background enforcer. Where the principal–agent relationship covers party-to-party transactions (including entities), trust and corporate law regulate relationships between the trustee and a beneficiary. In a donative trust relationship, the donor transfers to a trustee (fiduciary) a critical resource (whether tangible as land, or intangible as confidential information). This transfer legally binds the fiduciary to use the resource on the beneficiary's behalf. Unlike a principal–agent relationship, the beneficiary does not directly control or oversee the trustee.

Corporate law does not conform to either the agency or donative trust structure. Corporate law establishes its own variant though it is derived from donative trust. The corporation forms when individuals or contracting parties commit (by analogy, donate) resources to a joint effort. The corporate team members expect the board to transform their critical resources into the firm's core competencies and to enhance the firm's competitive capabilities. These trustees, then, act on the corporate team's behalf (beneficiaries) and augment their wealth-generating powers and distribute the benefits among team members. To enable the board to function as coordinator, corporate law establishes clear fiduciary (behavioral) expectations. In imperfect markets, corporate donors cannot write complete contracts and instead rely on fiduciary duties as gap fillers.

Although elastic, corporate duty of loyalty differs from good faith and fair dealing in relational contracting. Relational contracts, even when clearly tempered by good faith provisions, permit the contracting parties to act self-interestedly, even injuriously to the other, as long the contract countenances the questionable actions (Smith, 2002). When courts are asked to interpret a party's good faith actions, the weight does not favor either party. Rather, the courts seek out the mean between the two (Brudney, 1997). Hence, the distinction between corporate fiduciary loyalty and relational contracts remains (Smith, 2002).

If the courts permit corporate fiduciary unwinding, then, they lose their role in superintending director trustworthiness (Stout, 2003; Frankel, 1995). Corporate value-adding stakeholders would only have protection under relational contract's good faith standard. They would lose the court's interventions to shape directors' 'other-regarding' behavior (Rock & Wachter, 2001; Rock, 2000). Fiduciary duty cognitively biases judges (and, consequently, directors) to perceive directors as fiduciaries, as those who have a legal obligation to be trustworthy. The judges' cognitive bias encourages them to survey from the corporate case law best practices and to transmit them in each new ruling (Veasey, 2001, 2003). The courts' rulings, which include moral language, inform directors (as advised by legal counsel) on their responsibilities and cajole them to constrain their rational maximizing persona (Mitchell, 2001a, 2001b; Alexander, 1997).

Corporate law enables the firm. Fiduciary duty's legal definition and its sanctions for breach enable corporate stakeholders to deem directors' trustworthy and to transfer resources to their care. Directors coordinate stakeholder contributions as corporate trustees for the corporate constituents' benefits. Even though the law encumbers directors with responsibilities, the law cannot organize a new wealth-creating association. This occurs spontaneously, contractually, as each seeks to gain from joint production. As deals get struck and boards emerge as coordinators, a director community materializes, establishing a socially privileged group whose membership depends on each director's trustworthiness (Herman, 1981; Westphal & Zajac, 1995, 1997, 1998; Westphal, 1999). Those who violate this trust face communal sanctions, e.g., reputation loss, public shame, etc. The law codifies this community and promulgates evolving behavioral norms. Together, the statutory and the self-generative, can invest trustworthiness into a director's self-identity (Eisenberg, 1989, 1999; Mitchell, 2001a; Hardin, 2002; Cook, Hardin & Levi, 2005).

Fiduciary duty defines the coordinator's *focal good*. The coordinator acts 'selflessly' to secure the corporate team and to distribute neutrally its generated surpluses. The distributive standard proceeds from Pareto to Kaldor/Hicks efficiency and, if necessary, to a utilitarian cost/benefit outcome (Hardin, 2006). The director-community's collective function, to oversee the corporate sector's wealth-producing capabilities, engages the directorate in debates over a large social good, a social distributive justice standard. Democracy's basic values, liberty and equality, establish the options. The US federal government provides the stage.

4 Conclusion

Stakeholder theorists have often claimed that their insistence on integrating ethics into corporate strategy differentiates them from neoclassical economics (Freeman, Wicks & Parmar, 2004). To be sure, many economists stubbornly enforce the distinction between efficient and fair. However, economists who belong to the law and economics (Chicago School) movement, similarly, find the rigid separation artificial. They have waged a protracted intellectual campaign to integrate ethical norms and descriptive paradigms, distributive justice and Pareto efficiency (Yergin & Stanislaw, 1998). These libertarians did not have to go outside economic theory for an entry way into ethical reason: contract's underpinnings – autonomy, liberty, secure property rights – provided the materials that naturally led to a procedural justice standard (Hayek, 1944; Knight, 1947; Hayek, 1960; Posner, 1990; Nozick, 1974). Still, their reliance on *homo economicus* distances law and economics from stakeholder theory. Freeman and Phillips (2002) claim the libertarian terrain among stakeholder theorists. Yet, these two differ from the Chicago School by arguing for a complex human psychology and by suggesting that fairness – of a Rawlsian sort – be incorporated into the firm's contracts (Freeman, 1994).

These differing conceptions of human nature returned us the Carnegie Mellon managerial tradition. Our retrospective includes a prospectus on behavioral law and economics, which has done much to advance the CMU perspective. Behavioral economists and their legal scholar partners have generated a contrary archetype, *homo socius*, one that we argue 'naturally' inhabits to stakeholder theory.

Our argument devolves into five summary propositions. First, the transformation of *homo economicus* into *homo socius* permits the creation of a parsimonious firm. Team production, the behavioral law and economics' joint product, proceeds deductively to construct the firm and to analyze corporate law's supportive role. Second, team production and strategic management generate categories – value creation, unique risk and strategic information – for identifying the firm's 'core' wealth-producing stakeholders (Conner & Prahalad, 1996; Grant, 1996). This categorization brings stakeholder theory into the strategic management literature, with its emphasis on core competencies and resource-based competitive advantage. These categories do not displace stakeholder theory's well-established 'contingent' analytics, e.g., legitimacy, power, urgency and salience (Mitchell, Agle & Wood, 1997). The firm's dynamic development, its actions among various social and political arenas, resists a single managerial schematic. Still, ours provides a means for designating core competency salience by linking stakeholder analysis to resource-based economics. And our categories amplify the other important stakeholder identification method, the normative/derivative distinction (Phillips, 1997). Like ours, it uses contributions, benefits and harm. But, our procedure refines these terms by bringing stakeholder theory into the strategic management literature.

Three, corporate law has a greater importance in our synthetic paradigm than is normally the case among stakeholder theorists. True, stakeholder theorists speak of the firm as a bundle of rights and obligations (Donaldson & Dunfee, 1999), however, our model requires state incorporation charters and corporate laws as being essential to the US firm's constitution. Incorporation solidifies team production by requiring a board of directors whose members must exhibit other-regarding behavior. In turn, they set standards for their agents, senior managers, demanding them to be trustworthy (Whitener, Brodt, Korsgaard, & Werner, 1998). Our detailed account of the courts' assistance in coalescing corporate stakeholders brings an extra, empirical benefit: incorporation, as practiced in Delaware (and in most other states), conceives of the firm as a stakeholder association, rather than as a shareholder maximizing institution, as agency theory normatively instructs.

Fourth, team production (behavioral law and economics) identifies corporate boards as the corporate coordinator. Typically, stakeholder theorists speak of managers as the corporate coordination/control group. Of course, the separation of residual and control rights has allowed managers/senior executives to dominate the board and the board's nominating committee. But, even inside directors are encumbered with fiduciary duties.

Fifth, and finally, the corporate board fits within an interlocking network, generating a corporate directorate – a community that has eluded stakeholder theory. The recent reforms (NYSE, Sarbanes/Oxley) have changed this interlocking network's members and their identities. Where insiders once dominated boards, now outsiders do. When insiders predominated, they sat on the nominating committee to secure their control. Now, outsiders, primarily, current and retired CEOs, populate this committee. These new circumstances encourage board members to consider themselves as corporate sector stewards rather solely as the focal firm control group. This reformation reinforces the ability of the corporate directors to offer collective resistance challenges to managerial – now, collective CEO – control, even if this means punishing the few who perform inadequately (Khurana, 2002).

These concluding propositions contain rich research implications, of a theoretical, empirical and practical sort. We only consider here two, one empirical, one theoretical. Recent empirical work evaluating stakeholder management's impetus – whether it proceeds from ethical rules or from stratefic needs – have upheld the latter. This finding has disturbed some who find it difficult to reconcile stakeholder theory's ethical instructions – that stakeholders be treated as autonomous moral ends – with the market's preponderance to convert all into gain (Berman, Wicks, Kotha & Jones, 1999; Harrison & Freeman, 1999; Jones and Wicks, 1999). The anomaly vanishes if one considers managers constrained by market competition and 'coerced' into the old-fashion strategic (instrumental) way (Hendry, 1999). Still, the Kaldor/Hicks standard furnishes a reasonable limit on market instrumentality. And procedural processes do count in establishing a fairness-felt sense.

This conclusion, however, does not insinuate that managers are unable to act by non-market-generated norms. However, the possibility occurs in the political sphere where managers may lobby for policies to correct the market's 'unfair' consequences. These correctives may rely on direct redistribution or they may be regulatory initiatives to strengthen the bargaining position of the most disadvantaged groups. Of course, if managers have volition, they may simply affirm procedural justice, which, in effect, corroborates market outcomes. Historically, US corporate managers have demonstrated a preference for each. Between WWII and the late 1980s, managers promulgated a technocratic creed in which they conceived of the firm as a stakeholder coalition and public policy as means for correcting bargain advantages. By the early 1990s, managers had abandoned their neutrality and rallied to shareholder partisanship and to a collective preference for procedural justice. Thus, managers abandoned their former corporate social responsibility doctrine and had an indifferent view of two decades of stagnant wages and an expanding chasm between those who diversified portfolio investors and those who have not. In considering these alternative distributive justice options, our revised stakeholder theory permits agnosticism, as long as managers dissuade themselves from the creed of firm shareholder centrality. Still, we do have a decided preference for technocratic impartiality.

References

Alchian, A.A. and H. Demsetz (1972) 'Production, Information Costs, and Economic Organization', *American Economic Review*, vol. 62(5), pp. 777–95.
Alchian, A.A. and H. Demsetz (1973) 'The Property Right Paradigm', *Journal of Economic History*, vol. 33(1), pp. 16–27.
Alexander, G.S. (1997) *Commodity and Propriety: Competing Visions of Property in American Legal Thought, 1776–1970*. New Haven: Yale University Press.
Amit, R., P.J. Schoemaker (1993) 'Strategic Assets and Organizational Rent', *Strategic Management Journal*, vol. 14, pp. 33–46.
Aoki, M. (1984) *The Co-operative Game Theory of the Firm*. New York: Oxford University Press).
Arrow, K.J. and G. Debreu (1954) 'Existence of Equilibrium for a Competitive Economy', *Econometrica*, vol. 22, pp. 265–90.
Atiyah, P.S. (1995) *An Introduction to the Law of Contract*, 5th edn. Oxford: Clarendon Press.
Bainbridge, S.M. (2002a) 'Why a Board? Group Decision Making in Corporate Governance', *Vanderbilt Law Review*, vol. 55, pp. 3–55.
Bainbridge, S.M. (2002b) *Corporation Law and Economics*. Mineola, NY: The Foundation Press.

Barnard, C.I. (1938) *The Functions of the Executive*. Cambridge, MA: Harvard University Press.

Barney, J.B. (1991) 'Firm Resources and Sustained Competitive Advantage', *Journal of Management*, vol. 17, pp. 99–120.

Barney, J.B. (2001) 'Is the Resource-Base "View" a Useful Perspective for Strategic Management Research? Yes', *Academic of Management Review*, vol. 26, pp. 41–56.

Barry, B. (1995) *Justice as Impartiality*. New York: Oxford University Press.

Barry, B. (1989) *Theories of Justice*. Berkeley: University of California Press.

Bebchuk, L.A. (1989) 'Limiting Contractual Freedom in Corporate Law: The Desirable Constraints on Charter Amendments', *Harvard Law Review*, vol. 89, pp. 1820–60.

Bebchuk, L. and A. Cohen (2003) 'Firms' Decisions Where to Incorporate', *Journal of Law and Economics*, vol. 46, pp. 383–425.

Berman, S.L., A.C. Wicks, S. Kotha and T.M. Jones (1999) 'Does Stakeholder Orientation Matter? The Relationship Between Stakeholder Management Models and Firm Financial Performance', *Academy of Management Journal*, vol. 42, pp. 488–506.

Bhattacharya, R., T.M. Devinney and M.M. Pillutla (1998) 'A Formal Model of Trust Based on Outcomes', *Academy of Management Review*, vol. 23, pp. 459–72.

Blair, M.M. and L.A. Stout (1999) 'A Team Production Theory of Corporate Law', *Virginia Law Review*, vol. 85, pp. 247–328.

Blair, M.M. and L.A. Stout (2001) 'Trust, Trustworthiness, and Behavioral Foundations of Corporate Law', *University of Pennsylvania Law Review*, vol. 149, pp. 1735–810.

Bolton, G.E., and A. Ockenfels (1999) 'A Theory of Equity, Reciprocity and Competition', *American Economic Review*, vol. 92(4), pp. 727–44.

Bowles, S. (2004) *Microeconomics: Behavior, Institutions and Evolution*. Princeton NJ: Princeton University Press.

Bratton, W.W. and J.A. McCahery (2004) 'The Equilibrium Content of Corporate Federalism', ECGI Working At the beginning of this meeting Paper Series in Law, Number 23/2004.

Brudney, V. (1997) 'Contract and Fiduciary Duty in Corporate Law', *Boston College Law Review*, vol. 38, pp. 595–665.

Cary, William L. (1974) 'Federalism and Corporate Law: Reflections upon Delaware', *YALE Law Journal*, vol. 83, pp. 663–705.

Cheung, Steven N.S. (1983) 'The Contractual Nature of the Firm', *Journal of Law and Economics*, vol. 26, pp. 1–21.

Child, J.W. and A.M. Marcoux (1999) 'Freeman and Evans Stakeholder theory in the original position', *Business Ethics Quarterly*, vol. 9, pp. 207–23.

Clark, R.C. (1985) 'Agency Costs Versus Fiduciary Duties', in J. Pratt and R. Zeckhauser (eds), *Principals and Agents: The Structure of Business*. Cambridge, MA: Harvard Business School Press.

Coase, R.H. (1937) 'The Nature of the Firm', *Econometrica*, vol. 4, pp. 386–405.

Conner, K. and D.K. Prahalad (1996) 'A Resource-based Theory of the Firm: Knowledge versus Opportunism', *Organization Science*, vol. 7, pp. 477–92.

Cook, K.S., R. Hardin and M. Levi (2005) *Cooperation Without Trust?* New York: Russell Sage Foundation Press.

Cyert, R.M. and J.G. March (1963, 1992) *A Behavioral Theory of the Firm*, 2nd edn. Cambridge: Blackwell.

Dent, G.W., Jr. (1981) 'The Revolution in Corporate Governance, the Monitoring Board, and the Director's Duty of Care', *Boston University Law Review*, vol. 61, pp. 623–81.

Dodd, E.M. (1932) 'For Whom are the Corporate Managers Trustees?', *Harvard Law Review*, vol. 45, pp. 1145–63.

Donaldson, T. and T.W. Dunfee (1999) *Ties That Bind: A Social Contracts Approach to Business Ethics*. Boston, MA: Harvard Business School Press.

Easterbrook, F.H. and D.R. Fischel (1991) *The Economic Structure of Corporate Law*. Cambridge, MA: Harvard University Press.

Eisenberg, M.A. (1989) 'The Structure of Corporate Law', *Columbia Law Review*, vol. 89, pp. 1461–525.

Eisenberg, M.A. (1999) 'The Conception That the Corporation is a Nexus of Contracts and the Dual Nature of the Firm', *Iowa Journal of Corporate Law*, vol. 24, pp. 819–83.

Elster, J. (1992) *Local Justice: How Institutions Allocate Scarce Goods and Necessary Burdens*. New York: Russell Sage Foundation.

Englander, E.J. (1986) 'Technology and Oliver Williamson's Transaction Cost Economics', *Journal of Economic Behavior and Organization*, vol. 10, pp. 339–53.

Englander, E. and A. Kaufman. (2004) 'The End of Managerial Ideology: From Corporate Social Responsibility to Corporate Social Indifference', *Enterprise & Society*, vol. 5, pp. 404–50.

Fama, E.F. (1970) 'Efficient Capital Markets: A Review of Empirical Work', *Journal of Finance*, vol. 25, pp. 383–417.

Fama, E.F., and K.R. French (2004) 'Disagreement, Tastes and Asset Prices'. Unpublished paper.

Frankel, T. (1995) 'Fiduciary Duties as Default Rules', *University of Oregon Law Review*, vol. 74, pp. 1209–77.

Freeman, R.E. (1984) *Strategic Management: A Stakeholder Approach*. Boston, MA: Pitman.

Freeman, R.E. (1994) 'The Politics of Stakeholder Theory: Some Future Directions', *Business Ethics Quarterly*, vol. 4, pp. 409–22.

Freeman, R.E. and W.M. Evan (1990) 'Corporate Governance: A Stakeholder Approach', *The Journal of Behavioral Economics*, vol. 19, pp. 337–59.

Freeman, R.E. and R.A. Phillips (2002) 'Stakeholder Theory: A Libertarian Defense', *Business Ethics Quarterly*, vol. 12, pp. 331–49.

Freeman, R.E., A.C. Wicks and B. Parmar (2004) 'Stakeholder Theory and "The Corporate Objective Revisited." A Reply', *Organization Science*, vol. 15, pp. 364–9.

Fehr, E. and S. Gächter (2000) 'Fairness and Retaliation: The Economics of Reciprocity', *Journal of Economic Perspectives*, vol. 14, pp. 159–81.

Fehr, E. and K.M. Schmidt (1999) 'A Theory of Fairness, Competition and Cooperation', *Quarterly Journal of Economics*, vol. 114, pp. 817–68.

Gauthier, D. (1986) *Morals by Agreement*. New York: Oxford University Press.

Ghoshal, S. and P. Moran (1996) 'Bad for Practice: A Critique of the Transaction Cost Theory', *Academy of Management Review*, vol. 21, pp. 13–47.

Grant, R.M. (1996) 'Toward a Knowledge-based Theory of the Firm', *Strategic Management Journal*, vol. 17, pp. 109–22.

Greenfield, K. and P. Kostant (2003) 'An Experimental Test of Fairness Under Agency and Profit Constraints', *George Washington Law Review*, vol. 71, pp. 983–1024.

Grossman, S. and O.D. Hart (1986) 'The Costs and Benefits of Ownership: A Theory of Vertical and Lateral Integration', *Journal of Political Economy*, vol. 94, pp. 691–719.

Gulati, R. (1995) 'Does Familiarity Breed Trust? The Implications of Repeated Ties for Contractual Choice in Alliances', *Academy of Management Journal*, vol. 38, pp. 85–112.

Hardin, R. (1982) *Collective Action*. Baltimore, MD: The Johns Hopkins University Press.

Hardin, R. (1995) 'Efficiency', in R.E. Goodin and P. Pettit (eds), *A Companion to Contemporary Political Philosophy*. Oxford: Blackwell.

Hardin, R. (2002) *Trust and Trustworthiness*. New York: Russell Sage Foundation.

Hardin, R. (2003) *Liberalism, Constitutionalism, and Democracy.* New York: Oxford University Press.

Hardin, R. (2006) *Indeterminacy and Society.* Princeton, NJ: Princeton University Press.

Harrison, J. S., R.E. Freeman (1999) 'Stakeholders, Social Responsibility, and Performance: Empirical Evidence and Theoretical Perspectives', *Academy of Management Journal*, vol. 42, pp. 470–85.

Hart, O. (1990) 'Property Rights and the Nature of the Firm', *Journal of Political Economy*, vol. 98, pp. 1119–58.

Hayek, F. A. von (1944) *The Road to Serfdom.* Chicago: University of Chicago Press.

Hayek, F. A. von (1960) *The Constitution of Liberty.* Chicago: University of Chicago Press.

Hendry, J. (1999) 'Universalizability and Reciprocity in International Business Ethics', *Business Ethics Quarterly*, vol. 9, pp. 405–20.

Herman, E.S. (1981) *Corporate Control, Corporate Power.* Cambridge: Cambridge University Press.

Hoffman, E., K. McCabe, K. Shachat and V.L. Smith (1994) 'Preferences, Property Rights and Anonymity in Bargaining Games', *Games and Economic Behavior*, vol. 7(3), pp. 346–80.

Holmstrom, B. (1982) 'Moral Hazard in Teams', *Bell Journal of Economics*, vol. 13, pp. 324–40.

Horsey, H.R. (1994) 'The Duty of Care Component of the Delaware Business Judgment Rule', *Delaware Journal of Corporate Law*, vol. 19, pp. 971–98.

Jensen, M.C. (2002) 'Value Maximization, Stakeholder Theory, and the Corporate Objective Function', *Business Ethics Quarterly*, vol. 12, pp. 235–56.

Jensen, M. C., K.J. Murphy, E. Wruck (2004) 'Remuneration: Where We Have Been, How We Got to Here, What are the Problems, and How to Fix Them', Harvard Business School NOM Research Paper No. 04-28. Accessed at http://ssrn.com/abstract=561305.

Johnson, L. and D. Millon (2005) 'Recalling Why Corporate Officers are Fiduciaries', *William & Mary Law Review*, vol. 46, pp. 1597–653.

Jolls, C., C.R. Sunstein and R. Thaler (1998) 'A Behavioral Approach to Law and Economics', *Stanford Law Review*, vol. 50, pp. 1471–546.

Jones, T. and A.C. Wicks (1999) 'Convergent Stakeholder Theory in Management Research', *Academy of Management Review*, vol. 24, pp. 206–21.

Kahan, Dan M. (2001) 'Trust, Collective Action, and Law', *B.U. L. Rev.*, vol. 81 pp. 333–46.

Kahneman, D., J. Knetsch and R. Thaler (1986) 'Fairness as a Constraint on Profit Seeking: Entitlements in the Market', *The American Economic Review*, vol. 76, pp. 728–41.

Kay, N.M. (1997) *Pattern in Corporate Evolution.* New York: Oxford University Press.

Kaufman, A. (2002) 'Managers' Dual Fiduciary Duty: To Stakeholders and to Freedom', *Business Ethics Quarterly*, vol. 89, pp. 189–214.

Kaufman, A. and E. Englander (1993) 'Kohlberg Kravis Roberts & Co. and the Restructuring of American Capitalism', *Business History Review*, vol. 67, pp. 52–97.

Kaufman, A. and E. Englander (2005) 'A Team Production Model of Corporate Governance', *Academy of Management Executive*, vol. 19, pp. 9–22.

Kaufman, A. and L. Zacharias (1992) 'From Trust to Contract: The Legal Language of Managerial Ideology, 1920–1980', *Business History Review*, vol. 66, pp. 523–72.

Kaufman, A., L. Zacharias and M. Karson (1995) *Managers vs. Owners: The Struggle for Corporate Control in American Democracy.* New York: Oxford University Press.

Kaufman, A., C.H. Wood and G. Theyel (2000) 'Collaboration and Technology Linkages: A Strategic Supplier Typology', *Strategic Management Journal*, vol. 21, pp. 649–63.

Klein, W.A. and J.C. Coffee, Jr. (2004) *Business Organization and Finance*, 9th edn. Mineola, NY: The Foundation Press.

Khurana, R. (2002) *Searching for a Corporate Savior: The Irrational Quest for Charismatic Corporate CEOs.* Princeton, NJ: Princeton University Press.

Knight, F. (1947) *Freedom and Economics: Essays on Economics and Social Philosophy.* New York: Harper & Brothers.

Langbein, J.H. (1995) 'The Contractarian Basis of the Law of Trusts', *Yale Law Journal* vol. 105, pp. 636–43.

Langevoort, D.C. (2003) 'Agency Law inside the Corporation: Problems of Candor and Knowledge', *University of Cincinnati Law Review*, vol. 71, pp. 1187–231.

Lewicki, R.J. and B.Bunker (1995) 'Trust in Relationships: A Model of Trust Development and Decline', in B. Bunker and J. Rubin (eds), *Conflict, Cooperation and Justice.* San Francisco: Jossey-Bass.

Luo, Y. (2005) 'How Important are Shared Perceptions of Procedural Justice in Cooperative Alliances?', *Academy of Management Journal*, vol. 48, pp. 695–709.

Macey, J.R., G.P. Miller (1987) 'Toward of Interest Group Theory of Delaware Corporate Law', *Texas Law Review*, vol. 65, pp. 469–524.

Macneil, I.R. (1980) *The New Social Contract: An Inquiry into Modern Contractual Relations* New Haven, CT: Yale University Press.

Maitland, F.W. (1981) 'Trust and Corporation', in H.A.L. Fisher (ed.), *The Collective Papers of Frederic William Maitland*, vol. III. Buffalo, NY: Williams, Hein and Company.

Marens, R., A. Wicks (1999) 'Getting Real: Stakeholder Theory, Managerial Practice, and the General Irrelevance of Fiduciary Duties Owed to Shareholders', *Business Ethics Quarterly*, vol. 9, pp. 273–93.

McKnight, D.H. and L.L. Cummings (1998) 'Initial Trust Formation in New Organizational Relationships', *Academy of Management Review*, vol. 23, pp. 473–90.

Meckling, W.H. and M.C. Jensen (1976) 'The Theory of the Firm: Managerial Behavior Agency Costs and Ownership Structure', *Journal of Financial Economics*, vol. 3, pp. 305–60.

Mitchell, L. E. (2001a) 'The Importance of Being Trusted', *Boston University Law Review* vol. 81, pp. 591–617.

Mitchell, L.E. (2001b) *Corporate Irresponsibility: America's Newest Export.* New Haven CT: Yale University Press.

Mitchell, R.K., B.R. Agle and D.J. Wood (1997) 'Toward a Theory of Stakeholder Identification and Salience: Defining the Principle of Who and What Really Counts' *Academy of Management Review*, vol. 22, pp. 853–86.

Mohrman, S.A., S.G. Cohen, A.M. Mohrman Jr. (1995) *Designing Team-based Organizations New Forms for Knowledge Work.* San Francisco: Jossey-Bass.

Morrison, E.W. and S.L. Robinson (1997) 'When Employees Feel Betrayed: A Model of How Psychological Contract Violation Develops', *Academy of Management Review*, vol 22, pp. 226–56.

Nelson, R.R. and S.G. Winter (1982) *An Evolutionary Theory of Economic Change* Cambridge, MA: Belknap Press.

Nozick, R. (1974) *Anarchy, State and Utopia.* Oxford: Blackwell.

Olson, M. (2000) *Power and Prosperity: Outgrowing Communist and Capitalist Dictatorships* New York: Basic Books.

Penrose, E. (1959, 1995) *The Theory of the Growth of the Firm*, 3rd edn New York: Oxford University Press.

Phillips, R.A. (1997) 'Stakeholder Theory and a Principle of Fairness', *Business Ethics Quarterly*, vol. 7, pp. 51–67.

Phillips, R.A. (2003) ' Stakeholder Legitimacy', *Business Ethics Quarterly*, vol. 13, pp. 25–41.

Phillips, R.A., R.E. Freeman and A.C. Wicks (2003) 'What Stakeholder Theory is Not', *Business Ethics Quarterly*, vol. 13, pp. 479–502.

Posner, R. A. (1990) *Economics of Justice.* Cambridge, MA: Harvard University Press.
Post, J.E., L.E. Preston and S. Sachs (2002) *Redefining the Corporation: Stakeholder Management and Organizational Wealth.* Stanford, CA: Stanford University Press.
Prahalad, C.K. (1993) 'The Role of Core Competencies in the Corporation', *Research Technology Management*, vol. 36(6), pp. 40–7.
Rabin, M. (1993) 'Incorporating Fairness into Game Theory and Economics', *American Economic Review*, vol. 83, pp. 1281–302.
Raiffa, H. (1982) *The Art and Science of Negotiation.* Cambridge, MA: Belknap Press.
Rajan, R. and L. Zingales (1998) 'Power in a Theory of the Firm', *Quarterly Journal of Economics*, vol. 113, pp. 387–432.
Rawls, J. (1999) *The Theory of Justice*, revised edn. Cambridge, MA: Harvard University Press.
Rock, E.B. (1997) 'Saints and Sinners: How Does Delaware Corporate Law Work', *UCLA Law Review*, vol. 44, pp. 1009–106.
Rock, E.B. (2000) 'Fiduciary Duty, Limited Liability, and the Law of Delaware: Corporate Law as a Facilitator of Self Governance', *Georgia Law Review*, vol. 34, pp. 529–45.
Rock, E. and M.L. Wachter (2001) 'Islands of Conscious Power: Law, Norms, and the Self-governing Corporation', *University of Pennsylvania Law Review*, vol. 149, pp. 1620–99.
Rock, E. and M.L. Wachter (2002) 'Dangerous Liaisons: Corporate Law, Trust Law, and Interdoctrinal Legal Transplants', *Northwestern University Law Review*, vol. 96, pp. 651–72.
Romano, R. (1993) 'Competition for Corporate Charters and the Lesson of Takeover Statutes', *Fordham Law Review*, vol. 61, pp. 843–64.
Sen, A. (2002) *Rationality and Freedom.* Cambridge, MA: Harvard University Press.
Simon, H. (1955) 'A Behavioral Model of Rational Choice', *Quarterly Journal of Economics*, vol. 69, pp. 99–118.
Simon, H. (1959) 'Theories of Decision-Making in Economics and Behavioral Science', *The American Economic Review*, vol. 49(3), pp. 253–83.
Simon, H. (1976) *Administrative Behavior: a Study of Decision-making Processes in Administrative Organization*, 3rd edn. New York: Free Press.
Sitkoff, R. (2004), 'An Agency Costs Theory of Trust Law', *Cornell Law Review*, no. 69, pp. 621–48.
Smith, D. Gordon (2002), 'The Critical Resource Theory of Fiduciary Duty', *VAND. L. REV.*, vol. 55, pp. 1399–1467.
Stout, L. (2003) 'On the Proper Motives of Corporate Directors (Or, Why You Don't Want to Invite *Homo economicus* to Join Your Board)', *Delaware Journal of Corporate Law*, vol. 28, pp. 1–24.
Sundaram, A.K. and A.C. Inkpen (2004a) 'The Corporate Objective Revisited', *Organization Science*, vol. 15, pp. 350–63.
Sundaram, A.K. and A.C. Inkpen (2004b) 'Stakeholder Theory and "The Corporate Objective Revisited": A Reply', *Organization Science*, vol. 15, pp. 370–1.
Thaler, R. (2000) 'From Homo Economicus to Homo Sapiens', *Journal of Economic Perspectives*, vol. 14, pp. 133–41.
Tversky, A. and D. Kahneman (1974) 'Judgment Under Uncertainty: Heuristics and Biases', *Science*, vol. 185, pp. 1124–30.
Veasey, E.N. (2001) 'Should Corporation Law Inform Aspirations for Good Corporate Governance Practices – or Vice Versa?', *University of Pennsylvania Law Review*, vol. 149, pp. 2179–91.
Veasey, E. N. (2003) 'Policy and Legal Overview of Best Corporate Governance Principles' *Southern Methodist Law Review*, vol. 56, pp. 2135–46.

Wernerfelt, B. (1984) 'A Resource-based View of the Firm', *Strategic Management Journal*, vol. 5, pp. 171–80.

Wernerfelt, B. (1995) 'The Resource-Based View of the Firm: Ten Years After', *Strategic Management Journal*, vol. 16, pp. 171–4.

Westphal, J.D. and E.J. Zajac (1995) 'Who Shall Govern? CEO/Board Power, Demographic Similarity and New Director Selection', *Administrative Science Quarterly*, vol. 40, pp. 60–83.

Westphal, J.D. and E.J. Zajac (1997) 'Defections from the Inner Circle: Social Exchange, Reciprocity, and the Diffusion of Board Independence in U.S. Corporations', *Administrative Science Quarterly*, vol. 42, pp. 161–83.

Westphal, J.D. and E.J. Zajac (1998) 'The Symbolic Management of Stockholders: Corporate Governance Reform and Shareholder Reactions', *Administrative Science Quarterly*, vol. 43, pp. 127–53.

Westphal, J.D. (1999) 'Collaboration in the Boardroom: Behavioral and Performance Consequences of CEO–Board Social Ties', *Academy of Management Journal*, vol. 42, pp.7–24.

Whitener, E.M., S.E. Brodt, M.A. Korsgaard and J.M. Werner (1998) 'Managers as Initiators of Trust: An Exchange Relationship Framework for Understanding Trustworthy Behavior', *Academy of Management Review*, vol. 23, pp. 513–30.

Williamson, O.E. (1985) *The Economic Institutions of Capitalism: Firms, Markets and Relational Contracting*. New York: The Free Press.

Williamson, O.E. (1970) *Corporate Control and Business Behavior: An Inquiry into the Effects of Organization Form on Enterprise Behavior*. Englewood Cliffs, NJ: Prentice-Hall.

Winter, R.K. Jr. (1977) 'State Law, Shareholder Protection, and the Theory of the Corporation', *Journal of Legal Studies*, vol. 6, pp. 251–92.

Yergin, D. and J. Stanislaw (1998) *The Commanding Heights: The Battle for the World Economy*. New York: Touchstone.

5

Specific Investment and Corporate Law*

Margaret M. Blair and Lynn A. Stout

Introduction: Kuhn and corporate law

What is a business corporation? What purposes does and should it serve? These questions have been raised repeatedly by legal scholars, practitioners, and policy-makers for at least the past 150 years. Each generation has struggled to find acceptable answers.

In the last decades of the twentieth century, corporate theory has been dominated by an approach to these questions that can be called the principal–agent model.[1] According to this model, shareholders are the principals or ultimate 'owners' of corporations. Directors are agents for the shareholders and, as such, should be subject to shareholder control. Corporations are run well when directors run them according to a 'shareholder primacy' norm that requires directors to maximize shareholder wealth. When directors fail to do this, inefficient 'agency costs' result.

It is difficult to overstate the influence the principal–agent model has had on modern business thinking. This is especially true in the United States, where shareholder primacy has for years largely crowded out other notions of corporate purpose. Yet a new generation of legal and economic scholars has begun to question the principal–agent model as the best way to understand corporate law and to propose alternatives. After decades of intellectual hegemony, conventional shareholder primacy seems poised for decline.

In this essay we explore why. In particular, we explain that the principal–agent model is vulnerable for the simple reason that *it fails to explain many important aspects of corporate law*. During the heyday of shareholder primacy,

* Much of this essay has been extracted from a longer article written in honor of M.M. Blair and L.A. Stout (2006), 'Specific Investment: Explaining Anomalies in *Corporate Law*', *J. Corp. Law.*, vol. 31, pp. 719–44. An earlier version was presented at ADD CITE; the authors are grateful to participants in that workshop for their helpful insights and suggestions.

academics tended to react to these legal 'anomalies' either by glossing over them, or by arguing that corporate law needed 'reform' to bring it closer to the shareholder primacy ideal. Today many scholars are trying a different approach. Rather than trying to make corporate law fit the principal–agent model, they are searching for new models that better fit corporate law.

In the process, they are providing an object lesson in the nature of intellectual progress described in Thomas Kuhn's classic and much-cited *The Structure of Scientific Revolutions*.[2] As Kuhn observed, the world bombards us with information that is often puzzling, ambiguous, incomplete, even apparently contradictory. Somehow we must do our best to find meaning in the barrage of data. Kuhn argued that we make sense of the world by developing mental models about the way it works, theories about how certain causes lead to certain effects. At different times, for example, people have believed that infectious diseases were caused by witches, by night air, and by microbes.

Kuhn labelled these mental models 'paradigms'. According to Kuhn, once a society or culture embraces a particular paradigm as a way to explain a particular phenomenon, most of the individuals in that society will cling to the paradigm with remarkable tenacity. They will believe the paradigm to be a true and accurate description of the world even in the face of significant anomalies – empirical phenomena that cannot be explained by, or that even seem inconsistent with, the paradigm. Rather than reconsidering the paradigm, they overlook, dismiss as unimportant, or attempt to explain away the anomalies. Yet at some point, the anomalies may become so obvious and so troubling that a few individuals begin to study them. These individuals may develop a new theory that explains the anomalies, an alternate paradigm that does a better job of predicting what we see in the world. Often their ideas will be resisted by those who follow the original paradigm. Yet if the new paradigm does a better job than the old one of predicting what we actually observe, it will eventually win hearts and minds, and be accepted as correct. The old paradigm will come to be viewed as incomplete and outdated, a partial explanation at best.

During the sixteenth century, for example, many Europeans believed the sun revolved around the earth. This theory did a nice job of explaining why the sun appeared to rise in the East each morning and set over the western horizon each evening, but it could not explain the movements of the planets in the night sky. The Italian astronomer Galileo advanced an alternative model of a heliocentric universe that predicted not only the movements of the sun but also those of the planets. Not everyone appreciated Galileo's ideas at the time (he was investigated by the Inquisition and placed under house arrest for heresy), but today most educated people believe the earth does indeed circle around the sun.[3]

For most of the last three decades, corporate scholarship has been dominated by the powerful paradigm called the principal–agent model. This paradigm teaches that the concept of a corporate personality is not something to be taken seriously. Rather, a corporation is best understood as a nexus of private contracts. Chief among these contracts is the contract between the shareholders of the firm (often described as the 'principals' or 'owners' of the firm) and the directors and executive officers (usually described as the shareholders' 'agents'). The principal–agent model envisions this contract as an agreement that the directors and executives will run the firm in a fashion that maximizes the shareholders' wealth.

The principal–agent model maintained a firm grip on the corporate law literature throughout the 1980s and 1990s, and many influential academics still employ the model today. Yet even as a generation of experts embraced the principal–agent model, they could not help but observe, often with frustration, how many fundamental aspects of corporate law seemed inconsistent with the approach. The first section of this essay explores four of these fundamental corporate law anomalies: (1) corporate law does not grant shareholder the legal rights of principals nor burden directors with the legal obligations of agents; (2) corporate law does not treat shareholders of solvent firms as sole residual claimants; (3) far from being an empty fiction, legal personality is a key feature of the corporate form; and (4) corporate law does not impose any obligation on directors to maximize shareholder wealth.

Despite these obvious inconsistencies between theory and practice, until recently most corporate experts continued to accept the principal–agent model and to assume, consistent with this approach, that the maximization of shareholder wealth should be the corporate goal.[4] This sometimes-uneasy embrace of the shareholder primacy norm illustrates another of Kuhn's observations: intellectual progress must often await the arrival of new tools and technologies. The hypothesis that infectious diseases are caused by microbes rather than witches or night air, for example, could not gain widespread acceptance until the invention of the microscope, a technology that confirmed the existence of microbes by allowing scientists to observe them directly.

Similarly, corporate law scholars until recently lacked the theoretical tools necessary to explain the anomalies that are so obvious to informed observers. The principal–agent literature was the primary intellectual tool available to business scholars in the 1980s and 1990s, and they naturally tended to apply it liberally to many aspects of the corporate form. As the saying goes, when your only tool is a hammer, every problem tends to look like a nail.

More recently, however, theorists have begun to study and to write on a second economic problem that may be even more important to understanding the corporate form. This is the problem of protecting and encouraging 'specific' investments – specialized resources that achieve their highest value only when used in a particular process or project. The developing literature on the difficulties associated with fostering specific investment has created new theoretical tools that offer fresh insights into old puzzles in corporate law.

The second section of this essay explores how, in particular, two new ideas being developed on specific investment – work on team production and the emerging concept of capital lock-in (work we have contributed to elsewhere, both individually and together) – shed light on important features of corporate law that contradict the principal–agent model. With these new intellectual tools, modern corporate scholars are poised to take up where a previous generation of necessity left off. In the process, they will need to revisit the question of the proper social and economic role of business corporations.

1   The principal–agent model and the structure of corporate law

To understand the origins of the principal–agent paradigm of the corporation, we need to go back to a famous article published in 1976 by finance theorists Michael Jensen and William Meckling.[5] In *Theory of the Firm*, Jensen and Meckling argued that a firm should not be characterized as an entity that has its own goals and intentions (e.g., 'maximize profits'). Instead, a firm should be regarded as a nexus of contracts through which human actors – who do have goals and intentions – interact with each other. In particular, Jensen and Meckling said the most important contractual relationship in the firm was that between the primary investors or 'owners' of the business, and the professional 'managers' whom the owners hire to carry on the business on their behalf. (As this brief description suggests, Jensen and Meckling's analysis from its inception failed to reflect at least one reality of the modern corporation. As students who take corporate law quickly learn, corporations are not run by generic 'managers'. Rather, the law divides the task of running corporations among three categories of corporate participants – directors, officers, and shareholders – with each of these groups facing a different set of legal rights and responsibilities.)

The Jensen and Meckling article built on an important literature in economics dealing with problems that arise when firms are run not by their owners, but by professionals hired by the owners.[6] In particular, Jensen and Meckling suggested that whenever one person (a 'principal') hires another (an 'agent') to act on the principal's behalf, there will be inevitable 'agency costs' that arise because: (1) the agent might not always make the same choices as the principal; and (2) it is costly for the principal to try to monitor and control the agent to prevent this. The Jensen and Meckling approach highlighted the slippage between the principal's desires and the agent's actual choices, and the trade-off principals face between suffering the slippage or trying to control it through costly monitoring or incentive arrangements.

The agency cost model described the structure of certain types of contracts, but not the structure of firms in general, nor the structure of the unique type of firm called a public corporation. Nevertheless, many corporate scholars embraced their approach and, in applying it to corporations, concluded that the shareholders must be the 'principals' and directors and officers must be the shareholders' 'agents'. This idea had enormous appeal for a generation of business scholars who were confronted during the 1970s and early 1980s with the pressing question of what corporate law should require of executives and directors confronted with the newly popular practice of unsolicited tender offers.

In the early 1960s the economist Robin Marris had argued that, even though in theory corporate 'managers' might be tempted to let their personal concerns interfere with the maximization of shareholder wealth, if managers failed to maximize the value of a firm's shares in practice, an outside investor could make money by buying up the corporation's shares at a discount and replacing the managers or compelling them to maximize value.[7] Very soon after, the legal scholar Henry Manne proposed a similar idea, arguing that corporate managers would be driven to maximize share value by what he called 'the market for corporate control'.[8]

This argument, combined with the Jensen and Meckling theoretical framework, was seized upon by other corporate scholars as a rationale for arguing that corporate law ought to respond to the development of the hostile tender offer with rules that prohibited directors from resisting such offers. A substantial literature soon appeared arguing that directors, as 'agents' for the corporation's shareholders, ought to have a legal duty to manage the corporation to maximize share value, including acquiescing to any takeover that offered an immediate premium over the current market price of the shares.[9]

This example illustrates how enormously appealing the principal–agent model was to corporate scholars during the 1970s and early 1980s, when they were eager to find an approach that would allow them to make definitive policy judgments and recommendations about hostile tender offers. Nevertheless, there remained at least one glaring problem with simultaneously arguing that a corporation should be regarded as a nexus of contracts, and arguing that corporate law should require corporate managers to act on behalf of the shareholders who 'owned' the firm. The problem was that the nexus metaphor did not support the notion that the corporation was something that could be 'owned'.

Legal scholars Easterbrook and Fischel, two of the leading advocates of the 'law and economics' movement, soon fixed that problem. In a series of articles in the early 1980s they argued that while it did not make sense to speak of a nexus as having an owner, it was still conceptually useful and normatively correct to treat corporate directors and officers as shareholders' agents.[10] Easterbrook and Fischel asserted that when the various groups that participate in corporate production come together (groups that include, among others, creditors, suppliers, executives, employees, and shareholders) to interact through the nexus of contracts called 'the corporation', only one of these groups – the shareholders – contracts to be the firm's residual claimant.[11]

All other participants enter contracts that require them to be paid first, before the common stockholders can be paid. Since shareholders only get paid if the corporation produces a surplus over and above all its contractual obligations (according to the theory), shareholders have a strong incentive to see that this surplus, the 'profit' from the enterprise, is maximized. Thus, as holders of both residual claim rights and residual control rights, shareholders play a role similar to that played by the owner of an individual proprietorship, and it remains reasonable to refer to shareholders as 'owners' even though technically no one can own a nexus.[12]

The end result was the paradigm we call the principal–agent model of the corporation – an elegant theoretical framework for thinking about what corporate law should look like and what purposes it should serve. This framework was quickly adopted by mainstream scholars in the corporate law community, and it was in the context of this framework that a generation of theorists examined the corporate issues of the day, including the development of antitakeover defenses such as the staggered board and the 'poison pill', the structure and enforcement of directors' fiduciary duties, the best way to compensate directors and executives, and the nature and extent of shareholders' voting rights. Nevertheless, despite the conceptual beauty of the principal–agent framework, these attempts to apply the principal–agent model to the practice of corporate law highlighted how *the model did not fit quite right*. Despite decades of repeated calls for 'reform', the rules of corporate law and the realities of business practice stubbornly remained at odds with the principal–agent framework.

A.   Directors are not 'agents'

One of the most important ways in which corporate law departs from the predictions of the principal–agent model is that, unlike traditional principals, shareholders in publicly traded corporations have little control over who the directors are and no direct control over what the directors do. The rules of agency law provide that an agent owes her principal a 'duty of obedience'. Yet US corporate law does not require directors to follow shareholder mandates in any way. To the extent shareholders exercise any influence at all, it is only through two indirect and very dilute sources of power.

The first source of power is shareholders' very limited voting rights. Corporate law gives shareholders a right to vote on a slate of directors that has normally been selected by the existing directors (in extraordinary circumstances and at great personal cost, a disgruntled shareholder can propose an alternative slate). Once elected, it is the directors and not the shareholders who control the corporation and select and control the executive officers who run the firm on a day-to-day basis. Neither directors nor executives are required to do what the shareholders request. As a result it is directors, and not shareholders, who enjoy the legal right to set general business strategy and to control such key matters as the selection of executives and other employees,[13] the declaration and distribution of dividends,[14] the setting of directors' fees and employees' salaries,[15] and the decision to use corporate assets or earnings to benefit non-shareholder constituencies such as creditors, employees, the local community, or even general philanthropic causes.[16] Nor do the rules of fiduciary duty constrain directors in such matters. Although the duty of loyalty precludes directors from expropriating corporate assets for themselves,[17] as long as directors refrain from using their corporate powers to line their own pockets their decisions are protected from shareholder challenge by the doctrine known as the business judgment rule.[18]

The second weak and indirect source of power available to shareholders in a public corporation is their power to sell their shares. Normally the power to sell shares does not offer individual shareholders much protection from director incompetence for the same reason that the power to use emergency exits does not offer much protection to partygoers in a burning nightclub; neither strategy works well when everyone tries to employ it simultaneously. However, as both Marris and Manne pointed out in the 1960s, when shareholders sell *en masse* to a single buyer, whether an individual or another corporation, that single buyer can overcome the obstacles to collective action that plague dispersed shareholders in public firms and use voting rights to oust a recalcitrant board. The result (to use Manne's hopeful phrase) is an active 'market for corporate control'.

The principal–agent model gained much of its traction in the early 1980s, the peak years of the hostile takeover wars. In the decades since it has become clear that, like shareholders' voting rights, the 'market for corporate control' (at least in the United States) gives shareholders only a very weak and indirect source of influence over corporate boards. In particular, the widespread adoption of poison pills, staggered boards, and other anti-takeover defenses has made it possible for today's directors to fend off all but the most determined, wealthy, and patient bidders.[19] Moreover, by the late 1980s, case law and 'other constituency' statutes had affirmed directors' discretion to adopt these and similar devices in response to hostile takeovers, including their authority to use defenses to protect nonshareholder interests[20] and to protect 'long-run' corporate strategies (with the directors, of course, in charge of selecting the time frame for carrying out those strategies).[21]

Thus US corporate law today retains the same structure it had evolved before the rise of the principal–agent model: directors' legal powers and responsibilities do not resemble those of agents, but rather those of trustees. As corporate law guru and former Dean of the Harvard Law School Robert Clark has succinctly articulated, the actual authority structure of the corporation is as follows:

(1) corporate officers like the president and treasurer are agents of the corporation itself; (2) the board of directors is the ultimate decision-making body

of the corporation (and in a sense is the group most appropriately identified with 'the corporation'); (3) directors are not agents of the corporation but are *sui generis*; (4) neither officers nor directors are agents of the stockholders; but (5) both officers and directors are 'fiduciaries' with respect to the corporation and its stockholders.[22]

This description acknowledges in a forthright manner what many corporate scholars writing during the last part of the twentieth century tended to gloss over, dismiss as unimportant, or simply refuse to see. The claim that shareholders are 'principals' and directors are 'agents' contradicts the realities of corporate law.[23]

B.   Shareholders cannot demand dividends (and so cannot be sole residual claimants)

A second important anomaly of corporate law, closely related to the legal fact that corporate law does not give shareholders the control over corporations associated with the idea of 'ownership', is the fact that corporate law also does not grant the shareholders of a corporation that is not in bankruptcy the rights of sole residual claimants.[24] This economic reality is reflected in the corporate law rules surrounding dividends.

One of the most basic rules of corporate law is that only directors may cause the corporation to declare and pay dividends.[25] Moreover, they must do this acting as a body – no individual director has the authority to declare dividends by herself. This rule seems to strike a fatal blow to the notion that corporate law treats shareholders as sole residual claimants entitled to every penny of profit left over after the firm's contractual obligations to other groups have been met. To address this obvious point, corporate scholars defending the principal–agent paradigm typically argue that it still makes sense to view shareholders as the firm's sole residual claimants because, even if a corporation's profits are not paid out in dividends, they are preserved as retained earnings. Thus (the argument goes) retained profits increase the value of the firm, and with it, the market value of the shareholders' equity interest.[26]

The power of the principal–agent paradigm is such that is has led even sophisticated commentators[27] to overlook the rest of the anomaly – the retaining earnings argument does not work for the simple reason that earnings are an accounting concept controlled by directors, rather than shareholders. Even if a corporation is drowning in a flood of money, it remains up to the directors to decide whether and to what extent shareholders will share in that wealth through either dividends *or* an appreciation in the share price. This is because directors control dividends under the dividend rules, and also control earnings under the accounting rules. Earnings are nothing more than revenues minus expenses – and it is the directors, and not the shareholders, who determine the corporation's expenses.

The board of a firm that is making a surplus can choose to pass that surplus on to the corporation's shareholders. But it can choose instead to use the corporation's increasing wealth to raise employee salaries, buy the CEO an executive jet, build an on-site childcare center, improve customer service, or make donations to charity and the local community. Economic and legal reality simply does not track the principal–agent model. Many different groups are potential 'residual claimants' in corporations in the sense that they can share in the surplus created by the activities of the enterprise, including not only shareholders, but also creditors, customers, employees, and the community.

C. 'Legal personality' is a key feature of corporations

The nexus of contracts approach to the corporation implies that the notion that the corporation is a legal entity is not only a useless idea, but a misleading one – a corporation is only a web of explicit and implicit agreements among the various groups that participate in 'the firm'. This view has led economists and corporate scholars to downplay the importance of corporate personality and even to scoff at the notion that the corporation is an entity in its own right.[28] Nevertheless, legal personality remains an essential corporate characteristic. Indeed, it may be the most important characteristic to distinguish the corporate form from proprietorships and traditional partnerships.[29]

This is because entity status allows corporations to do something neither proprietorships nor traditional partnerships can easily do: shield the property used in the enterprise from the claims of equity investors, their successors and heirs, and their creditors.[30] At law, the corporation itself 'owns' all assets held in the corporate name. This is more than a mere convenience. It means that an equity investor who needs money cannot raise it by forcing the corporation to return her investment.

As section 2 will discuss in greater detail, this ability to 'lock in' corporate capital may be vital to understanding the evolution and success of the corporate form. In particular, it allowed public corporations to safely invest in what economists call 'specific' assets – infrastructure, machinery, processes, or relationships that are specialized to the enterprise and that would be worth far less if sold on the market for cash than they are worth when used in the firm.[31] Specific investments are often essential to long-term, uncertain, and complex economic projects (building railroads, developing new technologies, creating trusted brand names). Unfortunately, specific investment is easily discouraged when individual investors have a legal right to prematurely withdraw their contributions, and with it, the ability to threaten to withdraw in order to opportunistically 'hold up' their fellow investors and extract a larger share of the surplus generated by corporate activity. After investors have pooled their money to build a railroad, for example, it would cause enormous trouble if any of the investors were entitled to demand his or her money back.

The corporation's legal personality helps solve this problem by saying, in effect, that the railroad's assets belong not to the investors but to the railroad itself, and that only the railroad's directors – not its shareholders – may decide when to pull capital out of the enterprise to pay dividends, repurchase shares, or for any other purpose.

Incorporation accordingly means that individual equity investors in a public corporation can only get their money back by finding someone else willing to purchase their shares and their interest in the enterprise. Especially before the development of business forms like the limited partnership or limited liability company (LLC), this consequence of legal personality provided a key difference between partnerships and corporations. In traditional partnerships, each partner has the right at any time to withdraw her share of the assets from the firm.[32] Section 2 will discuss in greater detail how the corporation's ability to 'lock in' capital through its status as a legal personality may be of importance in explaining the rise of the corporation in the nineteenth century and the peculiar advantages enjoyed by corporations in encouraging long-term, complex economic projects.

D. Corporate law does not require shareholder wealth maximization

Finally, let us consider one of the most significant anomalies in corporate law to trouble scholars who follow the principal–agent model: the rules of corporate purpose. According to the principal–agent model, the purpose of the corporation is clear. Corporations exist only to maximize profits, and with them, the wealth of the shareholders who are said to be the firm's sole residual claimants. There is one obvious and dramatic problem with this claim, however. There is very little in US corporate law that supports it, and much that cuts against it.

Partnership law defines a partnership as an association for the purpose of earning business profits.[33] However, corporate law does not define the purpose of the corporation beyond restricting it to 'lawful' activities.[34] This means that corporate purpose remains, as a matter of law, an 'extremely varied, inclusive, and open-ended' concept.[35] Nevertheless, having only the principal–agent paradigm to work with, most corporate scholars writing in the waning years of the twentieth century tried to accommodate that perspective. While often recognizing how corporate law did not fit principal–agent analysis, many nevertheless ultimately accepted the idea that corporate directors should, as a normative matter, focus on maximizing value for shareholders. A classic example can be found in Robert Clark's leading treatise on US corporate law, which states that '[a]lthough corporation statutes do not answer this question explicitly, lawyers, judges, and economists usually *assume* that the *more* ultimate purpose of a business corporation is to make profits for its shareholders'.[36]

The main case Clark relied on in making this claim was, of course, the old chestnut *Dodge* v. *Ford* – a case nearly a century old, from a state unimportant to corporate law (Michigan), dealing with shareholder fiduciary duties in a closely-held (not public) company to boot.[37] Virtually every corporate scholar who has ever tried to argue that US corporate law follows shareholder primacy has been forced, like Clark, to base his or her argument on the dictum of the antiquated *Dodge* v. *Ford*. Yet ample modern case law confirms directors' legal freedom to divert corporate assets and earnings to creditors, employees, customers, the community, and even general charities.[38] Corporate law also clearly permits directors to require the corporation to obey laws and regulations even when violating the law would be more profitable for shareholders.[39]

This anomaly can be readily dismissed by those who want to dismiss it, because it is easy for corporate directors to (as Clark's treatise puts it) 'make the right noises' and claim that actions taken on behalf of nonshareholder constituencies also benefit shareholders 'in the long run'.[40] And if the directors themselves fail to advance this claim, it is also easy for a court, or a scholar, simply to advance the claim for them. Nevertheless, the outcome is clear. US corporate law does not follow the principal–agent paradigm on the question of corporate purpose.

2 Explaining anomalies: on specific investment, capital lock-in and team production

As has been detailed in section 1, there are many important ways in which the structure of US corporate law departs from the predictions of the principal–agent model. Although the misfit is obvious and in some cases dramatic, the reasons for the divergence remained unclear to a generation of theorists forced to work in a paradigm that treated common shareholders as the sole residual claimants in corporations. This paradigm in turn reflected legal scholars' enthusiasm for adapting the economic literature on the principal–agent problem to the institution of the public corporation.

In this section we suggest that a new paradigm is appearing in corporate law scholarship, one that offers to resolve many of the anomalies discussed in section 2. The new paradigm is emerging because corporate scholars have an intellectual tool to work with that they did not have a generation ago: a developing literature on the economic problem of encouraging and protecting specific investment. In several recent papers, economic and legal scholars (including ourselves, working both alone and together) have investigated how specific investment offers insights into a number of peculiar features of corporations that do not fit the principal–agent model, including their entity status and their director-dominated governance structure.[41] This growing literature suggests that the principal–agent model fails to predict many fundamental aspects of corporate law because it assumes that the only economic problem to be solved is the problem of getting directors and executives to do what shareholders want them to do.[42] Yet corporate law may to a very great extent be driven by the need to solve a different problem: the problem of encouraging essential specific investments in projects where contracting is incomplete because the project is complex, long-lived, and uncertain.

Corporations tend to be formed in order to pursue businesses that require large amounts of enterprise-specific assets, meaning assets that cannot be withdrawn from the enterprise without destroying much of their value. Specific assets can take a large variety of forms. For example, 'sunk-cost' investments in research, development, and business processes and relationships – money or time that has already been spent in the hope of earning future profits and is now 'water over the dam' – are specific. So are specialized machines and equipment that cannot be easily converted for other uses. Executives' and employees' acquisition of knowledge, skills, and relationships uniquely useful to their present firm, and of little value to other potential employers, are examples of investments in firm-specific 'human capital'. Developing customer loyalty, a trusted brand name, or a unique business process are all examples of specific investment.

Specific investment poses unique contracting problems. To understand why, consider the case of a group of investors who pool their money and intellectual talents to develop a cancer treatment. Once the money is spent and the research has begun, the investors' time and money has been transformed into an intellectual asset that, at least until it is patented and gets Food and Drug Administration approval, is largely specific to the enterprise. Neither the bottles and petri dishes in the lab, nor the lab notes, nor the records of the biologists and physicians who tested the treatment would have much value if not used by the company to get the patent and the FDA approval, and to manufacture and sell the drug. The investors get the greatest value from their investment by keeping their resources together until they can bring the whole project to fruition.

As a result, each of the investors must worry that if the business is formed as a traditional partnership – if there is no entity status and no capital lock-in – all of the investors are vulnerable to the possibility that the group might not hold together long enough to see the project through to its finish. Alternatively, and just as threatening, any one investor who provides a critical resource would be in a position to opportunistically threaten to withdraw his or her interest in order to coerce the others into giving up a larger share of any gains that flow from the joint project. Co-investors who contribute to projects requiring large amounts of specific investment accordingly can find themselves at risk from each other and from each others' successors and creditors. Unless the risks are controlled, the project may not be pursued in the first place.

This is where the new scholarship suggests that the creation of an incorporated legal entity with board governance can be useful.[43] If the investors form a corporation and take shares of stock in exchange for their contributions, the money that financial investors have put up, along with the scientists' work-in-progress and any patents obtained, belong to the corporate entity. The financiers cannot unilaterally withdraw their funding, nor can the entrepreneurs and employees unilaterally extract the value of their time and effort (much less their lab notes and intellectual contributions) unless such a break-up and liquidation of the firm is agreeable to the corporation's board of directors. The board in turn cannot be controlled by any one of the participants alone. All of the participants in the venture have to some degree 'tied their own hands' and made it harder to withdraw.[44] This seemingly self-defeating arrangement can in fact be self-serving if it encourages profitable joint investment in projects that require specific investments that could not otherwise be protected.

The problem of encouraging specific investment when corporate production requires different individuals to contribute different types of resources, such as a project that requires an executive's time, an entrepreneur' idea, and an investor's money, is often described as one of 'team production'. Building on the work of economists Armen Alchian and Harold Demsetz,[45] we define 'team production' as 'production in which 1) several types of resources are used . . . 2) the product is not a sum of separable outputs of each cooperating resource . . . [and] 3) not all resources used in team production belong to one person'.[46] Team production presents obvious problems of coordination and shirking, problems addressed by Alchian and Demsetz[47] and by Holmstrom[48] in early work proposing solutions that echo typical solutions to the principal–agent problem.

Then Oliver Hart and some co-authors began to look at the issue.[49] Although they did not use the language of team production, they considered a similar problem, and added an important additional confounding condition – the team members must make investments specific to the enterprise, putting them at risk if the enterprise failed or one team member attempted to hold up the others. Hart et al.'s addition may be vital to understanding corporations, because corporate production often requires a variety of 'stakeholder' groups to make specific investments that cannot be protected by formal contracts and that put them at risk if the business fails or they are forced to sever their relationship with the firm. Consider the executive who works long hours at a start-up company for below-market wages, or the customer who becomes adept at using a particular corporation's products, or the community that builds roads and schools to serve a company's factory employees.

Once again, however, the solution proposed by Hart et al. echoed the principal–agent model: at least one team member must have 'ownership' or 'property rights' over the team's joint output, meaning a residual right of control. This proposed solution was admittedly flawed: while such a property right would protect the team member who owned it, assigning the right to only one member of the team left the other members vulnerable. Hart et al. suggested this might be an inevitable difficulty with specific investment in team production, and that the best that could be done would be to assign the property right to the team member whose enterprise-specific investment was most 'important' in some sense.[50]

Rajan and Zingales then proposed an alternative solution. They noted that under Hart's solution, not only would team members who do not 'own' a right to the team's output have reduced incentives to make specific investments, but the owner might sometimes have a stronger incentive to opportunistically sell his control over the other team members (thereby capturing the value of any specific investments they had made) instead of completing the team and making specific investments himself. Their proposed solution to this problem was that all team members might be better off if they yielded control rights to an outsider.[51] In a detailed discussion elsewhere, we have expanded upon the Rajan and Zingales solution and suggested it provides a rationale for why people might choose to organize production through a corporation with entity status governed by a board of directors.[52]

In brief, forming a corporation requires the participants in that corporation to yield decision-making power over their ability to earn a return on their specific investments to a board of directors that is not, itself, a residual claimant in the firm.[53] Corporate participants yield power over their specific investments in the sense that, if they choose to withdraw from the firm, they must leave those investments behind or see their value destroyed. And as long as they stay with the firm, they cannot directly control how their (or other team members') specific assets are used, nor can they demand that the corporation pay for the value of those specific investments. As a result, the only way corporate participants can profit from specific investment in the company is by continuing their relationship with the corporate 'team' and hoping the board allocates to them some portion of the surplus generated by team production. Since the board is not itself a residual claimant and its members are precluded by fiduciary duties from expropriating the surplus for themselves (at least in their roles as directors), the board has no incentive to opportunistically threaten the value of team members' specific investment. And since the board at a minimum wants the team to stay together and to stay productive (thus assuring the continuation of the members' board positions), the board has some incentive to do this.

Space constraints preclude a full discussion here of how focusing on capital lock-in and specific investment in team production can explain a wide range of important phenomena in the business world, including the development of the corporate form,[54] the nature of directors' fiduciary duties,[55] the proper role of corporate counsel,[56] the rules of derivative suit procedure,[57] the regulation of takeover bids and antitakeover defenses,[58] and even bankruptcy reorganization[59] and the necessity of a corporate-level income tax.[60] Interested readers are invited to explore the large and growing literature on such topics. Below we simply note how these new intellectual tools promise to help us build a paradigm of corporate law that both explains and predicts the important anomalies discussed in section 1.

A.   Directors are not agents but 'mediating hierarchs' who protect specific investment in corporations and distribute the returns from that investment

Viewing corporations through the lens of capital lock-in and team production offers a variety of insights into the basic nature and structure of corporate law. One of the most important of these insights is an answer to the question of why, as discussed in section 1.A, corporate law does not treat corporate directors as agents who must do the shareholders' bidding but instead grants boards a remarkably wide range of autonomy and control over corporate assets. Board autonomy worsens the agency cost problem in corporations, because it means shareholders (and other stakeholders for that matter) have less leverage to pressure boards to maximize corporate returns. At the same time, both the capital lock-in approach and the team production model suggest that director authority in public corporations remains a "second-best" solution that provides offsetting economic benefits by encouraging and protecting specific investment in corporate production.

For example, capital lock-in theory explains that corporate law does not allow any individual shareholder or subgroup of shareholders to exercise direct control over the board for the simple reason that, if this were allowed, a shareholder with liquidity concerns (for example) could use that control to force the firm to sell essential specific assets at a loss in order to raise the funds necessary to buy out the shareholder's interest. Alternatively, and perhaps even more likely, the shareholder might opportunistically threaten to do this to try to force the other investors to agree to give the opportunist a larger share of corporate earnings.[61] The need to protect the company's specific assets thus explains why corporate law limits individual shareholders' power to control directors and to demand dividends, share repurchases, or other transactions that would threaten locked-in capital.

Relatedly, team production analysis emphasizes how shareholders' capital must be locked in and controlled by boards not only to protect shareholders' interests, but also to protect the interests of other team members that have made specific investments (e.g., employees, creditors, and customers who may have made past contributions of time and effort, invested in specialized relationships, skills, and loyalties, or acquired knowledge of particular firm processes and products). Shareholders cannot be allowed to directly control corporations because they are only one among the many groups that must yield control rights over the firm's assets and outputs in order to make credible commitments to other team members that they will not hold up the whole team to extract a larger share of the surplus.

Team production analysis accordingly can explain why, under the rules of corporate law, directors are not 'agents' of either subgroups of shareholders or shareholders as a class, nor of any other class of investors. Rather, as we have argued in some detail elsewhere,[62] directors are better described as 'mediating hierarchs' who must balance the competing needs and demands of shareholders, creditors, customers, suppliers, executives, rank and file, and even the local community, in a fashion that protects specific investments in the corporation and keeps the corporation alive, healthy, and growing. In other words, boards of directors, who alone are empowered to decide how to distribute the corporate surplus, should use this power to ensure that every vital team member gets at least enough of the surplus to keep that member motivated to stay with the team.

B. Many different groups make specific investments in corporations and are potential residual claimants

Once one acknowledges the legal reality that directors are not shareholders' agents, one must also accept that a second key component of the principal–agent model – the idea that shareholders are the sole residual claimants in firms – has no solid foundation. When corporate directors enjoy any significant discretion to decide how the corporation uses its assets, it becomes grossly inaccurate as a descriptive matter to assert that shareholders of a public corporation are the sole residual claimants of that firm.[63] To the contrary, shareholders are only one of many groups that may act as residual claimants or residual risk bearers in the sense that directors have authority to provide those groups with benefits (and sometimes to saddle them with burdens) above and beyond the benefits and burdens described in their formal contracts with the firm. For example, when a corporation is doing spectacularly well, it is common to see employees receive dental benefits and greater job security, executives get nicer offices and access to a company jet, bondholders get increased protection from insolvency, and the local elementary school get charitable donations of money and equipment. Conversely, these groups suffer along with shareholders when times are bad, as employees get stingier benefits, executives fly coach, debtholders face increased risk, pension funds fail, and the elementary school does without.

In reality directors simply do not behave the way the principal–agent model predicts they should. They reward many groups with larger slices of the corporate pie when the pie is growing, and spread the loss among many when the pie is shrinking. Far from providing evidence that directors are doing something wrong by imposing 'agency costs' on shareholders, this observation suggests directors may be doing exactly what team production analysis says they should be doing – acting as mediating hierarchs who balance the conflicting interests of the many members who make up a healthy, productive corporate team.

C. The concept of 'legal personality' plays an important economic role in protecting specific investment

One of the greatest weaknesses of the principal–agent model is its characterization of the firm as a nexus of contracts. As noted earlier, this idea is in tension with the claim that shareholders 'own' corporations, since it is difficult to envision how one might own a nexus. A second problem, however, is that the nexus metaphor does not give any guidance on where, exactly, the 'firm' begins and ends. If an executive who signs an employment agreement with Microsoft is 'in' the firm, what about the closely held corporation that signs an agreement to supply certain software programs? Are Microsoft and the closely held supplier one single company? What about the buyer who signs a contract to purchase a Microsoft product? Is the buyer part of Microsoft? Under the nexus approach, it is difficult to see where Microsoft ends and the rest of the world begins.

The capital lock-in approach may not, by itself, tell us what 'a firm' is, but it at least provides a way to define what 'a corporation' is. In brief, a corporation is a legal entity that can own property in its own name. This concept has economic as well as legal importance. As noted in the previous section, entity status allows a corporation to lock in resources so they can be converted safely to specific assets. Although one might imagine other legal mechanisms for achieving capital lock-in – say, a trust arrangement[64] – incorporation accomplishes the same result cleanly and simply.

Indeed, team production analysis suggests incorporation does more. By placing ownership of the firm's assets in the hands of the firm itself rather than in the hands of the firm's shareholders, incorporation encourages specific investments from other important groups that often participate in corporate production, including creditors, executives, customers, and rank-and-file employees. These constituencies become more willing to invest because they know that control over the corporation – and with it, control over their specific investments – now rests in the hands of a board, and not in the hands of shareholders who might opportunistically threaten to destroy their investment or exclude them from the firm in order to demand a larger share of any surplus. The result is a mutual 'hand tying' arrangement among the various groups that make specific investments in corporations – an arrangement that ultimately works to benefit all. This arrangement would be undermined by allowing any one of the team members to exercise direct control over the firm's assets.

Focusing on the problem of specific investment rather than the problem of agency costs accordingly allows us to see why corporate 'personhood' matters so much. Legal personality worsens agency costs. As Clark's treatise puts it, from a shareholder's perspective 'a major problem with legal personality as it has been developed for public corporations has been presented by the "hard to kill" character of the corporation'.[65] At the same time, this Frankenstein's monster aspect of incorporation may perform a vital economic function by protecting the value of shareholders' and other team members' specific interests in corporate production. To quote again from Clark's treatise, legal personality can 'safeguard going concern values'.[66]

D.   Corporate law leaves corporate purpose open to protect directors' role as mediating hierarchs

What does this all this imply for the fourth anomaly noted in this essay – the open-ended nature of the legal rules regarding corporate purpose? Interestingly, here capital lock-in and team production analysis give somewhat different, although in some respects complementary, answers.

The capital lock-in function of corporate law helps protect what Clark's treatise calls 'going concern' value for all corporate participants, not just shareholders. But capital lock-in theory, by itself, doesn't necessarily preclude a legal stance that emphasizes shareholder value maximization as the appropriate corporate goal. The team production approach, however, offers another and in many ways more intriguing explanation for the anomaly of open-ended corporate purpose. In brief, it suggests that the appropriate normative goal for a board of directors is to build and protect the wealth-creating potential of the entire corporate team – 'wealth' that is reflected not only in dividends and share appreciation for shareholders, but also in reduced risk for creditors, better health benefits for employees, promotional opportunities and perks for executives, better product support for customers, and good 'corporate citizenship' in the community.[67] To accomplish this, directors must have a wide range of discretion to balance competing interests in a way that keeps the team together and keeps it productive.

Team production analysis consequently warns against defining corporate purpose in a narrow fashion that would allow one or more members of the corporate team to challenge the board's authority and argue either that the board is pursuing the wrong goal, or that it is pursuing the right goal in the wrong way. Once we leave behind the narrow objective of maximizing share value, it is impossible for an outsider like a court to design an algorithm to measure whether a board is maximizing returns to the corporate team, and dangerous to invite courts to try. Allowing either shareholders or other stakeholders to claim in court that directors who are not violating their loyalty duties by using their corporate powers to enrich themselves are nevertheless acting with an 'improper purpose' simply invites corporate participants to try to extract wealth from other team members by waving the stick of personal liability over the directors' heads.

A corollary is that the corporate desideratum associated with the principal–agent model – 'increase share value whether this helps or harms other team members' – is a recipe for inefficiency. The team production approach undermines the principal–agent model's claim that corporations are governed well when they are governed in a fashion that maximizes share value. Rather, good governance means making sure the corporation survives and thrives as a productive, value-creating team – even though this is an objective that is difficult to measure, much less maximize.

It is important to note that the idea that corporate law does not require directors to maximize share value in no way implies that shareholders are worse off under corporate law rules that give directors such open-ended discretion. Team production analysis teaches that equity investors *as a class* are better off when corporate participants, including equity investors, lenders, employees, and entrepreneurs, have an organizational form available to them that allows them to cede power over corporate assets to the kind of director governance system provided by corporate law. Without director governance, these groups might not be able to overcome the risks of mutual rent-seeking created by complex, uncertain, and long-lived projects, and so might not pursue profitable projects in the first place.

Past and present business experience support this hypothesis. Nineteenth-century American business history is a story of entrepreneurs going to state legislatures in increasing numbers to seek permission to form corporations – corporations that outside investors purchased shares in and outside creditors loaned money to. The increasing popularity of this practice, even when it was much simpler and less costly to use partnership law to organize businesses, suggests that both the entrepreneurs, and the creditors and equity investors who financed their projects, found the arrangement valuable.[68]

Today we have even better evidence that incorporation and board governance serves the interests of shareholders and other corporate participants – evidence that was not available to scholars writing in the 1980s and even the early 1990s. In brief, US corporate law is mostly 'default rules', meaning that incorporators can modify the basic rules of corporate law by putting customized provisions in the corporate charter before the company 'goes public' and sells shares to outside investors.[69] If investors really wanted more power over boards, there is no reason why an enterprising entrepreneur who wanted to appeal to this desire could not add a charter provision that, for example, prohibited the board from adopting a 'poison pill' that would allow them to reject a premium takeover bid favored by the shareholders. Similarly, if outside investors really believed that requiring boards to pursue share value would make them better off, incorporators could put 'shareholder wealth maximization' in the charter as the corporate purpose.

Public corporation charters almost hardly ever contain such provisions.[70] Even more telling, recent empirical studies demonstrate that when promoters do tinker with charter provisions in the pre-IPO stage – exactly the stage at which they most need to appeal to outside investors – they almost always move in the *opposite* direction, adding provisions like a staggered board structure that insulates directors from shareholder influence even more than the default rules of corporate law already do.[71] Outside investors happily buy shares in these firms. This pattern suggests strongly that director discretion, including the discretion that comes from open-ended rules of corporate purpose, serves the long-run interests of 'the investor class' – even if it works against the interests of particular shareholders in particular firms at particular times. Capital lock-in and team production help explain why.

Conclusion

For most of the past three decades, US corporate law scholarship has been dominated by a single, widely accepted paradigm: the principal–agent paradigm. Yet US corporate law itself refuses, in many puzzling ways, to follow the precepts of the principal–agent model. These puzzling departures include such important anomalies as director governance; shareholder powerlessness to demand dividends; the importance of legal personality; and the open-ended rules of corporate purpose.

Nevertheless, until recently, many corporate scholars have chosen to continue to embrace the principal–agent approach for the simple reason that they lacked a compelling alternative. The result has been a literature that emphasized the agency cost problem and especially how director governance creates conflicts of interest between shareholders and directors, and that tended to be blind to the problem of specific investment and how director governance may temper potential conflicts between and among shareholders, executives, creditors, and others who make specific investments in corporations.

Today the situation has changed dramatically. Although the principal–agent model still has great influence, corporate scholars are involved in an escalating debate over the best way to understand the modern public corporation.[72] This debate increasingly recognizes the legal reality that public corporations are governed by boards and not by shareholders. It also recognizes recent developments in economic theory that teach that, in addition to the problem of agency costs, corporate production can raise important problems of encouraging specific investment.

These insights have inspired contemporary legal and economic scholars to explore new and different approaches to understanding the rules of corporate law. In this essay we have touched briefly upon two of these emerging alternative paradigms: the capital lock-in approach and the team production model. In exploring these alternatives, we are not suggesting that the original principal–agent model is always useless and should be discarded. For some corporate problems the principal–agent approach may be just as useful as the capital lock-in or team production approach, and considerably easier to apply. Similarly, Newtonian theory is just as useful as (and considerably easier to apply than) Einstein's theory of relativity for many problems in physics. Nevertheless, there are important phenomena in physics that can only be explained and predicted using Einstein's approach. And there are likewise important – indeed fundamental – phenomena in corporate law and practice the principal–agent model simply cannot account for.

In accord with Kuhn's thesis, these anomalies have attracted the attention of a new generation of corporate scholars. Rather than trying to minimize or ignore the poor fit between the principal–agent model and the rules of corporate law, they have instead sought to develop new models. They have been aided both by new theoretical tools, and by new empirical findings, that highlight the essential role specific investment can play in determining corporate structure. In the process, they are working toward new visions of the corporate purpose that go beyond the simple rubric of shareholder wealth.

Notes

1. Henry Hansmann & Reinier Kraakman, 'The End of History in Corporate Law', 89 *Geo L. J.* 439, 440–1 (2001) (arguing that academic, business and government elites now agree that 'the managers of the corporation should be charged with the obligation to manage the corporation in the interests of its shareholders ... and the market value of the publicly traded corporation's shares is the principal measure of the shareholder's interest'); see also R. Gordon Smith, 'The Shareholder Primacy Norm', 23 *J. Corp. L.* 277 (1998).
2. Thomas Kuhn (1996) *The Structure of Scientific Revolutions*, 3rd edn. Chicago and London: University of Chicago Press, p. 44.
3. Kuhn's book suggests humankind is a long way from a complete understanding of the universe, and in this sense all paradigms are to some extent social constructions and none are entirely 'correct'. Kuhn nevertheless clearly believes some paradigms are better than others at predicting real phenomena. Microbes are a better explanation for disease than witches, and it is more correct to say the earth revolves around the sun than vice versa.
4. See, e.g., Robert C. Clark (1986) *Corporate Law* (Little, Brown) (noting that U.S. corporate law fails to require directors to maximize shareholder wealth but stating this ought to be the corporate purpose).
5. Michael C. Jensen & William H. Meckling, 'Theory of the Firm: Managerial Behavior, Agency Costs, and Ownership Structure', 3 *J. Fin. Econ.*, vol. 4, pp. 305–60 (1976).
6. See e.g., Oliver Williamson, *The Economics of Discretionary Behavior: Managerial Objectives in a Theory of the Firm* (1964), and R. Marris, 'The Economic Theory of "Managerial" Capitalism', *Journal of the Royal Statistical Society, Series A (General)*, vol. 127(4) (1964), pp. 579–81.
7. See Marris, '"Managerial" Capitalism'.
8. Henry G. Manne, 'Mergers and the Market for Corporate Control', 73 *J. P. Econ.*, 110–20 (1965).

9. See e.g., Frank H. Easterbrook & Daniel R. Fischel, 'The Proper Role of A Target's Management in Responding to a Tender Offer', 94 *Harv. L. Rev.* 1161 (1981); Ronald J. Gilson, 'A Structural Approach to Corporations: The Case Against Defensive Tactics in Tender Offers', 33 *Stan. L. Rev.* 5, 819–91 (1981).
   The leap from viewing managers and directors as shareholders' agents to concluding that managers and directors must stand willing to sell out the corporation to a highest bidder requires one more assumption commonly accepted by proponents of law and economics. This additional assumption is that securities markets are both informationally and allocationally efficient, so that the market price of a company's shares reflects their 'fundamental' economic value. Although during the 1980s the idea of fundamental value efficiency enjoyed widespread support, in recent years it has been subject to both theoretical and empirical challenge, and many finance economists no longer accept it. See generally Lynn A. Stout, 'The Mechanisms of Market Inefficiency: An Introduction to the New Finance' 28 *J. Corp. L.* 633 (2003).
10. See, e.g., Frank H. Easterbrook & Daniel R. Fischel, 'Corporate Control Transactions', 91 *Yale L. J.* 698, 700–2 (1982); Frank H. Easterbrook & Daniel R. Fischel, 'Voting in Corporate Law', 26 *J. L & Econ.* 395, 395–427 (1983); Frank H. Easterbrook & Daniel R. Fischel, 'Two Agency-Cost Explanations of Dividends', 74 *Am. Econ. Rev.* 650 (1984). The ideas in these articles were later brought together in an influential book, Frank H. Easterbrook & Daniel R. Fischel (1991), *The Economic Structure of Corporate Law* (Harvard. University Press).
11. See id. at 11. Clearly most corporate participants do not actually bargain in this way, so the argument was an 'as if' argument of the type legitimized by economist Milton Friedman when he claimed that it is acceptable to argue that economic actors 'optimize' if the outcomes of their choices correspond to those that would obtain if in fact economic actors had consciously optimized. Milton Friedman (1966), 'The Methodology of Positive Economics', in *Essays in Positive Economics* (Chicago: University of Chicago Press), pp. 3–16, 30–43. Even if shareholders do not literally bargain to be residual claimants, the argument goes, if in fact we see shareholders play this role, the result is the same.
12. See Easterbrook & Fischel, *Economic Structure*, pp. 36–9, 185–91; see also Easterbrook & Fischel, 'Voting', p. 396 ('shareholders are no more "owners" of the firm than are bondholders, other creditors, and employees (including managers) who devote specialized resources to the enterprise').
13. Clark, *Corporate Law*, pp. 105–6. See, e.g., *Auer v. Dressel*, 118 N.E. 2d 590, 593 (N.Y. 1954) (holding that directors have no legal obligation to respond to shareholder resolution demanding reinstatement of dismissed officer).
14. Clark, *Corporate Law*, pp. 106, 594.
15. Ibid., pp. 106, 191. See, e.g., *In Re Disney Derivative Litigation*, No. Civ. A. 15452, 2005 WL 2056651 (Del. Ch. 9 August 2005).
16. Clark, *Corporate Law*, at pp. 105–6, 136–7, 681–2. See, e.g., *Credit Lyonnais Bank Nederland, N.V. v. Pathe Communications Corp.*, Civ. A. No. 12150, 1991 Del. Ch. LEXIS 215 (Del. Ch. Dec. 30, 1991) (upholding board discretion to pursue strategy that favored creditors' interests over shareholder's objections); *Shlensky v. Wrigley*, 237 N.E.2d 776 (Ill. App. Ct. 1968)) (upholding director discretion to pursue strategy that favored local community over shareholder's objections); *Theodora Holding Corp. v. Henderson*, 257 A.2d 398 (Del. Ch. 1969) (upholding director discretion to make philanthropic contributions over shareholder's objection).
17. Clark, *Corporate Law*, at pp. 141–2 (discussing duty of loyalty).

18. Ibid., 123–9 (discussing business judgment rule).
19. See Lynn A. Stout, 'The Shareholder As Ulysses: Some Empirical Evidence on Why Investors In Public Corporations Tolerate Board Governance', 152 *U. Pa. L.*, Rev. 667, 694–5 (2003) (discussing lack of active market for control); see also Lucian Arye Bebchuk Bebchuk et al., 'The Powerful Antitakeover Force of Staggered Boards: Theory, Evidence, and Policy', 54 *Stan. L. Rev.* 887, 890–1 (2002) (study finding that between 1996 and 2000, no hostile bidders succeeded against firms that had adopted staggered board structure).
20. See Smith, 'Shareholder Primacy', at 289 (discussing other constituency statutes); *Unocal Corp.* v. *Mesa Petroleum Co.*, 493 A.2d 946, 955 (Del. 1985) (discussing director discretion to consider interests of creditors, customers, employees, and community).
21. See *Paramount Communications, Inc.* v. *Time, Inc.*, 571 A. 2d 1140, 1151–5 (Del. 1989) (discussing directors' discretion to choose best "long-run" strategy). In an earlier case, the Delaware Surpeme Court had suggested that in limited circumstance directors might be required to maximize share price. See *Revlon* v. *MacAndres & Forbes Holdings*, 506 A. 2d 173, 176 (Del. 1986). *Paramount* and other subsequent cases make clear that directors can easily avoid being subject to *Revlon* duties. Stout, 'Shareholder as Ulysses', at p. 696.
22. See Clark (1985), 'Agency Costs versus Fiduciary Duties', in John W. Pratt & Richard J. Zeckhauser (eds), *Principals and Agents: The Structure of Business* (Boston, MA: Harvard Business School Press), pp. 55, 56.
23. Cf. Clark, *Corporate Law*, at p. 22 ('the relationship between shareholders and directors is not well described as being between principals and agents').
24. Nor is it clear shareholders enjoy this status even when the firm is in bankruptcy. Lynn M. PoPucki, 'The Myth of the Residual Owner', 82 *Wash. U. L. Q.* 1341, 1343 (2004) (empirical study finding that even in bankruptcy reorganization, 'no identifiable, single residual owner class exists').
25. Clark, *Corporate Law*, pp. 106, 594.
26. Ibid., pp. 594–602 (discussing Modigliani–Miller approach to irrelevance of dividend payouts).
27. See, e.g., Clark, *Corporate Law*, p. 594 (stating that directors and not shareholders control dividends) and at 18 (stating that 'it is the shareholders who have the claim on the residual value of the enterprise').
28. See, e.g., Easterbrook & Fischel, 'Economic Structure', p. 12 (arguing that '[t]he 'personhood' of a corporation is a matter of convenience rather than reality').
29. As late as 1986 the Uniform Partnership Act (UPA), which was the basis of most state law governing partnerships, was ambiguous on the question of whether partnerships had separate entity status. See UPA (1914), Sec. 6(1). The Revised Uniform Partnership Act (1997) clarifies that the default rule is that a partnership formed under the new act is given entity status. See Margaret Blair, 'Reforming Corporate Governance: What History Can Teach Us', 1 *Berkeley Business Law Journal*, 1, 1–44, text & notes 59–61 (discussing this evolution in the law and its implications).
30. See infra text accompanying notes 43–5, 65–7.
31. Oliver Williamson was among the first economists to explore the significance of investments in specific assets for the allocation of investment returns and the structure of ownership rights in long-term contracts. See, e.g., Williamson, 'Transaction-Cost Economics: The Governance of Contractual Relations', 22 *J. L. Econ.* 233 (1979). Margaret Blair (1995), *Ownership and Control: Rethinking Corporate Governance for the Twenty-first Century* (Washington, DC, The Brookings Institution)' pp. 249–71 highlighted the implications of specific investments in human capital for corporate governance.

32. See Clark, *Corporate Law*, at p. 19 ('Rarely do common shareholders in public corporations have a right to force the corporation to buy back their shares. Nor are they
able, on their own initiative, to force the company to liquidate and thus pay all the
shareholders. Consequently, there is no risk, as there is in a general partnership,
that the joint exercise of such a right by a number of investors will kill the enterprise. Corporations. . . . are more likely to preserve the going concern value of large
projects.')

33. Clark, *Corporate Law*, at p. 16.

34. See, e.g., Del. Code Ann. Tit. 8, Section 102(a)(3).

35. Clark, *Corporate Law*, at p. 17; see also id at 678 (noting that 'perhaps surprisingly,
the state business corporation statutes under which corporations are chartered generally do not say explicitly that the purpose of the business corporation is to make or
maximize profits'.)

36. Ibid., p. 17, emphasis added.

37. *Dodge* v. *Ford Motor Co.*, 170 N.W. 668 (Mich. 1919).
Contrary to the notion that corporate officers and directors have an enforceable duty
to maximize value for shareholders, liability is only very rarely imposed on directors
for anything other than breach of the duty of loyalty (that is, using their corporate
positions to line their own pockets, a practice which harms not just shareholders
but all the groups that participate in firms). Very few cases impose liability on directors for breach of the duty of care and, curiously, most of those cases were brought
on behalf of banks or other financial institutions in a situation where directors'
supposed lack of care harmed not shareholders but depositors or other creditors.
Thompson & O'Kelley (2003), 'Corporations and Other Business Associations: Cases
and Materials' (New York, Aspen Law and Business) pp. 233–4. Apparently, it is usually the bankruptcy trustee who pursues these cases.

38. Clark, *Corporate Law*, at 681–4.

39. Ibid., p. 686.

40. Ibid., p. 682.

41. See, e.g., 'Symposium: Team Production in Business Organizations', 24 *J. Corp. L.* 743
(1999); Steven A. Bank, 'A Capital Lock-In Theory of the Corporate Income Tax', 94
Geo. L.J. 889, 894 (2006); Margaret M. Blair, 'Locking In Capital: What Corporate Law
Achieved for Business Organizers in the Nineteenth Century', 51 *U.C.L.A. L. Rev.* 387
(2003); Margaret M. Blair & Lynn A. Stout, 'A Team Production Theory of Corporate
Law', 85 *Va. L. Rev.* 247, 275, 278 (1999); Margaret M. Blair & Lynn A. Stout, 'Director
Accountability and the Mediating Role of the Corporate Board', 79 *Wash. U. L. Q.*
403 (2001); Harold Demsetz, 'The Economics of the Business Firm: Seven Critical
Commentaries' 50–1 (1995); Henry Hansmann & Reinier Kraakman, 'The Essential Role
of Organizational Law', 110 *Yale. L. J.* 387 (2000); Peter Kostant, 'Exit, Voice and Loyalty
in the Course of Corporate Governance and Counsel's Changing Role', 28 *J. Socio-Econ.*
203 (1999); Lynn LoPucki, 'A Team Production Theory of Bankruptcy Reorganization',
57 *Vand. L. Rev.* 741 (2004); Lynn A. Stout, 'Bad and Not-So-Bad Arguments for
Shareholder Primacy', 75 *S. Cal. L. Rev.* 1189 (2002); but see Alan J. Meese, 'A Team
Production Theory of Corporate Law: A Critical Assessment', 43 *Wm. & Mary L. Rev.*
1629 (2002); David Millon, 'New Game Plan or Business as Usual? A Critique of the
Team Production Model of Corporate Law', 86 *Va. L. Rev.* 1001 (2000).
Basic corporate law casebooks also have begun to discuss the importance of specific
investment and director governance. See, e.g., Robert W. Hamilton & Jonathan
R. Macey (2005), *Cases and Materials on Corporations*, 9th edn (St Paul, MN: West
Group), pp. 22–5 (discussing team production model of corporation); Charles R.T.

O'Kelley (2003), Corporations and Other Business Associations, 4th edn (Aspen) (with Robert B. Thompson), p. 7 (discussing problem of team-specific investment). Stephen Bainbridge has also emphasized the importance of director governance for public firms, although for different reasons. See Stephen M. Bainbridge, 'Director Primacy: The Means and Ends of Corporate Governance', 97 *Nw. U. L. Rev.* 547 (2003).
42. See Margaret M. Blair, 'Human Capital and Theories of the Firm', in Margaret M. Blair & Mark Roe (1991), *Employees and Corporate Governance 7* (Washignton, DC: Brookings Institute) (discussing asymmetry of canonical principal–agent problem). See also Paul Milgrom & John Roberts, *Economics, Organizations, and Management* (Englewood Cliffs,. Prentice Hall, 1992), pp. 334–5 (discussing problem of getting employers to reveal accurate information so that employee incentive contracts can be enforced against them). Legal scholars rarely address the problem of mutual opportunism outside the close corporation context. See, e.g., Eric Talley, 'Taking the "I" out of "Team": Intra-Firm Monitoring and the Content of Fiduciary Duties', 24 *J. Corp. L.* 1001, 1015–21 (1999); Edward B. Rock & Michael Wachter, 'Waiting for the Omelet to Set: Match-Specific Investments and Minority Oppression in Close Corporations', 24 *J. Corp. L.* 913, 914–15 (1999).
43. See, e.g., Blair, 'Locking In', p. 391('The creation of a separate legal entity allows business organizers to partition the assets used in the business. . . . [This means] participants and third parties are assured that the pool of assets used in the business will be available to meet the needs of the business first (such as, to pay the claims of the business's creditors) before these assets can be distributed to shareholders'); Blair & Stout, 'Team Production', p. 292 ('the firm can hold title to the property, and can thereby function as the repository of all "residual" income from team production that is not actually paid out to team members').
44. See, e.g., Stout, 'The Shareholder As Ulysses', at 669 ('for some reason, participants in public corporations – including investors – *value* director primacy. Just as the legendary Ulysses served his own interests by binding himself to the mast of his ship, investors may be serving their own interests by binding themselves to boards'). Of course, this analysis does not apply to corporations that have a single shareholder. However, most corporations of any significant size have multiple shareholders, even when those shareholders may be relatively few in number.
45. See Armen Alchian & Harold Demsetz, 'Production, Information Costs, and Economic Organization', 62 Am. Econ. Rev. 777 (1972). Other scholars who have done important work on this idea include Bengt Holmstrom, 'Moral Hazard in Teams', 13 *Bell J. Econ.* 324 (1982); Oliver Hart, 'Incomplete Contracts and the Theory of the Firm', 4, *J. L. Econ. & Org.* 119 (1988); Sanford Grossman & Oliver Hart, 'The Costs and Benefits of Ownership: A Theory of Vertical and Lateral Integration', 94 *J. Pol. Econ.* 691, 693 (1986); Oliver Hart, 'An Economist's Perspective on the Theory of the Firm', 89 *Colum. L. Rev.* 1757 (1989); Oliver Hart & John Moore, 'Property Rights and the Nature of the Firm', 98 *J. Pol. Econ.*, 1119 (1990); Raghuram C. Rajan & Luigi Zingales, 'Power in the Theory of the Firm', 113 *Q.J. Econ.* 387 (1998).
46. Alchian & Demsetz, 'Economic Organization', at p. 779.
47. Ibid., p. 781.
48. Holmstrom, 'Moral Hazard', noted that *ex ante* agreements about the division of a surplus from production would give team members incentives to shirk and free ride on the efforts of fellow team members, while attempts to divide up the surplus *ex post* would lead to costly rent-seeking behavior. His proposed solution involved giving any surplus to an outsider not on the team unless the surplus was large enough to ensure that no team member had shirked. Such a solution provides

perverse incentives to the outsider to undermine the contract by bribing a team member to shirk. For a more complete discussion of the development of theoretical work in economics on team production, see Blair & Stout, 'Team Production', pp. 265–79.

49. See sources cited supra note 45.

50. See Hart & Moore, 'Property Rights', at 1149 ('[A]n agent is more likely to own an asset if his action is sensitive to whether he has access to the asset and is important in the generation of the surplus.')

51. See Rajan & Zingales, 'Power in the Theory of the Firm', at 422 ('[I]f all the parties involved in production (i.e. including the entrepreneur) have to make substantial specific investments over time, it may be optimal for a completely unrelated third party to own the assets. . . . [T]he third party holds power so that the agents critical to production do not use the power of ownership against each other').

52. See Blair & Stout, 'Team Production', at 276–87; see also Blair & Stout, 'Director Accountability'.

53. Blair & Stout, 'Team Production', at 274–7.

54. Blair, 'Lock-In'.

55. See Blair & Stout, 'Team Production', at 298–308.

56. See Kostant, 'Exit, Voice and Loyalty'.

57. See Blair & Stout, 'Team Production', at 292–7.

58. See Lynn A. Stout, 'Do Antitakeover Defenses Decrease Shareholder Wealth? The Ex Post/Ex Ante Valuation Problem', 55 *Stan. L. Rev.* 845 (2002).

59. See LoPucki, 'A Team Production Theory'.

60. See Bank, 'A Capital Lock-in Theory'.

61. As this discussion suggests, one can view capital lock-in primarily as a device that protects shareholders from the opportunism of other shareholders. We believe, however, that capital lock-in makes incorporation an attractive way to do business not only because it protects shareholders from each other , but also because it protects the interests of nonshareholder groups that have made specific investments in corporations that cannot be protected by formal contracts. For example, without capital lock-in, shareholders as a class might pressure directors to pay excessive dividends. (Shareholders with diversified portfolios are indifferent to increasing firm leverage, even though increasing risk threatens the interests of creditors, employees, and other corporate participants who cannot diversify their human capital or other specific investments in the company.) From an *ex ante* perspective, shareholders may benefit from yielding power over dividends to directors who owe fiduciary duties to the corporation as a whole, because ceding this power enables the shareholders as a group to make a more credible commitment not to strip assets out of the firm prematurely or injudiciously, in turn attracting the important firm specific investments of nonshareholder groups. This analysis can explain why corporate law grants directors the legal authority to ignore even a unanimous shareholder request for dividends.

62. See Blair & Stout, 'Team Production'; Blair & Stout, 'Director Accountability'.

63. See Blair & Stout, 'Team Production', at 250 ('Our analysis rests on the observation – generally accepted even by corporate scholars who adhere to the principal-agent model – that shareholders are not the only group that may provide specialized inputs in to corporate production. Executives, rank-and-file employees, and even creditors or the local community may also make essential contributions and have an interest in the enterprise's success' (footnotes omitted).)

64. Joint stock companies used by business people in the eighteenth and nineteenth centuries before the corporate form was widely accessible sometimes used complicated

trust arrangements to hold the assets used in the enterprise. This approach did not always achieve its intended purpose, as courts tended to treat such arrangements as a species of partnership and they would be broken up if a 'member' died or wanted out. See Blair, 'Lock-In', at 421–3 and sources cited therein.
65. Clark, *Corporate Law*, p. 762.
66. Ibid.
67. See, e.g., Blair, 'Reforming Corporate Governance' ('Management and boards of directors should understand their jobs to be maximizing the total wealth-creating potential of the enterprises they direct'); Blair & Stout, 'Team Production', at 271 (arguing that primary function of mediating hierarch is to exercise control 'in a fashion that maximizes the *joint welfare of the team as a whole*' (emphasis in original).
68. See Blair, 'Lock-In'; see also Margaret M. Blair, 'Reforming Corporate Governance', 1 *Berkeley Bus. L. J.* 1, 3 (2004) ('the decision of a firm's organizers to choose one organizational form or another, given the wide array of legal form choices available, should be taken as a signal that the organizers wanted the features of the form they choose . . . . In particular, . . .in choosing the corporate form, organizers opt into a series of rules and a body of law . . . that yields important decision rights to corporate directors').
69. See, e.g., Del. Code Ann. Tit. 8, Section 102(b)(3)(granting incorporators power to add charter provisions including 'any provision for the management of the business and for the conduct of the affairs of the corporation, and any provision creating, defining, limiting and regulating the powers of the corporation, the directors, and the stockholders....')
70. Stout, 'The Shareholder As Ulysses', at 699.
71. Ibid., at notes 73, 74 (citing studies). An even more extreme, if anecdotal example can be found in the case of the recent Google IPO, in which Google issued stock with reduced voting rights to public investors. The shares sold readily and appreciated in value despite the lack of control rights. See Lynn A. Stout & Iman Anabtawi, 'Sometimes Democracy Isn't Desirable', *Wall. St. J.* at B2 (10 August 2004) (discussing Google IPO).
72. See, e.g., sources cited in note 41.

References

Alchian, A. and H. Demsetz (1972) 'Production, Information Costs, and Economic Organization', 62 *Am. Econ. Rev.* 777.
Bainbridge, S.M. (2003) 'Director Primacy: The Means and Ends of Corporate Governance', 97 *Nw. U. L. Rev.* 547.
Bank, S.A. (2006) 'A Capital Lock-In Theory of the Corporate Income Tax', 94 *Geo. L. Rev.*
Bebchuk, L.A. et al. (2002) 'The Powerful Antitakeover Force of Staggered Boards: Theory, Evidence, and Policy', 54 *Stan. L. Rev.* 887, 890–1.
Blair, M. (1995) *Ownership and Control: Rethinking Corporate Governance for the Twenty-first Century*. Washignton, DC: Brookings Institution.
Blair, M.M. (1999) 'Human Capital and Theories of the Firm', in M.M. Blair and M. Roe, *Employees and Corporate Governance*. Washington, DC: Brookings Institution.
Blair, M.M. (2003) 'Locking In Capital: What Corporate Law Achieved for Business Organizers in the Nineteenth Century', 51 *U.C.L.A. L. Rev.* 387.
Blair, M.M. (2004) 'Reforming Corporate Governance', 1 *Berkeley Bus.L.J.* 1, 3.
Blair, M.M. and L.A. Stout (1999) 'A Team Production Theory of Corporate Law', 85 *Va. L. Rev.* 247, 275, 278.

Blair, M.M. and L.A. Stout (2001) 'Director Accountability and the Mediating Role of the Corporate Board', 79 *Wash. U. L. Q.* 403.

Clark, R. (1985) Agency Costs versus Fiduciary Duties, in Principals and Agents: The Structure of Business 55, 56 (John W. Pratt & Richard J. Zeckhauser eds.)

Clark, R. (1986) *Corporate Law*. New York: Little, Brown.

Demsetz, H. (1995) *The Economics of the Business Firm: Seven Critical Commentaries*. Cambridge: Cambridge University Press.

Easterbrook, F.H. and D.R. Fischel (1981) 'The Proper Role of A Target's Management in Responding to a Tender Offer', 94 *Harv. L. Rev.* 1161.

Easterbrook, F.H. and D.R. Fischel (1982) 'Corporate Control Transactions', 91 *Yale L. J.* 698, 700–2.

Easterbrook, F.H. and D.R. Fischel (1983) 'Voting in Corporate Law', 26 *J. L & Econ.* 395, 395–427.

Easterbrook, F.H. and D.R. Fischel (1984) 'Two Agency-Cost Explanations of Dividends', 74 *Am. Econ. Rev.* 650.

Easterbrook, F.H. and D.R. Fischel (1991) *The Economic Structure of Corporate Law*. Cambridge, MA: Harvard University Press.

Friedman, M. (1966) 'The Methodology of Positive Economics', in *Essays in Positive Economics*. Chicago: University of Chicago Press, pp. 3–43.

Gilson, R.J. (1981) 'A Structural Approach to Corporations: The Case Against Defensive Tactics in Tender Offers', 33 *Stan. L. Rev.* 5, 819–91.

Grossman, S. and O. Hart (1986) 'The Costs and Benefits of Ownership: A Theory of Vertical and Lateral Integration', 94 *J. Pol. Econ.* 691, 693.

Hamilton, R.W. and J.R. Macey (2005) *Cases and Materials on Corporations*, 9th edn.

Hansmann, H. and R. Kraakman (2000) 'The Essential Role of Organizational Law', 110 *Yale. L. J.* 387.

Hansmann, H. and R. Kraakman (2001) 'The End of History in Corporate Law', 89, *Geo L. J.* 439, pp. 440–1.

Hart, O. (1988) 'Incomplete Contracts and the Theory of the Firm', 4, *J. L. Econ. & Org.* 119.

Hart, O. (1989) An Economist's Perspective on the Theory of the Firm, 89 *Colum. L. Rev.* 1757.

Hart, O. and J. Moore (1990) 'Property Rights and the Nature of the Firm', 98 *J. Pol. Econ.*, 1119.

Holmstrom, B. (1982) 'Moral Hazard in Teams', 13 *Bell J. Econ.* 324.

Jensen, M.C. and W.H. Meckling (1976), 'Theory of the Firm: Managerial Behavior, Agency Costs and Ownership Structure', 3 *J. Fin. Econ.*, vol. 4, pp. 305–60.

Kostant, P. (1999) 'Exit, Voice and Loyalty in the Course of Corporate Governance and Counsel's Changing Role', 28 *J. Socio-Econ.*, 203.

Kuhn, T. (1996) *The Structure of Scientific Revolution*, 3rd edn. Chicago and London: University of Chicago Press.

LoPucki, L. (2004) 'A Team Production Theory of Bankruptcy Reorganization', 57 *Vand. L. Rev.* 741.

Manne, H.G. (1965) 'Mergers and the Market for Corporate Control', 73 *J. P. Econ.*, 110–20.

Marris, R. (1964) 'The Economic Theory of "Managerial" Capitalism', *Journal of the Royal Statistical Society*, Series A (General), vol. 127(4), pp. 579–81.

Meese, A. J. (2002) 'A Team Production Theory of Corporate Law: A Critical Assessment', 43 *Wm. & Mary L. Rev.* 1629.

Milgrom P. and J. Roberts (1992) *Economics, Organizations, and Management*. New Jersey: Prentice Hall.

Millon, D. (2000) 'New Game Plan or Business as Usual? A Critique of the Team Production Model of Corporate Law', 86 *Va. L. Rev.*, 1001.

O'Kelley, C.R.T. (2003) *Corporations and Other Business Associations*, 4th edn.

Rajan, R.C. and L. Zingales (1998) 'Power in the Theory of the Firm', 113 *Q.J. Econ.* 387.

Rock, E.B. and M. Wachter (1999) 'Waiting for the Omelet to Set: Match-Specific Investments and Minority Oppression in Close Corporations', 24. *J. Corp. L.* 913, 914–15.

Smith, R.G. (1998) 'The Shareholder Primacy Norm', 23 *J. Corp. L.* 277.

Stout, L.A. (2002) 'Bad and Not-So-Bad Arguments for Shareholder Primacy', 75 *S. Cal. L. Rev.* 1189.

Stout, L.A. (2002) 'Do Antitakeover Defenses Decrease Shareholder Wealth? The Ex Post/ Ex Ante Valuation Problem', 55 *Stan. L. Rev.* 845.

Stout L. A. (2003) 'The Mechanisms of Market Inefficiency: An Introduction to the New Finance', 28 *J. Corp. L.* 633.

Stout, L. A. (2003) 'The Shareholder As Ulysses: Some Empirical Evidence on Why Investors In Public Corporations Tolerate Board Governance', 152 *U. Pa. L. Rev.* 667, 694–5.

Stout, L.A. and I. Anabtawi (2004) 'Sometimes Democracy Isn't Desirable', *Wall. St. J.* at B2 (discussing Google IPO).

Talley, E. (1999), Taking the "I" out of "Team": Intra-Firm Monitoring and the Content of Fiduciary Duties, 24 *J. Corp. L.* 1001, 1015–21.

Williamson, O. (1964) *The Economics of Discretionary Behavior: Managerial Objectives in a Theory of the Firm*. Englewood Cliffs, NJ: Prentice-Hall.

Williamson, O. (1979) 'Transaction-Cost Economics: The Governance of Contractual Relations', 22 *J. L. Econ.* 233.

Part II

Normative Foundations of CSR as a Corporate Governance Model: Social Contract of the Firm, Reputations and Rational Agency

6
Corporate Social Responsibility in a Market Economy: The Perspective of Constitutional Economics

Viktor J. Vanberg

1 Introduction

Since Milton Friedman (1970) declared that 'the responsibility of business is to increase its profits' the literature on corporate social responsibility (CSR) has grown exponentially, and sorting out the variety of arguments that academic researchers on, and political advocates of, corporate social responsibility have advanced is a Sisyphean task.[1] Confining itself to a highly selective review, the purpose of the present paper is to identify and examine some of the more fundamental arguments by approaching the matter from the perspective of constitutional economics.

In his 1970 article Friedman restated an argument made earlier in his *Capitalism and Freedom* (1962). Commenting on the notion of 'social responsibility of business' Friedman noted there: 'This view shows a fundamental misconception of the character and nature of a free economy. In such an economy, there is one and only one social responsibility of business – to use its resources and engage in activities designed to increase profits so long as it stays within the rules of the game, which is to say, engages in open and free competition without deception or fraud' (ibid.: 133). It is Friedman's reference to the 'rules of the game' that invites revisiting the debate on CSR from the perspective of constitutional economics. At the heart of this debate is the issue of whether the responsibility of business in a market economy can be confined, as Friedman claims, to seeking profits *within the rules of the game* or whether it must include an explicitly 'social' component in the sense of a direct pursuit of 'socially desirable aims'. The purpose of this paper is to clarify some of the ambiguities that have clouded this issue.

2 The perspective of constitutional economics

Constitutional economics can best be described as the economics of rules (Buchanan, 1990; Brennan and Hamlin, 1998; Vanberg, 1998a). Its focus is on the role of rules in human social life, on the working properties of alternative rule regimes or, in F.A. Hayek's terms, on how the *order of rules* affects the resulting *order of actions* (Hayek, 1969). And its emphasis is on the distinction between two levels of choice, the constitutional level and the sub-constitutional level, or, in other words, between *choices among rules* and *choices within rules*. A principal interest of constitutional economics concerns the practical question of how people can improve the socio-economic-political arrangements within which they live by adopting better 'rules of the game'.

As a *theoretical science* constitutional economics seeks to provide insights into the systematic relation between the *order of rules* and the *order of actions*. As *applied science* it seeks to provide answers to the question of what rules of the social game are conducive to peaceful human coexistence and mutually beneficial cooperation. As theoretical science it is committed to *methodological individualism*, i.e. to explaining social phenomena in terms of the actions of individual human beings and of the combined effects of their interactions and co-operative efforts. As an applied science it is based on a *normative individualism* in the sense that the preferences of the individuals involved are taken as the measuring rod against which the 'desirability' of social transactions and rule-arrangements is to be judged.

As James M. Buchanan (1979) has emphasized, economics in general should be viewed properly as *the science of the gains from trade*, as the science that specializes in studying the means and ways by which people can reap mutual benefits from voluntary cooperation. While the traditional focus of economics is on voluntary market-exchanges as the paradigm case of mutually beneficial social transactions, constitutional economics extends the 'mutual gains from trade' notion to voluntary co-operation more generally understood, including arrangements for collective action, private and public (ibid.: 27ff.). It focuses, in particular, on the question of how people may realize mutual gains by 'exchanging' their *voluntary joint commitments to rules* (Buchanan, 1991: 81ff.). Or, in short, constitutional economics complements the economist's traditional focus on *mutual gains from exchange* by inquiring into how people may realize *mutual gains from joint commitment*, i.e. from jointly accepting suitable constraints on their behavioral choices.

In the case of market exchange the only conclusive evidence that can support the claim of *mutual* gains is that both sides *voluntarily agree* to the transaction, thereby indicating that, in their own judgement, they expect to be better off. In this sense, the economist's standard notion of the 'efficiency' of market outcomes is, in the last resort, derived from the presumption that they result from voluntarily agreed-on transactions. As Buchanan insists, consistency requires that the same reasoning be applied to all other forms of social cooperation, private and public. 'Efficiency' and mutual advantage can, in such cases too, ultimately be diagnosed only on the ground that all parties voluntarily agree on the desirability of the respective arrangements.

Because of its emphasis on *voluntary agreement* as the relevant criterion for the 'goodness' of social transaction or arrangements constitutional economics in the Buchanan tradition is often labeled *contractarian*.[2] The same label applies, in fact, no less to traditional economics insofar as its analytical focus is on *exchange contracts*, i.e. voluntary agreements on exchange transactions, as means of mutual improvement. What is distinctive about constitutional economics is its focus on *constitutional contracts* or *social contracts*, i.e. on voluntary agreements on rules, as means of mutual improvement. Because of its concern with constitutional or social contracts there is indeed a natural affinity between constitutional economics and the social contract tradition in moral philosophy, in particular modern contractarian approaches, such as John Rawls's *A Theory of Justice* (1971).

The remainder of this chapter is about applying the perspective that I have briefly sketched above to the issue of CSR in a market economy.

3 The market game and profit-seeking

With his characterization of the market as the 'game of catallaxy' F.A. Hayek has provided an instructive metaphor for how a market economy can be looked at from a constitutional economics perspective.[3] As he suggests, the working of the market can be understood best by looking at it as an 'exchange game', a game that 'proceeds, like all games, according to rules guiding the actions of individual participants' (Hayek, 1976: 71). From such a perspective the market can be defined as an institutionalized arena for exchange, an arena framed by rules and institutions that serve two related functions. Firstly, they serve to exclude coercion and fraud as strategies of enrichment and to ensure that, as far as this can be achieved under worldly conditions, transactions carried out in this arena are based on voluntary and informed agreement among the participants.[4] Secondly, they serve to maintain, again, as far as this can be achieved under worldly conditions, competition among the economic agents by preventing collusion and the acquisition of monopoly power. The reason for the participants to play the market game is, as Hayek emphasizes, that it is a wealth-creating or positive-sum game.[5] Participants can expect to realize overall better outcomes than they could expect from feasible alternative games, even if in the course of playing the game they may find themselves occasionally on the 'losing side', by strategic moves of their competitors or other events that run against their interests.[6]

To look at the market, as Hayek suggests, as a 'game' that is played according to certain rules helps to direct our attention to three issues that are of particular relevance in the present context, issues that I shall discuss here under the labels 'markets and profit-seeking', 'the effects of different rules', and 'different responsibilities'. To start with the issue of 'markets and profit-seeking', the essential feature of the market as an 'exchange game' is that playing the game successfully means to be able to provide goods or services for which others are willing to pay a price that covers the costs of producing them. Since what economists call *profit* is nothing other than the difference between the revenue earned from selling goods or services and the costs incurred in producing them,[7] profit can be said to be the measure of success in the market game.

The very point of the market game is to use competition in order to serve the participants' interests as consumers by disciplining their interests as producers. It is the discipline that this game imposes on producers that tends to ensure that resources are used in ways that make the greatest contribution to the satisfaction of human wants.[8] The market game induces the participants, on the one side, to seek to provide to others goods or services that are most valuable to them and for which they are, therefore, willing to pay, and, on the other side, to seek to provide these goods and services at the lowest possible costs. To the extent that participants are able to do so they play the game of catallaxy successfully, and the indication of their success is nothing other than their ability to earn profits.

Profit-seeking is, in the sense explained, inherent in the very logic of the game of catallaxy. Yet, profit-seeking in markets is, of course, not unconditional or unconstrained profit-seeking. It is profit-seeking within the constraints defined by the 'rules of the game', i.e. the rules of law and morals, and the constraints imposed on the market-players by competition.[9] The point that Adam Smith makes in one of his most often quoted phrase is that, if the baker, the butcher and the brewer are operating under the 'rules of justice' and under the constraints of competition, we can trust that their profit-earning interests will induce them to eagerly provide us with what we need for dinner (Smith, 1981: 26ff.). If, by contrast, they were to enjoy the privilege of a legally protected monopoly, their profit-seeking would surely not induce them to be equally eager to serve us.

4   The rules of the market game

It was Smith's important discovery that the market game solves the problem of inducing people to care for the needs of others in a much more effective way than all appeals to humans' altruistic inclinations have ever done. The 'social technology' by which the market game achieves this, is not to ask people to pursue other than their own interests, i.e. to act self-sacrificially, but to require them to pursue their own interests within what Smith called the 'rules of justice' and under the constraints of competition. It is because of the constraints that it imposes on the participants that the market game turns their profit-seeking efforts into services for other people's needs, most often the needs of persons of whom they have no direct knowledge and with whom they are connected only through the extended nexus of market exchanges.

'The effects of different rules' is an issue that Hayek addresses when he emphasizes the inherent connection between the working properties of market processes and the nature of the legal-institutional framework within which they operate. As he puts it:

> How well the market will function depends on the character of the particular rules. The decision to rely on voluntary contracts as the main instrument for organizing the relations between individuals does not determine what the specific content of the law of contract ought to be; and the recognition of the right of private property does not determine what exactly should be the content of this right in order that the market mechanism will work as effectively and beneficially as possible. (Hayek, 1960: 229)[10]

As noted above, it is not profit-seeking per se, operating under any kind of conditions that can be expected to make an economy function to the mutual benefit of all participants, but profit-seeking under appropriate rules. How effectively self-interest and the common interest are aligned depends on the 'quality' of the rules of the market game and their enforcement. Should market processes under given rules of the game systematically produce patterns of outcomes that the participants find undesirable,[11] there is reason to examine whether and how such undesirable outcome patterns could possibly be avoided by suitable changes in the rules of the game. To seek to correct for such 'defects' in the market game by asking market participants to limit their strife for profits beyond what the formal and informal rules of the game require cannot be a sensible strategy. If one chooses to play the market game for its overall beneficial working properties it can make no sense to ask the players in the course of the game not to aim at what indicates successful play, namely the earning of profits.

As important as it is to recognize the variability of the rules according to which the market game is played and the need to adapt them to changing technological and other relevant conditions, it is no less important to carefully distinguish demands for changing the rules that constrain profit-seeking in the market game from demands for changes that would transform the market game into an economic game of an entirely different nature. The difference between the two kinds of demands has to be kept in mind, for instance, in cases in which profit-seeking as such is the target of criticism and other criteria than profit are suggested as the proper criteria that should guide allocational choices.[12] To be sure, as citizens of political communities people may collectively choose whether they wish to play the market game or prefer to organize their economic activities on other principles than voluntary exchange, voluntary contracting and competition. Yet when making choices on how to organize their economy they should always be aware of the categorical difference between changing the rules for playing the market game and opting for changes that would transform the 'game of catallaxy' into a game of an entirely different nature. They should not under the pretext of modifying its rules unwittingly replace the game of catallaxy by a fundamentally different economic game, a game that they might not at all opt for if they were asked to choose it as an explicit alternative to the market game.

5   Constitutional and sub-constitutional responsibilities

Looking at the market in the spirit of Hayek's metaphor as an exchange game that is played under certain rules can, finally, help to direct our attention to the third of the three issues that I listed above and for which I chose the label 'different responsibilities'. This issue – upon which I already implicitly touched in the preceding remarks – concerns the need to clearly distinguish between two kinds of responsibility. This is, first, the players' *individual and separate responsibility* while playing the game, namely to abide by the legal and moral rules of the game. And this is, second, their *joint responsibilities* in defining and enforcing suitable rules of the game. If we are to apply labels, the first may be referred to as *sub-constitutional responsibility* and the latter as *constitutional responsibility*.

The rules of the market game do not fall from heaven and they are not, at least not all of them, self-enforcing. They need to be defined and adapted to changing circumstances, and they need to be enforced. This is a task that the players are neither authorized nor capable of performing in their individual and separate capacities. It is a task that they can fulfill only collectively, as an organized community through the political process.[13] While in playing the game they are fully legitimized to concentrate on playing the game success-fully, within the constraints defined by the rules, as members of the relevant political community they jointly share the responsibility for the quality of the rules under which they are playing or, in other terms, for the quality of the game they are playing. They exercise this joint responsibility through elected governments and legislatures. In more practical terms we can say, therefore, that it is the market players' responsibility to seek their advantage within the (formal and informal) rules of the game, and that it is the government's and the legislature's responsibility to establish and enforce formal rules that guide the players' advantage-seeking behavior in ways that result in desirable overall patterns of outcomes for all involved.

The joint responsibility that the participants face as members of a politically organized community is to define and enforce rules of the game that allow the market to work as effectively as possible as a wealth-increasing game to their mutual benefit. Rules that work out in mutually beneficial ways for all involved can be said to be in the participants' *common constitutional interests.*

The presence of such common constitutional interests does not per se generate an interest in working to get the respective rules adopted, nor does it automatically generate an interest in complying with these rules. There is, on the one hand, the conflict between *common constitutional interests* and *interests in privileges*. Their ambition to see rules adopted that favor their special interests or, in short, their privilege-seeking, may prevent the members of a group from reaching an agreement on rules that would serve their common constitutional interests and work to their mutual benefit. And there is, on the other hand, the difference between *constitutional interests* and *compliance interests*. Constitutional interests are about the rules by which one would like to play a game. Compliance interests are about whether in the course of playing the game there are incentives for players to deviate from the rules. Only in the case of self-enforcing rules does a constitutional interest automatically generate a compliance interest, i.e. an interest in acting in conformity with the rules by which one wishes the game to be played. In other cases the members of a community need to arrange for enforcement measures that bring their compliance interests in line with their common constitutional interests.

6 The corporation as a constitutional system

Corporations are organized units of cooperation that *internally* coordinate the activities of the participants in a centralized fashion on the basis of authority relations that define who is entitled to give orders on what to whom, and who is to follow such orders (Coase, 1937). Like organizations in general, corporations can be looked at as *constitutional systems* (Vanberg, 1992) in that they are based de facto on a 'constitution' that defines the terms under which the various parties participate in the joint corporate enterprise or, in other words, the rules and procedures by which their activities are coordinated. Since by their decision to join the corporate enterprise the parties agree to the terms of the constitution, the latter can be interpreted as a *social contract* entered into by all participants.

In a paper on 'Corporate Social Responsibility (CSR) as a Model of "Extended" Corporate Governance' Sacconi (2004) has applied such a contractarian outlook to corporations as constitutional systems to the CSR issue. As he puts it, he seeks to give 'a contractarian foundation to the concept of Corporate Social Responsibility' by interpreting the firm's 'system of corporate governance' as the product of a 'rational agreement' or a 'social contract' among 'all the firm's stakeholders' (Sacconi, 2004: 1ff.). The purpose of 'the constitutional contract of the firm', Sacconi (ibid.: 32) argues, is to define 'the institutional governance structure of the firm: that is, the complex set of rights which establishes legitimate claims (of various kinds) of both the stakeholders with ownership and control and the other stakeholders that in various ways participate in the firm or exchange with it' (ibid.: 32). The contractarian-constitutionalist outlook at the corporation that Sacconi suggests has apparent affinities to the constitutional economics perspective from which I approach the issue of CSR. Yet the interpretation of the contractual foundations of the corporation that I would like to suggest is somewhat different from his. Before I can specify the differences it is necessary to make a few clarifying remarks.

If confusion is to be avoided in applying a contractarian-constitutionalist perspective to the issue of CSR one must clearly distinguish between two kinds or two levels of 'social contracts'. This is, on the one side, the social contract among all members of a polity that establishes the rules of the 'economic game' to which all persons are subject who do business in the respective jurisdiction. And it is, on the other side, the various social contracts into which persons enter who, in the course of playing the 'economic game', establish, or participate in a corporation or any other joint enterprise.[14] The social contract at the societal level defines the rules according to which the economic game is to be played in a jurisdiction. It has systematic priority over social contracts of the second kind since it defines the constraints within which the latter may be concluded. If at the societal level the market-game has been chosen for a polity, this has implications for the kinds of 'constitutional contracts of the firm' that may be and will be chosen within the respective jurisdiction. The rules of the market game define the constraints under which potential alternative 'corporate governance systems' or corporate constitutions compete with each other in the sense that they may be found to be more or less conducive in helping players to play the market game successfully.[15]

Proper recognition of the fundamental distinction between the two levels or kinds of 'social contracts', namely the social contract that defines the rules of the market and the 'social contracts' by which corporations are constituted that operate within the market, requires one to pay attention to characteristic differences in the kinds of contractual relations and the various groups of persons that operate within the firm or interact with the firm, Sacconi appears to ignore these very differences when he describes the constitutional contract on which the corporation is based as a social contract among 'all the firm's stakeholders', and when he defines CSR as 'a model of extended corporate governance whereby who runs a firm (entrepreneurs, directors, managers) has responsibilities that range from fulfillment of the fiduciary duties towards the owners to fulfillment of analogous fiduciary duties towards all the firm's stakeholders' (Sacconi, 2004: 6). Quite apparently, as Sacconi (ibid.: 7) uses it, the term 'stakeholders' is meant to include everyone who, in whatever capacity, participates in the operation of a corporation, interacts with it, or is affected by its activities. While I agree that all these relations can be usefully analyzed from a contractarian-constitutionalist perspective, my emphasis is on the differences in the contractual relations between the various categories of 'stakeholders'.

7   Shareholders and stakeholders

As in Sacconi's case, the term 'stakeholder' is quite commonly used in ways that tend to obfuscate significant differences in the contractual relations between firms and various groups of persons that are classified under that label. In the context of the CSR debate the term is typically used to play down the difference between shareholders – that is, the owners of a corporation, and various other parties related to the corporation (Preston and Sapienza, 1990). What such use of the concept is supposed to suggest is, of course, that the responsibility of corporate executives or managers vis-à-vis the shareholders is just one among a number of 'responsibilities' that they owe to various other parties, including employees, customers, suppliers, the political community or the general public. That is, it is meant to support the claim that such views of CSR as Milton Friedman's represent an overly narrow conception of what 'socially responsible business' is about. As one inspects the stakeholder language more closely, though, this claim turns out to be based on little more than an ambiguous use of the term 'responsibility'. To be sure, if the term is used in a sufficiently diffuse sense, managers may well be said to have 'responsibility' not only vis-à-vis the owners of a corporation but to various other parties as well. Yet, using the term in such manner is to gloss over significant differences in what 'responsibility' means *in substance* when managers' relations to shareholders, employees, suppliers, customers, and other parties are concerned.

In terms of their relations to the corporation the various groups commonly subsumed under the 'stakeholder' label can be classified into three principal categories. There are, first, those parties who are with parts of their resources subject to the authority system of the corporation. These include, in particular, the shareholders who have put parts of their financial resources into a common pool where these resources are subject to collective decisions and are no longer under the original holders' individual and separate disposal. And it includes the employees who submit their labor, within defined limits, to the decision-making authority within the corporation. What is common to both groups is that, together with corporate executives or managers, they are parties to the 'social' or 'constitutional' contract that constitutes the corporation as an organized, corporate actor, i.e. as a team-production unit that allocates pooled resources under centralized direction.[16]

Understood in the sense outlined above, the 'constitutional contract of the firm' (Sacconi, 2004: 32) defines the terms under which the contributors of resources to the corporation's common resource pool participate in the joint enterprise. What is different between shareholders and employees is that the former, as owners and residual claimants, appoint the managers to direct the enterprise on their behalf, while the employees, as recipients of contractual income, are hired by the managers. That is to say, the managers are the shareholders' agents, they are not the agents of the employees.[17] While they owe 'responsibility' to both groups as defined in the implicit and explicit 'constitutional contract of the firm', their responsibility as agents vis-à-vis the shareholders is surely different from their responsibility as employers vis-à-vis the employees.

The second principal category of 'stakeholders' includes those parties who entertain market-exchange relations with the firm, such as the customers and the suppliers. Even if in cases of long-term contractual relations between a firm and its suppliers or customers the distinction may be less pronounced, there is a systematic difference between such market-exchange relations and the relations that exist between the participants in the firm's team-production process. Accordingly, the contractual foundation of the 'responsibility' that the managers owe the respective parties is different. In the case of customers and suppliers responsibility is defined by the implicit and explicit rules of the market-game and the specific contracts between the firm and its suppliers or customers; in the case of shareholders, employees and other participants in the team-production process it is the 'constitutional contract of the firm' that defines specific responsibilities. Finally, the third category of 'stakeholders' includes the political community and, in a sense, the general public. The political community in its capacity as the political authority over the jurisdiction within which the corporation operates is not a party to the 'constitutional contract of the firm' nor is it in a market-exchange to the firm.[18] It is the agency that is authorized to define the rules of the game that the firm must comply with when operating in the respective jurisdiction. Accordingly, the relation between the political community and the corporation is of a *political nature*. That is to say, the responsibility that the corporation or its managers owes to the political community is defined by the political constitution of the respective jurisdiction, i.e. by the 'social contract' that defines the rules according to which political authority is constituted and exercised in the jurisdiction. The relation between the corporation and the general public can be viewed as a part of this political nexus. How a corporation's conduct is perceived and judged by the public will indirectly impact on the political decision-making process, beyond the direct effects it may have on people's choices as consumers, employees or investors.

8   Corporate social responsibility and profit-seeking in the market game

In the case of an owner-operated firm the owner-operator clearly has 'responsibilities' vis-à-vis his employees, his customers, his suppliers, and the political community, where the substance of the respective responsibilities is defined by the different kinds of implicit or explicit contractual relations that exist between the owner-operator and the various groups. Yet, the owner surely operates the business not as an agent on behalf of his employees, his suppliers, his customers or the political community, but on his own behalf and in pursuit of his own interests. The measure of his success in the market game is his ability to earn a profit, where 'profit' is nothing other than the residual income that is left for him after he has paid the salaries to his employees, the bills of his suppliers, and the taxes to the political community.

It is difficult to see why there should be any relevant changes in the fundamental scheme of responsibilities as we move from the owner-operated firm to the manager-operated large corporation. What changes in the transition from owner-operated to manager-operated firms is that the owners appoint managers as agents to operate the business on their behalf, thereby adding a specific agency relation to the scheme of responsibilities. And the extent to which they can expect the managers actually to run the enterprise in ways that serve their, the owners' interests will largely depend on how well the overall rules of the market game and the terms of the corporate constitution allow them and motivate them effectively to control the management.[19] What surely does not change as we move from owner-operated to manager-operated firms is the fact that the measure of the firm's successful performance in the market game is its ability to earn a profit, and that the profit earned is nothing other than the residual that is left as compensation for the owners after the contractual obligations to all other parties have been met.

As indicated above, the argument that in a market economy the managers' task is to earn profits can be looked at from two angles that I propose to distinguish as the *system aspect* and the *agency aspect* of profit-seeking. The system aspect relates to the fact that, according to the logic of the market game, profit is the measure of successful performance in this game and that, accordingly, the ability to earn profits is the measuring rod for managerial performance. The agency aspect pertains to the fact that managers are employed by the firm's owners in order to run the firm in the service of their interest as *residual claimants*, i.e. as those participants in the joint enterprise who are compensated by the profits earned.

While the agency aspect of profit-seeking is mostly at issue among advocates and critics of CSR, it is in fact secondary or subordinate to the more fundamental system aspect that concerns the social advantages of the market game and the implications that follow as a matter of consistency if one chooses to play this game. The agency aspect is about the ownership structures established by the 'constitutional contract of the firm' which in turn, as noted above, derives its rationale from the logic of the market game. While the immediate reason for managers' profit-seeking is their contractual obligation as agents vis-à-vis the owners of the corporation, the more fundamental reason is the role that profits play as signposts in the game of catallaxy and the fact that the market game promises to produce more advantages for all participants than potential alternative 'economic games'.

Insisting on the systematic distinction between the shareholders as the owners and residual claimants and other groups of 'stakeholders' associated with or related to the firm is, of course, not meant at all to say that managers may safely neglect the interests of other 'stakeholders' in favor of the owners' interests. It is quite clear that managers cannot run a business successfully for long if they do not pay due attention to the interests of their customers, their employees, their suppliers, or the political community within which they operate. Nevertheless, just as there are, in the sense explained above, differences in the nature of the 'responsibilities' that they owe different groups of 'stakeholders', there are differences in the reasons why, and in the ways in which, managers have to take the interests of the different groups into account. In particular, there is a difference between their contractual obligation to serve the interests of the owners on whose behalf they manage the firm, and the kinds of constraints that induce them to take the interests of customers, suppliers, employees, or the political community into account. Serving the profit interests of the owners is what managers are hired to do as the owners' agents, and it is the direct criterion against which their performance is judged in a market economy. Paying due attention to the interests of the other parties is required of them not as a 'fiduciary duty' (Sacconi, 2004: 6) but as a constraint imposed on them by the nature of the market game, a constraint that they have to meet in order to be successful in serving the owners' profit interests.

Where the interests of the different groups are in conflict with each other – for example, consumer interests in low prices and employees' interests in high wages, or suppliers' interests in high prices for their inputs and owners' interests in profits – it is not the managers who are called upon to act as 'fair arbitrators', or at least no more than the owner-operator of a firm is called upon to arbitrate impartially between his own profit interests and the interest of other 'stakeholders'. Instead, it is the function of market competition to bring about a balance among these interests in ways that improve the prospects of all parties involved to benefit from this 'economic game' more than they could from a feasible alternative economic regime. This is the very point of the game of catallaxy that the owners of firms or their managers can concentrate on running the enterprise in a profit-generating manner, while the rules of the game and the forces of competition function as constraints that guide their profit-seeking ambitions in directions that serve the interests of others. It is not because they act as their 'fiduciaries' that the owners or managers of firms heed the interests of customers and suppliers, but because the constraints of the market game make it advisable for them to do so if they wish to operate successfully. And the same is true in essence for the interests of employees as well, even though, as noted above, there are significant differences between the nature of the employment relation and the market-exchange relations between the corporation and its customers or suppliers.

9 The rules of the market and the limits of knowledge

The virtue of the market game is not only that it economizes on people's benevolence by mobilizing the forces of self-interest in order to motivate people to care for the interests of others. It also relieves the participants of a task that would overcharge their limited cognitive capacities, namely to know how they may best contribute to the 'common good'. As F.A. Hayek has emphasized throughout much of his work, because of the limits of our knowledge and reason it is impossible for us to know all the direct and indirect consequences that result from our actions in a highly complex system such as an extended economy. It is therefore impossible for us to reliably judge on a case-by-case basis by which particular actions we may contribute most to the 'common good'. If we wish our interdependent actions to result overall in a desirable social order we must, so Hayek argues, rely on rules that guide our choices in ways that produce desirable patterns of outcomes, even if they cannot guarantee 'optimal' results in each and every case. Rules are adaptations to our 'inescapable ignorance of most of the particular circumstances which determine the effects of our actions' (Hayek, 1976: 20). They simplify our choice problems by reducing to manageable dimensions what we are required to take into account in making our choices.[20] In this sense the legal and ethical rules of the market game relieve the participants from the responsibility to consider all circumstances that might possibly be taken into account and all the consequences that might possibly follow from their actions – a responsibility that would be impossible to meet in a complex world – by focusing their attention on those consequences for which the rules of the game hold them accountable.

Of course, not just any kind of rules can be expected to work to the common benefit of the parties involved, and to know which rules will create a desirable overall order surely is for humans with limited cognitive capabilities a problem of no lesser magnitude than knowing all the effects of particular actions. The critical difference, though, is that with regard to the working properties of rules systematic learning from experience over time is possible. As different groups and societies have experimented throughout human history with different kinds of rules, experience with the kinds of outcome patterns that they tend to produce has been accumulated over time. In this sense the constitutive rules of the market game can be looked at as the product of an evolutionary process in which they have come to embody the experience of countless generations. It is not because we were intelligent enough to design them, but because we can rely on historical and contemporary records of how they work, compared to potential alternative systems of rules, that we have reason to trust in the capacity of the rules of the game of catallaxy to serve the common interest of the participants, allowing them to focus their attention on playing the game successfully within the constraints of rules, instead of burdening them with the unmanageable task of directly seeking the 'common good'.

The principal conclusion that follows from the foregoing discussion for the issue of CSR is that the very point of playing the market game is to dispense the participants from the responsibility to consider, in the course of playing the game, all of the consequences that their actions may possibly have for the 'common good', and to allow them, instead, to concentrate their attention on playing the game successfully within the constraints defined by its legal and moral rules. As noted above, the social responsibility for a well-functioning market game is 'divided' in the sense that there is a categorical distinction between the participants' individual and separate responsibility *in playing the game* and their joint responsibility *for the game*. Their social responsibility *in playing the game* is to pursue their ambitions in a fair, rule-abiding manner. Their social responsibility *for the game* is the responsibility they share as members of the respective political community and that they exercise through their government. It is their joint social responsibility to take care of the rules by which they play the game, and to see to it that rules are adopted and enforced that work out to their common benefit.

10   Varieties of corporate social responsibility: the 'soft' version

From the constitutional economics outlook at the market economy that I have discussed in the previous sections I shall examine some of the major demands on corporate behavior that have been made under the CSR rubric. As I shall seek to show, such demands can be classified into three major categories which I distinguish as the *soft*, the *hard*, and the *radical* version.

The distinction between the varieties of CSR demands that I wish to draw attention to is related to the distinction between the following three questions. This is, first, the question of whether or not the citizens of a polity wish to adopt the rules of the market game or some feasible alternative regime as the 'economic constitution' for their jurisdiction. This choice is to be made on prudential grounds, informed by the predictable working properties of the alternatives considered and in light of the informed common constitutional interests of the constituents. If the choice is made in favor of the market game, citizens have to decide on the specific rules under which they wish to play the market game. This is again a matter that they should decide on prudential grounds, in light of the predictable working properties of potential alternative rules. And there is, finally, the question of how the participants are supposed to behave in playing the market game, after they have opted for this game and have defined the specifics of the rules according to which they wish to play it. As I shall seek to show, what I call the *soft* version of CSR is concerned with the issue of how the participants should play the market game within given rules. The *hard* version is about the issue of how the rules of the market game should be defined. And the *radical* version is about the issue of whether it is the market game that should be played or some alternative economic game.

Like the other two versions of CSR the soft version suggests that for a corporation to act in a socially responsible manner means to 'work more consciously for the common good',[21] to do things not because they help to earn profits but because they serve broader 'social' purposes. What distinguishes advocates of the soft version from other CSR advocates is that they do not see a *fundamental* conflict between profit-seeking and social responsibility. They do not recommend abandoning the market game, nor do they call for a change in the legal rules of the game. They argue, instead, that by taking the interests of non-owning stakeholders properly into account managers promote the long-term success of the corporation and, thus, act in the interest of the shareholders.[22] The slogan that captures the spirit of their view is: 'Corporate social responsibility is good business!'[23] The business practice that they object to with their calls for CSR is, in effect, short-sighted, narrow-minded profit-seeking, and what they recommend as socially responsible business behavior is, in their view, nothing other than far-sighted, enlightened profit-seeking. CSR, so understood, is a matter of entrepreneurial prudence. It amounts to a business strategy that not only looks at immediate, short-term returns but also takes proper account of the long-term consequences that result from the ways in which customers and suppliers, employees, and the community are treated.[24]

Classifying corporate practices according to their compatibility with CSR-demands on the one side and with enlightened profit-seeking on the other side the matrix below (Matrix 1) represents the four combinations that are logically possible. The 'soft' version of CSR is concerned with the combinations that are marked as 'uncontroversial' cases.

Matrix 1

Corporate practices	In agreement with CSR-demands	In conflict with CSR-demands
In accord with 'enlightened' profit-seeking	Uncontroversial case	A
In conflict with 'enlightened' profit-seeking	B	Uncontroversial case

If they wish to achieve long-run business success managers are surely well advised to take into account the interests of the various parties on whose goodwill they depend, and to pay attention to the constraints that not only the formal rules of the game but also the ethical views that prevail in their relevant environment impose on their profit-seeking ambitions.[25] Yet, if – given the factual constraints of market competition and provided the rules of the game are effectively enforced – there are prudential reasons for managers to do the things that advocates of the soft version of CSR call for, it is not at all clear what the CSR philosophy is supposed to add to an appropriate understanding of the workings of markets. After all, the market game endogenously creates the incentives for the participants to learn how to play the game successfully. It punishes short-sighted profit-seeking strategies that harm a firm's long-term profitability and it rewards prudent, enlightened profit-seeking that keeps an eye on the firm's prospect to survive and prosper over time. If it aims at no more than reminding managers that prudent, far-sighted profit-seeking is better business than its nar-row-minded, short-sighted counterpart, CSR should properly be considered part of the ordinary job of business consultants. There would be little that an advo-cate of Friedman's view on CSR would have reason to disagree with. And there would be little justification for dressing CSR up as a moral or ethical doctrine that is needed in order to civilize an otherwise deficient market economy.

11   Varieties of corporate social responsibility: the 'hard' version

CSR becomes a more controversial matter where it amounts to demands for business practices that are in genuine conflict not only with short-sighted profit-seeking but with enlightened and far-sighted profit-seeking as well.[26] It is such demands that belong to what I call the 'hard' version of CSR. They are based on the diagnosis that profit-interests, even in their enlightened form, either induce corporate practices that are in conflict with the 'common inter-est' or prevent corporations from doing things that would be in the 'common interest'. In Matrix 1 the boxes A and B represent the cases that advocates of the hard version of CSR target with their demands for a more 'socially respon-sible' corporate conduct. They want corporate practices that belong in box A to be discouraged and those that belong in box B to be encouraged, opposed to the direction in which profit-incentives work.

The hard version of CSR raises two issues that need to be examined. The first has to do with the question of whether CSR-demands can actually be presumed to reflect the common interest of the citizens of a polity; the second has to do with the question of what the citizens should prudently do in those cases in which CSR-demands are found to be in their common interest.

The corporate practices that CSR-demands call for (or oppose) are typically claimed, either explicitly or implicitly, to serve (or to harm) the 'common good' or the 'public interest'. This claim can be interpreted, I suppose, as the conjecture that the corporate practices demanded serve (and the practices opposed harm) the *common interests* of the individuals concerned, such as, for instance, the citizens of a polity who collectively choose the rules to which cor-porations operating in their jurisdiction are subject.[27] It would surely be naïve to presume this conjecture to be actually true for each and every demand that may be voiced in the name of CSR. Rather, it needs to be examined whether the corporate practices that CSR-demands call for (or oppose) can indeed be expected to advance (or harm) the common interest or not. In other words, it needs to be examined whether demands voiced in the name of CSR may not in fact be 'inappropriate' moral demands in the sense that, if they were adopted as a general rule, they would produce overall consequences that are in conflict with the common interests of the respective citizenry. The matrix below (*Matrix 2*) represents the four combinations that may exist in the relation between CSR-demands and citizens' common interests.

Matrix 2

Corporate practices	Called for by CSR-demands	Rejected by CSR-demands
Serve the common interest	A	B
In conflict with common interest	C	D

Box A represents cases in which CSR-demands call for corporate practices that, under the given rules of the market game, would harm the profit-interests of firms adopting them, but would serve the participants' common interests. Box D represents the reverse case in which CSR-demands reject corporate practices that, again under the given rules of the market game, serve the profit-interests of firms adopting them, but are in conflict with the participants' common interests. In cases represented by boxes A and D citizens should pay attention to the respective CSR-demands and should look for ways to rectify the conflict between profit-interests and common interests that these demands identify. By contrast, boxes B and C represent cases in which following the advice that CSR-demands entail would be harmful to the common interest and in which citizens would be well-advised to discard such demands.[28] The critical question is, of course, how citizens should go about deciding on the merits or demerits of particular CSR-demands, an issue to which I will return below.

What should be done in cases in which there are good reasons to consider CSR-demands as 'appropriate' moral demands, i.e. as demands that point to actual conflicts between profit-interests and common interests? Calling on the players in the market game to behave in ways that systematically harm their profit-interests would mean to ask them deliberately not to seek to play the game successfully, an appeal that cannot make sense if one wishes to continue to play the market game. To be sure, where the market game produces patterns of outcomes that the participants consider undesirable, they have reason to look for a remedy. Yet, as I have argued above in my comments on 'different responsibilities,' the remedy must be sought in a suitable adjustment of the rules of the game. That is to say, the rules of the game must be (re-)defined in such a manner that the conflict between profit-interests and common interests is avoided or eliminated.

The remedy cannot be found in calling upon the players to sacrifice their own ambitions to play the game successfully in order to compensate for deficiencies in its rules.[29] Apart from its questionably effectiveness, the perverse effect of the attempt to correct for undesirable outcomes of the market game by such 'moral appeals' would be that those among the participants who are most receptive to such appeals would systematically lose out in market competition to those who are less so, in the end aggravating the problem rather than solving it.

12   Choosing the rules of the market game

As noted above, the very point of playing the market game in the first place is that the participants in their separate capacities can concentrate on playing the game successfully, in compliance with its legal and moral rules, while it is their joint responsibility to see to it that rules of the game are defined and enforced that produce overall desirable patterns of outcomes. As far as the legal rules are concerned this joint responsibility is exercised through government and legislature who are in charge of defining and enforcing an adequate legal framework, and who should adopt appropriate reforms in the rules of the game if the existing rules fail to do the task. As far as the informal rules of proper business conduct are concerned, the 'private' sanctions that the market participants impose on each other in playing the market game must provide sufficient incentives for compliance. In cases where these incentives turn out to be of insufficient force, and where the harmful consequences of non-compliance weigh heavily enough, the necessity may arise to formalize previously informal rules in legal terms and to give them the backing of the enforcement apparatus of the state.

The question remains of what role demands on business to act in 'socially responsible' ways are supposed to play in this scheme, beyond what the legal and informally enforced rules of ethical conduct do. One possible answer could be that the very point of the CSR movement is to create, for example, by public campaigns, incentives for corporate executives to act for the 'common good', incentives that are supposed to work as supplementary force exactly in those cases in which the constraints imposed by the legal apparatus and the informal rules of proper business conduct fail to guide the actions of the market-players in ways that reconcile profit interests and common interests.[30] The problem with this answer is, however, exactly the problem that I referred to above when I raised the issue of how the merits or demerits of particular CSR-demands are to be judged, i.e. how citizens are to know whether demands that are voiced in the name of CSR are actually conducive rather than harmful to the 'common good'.

To be sure, through their activities NGOs or other advocacy groups may well be able to create factual constraints for corporations that make it advisable for them to act in the ways that such groups define as 'socially responsible' corporate behavior.[31] They may, for instance, succeed – as Greenpeace did in the Brent Spar case – in mobilizing the pressure of public opinion to force corporations into compliance with their demands. For corporations to adopt the respective, supposedly 'socially responsible', practices becomes under such conditions a matter of entrepreneurial prudence. Yet, whether the practices 'enforced' in such manner actually serve the 'common good' is hardly ensured by the supposedly good intentions of the groups organizing the campaigns.[32] This question must be answered in light of the consequences that would, in fact, result if the supposedly 'socially responsible' corporate practices were adopted as a general rule – and these consequences may well turn out to be harmful. It is exactly the purpose of the elaborate legislative procedures that political communities employ for choosing the 'rules of the game' to ensure that rule-proposals are carefully examined in regard to their predictable impact before they are adopted, and to grant legitimacy to the rules that the members of the legislative assembly decide upon on behalf of the citizenry. As a rule, CSR-demands have not passed a comparable process of systematic examination, nor do they come with the legitimacy provided by a democratic legislative process or the legitimacy of the implicit consensus on which the commonly accepted informal rules of ethical conduct are based.[33]

To be sure, there is no reason to object as long as CSR-demands are advanced as contributions to the political discourse on which rules of the game a political community should adopt, and as long as they are subject to the same process of public examination to which all other legislative proposals are subject. Serious problems of 'constitutional prudence' and democratic legitimacy arise, however, where CSR-demands become a competing force to, and a substitute for, the formal legislative process by creating factual constraints that 'channel' corporate conduct in ways that CSR-advocates define as 'socially responsible' but that may well harm citizens' common interests. Citizens would be well-advised to set more trust in the ability of their established legislative procedures to define the rules of the game, and to improve these procedures where possible, rather than allowing self-appointed guardians of 'social responsibility' to set the standards against which corporate behavior is to be judged.

13 Varieties of corporate social responsibility: the 'radical' version

The two versions of CSR that I have discussed so far are related to the role that profit-seeking should be allowed to play in the market economy. The 'soft' version is about prudence in profit-seeking, it calls for far-sighted, enlightened by contrast to short-sighted, narrow-minded profit-seeking. The 'hard' version is about how profit-seeking should be constrained. It wants corporate behavior to be subject to constraints that go beyond the demands of current legal and ethical rules. The third, 'radical' version of CSR, in contrast to the first two, is about whether profit-seeking should be allowed to play a role at all. It amounts to an outright rejection of profit as a proper guide for economic activities and, thus, calls in effect for abandoning the market game in favor of a different kind of 'economic game' – even if advocates of the 'hard' version typically neither explicitly say so nor explicitly state how their envisaged alternative to the market game is supposed to function.

It is, in particular, the 'hard' version of CSR that is subject to Milton Friedman's (1962: 135) charge of being a 'fundamentally subversive doctrine'.[34] This charge is surely not meant to deny that it is up to the citizens of a democratic polity to decide whether or not they wish to adopt the rules of the market as their economic constitution. Nor can it be meant to deny that advocates of the 'hard' version are free to make their case against the market game in the debate on where the decision should go. Rather, I understand Friedman's charge to be meant as a warning against an erosion of the market economy that occurs in a tacit, concealed way. If citizens decide to adopt the market game, they cannot at the same time reject profit as the signal that guides economic activities. And the decision whether or not to adopt the market game should be made explicitly under due consideration of the overall working properties and merits of the market game compared to feasible alternative regimes. It should not be implicitly made under the false pretext of just requiring corporations to be more 'socially responsible'. CSR-demands that amount to a call for abandoning profit as the guiding signal in the economic game should be openly and explicitly presented as what in effect they are, namely calls to replace the market game by an economic regime of a different nature. And their advocates should be required to specify the nature of the economic regime that they wish to suggest as an alternative so that one can critically examine and rationally discuss whether the envisioned alternative can be expected, in light of our theoretical and empirical knowledge, to possess more desirable working properties than the market.

14   Conclusion: CSR as constitutional responsibility

The constitutional economics perspective that has informed the analysis developed in the preceding sections suggests that in examining the issue of corporate social responsibility in a market economy a careful distinction should be made between three questions. First, the question of whether the citizens of a polity wish to adopt the market game or some feasible alternative as the 'economic regime' for their jurisdiction. Second, the question of how they ought to specify the rules according to which they wish to play the market game. And, finally, the question of how the participants ought to behave in playing the market game, once its rules are specified. If a decision is made in favor of the market game straightforward implications for the CSR issue follow. In playing the market game the participants are allowed to concentrate on playing the game successfully and they are relieved from the responsibility to advance the 'common good' directly. The responsibility that they face in their individual and separate capacities is to play the market game in a fair manner, honoring its formally enforced legal, and the informally enforced ethical rules. In their capacity as members of the rule-choosing and -enforcing political community it is their joint responsibility to choose rules of the game that guide their individual and separate success-seeking efforts in ways that serve their common interests. In other words, they share a joint responsibility with regard to the cultivation and maintenance of an appropriate constitutional framework, a responsibility that one may call *constitutional responsibility*.

Just as individual citizens share in the constitutional responsibility for the legal-institutional framework and the ethical rules in their respective communities, corporations as 'corporate citizens' share in the constitutional responsibility for their legal and ethical environment. It is this constitutional responsibility that, I suppose, can truly be called corporate social responsibility. Corporations' longer-run business-prospects are critically dependent on the quality of the legal and ethical framework within which they operate. And the quality of this framework will depend on how well it is cultivated and maintained by the participants in the system. Meeting their constitutional responsibility to contribute to this task requires corporations not only to conduct their own business in ways that helps to sustain the existing legal and ethical framework, but also to contribute to the public-political discourse on how the rules of the game may be modified to better serve the common interests of all participants.

Notes

1. For a detailed review see Henderson (2001).
2. Buchanan (1991: 121f.): 'Contractarianism ... can be interpreted as little more than an extension of the paradigm of free exchange to the broader setting. ... By shifting "voluntary exchange" upward to the constitutional level of choices among rules, the consensual or general agreement test may be applied.'
3. On the term 'catallaxy' see Hayek (1976: 108ff).
4. Friedman (1962: 13): 'The possibility of co-ordination through voluntary co-operation rests on the elementary – yet frequently denied – proposition that both parties to an economic transaction benefit from it, *provided the transaction is bi-laterally voluntary and informed.* ... A working model of a society organized through voluntary exchange is a *free enterprise exchange economy* – what we have been calling competitive capitalism.'
5. Hayek (1976: 115): 'It is a wealth-creating game (and not what game theory calls a zero-sum game), that is, one that leads to an increase of the stream of goods and of

the prospects of all participants to satisfy their needs, but which retains the character of a game in the sense in which the term is defined by the *Oxford English Dictionary*: "a contest played according to rules and decided by superior skill, strength or good fortune".'

6. Hayek (1978: 137): 'The individuals have reason to agree to play this game because it makes the pool from which the individual shares are drawn larger than it can be made by any other method. But at the same time it makes the share of each individual subject to all kinds of accidents and certainly does not secure that it always corresponds to the subjective merits or to the esteem by others of the individual efforts.'

7. I leave aside here the difference between 'accounting profit', i.e. the difference between revenue and explicit costs, and 'pure economic profit', i.e. the difference between revenue and opportunity costs. The more intense market competition is the more speedily it will tend to erode pure economic profits while still allowing producers to earn accounting profits.

8. Individuals are involved in the market game in both capacities, as consumers as well as producers (i.e. as entrepreneurs, as investors, as employees, etc.). The question may be raised, therefore, why they should opt for the market game that favors consumer- over producer-interests. A. Smith considered the answer to this question to be self-evident: 'Consumption is the sole end and purpose of production; and the interest of the producer ought to be attended to only so far as it may be necessary for promoting that of the consumer. The maxim is so perfectly self-evident, that it would be absurd to attempt to prove it' (Smith 1981: 660). – From a constitutional economics perspective one could, nevertheless, answer this question by pointing out that an economic constitution that gives preference to consumer interests in competition is preferable for all persons involved over an economic constitution that accommodates protectionist interests of producers (Vanberg 2005: 39ff.).

9. This perspective on profit-seeking is in line, for instance, with such approaches in modern moral philosophy as D. Gauthier's (1986) theory of morality as 'constrained maximization'. According to Gauthier, moral conduct is about pursuing one's self-interest within moral constraints, not about acting against one's own interests.

10. Hayek (1948: 110ff.): 'That a functioning market presupposes not only prevention of violence and fraud but the protection of certain rights, such as property, and the enforcement of contract, is always taken for granted. Where the traditional discussion becomes unsatisfactory is where it is suggested that, with the recognition of the principles of private property and freedom of contract ... all the issues were settled, as if the law of property and contract were given once and for all in its final and most appropriate form, i.e. in the form which will make the market economy work at its best. It is only after we have agreed on these principles that the real problem begins.'

11. 'Systematically' produced undesirable outcome patterns are to be distinguished from the occasional undesired outcomes that players must unavoidably cope with in any game.

12. To this issue I shall return below when I examine more closely the different kinds of demands that are voiced under the CSR label.

13. Since Milton Friedman's argument on the issue of CSR is the reference point for my reasoning in this chapter it may be useful to quote what he has to say on the role of government in the market economy: 'The existence of a free market does not of course eliminate the need for government. On the contrary, government is essential both as a forum for determining the 'rules of the game' and as an umpire to interpret and to enforce the rules decided on' (Friedman 1962: 15). 'It is important to distinguish the day-to-day activities of people from the general customary and

legal framework within which these take place. The day-to-day activities are like the actions of the participants in a game when they are playing it; the framework, like the rules of the game they play. And just as a good game requires acceptance of the players both of the rules and of the umpire to interpret and endorse them, so a good society requires that its members agree on the general conditions that will govern the relations among them, on some means of arbitrating different interpretations of these conditions, and on some device for enforcing compliance with the generally accepted rules' (ibid.: 25).

14. Sacconi (2004: 13) appears to conflate these two kinds of social contracts when, in discussing the ethical criterion that he applies to 'the "social contract" among the stakeholders of the firm', he speaks of this contract as 'the agreement that would be reached by the representatives of all the firm's stakeholders in a hypothetical situation of impartial choice'. Sacconi (ibid.: 14ff.) draws a distinction between a 'first social contract' and a 'second social contract', but this distinction is different from the one I want to emphasize here.

15. This has, for instance, implications for the issue of 'distributive justice' within firms. In order for firms to operate successfully in their environment the internal system for the allocation of rewards obviously must be in line with the recipients' relative contributions to the joint enterprise's overall performance. In the absence of any clue to what the relative contributions are, market prices of inputs may be the best measure of input value one can get. They can, however, in fact do no more than reflect some average contribution value. In any particular case market-prices may be less or more than the actual contribution would merit.

16. For a more detailed explanation of this outlook at the firm as a 'corporate actor' see Vanberg (1992).

17. That would be different, of course, in a workers' cooperative in which the managers acted as the agents of the workers and where contributors of financial capital would be hired as recipients of contractual income by the managers.

18. A political community may, of course, be a shareholder or co-owner of a corporation and it may also purchase products or services from a corporation. But in this capacity its relation to the corporation is that of a shareholders or customer. What is of interest here is the relation between a political community *in its capacity as political authority* and a corporation.

19. The *Economist* (2005: 17) notes on this issue: 'In many of the corporate scandals of recent years, it has seemed that managers have acted as though they were accountable to nobody – not even, and in some cases least of all, to the firms' owners. This has been rightly recognized as a problem, and a lot of time and effort has been spent on trying to make accountability to shareholders – on matters such as executive pay – more effective. Muddled thinking on CSR, and on supposed accountability to non-owners, only makes it harder to put this right.'

20. Rules, as Hayek (1964: 11) argues, 'abbreviate the list of circumstances which we need to take into account in the particular instances, singling out certain classes of facts as alone determining the general kind of action which we should take'.

21. I am paraphrasing here John Mackey, the founder and CEO of Whole Foods who (in *Reason Online* 2005) says about his vision of CSR: 'The business model that Whole Foods has embraced could represent a new form of capitalism, one that more consciously works for the common good instead of depending solely on the 'invisible hand' to generate positive results for society.' – In commenting on his 'business model', Mackey (ibid.) expresses his conviction that it 'is simply good business and works for the long-term benefit of the investors'.

22. For a discussion of this view of CSR see e.g. L.E. Preston and H.J. Sapienza (1990) who conclude from their survey of empirical evidence: 'Moreover, most of these indicators of stakeholder performance are also associated with conventional measures of corporate profitability and growth. Thus, there is not in this data any significant evidence of strong trade-offs among stakeholder objectives.'

23. Kirk O. Hanson (*Stanford Business* 2000): 'I would say that most business ethicists in the United States spend their time trying to convince people that being ethical actually will help you win in the long run.'

24. T.J. Rodgers (*Reason Online* 2005): 'It is simply good business for a company to cater to its customers, train and retrain its employees, build long-term relationships with its suppliers, and become a good citizen in its community.'

25. Playing the market game in a 'fair' manner involves, in this sense, clearly more 'than mere obedience to the law's minimal demands' (McCann 2000: 111).

26. The EU Commission seems to come close to voicing demands of this kind when, in its Green Paper *Promoting a European Framework for Corporate Social Responsibility*, Brussels, July 18, 2001, it defines CSR as follows: 'By stating their social responsibility and voluntarily taking on commitments which go beyond common regulatory and conventional requirements, which they would have to respect in any case, companies endeavor to raise the standards of social development, environmental protection and respect of fundamental rights and embrace an open governance, reconciling interests of various stakeholders in an overall approach of quality and sustainability' (quoted from Sacconi 2004: 6).

27. The 'group' for which CSR demands are claimed to be in the 'common interest' may, of course, be more inclusively defined to include not only a particular polity, but several polities or, in the limit, the world community.

28. Corporate Social Responsibility Watch (http://www.csrwatch.com/) looks out for cases of CSR-demands that would fall into this category.

29. This issue has been explicitly discussed by Walter Eucken, the founder of the Freiburg school of law and economics (Vanberg 1998b). He emphasized that reconciling individual self-interest and common interest is the task of 'Ordnungspolitik', i.e. a policy that takes care of the institutional framework within which the market game is played. As he put it, 'the individuals should not be required to do what only the economic constitution can accomplish, namely to reconcile individual self-interest and common interest' (Eucken 1990: 368).

30. McCann (2000: 110): '(S)takeholder groups ... can easily mimic the ICCR's (Interfaith Center for Corporate Responsibility, V.V.) successful strategy of mobilizing religious communities to use their investment portfolios for leveraging various corporate social responsibility agendas through proxy battles and other insurgencies at annual shareholders' meetings. ... Top management is usually willing to negotiate with those who organize such efforts precisely because the one thing they abhor above all is bad publicity.'

31. As Doane (2005: 24), chair of the CORE (Corporate Responsibility) coalition of NGOs in the UK notes: '[T]here are some strong business incentives that have either pushed or pulled companies onto the CSR band-wagon. For example, companies confronted with boycott threats, as Nike was in the 1990s ..., may see CSR as a strategy for presenting a friendlier face to the public.'

32. As the *Economist* (2005: 9ff.) comments: 'Companies under NGO scrutiny have been dissuaded from investing in manufacturing operations in developing countries such as India or Bangladesh, or have decided to end such operations, faced with charges that they are employing "sweatshop labour". ... Many development NGOs

are pushing for labour standards that would mandate this kind of 'best practice', and want these standards written into future trade agreements. The evidence clearly shows that policies of this kind ... are not in the interests of the workers they purport to help. ... Capitulating to the ill-judged demands of the NGOs may be rational, profit-seeking behaviour on their (the companies', V.V.) part. But in this case, what is good for profits is bad for welfare.'

33. As the *Economist* (2005: 18) puts it: '[B]usinesses should not try to do the work of governments, just as governments should not try to do the work of businesses. ... Managers, acting in their professional capacity, ought not to concern themselves with the public good: they are not competent to do it, they lack the democratic credential for it, and their day jobs should leave them no time to think about it. If they merely concentrate on discharging their responsibility to the owners of the firms, acting ethically as they do so, they will usually serve the public good in any case. ... The proper guardians of the public interest are governments, which are accountable to all citizens. It is the job of elected politicians to set goals for regulators, to deal with externalities, to mediate among different interests, to attend to the demands of social justice, to provide public goods and collect taxes to pay for them.'

34. In her above (n. 31) quoted article, an article that appeared in a *Review* published by the Stanford Graduate School of Business, Doane appears to advocate the 'hard' version of CSR when she notes: '(U)ltimately, trade-offs must be made between the financial health of the company and ethical outcomes. ... Currently in Western legal systems, companies have primary duty of care to their shareholders, ... profit-maximization is the norm. So, companies effectively choose financial benefit over social ones' (Doane 2005: 24, 28).

References

Buchanan, J.M. (1979) 'What Should Economists Do?', in J.M. Buchanan, *What Should Economists Do?* Indianapolis, IN: Liberty Press, pp. 17–37.

Buchanan, J.M. (1990) 'The Domain of Constitutional Economics', *Constitutional Political Economy*, vol. 1, pp. 1–18.

Buchanan, J.M. (1991) *The Economics and Ethics of Constitutional Order*. Ann Arbor, MI: The University of Michigan Press.

Brennan, Geoffrey and Alan Hamlin (1998) 'Constitutional economics', *The New Palgrave Dictionary of Economics and the Law*, vol. 1, ed. P. Newman. London: Macmillan, pp. 401–10.

Coase, R. (1937) 'The Nature of the Firm', *Economica*, n.s.(4), pp. 386–405.

Doane, D. (2005) 'The Myth of CSR', *Stanford Social Innovation Review*, Fall, pp. 23–9 (www.ssireview.com).

Economist (2005) 'The Good Company. A Skeptical Look at Corporate Social Responsibility', *The Economist*, 22 January, pp. 3–18.

Eucken, W. (1990) (orig. 1952) *Grundsätze der Wirtschaftspolitik*, 6th edn. Tübingen: J.C.B. Mohr (Paul Siebeck).

Friedman, M. (1962) *Capitalism and Freedom*. Chicago and London: The University of Chicago Press.

Friedman, M. (1970) 'The Social Responsibility of Business is to Increase Its Profits', *The New York Times Magazine*, 13 September.

Gauthier, D. (1986) *Morals by Agreement*. Oxford: Oxford University Press.

Hayek, F.A. (1948) *Individualism and Economic Order*. Chicago: The University of Chicago Press.

Hayek, F.A. (1960) *The Constitution of Liberty.* Chicago: The University of Chicago Press.

Hayek, F.A. (1964) 'Kinds of Order in Society', *New Individualist Review*, vol. 3, pp. 3–12.

Hayek, F.A. (1969) 'Rechtsordnung und Handelnsordnung', in F.A. Hayek, *Freiburger Studien.* Tübingen: J.C.B. Mohr (Paul Siebeck), pp. 161–98.

Hayek, F.A. (1976) *The Mirage of Social Justice*, vol. 2 of *Law, Legislation and Liberty.* Chicago: The University of Chicago Press.

Hayek, F.A. (1978) 'Liberalism' in *New Studies in Philosophy, Politics, Economics and the History of Ideas.* Chicago: The University of Chicago Press.

Henderson, D. (2001) *Misguided Virtue – False Notions of Corporate Social Responsibility.* Wellington: New Zealand Business Roundtable.

McCann, D. (2000) 'Do Corporations Have Any Responsibility Beyond Making a Profit? A Response to Norman P. Barry', *Journal of Markets & Morality*, vol. 3, pp. 108–14.

Preston, L.E. and H.J. Sapienza (1990) 'Stakeholder Management and Corporate Performance', *Journal of Behavioral Economics*, vol. 19, pp. 361–75.

Rawls, J. (1971) *A Theory of Justice.* Cambridge, MA: Harvard University Press.

Reason Online (2005) 'Rethinking the Social Responsibility of Business, A *Reason* debate featuring Milton Friedman, Whole Foods' John Mackey, and Cypress Semiconductor's T.J. Rodgers', *Reason Online*, October. http://www.reason.com/0510/fe.mf.rethinking.shtml.

Sacconi, L. (2004) 'Corporate Social Responsibility (CSR) as a Model of "Extended" Corporate Governance', *Liuc Papers* no. 142, supplement, February.

Smith, A. (1981) *An Inquiry into the Nature and Causes of the Wealth of Nations.* Indianapolis: Liberty Press.

Stanford Business (2000) 'A Question of Ethics', Part 3, *Stanford Business*, November, vol. 69(1). http://www.gsb.stanford.edu/community/bmag/sbsm0011/feature_ethics3.html.

Vanberg, V.J. (1992) 'Organizations as Constitutional Systems', *Constitutional Political Economy*, vol. 3, pp. 223–55. (Reprinted in V.J. Vanberg (1994) *Rules and Choice in Economics.* London and New York: Routledge, pp. 125–43.)

Vanberg, V.J. (1998a) 'Constitutional Political Economy', in J.B. Davis, D.W. Hands and U. Mäki (eds), *The Handbook of Economic Methodology.* Cheltenham: Edward Elgar, pp. 69–75.

Vanberg, V.J. (1998b) 'Freiburg School of Law and Economics', in P. Newman (ed.), *The New Palgrave Dictionary of Economics and the Law*, vol. 2. London: Macmillan, pp. 172–9.

Vanberg, V.J. (2005) 'Market and State: the Perspective of Constitutional Political Economy', *Journal of InstitutionalEconomics*, vol. 1, pp. 23–49.

7
A Rawlsian View of CSR and the Game Theory of its Implementation (Part I): the Multi-stakeholder Model of Corporate Governance

Lorenzo Sacconi

1 Introduction

This is the first part of a comprehensive essay on the Rawlsian view of corporate social responsibility (in short, CSR). CSR is defined as a multi-stakeholder model of corporate governance and objective function based on the extension of fiduciary duties towards all of the firm's stakeholders (see section 2). A rationale for this idea is given firstly within the perspective of new institutional economic theory in terms of transaction costs efficiency. From this perspective, abuse of authority in regard to the non-controlling stakeholders emerges as the main unsolved problem, and makes it impossible to sever efficiency from equity within the domain of corporate governance (section 3). Intuitively, a Rawlsian principle of redress emerges as the natural answer to the legitimization problem of ownership and control rights allocations when, in order to provide incentives to one party (the incentive to undertake important specific investments), they give it a disproportionate advantage over other non-controlling stakeholders.

Moreover, in accordance with the prevailing opinion about its voluntariness, CSR is viewed here as a model of corporate governance that companies may undertake by autonomous self-regulation in terms of the explicit adoption of expressed self-regulatory norms and standards. This is to be understood as an institution in Aoki's sense of the term: i.e. roughly put, as a rule in the behavior of a group of players which is maintained through the repeated plays of a given game, thanks to a system of mutually consistent beliefs by players predicting each other's behavior and that induces them to act repeatedly according to the same rule. Because such an institution is self-supporting, it does not need a statutory law to be enforced; but neither can it be seen as the gracious, arbitrary and occasional concession of management discretion. With respect to Aoki's definition of institution, however, a proper understanding of CSR requires the addition of an explicitly expressed norm, including prescriptive principles and normative standards of behavior, which is to be accounted for in terms of the firm's stakeholders' *social contract* (see section 4).

The account of the social contract adopted here is Rawlsian. An impartial agreement is reached in an hypothetical original position by putting the parties 'under a veil of ignorance'. In our case, this is a matter of unanimous and impartial agreement among the corporate stakeholders that must be reached under a 'veil of ignorance' about the particular stakes that each of them holds (and with respect to any other personal traits). It takes place in the hypothetical bargaining that precedes the repeated non-cooperative game between the firm and each of its stakeholders. By this agreement, the principle of extended fiduciary duties and fair balance among different stakeholders is established as an explicit constraint on directors, managers, and in general on the party who controls discretionary decisions in the firm – a constraint that must prove to be effective throughout the repeated game between the firm and each of its stakeholders.

The bulk of this essay, in fact, is concerned with a game-theoretical explanation of the roles played by explicitly expressed norms and standards in so far as they are based on the *stakeholders' impartial agreement* (the social contract). Put briefly, the social contract on an explicit CSR norm performs essential functions in solving the basic game-theoretical problems faced in the implementation of the very broad idea of multi-stakeholder corporate governance (see section 5). These are:

- *construing* commitments to allow definition of a reputation game such that reputation effects can be attached to compliance with the CSR normative model;
- *selecting* just one of the many equilibria possible in such a game as the unique equilibrium *ex ante* acceptable by all under the condition of impartial and impersonal agreement;
- *refining* the set of possible equilibria so that only those reflecting conformist motivations deriving from the *ex ante* social contract are retained as true candidates for the *ex post* emergence of the equilibrium to which actual individual actions will converge;
- and, finally, to *predict* that the players' effective reasoning in the *ex post* implementation game will converge exactly to the equilibrium that would have been selected from the *ex ante* perspective, so that the social contract proves to be essential also to the generation of a mutually consistent beliefs system supporting CSR as an equilibrium institution.

The opening section part I of the essay focuses on the first role played by the social contract. Primarily, the social contract works as a gap-filling device with respect to the holes of incomplete contracts linking stakeholders (or at least the most essential of them) to the firm (section 5). In a context of the incompleteness of contracts and unforeseen contingencies, the repeated reputation game involving the firm (or those who control it) and each stakeholder would be badly specified because contingent strategies and commitment would be undefined with respect to unforeseen contingencies. In such circumstances the intention to accumulate reputation pursuant a strategy of stakeholders' fair treatment would be frustrated because there would be no standard of behavior whereby reputation could be assessed. Thus, at the outset of the stakeholders/firm interaction, a social contract must be established on a set of general and abstract principles of fair treatment, and precautionary (non-contingent) standards of behavior, which can be adapted to unforeseen contingencies: that is to say, capable of defining commitments neither meaningless nor void if unforeseen events occur. In the absence of such an explicit norm, no regularity of reputation-based behavior on the part of the firm could emerge through its interaction with stakeholders. In the presence of an unforeseen event, the only opportunity open to the party occupying the position of authority in the firm would be to take advantage of discretion. Abuse of authority would be the natural consequence. The *ex ante* social contract on a CSR norm is what enables completion of the *game form* of the reputation game involving the firm and its stakeholders through definition of the firm's types that carry out strategies with expected behavior in whatever state, even if unforeseen.

The further parts (part II, see Sacconi 2010, *infra*, and part III, see Sacconi 2011) of this essay illustrate other roles of a Rawlsian social contract over CSR norms. It may be useful here to provide the reader with an overview of how the whole argument will be worked out. A Rawlsian social contract, as said, makes it possible to describe the game so that several types of reputations, based on the full or less than full respect of the CSR model, may be developed even if unforeseen contingencies are involved (part I). But the Rawlsian social contract performs its main role in the second function discussed in part II of the essay: that is, the *ex ante* impartial selection of a unique equilibrium amongst the many possible in the repeated trust game involving the firms and its stakeholders. In this context it allows the impartial selection of just *one* fair reputation equilibrium amongst the many possible. Elaborating on Binmore's *Natural Justice* (2005) (but see also Binmore, 1987, 1991, 1994 and 1998) and its re-evaluation of John Rawls's egalitarian and maximin principle of justice within a game-theoretical perspective, this task is accomplished again from the *ex ante* (under the 'veil of ignorance') point of view, but in a way that allows to find out a unique course of action that satisfies the requirement of incentive compatibility (i.e. a Nash equilibrium) (see part II, *infra*). Further, an agreed CSR social norm aids reducing to *just two* the candidate reputation equilibria that *ex post*, in the real world interaction taking place beyond the 'veil of ignorance', may be played after an agreement (perhaps seen as cheap-talk and not-binding) over a general principle of fairness has been reached by the firm and its stakehold-ers (see part III Sacconi 2011 and Sacconi 2008). These equilibria are defined not as traditional Nash equilibria, but as psychological equilibria according to the theory of conformist preferences (Grimalda and Sacconi, 2005) developed along the lines of other behavioral game models (Geanakoplos, Pearce and Stacchetti, 1989; Rabin, 1993). It is argued that the behavioral model of con-formist preference is nothing more than the development of Rawls's theory of the sense of justice, and hence is a constitutive part of a Rawlsian theory of CSR, able to include not just the theory of choice under veil of ignorance in the original position, but also the neglected theory of *ex post* social contract sta-bility (Rawls, 1971; Sacconi and Faillo, 2010). Finally, given the psychological equilibria that remain candidate as possible results of the game, the social con-tract allows the initial players' beliefs to be identified and to be made credible over the possible game solutions wherefrom an equilibrium selection dynamic (representing the revision process of mutual expectation) singles out the game solution effectively carried out (my favorite equilibrium selection dynamics is the Harsanyi's *tracing procedure* – see Harsanyi and Selten 1988). For a large array of situations, that are cognitively the most reliable in case the players have *ex ante* agreed on a social norm or standard (even if the agreement is not bind-ing), the process selects an equilibrium corresponding to the normative model of multi-stakeholder fiduciary duties (see Sacconi 2008).

2   The definition of corporate social responsibility (CSR) as an 'extended' corporate governance model

For many authors, corporate social responsibility is related to the stakeholder perspective in strategic management (Freeman 1984; Freeman and Evans, 1989). In light of a well-known classification by Donaldson and Preston (1995), it may be suggested that CSR is a concept that fits naturally with the level of normative stakeholder theory (understood as a normative managerial theory). Taking the stakeholder theory seriously from a normative point of view, that is, from the point of view of the rights and legitimate claims of all company stake-holders, would imply that the company must be run in a 'socially responsible' manner. According to Freeman (Freeman, 1984; Freeman and Evans, 1989; Freeman and Ramakrishna Velamuri, 2006), however, 'social responsibility' is not the proper expression for normative strategic management within the stakeholder approach because it suggests a concern for 'society' which is col-lateral and not deeply integrated into the firm's proper economic nature and functioning. 'Stakeholder responsibility' would be the key concept, although many attempts to clarify what constitutes CSR could equally be considered ways to clarify the normative content of the stakeholder approach to strategic management of the modern corporation.

Nevertheless, even accepting that CSR essentially means corporate responsibility towards stakeholders, maintaining CSR only at the level of management (managerial values, methods, rules and practices) seems to be reductive (see also Trebilcock, 1993). Management works within the limits of some institutional corporate form, and under social norms concerning the firm's nature and obligations. It is constrained, for example, by fiduciary duties and the institutional goals of the firm, and furthermore by the exercise of residual control rights by owners (which may be more or less effective according to the company's legal structure). I hence suggest moving up to the higher level of the firm's institutional form and its governance structure, which also involves the choice of the company's objective function. Therefore, within the stakeholder approach, this essay will understand corporate social responsibility as the quality of an institutional form of the firm based on a norm (mainly an ethical norm, but which must nevertheless be complementary to the legal order) concerning its corporate governance and its objective function and – as a consequence – also its strategic management.

Let us therefore propose the following definition of CSR (see also Sacconi 2004, 2007, 2006, 2009):

CSR is a model of extended corporate governance whereby those who run a firm (entrepreneurs, directors, managers) have responsibilities that range from fulfillment of fiduciary duties towards the owners to fulfillment of analogous – even if not identical – fiduciary duties towards all the firm's stakeholders.

Two terms must be defined in order for the foregoing proposition to be understood clearly.

(a) Fiduciary duties. It is assumed that a subject has a legitimate interest but is unable to make the relevant decisions, in the sense that s/he does not know what goals to pursue, what alternative to choose, or how to deploy his/her resources in order to satisfy his/her interest. S/he, the *trustor*, therefore delegates decisions to a *trustee* empowered to choose actions and goals. The trustee may then use the trustor's resources and select the appropriate course of action. For a fiduciary relationship – this being the basis of the trustee's authority *vis-à-vis* the trustor – to arise, the latter must possess a claim (right) towards the former. In other words, the trustee directs actions and uses the resources made over to him/her so that results are obtained that satisfy (to the best extent possible) the trustor's interests. These claims (that is, the trustor's *rights*) impose fiduciary duties on the agent who is entitled with authority (the trustee) which s/he is obliged to fulfill (Flannigan, 1989). The fiduciary relation applies in a wide variety of instances: tutor/minor and teacher/pupil relationships, and (in the corporate domain) the relationship between the board of a trust and its beneficiaries, or, according to the predominant opinion, between the board of

directors of a joint-stock company and its shareholders, and, more generally, between management and owners (if the latter do not run the enterprise themselves). The term 'fiduciary duty' therefore means the duty (or responsibility) of exercising authority for the good of those who have granted that authority and are therefore subject to it.

(b) Stakeholders. This term denotes individuals or groups with a major stake in the running of the firm and that are able to influence it significantly (Freeman and McVea, 2002). A distinction should be drawn, however, between the following two categories:

(b1) Stakeholders in the strict sense. Those who have an interest at stake because they have made specific investments in the firm (in the form of human capital, financial capital, social capital or trust, physical or environmental capital, or for the development of dedicated technologies, and so on). They are investments that may significantly increase the total value generated by the firm (net of the costs sustained for that purpose), and which are made specifically in relation to *that* firm (and not any other) so that their value is idiosyncratically related to the completion of the transactions carried out by or in relation to that firm. These stakeholders are reciprocally dependent on the firm because they influence its value but at the same time – given the specificity of their investment – largely depend on it to satisfy their own well-being (lock-in effect).

(b2) Stakeholders in the broad sense. Those individuals or groups whose interest is involved because they *undergo* the 'external effects', positive or negative, of the firm's transactions, even if they do not directly participate in the transaction. Thus, they neither contribute to, nor directly receive value from, the firm.

It is now possible to appreciate the scope of CSR defined as an extended form of governance. It extends the concept of fiduciary duty from a mono-stakeholder setting (where the sole stakeholder with fiduciary duties is the owner of the firm) to a multi-stakeholder one in which the firm owes *all* of its stakeholders fiduciary duties (the owners included). Classifying stakeholders on the basis of the nature of their relationship with the firm must thus be regarded as an important device with which to identify these further fiduciary duties.[1]

3   A 'transaction-costs-economics' rationale for extending fiduciary duties

This section argues that extending fiduciary duties follows naturally from a critical understanding of the new-institutional view of the firm (see also Sacconi 2000, 2006, 2007, 2009). The bulk of this theory is an answer to the question: 'why does the firm exist?' It maintains that companies, and firms in general, are 'unified governance structures' devoted to the reduction of transaction costs that would otherwise materialize due to the imperfection of contracts (Williamson, 1975, 1986; see also Hansmann, 1996). Specifically, three well-known sources of costs are specified:

(i) First of all, *contracts are incomplete in the sense that some relevant contingencies are unforeseen,* so that concrete and contingent provisos cannot be explicitly written or implicitly agreed with reference to such unforeseen events.

Contract incompleteness is sometimes tamed by a much less deep and troublesome understanding of the subject: for modelling convenience, non-verifiability by a third party (i.e. a form of information *asymmetry* to the disadvantage of the judge or the external arbiter) plus the parties' complete knowledge of what may unfold is substituted for unforeseen contingencies in the proper sense (see Hart, 1995; Grossman and Hart, 1986; Hart and Moore, 1990; Tirole, 1999; Maskin and Tirole, 1999). The result is that the cognitive and epistemological bases of contract incompleteness (*bounded rationality*) are swept under the carpet. On the contrary, it must be reasserted that the explanation rests on the empirically grounded assumption that the contracting parties are cognitively unable to represent, describe and forecast some possible states of the world, and that these states are *relevant* to their relationship, in the sense that the contract's outcomes and payoffs are not independent or separable in their definition from the states of affairs wherein they occur. At least sometimes, unforeseen states shape the *meaning* of the outcomes that they obtain from the contract (for example, in terms of 'good' or 'bad' descriptions of such outcomes, and hence different preferences to the receiver).

(ii) After signature of a contract, *parties may carry out specific investments* which are also not contractible in any details: they may produce an unforeseen outcome, or their effects can materialize under unforeseen states of the world that cannot be *ex ante* described in such a concrete way that they are effectively includable in the contract through contingent provisos.

Specific investments change the contractual parties' relationship from one of indifference to one of strategic interdependence and bargaining over the surplus made possible by investments. In fact, what is typical of specific investments is that they increase (under some possible future state, not completely describable *ex ante*) the value of the transaction to the participant parties (to be precise, investments by a producer or a consumer, or both, may increase the value of the transacted item – a good, a service or whatsoever – to the consumer directly, and hence they increase also the potential value to the producer, in so far as he may claim a higher price or remuneration for contributing to provide it, and he is in fact needing, or preferring, higher remuneration if it is possible).

(iii)   The parties' behavior under incomplete contract is to some relevant extent 'opportunistic': in a situation of contract incompleteness, they would try to renegotiate or change the terms of the contract or threaten – unless they are allotted a larger part of (or the entire) surplus – not to complete the transaction in the future if the profitable opportunity to do so appears.

Opportunism typically takes place when specific investments by some parties have already been carried out and an unforeseen state of the world materializes such that these investments have potentially important consequences on the transaction values, even though such values cannot be made available without some decision under the control of an agent (not necessarily the one who made the investment) whereby s/he may act opportunistically in order to extract as much rent as possible from control over this relevant decision variable.

To say that behaviors can be opportunistic is not to imply that people always behave opportunistically and that agents have no other motive to act in different situations. It is simply to say that, *ceteris paribus*, under incomplete contracts (and specifically in the absence of any other agreed *ethical norm* underlying the incomplete formal contract or any other *social convention* among participants (Lewis, 1969)), with a surplus at stake as it is created by specific investments, there is a significantly positive probability of observing the onset of the typical selfish behavior called 'opportunistic renegotiation of an (incomplete) contract'. Altogether, these assumptions have important consequences as to the explanation of why the firm has emerged as an economic institution. Awareness of the possible renegotiation of incomplete contracts (which does not entail the prediction of concrete states of the world by the parties, but rather that they are *aware* of not being able to describe and foresee all possible future contingencies) induces the expectation that investments will be expropriated. This destroys incentives to make efficient investments, and hence a possible surplus value will not be created by intelligent prudent but cognitively limited agents (in the sense of their capacity to draw up complete contracts). Otherwise, if some party lacks even this basic degree of prudence, the instability of transactions generated by resentment at having been unfairly exploited will be observed. Note that the inefficiency effect of excepted opportunistic behaviors is closely bound up with the expectation by those making specific investments that they will be unfairly harmed. Harm is seen as deriving from *expropriation* of a fair share of the benefit to which they believe themselves entitled (whatever the holes in the contract) because of their contribution to the surplus's generation.

Against this background, the firm enters the scene as a unified *governance structure* able to alleviate the problem. Its institution, by giving ownership of physical assets to one party in the contract, also allocates to this party (and more in general to one stakeholder category among the many involved in a complex web of related transactions) the residual right of control, i.e. it gives that party the right to make discretionary choices on the *ex ante* non-contractible transaction variables. (For example, either the decision whether or not to carry out a specific investment or – once an investment has already been made – decisions essential for the investment to achieve its goal, which may affect the transaction value.) Since these decisions may entail actions performed by individuals other than the right-holder, for a residual decision right to be effective it must entail *formal authority* over the firm, i.e. the owner's authority to see decision variables – residual with respect to those inserted in the written contract – carried out according to his/her will, independently of any specific agreement on the precise case in point and just because the right-holder 'says so'. Formal authority in fact provides those who undergo the authority relationship with pre-emptive reasons to act (Raz, 1999); reasons that (within the legitimate range of authority exercise) replace other reasons to act without any need to enter in balance with them. However (given that authority is not merely power exerted by means of a threat to use force and violence), it is not obvious how this could be so. The explanation is that the preemptive nature of the authority's reasons to act results from some voluntary acceptance or *legitimization*. Thus, in order to enter into a formal authority relation, a party B must accept that another party A – who is in the authority position – makes decisions which are taken by B in general (within the range of legitimate A's authority) as the premise of B's deliberation process – i.e. neither executed for the convenience of the specific case in point, nor just because of the threat of punishment in case of non-compliance. This, of course, confronts the owner with the challenge of justifying (legitimating) the firm's authority structure, and explaining why a given residual right of control allocation should be accepted by those who will then be required to obey its exercise.

But before turning to this aspect, let us recall why the allocation of residual rights of control to a single party may be efficient. In essence, a party holding control over the non-contractible decision variables of the contract will be protected against the other parties' renegotiation threat, so that its investments are safeguarded against the opportunism of the other stakeholders. This assurance of the party being able to benefit from its own investments is a sufficient reason to invest in some relevant aspect of transaction at an efficient level. Since the protection of specific investments enhances efficiency, this is the basis for a transaction costs efficiency explanation of the firm. If the specific investment of agent A is by far the most important in terms of specificity, A is the natural candidate for the allocation of ownership and control.

However, this is only a two-tier explanation of why the firm exists. In fact, even if this is an efficiency reason for the institution of a hierarchical relationship between the party making specific investments and any other party, it is not

166 of CSR and Game Theory (Part I)

enough to cope with the fairness and distributive concerns that underlie the non-controlling stakeholders' decision to accept the authority of a party holding the right of control if also these stakeholders invest idiosyncratically.

Consider that only in very special cases can the firm be understood as a way to regulate transactions among stakeholders in a network wherein only one of them has an idiosyncratic relation with the transaction under consideration, whereas all others are indifferent about whatever transaction in which they may be involved. In general, the firm makes sense as 'team production', that is, as a team wherein many stakeholders cooperate by means of some joint and coordinated activity for the production of a joint surplus – which can be translated into the view of the firm as a productive coalition with a super additive output function. Being part of the team or otherwise is not a matter of indifference to each potential team member. An interesting result in the theory of the firm is the unification of team production with the new-institutional idea that specific investments are typical conditions for the emergence of the firm (see Blair and Stout, 1999, 2006; Rajan and Zinagles, 1998, 2000; but see also Aoki, 1984; Sacconi 1991, 1997 and 2000 for a previous formulation of a similar view). On this unified view, team production generates a surplus on each individual's production due to cooperation among the team members; but cooperation – and its joint output – arises from a joint activity made possible by their complementary specific investments, and especially by specific investments made at the moment of joining the team. Hence, the firm becomes a typical case of team production among many holders of specific investments (who are also stakeholders in the strict sense), with some other stakeholders potentially subject to the (negative or positive) externality deriving from it. Stakeholders in the strict sense are those who are materially in the position to make specific investments or who, owing to their control over essential but non-contractible decisions, are themselves essential for the success of other stakeholders' investments. By way of example, consider employees, both highly qualified and otherwise, who develop and learn firm-specific skills, competencies and behavioral codes which make their productivity for a given firm higher than any others (and who may also be idiosyncratically related to a place where the team operated due to sunk costs already incurred to become productive in that location). Or stakeholders in the strict sense may be raw materials and instrumental goods providers or technology developers who sell materials, goods or equipment specifically devoted to a specific firm's production process (materials, goods or equipment that would not be provided by the general market). Or they may be capital goods investors who immobilize a large amount of money in the acquisition of complex equipment and technologies or employee training, all items with highly delayed returns on costs. Consider also consumers who invest time and effort in collecting information on goods and services that may be idiosyncratically tailored to their personal non-standardized preferences, and in developing trust relationships with sellers. They expect to profit in the future from this knowledge and social capital investment by being furnished with the idiosyncratic good or service on a trust basis, which prevents them from adding new information and search costs at any further purchase. All these investments attach surplus value to cooperation among stakeholders.

Note that team production is usually related to the idea of the firm as a *nexus of contracts* (Alchian and Demsetz, 1972) with one actor (the owner) in the special position of a central contracting party with discretion over terminating any particular contract without terminating the life of the entire team. On the unified view, these contracts must be incomplete, so that the owner placed at the center of the nexus of contracts – *pace* Alchian and Demsetz – necessarily exercises authority over members of the team. In fact, s/he holds discretionary power over non-contractible decision variables essential for the possibility that each contracting party, after investing idiosyncratically in the team, may benefit from its participation.

But consider what is meant by having residual right of control and authority over decision variables that concern any stakeholder's relation with the team. According to the standard theory, the owner may terminate any stakeholder's relation with the team by excluding it from the physical assets if it does not perform the requisite actions and relinquishes any claim over the surplus. Actually, this may be an oversimplification of the reasons for a formal authority to be able to work. However, assume that formal authority annexed to ownership in one way or another entails that *ex ante* non-contractible decisions are resolved in the owner's favor. These decisions affect the surplus distribution generated by all specific investments. In brief, player A (the authority) will not allow player B (the non-controlling stakeholder) to benefit sufficiently from his/her investment to be able to repay its cost unless s/he accepts that A appropriates the surplus. Thus, the party holding residual control is in a position to claim the full surplus by expropriating other stakeholders' returns on investments.

Summing up, if fiduciary duties are only attached to ownership, while the non-controlling stakeholders are still left unprotected through incomplete contracts, then neither ownership nor contracts insure them against opportunism that will deprive them of any benefit deriving from their cooperation throughout the firm. Residual control, by affecting surplus appropriation, can then generate distribution schemes such that the surplus is entirely appropriated by the owner no matter what contribution other stakeholders have made to surplus generation – stakeholders which are left at the level where they barely cover investments costs. This is what I call 'abuse of authority'.

When stakeholders are sufficiently aware of such a prospect, they will prevent this risk by not entering the authority relation, so that the firm does not form even if 'team production' could be an efficient way of organizing. Alternatively, once they have entered, stakeholders will under-invest in their specific contribution (note that standard theory assumes that residual control is relevant for decisions that affect the possibility of an investment achieving its goal when the state of world is favorable, whereas the decision to invest as such remains up to any single stakeholder). This is why control structures are always second best: abuse of authority induces some to over-invest, others to underinvest. Again a governance structure inefficiency is strictly connected with the expectation of unfair behavior.

The threat of authority abuse does not forestall the need – simply for incentive reasons – of giving residual control to the stakeholder responsible for the most important specific investment, granted that by assuming the governing role he does not incur governance costs high enough to dissipate the wealth created by efficient investment in the assets he holds. Nevertheless this should not prevent the non-controlling party from benefiting fairly from their specific investments and the joint generation of surplus. Obvious here is a first reference to the Rawlsian maximin principle as the proper balancing criterion among different stakeholders' claims. Owing to mere incentive reasons, those who are in the position to carry out the most important investment must be granted the opportunity to benefit from it by holding residual control which, in general, will induce inequalities between them and other stakeholders to the advantage of the former. However, since the firm is a joint venture for mutual advantage, disadvantaged non-controlling stakeholders must also benefit from cooperation. This grants them the right to veto any control structure if it is not also the better one for the worst-off stakeholder with respect to all the available alternatives (including also the case that they take over control and the disadvantaged stakeholder position is taken by some other stakeholder). To legitimate a unilateral control structure, wherein ownership is held by the stakeholder undertaking the most important investment – which also gives him the opportunity to abuse non-controlling stakeholders – the implementation of a redress principle is necessarily required. This entails that also the non-controlling stakeholders can reach a position better than those possible under any other possible control structure arrangement. My suggestion is therefore to understand CSR as this Rawlsian governance structure.

When CSR is viewed as 'extended governance', it completes the firm as an institution for the governance of transactions (see Sacconi, 2000). The firm's legitimacy deficit (whatever category of stakeholders is placed in control of it) is remedied if the residual control right is accompanied by further fiduciary duties owed the subjects not controlling the firm and at risk of authority abuse. At the same time, this is a move towards greater social efficiency because it reduces the disincentives and social costs generated by the abuse of authority. From this perspective, 'extended governance' should comprise:

- the residual control right (ownership-based) allocated to the stakeholder with the largest investments at risk and with relatively low governance costs, as well as the right to delegate authority to professional directors and management;

- the fiduciary duties of those who effectively run the firm (directors and managers) towards the owners, given that these have delegated control to them;
- the fiduciary duties of those in a position of authority in the firm (the controlling owner and/or delegated directors and managers) towards the non-controlling stakeholders, that is
  - the obligation to run the firm in a manner such that these stakeholders are not deprived of their right to participate in the surplus distribution as it is cooperatively generated by their specific investments and their joint actions – so that the company distributes to each *strict-sense-stakeholder* a 'fair share' of the surplus (acceptable by whatever stakeholder in an impartial agreement), while the broad-sense stakeholders are immunized against negative externalities;
  - the duty of effective accountability to the non-controlling stakeholders in terms of reporting relevant information in a veracious, transparent and understandable way about the accomplishing of tasks related to their legitimate interests and rights (as defined at the previous point),
  - and the right of these stakeholders to be represented in corporate bodies where they can exercise effective supervision over the owner's, directors' and managers' compliance with their fiduciary duties – as defined to the previous two points – owed to non-controlling stakeholders (for example representation through independent members of a supervisory body not appointed as representatives of shareholders but as advocates of the non-controlling shareholders' points of view).

According to this revision of the corporate governance structure, boards of directors or managers appointed by owners owe a *special* fiduciary duty to the 'residual claimants' who have directly delegated authority to them (*via* a narrow fiduciary proviso). This duty applies, however, only under the constraint that the more *general* fiduciary proviso relative to *all* the stakeholders is accomplished – which is specifically defined *via duties owed to non-controling stakeholders.*

Moreover, the extended fiduciary duties model of corporate governance redefines the firm's objective function (more about this in Sacconi 2004, 2007, 2006, 2009). This can be reconstructed by a three-step decision rule that moves from the most general condition to the most specific one:

(i) Run any corporate activity in the way that minimizes negative externalities affecting stakeholders in the broad sense by preventing any corporate action from bringing about not repayable damages, such as those caused to the global environment, or compensating them in kind as they materialize, also before any legal suit for damages is started;

(ii) Identify the feasible set of agreements compatible with the maximization of the joint surplus and its simultaneous fair distribution, as established by the impartial cooperative agreement among the stakeholders in the strict sense (more on this in Part II);

(iii) If more than one option is available in the above-defined feasible set, choose the one that maximizes the *residual* allocated to owners (for example, the shareholders).

The rest of this essay concentrates on an argument in favor of this extended governance structure and objective function, taking seriously (at least from the abstract perspective of game theory) the challenge that any proposal for reform must prove to be implementable.

4   CSR as an 'equilibrium institution' based on the social contract of the firm

A common tenet concerning CSR is that it should go beyond what can be required of companies by statutory laws and that it involves a certain degree of voluntarism and self-regulation. However, discretion is quite different from effective self-regulation, in that it does not entail any *rule* (either internal or external, enforced or self-enforced, legal or moral). Moreover, self-regulation may be understood in rather different ways: (i) as the case of an organism (the firm) endowed with its own 'natural' (so to speak 'unchosen') internal regularity of functioning, whereby its behavior is completely endogenously directed, without any need for interaction with other agents, either to agree on or at least to abide by any social norm at any time; or (ii) as the output of an agreement (explicit or implicit) among individual members of more or less extensive social groups – whereby they establish and adhere to an expressed (in language) set of principles or rules, with a normative content that they understand and which gives them guidance by vetoing some actions and recommending others such a rule, but which is *not enforced* by any external authority imposing sanctions because this is instead performed through the voluntary adherence of the individual members of the relevant social group to the principles expressed (Posner, 2000). The self-regulatory nature of CSR is understood here in accordance with the second view. In particular, let us state the following definition of a CSR effective self-regulation (Clarkson, 1999; Sacconi, De Colle and Baldin, 2003; Wieland 2003):

(a) CSR is established by social norms such as multi-stakeholder governance codes and management standards, not merely managerial discretionary decisions;

(b) These include normative utterances: general abstract principles and preventive rules of behavior concerning fiduciary duties, general statements of the fair treatment principle for each company stakeholder, principles of inter-stakeholder justice and fair balancing, precautionary rules of behavior in any critical sphere of potentially opportunistic behavior between the firm and some of its stakeholders – so that fiduciary duties and related rights are put in practice by standard precautionary rules of conduct that pre-empt opportunistic behavior in typical critical situations;

(c) Such norms are agreed upon by both firms and stakeholders through (voluntary) forms of multi-stakeholder social dialog (which simulates the idea of a 'small scale social contract' among them);

(d) Nevertheless, these normative contents and standards of behavior are self-imposed by firms on themselves without external legal enforcement, but instead by means of the internal adoption of statutes and codes of ethics reshaping the corporate governance and participatory structures, self-organization, training, auditing and control, which are compatible with voluntariness at the corporate level; and only on the basis of the consequences that non-conformity my induce for the stakeholders/firm interaction;

(e) The previous self-enforcement approach does not prevent self-regulation from being monitored and verified by third-party independent civil society bodies (which do not have conflicts of interest with their mission of impartial overview over companies voluntarily subjected to self-regulation); this enhances the level of information and knowledge whereby stakeholders define their expectations about the firm's conduct. By contrast, this monitoring, verification and rating of conformity levels may be strictly necessary due to the typical information conditions wherein CSR social norms and standards are established.

Of course, effective CSR self-regulation is a viable option only within an institutional and legal environment that does nothing to obstruct it. Such obstruction would occur in the case of overly narrow definitions of the firm's objective function such as that prescribing shareholder value maximization as the company's only goal – as today is to be found in many company laws at international level.[2] If maximizing the joint stakeholder value conflicted even in the very short run with immediate shareholder value maximization, these laws would prevent the board from deciding to balance stakeholders' interests according to the social contract view, which implies a constrained maximization view (that is, constraining shareholder value maximization with the condition of the simultaneous maximization of other stakeholders' utility according to a bargaining solution) (for more on this, see Sacconi 2006a,b, 2009).

This is a good reason (in order properly to assess the implementation and stability of a CSR norm) to admit a sort of hypothetical 'state of nature' benchmarking into the assessment of institutions. It logically precedes histori-cal legal constructs that without necessity may legally obstruct by design (or due to contingent historical equilibrium paths) the emergence of such a normative model. Thus, admitted that company laws do not obstruct proper self-regulation, the thrust of my argument is that the endogenous beliefs, motivations and preferences of economic agents (companies and stakeholders) are the essential forces driving the implementation of the CSR model of multi-stakeholder governance. If this is true, there will be plenty of reasons – not only normative but also from the incentive compatibility and stability viewpoints – to promote reforms that enable companies to adopt governance structures, management systems and organization designs consistent with the CSR model.

Making sense of CSR as a self-regulatory explicit social norm requires a definition of *institution* different from a simple consideration of existing formal-legal orderings. Here Aoki's *shared-beliefs cum equilibrium-summary-representation* view of institutions seems to furnish an essential part of the appropriate institution concept. According to this view, an institution is 'a self-sustaining system of shared beliefs about a salient way in which the game is repeatedly played' which is a rule not in the sense of 'rules exogenously given by the polity, culture or a meta-game', but in the alternative sense of 'rules as being endogenously created through the strategic interaction of agents, held in the minds of agents and thus self-sustaining – as the equilibrium-of-the-game theorists do. In order for beliefs to be shared by agents in a self-sustaining manner ... and regarded by them as relevant ... the content of the shared beliefs' must be 'a *summary representation (compressed information)* of an equilibrium of the game (out of the many that are theoretically possible). That is to say a salient feature of an equilibrium may be tacitly recognized by agent or have corresponding symbolic representation inside the minds of agents and coordinate their beliefs' (Aoki, 2001, p. 11).

The self-enforceability condition of Nash equilibria is implicit in the above definition. A *compressed summary representation* of information about the way a game has been played repeatedly and regularly is not a complete description of all of the histories of the repeated game under any contingency. Nevertheless, it is a summarizing pattern (a model resident within the players' minds, i.e. a *mental model*) containing salient features of the players' equilibrium action profile that has been played in the game so far and which are sufficient to define reciprocal expectations and beliefs concerning each other's actions from now on. Given this mental compressed representation, boundedly rational players – without complete information – derive beliefs about how any other player currently plays the repeated game. And these beliefs are both *shared* – in the sense that any two players make the same prediction about any other player involved – and *consistent* – in the sense that beliefs whereby any player derives his choice also cohere with his prediction of beliefs whereby other players derive their choices. These beliefs replicate the prediction that a particular equilibrium will be played among the many possible, and it is from such beliefs that all players derive their best actions. Because these actions are best against beliefs, and these beliefs correctly summarize current behaviors, these actions are also the best responses to the other players' actual actions as these are represented by beliefs. Then the derived action profile satisfies the typical Nash equilibrium condition.

This clarifies why the belief system is *self-sustaining*. The resulting equilibrium profile, as it is generated by best responses to beliefs, also replicates the same behavior that the compressed information summary in fact represents – that is, it exhibits the same salient characteristics as summarized in that compressed information representation. Hence, it cannot but replicate the same summarized information on how the game is played, and hence support the same beliefs system.

The *beliefs/compressed information summary representation* pair is an institution *not* in the sense of a 'rule of the game' exogenously imposed on the players' choices by some physical or technological feature of the environment, or by any further external institution or authority. These rules are useful to define the *game form*, that is, the objective set of constraints and opportunities within which the game is played. But the *beliefs/compressed information summary representation* pair instead defines an institution as the endogenous rule of behavior emerging from how the game is played. In fact, *given* the game form, the beliefs system describes a regularity of behavior resulting from the players' choices that they represent in their minds and replicate in response to that representation. Thus, the *belief system* replicates itself *endogenously*.

One important consequence of Aoki's view is the following. A statutory law passed by a parliament or another legislative body, even though it may explicitly settle rights and duties, if there is *no* shared belief that it will be complied with by those who 'should', it is not to be considered an *institution*. Instead, the ongoing practice of violating the statutory law could be considered the 'true' institution of the relevant action domain (Aoki, 2001).

Nevertheless, at first glance, this definition has one major drawback. Institutions thus defined seem to be devoid of any significant normative meaning and force. On the contrary, institutions like constitutions or laws, ethical codes, shared social values, organizational codes of conduct and procedures have primarily a prescriptive meaning (in the case of ethics such meaning requires 'universalizability' (Hare, 1981)) – that is, they are action guides and not simply a description of the state of affairs. They tell agents what must or must not be done in different circumstances. Institutions in the above game-theoretical definition may seem to give an indication about the best action of each player only *ex post* – that is, once the participants have chosen their actions and have shared knowledge that they have already reached an equilibrium state in their choices. The institution (beliefs system and the relative compressed information representation) tells players only to maintain the existing pattern of behavior because it is an equilibrium supporting the existing beliefs system. An institution such as this seems to have no normative content. It is based on a summary of how the game has been played in the past and consists of a set of mutually consistent predictions of how the game is currently being played and will be played in the future.

But why then would institutions be as they are? Why would they contain principles and norms (moral, legal, social or organizational) explicitly formulated in sentences through utterances whose meaning is not mainly a *description* of how people normally act (even though they can also contain descriptions) but a prescription of how they *must* or *must not* behave? There is no reason why what the addressee *must* do according to a norm corresponds to what – before the utterance of these prescriptive sentence – s/he de facto does. A norm (as a component of an institution) is not *falsified* by the observation that people do not conform to it, even though it can be thus recognized as ineffective (and discarded as an institution in the proper sense). The point is that a necessary component of the belief system defining an institution must not merely replicate the description of behavior in a given action domain; it must instead prescribe it independently of the description of the ongoing course of action. In other words, it rests on some a priori standpoint. Arguably, this is a *necessary* although not sufficient condition for an institution to exist (for sufficiency, the beliefs equilibrium definition must be met).

Moreover, a norm is sometimes explicitly introduced in order to change the received behavior and to set up an institution to regulate a given domain of actions. It thus provides guidance for action choices in the given domain when the players' summary compressed representation of information about how they have acted cannot replicate the required change. Because it is a theory of institutional change, Aoki's theory provides an answer to this question. The problem under consideration is twofold:

(i) the problem of equilibrium selection within a given game form, where an old equilibrium path (old institution) has been abandoned for whatever reason and a new equilibrium path (new institution) has to be reached by all the players, even though it has not yet been stabilized among them; and secondly;

(ii) the problem of achieving such a new equilibrium actions profile supported by a stable and shared beliefs system (a new institution), when the underlying action domain changes because environmental or technological changes have been introduced, or some further action opportunity is simply discovered by players and represented for the first time in their subjective mental model of the game.

To these distinct but interlocked questions Aoki gives an answer based on the idea of the 'salience' of some game feature, which is not understood as mere description of a characteristic. That is to say, it is not confined to the condition that players' beliefs contain the description of a salient characteristic of how they have acted in the past and that they transfer into a prediction of how they will act in the future. Here, the genuine *guidance* function of a normative beliefs system emerges. And it is part of the explanation of why that beliefs system is widely accepted by every participant in the action domain, so that it is recognized as 'salient' or 'prominent' – i.e. so that everybody knows that others also accept it and use it to assess each other's behavior. It thus gives players reasons to coordinate (so to speak 'for the first time') on a specific equilibrium profile, inter alia, given that many are possible, also in cases when the domain of action changes or is enriched by new opportunities.

> The point is that some symbolic system of predictive/*normative* beliefs [emphasis added] precedes the evolution of a new equilibrium and then becomes accepted by all the agents in the relevant domain through their experiences. It could be 'unsettled culture or ideologies – explicit articulated highly organized meaning systems – that may establish new styles or strategies of actions ..., an entrepreneur's vision that may trigger certain action that eventually remove the limits of organizational capabilities and environmental constraints ... or even the political program of a subversive political party ... bounded rational individual agents form their own subjective models of the game that they play' ... so that the mechanism of institutional change is seen "a process of revision, refinement and inducement if mutual consistency of such model incorporating a (common) representation system. (ibid., p. 19)

These examples of symbolic systems of normative and predictive beliefs are introduced as possible empirical explanations of how an equilibrium may become focal before it is stabilized by customary behaviors and beliefs. Clearly, however, this view presumes that these beliefs exercise a *justificatory force* able to induce the *general acceptance* of a new equilibrium in a given domain, so that – but only later on – it becomes the 'salient' basis for reciprocal prediction of all of the participants' actions.

Thus, a second component of a proper definition of institution – integrating Aoki's definition – is the mental representation of a norm, necessarily expressed by utterances in the players' language (oral, written or simply mentally represented) concerning rights and duties, values and obligations, which needs to have a prescriptive and universalizable meaning able to *justify* its shared acceptance by all participants in a given interaction domain. Because it is *ex ante* accepted by all players, it enters their shared mental model (Dezau and North, 1994) of how the game should be played and hence becomes the basis for their coordination on a specific equilibrium under a given action domain.

The key point is then explaining *how* a normative system of beliefs, preceding the evolution of the corresponding equilibrium, *becomes accepted by all agents* in the relevant domain. And to be useful for the purposes of this essay, this explanation should make sense of a CSR norm accepted by all the corporate stakeholders and those in the position of authority in the firm.

To my knowledge, the best justificatory account for norms on the responsible exercise of authority, entailing *ex ante* shared acceptance, is the *social contract model*. Contractarian norms result from a voluntary agreement in an hypothetical original choice situation which logically comes before any exogenous institution is over-imposed on a given action domain, or before any institution (in the equilibrium sense) has yet emerged. Thus a norm (and the institution that may encapsulate it) arises and can be maintained only because of the voluntary agreement and adhesion of agents. To define the agreement on a justifiable norm, any social contract model sets aside threats, fraud and manipulation resources that would render the parties substantially unequal in terms of bargaining power. In addition to the normative reason for doing so, such initial conditions would need an explanation in terms of a previously reached equilibrium in a game of threats played in the relevant domain, or would be seen as the effect of institutions already existing in some adjacent domain that give some players more strength than others. The hypothetical choice under the original position proceeds as if these contingencies were arbitrary and irrelevant to the proper calculation of the social contract.

The idea of a 'fair agreement' thus becomes intuitive: the agreement must reflect only each participant's rational autonomy, decision-making freedom and intentionality, which are assumed to be *equal* in weight among the participants in the contract. (This can be disputed on an empirical basis, but *in principle* the idea is to skip any morally irrelevant difference among participants.) The agreement thus gives equal consideration and respect – i.e. equal treatment – to reasons, interests and decisions put forward by each participant in the contract, because a voluntary and unanimous agreement among autonomous choosers necessarily equally reflects the reasons to enter the agreement by each and all of them.

It is not only the initial creation of norms and institutions that is seen by the social contract model as a matter of unanimous agreement among autonomous agents. In addition, their implementation is understood as being a matter of voluntary adhesion. Thus, the endogeneity of institutions with respect to the agents' strategic interaction is respected at both stages: an institution is endogenous to the *ex ante* players' strategic interaction understood as *rational bargaining* among equally situated rational agents, i.e. it can be started only by the unanimous individual players' decision to enter a voluntary agreement. Moreover, the *ex post* implementation of an institutional arrangement is also seen as the composition of the autonomous decisions that players make in their strategic interaction, whereby they chose whether or not to comply with the social contract by carrying out decisions that reflect the whole set of their reasons and motives to act.

In order to accomplish these tasks, the social contract model must operate in two different but necessarily related directions. Entering *ex ante* and adhering *ex post* to the agreement on principles and norms for institutions are distinct decision problems, with quite different logics of choice, but which nevertheless must be solved in a mutually consistent way and within a unified view. The choice of entering the contract must provide a justification for norms and institutions. The form of this justification is the impartial rational agreement of all the concerned stakeholders. It is appropriate here to give weight only to considerations relevant to the rational decision to enter an impartial agreement, which is provisionally assumed to be possible since all of the parties involved are hypothetically assumed to voluntarily participate in a *thought experiment*. Hence preventing cheating and defection is not the focus of the decision logic employed to calculate the agreement, even though these considerations may be essential in defining the feasible outcome set from which the agreement should be selected. What is relevant here is the opportunity offered by an unanimous agreement to improve to mutual advantage the state of affairs with respect to the 'state of nature' that would result from cooperation failure. Moreover, such a mutual improvement and advantage must itself be recognized as acceptable by equally autonomous, free and rational participants in the bargain – so that it must not only be *mutual* in the sense that whatever improvement one party gains over the state of nature status quo necessarily corresponds to *some* improvement in another's. In addition, it must also treat participants symmetrically, so that they can accept such an agreement proposal of mutual advantage form an impartial standpoint.

Quite different is the decision logic of the *compliance problem*. When we move from the *ex ante* to the *ex post* perspective, we ask whether an agreement reached can also be complied with by the same players who have agreed upon it. This is a different problem because the game logic of compliance differs from that of entering a cooperative agreement. It is instead the logic of an *ex post* non-cooperative game in which the players decide separately but interdependently whether or not to comply with the *ex ante* agreed contract. From this perspective, the question is not so much whether the contract provides reasonably high joint benefits and distributes them in an acceptably fair way; rather, the question is mainly whether there are incentives for cheating on the counterparty to the agreement, given the expectation that s/he will abide by the contract.

Social contract models convincingly answer the *ex ante* decision problem, but are typically at odds with the compliance problem. This difficulty also applies to the most elaborate social contract theories that have made significant steps towards a unified view of both aspects (see Rawls (1971) and Gauthier (1986)).

Binmore also provides a unified view of the two problems according to the social contract model (see extensively part II of this essay). On the other hand, Aoki's institution definition guarantees that, if the agreed norm is represented within the players' minds by summary information about a 'salient' equilibrium profile and thus generates a system of predictive and normative beliefs, then the compliance problem is also amenable to solution, since it will satisfy the equilibrium condition. Thus, taking jointly the two requirements – (i) acceptability of the normative content of an institution through a social contract and (ii) a shared belief system based on the compressed representation summary of an equilibrium – seems to provide the comprehensive definition of institution needed here.

There are many different accounts of the social contract model. For example, the accounts of both Rawls and Gauthier are compatible with what has been said thus far. However, Rawls's idea of the original position is central to the purpose of this essay. It is a choice condition requiring unanimous agreement under a 'veil of ignorance' concerning any detail of each participant's personal identity and social position. To be clear, I mean by a 'veil of ignorance' radical uncertainty about the mappings that would identify each participant in the original position with a particular set of personal attributes such as strategies and payoffs that would represent his personal characteristics and social position under different contingencies. The veil of ignorance creates an impersonal and impartial standpoint whereby an agreement is unanimously workable because each participant's separate standpoint becomes identical with that of all the others. In other words, behind the 'veil of ignorance' each individual is ready to take symmetrically the position of any other and to replace his/her initial personal standpoint with that of everybody else. Under these symmetrical exchanges of position, whereby everyone assesses acceptance of any given set of normative statements, they reach an agreement that reflects a reasonable impartial combination of all the reasons to act that they consider in turn. Importantly, the agreement accepted by each of them cannot but be unanimous, for the symmetrical replacement of personal positions is carried out in identical ways by all of the involved parties, so that they are identically situated in their exercise of institutional assessment.

Thus, it is the agreement under the veil of ignorance among all the corporate stakeholders that should generate the shared acceptance of CSR as a social norm corresponding to a particular equilibrium among the many possible. Since it is a 'thought experiment', it would impress the players' minds with a mental model of how the game should be played and generate an identical 'salient' aspect of their interaction that would favor effective coordination over a specific equilibrium point to be played by the choice of each action. When the shared system of mutually consistent beliefs has been formed for the first time, it will allow for mutual predictions and the generation of an equilibrium that also confirms the same beliefs set. The summary information compressed into a mental representation of the regular players' behavior throughout the repetition of the game, generated by *ex ante* acceptance of the normative beliefs that a particular equilibrium is to be played, can then be understood as an institution. It is now argued that CSR is the social norm in the corporate governance domain that satisfies this definition.

A social contract explanation is a *zero-level* explanation which in fact assumes as its starting point the 'state of nature' hypothesis. It is more fundamental than, and prior to, any consideration of complementarities between a CSR model of corporate governance and institutions belonging to different domains. And it also logically precedes any assessment of how institutional changes in other domains – such as labor law, the industrial relation system, or, in general, the political system – may ease the introduction of CSR. In fact, assume that a social contract among all the company stakeholders induces them to build CSR as an institution which is not only impartially acceptable to stakeholders but also self-sustainable – admitted that it is neither obstructed by prohibitions in the legal system nor incentivized by other institutions or regulations. Such a normative model is the natural candidate for a legal reform of statutory company laws and corporate governance regulations because it has already proved to have endogenous forces of its own pushing toward its institution.[3]

5 The four roles of a social contract on CSR norms

To understand why the stakeholders' social contract on a CSR norm explicitly stated through utterances in normative language is so essential for the endogeneity and self-sustainability of the corresponding behavior and expectations (e.g. an institution in Aoki's sense), we must consider the *roles* performed by voluntarily agreed explicit norms. But let us first model the relationships between the firm and each of its stakeholders as a case of the well-known *trust game* (TG) – a formal context wherein these roles can be better situated (see Figure 7.1) (Fudenberg and Levine, 1989; Fudenberg and Tirole, 1991). A stakeholder A may or may not enter into a specific relationship with the firm. The firm is here identified with the particular stakeholder B who owns its physical assets and hence exercises control on some discretionary decision variables that affect the mutual opportunity to profit from the stakeholder A's (and maybe his/her own) specific investment and cooperative decision to enter the relationship. Hence, in the trust game, what stakeholder A may or may not enter is a fiduciary relation with those in a position of control (synthetically called 'the firm'). By entering, it is assumed that the stakeholder makes a specific investment that renders his/her relationship with the firm idiosyncratic, but also makes possible a surplus deriving form this relationship. On the other hand, the position of the firm's owner in the game makes explicit the possibility that s/he may abuse his/ er authority toward the non-controlling stakeholder. The owner may or

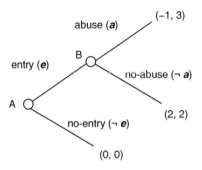

Figure 7.1   One-shot Trust Game in extensive form

may not abuse the stakeholder's trust. In the case of abuse, the owner appropriates all of the surplus generated by specific investments and gets 3, leaving the stakeholder with only the cost of its investment (-1). If the owner does not abuse, there is a mutually beneficial sharing of the surplus for both the players (2, 2) that reflects their joint contribution to 'team production'. As well known, this game has a single Nash equilibrium, the Pareto-inefficient outcome corresponding to the payoffs vector (0, 0). Since the firm B will necessarily abuse ('abuse' is its dominant strategy), the stakeholder A will not enter.

But matters may change substantially if the TG is infinitely repeated between a single long-run player B, in the institutional role of the firm, and an infinite series of short-run stakeholders seen as players $A_1,...,A_n$ (where n goes to infinity). At each stage game (repetition) a player in the role of A_i has a short-run strategy choice at hand: whether or not to enter, given the consideration of the previous story of how the game has been played until the stage where s/he is required to make his/her decision. On the other side, the long-run B player has to make a choice among long-run strategies which at each repetition select a concrete action (abuse, not abuse or a random mechanism to mix the two probabilistically) as a function of the story of the game until each possible stage. Note that because B chooses at each stage, a long-run player's strategy is a rule for making such selection at each stage given any story of the game at whatever stage. Thus, a long-run strategy considered as a whole accounts for every possible story of whatever length according to which the game might have been played at each stage. As a consequence, each mono-periodical short-run stakeholder A_i (for whatever value of (i) has a payoff function defined on the outcome of the specific stage at which s/he participate in the game. Otherwise the long-run player B's payoff function is the infinite summation of each payoff s/he gets at any stage multiplied by a discount factor δ ($0 \leq δ \leq 1$) reflecting player B's impatience or short-sightedness. Under convenient conditions, such a payoff is the *limit of the mean* payoff associated with the loop of whatever length (going to infinity) into which player A's strategy enters again and again along its repetition, given the short-run players' strategy choices (i.e. loops generating identical series of stage game payoffs). Let us assume that the discount factor δ is not 'too small' with respect to the ratio between: (i) how much player B in a single case forgoes by not abusing player A_i instead of taking the opportunity to exploit him/her; and (ii) how much s/he forgoes at each successive stage by receiving the payoff associated with non-entrance by player A_i instead of the payoff of mutual cooperation.

The game is qualified as 'incomplete information game' in a distinct sense. Short-run players A_i are *uncertain* about the rationality of player B (i.e. criterion of choice) so that they take as possible different player B types, where types identify the long-run strategies played by B. This is to be understood in the sense that players $A_1,...,A_n$ take it for granted that player B is irrevocably committed or disposed to play some specific behavior rule – which consists of a specific repeated strategy – but is also uncertain about which among the many possible such commitments he chooses. Thus player B is deemed to be a not completely strategically rational agent because s/he would stick to a rule of behavior independently of player A's choice. This is only the way that players $A_1,...A_n$ think about the game, however. Indeed, player B is nevertheless completely strategically rational and informed, so that s/he will decide his/her strategy without any sense of absolute commitment, and only on the basis of his/her best prediction of strategy choice by players $A_1,...,A_n$. This in turn is based on his/her understanding of how the short-run players' beliefs change from one repetition of the game to the next.

Player B's reputations are the probabilities attached by players A_i at each stage to B's types, whereas types are stereotyped commitments on player B's rules of play (strategies). Changes in reputations are a function of the repeated observation of how stages games have been played by B, and of the stage game outcomes and their comparison with what a given commitment would have entailed (contingently on also the behavior of players A_i). Each player A_i is assumed to update, by means of the Bayes rule, the initial probabilistic beliefs shared by all players A_i concerning player B's types. Repeated observations of 'not abuse' will augment the *ex post* probability of any B's strategy (pure or mixed) that does not abuse at all or abuses very slightly. Whereas such observations will falsify the hypothesis that player B is the abusive type, or they will reduce the probability of any significantly abusive B's mixed type. Player B supports his/her reputation of being a given type by continuing to play stage game moves which are consistent with the type.

Under these not innocuous assumptions it is well known that a whole set of new equilibria becomes possible in the repeated trust game. In particular, this set of equilibria (consisting of repeated short-run strategies chosen by players $A_1,...,A_n$ paired with a long-run player B's strategy) is bounded from above by the equilibrium wherein player B plays his Stackelberg strategy, and from below by the equilibrium in which no player in the role of A_i enters throughout the game repetition (Fudenberg and Levine, 1986; see also Fudenberg and Tirole, 1991). It is important to achieving an understanding of how spontaneous cooperation can arise between the firm and its stakeholder that if only pure strategies are considered, then a repeated B's decision not to abuse will eventually induce entrance by every short-run player A_i (after some periods spent on accumulating reputation). If the discount factor is not too low, continuing to play no abuse is also player B's best response, so that repeated non-abuse and substantial entrance by players A_i will be an equilibrium of the game. This is the typical 'good reputation' equilibrium which is typically advocated by those who are 'optimistic' about spontaneous cooperation between the firm and its stakeholder.

Against the background of this concise representation of the stakeholder/firm interaction, we may understand the *four roles* of a social contract on a CSR norm expressing player B's fiduciary obligation not to abuse player A's trust.

- The *cognitive-constructive role*, which answers the question about *how* the firm *works out* the *set* of commitments that it *can* undertake with respect to generic states of the world that it is aware of not being able to predict in any detail, and therefore *what* types of *possible* equilibrium behavior the firm can work out so that stakeholders may entertain expectations about them;
- The *normative role*, which answers the question about what (if any) pattern of interaction the firm and its stakeholders must a priori *select* from the set of possible equilibria to be carried out *ex post* (according to the answer given to question a), if they adopt an *ex ante* standpoint ('under the veil of ignorance') enabling an agreement to be reached from an impartial point of view;
- The *motivational role*, which answers the question about *what* and *how many* equilibrium patterns of behaviors, amongst those that may emerge *ex post* from the interaction between firm and stakeholder, would retain *their motivational force* if firm and stakeholder were able to agree in an *ex ante* perspective on a CSR norm along the lines of question (b);
- The *cognitive-predictive role* concerning how the *ex ante* agreement on a CSR norm *affects* the beliefs formation process, whereby a firm and its stakeholders cognitively converge on a system of mutually consistent expectations such that they reciprocally predict from each other the execution of a given equilibrium in their *ex post* interaction (given that more than one equilibrium point still retains motivational force). The question to be answered by this function is 'Does the norm shape the expectation formation process so that in the end it will coincide with what the *ex ante* agreed principle would require of firm and stakeholders?'

6 The cognitive/constructive role of the social contract

The second role is *the focus* of part II of this essay, where the main contribution of the Rawlsian view is discussed (see Sacconi 2010, *infra*). I have discussed at length the first role elsewhere (Sacconi 2000, 2006a, 2007b, 2008), so here I may briefly summarize the main argument with reference to the repeated trust game.

To enable the reputation cumulative process, the firm should commit to a strategy carried out with specific unambiguous and verifiable actions at each stage game according to a conditional rule. *The* stage game choice induced by a strategy is specified with respect to every possible story of the game – that is, with respect to all the possible state of the world wherein the game has been played until the current stage, for whatever stage. This means that, given a player B's strategy, every player A_i at any stage t is capable to predict how player B will play at any stage (given any previous possible story).

Consider, however, that modeling the firm like this entails assuming a context of incomplete contracts, which we interpret in its genuine nature as the existence of unforeseen and unforeseeable states of the world (Kreps, 1992). Complete contracts between two parties would be agreements on pairs of contingent strategies, one for each party. In our case these would at least make it possible to say how the firm will act in whatever state of the world that may unfold through all the game repetitions. With contract incompleteness, by contrast, some states of the world are unforeseen. Hence it is impossible *ex ante* to define how any *contingent* strategy will behave when an unforeseen state of the world arises at some repetition of the game. In fact, under incomplete knowledge, contingent contractual commitments are mute, or not even specified, on the unforeseen states, and this implies that also commitments to specific contingent strategies that the firm B may undertake toward its stakeholders A_i will be unspecified.

But a type's reputation depends crucially on verification of the correspondence between the game outcome in a given state and the commitment to be fulfilled by the type in the same state, which entails an expected outcome for that state under the given type (also contingent on player A_i's choice). When a state of the world is unforeseen, a concrete contingent strategy cannot be *ex ante* specified as to its possible occurrence. Thus no contingent commitment can *ex ante* be undertaken with respect to unknown states of the world. From this it follows that there is no basis for saying whether '*what had to be done has been done*' (Kreps, 1990). Commitments are emptied by cognitive gaps in relation to states that stakeholders and the firm cannot *ex ante* concretely describe. These cognitive gaps give *no* basis for reputation as modeled as the probabilistic updating of initial beliefs associated with commitments calculated in function of stage-by-stage observation of whether or not actions prescribed by commitments are performed at any stage of the game.

In more general terms, the problem is essentially one of the incomplete specification of the *game form* and, in particular, of the strategy set (type set) and outcome functions (which map strategy combinations to payoffs for each state of the world at each stage). But without types uniquely related to commitments to strategies, no reputation effects are possible. Thus an 'existence of the equilibrium' problem arises. Players cannot calculate the equilibrium strategies of the reputation game because their commitments are unspecified with respect to unforeseen states of the worlds. Put differently, they lapse into a state of cognitive unawareness of the equilibrium strategies that would support any level of mutual cooperation amongst the players.

The picture changes if the social contract has been introduced *ex ante* on a norm understood as the firm's constitution stating its fiduciary duties towards all of the stakeholders in terms of general and abstract principles and precautionary rules of behavior. It predefines the standard conducts to be carried out if some principle is placed at risk of violation by the occurrence of whatever (even if unforeseen) state of the world. What is crucial here is that the social contract introduces explicit norms (general and abstract principles and precautionary rules of behavior) that are established without *ex ante* complete knowledge of all future states of affairs. In general, this is the role of constitutional principles in legal orders, and specifically the role of universalizable principles in ethical codes.

Once a social contract has been introduced, there will be universalizable, general and abstract principles and precautionary rules of behavior to which stakeholders and the firm have agreed without being contingent on any concrete and complete *ex ante* description of future states of affairs; and these principles can be taken as benchmarks with which to assess the firm's behavior also when unforeseen states arise (as Kreps suggested in respect of corporate culture principles but mistakenly restricting them to cultures rather than to ethics – see Kreps, 1992 and Sacconi, 2000). In so far as the agreement is worked out through counterfactual reasoning under a hypothetical original choice situation, and concerns general and abstract universalizable principles – by definition independent from any concrete description of details about the players' positions and any other concrete contingency – the principles agreed are adaptable to a wide array of situations. The social contract thus plays a cognitive role as a *gap-filling device* (Coleman, 1992) which establishes the *types* of behaviors that stakeholders can expect from the firm in situations where contracts fail owing to the absence of conditional provisos constraining residual decisions.

This cognitive function is primarily *constructive*. The *game form* (Aoki, 2007) is badly specified under unforeseen situations, because contingent strategies for such states are unspecified. Norms nevertheless allow a default inference to be made on how the honest type of firm will behave under these circumstances. These 'strategies' are not defined contingently on states of the world that the parties are unable to write down in the contract or are even unable to foresee. These default rules are based on the satisfaction of a *fuzzy* membership condition of states with respect to the domain of abstract, general and universalizable ethical principles that are *ex ante* known (because they are agreed through the social contract) (Sacconi, 2000; Zimmerman, 1991; Sacconi 2007b). Membership is always *ex post* verifiable through a shared understanding of the inherent vagueness of unforeseen contingencies with respect to the principle. Once these norms have been stated *ex ante* in terms of precautionary standards of behavior, it is possible to say how the firm is expected to behave in whatever unforeseen state that may put a general principle at risk, until contrary proof is given that the principle does not apply to the new situation. In other words, the firm types implementing or otherwise strategies of conformity to norms are described. Explicit norms then complete the description of the game form by substituting default rules of behavior for conditional strategies. What is involved here is not inductive learning about the probability of an already given set of possible but uncertain set of types, but the conception of the type set itself that contributes to an (approximate) description of what may occur in the future. Accordingly, the social contract role is *constructive*. Through the agreed statement of norms, firms and stakeholders *construct* an approximate model of the game that they will play in states of the world that they are ex ante unable to describe in every detail.

Nevertheless, the cognitive (and constructive) function of norms takes us only half-way into our argument. A well-conceived game form makes it possible to define the players' strategy combinations and equilibria wherein the firm may be described as acting in support of its reputation, so that after some time stakeholders will begin to trust it. Under the usual condition of the long-run player's non-myopia, these equilibrium combinations include the firm's continuing not to abuse and the stakeholders' continuing to enter the relation with the firm. Nevertheless, in general, this will be *just one* of the many possible reputation equilibria of the game. Other equilibria will entail strategies of random compliance with the norm by the firm (a mixed repeated strategy) such that the stakeholder's best response is to yield to the firm's strategy (entering throughout all the game repetitions and enduring consequences from the firm's partial abuse). Among these equilibria (see Figure 7.2, where the equilibrium set X of the repeated TG is depicted as the dashed area, and note in particular the equilibrium with average discounted payoffs (0, 2.66)), one is the *Stackelberg equilibrium*, this being the equilibrium that the firm would select if it committed unilaterally to its preferred *mixed type* and induced stakeholders to play their best responses to such an irremovable commitment. (Note that in a non-cooperative repeated game such an irremovable commitment can only be 'simulated' by the firm with the accumulation of a reputation of being such a type, so that stakeholders play their best responses whereby the firm must respond by fulfilling the commitment.) Under such an equilibrium, the firm must have been able

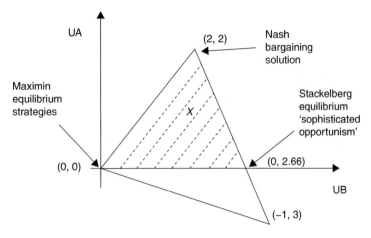

Figure 7.2   Equilibrium set X of the repeated TG

to accumulate a reputation for a mixed level of abuse which leaves stakeholders indifferent between entering or not entering – so that by entering a very large part of the potential surplus is appropriated by the mixed type firm.

There is no reason to assume that, because the Stackelberg equilibrium is one of the possible Nash equilibria, it must necessarily be the one selected. Yet there are also strong reasons to believe that in so far as no other element is introduced into the picture, player B will engage in maneuvers to develop a reputation that will allow him/her to select exactly this equilibrium, which gives him/her the highest payoff within the equilibrium set. To sum up, when a repeated reputation game is constructively defined in terms of strategies that abide or otherwise with the *ex ante* agreed CSR norm, the game will have too many equilibrium points, not just the 'socially preferable' equilibrium where the firm abstains from abusing stakeholders and cooperates with them at any stage. Then the typical game-theoretical problem of *multiple equilibria* arises.

Before going a step further, however, note that we have already obtained an important result – even if it is an admittedly partial one. It follows naturally from what has been said about the *constructive role* of explicitly agreed CSR social norms (and the related *multiplicity* problem) that effective self-regulation should not be confused with the standard economic view that if CSR is to emerge as an equilibrium behavior from endogenous incentives, its driving force must simply be 'enlightened self-interest in the long run'. According to this view, a self-interested entrepreneur who owns the firm, and cares only for his/her own self-interest in the long run (or, if s/he does not own the firm personally, cares for the self-interest of all the company shareholders), would adopt behavior that spontaneously satisfies the company stakeholders' interests with no need to single out a principle of fairness, either to agree on any social contract or to state explicitly any charter on the firm's fiduciary duties to stakeholders. Self-interest in the long run – or, more concretely, maximizing total shareholder value in the long run – would naturally guarantee that the treatment of corporate stakeholders will fulfill their interests and claims, thus making any explicit statement of extended fiduciary duties superfluous. As a consequence, the only goal that should be specified as the proper constraint on managerial and entrepreneurial discretion in the management of the firm is the coherent pursuit of shareholder value in the long run. The stakeholders' legitimate interests would be satisfied simply as a side-effect of this main goal, because they are related to it through a means–end relation. Hence whilst stakeholders are to be taken into account by the corporate strategy in the domain of *means*, only shareholders are recognized as sources for corporate *ends*.[4] This view, of course, does not recognize any need for a norm that explicitly states a principle of fair balancing amongst stakeholders, even if it may be understood as not externally enforced but as self-imposed through self-organization by those in an authority position in the firm.

From what we already know, however, this 'self-interest-in-the-long-run' view is clearly untenable. First of all, without the explicit statement of a CSR norm – based at least hypothetically on agreement by the company stakeholders reached under ideal conditions of impartial bargaining – a long-run self-interested corporate strategy simulating the discharge of fiduciary duties owed to stakeholders may simply not exist (or, alternatively, be something that the firm cannot be aware of at all). This is implied by the case just discussed of unspecified game form. Under incompleteness of contracts, and without the protection of a constitution charter or a code of ethics stating general abstract principles and prophylactic rules of behavior about the fair treatment of stakeholders, no conditional commitment is defined with respect to unforeseen states of the world. Thus, the firm cannot accumulate reputation due to its expected behavior in these states.

Moreover, if such behavior in the long run could be worked out as something of which the firm might be aware (and this will happen when a CSR norm is given), nevertheless other behaviors in the long run could also be worked out by the company, such that they provide very limited and minimal satisfaction of the stakeholders' claims for fair treatment. These further behaviors would not only be preferable to the firm's owners; they would also command a certain acquiescence by the stakeholders – which could be made indifferent between the prospects of giving in to these firm's opportunistic strategies or refraining from entering any relationship with it. We must conclude that the simple self-interest in the long-run view, translated into shareholder value in the long-run doctrine, would imply a considerable violation of stakeholders' legitimate claims and an abuse of ownership-based authority.

By contrast, the self-regulatory view defended here requires the establish-ment of explicit norms arrived at by social dialog and multi-stakeholder agree-ments, and taking the form of CSR governance codes or management standards voluntarily accepted by firms because they contain and specify the terms of the ideal and fair social contract between the firm and its stakeholders. They are explicitly formulated in language (written or oral) and their utterances state the extended fiduciary duties and obligations that the firm owes to its stakeholders. At the same time they are adhered to voluntarily. And, as far as enforcement is concerned, they are not imposed by external legal sanctions but instead through endogenous social and economic sanctions and incentives. In this sense they are self-enforceable explicit norms put into practice essentially by means of endogenous economic and social forces such as reputation effects and conformity. As a matter of fact, such a norm will correspond to just one equilibrium among the many possible (see again Figure 7.2; it is quite obvious that a norm of fair treatment will require play of the repeated strategy equilib-rium with average discounted payoffs (2, 2)). Part II will show that the social contract on an explicitly expressed CSR standard and norm also performs a normative role by providing an *ex ante* guide for the solution of the equilibrium selection problem.

Notes

1. At first glance, one might object to the idea that many stakeholders, in both the 'strict' and 'broad' senses, do not have relations with a firm such that they formally delegate authority to those who run it (for example, they do not vote). The consequence is that the fiduciary duties as defined earlier do not apply to them. In the model of the social contract as a hypothetical explanation of the origin of the firm, however – see section 5.2 – all of the stakeholders participate in the 'firm's second social contract'. The conse-quence is that their trust constitutes the authority of the firm's owner and manager. This also explains how the latter's authority may be accepted by these subjects. Moreover, the hypothetical social contract is typically used to explain how authority – that is, legitimate power – may come about at both the political and organizational levels; see, for example, Green (1990), Raz (1985) and Watt (1982). For a discussion of managerial authority, see MacMahon (1989) and Sacconi (1991).
2. However, consider debates on the business judgment rule in relation to its consist-ency with 'team production theory' as inherent in the American tradition of com-pany law (Blair and Stout, 1999; Meese, 2002), but also see the recent UK company law reform – especially the introduction of the directors' obligation to run the com-pany '*in the way he considers, in good faith, would be most likely to promote the success of the company for the benefit of its members as a whole, and in doing so have regard*' ... for the interest of stakeholders other than the 'members' of the company (employees, customers, suppliers, communities and others), for the impact on the environment, and the company reputation conditioned by these relationships, which moreover states that when these further purposes are to be considered, beyond the interest of shareholders, the meaning of '*promoting the success of the company in the interest of its members*' must be understood as if it included the pursuance of also these further

purposes and interests (the 2006 UK company law reform, Art. 172). Such an enlarge-ment of the purposes that directors must pursue as the definition of the company success concept effectively opens the way to effective CSR self-regulation.

3. Aoki pays much attention to institutions of different level ('generic, substantive and operational') and their mutual complementarities (Aoki 2007a, 2002). On the contrary, my view of CSR as a corporate governance institution emerging form the firm's social contract is a 'state of nature' explanation such that other institutional levels do not significantly affect the interaction among stakeholders, and between the stakeholders and the firm (see also Sacconi 2000, 2006a,b, 2009). Admittedly, there are benefits and costs in both the modeling strategies. I maintain that there is an advantage in being able of considering what would happen in case the law in general made room for the firm's social contract among all its concerned stakehold-ers seen as an endogenous institution-making process, including both the *ex ante* settlement of a set of explicit norms and the solution of the *ex post* compliance and equilibrium selection problem. Nevertheless, in order to model the stakeholders' social contract on the firm's control and accountability structure as a governance institution, there is no need to consider it as a completely isolated object lost in a institutional vacuum. It is enough to borrow the idea of 'morally free zone' – as it was re-elaborated by Dunfee and Donaldson (1995) in quite a different way with respect to the original version given by David Gauthier (1986). 'Small-scale social contracts' at industry, local or sectional levels are explicitly allowed by hyper-norms that are the object of the 'general social contract'. The general social contract leaves inten-tionally room to them due to the parties' awareness of bounded moral knowledge and rationality. However, by contrast also with Dunfee and Donaldson's view, the small-scale social contract of the firm is here explicitly modeled as the result of an *ex ante* bargaining between stakeholders under the 'veil of ignorance' (see also part II), and not just as an *ex post* equilibrium institution. Whereas the equilibrium condi-tion was also true of the local norms' definition in Dunfee and Donaldson's ISCT, seeing them as 'approved social convention', that theory was unable to provide a proper social contract model for the emergence of local norms – i.e. to explain them in terms of an impartial agreement among the firm's stakeholders on constitutional general principles and preventives rules of behavior. This is provided by the Rawlsian view of CSR.

4. This is probably the opinion of Jensen when he says 'Indeed, it is a basic principle of enlightened value maximization that we cannot maximize the long-term market value of an organization if we ignore or mistreat any important constituency. We cannot create value without good relations with customers, employees, financial backers, suppliers, regulators, and communities. But having said that, we can now use the value criterion for choosing among those competing interests. I say "competing" interests because no constituency can be given full satisfaction if the firm is to flourish and survive' (Jensen 2001). See also Sternberg (1999).

References

Alchian, A. and H. Demsetz (1972) 'Production, Information Costs and Economic Organization' *American Economic Review*, vol. 62, pp. 777–95.

Aoki, M. (1984) *The Cooperative Game Theory of the Firm*. Cambridge: Cambridge University Press.

Aoki, M. (2001) *Toward a Comparative Institutional Analysis*. Cambridge, MA: MIT Press.

Aoki, M. (2007a) 'Three-Level Approach to the Rules of the Societal Game: Generic, Substantive and Operational' paper presented at the conference on 'Changing Institutions (in Developed Countries): Economics, Politics and Welfare', Paris, 24–5 May.

Aoki, M. (2007b) 'Endogenizing Institutions and Institutional Change', *Journal of Institutional Economics*, vol. 3, pp. 1–39.

Binmore, K. (1987) 'Modeling Rational Players', *Economics and Philosophy*, 1(3), pp. 9–55 and 2(4), pp. 179–214.

Binmore, K. (1991) 'Game Theory and the Social Contract', in R. Selten (ed.), *Game Equilibrium Models II, Methods, Morals, Markets*. Berlin: Springer Verlag.

Binmore, K. (1994) *Game Theory and the Social Contract (Vol. I): Playing Fair*. Cambridge MA: MIT Press.

Binmore, K. (1998) *Game Theory and the Social Contract (Vol. II): Just Playing*. Cambridge MA: MIT Press.

Binmore, K. (2005) *Natural Justice*. Oxford: Oxford University Press.

Blair, M. and L. Stout (1999) 'A Team Production Theory of Corporate Law', *Virginia Law Review*, vol. 85(2), pp. 248–328.

Blair, M. and L. Stout (2006) 'Specific Investment: Explaining Anomalies in Corporate Law', *Journal of Corporation Law*, vol. 31, pp. 719–44.

Clarkson, M. (1999) *Principles of Stakeholder Management*. Toronto: Clarkson Center for Business Ethics.

Coleman, J. (1992) *Risks and Wrongs*. Cambridge, MA: Cambridge University Press.

Dezau, A. and D. North (1994) 'Shared Mental Models: Ideologies and Institutions', *Kyklos*, vol. 47, pp.1–31.

Donaldson, T. and L.E. Preston (1995) 'Stakeholder Theory and the Corporation: Concepts, Evidence and Implication', *Academy of Management Review*, vol. 20(1), pp. 65–91.

Dunfee, T. and T. Donaldson (1995) 'Contractarian Business Ethics', *Business Ethics Quarterly*, vol. 5, pp. 167–72.

Faillo, M. and L. Sacconi (2007) 'Norm Compliance: The Contribution of Behavioral Economics Models', in A. Innocenti and P. Sbriglia (eds), *Games, Rationality and Behavior*. London: Palgrave Macmillan.

Flannigan, R. (1989) 'The Fiduciary Obligation', *Oxford Journal of Legal Studies*, vol. 9, pp. 285–94.

Freeman, R.E. (1984) *Strategic Management: A Stakeholder Approach*, Boston, MA: Pitman.

Freeman, R.E. and P. Evans (1989) 'Stakeholder Management and the Modern Corporation: Kantian Capitalism', in T.L. Beauchamp and N. Bowie (eds), *Ethical Theory and Business*, 3rd edn. Englewood Cliffs, NJ: Prentice Hall.

Freeman, R.E. and J. McVea (2002) 'A Stakeholder Approach to Strategic Management', Working paper No. 01-02, Darden Graduate School of Business Administration.

Freeman, R.E and S. Ramakrishna Velamuri (2006) 'A New Approach to CSR Company Stakeholder Responsibility', in A. Kakabadse and M. Morsing (eds), *Corporate Social Responsibility Reconciling Aspiration and Application*, London: Palgrave Macmillan.

Fudenberg, D. and D. Levine (1986) 'Limit Games and Limit Equilibria', *Journal of Economic Theory*, Elsevier, vol. 38(2), pp. 261–79.

Fudenberg, D. and D. Levine (1989) 'Reputation and Equilibrium Selection in Games with a Patient Player', *Econometrica*, vol. 57, pp. 759–78.

Fudenberg, D. (1991) 'Explaining Cooperation and Commitment in Repeated Games', in J.J. Laffont (ed.), *Advances in Economic Theory*, 6th World Congress. Cambridge: Cambridge University Press.

Fudenberg, D. and J. Tirole (1991) *Game Theory*. Cambridge, MA: MIT Press.

Gauthier, D. (1986), *Morals by Agreement*. Oxford: Clarendon Press.

Geanakoplos, J., D. Pearce and E. Stacchetti (1989) 'Psycological Games and Sequential Rationality', *Games and Economic Behavior*, vol. 1, pp. 60–79.
Green, L. (1990) *The Authority of the State*. Oxford: Clarendon Press.
Grimalda, G. and L. Sacconi (2005) 'The Constitution of the Not-for-profit Organisation: Reciprocal Conformity to Morality', *Constitutional Political Economy*, vol. 16(3), pp. 249–76.
Grossman, S. and O. Hart (1986) 'The Costs and Benefit of Ownership: A Theory of Vertical and Lateral Integration', *Journal of Political Economy*, vol. 94, pp. 691–719.
Hansmann, H. (1996) *The Ownership of the Enterprise*. Cambridge, MA: Harvard University Press.
Hare, R. M. (1981) *Moral Thinking*. Oxford: Clarendon Press.
Harsanyi, J.C. (1977) *Rational Behaviour and Bargaining Equilibrium in Games and Social Situations*. Cambridge, MA: Cambridge University Press.
Harsanyi, J.C and R. Selten (1988) *A General Theory of Equilibrium Selection*. Cambridge, MA: MIT Press.
Hart, O. and J. Moore (1990) 'Property Rights and the Nature of the Firm', *Journal of Political Economy*, vol. 98, pp. 1119–58.
Hart, O. (1995) *Firms, Contracts and Financial Structure*. Oxford: Clarendon Press.
Hobbes, T. (1994) *Leviathan*, English edition With Selected Variants from the Latin Edition of 1668, edited by Edwin Curley. Indianapolis, IN: Hackett Publishing Company Inc.
Jensen, M.C. (2001) 'Value Maximization, Stakeholder Theory, and the Corporate Objective Function', *Journal of Applied Corporate Finance*, vol. 14(3), pp. 8–21.
Kalai, E. and M. Smordinski (1975) 'Other Solution to Nash's Bargaining Problem', *Econometrica*, vol. 43(3), pp. 880–95.
Kreps, D. (1990) 'Corporate Culture and Economic Theory', in J. Alt and K. Shepsle (eds), *Perspectives on Positive Political Economy*. Cambridge: Cambridge University Press.
Kreps, D. (1990) *Games and Economic Modelling*. Oxford: Oxford University Press.
Kreps, D. (1992) 'Static Choice in the Presence of Unforeseen Contingencies', in P. Dasgupta, D. Rae, O. Hart and E. Maskin (eds), *Economic Analysis of Markets and Games*. Cambridge, MA: MIT Press.
Lewis, D. (1969) *Convention: A Philosophical Study*. Cambridge, MA: Harvard University Press.
Maskin, E. and J. Tirole (1999) 'Unforeseen Contingencies and Incomplete Contracts', *Review of Economic Studies*, vol. 66, pp. 83–114.
McMahon, C. (1989) 'Managerial Authority', *Ethics*, vol. 100, pp. 33–53.
Meese, A.L. (2002) 'The Team Production Theory of Corporate Law: A Critical Assessment', *William and Mary Law Review*, vol. 43, pp. 1629–39.
Nash, J. (1950) 'The Bargaining Problem', *Econometrica*, vol. 18, pp. 155–62.
Posner, E.A. (2000) *Law and Social Norms*. Cambridge, MA: Harvard University Press.
Rabin, M. (1993) 'Incorporating Fairness into Game Theory', *American Economic Review*, vol. 83(5), pp. 1281–1302.
Rajan, R. and L. Zingales (1998) 'Power in a Theory of the Firm' *Quarterly Journal of Economics*, 113.
Rajan, R. and L. Zingales (2000) 'The Governance of the New Enterprise', in X. Vives (ed.), *Corporate Governance: Theoretical and Empirical Perspectives*. Cambridge: Cambridge University Press.
Rawls, J. (1971) *A Theory of Justice*. Oxford: Oxford University Press.
Rawls, J. (1993) *Political Liberalism*. New York: Columbia University Press.
Raz, J. (1985) 'Authority and Justification', *Philosophy and Public Affairs*, vol. 14(1), pp. 3–29.

Raz, J. (1999) *Engaging Reason: On the Theory of Value and Action.* Oxford: Oxford University Press.

Sacconi, L. (1991) *Etica degli affari, individui, imprese e mercati nella prospettiva dell'etica razionale.* Milano: Il Saggiatore.

Sacconi, L. (1997) *Economia, etica, organizzazione.* Bari: Laterza.

Sacconi, L. (2000) *The Social Contract of the Firm: Economics, Ethics and Organisation.* Berlin: Springer Verlag.

Sacconi, L., S. De Colle and E. Baldin (2003) 'The Q-RES Project: The Quality of Social and Ethical Responsibility of Corporations', in J. Wieland (ed.), *Standards and Audits for Ethics Management Systems: The European Perspective.* Berlin: Springer Verlag, pp. 60–117.

Sacconi, L. (2006a) 'CSR as a Model of Extended Corporate Governance, an Explanation Based on the Economic Theory of Social Contract, Reputation and Reciprocal Conformism', in F.Cafaggi (ed.), *Reframing Self-regulation in European Private Law.* London: Kluwer Law International.

Sacconi, L. (2006b) 'A Social Contract Account For CSR as Extended Model of Corporate Governance (Part I): Rational Bargaining and Justification', *Journal of Business Ethics,* vol. 68(3), pp. 259–81

Sacconi, L. (2007a) 'A Social Contract Account for CSR as Extended Model of Corporate Governance (Part II): Compliance, Reputation and Reciprocity', *Journal of Business Ethics,* vol. 75(10), pp. 77–96.

Sacconi, L. (2007b) 'Incomplete Contracts and Corporate Ethics: A Game Theoretical Model under Fuzzy Information', in F. Cafaggi, A. Nicita and U. Pagano (eds), *Legal Orderings and Economic Institutions.* London: Routledge.

Sacconi, L. (2008) 'CSR as Contractarian Model of Multi-Stakeholder Corporate Governance and the Game-Theory of its Implementation, University of Trento – Department of Economics Working paper N.18

Sacconi, L. (2009) 'Corporate Social Responsibility: Implementing a Contractarian Model of Multi-stakeholder Corporate Governance trough Game Theory', in J.P. Touffut and R. Solow (eds), *Does Company Ownership Matter?,* Centre for economic Studies Series. London: Edward Elgar Publishing.

Sacconi, L. (2010) 'A Rawlsian view of CSR and the Game Theory of its Implementation (Part II): Fairness and Equilibrium', in L. Sacconi, M. Blair, E. Freeman and A. Vercelli (eds), *Corporate Social Responsibility and Corporate Governance: The Contribution of Economic Theory and Related Disciplines.* London: Palgrave Macmillan.

Sacconi, L. (2011) 'A Rawlsian View of CRS and the Game of its Implementation (Part III): Conformism and Equilibrium Selection', in L. Sacconi and G. Degli Antoni (eds), *Social Capital, Corporate Social Responsibility, Economic Behavior and Performance.* London: Palgrave Macmillan (forthcoming).

Sacconi, L. and M. Faillo (2010) 'Conformity, Reciprocity and the Sense of Justice. How Social Contract-based Preferences and Beliefs Explain Norm Compliance: the Experimental Evidence', *Constitutional Political Economy,* vol. 21(2), pp. 171–201.

Sternberg, E. (1999) 'The Stakeholder Concept: a Mistake Doctrine, Foundation for Business Responsibility', Issue Paper no. 4, November. Available online at http://papers. ssrn.com/sol3/papers.cfm?abstract_id=263144.

Stout, L. (2006) 'Social Norms and Other-Regarding Preferences', in J.N. Drobak (ed.), *Norms and the Law.* Cambridge: Cambridge University Press.

Tirole, J. (1999) 'Incomplete Contracts: Where do We Stand?', *Econometrica,* vol. 69(4), pp. 741–81 .

Tirole, J. (2001) 'Corporate Governance', *Econometrica*, vol. 69(1), pp. 1–35.
Trebilcock, M. (1993) 'The Corporate Stakeholder Conference', *University of Toronto Law Journal*, vol. 62(3), pp. 297–793.
Watt, E.D. (1982), *Authority*. London: Croom Helm.
Wieland, J. (ed.) (2003) *Standards and Audits for Ethics Management Systems: The European Perspective*. Berlin: Springer Verlag.
Willamson, O. (1975) *Market and Hierarchies*. New York: The Free Press.
Willamson, O. (1986) *The Economic Institutions of Capitalism*. New York: The Free Press.
Zimmerman, H.J. (1991) *Fuzzy Set Theory and Its Applications*, 2nd revised edn. Dordrecht and Boston: Kluwer Academic Press.

8
A Rawlsian View of CSR and the Game Theory of its Implementation (Part II): Fairness and Equilibrium

Lorenzo Sacconi

1 Introduction

This is the second part of an comprehensive essay of the Rawlsian view of corporate social responsibility (CSR thereafter) understood as an extended model of corporate governance and objective function, based on the extension of fiduciary duties owed to the sole owner of the firm to all the company stakeholder (for this definition see part I, Sacconi, 2010a, *infra*). As in the first part, CSR is also understood as a self-sustaining institution – i.e. as a self-sustaining system of descriptive and normative beliefs consistent with the equilibrium behaviors performed repeatedly by agents in the domain of action of corporate governance (firms and their stakeholders). But equilibria are multiple in the game representing the strategic interaction among the firm and its stakeholders – modeled as a repeated trust game or some similar 'social dilemma game' (Ostrom, 1990). Thus asserting that CSR satisfies the Nash equilibrium condition as an institution is not enough. There is also an equilibrium selection problem. This the place where the Rawlsian social contract (Rawls, 1971, 1993) enters again the picture by performing its main role as normative equilibrium selection device from the *ex ante* perspective: that is, the *ex ante* impartial selection of a unique equilibrium amongst the many possible in the repeated trust game involving the firms and its stakeholders. Note that this was its second role previously suggested (see section 5 part I, and left to this part where it is treated at length), as distinguished from the role of shaping the players' expectations so that in the *ex post* perspective they are able to predict the agreed solution as the result of a cognitive process of beliefs convergence to the equilibrium, which is focused on in part III, (see Sacconi, 2011 and Sacconi 2008).

To this end (in section 2) I shall discuss at length the rehabilitation of the Rawlsian maximin principle provided by Ken Binmore's game-theoretical reformulation of the social contract (Binmore, 1984, 1989, 1991, 1994, 1998, 2005).

Contrary to the belief that Rawls's view was utopian, it is shown that the maximin principle provides the best account of the social contract under the assumption that in a 'state of nature' any agreement on principles for institutions must be self-sustainable. In other words, to be self-sustainable and incentive-compatible, the agreement must be egalitarian, or in the best interest of the worst-off player.

Such an unconventional result has overarching implications also for the constitutional contract on the firm's governance and control structures. This is a theory to make sense of the idea of extended fiduciary duties put forward in previous works (Sacconi, 1997, 2000, 2006a,b, 2007). Its main point was that the stakeholders' constitutional agreement (seen as the rational solution of an original bargaining game) will complement the efficient control structure with further social responsibilities toward non-controlling stakeholders, enabling them to participate in the surplus created by joint production through a redress rule against the abuse of authority (section 3). However, when a constitutional bargaining situation is considered such that the only feasible constitutions are allocations of exclusive property and control rights, a strong imbalance of bargaining power is inevitable, so that asymmetry in the final surplus distribution will reflect the asymmetry of decision rights. Then, an outcome corresponding to the arrangement of rights (ownership and control rights plus redress rights with the attached fiduciary duties) that immunizes non-controlling stakeholders against abuse of authority, and gives them an opportunity to participate in the surplus created by joint production, may not belong in the equilibrium space of the constitutional choice game (section 4). This means that the outcome of such a redress mechanism cannot be obtained in equilibrium (violating the self-sustainability condition).

The idea is that each constitution corresponds to a set of feasible (equilibrium) outcomes, and each of them comprises a post-constitutional bargaining solution within its feasible set of outcomes. Different constitutions – as they allocate rights of control to one player or another – will have post-constitutional bargaining solutions differently favorable to one or another player, but not equally favorable to all. Agreement at the constitutional stage selects the allocation of exclusive rights of ownership and control endowed with the most efficient post-constitutional solution in terms of incentives for the accomplishment of specific investments and in terms of wealth maximization. Players who forgo control in order to make agreement on the most efficient control structure possible, then need to be redressed through fiduciary duties. Implementation of such duties is an outcome coinciding with an equitable compromise (a linear combination) of the post-constitutional rational solutions preferred by different stakeholders as they relate to different allocations of rights, some in favor of one stakeholder, some in favor of another. But when the assumption is made that the only feasible outcomes (corresponding to equilibria) are those belonging to the outcome set of constitutions asymmetrically allocating ownership and control rights, then the quite obvious possibility arises that the symmetric outcome of an equitable redress mechanism does not correspond to any feasible outcome.

Many scholars of corporate governance accustomed to accepting second-best solutions would then be ready to give up fairness and extended fiduciary duties in order to achieve nothing more than the most efficient constitution of the firm. Remarkably enough, application of the Rawls–Binmore theory to the social contract on corporate governance structures yields quite the opposite suggestion (see section 5). In order to be consistent with the requirement of self sustainability, the impartial agreement must select the constitution with the best egalitarian solution among all the alternative feasible constitutions. That is to say, a constitutional arrangement must be chosen such that, within its feasible outcome set, the solution that maximizes the position of the worst-off stakeholder is accepted because this is the best egalitarian solution with respect to all the egalitarian solutions available under alternative constitutions. Pareto dominance, as a principle of unanimous agreement, is therefore to be applied only to the comparison of feasible egalitarian solutions under alternative constitutions. The social contract will select the constitution with the relatively most Pareto-efficient egalitarian solution. What is most important here is that this result follows straightforwardly from the requirement that the social contract should select an outcome belonging to the set of (impartial) equilibria, i.e. a self-sustaining institution.

Moreover, the Rawlsian theory of corporate governance refutes much of the traditional wisdom in the domain of corporate governance as it has been viewed by both new institutional economics and law & economics (section 6). Quite unconventionally again, fairness precedes both efficiency and welfare maximization (contrary to Kaplow and Shavell), and it also precedes aggregate transaction costs minimization (against Hansmann 1988, 1996). Even libertarians like Hayek's followers – who typically believe that rules of behavior should spontaneously emerge from endogenous motivations respecting free choice – will have to concede that under the simple ethical constraint of impartiality egalitarianism is a natural consequence of the self sustainability of institutions in the domain of corporate governance.

2   Normative selection of an equilibrium: Binmore vindicates Rawls

By 'normative role' I mean the function of a contractarian fairness principle in giving impartial reasons for singling out a unique equilibrium solution amongst the many possible. Note that the normative principle is here used to choose an equilibrium point within the equilibrium set of the game to be played afterwards in the implementation phase. The perspective is still that of an *ex ante* impartial choice, but it now concerns equilibria, that is, game solutions that are self-enforceable.

In order to accomplish this endeavor a social contract theory is needed as an *ex ante* equilibrium selection tool. Ken Binmore has provided such a theory as a game-theoretical reinterpretation of John Rawls's famous maximin principle of justice (Binmore, 2005).[1]

2.1   The game of life

The social contract on constitutional principles takes place against the background of a *state of nature* called the 'game of life' (Binmore 2005). Assume for simplicity that there are two players; and then that it is a repeated game, for example a repeated asymmetrical prisoner's dilemma (PD) or something similar (for example, a repeated Trust Game, whereby the second player has an advantage over the first because he may abuse her trust, whereas she can only protect herself by refraining from any cooperation). Its payoff set is a convex-compact space resulting from attaching the players' average discounted payoff to each repeated game strategy profile mixing both players' cooperation and cheating in whatever proportion along the repetitions of the stage games. To exemplify, the payoff space represents outcomes of profiles whereby both players completely cooperate, they both never cooperate, they choose cooperating and cheating with the same frequency, as well as profiles whereby one party adopts cooperation more frequently (in whatever proportion) than the other and vice versa. As a whole, the payoff space (in terms of average discounted payoffs) amounts to the set of all the convex combination in whatever proportion of the stage game pure payoff vectors. According to the folk theorem, the equilibrium set of this game again in terms of average discounted payoffs is represented by an extensive region of the convex compact payoff space (see Fudenberg and Tirole, 1991).[2] On the south-west side of the payoff space (possibly at the utility axes' origin), in correspondence to the profile 'never cooperate throughout all the repetitions', there is the worst possible equilibrium point for both the players. The payoff space's region to the north-east of this point is made up of points corresponding to equilibrium strategy profiles affording the players any non-negative surplus over the worst possible equilibrium result. In this perspective, the social contract works as a way to single out principles able to select just one amongst the many equilibrium profiles of the repeated game, affording some mutual advantage to both the players.

To keep things simple, let us again assume that there are only two players. The repeated game is played by player 1 in the role of Adam, A for short, and player 2, in the role of Eve, E for short. Adam is systematically in an advantageous position over Eve because of some natural or historical brute fact (natural power, brute force). Hence the repeated game equilibrium set is Z_{AE} (from the

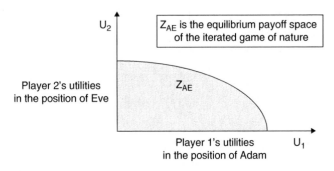

Figure 8.1   The repeated game equilibrium set Z_{AE}

name of the players – Adam and Eve; see Figure 8.1), which is an asymmetric space. This means that within the equilibrium set Z_{AE} of the repeated game there are equilibrium pairs advantaging A over E or E over A in the relative sense; but in the absolute sense the equilibrium pairs preferred by player A give him much higher payoffs than those given to player E by the equilibrium pairs she prefers. The best chances of profiting from the game are quite different for the two players. In other words, there are many outcomes in which Adam gets a much higher payoff than Eve, whereas symmetrical outcomes, giving Eve a similar higher payoff, are not possible.

The *game of life* is repeated in the long run. As it is repeated, some details may occasionally change as new generations of players join. Thus, there is a chance that a player 1 is sometimes called upon to play in the position of Eve, while a player 2 is called upon to play in the position of Adam. Evolutionary games typically select players at random from given populations (viz. players from population 1 and players from population 2) to play any role in each repetition of a given. The situation is such that throughout the evolutionary history of humankind or societies, players that usually play as weak stakeholders may also sometimes (even though with small probability) occupy the role of the owner of a firm and vice versa. Consider that player 1's progeny consists of many more players taking the role of Adam with respect to Eve but, due to a mutation at some point in time, Mother Nature has selected for a while only player 1's sons to play the role of Eve. By chance, these Eves may play against player 2's heirs, who are Adams. Hence player 1 and player 2 have undergone a permutation of their roles across these game and they may retain memories of this position exchange through their evolutionary history. This is the evolutionary basis for the capacity to assume the other's perspective and develop empathetic preferences. Put in neuroscience language, player A's 'mirror neurons' fire when A sees poor E getting such a modest payoff x that it as if it was player A himself who had received that same payoff x.

2.2   The game of morals

All this is simply preparatory (i.e. gives an evolutionary basis) for introduction of the social contract as an *ex ante* generally acceptable and stable equilibrium selection mechanism. Following the Rawlsian idea of a hypothetical 'original position', Binmore calls the relevant choice situation 'the game of morals', which re-elaborates the game of life from an impersonal, empathetic and impartial perspective (Binmore, 2005). It is a hypothetical choice situation whereby each player consider the entire set of possible equilibrium outcomes of the repeated game as if he/she were able to occupy each role (Adam or Eve) under each outcome and to receive each possible role-related payoff from each outcome. Consequently, neither of the players identifies with his/her role, and each of them (player 1 or 2) takes it for granted that there is an equal chance of occupying the positions of both A or E interchangeably. These are the typical assumptions made when the original position is seen as a choice under the 'veil of ignorance'. However, there are distinct hypotheses that must be introduced step by step.

2.3   Impersonality and interchangeability of the players' positions

First of all, impersonality is the capacity to consider not just one's own narrow personal point of view and to assume every possible personal perspective when assessing the outcome space – i.e. both players 1 and 2 view the decision problem from the personal perspectives of both Adam and Eve. This requirement is captured by the geometrical construction of a payoff space translation with respect to the Cartesian axes representing player 1 and 2's utilities (payoffs) respectively. Given the initial payoff space Z_{AE}, the translation generates a new payoff space Z_{EA}. For each 'physical' outcome of the original game (represented by a point in Z_{AE}) this translation generates an outcome (a point in Z_{EA}) with the players 1's and 2's social and personal positions (A and E respectively) symmetrically replaced. So that player 2 (ex-E, now in the role of A') obtains exactly the outcome that was got by player 1 in the role of A 'before the translation', whereas player 1 (ex-A, now in the role of E') gets exactly the outcome that were got by player 2 when s/he was in the position of E. Hence, for every equilibrium point in the original outcome set Z_{AE}, whatever the equilibrium outcome afforded to player 1 in the initial representation, the same outcome will be afforded to player 2 under the translated outcome set Z_{EA}, and vice versa (see Binmore, 2005).

2.4   Empathetic preferences and interpersonal utility comparisons

However, one point must be raised here. Players 1 and 2 are just labels for individual players, but a complete description of a player's preference can only be given when s/he takes a particular social role and personal position as Adam or Eve. In assuming the role/position of Eve, player 1 (normally Adam) tests his psychological capacity for empathetic identification with the preferences held by player 2, who usually plays in the role/position of Eve.

Consider first what is not an exercise of empathy (but autism – as Binmore suggests, see Binmore, 2005). Although player 2, now in the role A', receives the consequences of player 1 when he was A, she is incapable of evaluating them in terms of the same preference as player 1's in the role of A, and to compare these preferences and their utility measure with the preferences he had in the role of E. On the contrary, she keeps the preferences and utility measure she had when she was in the role of E. Hence the translated Z_{EA} need not be a symmetrical image of Z_{AE}.

However, this is not the proper manner to construct the original position, which is designed to enable the players to exercise their capacity for empathetic identification. What is required of player 1, while he is E', is to understand what it means for player 2 to be in the E role with her own preferences, and vice versa. Under empathetic preference, player 1 (respectively, player 2), when he (resp. she) takes the position E' (resp. A') experiences being in this position with the preference that another player had when she (he) was in position E (resp. A). They thus carry out interpersonal comparisons of utility, which means that player 1, in the roles of both A or E', uses the same utility unit to represent and compare his *empathetic* preferences with his *personal* preference between the two positions (see Harsanyi 1977). The capacity for empathetic preference is a distinctive trait that makes human psychology what it is. Binmore assumes (and I follow him) that biological evolution has equipped us not only with a capacity – maybe our "mirror neurons" – for empathetic introspection and simulation but also with the competence to represent different individuals' preferences in a fairly similar manner, that is, by means of fairly similar utility units (Binmore 2005).

What we have now are two spaces X_{AE} and X_{EA}, one the *symmetrical* image of the other (see Figure 8.2). Space X_{EA} results from the *symmetrical* translation of all points of the first space into (symmetrical) points of the second. Recall that in the game with payoff space X_{AE} player 1 is A (with payoff measured on the horizontal axis), and player 2 is E (with payoff measured on the vertical axis). Under the translation, player 1 (ex A) becomes E' (with utilities identical to E) and player 2 (ex E) becomes A' (with utilities identical to A). Owing to the symmetry of the translation, for each outcome x in X_{AE}, where the two players get payoff x_A, x_E, respectively for player 1 and 2, we may find within the space X_{EA} a point $x' = (x'_{E'}, x'_{A'})$ where payoffs are simply exchanged between the players 1 and 2, i.e. such that player 1 gets $x'_{E'} = x_E$, and player 2 gets $x'_{A'} = x_A$. Hence, exactly what was got by player 1 (as A) now belongs to player 2 (as A'), while the payoff got before by player 2 (as E) is now obtained by player 1 (as E').

2.5   Impartiality and solution invariance

This construction allows each player to put himself into the shoes (A or E roles) of the other player and vice versa. But now that the players are *impersonal* – that

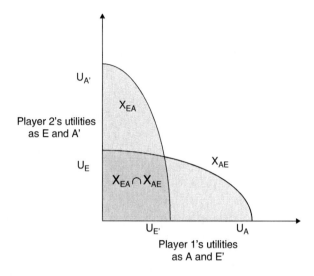

Figure 8.2 Symmetric translation of the payoff space X_{AE} with respect to the individual utility axes, so that the utility function U_A is replaced by $U_{A'} = U_E$ and vice versa

is, they properly (empathetically) consider the decision problem from every personal point of view, but do not identify themselves with whatever personal perspective – what is required is that they give an *impartial* solution to the problem; a solution that is not biased to the advantage of either player, and does not put any personal role in a position of differential advantage with respect to others. A natural consequence for the equilibrium selection problem is that the solution must have some *invariance* under the position replacement, so that the player can continue to recognize and choose it in both positions. Impartiality thus simply implies that the solution must be invariant under this payoff space translation, because the solution has to be accepted by each player under both the roles s/he will occupy, i.e. it cannot be contingent on a particular role-position s/he occupies. This seems to mean that each player must get from the solution the same 'acceptable' payoff whatever the role (A or E) he takes, i.e. whatever the party's position he takes in the game. Thus an *impartial* solution is an equilibrium point that allows each player to achieve a payoff which is invariant, whatever the role the player happens to occupy. By contrast, a solution (given a particular representation of the game payoff space) is said to *depend* upon the *particular personal and strategic position* that players hold in the game if implementing the corresponding equilibrium yields payoffs that the players could not obtain if the same equilibrium point were implemented under the symmetric translation of the payoff space – that is, under the symmetric replacement of the players with respect to each outcome. Translation invariance must be satisfied in order for the equilibrium point selected to be normatively considered *the solution*.

It is fairly clear that this property is satisfied if the initial payoff space X_{AE} is restricted to the bisector of the Cartesian plan, that is, if the outcome space is constrained to satisfy the condition that any outcome is mapped onto itself by a symmetric translation of the outcome space with respect to the Cartesian axes. But, of course, this is very far from being the general case (consider, however, section 5 where this case is relevant). In general, a payoff space, whether symmetrical or otherwise, will contain many outcomes that under a payoff space symmetric translation will be mapped onto another point in the Cartesian plan by inverting individual payoffs in the payoff vector. In other words, invariance would require a solution to be located on the bisector, which seems at first glance to be a very restrictive condition with respect to payoff spaces in general.

To be sure, symmetric and asymmetric payoffs spaces are not on an equal footing in this respect. A symmetrical outcome space can be simply assumed to have a symmetrical solution. When an outcome space is perfectly symmetrical, there is no reason to imagine that there are major differences between the players. Nor there is any need to impose explicit impersonality and impartiality between players who are completely equal in any respect: they will directly jump to the egalitarian solution, which is typically on the bisector where any symmetric translation of the outcome space will result in outcome invariance (this was also John Nash's intuition, see Nash (1950)).

But now assume that the equilibrium space is asymmetrical, as X_{AE} in fact is. Why not admit that, without an explicit requirement of impartiality and impersonality, unequal self-interested players would produce by their bargaining process whatever result other than a perfectly equal one? Thus, assume that any player would *ex ante* accept (under a given representation of the payoff space) any equilibrium point but an egalitarian one as the solution. Under the payoff space translation X_{EA} this equilibrium point translates into a *different* point outside the original payoff space. Once the player positions have been exchanged, the payoff space translation identifies a point corresponding to the same equilibrium, but this point (a payoff vector) does not afford each player the same payoff as before (simply because it replaces the payoff of the previously 'fortunate' player with that of the previously 'unfortunate' one, and vice versa). Thus the solution cannot be invariant.

2.6   Veil of ignorance, and equally probable mixtures

The invariance condition in the case of a large space with numerous asymmetric outcomes is regained by introducing another step in the construction of the 'original position', i.e. by imposing (following Harsanyi and not Rawls on this point) the probabilistic interpretation of the 'veil of ignorance'. The veil of ignorance, according to this version (see Binmore, 2005), consists of complete (probabilistic) uncertainty about the roles of players 1 and 2 (A or E) in the game, i.e. complete uncertainty about which of the two asymmetric spaces, X_{AE} and X_{EA}, will actually take place. This amounts to saying that each space has probability ½ to represent the actual outcome space of the game. If the players were required to choose a joint strategy that produces the outcome x in the outcome space X_{AE}, they would consider that this choice will achieve the outcome x only with probability ½, whereas it may also achieve by probability ½ the symmetric outcome x' where the players' positions are mutually exchanged.

The probabilistic version of the veil of ignorance implies that when a player chooses in the original position s/he must always account for the expected value of any decision. For any selection of a particular equilibrium point, this amounts to always considering the equally probable mixture of the payoffs s/he gets under that particular outcome and its symmetric translation. We are thus back to the 45° bisector, where all the expected values of equally probable mixtures of symmetric outcomes belonging to spaces X_{AE} and X_{EA} do in fact lie.

This is what gives invariance to the solution also in the case of an initially asymmetric payoff space: when a player considers as the candidate solution an equilibrium point s in X_{AE}, s/he must also account for its translation s' into X_{EA}, and in fact s/he takes as the actual candidate solution payoff the mid-point on the straight line representing the linear combination of the two outcomes s and s'. What matters for this choice is the expected value of the equally-probable combination of his/her payoff for the equilibrium s in X_{AE} and his/her payoff for its symmetric translation s' in X_{EA}.

2.7 Feasibility

Decision-making under the veil of ignorance raises the further question as to whether equally probable combinations of symmetric outcomes are themselves *feasible* terms of agreement. The question is whether is it feasible to agree on a jointly randomized pair of strategy combinations that generates two outcomes with the same probability, in such a way that one may consider at least *ex ante* the expected value as the utility that one will actually receive from selecting the joint strategy combinations. This makes sense only if one is confident that, whatever outcome may be selected by the random device attached to the pair of strategy combinations (or outcomes), it will be put into practice. Put differently, whatever outcome is selected, it will be automatically enforced. The opposite hypothesis is that when the time at last arrives that the agreement must be implemented by a random choice of the actual outcome, if the selected outcome does not satisfy a player, the latter can renegotiate it. Typically, player 1, when by chance an outcome is selected in which he is E', may ask to renegotiate the outcome selected in order to have a new chance of occupying the luckiest role of A as an outcome is selected. After all, in the game of life he *de facto* plays in the role of A (see Binmore 2005).

The question would be simply solved if the mid-point of the probabilistic mixture was an equilibrium point on its own. If in correspondence to this mid-point there is an equilibrium point formed of strategies (pure or mixed) that in practice the players may adopt in the *ex post* game, then that equilibrium can be selected in order to generate an impartial solution. I would say that this is not beyond any doubt, for player could maintain doubts about the obedience of other real-life players to an action dictated by the random mechanism. However, there is no incentive in this case to defect from the outcome selected by the random mechanism. The case is different if the 'mid-point' results from the convex combination (joint randomization) of two points each alternatively belonging to one of the two basic payoff spaces, but it actually falls outside both the basic spaces and their intersection. Certainly, such mid-points of equally probable mixtures falling outside both the space X_{AE} and X_{EA} cannot be equilibria in the 'game of life'.

2.8   The *Deus ex machina* hypothesis

Here a basic methodological decision must be made. Joint randomization is an admissible operation within the context of cooperative games, where joint strategies (plans of action) can be always randomized by an interpersonally valid random mechanism without fear that individual players will act according to separate mixed strategies in practice. But cooperative games assume that an exogenous mechanism will enforce whatever agreement on any jointly randomized outcomes: this amounts to what can be called a *Deus ex machina* hypothesis.

At the methodological level, however, the modeller must decide whether or not it is appropriate to assume – or whether or not the players actually believe in – the existence of God as an external enforcer for whichever agreement to which the players subscribe in the 'original position'. If God exists, then the outcome space will expand significantly because it will also include all the linear combinations of any pair of points in X_{AE} and X_{EA}, i.e. the bargaining game in the original position will become the convex hull of all the points in the union of X_{AE} and X_{EA} – which is necessarily a symmetric space of expected payoff (see Figure 8.3).

In this case there is an open choice among a wide variety of principles. For example, the utilitarian solution seems reasonable because it suggests taking as the solution the point in each space where the utility sum is maximized, and then considering their mean value. We thus do not have to concern ourselves with what the players will do when the veil of ignorance is removed and hence face the situation where one player is reduced to extreme poverty in order to maximize the utility sum.

We are looking for contractarian principles. Assume that under each representation of the payoff space players agree by rational bargaining on the relevant Nash bargaining solution. Hence, the equally probable combination of the two Nash bargaining solutions (NBS), each belonging to space X_{AE} or X_{EA}

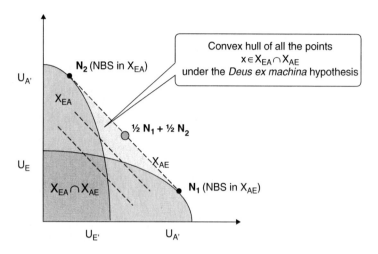

Figure 8.3 Veil of ignorance under convexity

respectively, seems to be the obvious candidate. This means that player 2 will take it for granted that s/he will be afforded the payoff resulting at the mid-point along the straight line joining his/her payoffs at the two NBS, N1 and N2, each belonging to the relevant payoff space X_{AE} or X_{EA} respectively. What s/he gets in fact is his/her expected payoff at the point $½ N1 + ½ N2$, a point that requires the presence of a *Deus ex machina* to be implemented because it does not belong either to X_{AE} or to X_{EA}.

Nevertheless, believing that God will always be ready to play the role of an exter-nal enforcer is not the most appropriate hypothesis for a decision in the original position. The idea of a 'state of nature' would be pointless in this case. In fact it means maintaining that only agreements corresponding to equilibrium points of the underlying non-cooperative game of life can be expected to be implemented, because they are self-sustaining and does not require any previous authority to impose them. In other words, the game considered here is non-cooperative. Thus one is *not* allowed to generate from the original outcome space and its symmetric translation the convex hull of all their components (see Binmore, 1987).

It follows that both the equally probable combinations of the Utilitarian and the Nash bargaining solutions are ruled out because they do not belong to the payoff space intersection $X_{AE} \cap X_{EA}$.

To explain, assume that a random mechanism is agreed upon, and it ran-domly selects the payoff distribution corresponding to N2 where player 1 is in the role of E'. Since, in the actual game of life player 1 is in fact occupying A's role, he can decline to comply with the randomly selected solution N2 because it is not enforced by itself. Thus, in the event that the players agreed on the NBS equally probable combination under the veil of ignorance, this would simply amount to player 1 getting his Adam's payoff for N1 with probability one, because his alternative N2 payoff (Eve's payoff) cannot be enforced if it is selected. If the coin was to fall on the side that would dictate the payoff of A' to player 2, player 1 would simply refuse to comply by asserting that his actual role in the *game of life* is playing as A. Why, then, should player 2 enter the original position. It seems cheap talk without any relevance to the players' actual behavior. Summing up, there is no scope for agreeing under the veil of ignorance on outcomes that cannot be enforced.

2.9   No Deus ex machina

Contrary to the conventional wisdom, this does not require giving up either the original position or the veil of ignorance. Binmore suggests retaining symmetric payoff translations (impersonality), empathetic preferences and equally probable mixtures (impartiality), but to skip the hypothesis of a *Deus ex machina* ready to serve as an external enforcer, thus adding the requirement of *self-sustainability* (Binmore 2005). This consists of restricting the selection of the acceptable solution only to within the *intersection* of the original outcome space and its symmetric translation i.e. $X_{AE} \cap X_{EA}$. Any selection within this set, in fact, does not create the feasibility problem just considered because any point in the intersection set corresponds to an equilibrium point that is always existent as long as it belongs to both the original and the translated outcome sets, viz. an equilibrium outcome that would always materialize if either X_{AE} or X_{EA} were actually the case.

Thus one way to satisfy the condition of solution invariance under the symmetric replacement of players with respect to the payoff space follows quite naturally. As before, the veil of ignorance entails considering as admissible only equally probable mixtures of each player's payoffs derivable from an equilibrium point and its symmetric translation. Necessarily, the solution will be a point on the 45° straight line (the bisector) connecting the origin of the intersection space $X_{AE} \cap X_{EA}$ to its north-east frontier, where all the admitted equally probable mixtures lie (see Figure 8.4). Each outcome resident on the bisector is invariant under the symmetric translation of the outcome space. But each of such 'mid-points' also necessarily identifies one equilibrium that the players can *ex post* achieve by a feasible pure or mixed strategy as long as it belongs to the intersection set $X_{AE} \cap X_{EA}$.

Moreover, consider that the space $X_{AE} \cap X_{EA}$ is also a symmetric space on its own. It is, in fact, the collection of all those pairs of symmetrical points – like x and y generated one from the other by a symmetrical payoff space translation – which are at the same time elements of both the spaces X_{AE} and X_{EA} separately. Thus $X_{AE} \cap X_{EA}$ coincides with the symmetric sub-set of each space X_{EA} and X_{EA}.

Given the symmetry of the payoff space, bargaining theory becomes extraordinarily simple. The bargaining solution must be taken on the 45° bisector

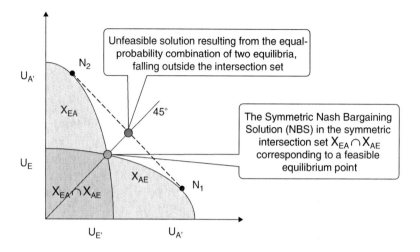

Figure 8.4   Egalitarian feasible solution and efficient unfeasible solution

deriving from the origin at the point where it intersects with the north-east boundary of the payoff space. Being on a straight line deriving from the status quo and pointing north-east simply means that the solution provides mutual gains to both the players with respect to the status quo. Being on the bisector means that mutual gains are equal. This depends on the symmetry of the payoff space. Given any agreement on which a player may insist, there is a symmetric agreement in the same outcome space, with the same payoffs exchanged between the players, on which the other party may insist as well. The reasons for insisting on each side are equally strong (under whichever definition) and would be perfectly balanced. It is then reasonable to expect rational bargaining to lead to an agreement located at the midpoint of the linear combination joining any symmetric pair of possible agreements. Lastly, that the solution is at the intersection point with the north-east boundary simply implies Pareto optimality – which means that equal mutual gains must be as high as possible.

All of these qualifications seem very natural for the selection of a single equilibrium point within the intersection set $X_{AE} \cap X_{EA}$ given its symmetry. The result is the Nash Bargaining Solution (NBS) for the special case of a symmetrical payoff space, which is also the same as the *egalitarian solution*: the surplus over the status quo point is distributed to players in (feasible) maximal equal shares. Since, in our construction, we have assumed interpersonal utility comparability, this means that the players get substantially the same amount of welfare or the same level of needs satisfaction over the status quo.

2.10   General validity of the egalitarian solution

However, our starting point was not a symmetric payoff space. Hence the decision to restrict the solution to the symmetric intersection set $X_{AE} \cap X_{EA}$ must rest on some reasons direct or indirect in favour of *egalitarianism*. To appreciate this, consider that egalitarianism requires that if it is wanted to reach an agreement under the 'original position', the agreed solution must be such that the players' payoffs are invariant to the symmetrical permutation of the players' positions and roles. The solution is a point in the payoff space such that the individual payoff allotted to each player must remain perfectly unchanged under the symmetric translation of the payoff space with respect to the players' utility-Cartesian axes.

This invariance condition is much stronger than the simple requirement that the *solution concept* (and its corresponding maximum value, i.e. the maximal value resulting from aggregation from whatever social welfare function) be invariant under the mutual replacement of players with respect to their roles and positions. In this second case, whereas the value of the solution function would remain unchanged (for example, the outcome where the Nash bargaining product is maximal is invariant to any independent affine utility transformation of the payoff space and hence also to its symmetrical translation from X_{AE} to X_{EA}), the payoff allocated to each player would vary according to the translation. Hence, in general, players would not preserve the same payoffs that they had before the replacement.

By contrast, the egalitarian solution amounts to saying that the anonymity of social roles does not justify any inequality of distribution. 'Who gets what' cannot depend on who gets the social role of Adam or Eve, no matter that the assignment of social roles is anonymous, and both player 1 and player 2 think it equally possible to be in A or E's roles. Egalitarianism seems to rest on a more basic idea of equality among people, which is antecedent to the differences (utility function, strategy set, etc.) associated with their A or E social roles. It seems to reflect a basic feature of the original position where all these difference are weighted out. Only perfect equality is acceptable in the original position because if all the positions must be mutually interchanged, nobody is able to claim a payoff that others could not also claim. And in case the claims each player would make from any different standpoints were mutually incompatible, they should be compromised by an equally probable mixture of the two.

However, the *egalitarian distribution* does not necessarily follow directly from the *equality* of participants in the original position. The main argument in its favor is indirect. Stability, which is not an ethical assumption, is sufficient here. In fact, in order to make such agreement *credible*, it may be constrained to belong to the symmetric subset of the two equally possible spaces of claimable outcomes. Owing to the symmetry of this space the solution is necessarily egalitarian. But what requires a symmetric payoff space, which in turn implies egalitarianism, is the *ex post* feasibility and stability of outcomes. Hence *stability* plus *impersonality* (symmetric interchangeability) and *impartiality* (equally probable mixtures) leads to the egalitarian solution.

2.11 Rawls vindicated also to non-Kantians

By this route Binmore vindicates Rawls and his proposal of the maximin principle as a choice rule in the original position also when it is seen in the apparently alien context of a game-theoretic social contract (Binmore, 1991, 1998, 2005). In fact Eve's payoffs, those allotted to the disadvantaged player, are maximized within both the payoff spaces X_{AE} and X_{EA}. When players 1 and 2, through their position permutation, take Eve's role under the alternative label of E and E' respectively, they both have their payoffs maximized.

It should be noted, however, that the *egalitarian* and *maximin solutions* are based neither on a direct intuition in favor of such payoffs distributions nor on an extreme form of risk aversion (as Rawls himself seemed to think). According to Binmore, they depend on the requirement of the *ex post stability* of any agreement reached in the original position when joined with the genuine ethical requirements of symmetrical place permutation of players, veil of ignorance and the capacity for empathetic preferences (Binmore 2005).

In essence, an agreement in the original position must be taken *seriously*. Each player – the disadvantaged one in particular – is thus entitled to decline an agreement that renders the impersonality and impartiality of the solution purely illusory due to its *ex post* instability. Solution invariance under the exchange of the players' position with respect to the payoff space, and equally probable mixtures of symmetric outcomes, are hypotheses that any credible agreement in the original position must satisfy *effectively*, rather than fictitiously. But this would not be possible if the agreement fell outside the intersection set wherein all agreements can be implemented in equilibrium. Hence, the disadvantaged player has veto power over such an illusory agreement. This point resembles the one that Rawls made by stating that in the original position – due to the recognized moral arbitrariness of inequality in general – the disadvantaged party also has *veto power* over all the inequalities that do not maximize his/her benefit. Here, alternatively, s/he has the capacity to veto every agreement that cannot be trusted as fair because its implementation will necessarily turn out to be biased in favor of the advantaged player.

3 Constitutional contract over the control structure of the firm

What does this Rawlsian social contract theory tell us about the selection of a CSR model of corporate governance and a firm control structure? In order to give an answer I need to return to the theory of constitutional contract on control structures of the firm, which was at the basis of my previous definition of the normative multi-stakeholder model of corporate governance (see Sacconi, 1991, 1997, 2000, 2006a,b, 2007a, 2008). It is a contractarian theory of an *ex ante* choice concerning the control structure of the firm seen as the firm's 'constitution' (see also Vanberg, 1992). The model rests on the analogy between social contract theories used to justify on one hand the legal ordering by constitutional contract (Buchanan, 1975; Brock, 1979) and the mutually advantageous moral rules of a society 'by agreement' (Gauthier 1986), and on the other hand the economic theory of the efficient control structure of the firm based on the idea of contractual incompleteness (Williamson, 1975; Grossman and Hart, 1986; Hart and Moore, 1990; Hart, 1995).

3.1   A multi-stage decision model

As far as the latter is concerned, this model is a multi-step decision model with timing, involving the potential members of a productive coalition S. At time t = 1 the allocation of rights is decided, and this determines the control structure exerted over the productive coalition S. At this step, however, not only are the ownership structure and the related residual rights of control allocated but also any other right and responsibility owed to non-controlling stakeholder such that they give them any level of protection against the 'absolute power' of those in the position to make residual decisions (here there is a departure from the standard incomplete contract model).

At time t = 2 the right-holding individuals (both owners and non-owners) take specific investment decisions with a view to the completion of subsequent transactions. Such investment decisions cannot be required in the ex ante contract because they cannot be *ex ante* described in a formal contract.

At time t = 3 events may occur which are also unforeseen by the initial contract. These events reveal the possibility of further decisions that may be essential to the value of investments already undertaken. For example, these decision are essential for implementing some technical innovation that the foregoing investment has made possible. Such decisions may physically pertain to one player or another. However, '*ex ante*' rights allocate control over these decisions in an indirect way. A party in the position of an authority in the firm may order those parties who do not formally control the firm but are in the physical condition to implement decisions, to execute actions chosen by the first party. In this way, an investment – when introduced at time 2 – is exploited so as to derive surplus value from it.

At time t = 4 a new bargaining game begins, defined for each allocation of rights, given whatever investment decisions were taken at time 2. Time 4 bargaining concerns decisions revealed as possible at step 3, according to control rights and responsibility. How time 4 bargaining is resolved depends on the allocation of rights at time 1. Thus, according to the firm's constitution, ex post bargaining will be in favour of one or other of the participants, in the sense that these will be able to appropriate shares of the corporate surplus depending on how may rights (ownership, control, protection, verification, accountability etc.) they have acquired at step 1.

Here the analogy with constitutional economy theory emerges: in fact, the overall collective decision problem is modeled as a compounded two-step bargaining game: an *ex ante* constitutional bargaining game G_C on the 'constitution' and an *ex post* 'post-constitutional' bargaining game G_I on the collective agreement concerning the surplus's distribution amongst the coalition S members. First, the constitutional bargaining game G_C is carried out (at time t = 1), when what is at stake is a 'constitution': i.e. a subset of the logically possible strategies open to each player at time 1 is singled out. This set will constrain the bargaining strategy set open to each player at the post-constitutional stage. Because it is a restriction on the initial set of strategies, and defines a subset of strategies available to each player, it can be understood as a 'constitution', that is, a delimitation of the natural liberties of each player that institutes the correlated set of rights and responsibilities held by all the other players. The not obvious point here is that the first agreement concerns not just a single joint strategy profile, but a set of possible joint strategies. Accordingly, the G_C game is a game that does not single out a joint strategy but an entire set (subset) of joint strategies that could constitute the possible actions and agreements allowed by the given constitution. Second, a subsequent bargaining game is played (at time t = 4) within the limits of the given constitution, and wherein the players make a choice among the available joint strategies allowed by the agreement reached at the constitutional step.

The constitutional economics aspect of the model introduces an *ex ante* social contract on the allotment of rights at step 1 as a bargaining game; whereas bargaining was admitted by the incomplete contract model only at step 4 (where also the constitutional economics model posits the post-constitutional bargaining) so that the *ex ante* decision remained quite unspecified – a somewhat mysterious collective decision based on the intent to minimize transaction coasts.

However, the analogy with the incomplete contract model explains why the constitutional contract is a two-stage decision. The social contract is incomplete: it cannot provide for whatever particular decision in detail. On the contrary, it only provides for the *ex ante* assignation of decision rights. In the second stage, therefore, decision rights influence the post-constitutional division of the surplus by means of post-constitutional bargaining, after investments have been undertaken and also after new decision opportunities have been revealed.

Nevertheless, as in much of the incomplete contract literature, here the simplifying assumption will be made that a resolution in terms of surplus division can be assigned to each constitution at the first stage, so to speak. Given each constitution, players can forecast the single post-constitutional solution for that constitution in terms of post-constitutional bargaining: a fact that the player can assess by looking onward from the first stage in order to decide the constitution on which s/he wants to agree. Put simply, at the first step the game is split into numerous subgames, each defined in terms of a given subset of the basic strategy space. Then a solution is computed for each subgame. Hence the overall range of the subgame solutions is assessed and the different *ex post* solutions are compared at the constitutional stage (*ex ante* decision) in order to give a basis for the constitutional choice in terms of each constitution's outcome. This is a strong simplification indeed, because it should be admitted that, owing to proper contract incompleteness, the realization of the possible available amounts of surplus (and hence the payoff value related to each concrete joint strategy) must be learnt only after specific investments have been made, and after the revelation of unforeseen events that allow surpluses to be made out of investments. These facts, because they cannot be included in the contract, would be unforeseen at the first stage, and hence would not allow the onward assessment of alternative constitutions in terms of their final payoffs distribution.

This would require modeling the constitutional contract as a choice with vague payoff variables (maybe fuzzy payoffs) – which is also consistent with our solution of the constructive/cognitive problem in part I of this essay (see Sacconi 2010a, *infra*). – i.e. the specification of the vague game form of the underlying trust game played by stakeholders and firms under unforeseen contingencies. In fact, in that unforeseen events are defined as fuzzy sets, understood as application domains (sets) for principles of behavior (corresponding to strategies) contingent on unforeseen states, the players' payoffs attached to joint strategies can be modelled in a similar way. Because these payoffs are functions of unforeseen events, they could become vague variables. For simplicity, however, I set this point aside for the moment by assuming that, even if in a vague way, players have a fairly good understanding of the payoff space of the constitutional choice game as a set of outcomes each associated (vaguely to a certain degree) with (many) possible constitutions (subset of the initial strategy space) (Kreps, 1990; Zimmermann, 1991; Sacconi, 2000, 2007).

3.2   The 'state of nature' game

Having assumed that the constitutional choice is about rights and restrictions on the admissible sets of free actions and their outcomes, where do these actions and outcomes come from? The answer is (in part) from the 'state of nature'. Many of the possible constitutional outcomes, based on the use of some action capabilities by players, are state-of-nature outcomes virtually already possible in the case that these actions were adopted. They are not *all* state-of-nature possible outcomes simply because, in the constitutional phase, we can devise many intermediate cooperation modes that we did not appreciate in the rough picture of our actions opportunity in the state of nature (for example, the opportunity to randomize between two possible agreements). Nevertheless, most of these outcomes and strategy profiles were already possible in the state of nature.

Thus before the constitutional game is played, we must consider the state-of-nature game G_N. This is a generic game with a finite number of players (at least two) and any finite number of pure strategies, which is a generalized form of PD or social dilemma. In this game, players have any degree of liberty allowing them to cooperate or act favourably towards each other, or to defect from any degree of cooperation, cheating and using offensive or defensive action one against the other. The salient aspect of this game is that players (without any constraint or obstruction, external or internal, physical, legal or motivational) are able to resort to any level of 'natural' liberty. At the same time, the only equilibrium point in this game played as a *one-shot game* is a combination of pure strategies d* that represents an extremely poor and mutually unprofitable state of interaction in which they do not restrain in any significant way activities aimed at appropriating other natural endowments. Not only are they unable to cooperate, but the logic of choice induces them to adopt actions able to steal any benefits from the counterparty if s/he is ready to act kindly toward them. As a matter of fact, this is a Hobbesian 'state of nature', with an unique equilibrium solution wherein the conduct of players' reciprocal business relations render their lives 'solitary, poor, nasty, brutish, and short'. It has to be understood as a market interaction characterized by any sort of contract failure and incompleteness leading to very high transaction costs which makes almost impossible to attain in equilibrium mutually advantageous exchanges.

The outcome space P_N of the state-of-nature game G_N is shown in Figure 8.5. This includes a large number of discrete outcomes because it represents many possible levels of mutual or unilateral cooperation and defection, friendly or aggressive attitudes in the conduct of many business activities by the two players. What matters in this representation is that the unique equilibrium point is interior to the payoff space, which is pushed towards the origin (in order to avoid the extreme but not completely unreasonable possibility that they may also get negative payoffs in the one-shot version of this game) but (as

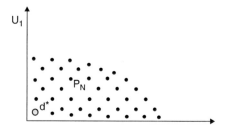

Figure 8.5 The 'state of nature' game

in Hobbes's state of nature) is equally bad for everyone. Formally, the unique equilibrium d* is Pareto-suboptimal.

3.3   The 'all possible constitutions' game

Let us move from this payoff space to the constitutional choice-game G_C payoff space. Firstly, the G_C outcome space P_1 consists of the symmetrical 'state of nature' equilibrium d*, taken as the status quo where the game would remain if the players were incapable of reaching any agreement, plus the other 'state of nature' possible outcomes and all their (convex) combinations as outcomes of possible enforceable agreement (see fig. 8.6). This means that agreements on constitutions can generate all the outcomes that were previously only 'virtually' possible, and also all their convex combinations that were not allowed in the state of nature. In fact, the state of nature is a *non-cooperative* game, whilst the G_C is a *cooperative* bargaining game. Given any pairs of pure joint strategies (each corresponding to a profile of individual pure strategies), a cooperative game admits joint randomizations on such pairs that generate jointly randomized joint strategies or (to put it differently) mixed joint strategies as additional possible agreements of the bargaining game. Such jointly mixed joint strategies are effective in this game because any joint strategy (pure or mixed) can be enforced. That is, given agreements on two pure strategy combinations, a randomizing mechanism may dictate which of the two will be implemented without fear of individual defection from the selected combination. This defines the outcome space of G_C as, at least, the convex hull of the state-of-nature game outcomes.

A legitimate question is how the cooperative game G_C could ever emerge from the non-cooperative G_N. The answer is that G_C is a 'thought experiment' that players may conduct at any time when, in order to devise a *justifiable*

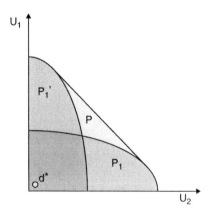

Figure 8.6   The G_C payoff space

escape to the suboptimality of G_N solution d*, they are willing to suppose that a solution can be given by agreement – that is, by admitting that they are able to subscribe to whatever agreement without the fear that any player (him/herself included) may fail to comply with it. Hence, in moving forward from the state of nature game G_N to the constitutional choice game G_C it is not necessary to assume that the underlying real world situation has been changed substantially. Simply, we assume that players may *frame* it as *different* games. Firstly, as a non-cooperative game G_N. Secondly, as a cooperative bargaining game G_C generated form the same physical action set and possible outcome set as G_N but with a major framing difference: the assumption that 'whatever agreement is reached by players can be automatically enforced'. This can be understood as taking a different perspective or point of view on the game, starting from the question 'What constitution would we *fairly* agree granted that our agreements were enforceable?', which entails a completely different but internally consistent frame of the game with respect to the case of G_N.

However, this different framing of the situation allows us to enlarge the outcomes space even further. Because the players are considering 'all the possible' cooperative agreements, their imaginations must not be limited by their real-life power relations. They can decide to subscribe to whatever terms of agreement. This introduces a second step in the definition of the outcome space of the constitutional choice game – i.e. assuming that the G_C game outcome space is in general symmetrical and convex for whatever configuration of the outcome space of the basic state-of-nature game G_N. As far as symmetry is concerned, we proceed as follows. Players considering all the logically possible agreement, given a basic state-of-nature outcomes set, can account not just for all the probabilistic mixtures of possible agreements represented in P_1 but also for those resulting from a symmetric translation P_1' of the outcomes space with respect to the Cartesian utility axes, i.e. from the idea that they can also agree to exchange each other's positions with respect to any possible agreement directly accounted for by outcomes of the basic game. Recall that G_C derives from G_N as a 'thought experiment' intended to devise a *justifiable* agreement enabling the players to escape from the suboptimal equilibrium d* of G_N. The need for justification (or impartial justification) is what entails that the G_C outcome space accounts for not just the convex combinations of the basic game possible outcomes, but also for the symmetric translation of these outcomes with respect to the Cartesian axes representing the players' utility payoffs. Once all these possibilities have been taken in account, also all the linear combinations among all the resulting symmetrical points are allowed, so that the space is also convex as in standard cooperative bargaining game theory. What results is a convex symmetrical outcome space P resulting from the more basic outcome space P_1 (see Figure 8.6). Note that because the status quo d* was already on the bisector, it remains unvaried under the payoff space

translation (otherwise we would have taken as the relevant *status quo* the convex combination of the original one and its symmetrical translation).

As we already know, the distinctive feature of the constitutional choice
game is that it seeks a solution understood as an *optimal* (in a sense to be clari-
fied) *subset* of the possible agreements in G_C. Players simply choose a subset I_i
of the joint strategies set I admissible in G_C. Each subset of the G_C strategies
space is a limitation on the players' choice freedom. Thus, the choice of any
subset coincides with the choice of a 'constitution'. Each subset (constitution)
in turn defines a cooperative subgame G_i whose outcome space P_i is a subset
of the outcome space P of G_C. These subgames may be understood as post-
constitutional coalition games in which the players negotiate on how much
they obtain from cooperation according their 'constitutional rights'. Hence,
each post-constitutional subgame G_i is constrained by the constitution (its
set of possible strategies) chosen in G_C. Formally, the outcome space P of the
constitutional choice game G_C is the union of all its possible subsets $P_1.....P_n$
(see Figure 8.7 for a case where seven payoff subspaces of P are represented),
and the decision problem in G_C concerns the selection of the 'best' subset of P
(Nash, 1950).

3.4   A backward-induction solution of constitutional choice as a sequential game

How must the best constitutions be identified? Recall that even if the constitution is selected as a set of joint strategies, nevertheless, for each subgame
constrained by a specific strategy set, we assumed that from the constitutional point of view players may learn the unique bargaining solutions of the
post-constitutional games. They thus use this information to select the best
constitution. Every outcome subset reduces to the unique outcome coinciding
with the subgame solution relative to that particular subset, and these solutions are compared in terms of the relevant constitutional property.

As a whole, this amounts to saying that players take part in a sequential game
in two steps so that the constitutional contract can be worked out by backward
induction. Given the complete description of all the possible subgames, players
start to solve the game from its second step, i.e. by solving each post-constitutional game G_i defined for each possible constitution (each possible subset of
the outcome space). Given each subgame hypothetically, the players calculate
the payoff assigned to them by the *Shapley value*, which is the relevant solution
concept for n person cooperative coalition games

$$V_i = \sum \left[(s-1)! \frac{(n-s)!}{n!} \right] [v(S) - v(S - \{i\})]S$$

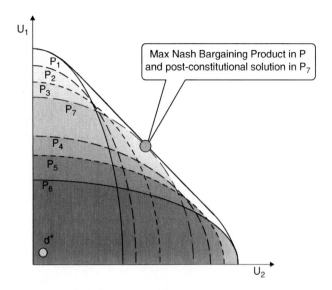

Figure 8.7   Possible payoff spaces of post-constitutional subgames

(note that in two-player bargaining in which the coalition structure reduces to the 'solo-coalitions' and the 'total-coalition' of two players, this reduces to the Nash bargaining game taking the 'solo-coalition' as the status quo d*). For each subgame G_i there is thus a well-defined solution σ_i of the coalition problem such that $\sigma_i \geq d^*$. Then, moving backwards, the players solve the first-stage constitutional choice game. Because the G_C solution is a social contract, it must be the unanimous choice of a unique constitution by all the members of S. If this agreement is not reached, players are doomed to play the unprofit-able 'state of nature' game with solution d*. Since G_C is a typical cooperative bargaining game, the most accredited solution is the Nash bargaining solution (N.B.S), which follows from different sets of very general rationality postulates (Nash, 1950; Harsanyi–Zeuthen, 1977):

$$\text{Max } \Pi_i(U_i - d^*_i)$$
$$\sigma i \in I$$

In G_C the NBS must be found within the symmetrical outcome space **P** gener-ated by the power-set **I** of all the *logically possible* subsets of the strategies set I of G_C itself. All the points in this space are understood as being solutions for possible post-constitutional games. What is remarkable is that this payoff space **P** is the same as the payoff space P assigned to G_C when seen as a bargaining game directly played on possible agreement concerning specific joint strategies included in the set I. The NBS hence selects a constitution such that the relevant post-constitutional game will distribute equal parts of the cooperative surplus calculated with respect to the entire G_C outcome space P (= **P**). In other words, the constitution chosen in G_C will have a post-constitutional solution coinciding with the maximization of the Nash bargaining product also relative to P. In our example (where for simplicity we exemplify only seven subsets of P), the selected constitution is identified by the space P_7, wherein the Nash bargaining solution coincides with the NBS valid for the 'all-encompassing' space P.

3.5   Distributive justice interpretation

The sequential bargaining game solution can be given an intuitive ethical interpretation not only because of the symmetrical shape of the bargaining game, but also on the basis of the correspondence between each of the two concepts of solution that I have employed and the intuitive principle of justice appropriate to the respective bargaining phase in question. The solution to each post-constitutional game according to the Shapley value can be interpreted as an application of the principle of *remuneration on the basis of relative contribution*. The Shapley value is in fact the linear combination (weighted with equal probability assigned to all the coalitions with the same number of members) of the marginal contributions that an individual can make to all the coalitions. On the other hand, the Nash bargaining solution – provided that the units of measure for the individual utilities are assumed to be interpersonally calibrated (which is not required for simple calculation of the Nash bargaining solution) – can be interpreted as an equivalent solution to the distribution proportional to relative needs, that is, proportional to the relative intensity of marginal utility variations comparison for the players at the point where the solution falls. In fact, the ratio in which the shares of the surplus are distributed under the Nash bargaining solution is proportional to the ratio between the marginal variations in the players' utilities $\partial U1/\partial U2 = -a1/a2$. Thus, once the utility units have been interpersonally calibrated, so that each unit expresses the same magnitude of preference for both the players, the ratio between their marginal variation measures the players' relative needs at the solution point (see Brock, 1979; Sacconi, 1991, 2000, 2006b).

The twofold distributive justice characterization of the bargaining solutions matches the different nature of the problems of collective choice modeled by the post-constitutional games, on the one hand, and the constitutional choice game G_C on the other. Before the parties play a post-constitutional subgame, they undertake their specific investments bearing in mind the guarantees offered by the constitution in regard to their possibilities of reaping the benefits of cooperation. They then calculate the effect of their participation in each possible sub-coalition of S, and finally contract with S the part due to them for concluding an agreement which will enable S to pursue its best joint strategy, associated with which is a super additive production function (or characteristic function).

The solution of each subgame distributes benefits to which the players have already contributed through their investment decisions and through their decision to join the coalition S. Therefore appropriate at this point is the distribution criterion based on *relative contribution* or, put otherwise, *relative merits*. Instead, in the case of the constitutional bargaining game G_C, none of the parties subscribing to the agreement has yet contributed anything, so that in this case the merit or relative contribution criterion does not seem to be a valid criterion of distributive justice. Chosen in G_C is the constitution on the basis of which the investment decisions will be taken. What the various players will be willing to contribute depends on which constitution is chosen. These rights-for-incentives, however, must be incorporated into an agreement among participants in the constitutional bargaining phase which considers only what is relevant from their current point of view. In the absence of any relevance of merit, in this case only *needs* can matter for the players' agreement. Hence an appropriate criterion for the solution will refer to the *relative needs* of the parties in regard to what will subsequently enable them to contribute to joint production.

3.6 Dealing with exclusive property rights

Thus far *every logically* possible constitution for the productive organization has been considered to be equally feasible. This case can be called *Utopian*, because any constitutional design can be devised out by the players' imaginations, without any constraint in terms of 'institutional feasibility'. This amounts to saying that, for example, property rights may be allotted amongst players as if they were a continuous variable based on some qualitative object or property (i.e. control over a good or an action) indefinitely divisible amongst them, so that rights can be distributed in whatever proportion among all the players. Non-separable discrete objects are completely excluded in this case.

However, more realistic is the hypothesis that only certain kinds of restrictions (constitutions) on the set of all the possible joint strategies of G_C are 'institutionally feasible'. Specifically, only 'exclusive' allocations of property rights on all the physical assets of the firm may be institutionally feasible. For example, control structures could allow the assignation of authority (residual decision rights) to some party or another, but not any intermediate or equal degrees of authority to all parties – understood as whatever splitting of the same decision right on the very same asset. (Note, however, that this does not imply that other rights combinations are impossible, for example ones complementing a residual decision right held by a party with a responsibility or an accountability duty owed to those who do not hold that right.) If these indivisibilities are admitted, the NBS relative to the all-inclusive payoff space of G_C may not coincide with the solution of any of the institutionally feasible subgames, since the choice must fall within the set of *institutionally feasible solutions*, which will not coincide with the entire payoff space P.

A reasonable interpretation is that 'realism' constrains desirable normative properties such as ideal social efficiency and fairness. (In fact, it is a standard assumption in transaction cost economics that governance and authority costs entail that any whatever governance structure is second-best. Moreover, we know that this occurs because of abuse of authority and unfairness under each exercise of ownership as an exclusive right.) Thus feasible subgames are assumed to have outcome spaces that coincide with only a few of the proper subsets of the all-encompassing outcome space P. The resulting candidate set of constitutions (deriving from the post-constitutional solutions of feasible subgames) is defined as a set of second-best solutions with respect to the outcome space P.

Consider a two-player case (see Figure 8.8). There is one feasible constitution G_1 (which assigns ownership to player 1) with payoff space P_1, whose solution is more efficient than that of the alternative feasible constitution G_2 with payoff space P_2 (which assigns ownership to player 2). Since these constitutions give complete control to one player or another, but not to both, it is natural that such constitutions should also assign a significant advantage to owners in terms of the surplus shares that they may appropriate. Assume that there are not other institutionally feasible constitutions of the control structure in terms of property rights allotment. Both the feasible constitutions have second-best solutions with respect to the all-encompassing space P. Efficiency is here understood as proximity to the Pareto frontier, i.e. how large the aggregate surplus is under the two ownership allocations. In *ex post* efficiency terms, ownership should be given to player 1 (which entails availability of a Kaldor–Hicks side-payment that would allow a shift from one solution to the other but not vice versa). However, under the G_1 game we may predict a significant level of abuse of authority by player 1 as s/he appropriates an unjustly large share of the surplus. Why should player 2 agree to such a control structure?

The only way to legitimize such an inequality into the distribution of property rights by *ex ante* agreement is for player 1 to render it acceptable from the *ex ante* perspective also to player 1, who will be disadvantaged under such a control structure. Player 1 must then take account of player 2's claims and compensate him/her for the prospective abuse of authority and injustice that s/he will suffer under player 1's control. The agreed control structure must then provide for player 1 a constitutional commitment to implement a utility side-payment drawn from the surplus that s/he will appropriate under his/her control of the firm's assets and transferred to player 2: the utility side transfer will continue until player 2's fair claim of redress has been satisfied so that the most efficient control form is accepted by unanimous agreement.

But what is the fair and efficient amount of the side utility transfer from 1 to 2?

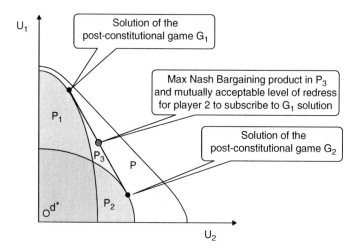

Figure 8.8 Constitutions pay-off spaces under feasibility

The problem is that at first glance we do not have a Pareto convex frontier along which the players can move until they reach a mutually acceptable bargain. But we can provide it by construction as follows. There are two payoff spaces, each relative to an institutionally feasible constitution (set of strategies). The constrained constitutional imaginations of the players can be simply used to allow any convex combination of each pair of possible agreements, where one agreement in each pair belongs to a different feasible strategy set respectively. In particular, we focus on all the convex combinations of the two post-constitutional subgame solutions and interpret such convex combinations as random mechanisms implementing each of the two solutions with given probabilities. The set of all these convex combinations defines the relevant north-east frontier of the payoff space P_3 worked out by taking the convex hull of outcomes belonging to spaces P_1 and P_2 associated with the feasible constitutions. The rational utility side transfer is identified by the point where NBS is maximized along the north-east frontier of the outcome space P_3. In order to allow the acceptance of the solution reachable under subgame G_1, player 1 must then *ex ante* commit him/herself to transferring to player 2 an *ex post* side-payment such that the surplus shares will be equal to those that will maximize the NBS calculated with respect to P_3 (see again Figure 8.8), which is the same as allowing an appropriate random mechanism to make the choice between the two relevant subgame solutions.

Thus, even in the context of this reduced set of feasible constitutions, we can identify a unique solution for the firm's constitution: the most efficient control structure plus the mutually acceptable (from the constitutional perspective) level of redress for the disadvantaged party.

3.7   Institutional feasibility

Institutional feasibility, as I have implicitly understood it in the previous sub-section, is a twofold condition:

(a) Institutional feasibility means 'a consistent manner to introduce constraints on the complete players' natural capabilities to act' (held by some or all of them), and thus to assign different players' rights and responsibilities. Here 'consistent' must be understood not in a pure mathematical sense but in terms of compatibility with our best knowledge about norms, institutions and legal orders as matter of facts and values.

For example, assigning ownership – residual right of control – to all the interested stakeholders in the same measure, or giving each of them the same right, could be *inconsistent* with *facts* about the non-divisibility of assets or rights over some assets. By contrast, allotting control rights so that one stakeholder is given the right to take residual decisions, while another stakeholder is given protection against some extreme form of that decision, could be "consistent". So that the latter is given the following rights: (i) to ask the first stakeholder to account for his decision; and (ii) to be redressed under certain conditions. The 'impossibility of social choice' (Arrow, 1951) is an example of inconsistency related to certain mechanisms of collective choice that presupposes certain decision rights of the society's members plus ethical and structural assumptions concerning the mechanism that represents some facts and values about social choice. More generally, institutional consistency requires us to have discovered an institutional arrangement consistently describable in our normative language and which can prescribe the allocation of decision rights and responsibility among the players that does not clash with our best knowledge of the subject matter. One might say that the highly fine-tuned and continuous allotments of decision rights entailed formally by taking as the basis for the constitutional choice all the logically possible subsets of the payoff space P is not institutionally feasible because we still have not designed in practice a plausible legal order able to allot legal rights in this continuous and fine-tuned mode. Thus, whereas in the mathematical model we may think of infinite subsets of the outcome space P, and we can think of moving from one subset to another by a continuous marginal change in the distribution of rights, on the contrary, within the language of institutions, we may only face a description of discrete objects permitting only rough divisions into discrete "pieces of rights" held on such objects. Some rights can be indivisible and not sharable, whereas they can be counteracted by different rights, also indivisible but consistently able to curtail the first right abuse. Even if this second institutional structure may be consistent, there is no reason to say that it does not entail a loss in terms of ideal efficiency and fairness. Indeed, the perfect divisibility of property rights would give a perfect modulation of investment incentives to all the players in proportion to the importance of these investments for social surplus production, whereas the feasible arrangement may be less fine-tuned to this purpose. Moreover, it is fairly obvious that institutional feasibility, by requiring the assignation of authority to one party and submission to the authority of another party, has unequal payoff distributions.

(b) Institutional feasibility entails a sufficient level of effectiveness, i.e. a control and governance structure which can be intended as a protection of some rights or interests is feasible only if it can be put into practice effectively.

This condition has various interpretations. The most obvious one is to equate effectiveness with self-interested incentive compatibility in the pure game-theoretical sense. Thus, the agreed solution should be required to correspond to a pre-existing equilibrium point in the underlying game (the state of nature) which implements the agreement. However, in our case – where the state of nature is seen as a one-shot game – this interpretation cannot work, because only the status quo d* corresponds to a pre-existing equilibrium point of the 'state of nature' game. One possible way to introduce this type of effectiveness would be to assume that G_N is an infinitely repeated game, so that each one-shot game outcome may be reached in equilibrium as the average payoff of an appropriate combination of repeated strategies.

Nevertheless, the use of this strict notion of incentive compatibility is not necessary in order to account for institutional effectiveness. As an alternative explanation, consider only those constitutions which define allotments of decision rights such that a bargaining subgame within these agreed constitutional constraints is supported by motivations sufficiently strong to induce players to stay within the limits of that agreement. In other words, effectiveness comes about if the constitution distributes rights and action opportunities in such a way that players in the corresponding subgame will reach agreements that are effective causal factors in inducing intrinsic motivations to implement that same agreement. The difference, of course, is in the role that constitutions as such may play in generating incentives and motivations that are effective in the implementation phase. There is no need to make a choice between these two interpretations at this stage (however this line of though will be undertaken in Part II of this essay, see Sacconi 2011).

Thus far, we can maintain that effectiveness is a constraint on the 'all possible constitutions' set P, so that only proper subsets are feasible (which entails that the effective constitutions outcome spaces are proper subsets of the all-encompassing space P, and because these subsets will not include the north-east boundary of space P, in general they are quite obviously *second best* in terms of efficiency). However, it is not obvious what this means in term of fairness.

4 Difficulties in the constitutional contract of the firm

Constitutions are not simply logically possible but also institutionally feasible if their design is 'consistent', and some mechanism (able to carry out their constitutional agreement) exists. The mechanism may be of any nature, internal or external, legal, social, moral or psychological. Simply, there must be positive inducements or negative sanctions (internal or external, material or psychological) able to induce individuals to comply with the agreement, which may operate through the legal system, the social acceptance mechanism, or through internal motivations like moral sentiments, the sense of moral obligation, or the belief that God will condemn us to Hell.

That assumption was implicitly made when the idea of an *ex ante* grand social contract on the constitution of the firms was introduced, and which was admitted to be about all of the logically possible institutional arrangements of the control structure and other legal rights. Then, by dealing with exclusive property rights alone, I have simply constrained this hypothesis to hold only for a subset of the logically possible institutions, i.e. for the subsets in which property rights are exclusively assigned to one or another stakeholder. This intentionally makes the problem of designing a multi-stakeholder control structure of the firm more realistic and serious, because we cannot now rely on an all-encompassing institutional structure in which every stakeholder is granted an equal proportion of control rights. Hence we need to define the redress duties or responsibilities owed to those stakeholders that cannot share rights of control.

In the context of the theory of the firm, this line of reasoning could be pursued with few difficulties, because some parts of the institutional system can be presumed to be already enacted before the social contract of the firm occurs. Hence it is admissible that at least some institutional arrangements that are deliberate through the social contract of the firm may also be externally enforced by some other mechanism (social or legal) which pre-exists the firm itself. Nevertheless, I do not want to rely too much on these presumptions, because the basic thesis of this essay is that the CSR model of corporate governance is self-enforceable, and hence can rest primarily on endogenous forces.

The following question must then be asked: 'How self-sustaining is a solution that, given two feasible arrangements of property rights, defines a side-payment from the owner to the non-owner in order to redress the abuse of authority that will take place under each feasible institutional structure of control?' Recall that the exact dimension of this side-payment was identified through the construction of a small-scale constitutional choice problem, i.e. the convex combination of the two sets of outcomes admitted by the outcome space of the two institutionally feasible subgames, and by the straight line joining their NBS. In other words, this implies resolving the problem of collective choice within the linear combination of the two bargaining solutions, one for each subgame.

But we must now address a problem: this linear combination does not necessarily satisfy the same assumptions that we made for the two institutionally feasible subgames. Hence its agreed solution on the north-east frontier of the convex combination of their payoffs spaces does not need to be feasible. How can we deal with this difficulty? And must a proper escape from the feasibility problem compromise the request for fairness and accordance with intuitive principles of justice in the constitutional choice on control structures? Of course, any successful attempt to solve this difficulty will contribute essentially to the very basis of the idea that CSR is a governance system not externally imposed by the law but implementable as a self-enforceable social norm incorporating the normative requirements of contractarian ethics. To be sure of the relevance of these questions, let us look at the institutionally feasible solution more carefully, with the aid of some geometry (see Figure 8.9).

Figure 8.9 shows a line segment joining points S_1 and S_2 and that represents the linear combination of the two bargaining solutions relative to subspaces P_1 and P_2 respectively. Along this line segment, there are all the possible probabilistic combinations of S_1 and S_2. Also represented are all the possible utility side-payments which, given solution S_2 – the more efficient one and nearest to the north-east frontier – may be agreed to redress player 1's loss for agreeing to give up control over the firm. The utility transfer in L is calculated as the constitutional agreement within P_3, i.e. a subset of the all-encompassing payoff space P, which is constructed as the convex hull of the subgame spaces P_1 and P_2 representing institutionally feasible subgames. The status quo is assumed to be at the origin. Hence, L is the NBS of P_3, and thus is also proportional to relative needs contingent to this subspace P_3. This last property may be seen by considering that the slope of the line segment joining S_1 and S_2 is the same, with inverse sign, as the dashed line joining the origin (status quo) and L, where it is incident on S_1S_2, which in fact is the frontier of the convex (compact) space P_3.

Two points are raised by this case:

(i) *Instability of the equitable institutional arrangement.*
 The institutional mechanism granting that player 1 will agree *ex ante* to enter a control structure that legitimizes player 2's control, and also allowing him to profit considerably from control, is the utility-side payment represented by L on S_1S_2. But whereas P_1 and P_2 are assumed to be institutionally feasible subgame payoff spaces, i.e. to have bargaining solutions that are enforced by some mechanism or motivation, the same does not hold for any points in P_3 lying outside the union of P_1 and P_2. Combining points like S_1 and S_2 does not ensure that the resulting linear combination lies inside the institutionally feasible set of solutions. The linear combination may give rise to outcomes that are not enforceable; and this is exactly the case when, as for L, the point representing the optimal redress lies outside the P_1 and

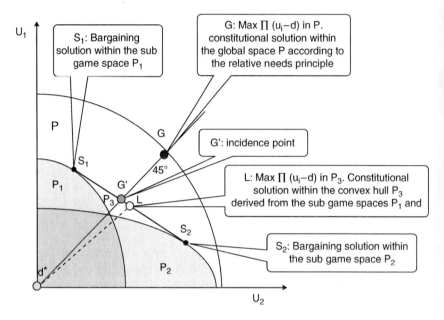

Figure 8.9 Alternative bargaining solutions, feasible and unfeasible

P_2 union. What will make point L feasible? Notice that L is an *ex ante* social contract on the institutional structure of the firm which would induce the players to give their *ex ante* consent to entering the institutional arrangement of the firm. Nevertheless, it does not necessarily coincide with any solution of the *ex post* implementation problem, and is therefore unstable. On anticipating such instability, player 2 would not effectively endorse such an agreement. But then on what should they reach an agreement?

(ii) *Divorce between local and global justice.*

Global justice is represented by point G in Figure 8.9, where the NBS relative to space P is located. Here the institutional structure is arranged so that it reflects a measure of relative needs with respect to the all-encompassing space of possible institutions P such that it is uniquely reflected by the NBS's distribution of payoffs. This space is properly understood to be symmetrical in so far as any logically possible allocation and distribution of control rights is taken into consideration. In fact, the dashed line segment from the origin to G has the same slope (with inverse sign) as the tangent to the north-east boundary of P at the incidence point G. Because point G lies outside any institutionally feasible subgame payoff space such as P_1 and P_2, we recognize that this solution is merely utopian. Nevertheless, the line segment joining the status quo to G represents the distributive proportion that would incorporate the relative needs principle with respect to the 'global' payoff space P. The point G' at which this line segment crosses the north-east boundary of P_3 (incidence point) is hence a natural candidate for the agreement according to the constitutional choice principles, the one that mostly approximated the global justice solution (call it *constrained global justice*). Here payoffs are allotted so that the relative needs principle is satisfied not so much with respect the contingent subspace P_3 as with respect to the set of possible institutional alternative P in general. This would be a natural requirement derived from the general theory of constitutional choice: select the subgame with a payoff space such that its bargaining solution is the one closest to the point where NBS is maximized on the all-encompassing payoff space P. In other words, select a subgame such that its own bargaining solution lies on the line segment joining the status quo to G, as near as possible to G (that is as mutually advantageous as possible). If there are no such subgames, take as an acceptable level of redress to the disadvantaged party the point within the convex combination of feasible subspaces that lies on the line segment joining the status quo to the global justice point G. By contrast, L is a *local justice* solution: it allots payoffs in such a way that the relative needs principle is respected only with reference to the contingent subset of institutionally feasible subgames.

Which of the two should prevail? Intuition helps only when we consider extreme cases. Let us therefore concentrate on the case where local justice diverges from global justice owing to the asymmetrical shape of all the institutional feasible subsets and hence also to their convex combination. Figure 8.10 illustrates this case: P is symmetric, but both its institutionally feasible subsets are rather asymmetrically placed in the region where player 1 always fares somewhat better than 2 (incidence point). In a sense, this means that only property rights assignations to player 1 are allowed – which gives player 1 a plain advantage – even if these regimes may be more or less favorable also to player 2 (i.e. they leave player 2 unprotected at different levels against player 1's discretion). Within this subset of institutions, the subgame corresponding to the outcome space P_1 has a solution nearest to the Pareto frontier of P. This means that there are Kaldor–Hicks side-payments that allow reaching the solution P_1 form the solution P_2 but not vice versa. Moreover, there is an arrangement in which player 1 partially redresses the imbalance in the payoff distribution generated by the most extreme form of ownership in favour of player 1 by a utility side-payment in favor of player 2, calculated as the bargaining solution within the bargaining subset P_3 derived from the convex combination of P_1 and P_2. Nevertheless, this seems to be a caricature of the redress principle: the best feasible case for player 2 – the solution under P_2 – has

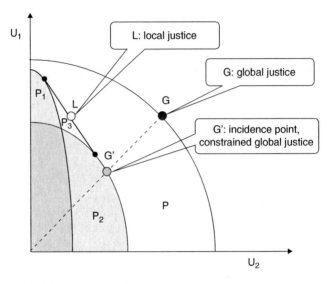

Figure 8.10 Global justice and local justice

already asymmetrically shifted in favour of player 1. Indeed, drawing the convex combination of spaces P_1 and P_2 simply induces a compromise between two solutions both to the advantage of player 1; and any whatever linear combination of these solutions will shift the final result even more toward player 1's advantage than will taking the solution directly in P_2. So why should player 2 not insist on the less efficient but nevertheless feasible solution in P_2?

Global justice here seems to prevail over the alternative. Following the straight line joining the status quo to the global justice solution G in P, the north-east boundary of P_2 is crossed in G'. Because P is a perfectly symmetric payoff space, this happens along the 45° straight line. Hence the solution G' is egalitarian and also proportional to relative needs in a global sense. By contrast, the locally fair solution L, located on the north-east boundary of P_3, seems excessively to reflect the arbitrary fact that only institutions that favor player 1 are feasible.

Apparent realism would mistakenly suggest abandoning global justice for local justice, but this is not the case. G' lies on the boundary of the payoff space of a subgame pertaining to a feasible institution, while this is not the case of L, which lies outside any feasible payoff space. Hence proper realism would suggest proceeding the other way round, and admitting an allocation of control rights compatible with selecting the approximation to utopia G'. Thus both the ethical intuition of distributive justice and the requirement of *ex post* stability seem to suggest a reformulation of the 'non-utopian' version of the firm's constitutional contract. Rawlsian contractarian theory, as already illustrated, provides this reformulation.

5   The Rawlsian theory of corporate governance and control

As already discussed, for whatever (repeated) game, based on a constituent *social dilemma* game, however endowed with an asymmetrical equilibrium (convex) outcome space, the Rawls–Binmore social contract always selects a non-cooperative Nash equilibrium coinciding with an application of the Rawlsian maximin principle of welfare distribution. It is computed as the egalitarian solution within the symmetrical intersection set generated by the original (equilibrium) outcome space and its symmetrical translation with respect to the Cartesian axes, i.e. the Nash Bargaining Solution (NBS) computed with respect to this symmetrical payoff subspace.

5.1   Egalitarianism and constitutional choice amongst different control and governance structures

From this general result let us return to the constitutional choice of a governance and control structure of the firm. Consider two different institutionally *feasible* subsets derived from the all-inclusive set of the possible governance and control structures. I interpret this hypothesis as stating that, by proper design of the related corporate constitutions, we find two outcome spaces – subsets of the all-inclusive outcome space – corresponding to non-cooperative Nash equilibria sets (in the sense of the Rawls–Binmore theory). Given that such equilibria can only derive from the outcome space of an underlying non-cooperative game, it follows that we are necessarily considering constitutions whose outcomes belong as proper subsets to the equilibrium set of the 'state of nature' game played as a *repeated* game. In other words, by proper design we are able to select outcome spaces that are different subsets of the basic outcome space P_N of Figure 8.5 (according to the *folk theorem*, the region lying between the status quo d* and the north-east frontier of the convex and compact envelope of outcomes depicted in P_N is the equilibrium set of the repeated basic game G_N).

Taking such two outcome sets as the starting point, the 'veil of ignorance' hypothesis is introduced with respect to each of them – i.e., the hypothesis that players consider *each* feasible constitution from an impartial standpoint by allowing the mutual replacement of the roles (and utility function) that they play under each constitution. Not only is the basic outcome space symmetrically translated, but also *each* feasible subset – candidate for the outcome space of an acceptable constitutionally subgame – must be considered impartially. This means that a symmetrical translation with respect to the Cartesian axes is taken for *every* candidate outcome space, and an acceptable solution is accounted for in terms of candidate solutions that are invariant under the symmetric translation of the respective outcome spaces.

Hence, what we relinquish are not impartiality and empathy but only the possibility to take for granted the feasibility of every convex combination of feasible outcome spaces. This is a requirement of realism that reminds us that the implementation of whatever constitution we could devise by institutional imagination is constrained by feasibility. Proposition I logically follows.

PROPOSITION I:

Given any pair of feasible convex outcome subspaces P_1 and P_2, relative to a pair of constitutions and their respective post constitutional cooperative games, if the 'veil of ignorance' hypothesis is introduced, but the *'Deus ex machina'* hypothesis is rejected, then the Constitutional Choice selects a constitution corresponding to the bargaining subgame endowed with a feasible outcome subspace P^* such that the *egalitarian solution* in P^* dominates any other egalitarian solution belonging to the alternative feasible subspace.

More specifically, given any two feasible convex outcome sub-spaces P_1 and P_2 and their symmetric translations P_1' and P_2', *no matter how other characteristics of the relevant spaces are established,*

$$\sigma_2^* > \sigma_1^* \quad \text{if and only if } P_1 \cap P_1' \subset P_2 \cap P_2'$$

where σ^* is the egalitarian solution within the respective outcome space P_i and the order relation $>$ should be understood as *strictly superior unanimous acceptance* (strong Pareto dominance). Thus inclusiveness of the symmetric intersection is the only property relevant to the constitutional choice of subgames (see Figure 8.11 for an example).

From a purely formal standpoint, this proposition is fairly trivial. Recall the relation $>$ between points s and s', representing players' payoff pairs on the Cartesian plane, is *strong Pareto dominance* (i.e. if s' $>$ s then in s' both players' payoffs are greater than in s). If we take two payoff spaces S and S', both symmetric and convex, such that S $\subset$ S' (S is a proper subset of S'), and two points $\sigma \in$ S and $\sigma' \in$ S' respectively equal to the loci where the bisector of the Cartesian plane intersects the north-east frontiers of S and S' (i.e. they are the *egalitarian solutions* relative to spaces S and S' under the condition that $\sigma \in$ S' but $\sigma' \notin$ S), then the relation $\sigma' > \sigma$ holds *necessarily* for these points. In fact, all points taken along the bisector are strictly increasing toward north-east as a function of the players' pairs of (identical) increasing payoffs. Since the two egalitarian solutions σ and σ' coincide with two of those points – not identical given $\sigma' \notin$ S – they are also ordered in the same way.

In other words, if two symmetrical payoff spaces S and S' are defined so that S ⊂ S' and each point s' ∈ S' is a function of the same increasing monotonic – symmetry and convexity preserving – transformation of a pair of players' payoffs corresponding to a point s ∈ S, then also the egalitarian solution point σ' ∈ S', which lies on the bisector, will be a monotonic increasing transformation of the egalitarian solution point σ ∈ S, which also lies on the bisector – that is, σ' > σ.

Of course, the intersection between any generic convex space and the space generated by its symmetrical translation with respect to the Cartesian axes is also a symmetric space. Thus, when many intersection sets are generated by this operation from generic convex spaces, an entire collection of symmetric spaces results so that they are related to each other by set theoretic inclusion. It follows that Pareto-dominance among egalitarian solutions, each belonging to a different payoff space, is monotonically related to how much inclusive these symmetric intersection sets are.

From a substantive point of view, however, it is important that Pareto-dominance *only* between egalitarian solutions should be considered as the decisive condition for the unanimous choice of constitutions, *no matter how other characteristics of the payoff spaces are settled*. From this perspective, the proposition states that the level of unanimous acceptance of a constitution (and hence its outcome) dominates the level of acceptance of another constitution only if its egalitarian solution is Pareto-superior to the egalitarian solution of the alternative, no matter what the same Pareto dominance relation states about other points in the respective payoff spaces. From sections 2 and 3 we know that this restriction of unanimous acceptance to egalitarian solutions rests on a concern for *impartial feasibility*, i.e. an individual rationality criterion (equilibrium) under the hypothesis of impartiality (veil of ignorance), rather than for maximizing some welfare aggregate. We choose then the most efficient (in the Paretian sense) point within the collection of egalitarian solutions, which are monotonically ordered according to the inclusiveness of the respective intersection sets, since this restriction guarantees satisfaction of an ex post stability condition granted that the decision must be *ex ante* impartially acceptable under the 'veil of ignorance'.

To illustrate proposition I, consider Figure 8.11. The 'all-encompassing' outcome space P represents all the logically possible ways to cooperate on choice of a constitution. It is assumed that no equilibrium points exist that are able to implement all outcomes in P, and in particular there is no such equilibrium corresponding to the utopian solution U in P, i.e. its symmetric NBS. Thus, our attention is restricted to two subspaces, P_1 and P_2, which are *feasible* subsets of P. These subsets are construed so that they can be also understood as proper subsets of the convex equilibrium space P_N of the 'state of nature game' played as a *repeated* game.

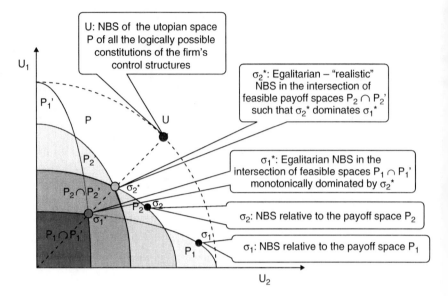

Figure 8.11   Egalitarian solutions monotonically ordered according to the inclusiveness of the respective intersection set

Because they are related to the asymmetrical space P_N embodying natural inequalities between the two players, both spaces P_1 and P_2 are asymmetrical and give some advantage to player 2, but at different levels. In comparison with P_2, P_1 is a more asymmetric outcome space with a cooperative solution σ_1 of the post-constitutional cooperative game quite near to the north-east frontier of P. In terms of NBS or other welfare measures, this entails that this post-constitutional game would produce a larger amount of aggregate utility as solution – i.e. compared with P and P_2, the solution σ_1 of P_1 is *second-best* in term of efficiency (again taking the utopian solution of P as the first best), even though the aggregate value is quite unfairly distributed. P_2 on the contrary entails a cooperative solution σ_2 of the cooperative post-constitutional subgame which is *third-best* in terms of efficiency. However, because its solution σ_2 lies nearer to the bisector joining the origin with the egalitarian solution U, it would distribute payoffs in fairer shares. Recall that according Rawls-Binmore theory a constitution needs to be found by impartially acceptable choice. In other words, i.e. a constitution must be chosen with an invariant solution under the symmetric replacement of the players' roles, which at the same time must be *ex post* stable (equilibrium). Picking solution σ_1 or σ_2 as such is thus ruled out. But feasibility also debars us from any arbitrary operation on the convex combination of spaces P_1 and P_2. So what properties does constitutional choice impose on the final payoffs in terms of *ex post* distribution? And which outcome space corresponds to the selected constitution?

For each feasible outcome space, Figure 8.11 also shows the respective symmetrical translation P_1' and P_2'. Assuming that no convex combination of P_1 and P_1', and P_2 and P_2' can be generated, we must focus on the respective intersection sets $P_1 \cap P_1'$ and $P_2 \cap P_2'$, where it is clear that the former is a proper subset of the latter. Both intersection sets are symmetrical spaces, and have symmetrical NBS equal to the egalitarian solutions σ_1^* and σ_2^* belonging to P_1 and P_2 respectively and lying on the bisector. Both these solution are impartial because they are invariant under the players' role replacement. But they are also *feasible*, given that all the points included in these intersection sets are equilibrium points of the underlying 'state of nature' game, so that any convex combination of outcomes falling *within* a symmetric intersection set would be implementable in equilibrium. Any agreement within each of these sets would not be ruled out by unfeasibility if one player's role were interchanged with the other, since the resulting agreement would nevertheless be an equilibrium. However, the symmetrical intersection set $P_2 \cap P_2'$ strictly includes $P_1 \cap P_1'$, so that the egalitarian solution within P_2 strictly Pareto-dominates the egalitarian solution relative to P_1.

Figure 8.11 shows why. The more asymmetric a payoff space and the more unequal its post-constitutional NBS with respect to the available alternative, the less inclusive is its intersection set, and the less unanimously acceptable (in term of constrained Pareto dominance) its egalitarian solution.

Summing up, constitutional choice falls on the constitution with outcome space P_2, which would have a post-constitutional bargaining solution σ_2 (as far as the pure exercise of ownership and control rights is considered). But in order to make such a constitution impartially acceptable and at the same time to preserve its *feasibility* of, the constitutional choice requires an *ex post* redistribution with respect to the solution σ_2 belonging to P_2 such that the egalitarian solution σ_2^* in P_2 is *de facto* implemented. Thus *egalitarian redress* of the disadvantaged stakeholder is the main constitutional constraint on implementation of the constitution of ownership and control rights denoted by P_2. It entails maximizing the benefit of player 2, who even under this less unfair constitution still occupies the role of the disadvantaged player. Note that because the dominant egalitarian solution is an equilibrium of the underlying game, reaching an agreement on the redistributive mechanism is not 'wishful thinking'. No constitutional agreement may be acceptable without the *ex ante* acceptance of such an egalitarian condition, and the selected egalitarian solution – admitted that it coordinates expectations also in the post-constitutional game – is also *ex post* stable as it is a Nash equilibrium.

5.2   Global justice overrides local justice

Thus far we have been concerned only with the *instability of the equitable institutional arrangement* problem. Let us now turn to the second problem: the divorce between global and local justice in the choice of the firm's constitution. The Rawlsian theory of corporate governance solves this problem because neither global justice nor local justice as such simply succeeds; but considerations from global justice make it possible to derive an approximation to global justice that always overrides local justice. In fact, the egalitarian solution is always on the bisector where also the global justice solution lies, and given any two different feasible payoff subspaces, and the symmetrical intersection sets that they generate with their symmetric translation, their egalitarian solutions always stand in a relation of monotonic dominance of one over the other. Thus the Pareto-dominant egalitarian solution provides the best feasible approximation to global justice. No room remains for considerations of local justice, which are rebutted simply by the unfeasibility of the collateral utility transfer mechanism.

To see why, for the moment discard the strict concern for adherence of the feasible payoff subspaces to the underlying state-of-nature equilibrium space, and allow constitutions to be *feasible* in a less constrained sense, so that effectiveness may be granted by hypothesis to whatever subset of the all-encompassing space P. In this light we can reconsider the cases of Figure 8.9 and Figure 8.10 (see Figure 8.12 and Figure 8.13 respectively).

In Figure 8.12, P_1 and P_2 are two outcome spaces corresponding to institutionally feasible constitutions such that either player 1 or player 2 is alternatively advantaged (by alternative assignments of exclusive property rights). Note that this presumes that feasible institutions do not coincide with state-of-nature equilibria, or – put differently – players are able to generate other equilibria or stable configurations of play through their institutional imaginations and artifice. This figure also considers the spaces P_1' and P_2' resulting respectively from the symmetric translation of space P_1 and P_2 with respect to the Cartesian axes. The intersection between space P_1 and its translation P_1' entirely includes the intersection between space P_2 and its translation P_2'. Thus its egalitarian solution E_1 dominates the second E_2. It is noticeable that what was said to be a local justice solution L is no longer affordable because it is infeasible. What about the egalitarian solution G' previously called 'approximation to global justice' because it was resident on the bisector where also the utopian solution U lies? Even though it is Pareto-dominant over the alternatives, it is nonetheless ruled out because it is unaffordable due to unfeasibility. However, the Rawls–Binmore solution E_1 provides a new second-best approximation to global justice which is compatible with feasibility.

The case of Figure 8.13 is somewhat clearer in terms of its implications for the problem of global vs local justice. We started with two feasible outcome spaces P_1 and P_2, both benefitting player 1 at different levels. This case can be regarded as one where ownership is always allotted to player 1, granting some degree of abuse of authority to player 1. But under the constitution corresponding to the outcome space P_2, player 1's residual right of control is

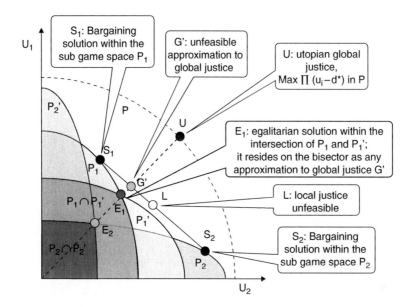

Figure 8.12   The Pareto-dominant egalitarian solution dominates local justice

moderately constrained. All of this can be seen by looking at the respective post-constitutional bargaining solution annexed to the two constitutions (S_1 and S_2). In order to redress such unfairness of the feasible solutions, the local justice collateral utility transfer L and the constrained global justice solution G' (belonging directly to the feasible space P_2) have been proposed. The latter coincides exactly with the egalitarian solution E selected by the Binmore–Rawls social contract, because it was already the egalitarian solution selected by the incidence point of the bisector on P_2 frontier, which is the most symmetrical payoff space among those considered here. By introducing into Figure 8.13 also the symmetrical translations of spaces P_1 and P_2, accounting for considerations of impartiality and 'veil of ignorance', the intersection set $P_2 \cap P_2'$ results more comprehensive than $P_1 \cap P_1'$; hence its egalitarian solution is dominant. Again, the local justice solution is unaffordable because it does not belong to any feasible payoffs space. I do not have to deal with its anti-intuitivism from the distributive justice point of view (it redresses player 2 less than does solution S_2). Feasibility already rules out it from the outset.

6   Challenging received wisdoms

Some corollaries are required to illustrate the relevance of the main proposition given in the previous section to the economics of institutions and in particular

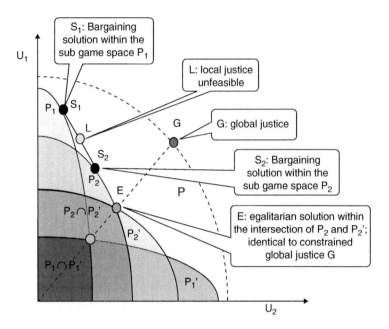

Figure 8.13   Unfeasibility of local justice, approximate global justice coincides with the dominant egalitarian solution

to the selection of the firm's governance and control structures. They concern two typical positions playing important roles in the literature on institutions design: the aggregate welfare maximizer and the libertarian one.

6.1   Fairness vs welfare?

Consider two feasible outcome spaces P_1 and P_2 such that P_1 includes both the maximal utilitarian solution and the best solution in terms of Kaldor–Hicks efficiency. Nevertheless, P_2, with its symmetric translation P_2', generates an intersection set which strictly includes the intersection of P_1 and its own symmetric translation P_1'. Then, any rational constitutional choice must prefer the constitution of the firm corresponding to the outcome space P_2 – no matter what the efficiency properties of P_1.

Assume that the Utilitarian and Kaldor–Hicks solutions do not coincide with the egalitarian solution of any relevant outcome space P_i as such. We are thus in a situation such as depicted by Figure 8.13, where the quite unequal NBS solution S_1 in P_1 is the also the one that satisfies both the foregoing welfarist conditions. Since a constitutional choice must be reached under the "veil of ignorance", a natural way to preserve this solution would be to take the equally probable lottery between this solution treated as a point belonging to the original space P_1 and its realization under the symmetric translation in space P_1'.

But without the *Deus ex machina* assumption, a convex combination of these symmetric Utilitarian or Kaldor–Hicks solutions does not generate any feasible outcome. On the other hand, the feasible intersection of $P_1 \cap P_1'$ is Pareto-dominated by $P_2 \cap P_2'$, so that P_1 cannot be constitutionally chosen. An efficiency criterion (Pareto dominance) is then decisive for the unanimous acceptance of a constitution in so far as it is *restricted* to comparison between egalitarian solutions. Hence, *equity constraints efficiency*. It follows that

COROLLARY 1: Equity comes before efficiency.

Often the quest for social efficiency does not extend to requiring satisfaction of the demanding standard of utilitarianism. Many *law & economics* analysts are sufficiently content with wealth maximisation taken as a proxy for the more demanding utilitarian requirements. But wealth maximisation as a solution concept performs no better than the former two in the context of constitutional choice (for example in *fig. 8.13* the space P_1's solution S_1 also maximises the payoffs sum understood in simple monetary terms). Joint feasibility and impartiality rules out wealth maximisation. Even if it may sound iconoclastic to the standard theorizing in law and economics, the following proposition naturally obtains.

PROPOSITION II:

In order to select an institutional form of corporate governance under the constraint of being ex post stable – i.e. implementable by an equilibrium point – do not bother with welfare maximization or its proxy, wealth maximization. Instead, look for the best 'egalitarian solution', in the qualified sense of being the best monotonic Nash bargaining symmetric solution among those related to the symmetric intersection sets resulting from symmetrical translations of the outcome equilibrium sets annexed to feasible constitutions.

Students of corporate governance may be struck by this result, which contradicts many of the subject's basic credos – as they have been extensively elaborated by, for example, Kaplow and Shavell.[3] Let us quote them extensively:

Our argument for basing the evaluation of legal rules entirely on welfare economics, giving no weight to notions of fairness, derives from the fundamental characteristic of fairness-based assessment: such assessment does not depend exclusively on the effects of legal rules on individual's well-being. As a consequence, satisfying notion of fairness can make individual worse-off, that is, reduce social welfare. Furthermore, individuals will be made worse off overall whenever consideration of fairness leads to the choice of a regime different from which would be adopted under welfare economics because by definition the two approaches conflict when a regime with greater overall well-being is rejected on grounds of fairness. (p. 52) ... This thesis is particularly compelling because also in important and simple situations, i.e. 'symmetric' contexts – those in which all individuals are identically situated – it is always the case that everyone will be worse off when a notion of fairness leads to the choice of different legal rule from that chosen under welfare economics. (p. 52)

The violation of strong Pareto optimality (choosing a rule under which everyone is worse off) is particularly unacceptable in such a symmetric context. In order to avoid such a risk, the conclusion is that no institutional regime should be chosen primarily on the basis of fairness; or better, fairness as an independent criterion with respect to aggregate welfare maximization must have no role to play in the choice of institutions.

On the contrary, given the previous analysis, it may be shown that:

(i) In the simplest symmetrical cases, egalitarianism and strong Pareto optimality always go hand in hand;

(ii) In most cases where only asymmetric payoff spaces are feasible, but individuals are symmetrically situated by imposition of the 'veil of ignorance' (the typical case of symmetric situation also for Kaplow and Shavell) it is very reasonable to put maximization of aggregate welfare completely aside in order to maintain egalitarianism, without any contradiction of 'general acceptance' understood as a strong Pareto condition;

(iii) Even in the special case where the legal regimes under assessment correspond to a feasible payoffs space that renders egalitarianism Pareto-dominated, egalitarianism has reasonable priority over welfare maximization as the criterion for identifying the payoffs allocation that should be generated in order to make such a regime acceptable. It constrains Pareto improvements reasonably acceptable by all players to be consistent with the *least* deviation from perfect egalitarianism; moreover, it reasonably debars players from reaching solutions of welfare maximization that would be naturally acceptable if no weight were given to fairness.

Before arguing in favor of these propositions, let us recall that Kaplow and Shavell define a fairness principle as an assessment criterion not consequentialist and not entirely based on personal well-being measures, i.e. not entirely reducible to an assessment of the individuals' subjective welfare perceptions annexed to consequences that happen to each individual under such a legal rule.[4] Thus a fairness principle is an assessment criterion $Z(x)$ where x is a legal regime, or rather a state of affairs described in terms of individual actions regulated by the relevant regime, but not necessarily (and only) their consequences.[5] Thus Z is not reducible to a description of personal well-being levels or utilities and their aggregation (summation or multiplication or whatsoever) because it evaluates x in terms of other characteristics – for example, fairness, rights or duties. Egalitarianism falls within this assessment category: it accounts for the state x in terms of a ratio between agents' payoffs, which admittedly presupposes a description of personal utilities but says more. It states how equal is the *proportion* between players' payoffs, whatever they are in absolute terms. It is a *relation* not reducible to a measure of how well individuals fare as distinct persons or as an aggregate.

Be warned that Kaplow and Shavell's argument is tricky. Fairness considerations are accommodated by welfare maximization because individuals possibly develop a *taste* for fairness.[6] Thus fairness becomes an object of preference exactly like any other consequence or good whereby it can be accounted through the personal subjective well-being that individuals attach to this taste. No doubt, the formal treatment of preferences can be extended to make room for fairness principles as motives to act and represent them through utility functions (for a proper enlargement of the motives to act represented by utility functions see part III of this essay). But calling a *taste* the motivational importance that we give to adhering to principles is quite at odds with intuition. In fact, there is no reason to reduce preferences – i.e. binary relations expressing whatsoever *betterness* judgment consistent with behavior (see Broome, 1999) – to the idiosyncratic case of *tastes*.

It is also noticeable that this immunization move entails that Kaplow and Shavell's theory is virtually devoid of any empirical content (and perhaps paradoxical). Assume that most people are convinced of the view that Kaplow and Shavell wish to confute. Nearly everybody prefers to assess legal regimes by fairness principles not completely dependent on individual well-being – for example, by using equality as a choice criterion. Since they prefer to perform assessments of this kind, Kaplow and Shavell would say that the people have a taste for fairness, and hence that people's welfare is maximized by assessing legal regimes on the basis of a criterion that gives no essential relevance to welfare maximization. Given such a social preference, Kaplow and Shavell would conclude that legal regimes are chosen solely on the basis of considerations of personal well-being and welfare maximization, even though the actual assessment of legal rules accommodated by their own theory rests on fairness principles which do not primarily refer to personal well-being. Could one say that such a theory is useful in any sense? Defining a different social choice rule consistent with the fact that individual utilities are functions (also) of fairness principles – appropriately understood as measures of the motivational strength of individuals' adhesions to fairness principles – would be more useful than collapsing everything into generic welfare maximization.

However, let us set aside these comments and take Kaplow and Shavell's thesis at its best. How would it work in our context of constitutional choice on intuitional regimes of corporate governance and control? It is clearly irrelevant in the simplest case where only constitutions represented by symmetric payoff space are feasible. Such constitutions are increasingly ordered in terms of Pareto dominance by inclusiveness of their payoff spaces; and the acceptability of their egalitarian solutions monotonically depends on the inclusiveness ordering defined on spaces. In this case, there is no divorce between egalitarianism and efficiency. Given the perfect equality of players, no reasonable bargaining theory may ask players to accept any solution except the symmetrical one. At the same time, the intuition that the solution must fall on the bisector is simply completed by the requirement that it also resides on the payoff frontier. As this is true under any initial symmetric feasible payoff space, it is also true under any symmetrical translation of the payoff space which cannot destroy the original symmetry of the situation. In fact, impersonality and the veil of ignorance, operationalized through symmetric translation of the payoff space, map the space onto itself, generating a perfectly identical payoff space. Players are perfectly identically situated and see the solution in exactly the same way under the roles of both players. Solution invariance under symmetric translation of the payoff space (which is the egalitarian requirement derived from impersonality and impartiality) is naturally satisfied by keeping to the symmetric solution that already proved intuitive given the initial payoff space representation. Even though egalitarianism is defined in term of the payoffs *ratio* (1/1), not a specific allocation of any welfare amount, it is not inconsistent, but rather perfectly compatible, with 'general acceptance' as Pareto dominance because it requires taking the intersection of the bisector with the north-east boundary of the payoff space as uniquely defined solution.

However, Kaplow and Shavell's thesis seems rather relevant to cases where the only outcome spaces corresponding to feasible constitutions are asymmetrical and reflect inequalities among players. Players can then be identically situated with respect to the decision problem precisely because of the symmetrical translation of the payoff space that allows the mutual replacement of their personal and position-relative points of view, and the introduction the veil of ignorance in order to seek a solution which is impartial and independent from any personal perspective. Owing to feasibility and the *No Deus ex machina* assumption, identically situated players must choose the solution from within the intersection set and pick it up on the bisector. Thus, in the case of two possible feasible constitutions, no matter what their further efficiency properties, the one with highest egalitarian solution must be chosen – because it is identified by a monotonic function of symmetrical intersections sets inclusiveness. No doubt, this solution will not generally satisfy most of the usual welfare maximization concepts, such as utilitarianism, or the largest Nash bargaining product with respect to alternative feasible constitutions. Moreover, such welfarist solutions could be easily reached from the egalitarian solution through Kaldor–Hicks utility side-transfers that testify to the social efficiency of these further solutions.

Nevertheless, there are very good reasons for not accepting these solutions instead of the best egalitarian one. These reasons are *feasibility* together with the *'veil of ignorance'* and awareness that there is *No Deus ex machina* able to enforce any agreement that players may reach in the constitutional choice context. Impartiality and impersonality (underlying the veil of ignorance) are independent of personal well-being and they constrain the solution to be on the bisector. Feasibility, together with the *No Deus ex machina* hypothesis, requires that such a solution must be reached within the intersection set. Quitting this outcome set in order to reach the welfare-maximizing solution would simply mean that one party can impose looking at the solution solely from his/her point of view, because s/he is effectively the stronger player in the actual game of life. Conversely, looking at the solution from the perspective of the symmetrically translated payoff space would be considered pure wishful thinking. But the egalitarian solution within the intersection set is also feasible, i.e. it corresponds to an equilibrium under both the payoff spaces representations. Its implementation is incentive compatible whatever personal role is taken by players. This impartial realism overrides the claim of the fortunate player to profit unilaterally from his strongest position. For an example see Figure 8.13, where S_1 in P_1 is both the utilitarian solution and the highest value of the Nash bargaining product among any feasible spaces; but nevertheless the chosen constitution is P_2 because its egalitarian solution is better. What about acceptability in terms of making all players worse off or better off? No solution Pareto-dominates the alternative; hence there is no room for asserting that egalitarianism worsens each player's position. It is true that a Kaldor–Hicks utility transfer could improve player 2's position if he agreed to switch from the egalitarian solution to S_1. But why should s/he accept this change rather than any other one more sensitive to fairness considerations?

In order to clarify this point, consider the third case illustrated in Figure 8.14, which is also the most problematic from the egalitarian point of view. The feasible payoff space P_1 is so asymmetric that by considering its translation P_1', the intersection set is a very narrow region of the plan and the egalitarian solution in $P_1 \cap P_1'$ proves to be Pareto-dominated by S_1, where both the maximal utilitarian solution and the maximum Nash bargaining product reside, with respect to any other feasible outcome. This seems to be a case where keeping to fairness makes all players worse off, which – according to Kaplow and Shavell – is unacceptable. In fact, player 1 could try to convince player 2 to relinquish egalitarianism with the reasonable argument that there is a mutual advantage in switching to S_1. To be sure, this would entail also relinquishing adhesion to principles of impersonality and impartiality, because accepting S_1 means selecting the bargaining solution rationally reachable by playing the post-constitutional bargaining game related to space P_1 as a separate game, without any pretence of choosing a solution under a veil of ignorance. But in

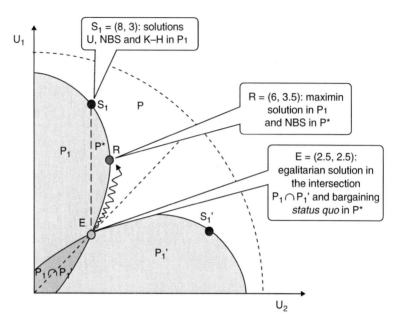

Figure 8.14   The maximin solution as Pareto improvement from Egalitarianism

the end, why defend impersonality and impartiality if these principles condemn everybody to having the worse?

But this is not the case. On the contrary, giving egalitarianism priority
over welfare maximization is perfectly reasonable because it allows mutually
acceptable Pareto improvements with respect to the egalitarian solution itself.
Egalitarian solutions constrain Pareto efficiency in so far as egalitarianism is
taken to be the proper starting point from which acceptable Pareto improvements are calculated. This solution is the maximin point R on the north-east
frontier of the space P_1, where player 2's payoffs (the disadvantaged player) are
improved as much as possible, no matter what the marginal payoff improvement of player 1 (who for each player 2's improvement obviously fares better
than player 2 him-/herself). According to this solution, Pareto improvements
with respect to E are achieved by moving along the frontier of P_1, and they end
as soon as no better improvement in player 2's payoff is possible. This solution
dominates E, but it makes sense only because E is taken to be the appropriate
status quo from which the Pareto improvements process is started.

Assume that E is initially accepted owing to impersonality and impartiality
seen as independent (from personal well-being) conditions, under the additional assumptions of feasibility and *No Deus ex machina*. Then, player 1 proposes to player 2 a switch from E to S_1 for reasons of mutual advantage. Player

2 can reply that it is also unfair not to consider the alternative Pareto-dominant solution S_1', that would advantage her rather than player 1 if the symmetrical translation P_1' were assumed as the payoff space from which to select the solution. Thus she suggests that some compromise between the two solutions S_1 and S_1' should be agreed upon in order to improve over E. However, player 1 may insist that seeking a solution in P_1' is pointless: space P_1' is only a virtual, conjectural payoff space admitted for convenience of the veil of ignorance exercise, but only P_1 is the relevant payoff space of the game players will actually play. Agreeing on S_1 prevents mere cheap talk because it entails reaching an equilibrium point that will be executed in the implementation stage. By contrast, if an agreed random mechanism were to select the corresponding solution S_1', player 1 could simply veto its implementation. Since all this is common knowledge, it can be also anticipated by both the players at the stage where they are to select a proper constitution by the social contract. In other words, S_1' is outside the feasible agreement set that they can reach at this stage because player 1's *actual* concession limit does not extend to include S_1'.

Note that all of these are arguments of rational bargaining. Hence, by similar argument, player 2 can recall that the solution E, being itself an equilibrium point lying within both spaces P_1 and P_1', is the status quo of a bargaining game seen as a second thought in the constitutional choice. In fact, E has been accepted at least as a first step in the selection of the solution; so it is the outcome that will be effectively implemented if the players do not agree to any further improvement of E. By sticking to E, player 1 can effectively veto any unacceptable change to the constitutional solution. What results is a new bargaining problem which takes E as the status quo that delimits the set of possible agreements as those included within the players' concession limits on the Pareto frontier of P_1.

A peculiarity of the new bargaining problem is that the status quo point E defines as the relevant bargaining set the outcome subspace P*. In P*, the players' incentives to reach an agreement are different. Whilst player 2 is restricted to claiming only her minimal acceptable payoff fixed at E (e.g. *2.5*), on the other hand a very large surplus appropriable by player 1 is created (e.g. *8.5*). Any movement from that position in order to improve player 2's payoff entails a trade-off (a conflict) between player 1 and player 2. By contrast, restricting player 1 to claiming only her minimal acceptable payoff set at E (*2.5*) is of no value to player 2. Moving from this position along the payoff frontier in order to improve player 1's payoffs on the status quo is also in the best interest of player 2. She fares better and better by also raising player 1's payoff until player 2's maximum possible payoff in P* is reached at R = (*6, 3.5*). This means that player 2 is a much more profitable bargaining partner for player 1 than the other way round, because there is much less bargaining attrition in reaching player 2's most desirable agreements – which are also desirable to player 1 – than player 1's most desirable agreements. In other words, player 1 is much readier to satisfy player 2's claims to improve her payoff than player 2 is in regard to player 1, since in order to satisfy player 1's most desired claim, s/he needs to forgo any possible improvements, whereas player 1 does not face any payoff renunciation by satisfying player 2's highest claim. This clearly reflects upon the Nash bargaining solution relative to the bargaining sub-problem (E, P*) because it coincides with the maximin point R, where the disadvantaged player 2's payoff is maximized.

Consider again the numerical example of Figure 8.14. Payoffs at S_1 are *(8, 3)* for player 1 and 2 respectively. Both the utilitarian solution *(11)* and the Nash bargaining product (24) are maximal at S_1 with respect to the entire P_1 space. But now impose E as the status quo of a new bargaining problem with the subspace P* as the appropriate bargaining set. Players' payoffs at E are *(2.5, 2.5)*. Then at the maximin point R = *(5, 3.5)* the Nash bargaining product is greater than at S_1:

$$(6 - 2.5) \times (3.5 - 2.5) = 3.5 > (8 - 2.5) \times (3 - 2.5) = 2.75$$

Thus the players would accept the point R as the constitutional choice of the final payoff allocation that must be carried out by selecting the constitution corresponding to P_1, which entails a redress (from *3* to *3.5*) of player 2 with respect to the solution S_1 reachable in the relevant post-constitutional bargaining game. This shift of the bargaining solution is entirely caused by taking the egalitarian solution E as the appropriate status quo of the second bargaining step in constitutional choice, an assumption due to impersonality and impartiality considerations that are independent of personal well-being. True, this induces setting aside welfare maximization solutions belonging to P_1. However, it does not contradict Pareto-dominance at all, because the solution R Pareto-improves on E; or rather, it is the only acceptable Pareto improvement attainable by rational bargaining from E.

Summing up, fairness precedes efficiency in that it establishes the relevant status quo from which the proper Pareto improvement can be calculated. Moreover, it constrains such improvements to converge to the maximin solution R, so that no Pareto-efficient improvement is admitted whenever there exists another that would reduce the distance from perfect egalitarianism more (indeed R is the point belonging to the Pareto frontier of P_1 nearest to the bisector).

6.2   Just minimizing transaction costs?

Much closer to the corporate governance literature is Hansmann's theory of 'ownership of the firm', which is based on the principle that a single stakeholder class should be given property and control over the firm when this regime minimizes the aggregate value of transaction costs resulting from the summation of governance costs held by the controlling party and the aggregate contract costs held by all the remaining (non-controlling) stakeholders (see Hansmann, 1988, 1996). This is also an aggregate efficiency or wealth maximization criterion seen as a proxy for the utilitarian solution. Hence it is set aside by Rawlsian theory as a solution for the constitutional choice of corporate governance institutions.

Let us assume that each post-constitutional game played under its relevant constitution generates aggregate costs allocations according to Hansmann's formula, and that one particular ownership regime minimizes them. Player 1 could bear the minimal governance cost with respect to any other player, and also his governance costs could be smaller than his contract cost, so that giving him control over the firm would certainly reduce overall costs with respect to a situation of 'no corporate ownership and control' – admitted that it does not increase other players' contract costs too much. This can also minimize the overall costs if player 1's contract costs, replaced by his minimal governance costs, are higher than other players' contract costs. Nevertheless, this solution could also not be Pareto-dominant with respect to a more costly institutional alternative if player 1's ownership and control regime were more abusive in terms of player 2's contract costs rather than player 2's control regime in terms of player 1's contract costs (induced by player 2's abuse). This may hold even though, by substituting her 'natural' contract costs with her governance costs, player 2 could only gain a small improvement in terms of efficiency. For example, assume that in a 'state of nature' of no ownership and control over the productive organization where business relations are only subject to incomplete contracts, players 1 and 2 bear contract costs (7, 7) respectively. Giving ownership and control to player 1 would replace his contract costs with the minimal governance cost 1, but owing to his abuse of authority such a control structure would only slightly reduce player 2's contract costs to 6. On the other hand, giving ownership to player 2 would give more protection to player 1 by reducing his contract costs to 5, but it would inefficiently replace player 2's contract costs with her high governance costs set at 4. Overall, transaction costs under player 1's control score 7 and are minimal, whereas the 'state of nature' badly scores 14 and player 2's control scores 9. Nonetheless, there is no reason for player 2 to agree to give control to player 1 rather than claiming control for herself, as long as her cost amount to 4 by controlling and to 6 by not controlling.

The natural response would be to resort to a Kaldor–Hicks efficient side-payment that would immunize player 2 under player 1's control against the effect of his authority abuse, so that her contract costs are kept below 4. But, of course, in our context the question arises of whether or not this side-payment may fall within a feasible outcome set. Giving so much authority to party 1 under the non-credible promise that he will repay player 2 in the future for his authority abuse may not correspond to any feasible (equilibrium) solution in the *ex post* perspective.

According to Rawlsian theory, in this situation it may be necessary to choose a different governance structure; for example, by giving control to player 2 if this structure may have a better egalitarian effect on the allocation of payoffs. This happens if this better (in the Paretian sense) egalitarian allocation: (i) is an equilibrium point resident within the intersection set of the payoff space corresponding to the less efficient governance structure (player 2 control) and its symmetrical translation; and (ii) it can be reached from the cost allocation of the post-constitutional game (e.g. the cost allocation (5,4)) by moving within the equilibrium set of the game. In fact, whereas the first side-payment could be unfeasible, this redress mechanism in favor of player 1 corresponds to an equilibrium point and is therefore perfectly implementable.

6.3   Really is social justice a mirage?

There are other commonplace tenets in the field of the economics of institutions that the Rawlsian theory calls into question. Most of the new-institutional theorizing on the governance and control structures of the firm (and other institutions) is based on the implicit postulate that institution design cannot go further than prescribing outcomes interpretable to a certain extent as *spontaneous orders*, or at least as corresponding to outcomes that could be achieved by a spontaneous order. Hayek would certainly see commercial law and corporate governance codes, institutions and principles as sets of norms resulting as spontaneous orders from evolution (see also Vanberg's idea of corporations as constitutional contracts; Vanberg 1992).

Only spontaneous orders are self-enforcing norms – that is, they do not require the intervention of an external *Deus ex machina* that would heavily constrain individual freedom. This responds to a demand for stability. But this statement points out a concern for freedom of choice. It is the same, but in milder form, as the requirement that any institutional design must be 'incentive compatible' – incentives are only relevant to decision makers who are at a certain level free to choose.

Often, this is not just a descriptive belief concerning the fact that economic agents are more or less free and hence able to circumvent any strict regulation that does not provide for an equilibrium property. It is also a normative presumption that freedom of choice must be respected. Now take this normative value as granted and understand it as the central concern of the libertarian standpoint. Our theory has unexpected implications for mild libertarians as well.

Corollary 2: Mild libertarians cannot but be egalitarians.

A mild libertarian would not reject the contention that individual agents must enter the 'original position under the veil of ignorance'. Granted the priority of freedom and spontaneous order, s/he would take the veil of ignorance standpoint at least in order to make an impartial assessment of possible spontaneous order outcomes and to voluntarily agree on such an outcome that is also invariant under the symmetrical permutation of players' roles.

However, constraining the libertarian position with a concern for impartiality, plus the concern for *ex post* stability (no *Deus ex machina*), has dramatic consequences for the libertarian point of view. Freedom requires spontaneous order (equilibrium), but constraining it by impartiality entails that the only admissible subset of spontaneous orders is the symmetric intersection of the equilibrium set with its symmetric translation. Thus only governance and control structures providing for an egalitarian payoffs distribution (at least in term of redress) are acceptable. Once the 'spontaneous order' outcome space has been restricted to the symmetrical subset resulting from the intersection of the original space and its symmetrical translation, the egalitarian solution is the only one acceptable through the players' free agreement.

Libertarians such as Hayek (1973) and Nozick (1974) have militated strongly against any redistributive notion of social justice. But far from ostracizing the 'mirage of social justice', even in the small-scale society constituted by the stakeholders of a firm, a moderate impartial libertarian *cannot but be egalitarian* in the selection of the firm's governance structure.

7 Unique *ex ante* equilibrium selection in the repeated Trust Game and end remarks

Let us return to the problem of the *ex ante* justification of a particular equilibrium as raised in part I of this essay. The 'game of life' played by the firm and its stakeholders was then represented as a repeated Trust Game (TG) where the entire positive region of the payoff space is constituted by Nash equilibria. In this second part, I have been concerned with a generalization of this case by taking the constituent game played by the firm (Adam) and the stakeholder (Eve) as a generic social dilemma resembling an asymmetric prisoners' dilemma (PD) with an enlarged set of pure strategies. The basic difference is that, in the TG, only one side (the firm) can profit from abusing the other player's trustworthy behavior, whereas the only profitable payoff for the stakeholder is reaching the symmetrical cooperation outcome (2,2) when – as usually assumed – it exists. In a typical PD representation of the stakeholder/firm interaction, the two parties would have symmetric abilities to cheat one another. The asymmetric PD-like social dilemma here assumed was midway between the two. Eve (the stakeholder) is allowed some defection opportunity from the contract, even though non-cooperative resources with which to take advantage of the other side's cooperation are in general more profitable to the stronger player Adam (the firm) – what in fact represents in our situation the 'game of life' imbalance of power, and also captures the effects of abuse of authority in the stakeholder/firm interaction. But we can now come back to the trust game,

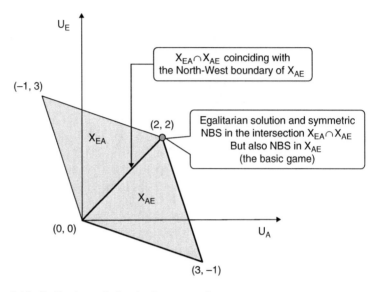

Figure 8.15   Egalitarian solution in the repeated trust game

which was assumed to be the simplest and most typical formal representation of the implementation problem related to a CSR social norm based on the social contract of the firm, because this problem is addressed through the firm and its stakeholders' strategic interaction.

It is remarkable that Rawlsian theory gives a particularly simple and compelling solution to the *ex ante* equilibrium selection problem when the repeated TG is considered. The requirement of selecting a solution within the intersection of the basic outcome space X_{AE} (see Figure 8.15) and its symmetric translation is sufficient for singling out a unique solution, once the obvious Pareto dominance condition has been granted, which cannot but be the egalitarian Nash bargaining solution of the original game. In order to achieve this result, we need not concern ourselves with the complex construction of equally probable linear combinations between outcomes resident in a payoff space and its translated version – which is typical of the probabilistic interpretation of the veil of ignorance. Only relevant assumptions are *impersonality* (the capacity to permute the individual players' points of view) plus *feasibility* (to stay within the intersection set generated through impersonality), so that the solution must reside within the intersection set generated by rotation of the payoff space X_{AE} around its north-west boundary. But the intersection set is quite peculiar in this case. It coincides exactly with the north-west boundary itself of the payoff space, which lies on the bisector. Because it is reduced to a segment of the 45° line, the solution cannot but be the only point on this line segment belonging to the Pareto frontier, i.e. the symmetric Nash bargaining solution (2,2).

Thus applying the 'veil of ignorance reasoning' without a *Deus ex machina* provides a reason for selecting the intuitively fair outcome (2,2) of the Trust Game.

Note that the key point in arriving at this conclusion is simply that an impartial exercise of choice (replacement invariance) must select an equilibrium point *within* the intersection set; that is, an equilibrium point that necessarily exists and is therefore implementable by each player whatever the position he or she occupies in the *ex post* perspective. A stability condition (the solution must lie in the set of those points that correspond to *ex post* implementable equilibria) linked with the weak fairness condition of invariance to players' replacement is sufficient to derive the egalitarian solution. Thus, the social contract as an explicit normative method of impartial reasoning helps resolve the multiplicity problem from the *ex ante* perspective in an extremely simple way in the repeated Trust Game.

However, this result should not be overemphasized as far as the equilibrium selection problem is concerned. What would effectively solve the multiplicity problem is an equilibrium selection theory able to predict the *ex post* game equilibrium solution so that it is consistent with the *ex ante* solution identified. In other words, selection is *ex post* effective only if it gives reasons to act that fit the *ex post* reasoning context. *Ex post*, only common knowledge of the solution – that is, a system of mutually consistent expectations converging on the prediction of a uniquely determined equilibrium point – conveys to each player the appropriate reason to act, because choosing an equilibrium strategy amongst many others requires having a clear prediction of other players' behavior and beliefs. However, from that in the *ex ante* perspective a solution is invariant to the players' position replacement, there is no logical reason to conclude that that solution will be effectively implemented. The reason that justifies a particular decision in the *ex post* game is knowledge of what the players will effectively do. Moreover, this knowledge about the other players' decisions must be consistent with their being symmetrically able to predict the others' behavior and to choose their best response to those predictions. Therefore, it is not the impartial selection of a desirable *ex ante* solution, but the knowledge of other players' *de facto* behaviors that provides the proper reason for acting in the *ex post* context. Moreover, there is no logical implication from what is fair *ex ante* selection (even if it falls on an equilibrium point) as to what other players will actually do. Maybe they will act in accordance with the principle, maybe not. The fair *ex ante* agreement, or impartial choice, does not gives us common knowledge of the *ex post* behavior of players. If, however, one does not know how other players will behave, one has no reason to play a given strategy, even though the fair solution is part of an equilibrium point.

This is not to say that the *ex ante* agreement on an impartial solution does not provide any cue to believe that players will act according to the same principle in the *ex post* interaction. But this is simply a matter of fact, or of cognitive psychology, not a matter of logic. Common knowledge, on the contrary, is a matter of epistemic logic: this means recursive group knowledge of what everybody knows to be true (a *truism*).[7] It is the case that a given equilibrium is *commonly known* to be played only if each player has many layers of knowledge about every other player's action, beliefs, beliefs about beliefs, and so on, that are consistent and justify the prediction that this equilibrium will be played. This state of knowledge can be approximated by a theory of belief formation that at last leads us to a stable prediction of any other player's equilibrium choice and belief (see Sacconi 2011). *Ex ante* selection, on the contrary, does not predict how one will actually decide; it only answers the question of what equilibrium *should* be chosen, because it is invariant under the individuals' position replacement. The step from an answer to the question of which equilibrium is *fair* to an answer to the question of how players will *actually* behave is a *default inference* that some player may in fact make; but this is just a possibility. Thus, from the perspective of the *ex post* game, there is still much to do before the multiplicity problem is solved.

Notes

1. This section presents my own account of Binmore's theory. Because it has evolved over time (Binmore 1984, 1989, 1994, 1998, 2005), I do not claim that my treatment is entirely consistent with all of the theory's statements, especially with its multifaceted attempt to give biological and evolutionary foundations to the Rawlsian social contract. But it is the best way for me to make sense of it, and to put it at the basis of my own revision of the theory of constitutional choice on corporate governance structures. Even if reference could be made to many of Binmore's papers and books, and especially to his first paper 'Game Theory and the Social Contract' (1984), I will confine my references in this section mainly to the last one (Binmore 2005).
2. For an example, in the case of the repeated trust game see Figure 7.2 in part I.
3. For a detailed exposition of how the dogmas of the overriding ness of welfare maximization and efficiency over fairness permeate all the economics of institutions, see Kaplow and Shavell (2002).
4. See Kaplow and Shavell (2002).
5. Ibid.
6. See op. cit. pag. 78.
7. The *ex post* rationality of the Nash equilibrium – implied by the notion of common knowledge – was already clear in Lewis (1968), who also suggested that an agreement could give an empirical explanation of how a state of common knowledge could emerge. He, however, focused on the different cognitive phenomena of salience. On the game-theoretic definition of common knowledge, see Binmore and Brandeburger (1990) and Kreps (1990); on the epistemic logic of common knowledge, see Fagin, Halpern, Moses and Vardi (1996).

    On the selection of Nash equilibria based on common knowledge of the unique solution see Harsany and Selten (1988).

References

Arrow, K. (1951) *Social Choice and Individual Values*. New York, Wiley (Italian translation: *Scelte sociali e valori individuali*. Milano: Etas libri, 1977).

Binmore, K. (1984) 'Game Theory and the Social Contract' ST/ICERD Discussion Paper (84/108), LSE , London.

Binmore, K. (1987) 'Modeling Rational Players', *Economics and Philosophy*, vol. 1(3), pp. 9–55 and vol. 2(4), pp. 179–214.

Binmore, K. (1989) 'Social Contract I: Harsanyi and Rawls', *The Economic Journal*, Vol. 99, No. 395, pp. 84–102.

Binmore, K. and A. Brandenburger (1990) 'Common Konwledge and Game Theory', in K. Binmore, *Essays on the Foundations of Game Theory*. Oxford: Basil Blackwell.

Binmore, K. (1991) 'Game Theory and the Social Contract', in R. Selten (ed.), *Game Equilibrium Models II, Methods, Morals, Markets*. Berlin: Springer Verlag.

Binmore, K. (1994) *Game Theory and the Social Contract (Vol. I): Playing Fair*. Cambridge MA: MIT Press.

Binmore, K. (1998) *Game Theory and the Social Contract (Vol. II):Just Playing*. Cambridge MA: MIT Press.

Binmore, K. (2005) *Natural Justice*. Oxford: Oxford University Press.

Buchanan, J. (1975) *The Limits of Liberty*. Chicago: The University of Chicago Press.

Brock, H. (1979) 'A Game Theoretical Account of Social Justice', *Theory and Decision*, vol. 11, pp. 239–65.

Broome, J. (1999) *Ethics Out of Economics*. Cambridge: Cambridge University Press.

Fagin, R. J.Y. Halpern, Y. Moses and M.Y. Vardi (1996) 'Common Knowledge: How you have it, now you don't' in Intelligent Systems: A Semiotic Perspective, Proc. 1996 Int. Multidisciplinary Conf., vol. 1, pp. 177–83.

Fundenberg, D. and J. Tirole (1991) *Game Theory*. Cambridge, MA: MIT Press.

Gauthier, D. (1986) *Morals by Agreement*. Oxford: Clarendon Press.

Grossman, S. and O. Hart (1986) 'The Costs and Benefit of Ownership: A Theory of Vertical and Lateral Integration', *Journal of Political Economy*, vol. 94, pp. 691–719.

Hansmann, H. (1988) 'Ownership of the Firm', *Journal of Law Economics and Organization*, vol. 4(2), pp. 267–304.

Hansmann, H. (1996) *The Ownership of the Enterprise*. Cambridge, MA: Harvard University Press.

Harsanyi, J.C. (1977) *Rational Behaviour and Bargaining Equilibrium in Games and Social Situations*. Cambridge, MA: Cambridge University Press.

Harsanyi, J.C and R. Selten (1988) *A General Theory of Equilibrium Selection*. Cambridge, MA: MIT Press.

Hart, O. (1995) *Firms, Contracts and Financial Structure*. Oxford: Clarendon Press.

Hart, O. and J. Moore (1990) 'Property Rights and the Nature of the Firm', *Journal of Political Economy*, vol. 98, pp. 1119–58.

Hayek, F.A. (1973) *Law, Legislation and Liberty*. Chicago: University of Chicago Press.

Kaplow, L. and S. Shavell (2002) *Fairness versus Welfare*. Cambridge, MA: Harvard University Press.

Kreps, D. (1990) 'Corporate Culture and Economic Theory', in J. Alt and K. Shepsle (eds), *Perspective on Positive Political Economy*. Cambridge: Cambridge University Press.

Kreps, D. (1990) *Games and Economic Modeling*. Oxford: Oxford University Press.

Nash, J. (1950) 'The Bargaining Problem', *Econometrica*, vol. 18, pp. 155–62.

Nozick, R. (1974) *Anarchy, State and Utopia.* New York: Basic Books.

Ostrom, E. (1990) *Governing the Commons.* New York: Cambridge University Press.

Rawls, J. (1971) *A Theory of Justice.* Oxford: Oxford University Press.

Rawls, J. (1993) *Political Liberalism.* New York: Columbia University Press.

Sacconi, L. (1991) *Etica degli affari, individui, imprese e mercati nella prospettiva dell'etica razionale.* Milano: Il Saggiatore.

Sacconi, L, (1997) *Economia, etica, organizzazione.* Bari: Laterza.

Sacconi, L. (2000) *The Social Contract of the Firm: Economics, Ethics and Organisation.* Berlin: Springer Verlag.

Sacconi, L. (2006a) 'CSR as a Model of Extended Corporate Governance: An Explanation Based on the Economic Theory of Social Contract, Reputation and Reciprocal Conformism', in F. Cafaggi (ed.), *Reframing Self-regulation in European Private Law.* London: Kluwer Law International.

Sacconi, L. (2006b) 'A Social Contract Account For CSR as Extended Model of Corporate Governance (Part I): Rational Bargaining and Justification', *Journal of Business Ethics,* vol. 68(3), pp. 259–81.

Sacconi, L. (2007a) 'A Social Contract Account for CSR as Extended Model of Corporate Governance (Part II): Compliance, Reputation and Reciprocity', *Journal of Business Ethics,* vol. 75(1), pp. 77–96.

Sacconi, L. (2007) 'Incomplete Contracts and Corporate Ethics: A Game Theoretical Model under Fuzzy Information', in F. Cafaggi, A. Nicita and U. Pagano (eds), *Legal Orderings and Economic Institutions.* London: Routledge.

Sacconi, L. (2008b) 'CSR as Contractarian Model of Multi-Stakeholder Corporate Governance and the Game-Theory of its Implementation, University of Trento – Department of Economics Working paper No. 18.

Sacconi, L. (2009) 'Corporate Social Responsibility: Implementing a Contractarian Model of Multi-stakeholder Corporate Governance trough Game Theory', in J.P. Touffut and R. Solow (eds), *Does Company Ownership Matter?,* Centre for Economic Studies Series. London: Edward Elgar Publishing.

Sacconi, L. (2010a) 'A Rawlsian View of CSR and the Game Theory of its Implementation (Part I): The Multistakeholder Model of Corporate Governance', in L. Sacconi, M. Blair, E. Freeman and A. Vercelli (eds), *'Corporate Social Responsibility and Corporate Governance: The Contribution of Economic Theory and Related Disciplines'.*

Sacconi, L. (2011) 'A Rawlsian View of CRS and the Game of its Implementation (Part III): Conformism and Equilibrium Selection', in L. Sacconi and G. Degli Antoni (eds), *Social Capital, Corporate Social Responsibility, Economic Behavior and Performance.* Basingstoke: Palgrave MacMillan London (forthcoming 2011).

Vanberg, V.J. (1992) 'Organizations as constitutional systems' *Constitutional political Economy,* vol. 3(2).

Willamson, O. (1975) *Market and Hierarchies. New* York: The Free Press.

Zimmerman, H.J. (1991) *Fuzzy Set Theory and Its Applications,* 2nd revised edn. Dordrecht and Boston: Kluwer Academic Press.

9
When Reputation is not Enough: Justifying Corporate Social Responsibility

Luciano Andreozzi

1 Introduction

In a survey on corporate social responsibility (CSR) published in 2005, *The Economist* issued a series of articles that were sternly critical of the idea that firms should commit themselves to explicit codes of ethics. One of the main arguments, repeated on several occasions in the survey, is the familiar one based on the invisible hand, which was originally proposed by Friedman (1970). According to this argument the market economy has proved to be an extremely efficient mechanism for producing and allocating resources. Although advocates of CSR rarely contest this point, they seem to believe that this success has been obtained despite the fact that the market's actors, for example large corporations, usually consider only their own profits when making their decisions. *The Economist* believes that quite the contrary is true: markets achieve such astonishing performances *just because* each agent only minds his own business. Which implies that if firms take ethical codes seriously, as opposed to merely paying lip service to them, the capacity of capitalism to generate wealth could be severely impaired.

A superficial knowledge of modern economics suffices to realize that many hypotheses must be introduced before such a bold statement becomes acceptable. Markets reconcile the pursuit of individual profit with social welfare only when they are close to being perfectly competitive. This requires that such imperfections as monopoly power, public goods, externalities and asymmetric information are small enough to be assumed away. When they are not, there is room for non-selfish motives to play a positive role in improving markets' performances.

Take trust, for example. When goods are traded on the spot and there is no asymmetric information, buyers need not trust sellers and the market would work fine even among sociopaths devoid of any moral sense (Gintis, 2007). Unfortunately, not all markets work this smoothly. In the presence of asymmetric information, or when goods are delivered after the payment is made, buyers need to trust sellers that the goods they purchase are of the agreed upon quality, and that they will be delivered in the due time. Many years ago, Arrow (1974) equated trust to 'an important lubricant of a social system'. 'Trust and similar values, loyalty or truth-telling, are examples of what the economist would call "externalities." They are goods, they are commodities; ... they increase the efficiency of the system, enable you to produce more goods or more of whatever values you hold in high esteem' (p. 23).

Of course, *The Economist*'s journalists know enough economics to anticipate this line of attack and have a prompt reply. Purely self-interested agents will show no concern for trustworthiness or fairness only in those circumstances in which they think they can get away with it. This is typically the case when one's reputation is not at stake, for example because one knows that he will not deal again with the person he is cheating. When a seller interacts with a buyer every day, however, she will have a reason not to cheat today because she knows that she is going to meet the same customer tomorrow. All it takes to generate virtuous behavior is enlightened self-interest, which includes the ability to foresee the consequences of one's own actions and to pay attention to future profits. According to *The Economist*, self-interest so defined is the main ingredient of a well-functioning market and must not be confused with 'greed'.

> Greed, in the ordinary meaning of the word, is not rational or calculating. Freely indulged, it makes you fat and drives you into bankruptcy. The kind of self-interest that advances the public good is rational and enlightened. Rational, calculating self-interest makes a person, or a firm, worry about its reputation for honesty and fair dealing, for paying debts and honouring agreements. It looks beyond the short term and plans ahead. It considers sacrifices today for the sake of gains tomorrow, or five years from now. It makes good neighbours. (*The Economist*, 2005)

The negative lesson of this line of thought for CSR is easily drawn: if fair and trustworthy behavior is just one form of self-interest, then there is no apparent need to give it a different name. A butcher who refrains from selling rotten meat to his recurring customers is only serving his own (long-run) interest, and this decision deserves to be labeled as 'ethical' no more than his decision to periodically renovate his shop to make it amenable to the clientele.

This kind of argument echoes some positions that are well established within the economic profession. For example, E.O. Williamson notes that '... it is redundant at best and can be misleading to use the term "trust" to describe commercial exchange for which cost-effective safeguards have been devised in support of more efficient exchange. Calculative trust is a contradiction in terms' (Williamson, 1993: 463).

In this article Williamson uses the word 'trust', and its companion 'trustworthiness', with their normative content. You trust somebody if you believe that he will not abuse your trust even if it were not in his strict self-interest to do so. When being trustworthy goes hand in hand with self-interest, this normative content disappears.

Proponents of CSR thus face a dilemma which is deeply rooted in all forms of moral reasoning.[1] If a code of ethics only prescribes choices that are compatible with enlightened self-interest, it is at least hypocritical to mask it with anything different from normal decency and prudence. On the other hand, most observers who are not directly involved in the CSR business are rightly sceptical about the ability of large corporations to commit to practices that systematically hurt their own ability to produce profits, even when this would enhance society's overall welfare. A strong version of CSR (which prescribes non-optimal choices in the name of society's welfare) looks impracticable. A weak version (which only prescribes prudent and optimal choices) looks useless at best.

This chapter addresses these criticisms of CSR on the basis of a slightly less superficial knowledge of modern economic theory. To this end, we shall build on one of the most comprehensive game-theoretical accounts of CSR, that due to Sacconi (2000). Sacconi uses standard results in the theory of repeated games, among which is the so-called *folk theorem*, to show that a rational firm has incentives to adopt (and respect) a code of ethics. At first sight this approach can be criticized by the same arguments we found in *The Economist*'s survey: the use of repeated game considerations introduces just the concern for one's future reputation that makes redundant any appeal to ethics. However, it is a consequence of the folk theorem that repeating a game among the same players produces an enormous number of equilibria, some of which are efficient while others are not. Moreover, fair and trustworthy behavior will be observed in some of the efficient equilibria, but not in others.

The main point of this chapter is that repetition per se is not sufficient to guarantee the emergence of behavior that incorporates normative requisites such as honesty, trustworthiness and the like. Hence, while trust and trustworthiness are *possible* outcomes of reputation, they are by no means the only ones. To make this point we shall propose an extremely simplified evolutionary model based on the repetition of the so-called Trust Game, involving a population of firms and a population of customers. We show that many stable states exists, some of which only contain fair and trustworthy firms, while others contains firms that are moderately dishonest but are still able to induce customers to trust them. This result suggests a possible refinement of the model proposed by Sacconi (2000), in which the code of ethics is viewed as a coordination device. A code of ethics might be viewed as signals firms send in order to better coordinate with their customers on one of the many equilibria of the repeated game they play.

The chapter proceeds as follows. Section 2 introduces and illustrates informally the model that will be discussed throughout. Section 3 discusses and criticizes Sacconi's approach to CSR based on reputation. Sections 4 and 5 introduces the repeated Trust Game and set the stage for the main result of the chapter. Section 6 contains this result: we prove that honest firms that implement a code of ethics might survive in an evolutionary environment, although there are other stable states in which honesty and trustworthiness are not observed. Section 7 discusses the relevance of this result to CSR and offers some conclusions.

2 Reputation and cooperation

This chapter revolves around the simplest situations in which asymmetric information produces a market failure. A firm sells a good whose quality cannot be assessed by customers before the purchase. So customers must trust the firm not to lie about the real quality of the good, and the firm has an incentive to cheat, that is to sell low-quality goods as if they were high quality. Most of the literature on asymmetric information is concerned with the incentives firms have to behave honestly. Once a way is found to induce firms to become trustworthy, consumers' trust will soon come about. As Hardin (2002) puts it, 'trustworthiness begets trust'.

The standard solution to this problem is represented by reputation: if a customer repeatedly interacts with the same firm, the firm will find it worthwhile not to abuse his trust today, in order to have him trusting tomorrow. This argument has an intuitive appeal to it, but neglects one crucial aspect: for the reputation incentive to work, it must be the case that customers be ready to end a relationship with the firm at the first instance of dishonest behavior. This might be an empty threat, though, as it might be costly to carry on. Consider the following example, discussed by Stiglitz:

> If a Chinese restaurant that cheats me by providing an inferior meal (relative to what I had come to expect) has a locational advantage for me, is there any reason I should refuse to go there simply because he has cheated me once? Only if I thought that he was likely to cheat me again. [...] On a priori grounds, then, it is not obvious that it is in the interest of customers who have been cheated by firms selling shoddy products [...] to punish the cheaters. But if they do not punish cheaters, individuals will have no incentive not to cheat, and reputation becomes an ineffective mechanism for enforcing honesty. (Stiglitz, 1989)

So you dined ten evenings at the same Chinese restaurant and have always received impeccable treatment. Should you quit going there just because of one bad meal? Of course, the answer is affirmative if there is no cost to you in doing so, perhaps because there is another, identical Chinese restaurant just round the corner and you know it will treat you handsomely. But if the closest restaurant (of any kind) is ten blocks away, you might consider that being cheated once every ten times is not too bad a deal, and will continue to go there in the future. However, if you are willing to tolerate one bad meal in ten, then the Chinese restaurant will have no reason not to cheat you at least once every ten evenings.

Notice that this argument does not prove that reputation is unable to sustain *some* form of cooperation. While you might find it convenient not to quit the relationship if you are cheated once every ten times, you will surely quit immediately if you expect to be cheated every day. (This assumes that the value of a bad meal is below its cost for you, so you would not tolerate a bad meal every evening. More on this in the next section.) Customers might lack an incentive to enforce *perfect* honesty, but they will surely enforce at least a minimum level of cooperation on the side of the firm.

The problem with reputation, then, is not that it fails to sustain a Pareto improvement with respect to the no-trust condition. Rather, it is its inability to sustain 'honesty' and 'trustworthiness' in the way they are usually defined. This problem resurfaces in all treatments of trust in the economic environment. For example, Horner (2002) notices that the main problem in explaining firm's good behavior in the face of opportunity to cheat is that

> [a] consumer's refusal to purchase from a firm that has sold her a low-quality good must also be rational. In particular, it must be optimal for a consumer to end a long relationship with a firm she had considered trustworthy after perhaps just a short string of bad experiences. (Horner, 2002: 644)

In Horner's model, this problem is solved by competition. When there is a population of firms competing for customers, there is an equilibrium in which all firms are honest because customers have no costs in switching to other (honest) firms. In his approach, 'competition helps preserve reputations', because it 'endogenously generates the outside option for consumers that is necessary to keep firms on their toes, as it gives consumers the power of choosing between the offerings of rival suppliers whose prices adjust to their reputation' (p. 656).

These models, interesting as they are, seem to offer only a partial solution to the original problem posed by Stiglitz. In fact, their optimistic conclusions about the viability of trustworthiness depend on the crucial hypothesis that there is competition among firms, so than none of them has market power. In the next sections we shall follow Sacconi (2000) in modeling CSR as a solution to problems created by markets characterized by asymmetric information *and*

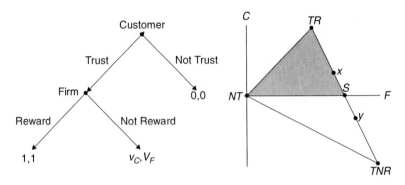

Figure 9.1 The Trust Game (left) and the space of feasible payoffs (right). $V_F = 2$, $v_C = -1$

lack of competition. An important consequence of this choice is that punishing a dishonest firm always has a cost for the consumer. We shall show that this approach involves a problem of equilibrium selection, which we shall address, using an evolutionary approach, in sections 5 and 6.

3   A long-run firm against a population of short-run customers

In discussing the relevance of trust and reputation for 'corporate culture', Kreps (1990) introduced the Trust Game, which is represented in Figure 9.1, on the left. In the version presented here, a player (the Customer) moves first and decides whether to Trust (T) a Firm or not (NT). Then the Firm decides whether to Reward (R) or Not Reward (NR) the Customer's trust. The payoffs are such that $V_F > 1 > 0 > v_C$, so that (NT, NR) is the only subgame perfect equilibrium of the game. This equilibrium is clearly inefficient, as both players get zero, while they could have obtained one by choosing T and R.

This need not be the outcome of the game if we imagine that the Firm plays more than once and hence has the possibility of building a reputation for trustworthiness. In a pair of classical papers published almost two decades ago, Fudenberg and Levine (1989, 1992) introduced a model in which a single long-run player interacts with a population of short-run players (see Fudenberg and Tirole, 1990, chapter 9 for a textbook treatment). In this model, the stage game (for example, the Trust Game) is played repeatedly, but while one of the two positions of the game is occupied always by the same agent, the other position is occupied by a succession of agents drawn by a population of identical players. Before playing the game, the selected short-run player observes the strategy the long-run player has chosen in all the rounds she played before against other short-run players. The idea is that while one of the two players must consider the effects of his current choices on his future reputation, the short-run players are only concerned with their current payoffs, and therefore play a best response to whatever (mixed) strategy they expect the long-run player to choose.

The final ingredient of the model is a degree of incomplete information. The short-run players are unsure about the real payoffs of the long-run player. As in standard models of this kind, short-run players assign a non-zero probability to the fact that the long-run player could be of several different types θ_i, each type being characterized by a different payoff function. Since short-run players are rational, they update their probability distributions on the possible types applying Bayes' rule to the observed behavior of the long-run player.

This model makes a stark prediction concerning the outcome of the game: the long-run player can obtain a payoff that approximates the payoff he would obtain if he could play the game as a Stackelberg leader, that is the same payoff he would get by pre-committing to use one of the (possibly mixed) strategies of the game. To get a feeling of how the proof of this result works, consider first the Stackelberg version of any game Γ (Myerson, 1997). The Stackelberg version of Γ is obtained by having one of the players (the leader) to choose first his strategy, and the other player (the follower) to choose after having observed the choice made by the first one. We shall refer to these strategies as the leader and follower's strategies and we shall indicate them as S_L and S_F respectively. If there is more than one best reply to S_L (a case we shall deal with in a while), S_F is the one that yields the highest payoff *to the leader*.

There is a close connection between the Stackelberg version of a game and its repetition between long-run and short-run players. To see this, suppose that the short-run players initially believe, with strictly positive probability, that the long-run player could be of type θ_S, the *Stackelberg type*, for whom the strategy S_L is dominant. The intuition behind the proof is that if the long-run player is sufficiently forward looking, he will mimic the behavior of a θ_S player, playing S_L at each interaction. This will induce the short-run players to believe that he is of type θ_S, which will make S_F the best response for them. After at most a finite number or rounds, the short-run players will thus start playing S_F and therefore the long-run player will obtain his Stackelberg leader's payoff.

Sacconi (2000) applies the logic of these models to the Trust Game and reasons as follows. Suppose the Trust Game is played repeatedly by a single firm and a succession of customers each of whom only plays once, having observed how the firm has treated all the preceding customers. Customers might believe (initially with a very small probability) that the firm is honest (type θ_H). An honest firm has payoffs such that playing Reward is the dominant strategy (that is $V_R < 1$). A long-run firm that is not honest in this sense (so that $V_R > 1$) might find it convenient to imitate the behavior of an honest firm (playing R with each customer) in order to induce all subsequent customers to play T. Playing NR once would reveal its real type, and will induce all the subsequent customers to play NT.

This argument is not entirely convincing for the following reason.[2] Consider the Stackelberg version of the Trust Game in which the Firm acts as a leader. Choosing R is the Firm's Stackelberg strategy if one assumes that the Firm can only choose pure strategies. If Firm can commit to use a mixed strategy, however, the optimal choice would be to play R with the minimum probability that induces the Customer to play T, that is, $q = 1/(1 - v_C)$. By playing this strategy, the Firm makes the Customer just indifferent between T and NT, but since we stipulated that the follower breaks an eventual indifference in favor of the leader, the Customer will play T.[3] The payoff pair corresponding to this strategy combination is the point S in Figure 9.1.

Commitments to mixed strategies are unrealistic in one-shot games. However, in the repeated setting discussed by Sacconi (2000) it is absolutely realistic to assume that short-run players can observe the long-run player's mixed strategies. In fact, the mixed strategy played by the Firm has a natural interpretation in the frequency with which the two strategies have been played in the past, that are observed by the customers. There is nothing unrealistic in assuming that a customer who has observed the Firm to play Reward approximately one-half of the times will expect it to do the same in the current round. A long-run Firm will thus find it convenient to alternate (randomly) between Reward and Not Reward in such a way to give the Customer the minimum incentive to play Trust.

If anything, commitment to a pure strategy is even less credible than a commitment to a mixed strategy. Fudenberg and Levine (1992) provide the following justification for considering commitment to mixed strategies, which is worth quoting because it repeats, almost word by word, the canonical example of entry deterrence games, the considerations Stiglitz made about his example with the Chinese restaurant.

An additional reason for interest in mixed-strategy reputation is that they allow the short-run players to update their beliefs in a way we find more plausible: if the only commitment types are those who always fight, then if the incumbent ever accommodates he is thought to be weak, regardless of how many times he has fought in the past. We find it more plausible that an incumbent who has fought in almost every previous period will be expected to fight again with high probability, and our model allows that conclusion. (p. 562)

Similarly, a Firm that has played Reward in all the previous periods cannot be believed to play Not Reward with probability one after the first time it has played Not Reward. Once this unrealistic element has been removed from the model, there is no reason to believe that standards models of reputation formation single out perfect trustworthiness as the only outcome of the repeated Trust Game.

4   The (symmetrically) repeated Trust Game

The result obtained in the previous section is due to the asymmetry in the interaction structure. The fact that the Firm can appropriate the entire surplus from the transaction (leaving the customer with the value of his outside option, namely zero) is a consequence of the fact that only one of the agents (the Firm) is able to build a reputation. In this and the following sections we explore the possibility that a more equitable outcome might emerge when *both* players care about their reputation, because both of them play more than once the same game against the same opponent. This structure of interaction resembles more closely the original Stiglitz example of the Chinese restaurant with a loyal clientele.

Suppose thus that the Trust Game is played repeatedly by the same two players. Depending on the strategies chosen by the two agents at each round of the game, a stream of payoffs (π_C^t, π_F^t) is generated, where $t = 1, 2, \ldots$ is the round and π_i^t is the payoff player $i = F, C$ obtains at round t. These streams of payoffs are evaluated by means of the average discounted criterion, that is,

$$\pi_i = (1 - \delta) \sum_{t=1}^{t=\infty} \pi_i^t \delta^{t-1}$$

where δ is the common time discount factor. The folk theorem for repeated games states that any pair of payoffs that Pareto dominate the vector $(0, 0)$ can be obtained in a subgame perfect equilibrium, provided that the players are sufficiently patient. The content of this proposition is illustrated by the picture on the right of Figure 9.1. The shaded area represents all pairs of feasible payoffs that Pareto dominate the payoffs corresponding to the Nash equilibrium outcome. The folk theorem ensures that, if the two players are sufficiently patient, for any point (π_C, π_F) in the shadowed area there is a pair of strategies for the repeated game that guarantee the two players payoffs (π_C, π_F) and that form a subgame perfect Nash equilibrium.

The intuition behind the folk theorem is straightforward. Consider, for example, the payoff pair $(1, 1)$. The two players could obtain a stream of payoffs whose present value, evaluated with the average discount criterion, is $(1, 1)$ by playing (*Trust, Reward*) for the entire duration of the game. This outcome can be sustained as a subgame perfect equilibrium, because the Customer can threaten the Firm to play *NT* forever, in case the Firm plays *NR* once. (Notice that this strategy is not available in the model discussed in the previous section, because in that model there is a new customer in each period.) If the Firm expects the Customer to play this strategy, and is sufficiently patient, it is obviously in its interest to play Reward throughout.

There are many other efficient Nash equilibria in addition to the one just described, however. The payoff combination x in the picture is obtained by having the Customer always trusting the Firm and the firm abusing her trust once every three rounds. The reason why this strategy can form an equilibrium is that the Customer prefers to play T, being cheated once every three rounds, rather than paying NT. However, if the frequency of NR becomes too large, then there is no way to ensure that the Customer will continue to play Trust, because his payoff will be smaller than zero. This is the case for a point like y that can be obtained by having the Firm to play Reward only once every three rounds. The threshold that separates the payoff pairs that can be sustained by equilibrium strategies from those that cannot is precisely the Stackelberg strategy discussed in the previous section, which corresponds to the point S in Figure 9.1. At variance with the reputational model presented in section 3, the folk theorem lends *some* support to the idea that fairness and trustworthiness can be the upshot of purely enlightened self-interest. The trouble with this result is that it is compatible with too many outcomes. Except for the exploitative outcomes in which the Customer obtains less than zero, all other outcomes can be sustained as equilibria.

5   A simplified repeated Trust Game

A standard trick to cope with the enormous number of Nash equilibria in repeated games is to resort to learning and evolution. Instead of imagining that a single Firm and a single Consumer decide once and for all the strategy to employ in a repeated game, evolutionary models assume that the same (repeated) game is played over time by agents drawn from populations of identical Firms and Consumers. Each agent adopts a strategy to use in his interaction with other agents, occasionally revises his choice and, if necessary, switches to another strategy. While agents are not assumed to be rational in a game-theoretical sense, it is assumed that they can learn from experience, so that they will tend to switch from strategies that yield low payoffs to those that yield higher payoffs.

In this and the following section we shall sketch an extremely simplified evolutionary model for the repeated Trust Game. This section is preparatory. We shall only provide a drastically simplified list of possible strategies for the Firm and the Consumer to use in the repeated game, and provide some justification for our choice. We also characterize the set of Nash equilibria for this simplified version of the repeated Trust Game. In the following section we shall discuss the application of the evolutionary approach to this game.

The strategy set for the two players is restricted as follows. For the Customer:

- *Never Trust* (*N*). This strategy plays NT throughout.
- *Always Trust* (*A*). This strategy always plays T, irrespective of what the Firm does.

- *Grim Tolerant* (GT). This strategy starts with T and continues to play T as long as the Firm has played NR more than once in the last three rounds. It reverts to perpetual NT if the firms plays NR more often than that.
- *Grim Strict Honesty* (GSH). This strategy starts with trusting and keeps to play T as long as the Firm has never played NR. It reverts to perpetual NT after a single occurrence of NR.

For the Firm:

- *Dishonest* (D). This strategy never plays Reward.
- *Moderately Dishonest* (MD). This strategy plays NR once every three rounds, starting with two rounds of R.
- *Honest* (H). This strategy always plays R.

The approach to repeated games consisting in a restriction to a small set of strategies is quite common, especially in the biological literature. There are obvious drawbacks in this choice, but also some advantages. For example, it makes it possible to obtain analytical results that would be impossible to obtain without such a restriction. In our selection of strategies we have included those that can implement three Nash equilibria for the repeated Trust Game. N and D correspond to the Nash equilibrium in which there is neither trust nor trustworthiness. H and GSH implement the Nash equilibrium in which the Firm plays R at each round because it fears the Customer's retaliation after the first NR. Finally, GT and MD implement the Nash equilibrium in which the Firm cheats once every three rounds, because the Customer is willing to tolerate that. In this equilibrium (whose payoffs correspond to point x in Figure 9.1) we observe trust (because the Customer plays T at every round), but not trustworthiness, because the Firms fails repeatedly to reward the Customer's trust.

Table 9.1 represents the normal form associated to a repeated Trust Game in which the strategy set is restricted to the seven strategies described above. The computation of the payoffs in each cell is straightforward. For example, a match involving a customer that plays N produces a constant flow of zeroes for both players, irrespective of the strategy chosen by the firm. Similarly, against a firm that plays H, all costumers who trust will get the same payoff, i.e. one, irrespective of the strategy they play, either A, GT or GSH. It is slightly more complex to compute the payoff streams when a firm that plays MD is involved. The basic ingredient are the terms $(1 + \delta + V_f \delta^2)$ and $(1 + \delta + v_C \delta^2)$. These are the payoffs the firm and the customer obtain during a cycle of three rounds in which the outcome has been (T, R) for the first two, and (T, NR) in the third. When a MD Firm encounters a Customer who plays AT or GT, the firm will receive $(1 + \delta + V_f \delta^2)$ every three rounds, so its present value (calculated

Table 9.1 A simplified repeated Trust Game

	Dishonest (D)	Moderately Dishonest (MD)	Honest (H)
Never Trust *(N)*	0, 0	0, 0	0, 0
Always Trust *(A)*	v_C, V_F	$\dfrac{(1+\delta+v_C\delta^2)}{(1-\delta^3)}(1-\delta), \dfrac{(1+\delta+V_F\delta^2)}{(1-\delta^3)}(1-\delta)$	1, 1
Grim Tolerant (GT)	$v_C(1-\delta), V_F(1-\delta)$	$\dfrac{(1+\delta+v_C\delta^2)}{(1-\delta^3)}(1-\delta), \dfrac{(1+\delta+V_F\delta^2)}{(1-\delta^3)}(1-\delta)$	1,1
Grim Strict Honesty (GSH)	$v_C(1-\delta), V_F(1-\delta)$	$(1+\delta+v_C\delta^2)(1-\delta), (1+\delta+V_F\delta^2)(1-\delta)$	1,1

with the average discount criterion) is $(1+\delta+V_F\delta^2)(1-\delta)/(1-\delta^3)$. The same applies, *mutatis mutandis*, to the Customer. When a *MD* firm encounters a customer who uses *GSH*, $(1+\delta+V_F\delta^2)$ will only be obtained for the first three rounds, which will be followed by an infinite stream of zeroes, so that its actual value is just $(1+\delta+V_F\delta^2)(1-\delta)$.

Our main result is based on the following technical condition:

Assumption 1. We assume that $\delta \in ((V_F-1)/V_F, -(1+\sqrt{1-4v_C})/2v_C)$, which requires that $(V_F-1)/V_F < -(1+\sqrt{1-4v_C})/2v_C$.

Consider first the condition $\delta > (V_F-1)/V_F$. This assumption insures that the payoff a firm obtains playing Reward in every round (strategy *H*) is larger than the payoff the same firm could obtain by switching to *NR* at the first round (strategy *D*), assuming that the consumer will punish the latter behavior by switching to perpetual *NT* (which happens if the consumer uses either *GT* or *GSH*). This is the standard hypothesis that the value of future payoffs obtained through cooperation should be large enough to offset the temptation to cheat at the first round.

The condition $\delta < (1+\sqrt{1-4v_C})/2v_C$ insures that a Consumer prefers to be cheated once every three rounds, rather than not trusting at all. Notice that the discount factor δ must be *small*. The reason is that the customer must tolerate a negative payoff, v_C, after three rounds from the first one. A Consumer will accept to be cheated once every three rounds only if she gives sufficiently *little* weight to future payoffs.

We are now ready for the first result of this chapter.

Proposition 1. In the restricted version of the repeated trust game represented in Table 9.1, the only Nash equilibrium that survives elimination of weakly dominated strategies is (*GT, MD*).

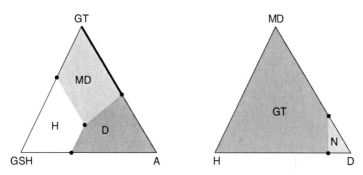

Figure 9.2   Best responses for the repeated Trust Game. Sender (left) and Receiver (right)

Proof. ■ First notice that the second part of Assumption 1 ensures that $(1+\delta+v_C\delta^2)>0$. Since $\delta \in (0, 1)$, it follows that

$$\frac{(1+\delta+v_C\delta^2)}{(1-\delta^3)}(1-\delta) > (1+\delta+v_C\delta^2)(1-\delta)$$

which implies that *GT* weakly dominates *GSH* (because it gets the same payoff against *H* and *D*, and a strictly larger payoff against *MD*). If one eliminates *GSH*, *MD* weakly dominates *H*, because $(1+\delta+V_F\delta^2)>1$. On the other hand, *GT* weakly dominates *AT*, because $v_C(1 - \delta)>v_C$ (recall that $v_C<0$). If one eliminates *AT*, *MD* weakly dominates *D*, because the assumption $\delta>(V_F - 1)/V_F$ implies that $V_F(1 - \delta)<1<1+\delta+V_F\delta^2$. Finally, once D has been eliminated, GT dominates N. ■

The game has other equilibria, besides *(GT, MD)*. The left-hand side graphics in Figure 9.2 depicts all possible mixed strategies for the Customer, in which the probability of playing *N* is set equal to zero. The corners of the triangle represent the three remaining pure strategies *A*, *GT* and *GSH*. The triangle is divided into three areas, depending upon the Firm's best response. In the white area, the probability with which the Customer enforces perfect honesty (i.e. plays *GSH*) is large enough to make honesty (strategy *H*) the best policy for the Firm. In the lightly shaded area, the probability with which the customer tolerates some dishonesty, but not complete dishonesty (strategy *GT*), is large enough to make moderate dishonesty (*MD*) the best policy. Finally, in the darkly shaded area the Customer is willing to tolerate even complete dishonesty with such a large probability that being completely dishonest (*D*) is the best policy.

The diagram on the right depicts the possible mixed strategies for the Firm. In the lightly shaded area the Firm is dishonest (strategy *D*) with such a high probability that the Customer's best reply is never trust (*N*). In the darkly shaded area, the probability with which either *MD* or *H* are used is sufficiently high to make

GT the best reply. Notice that there are no areas in which *A* and *GSH* are best replies, which reflects the fact that these strategies are weakly dominated by *GT*.

With the help of these pictures it becomes easy to characterize all (sets of) Nash equilibria of the game. First, there is the set we will denote E_{NT}, in which the Firm chooses a mixed strategy in the *N* area in the right triangle, and the customer plays *N* with probability one. It is easy to check that all those are Nash equilibria, because when the customer plays *N* the Firm gets zero independently by the strategy it uses. On the other hand, by definition, *N* is the customer's best reply to any mixed strategy in the *N* area of the right triangle.

Second, there is the set of equilibria E_H in which the Firm chooses *H* with probability one and the Customer chooses a point within the *H* area in the left triangle. In each of these equilibria the Firm prefers to be honest because it believes (correctly) that the customer will stop playing trust with sufficiently high probability after the first time *NR* is played. On the other hand, when the Firm chooses *H* with probability one, the Customer is indifferent among *AT*, *GT*, *GSH* (which are strictly preferred to *N*), so that playing any mixture of these strategies is a best reply.

Finally, there is a third set of Nash equilibria E_{MD}, in which the Firm chooses *MD* with probability one and the Customer chooses any point on the thick segment in the right triangle. In all these equilibria the Firm is moderately dishonest and the Customer tolerates this dishonesty, although it will punish a completely dishonest behavior with a probability that is sufficiently high to induce the Firm to choose *MD* rather than *D*. The pure strategy Nash equilibrium (*MD*, *GT*) described in Proposition 1 belongs to E_{MD}: it corresponds to the *GT* corner in the left triangle (which belongs to the thick segment) and the *MD* corner in the right one.

The intuition behind Proposition 1 is straightforward. The equilibrium (*GPH*, *H*) in which perfect honesty is observed requires that a customer stands ready to punish the Firm after the first time the latter plays *NR*. However, against an honest Firm, a Customer has nothing to lose in adopting a more tolerant strategy (*GT*) which allows for some dishonesty, because the honest Firm will never exploit this possibility. On the other hand, against a moderately dishonest Firm, *GT* yields strictly larger payoffs than *GSH*, because trusting and being cheated once every three rounds is still better than never trusting. This is the reason why the perfect honesty equilibrium (*GPH*, *H*) requires the Customer to use a weakly dominated strategy.

Things are different with the equilibrium in which the Firm is moderately dishonest (*GT*, *MD*). This equilibrium is based on the threat that the Customer will quit trusting if the Firm fails to play *R* at least twice every three rounds. Also in this case, against a Firm that plays *MD*, a Customer has nothing to lose in switching to a strategy that tolerates even less cooperation, that is to strategy *A*. However, *A* does not weakly dominate *GT*, because it yields a strictly lower payoff against D. This is a way to reformulate what we said in the Introduction: while it might pay to tolerate some dishonesty, it surely does not pay to accept a completely dishonest behavior.

6 The evolution of trusting behavior

The fact that equilibria in E_H and E_{NT} do not survive elimination of weakly dominated strategies cannot be taken as a proof that they will not be observed in reality. A large literature that starts with Binmore et al. (1995) has shown that the forces of learning and cultural evolution are ineffective in eliminating weakly dominated strategies.

In this section we shall imagine that the repeated Trust Game is played repeatedly by agents drawn at random from two populations F and S. Each agent can only adopt one of the seven strategies introduced above. Let p_i be the fraction of the C population that adopts strategy $i \in \{NT, AT, GT, GSH\}$, while q_j is the fraction of population F that adopts strategy $j \in \{D, MD, H\}$. The *state* of the two populations is the strategy distribution (p, q).

Within each population the fraction of agents using a pure strategy changes according to the *replicator dynamics*:

$$\frac{dp_i}{dt} = p_i(\pi_C(i,q) - \bar{\pi}_C(p,q))$$
$$\frac{dq_j}{dt} = q_j(\pi_F(j,p) - \bar{\pi}_F(p,q))$$

(1)

In the first equation, $\pi_C(i, q)$ is the payoff strategy i obtains in the C population when the state of the F population is q, while $\bar{\pi}_C(p, q)$ is the average payoff in the C population when the states of the two populations are p and q. The same applies, *mutatis mutandis*, for the second equation. The idea behind the replicator dynamics is that successful strategies tend to displace less successful ones. This might reflect either a process of differential reproduction (for example, firms with lower payoffs will tend to get bankrupt more often than those with higher payoffs) or a process of learning (customers and firms tend to imitate the behavior of the most successful agents in their population). Whatever the reason, the replicator dynamics postulates that over time those strategies that score above average within the relevant population will be more represented, while those that score below average will tend to disappear.

We are now ready for the second proposition of this chapter:

Proposition 2. The Nash equilibria (GSH, H), (GT, MD) and (N, D) are stable (although not asymptotically stable) under the replicator dynamics (1).

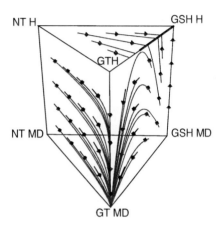

Figure 9.3 Orbits generated by the Replicator Dynamics on the simplified Trust Game

Proof. This proposition is an immediate consequence of Somanathan (1997), Theorem 1. The interested reader can easily check that all conditions stated in that theorem are met by the game in Table 9.1. ■

Figure 9.3 provides a visual representation of this proposition. It represents several orbits generated by the replicator dynamics on the repeated trust game. To visualize the dynamics in a three-dimensional space, we restricted our attention to orbits originating from initial states in which only three strategies (N, GT and GSH) are represented in the C population, and two strategies (H and MD) are represented in the F population. The base of the polyhedron represents all possible distributions among NT, GT and GSH for the C population, while the height of the polyhedron represents the frequency of H players in the F population. The corners of the polyhedron are the states in which both populations are entirely composed by the same strategy. For example, in the corner labelled GSH/H the F population is entirely made by H players, while the C population is entirely made by GSH players.

The corner GT/MD belongs to the set of Nash equilibria E_{MD}, while the thick segment belongs to the set of Nash equilibria E_H. The content of Proposition 2 is revealed by the fact that all the orbits that start close enough to the corner GT/MD converge to it. It is also shown by the fact that the orbits that start sufficiently close to the thick segment converge to it. It follows that for any point x which is sufficiently close to the vertex GSH/H, there is a neighborhood such that if the orbit starts in that neighborhood it will not go too far from x. In this sense, the point GSH/H is stable.

Readers who are familiar with the evolutionary approach to punishment-based cooperation will have recognized the logic behind this result. Consider any point in the thick segment. The percentage of GSH players is large enough to make *H* the best reply. We know from the previous section that *GSH* is weakly dominated by *GT*: tolerating some dishonesty is a better policy than insisting on always obtaining *R*. The reason why *GSH* players are not eliminated from the *C* population is that when all firms are honest, *GHS* players and *GT* players obtain the same payoff, because there are no dishonest firms in the F population to punish. Intuitively, being ready to punish dishonesty has little cost when dishonest behavior is rare. On the contrary, when most of the consumers punish moderate dishonesty, an honest firm that plays *H* obtains a substantially larger payoff than a moderately dishonest firm that plays MD. So while consumers who enforce perfect honesty will be subject to only a moderate pressure, the pressure on moderately dishonest firms is substantial.

7 Concluding remarks on reputation and CSR

We are now in a better position to evaluate *The Economist*'s claim that codes of ethics are useless, because they only prescribe choices that rational firms would take anyway out of a concern for their own reputation. Such a position is clearly dictated by the standard approach to the evolution of trustworthy behavior based on the repeated Prisoner's Dilemma or the repeated Trust Game. In fact, most of the models discussed in the literature are focused on the two polar cases in which a firm (or any other trustee, for that matter) is either completely trustworthy, or absolutely dishonest. (See, for example, the survey on trust in James, 2002.) The choice a firm faces is thus between being honest and trusted or being dishonest and not trusted. Since the first condition is preferable (for the firm itself) to the second, one might be under the (wrong) impression that there is no conflict between trustworthiness and long-run self-interest, which in turn would make redundant any appeal to ethics.

This approach fails to account for the full force of the folk theorem. (Notable exceptions are Miller, 1992, 2001.) In fact, repeating the Trust Game generates many other equilibria beside these two. In some of these equilibria, customers learn to trust moderately dishonest firms, because trusting them is better than not trusting at all. In the previous section we have shown that these equilibria can be stable under the replicator dynamics, just like the equilibrium in which the firms are perfectly honest.

The relationship between trustworthiness and reputation is thus less direct than some simplified models widely discussed in the literature would suggest. The decision of a firm to became 'honest' (i.e. to adopt strategy *H* in the model above) cannot be seen exclusively in terms of enlightened self-interest. There are other strategies (for example, *MD*) which would induce the customers to trust anyway and would yield a larger payoff to the firm. Similarly, the decision of a customer to abandon a firm after the first misbehavior cannot be conceived only in terms of a strict self-interested calculation. In fact, enforcing perfect honesty (strategy GSH) is weakly dominated by tolerating *some* dishonesty (strategy *GT*). What we want to suggest by way of conclusion is that if firms and customers converge towards the 'perfect honesty' equilibrium, is because they share a common understanding that that is the 'right' or 'fair' way to play the game. An explicit code of ethics is the signal a firm sends that this is actually the case.

Notes

1. One of the best presentations of this dilemma in moral philosophy is Gauthier (1968, chapter 1). 'What theory of morals can ever serve any useful purpose, unless it can show that all the duties it recommends are also the true interest of each individual? David Hume, who asked this question, seems mistaken; such a theory would be too useful. Were duties no more than interest, morals would be superfluous' (p. 1).
2. In addition to the problems mentioned in the text, some issues are raised by the logic of reputation formation to extensive form games like the Trust Game. One has to take into account, for example, that the prior probability of the firm being honest might be so small that customers prefer to play Not Trust. When this is the case, the Firm's behavior is not observable, so that it becomes impossible to build a reputation for trustworthiness. See Fudenberg and Levine (1992).
3. The logic of this assumption is that by playing R with a probability slightly larger than $1/(1 - v_C)$, the Firm can make T be strictly better than NT for the Customer.

References

Arrow, K.J. (1974) *The Limits of Organization*. New York: W.W. Norton.
Binmore, K., L. Samuelson and J. Gale (1995) 'Learning to be Imperfect: The Ultimatum Game', *Games and Economic Behavior*, vol. 8, 56–90.
Friedman, Milton (1970) 'The Social Responsibility of Business is to Increase Its Profits', *The New York Times Magazine*, 13.
Fudenberg, D. and D.K. Levine (1989) 'Reputation and Equilibrium Selection in Games with a Patient Player', *Econometrica*, vol. 57(4), 759–78.
Fudenberg, D. and D.K. Levine (1992) 'Maintaining Reputation when Strategies are Imperfectly Observed', *Review of Economic Studies*, vol. 59, 561–79.
Fudenberg D. and Jean Tirole (1991) *Game Theory*. Cambridge, MA: MIT Press.
Gauthier, D. (1986) *Morals by Agreement*. Oxford: Clarendon Press.
Gintis, Herbert (2007) 'Game Theory and Human Behavior', mimeo.
Hardin, Russell (2002) *Trust and Trustworthiness*. New York: Russell Sage Foundation.
Horner, J. (2002) 'Reputation and Competition', *The American Economic Review*, vol. 92(3), 644–63.
James, Harvey S. (2002) 'The Trust Paradox: A Survey of Economic Inquiries into the Nature of Trust and Trustworthiness', *Journal of Economic Behaviour and Organization*, vol. 47, 291–307.
Kreps, D. (1990) 'Corporate Culture and Economic Theory', in J.E. Alt and K.A. Shepsle (eds), *Perspectives on Positive Political Economy*. Cambridge: Cambridge University Press.
Miller, G. (1992) *Managerial Dilemmas: The Political Economy of Hierarchy*. Cambridge: Cambridge University Press.

Miller, G. (2001) 'Why is Trust Necessary in Organizations?', in K.S. Cox, *Trust in Society.* New York: Russell Sage Foundation.

Myerson, R. (1997) *Game Theory: Analysis of Conflict.* Cambridge, MA: Harvard University Press.

Sacconi, L. (2000) *The Social Contract of the Firm: Economics, Ethics and Organization.* Berlin: Springer.

Somanathan, E. (1997) 'Evolutionary Stability of Pure-Strategy Equilibria in Finite Games', *Games and Economic Behavior,* vol. 21, 253–65.

Stiglitz, Joseph E. (1989) 'Imperfect Information in the Product Market', in R. Schmalensee and R.D. Willig (eds), *Handbook of Industrial Organization,* vol. I. Amsterdam: Elsevier Science, pp. 771–847.

The Economist (2005) 'Profit and the Public Good', 20 January.

Williamson, O.E. (1993) 'Calculativeness, Trust and Economic Organization', *Journal of Law and Economics,* vol. 36, pp. 453–86.

10
Rational Association and Corporate Responsibility*

Bruce Chapman

1 Introduction

It is a widely held view that limited liability, where the personal assets of shareholders in a corporation are insulated from any claims made by creditors against the corporation, is a kind of special 'concession' made to these investors. Apparently, the default position against which this concession operates is that, more normally, these investors, as owners, would be *personally* responsible for the conduct that they effect through the corporate form.[1] However, either for what some might cynically think are political reasons (for example, large and powerful investors have managed to lobby for favorable legislation exempting them from personal responsibility), or for what others would argue are good economic reasons (for example, it would be difficult to amass large amounts of capital and have an active market for shares without limited liability), virtually all western economies have adopted a rule limiting the personal liability of investors in corporations. Any thought that liability should cease at the boundary of the corporation, because it is the *corporation* that has acted, and not the investors, plays no serious role in these arguments.

Even when the idea of a concession is resisted, and the idea of a political 'quid pro quo' argued for in its place, the ontological presupposition that informs the argument is that the only real actors worth considering are the corporate investors and their various creditors, creditors that might have dealt with these investors either directly (that is, personally, or not through the

* This chapter was originally prepared as a paper for the Conference on 'Corporate Social Responsibility and Corporate Governance', sponsored by the Institute for Economic Affairs, and held at the Department of Economics, University of Trento, Italy, in July 2006. I am grateful to my commentator Giuseppe Bellantuono and my colleague Ian Lee for very helpful comments on an earlier draft. Research for this work was supported by a grant from the Social Science and Humanities Research Council of Canada.

corporation) or indirectly (that is, through the corporation or 'behind the corporate veil'). For example, in the recent literature on 'asset partitioning', the argument is that the creditors of the corporate enterprise have limited their claims to the assets of the enterprise (defensive asset partitioning, or limited liability) and, in exchange, the law has protected the assets of the enterprise for the benefit of its creditors from the claims of the personal creditors of the investors (affirmative asset partitioning).[2] Again, although one can imagine that there might be cynical accounts of this bilateral political exchange, just as there were for the idea of a unilateral legislative concession, the more usual argument is that these different forms of asset partitioning can be economically justified as investment arrangements that the different investors and creditors would require as they individually transact with one another in quite different economic situations. It would be particularly difficult, for example, for the creditors dealing with an investor who owned some enterprise in Italy to be secure in, or knowledgeable about, the risks of advancing credit to that enterprise if every personal creditor of that same investor in Germany or Holland could lay claim to the assets lent to the Italian enterprise to satisfy their own personal claims against that investor. And the exchange of shares in the enterprise would be complicated by the fact that the value of the shares would vary with the identities of the investors holding them (and, more specifically, with what these different investors might be doing with their personal lines of credit). Affirmative asset partitioning, as a matter of organizational law, goes a long way towards reducing those risks and assuaging those fears. It would be far too difficult, the argument goes, for the different investors and creditors to arrange, to their mutual benefit, the same sorts of legal protections contractually.

Of course, asset partitioning, and the owner-shareholder and entity shielding that goes along with it, would be quite a natural consequence if we were prepared to think of the corporation as a rational agent distinct from its shareholders. It does not occur to us that we have to defend the idea that *your* personal assets are not available to *my* creditors, and vice versa, for example. We are separate rational agents, each with our own responsibilities and liabilities. You own, and are responsible for, what is yours, and I own, and am responsible for, what is mine. Nothing could be simpler.

But it will be suggested that all is not quite so simple if we are acting together, for example, in partnership. Then our joint action *does* attract a special kind of joint and several liability for each of us personally. Your personal assets *are* available to the claims of *our* creditors (or the creditors I have attracted when I have acted as your partner). So, some might argue that even if we concede the possibility of corporate action as a form of joint action distinct from individual action, we still need the economic arguments to sensibly distinguish the sort of joint action that occurs under partnership, and which attracts joint and several personal liability there, from that which occurs under the corporate form and which there allows for asset partitioning.

However, in this chapter I continue to press the claim that the economic arguments for asset partitioning are not strictly required for distinguishing the corporation. The idea of the corporation as a rational actor, distinct from its shareholders, will still do. However, what *is* required is a richer and more developed conception of rational agency, a conception that I have been developing elsewhere in a more individualistic context. A rational actor is an agent that is responsive both to reasons *and* to the normative requirements of practical rationality.[3] I will explain this distinction more fully in section 2, but here it will suffice to say that the normative requirements of rationality require an agent to respect prior commitments that it has made in a way that merely acting for reasons does not. The understanding of rational agency that is typically used in economics limits it to conduct that is responsive to reasons alone. This explains why individuals, under the familiar backward induction arguments, have difficulty keeping to their prior commitments (e.g., making credible promises or threats) unless there are ongoing (typically, 'long-run' or reputational) reasons (usually grounded in welfare or preference maximization) to do so. In the context of joint action, this thinner conception of rational agency shows up institutionally in the idea of partnership, where individual investors, motivated only by preference or profit maximization, are entitled, without any burden of commitment, to withdraw their capital from the partnership on demand. There is, as some would put it, no 'capital lock-in'.[4] However, the richer conception of rational agency, which in this more collective context I call rational association, is exemplified by the corporation, where capital lock-in, and its kindred idea of (affirmative) asset partitioning, is the norm.

My argument does not deny that there might be economic benefits for individual investors (and their creditors) that follow from asset partitioning. But it should suggest that these are the incidental effects of, and not the rationale for, the corporate form. The rationale is in the fact that collectives, once incorporated as a body, can act rationally and independently of the shareholders that make them up. In other words, they can act as rational associations. Not surprisingly, therefore, their assets, and only their assets, are their own.

But some might wonder what advantage there is in approaching the problem this way rather than by way of the economic arguments emphasizing the benefits for shareholders. The reason is that the argument from rational association carries implications that go further than asset partitioning. Not only are shareholders to enjoy the benefits that flow from limited liability and entity shielding, under rational association they are also committed to other stakeholders in a way that limits what they can rationally do to maximize their profits. The explanation for this goes back to the idea that a rational agent, richly understood, acts under reasons *and* in accordance with the normative requirements of practical rationality. The latter, we shall see, imposes rational obligations that extend beyond the maximization of profit. Thus, the argument from rational association that I offer here links the benefits that flow from asset partitioning (which most economic arguments readily accept) to the burdens that follow from a broader set of corporate obligations to non-shareholder stakeholders (which most economic arguments are reluctant to accept).

The argument is organized as follows. In section 2 I explain what I mean by the distinction between reasons and the normative requirements of practical rationality and show, in the context of individual action, how the combination of the two offers a sensible approach to dealing with the problem of rational commitment and backward induction. In section 3 I move to the context of joint action and show how there can be a sharp discontinuity between what comprises rational conduct for an individual and what comprises rational conduct for the corporate entity of which that individual is a member. This will secure, I will argue, two distinct ideas, first, that the corporation can act independently of the individuals that make it up and, second, that rational conduct for the separate corporation will often be in the name of prior commitments or decisions that the corporation has made, and even when these prior commitments rationally entail decisions that no individual (or shareholder) would now support as a matter of current preference (or profit maximization). Finally, in section 4 I provide an example, using the backward induction argument, of how shareholders as owner investors in the corporation are properly constrained under the idea of rational association to respect their prior commitments to other stakeholders and to limit their profit maximization. The example is developed in the context of a takeover, an 'end game' situation where shareholders are most tempted to defect on prior commitments (exiting the firm into an anonymous market without loss of reputation) and where the backward induction argument is most applicable. The paper concludes in section 5.

It is worth making one final introductory comment before proceeding to the substantive argument. The idea that the corporation is a rational association organized around some purpose other than profit maximization will no doubt strike some as fanciful. However, this would be to misread what is being argued here. I accept the view that the corporation is an organization typically dedicated to the making of profit. I only argue here that the corporation is a *rational association* for the making (under this characterization, I would even accept 'maximization') of profit. This is a characterization that sensibly places the for-profit corporation between the partnership (a form of organization that is profit maximizing, but not rationally committed) and the non-profit corporation (one that is rationally committed, but not profit-maximizing). Thus, the richer conception of rationality or rational association that informs the particular arguments in this chapter also goes some way to providing a more general taxonomy of the different forms of enterprise that we observe.

2   Reasons, the normative requirements of practical rationality and rational commitments

It is tempting to think that it cannot be rational to do something that on balance you have reason *not* to do. If practical rationality simply *is* acting for reasons, then this would surely follow. If there is no space between what rationality requires you to do and what reasons tell you to do, then the possibility of acting rationally, but contrary to the balance of reasons, is simply precluded.

The economist's theory of rational choice would seem to have this view of how rationality structurally relates to reasons. According to rational choice theory an agent may have any number of different reasons which ultimately give rise, on balance, to preferring to do *x* rather than *y*, and rationality consists in following that preference. It would be irrational, in other words, to act contrary to some preference or the reason (or balance of reasons) that lies behind it.

Of course, the economist or rational choice theorist also talks about choices or preferences being rationally consistent, for example, that they satisfy transitivity or some analogous revealed preference axiom.[5] But this idea only follows from the more basic one that that choice should accord with preference or the reasons that support preference. For example, suppose that an agent had, or had revealed by choice, preferences that were intransitive, say, *x* preferred to *y*, *y* to *z*, and *z* to *x*. Then it would be impossible for this agent to choose from the set (*x*, *y*, *z*) without choosing contrary to some preference or the requirements of some reason. Thus, the basis for insisting on this rationality condition across different choices is really only to preserve the possibility that many would suggest is essential to the exercise of practical rationality, namely, that in every choice an agent must act only and always on the balance of reasons.

However, in recent times the idea that rationality consists only in acting according to the balance of reasons has come into question.[6] In addition to reasons there are also, it is said, the normative requirements of practical rationality. Where reasons go to a relation that should exist between some attitude (e.g., a belief, intention, desire) that an agent has and some fact about the agent's situation, the normative requirements of practical rationality go to the relation that should exist between (or among) those attitudes themselves. Indeed, the normative requirements of practical rationality hold in complete abstraction from an agent's situation, something that makes these requirements *strict*. In this respect they are stronger than reasons which only hold *pro tanto* (i.e., have weight). For example, one should not, as a matter of strict rationality, believe both *p* and *not-p*; this requirement holds regardless of the truth of *p*, or regardless of one's situation (i.e., it is not merely a matter of weight). If you believe both *p* and not-*p*, then, strictly, you are not as you should be as a matter of rationality. On the other hand, if everything that you have learned in school tells you that *p* is true, then that is a very strong (or weighty) reason for believing *p*. However, you are not strictly required by this reason to believe *p*. For example, this reason would only hold *pro tanto* (i.e., not strictly) against the fact (or other reason) that some very credible expert has just told you that not-*p* and might very well be outweighed by that fact.

Reasons, however, because they go to a relation between an agent's attitude and an agent's situation, are stronger than the normative requirements of practical rationality in one respect: they are independent or detachable from the other attitudes held by the agent. By contrast, the normative requirements of practical rationality are only relative, not independent: they only hold for an agent for a given attitude *if* the agent holds some other attitude that implicates the first as a matter of practical rationality. If one ceases to hold that other attitude, then the rationality requirement says nothing about holding the first. Thus, one is not strictly required as a matter of rationality to relax any one attitude in particular. Some analysts capture this idea by saying that, whereas reasons have 'narrow scope' (in being detachable and applicable to particular attitudes the agent has), the normative requirements of practical rationality only have 'wide scope' (in not being capable of such particular, and often helpful, resolution).[7]

Now, the possibility that there is more to practical rationality than acting for reasons opens up the possibility that, contrary to the rational choice account (which bases rational conduct on reasons alone), one *can* act rationally but contrary to the balance of reasons. More specifically, one can intend, decide, or commit to do what one has reason not to do. Note that this is not the same as saying that one can have *reason* to intend, decide, or commit to do what one knows one will have reason not to do. *That* possibility is easily admitted by anyone, including the rational choice theorist, who has considered the problem of rational commitment. For example, I can have a reason to make a promise to do *x* if you do *y* even though I know I will have no reason actually to execute on that promise when the time comes for its performance. The reason for me *to promise x* is that I am better off with your doing *y*, even after incurring the costs of my doing *x*, and my promise helps to accomplish that. The reason *not to do x* is that I am (again) better off not doing something that is costly for me to do if there is no further benefit to be secured by actually doing it. Indeed, this familiar example shows simply, but importantly, that the very *same* reason *R* (here, a consideration of my own welfare) can be the reason why I both make the promise *and* fail to perform it.

As I say, this is all quite familiar. But, if reasons are all there is to rationality, the problem of credible commitments begins to loom large. For if I know that I am rational, and it is irrational to do some *x* that I know I will have reason not to do, then I know that I will not do *x* and, therefore, I cannot credibly promise (to others), or even credibly intend or decide (to myself) to do *x*.

This undermines, by way of the usual backward induction argument, the reason that I have for making the commitment in the first place. However, if there is more to rationality than acting for reasons, then my knowledge of my rationality, together with my knowledge that I will have reasons not to execute on my commitments, is *not* sufficient for me to know that I will not actually do what, with reason, I have decided, intended, or committed to do. For now I can think about executing on the commitment as a matter of normative requirement, not reason, and still be acting in accordance with practical rationality. Thus, the backward induction argument cannot so easily go through. Specifically, I can now decide, intend, or commit to do *x* (something that I have reason to do), even though I know I have reason not to do *x* when the time comes for its performance, because now I cannot know (since reasons are not all there is to practical rationality) that I, being rational, will not do it.

But now I want to argue for something even stronger, namely, that in addition to being able to *form* the prior intention, there are also at least some circumstances in which an agent should also *act* upon that intention, even if so acting is contrary to reasons or preferences that the agent has at the time. It is worth noting, first, that this needs to be argued for, as it does not follow immediately from the mere fact that having adopted an intention, or having made a decision, to do some act that an agent should, as a matter of rationality, actually do it. For recall that the normative requirements of practical rationality, while strict, were only relative. Only *if* one had some particular attitude, say the intention to do *x*, would one, say, be implicated by these requirements to have some other attitude, say, the derivative intention to do *y*. For example, suppose that Oliver has formed the intention (or decided) to meet Lorenzo in Trento tomorrow at noon. He believes that the only way for him to do so is by flying to Verona tonight. It follows then that he must intend (or decide) to fly to Verona tonight. That is a derivative intention that follows as a matter of normative requirement from his primary intention and his belief. If he continues to have that primary intention and that belief, then, if he does not have the derivative intention, he is not, strictly, as he should be. But suppose that he discovers a reason for not having that derivative intention. Perhaps he learns that there is a one-day strike by the air controllers at Verona airport, something which makes flying into Verona less safe. Now he has a reason not to intend or decide to fly to Verona tonight. But this conflict between what he has reason to do, and what he is committed to doing as a matter of normative requirement, is easily solved. Because the normative requirements of rationality, while strict, are only relative, he can simply repudiate his primary intention or decision to meet Lorenzo. (I am assuming that he cannot so easily change his belief.) Then he can satisfy his (new-found) reason for not flying into Verona *and* also be exactly as he should be as a matter of strict normative requirement.

Does this mean that one's primary intention to do some action x should always give way to reasons not to do x? If that were so, then there would be no real force in the normative requirements of practical rationality. Reasons would govern rational conduct whenever there was a conflict between reasons and normative requirements, exploiting the merely relative (wide scope) nature of the latter to secure the particular (narrow scope) independence of the former. We would be back to the model of reasons so familiar to rational choice theory and the (perverse) backward induction that it recommends.

However, this unhappy result can be avoided if we distinguish two different scenarios. In the example above, Oliver only learned about the air controllers' strike *after* he had decided to meet Lorenzo in Trento tomorrow at noon. Thus, there was new information that truly was not accounted for when he made the earlier commitment. In this sort of situation it does seem irrational, indeed, it seems almost thoughtlessly mechanical, to go ahead and act (or, more accurately, to form the derivative intention to so act) on a prior intention without allowing this new unanticipated reason to have any impact. After all, it is a mistake to think that the whole of practical rationality is action according to normative requirements. There is also rational repudiation of prior intentions in the face of independent reasons.

But now consider the second possibility. Suppose that Oliver had known about (and fully appreciated) the risk of flying to Verona tonight when he first formed the intention or decided to meet Lorenzo in Trento tomorrow. Then, surely, we are entitled to wonder a little about Oliver if he changes his prior intention and fails to appear at the meeting with Lorenzo. After all, although there is a reason for his not flying to Verona tonight, this reason was already anticipated and accounted for when he came to form his prior intention. So nothing has changed. Thus, Oliver is *changing* his prior intention or commitment *without* any good (in the sense of 'unaccounted-for') reason for doing so, and this seems irrational. After all, just as it is a mistake to think that the whole of practical rationality is action according to normative requirements, so too is it a mistake to think that the whole of it is action according to reasons. And once these reasons have already been accounted for, there seems only to be the normative requirements of practical rationality to be considered. Rationally, Oliver should not repudiate his prior intention on the basis of reasons that have already figured in his decision. At least this much, I argue, is the stuff of rational commitment.[8]

It should be clear that the second scenario is the one most directly applicable to the backward induction problem that argues against the possibility of making rational commitments. For, if there is more to practical rationality than acting in accordance with the balance of reasons, and in particular if there is the practical rationality of acting under normative requirements as well, then there is, as I have already argued, the rational possibility of *forming an intention* to do what one knows (precisely because one has anticipated the reason) one will have reason *not* to do. So, more specifically, there is the possibility of forming the intention to carry out a promise even if one knows, when it comes time to carry out this intention, that it will be contrary to one's preferences (or reasons) to do so. The important point is that these countervailing preferences have already been accounted for when the prior intention was formed. Further (and this is what we have just now added), *having formed the prior intention to carry out the promise, and without any truly independent (i.e., not already anticipated and accounted for) reasons for repudiating it, it only remains to meet the normative requirements of practical rationality in actually carrying through on these prior intentions in one's derivative intentions and, ultimately, in one's actions.* This is, of course, what the alternative, richer account of the rational actor was meant to provide for. It now remains to take this account from the individual context to the context of joint and corporate action, something that I turn to in the next section.

3   Rational association

In this section I argue that the same account of rationality that I have developed for individuals in the last section can sensibly be predicated of a group of individuals acting together as a body. I call such a body a rational association and will argue in the next section that the for-profit corporation, at least if it is truly *committed* to the making of (maximum) profits, is one example of such a rational association. The non-profit corporation (for example, one committed to some charitable purpose) is another. A partnership, I will suggest, is an association (also typically oriented around the making and sharing of profit across its members) in that there is shared agency, but it is not a *rational* association constrained by these sorts of prior commitments.[9]

To make this section's argument I need to make two distinct points. First, I need to show that there can be a sensible conception of group agency that is not reducible to the acts of the individuals that make up the group. Then, second, I need to show that at least some groups sometimes are plausibly subject to the rational pull of prior commitments, that is, to the normative requirements of practical rationality.

To see the first point, consider the following simple (and, admittedly, slightly artificial) example.[10] Imagine that there is a corporation owned by three individual investors (or three groups of such investors), A, B, and C, with equal voting rights deliberating over whether the corporation should install some sort of safety technology in its workplace. (That the shareholders might themselves be deliberating over this matter is what, in part, makes the example artificial; more likely some management team would have the decision delegated to them.[11]) Each and every shareholder agrees that it would be negligent not to install the technology if and only if the costs of installation are small compared to the expected losses to workers of not installing it, that is, if B < P × L, where B is the cost of installing the technology, P is the probability of an injury, and L is the loss should an injury occur.[12] Shareholder A considers the probability of injuries to be very large and, therefore, believes that the technology should be installed even though the cost is high and the injuries, when they occur, are not likely to be serious. Shareholder B thinks the probability of injury is low, but that the injuries, when they occur, are likely to be very serious. Thus, she too would choose to install the technology even though she concedes it is expensive. Finally, Shareholder C is inclined to think that both the probabilities and seriousness of injuries are likely to be small, but agrees to the proposed installation because, in his view, it is not very costly. These three views are summarized graphically below in Table 10.1. (For purposes of illustration I have assumed that the above quantitative formula effectively reduces to the more categorical rationality requirement 'Answer Yes to (4) if and only if you answer Yes to at least one of (1), (2) or (3); otherwise answer No').

Each shareholder in this corporation can honestly say that it is her view (or preference) that the technology should be installed. And if there was a vote on this as an *outcome*, the vote in column (4) would be correspondingly unanimous in the corporation that the technology be installed. However, suppose instead that there was a separate vote on each of the *issues* that are rationally relevant to that outcome, namely, on each of the issues in columns (1), (2) and (3). Then a majority of the shareholders would answer No to each of the issues, a set of votes that appears *rationally* to commit the corporation as a whole to not installing the technology, even though each and every individual could still honestly say that her voting across the issues (and her preference) was for

Table 10.1   Shareholders' assessments of the probability and seriousness of injury

	1. Is the probability of injury large?	2. Is the loss serious in the event of injury?	3. Is the cost of installation small?	4. Should the technology be installed?
Shareholder A	Yes	No	No	Yes (because Yes to (1))
Shareholder B	No	Yes	No	Yes (because Yes to (2))
Shareholder C	No	No	Yes	Yes (because Yes to (3))
Majority View	No (2:1)	No (2:1)	No (2:1)	Yes (for different reasons) (3:0)

installation. This difference between what is the majority view coming *down the last column* (4), and what is the rational implication of the different majority views in columns (1), (2) and (3) as we combine them *across the last row*, is what gives rise to the judgment aggregation paradox.

Now suppose that there was a workplace accident and that a court has determined that the failure to install the technology is its negligent cause. It would seem odd to say that *any* one of the shareholders should be held personally responsible for what has happened here. Each investor voted Yes on one of the issues and, therefore, each can honestly say that he or she wanted, and even chose, to install the technology. On the other hand, it does seem that a judgement of responsibility, and the liability that it entails, is appropriately predicated of *some* actor in this situation. After all, the decision not to install the safety technology was not the result of some random concatenation of unrelated events, but came about after some deliberation within the corporation on that very issue, and a court has now determined that the failure to install the technology was the negligent cause of the accident. So a natural implication of all this is that the corporation, and not the individual shareholders, should be held responsible. Thus, there seems to be a way of thinking about *collective* or *corporate* liability (and the limited personal liability that goes with it) that cannot be reduced to, or built out of, any sensible notion of individual shareholder liability.[13]

Now one might wonder if a corporation would ever make decisions in this way. It might be suggested, even if we could get past the thought that shareholders do not typically vote on these matters, that, if they did, they would vote directly on the final outcome ('Should the technology be installed?') and not indirectly on the more specific issues that combine rationally to determine that outcome (that is, the separate questions in columns (1), (2), and (3)). And if that were so, then the discontinuity between what each one of them thinks and chooses as individuals ('The technology should be installed') and what the corporate entity appears to think or choose would not arise since that same outcome would also be the one unanimously chosen by the corporation.

However, it will not always be the case that the different issues rationally implicating an outcome will arise simultaneously in a way that allows the voters to bypass the issues and go directly to a vote on the outcome. The issues might arise sequentially, where each corporate voter votes his opinion on the issue as it comes up. And this is where the normative requirements of practical rationality again begin to loom large – the second point I need to make in this section.

We can imagine, for example, a corporate version of the prior intention/belief/derivative intention problem that arose for our friend, Oliver, in the last section. Suppose the overall issue is again workplace safety. Two of the three shareholders are agreed that workplace safety is a priority for the corporation and have voted at t_1 to make it one. Further, after conducting some research into the matter of safety, there is a majority view (now a matter of belief) that the only effective way to address the issue is by adopting technology T when it becomes available at a reasonable price P. The corporation has now adopted this view at t_2. And now, at t_3 safety technology T has dropped to price P.

Is the corporation not now committed to adopting the technology? It would seem so. The views of the three shareholders are summarized in Table 10.2. Note that the column (1) question is analogous to asking the corporation to form a prior intention, the column (2) question to asking for a corporation's belief, and the column (3) question to asking whether the corporation has the (derivative) intention to buy the technology now.

Had all these issues come up at once at t_3, it might have been possible for the corporation to present a perfectly rational face to the world by simply voting No on the final outcome in column (3). Certainly that is what the majority view of the outcome is at t_3, based on reasons that each individual voter has in columns (1) and (2), reasons that might well persist into time t_3. And without any prior decisions pulling in the opposite direction, perhaps there is nothing to attend to but *the reasons* (albeit, quite different, even contradictory, reasons) the majority now has (at t_3) for not adopting the technology. But, given the decisions that have already been made by the corporation at t_1 and t_2, it is not where the *normative requirements* of practical rationality now take us. Just like Oliver, who adopted a prior intention to meet Lorenzo in Trento at noon tomorrow, and who would appear to be acting somewhat erratically and irrationally if he simply repudiated that earlier decision without any new (i.e., unanticipated and unaccounted for) reason for doing so, so too this corporation, having adopted workplace safety as a priority, and having exercised its best judgment that technology T at price P was the best means to meet this priority, would be acting irrationally and erratically if it failed to execute on this priority when the price of the technology T actually dropped to the price P as it had anticipated it might.

Table 10.2 Shareholders' views about the adoption of technology

	1. Is workplace safety a priority for the corporation?	2. Is the only way to address workplace safety to adopt technology T at price P?	3. Should we adopt technology T now that it is available at price P?
Shareholder A	Yes	No	No
Shareholder B	No	Yes	No
Shareholder C	Yes	Yes	Yes
Majority View (at each time t)	Yes (2:1 at t_1)	Yes (2:1 at t_2)	No (2:1 at t_3)

It is worth emphasizing that to hold the corporation to what is entailed, rationally, by its earlier decisions is to hold it to a decision that is not responsive to what the majority most wants to do *at t_3*. Indeed, a slightly more complicated example – say, a diachronic version of the one discussed in Table 10.1 – could have shown that the corporation might be rationally committed by its prior decisions to what *no* individual in the group wants to do at t_3. But this, I suggest, is simply what it means for a corporation, and its members (*qua members*), to offer a rational face to the world. A corporation that sought merely to be responsive to majority reasons at any point in time, for example, to what the majority most wanted, or most had reason to do at t_1, at t_2, *and* at t_3, without any view as to how these different decisions, in combination, formed a coherent purpose or plan, would not be taken seriously as an ongoing entity with which it was sensible (or safe) to deal.

Of course, this is not to say that a corporate plan or purpose should be beyond revision. At a minimum, our earlier discussion of rationality as comprising both the normative requirements of practical rationality *and* reasons suggests that it would be thoughtlessly mechanical to carry on with the corporate plan without any possibility of revision in the face of new and unanticipated information. But a corporation, even in that sort of case, should probably not make the revision of its plan a matter of easy routine (e.g., always repudiating its prior t_1 commitment in light of what it most wants to do at t_3). Again, to do so would undermine its credibility as an ongoing agent committed to those with whom it must deal.[14]

These final remarks will suggest, unfortunately, that the most conventional of economic models, namely, those that argue that there are only individual agents acting through the corporate form and no such thing as rational associations, can account for all that is required here. For example, so long as we allow shareholders in the corporation to be more sophisticated and, more particularly, to be concerned with how their short-run conduct might impact their long-run *individual* reputations with corporate creditors, then everything alluded to in the previous paragraph is easily accounted for. We need no fanciful discussions of an entity distinct from the individuals who are its members and certainly no discussion of an entity's rational face on the world distinct from the concerns that individual shareholders will have for their own ongoing reputations. Or so the argument will go.

However, I now want to suggest that this is only a more sophisticated version of the same mistake that fuels the backward induction argument and all the perversity that this more impoverished model of rationality entails. The hard truth is that a corporation formed only out of the reason-maximizing motivations of shareholders, even where these shareholders are sophistically oriented to how their reason-maximizing conduct impacts on their long-run reputations, is a corporation inadequately committed to achieve what the economic model most wants it to achieve. What is required is a rational association, that is, an association constrained both by reasons *and* by the normative requirements of practical rationality. Of course, a rational association committed as an association to the maximization of profit for shareholders will do (indeed, this sort of commitment will be required for most economic understandings of the for-profit corporation), as long as it also shows these sorts of commitments. (This, I suggest, is realized at least in part by the economist who accounts for the economic advantages of asset partitioning and capital lock-in within a corporation.) What will *not* do is a motivation, even a sophisticated motivation, limited to the maximization of profit *without* those commitments. This, alas, is the sort of corporation most often discussed in the economic literature, when the corporation is likened merely to 'a nexus of contracts' that somehow links the different transactions that take place between the individuals who make up the corporation as stakeholders.[15] I argue for the inadequacy of this account in the next section.

4   A problem with a non-rational association of corporate stakeholders

The most obvious difficulty with employing the idea of reputation as a device to explain the rationally sophisticated reason-maximizing (specifically, profit-maximizing) behavior by shareholders is that there is at least one important context where reputation seems to have little theoretical bite. In a takeover situation, where the target shareholders are exiting the corporation and being replaced by acquiring shareholders, there is at least the potential for a serious end game problem. (An end game is the predictable last game, or interaction, between players in a repeated interaction; repeated interactions, not necessarily between the same players, are typically required for modeling the impact on subsequent play of a reputation determined by earlier play in the game.) In the case of an acquisition of a widely held corporation the various target shareholders will be selling into an anonymous market and, therefore, without loss of individual reputation on this transaction, the final transaction they will have (if they sell all their shares) with other corporate stakeholders in the firm. This means that concern for reputation will set few constraints on their behavior around the takeover transaction, something that can be problematic.

To see this, consider the following scenario and how it might be represented.[16] Suppose that there is a corporation in which there is much protracted bargaining between management and employees. There is an attempt to work out every detail in advance, and there are high costs of transacting in this way, both in terms of the direct costs involved in negotiation and drafting and in terms of the psychological and emotional drain on the parties working in such an adversarially charged atmosphere. Call this status quo social state *x*. Suppose that it is agreed that it might be better if the managers and the employees met on their own without all the lawyers, proceeding less 'legalistically', and trusting that they will be able to work out problems as they meet them on the basis of some much more general and implicit 'understanding' of appropriate behavior. Call this social state y, and suppose that it is better than x for employees, managers, and shareholders alike. Certainly this seems plausible, especially if one thinks of the adversarial process as consuming resources that could otherwise be shared across all three groups of stakeholders.

However, the employees begin to worry that a large share of the savings in social state y are provided by them in the form of wages the payment of which is deferred until the corporation has proven itself to be more profitable as a consequence of the change from social state x to social state y. Specifically, they are fearful that these deferred wages might attract, and be appropriated by, a corporate acquirer who would not (at least on the kind of individualistic analysis presented so far) feel bound by any (non-legally enforceable) prior understandings to which it had not agreed. Call this possible outcome, where the deferred wages are appropriated by the acquirer, social state z, an outcome worse for the employees than social state x, but one which is better than x for both the shareholders (selling into this opportunistic acquisition) and the managers (who sell their cooperation in the takeover by securing a share of the gain that is otherwise split between target and acquiring shareholders).

But the employees are not without their own devices. Confronted with the threat of such a takeover, they might propose to the managers that the employees take a large equity stake in the corporation in the form of some employee stock ownership plan (or ESOP). Call this social state w. Such a stake gives the employees some voice in the running of the corporation (even if, typically, it is only through a trustee) and, as a defensive tactic against corporate acquirers, it has proven to be both effective and acceptable to the courts.[17] Of course, social state w requires the employees to be even more specifically invested in the corporation than they already are with all their human capital. So, it is for them (for reasons of risk aversion) an inferior social state to either social state x or y. Nevertheless, it is clearly better for them than social state z, where their deferred wages are threatened with appropriation by an opportunistic acquirer. Management prefers social state w most of all; in w they would have a legally effective defensive tactic against virtually all takeovers and, therefore, the sort of job security they have always coveted. Shareholders would consider w the worst of all possible outcomes for exactly the same sorts of reasons; such job security would undermine the incentive that management has for the efficient running of the firm by isolating it from the disciplinary effects of the market for corporate control.

The preferences of these three different corporate stakeholders (managers, shareholders, and employees) over these four possible social states, w, x, y, z, are presented in summary form in Figure 10.1 (reading the social states in decreasing order of preference from top to bottom for each stakeholder). The astute observer will notice that this particular preference profile is the one that can generate a majority voting paradox, given an even distribution of voting power across the three groups. But voting is not strictly required for there to be a problem. More generally, if managers and shareholders form a decisive coalition for choosing social state z over social state y (as they do if managers, in the course of a takeover, owe their fiduciary obligations *only* to shareholders[18]), and if managers and employees can form a decisive coalition for the choice of w over z, that is, for the adoption of an ESOP in the face of such a takeover threat (as they can if the law supports the use of this particular defensive tactic[19]), then it seems plausible that any movement to social state y from x, the status quo, will have a tendency to lead on, by way of these two decisive coalitions, to social state w. But this is the worst possible outcome for the shareholders. So it is hard to think that shareholders would support any initial move away from the status quo x that leads, ultimately, to w. (And, if there was any such move away, then they would press for a return to the status quo in a way analogous to the majority voting cycle that more conventionally illustrates the social choice problem here.) Moreover, the reluctance to make such a move is something that they share with the employee group. So, unless managers can fashion this move from x to y on their own, it seems that a move from the status quo x, with all its costly bargaining, is unlikely, this despite the fact that every one (except, perhaps, the lawyers) is better off in y than x.

If we represent this situation in Figure 10.2 as a centipede game[20] (for three players), then we can see that the above argument essentially involves using backward induction to solve that game in a way that is now conventional within economic theory. At each of the three nodes in the game a different

Managers	Shareholders	Employees
w	z	y
z	y	x
y	x	w
x	w	z

Figure 10.1 Stakeholders' preference orderings for four social states resulting from four different collective decision methods

Note: x = the status quo explicit and costly bargaining; y = less legalistic and less adversarial bargaining; z = threat of acquisition and deferred wages; and w = adoption of ESOP as a defensive tactic.

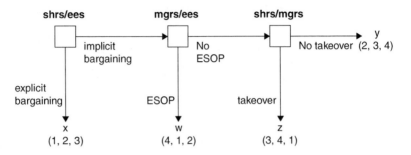

Figure 10.2   A centipede game
Note: payoffs in parentheses are ordinal and are for (managers, shareholders, employees)

possible corporate coalition is decisive for choice at that node. For example, at the extreme right-hand node, a coalition of managers and shareholders chooses between No Takeover (moving across) and Takeover (moving down). At the middle node the coalition of managers and employees is decisive for the rejection (across) or adoption (down) of an ESOP. And, finally, at the left-hand node, the coalition of shareholders and employees is decisive for the choice between adopting implicit bargaining (across) or more costly explicit bargaining (down). The four different outcomes or social states are the four different points at the end of each one of the arrows. The payoffs for the three different stakeholder groups in the four different outcomes are represented in the parentheses in this order: (managers, shareholders, employees). These payoffs are of ordinal significance only and can be read directly off Figure 10.1 with the most preferred (top) social state for any stakeholder receiving a payoff of 4 and the least preferred (bottom) social state a payoff of 1.

It is easy to show the backward induction. The coalition of shareholders and managers at the right-hand node enjoy higher payoffs in *z* than *y* and, therefore, presented with that choice, would choose *z*. Moreover, this is perfectly predictable given the usual game-theoretic assumptions about common knowledge of both the game and the rationality of the players. So the coalition of managers and employees who choose at the middle node will 'solve' for *z* as the outcome at the right-hand node and will now consider how that outcome (the outcome from this coalition moving across at the middle node) compares to *w*, the outcome which results from this coalition moving down. Examination of the payoffs shows that social state *w* is clearly better than *z* for this coalition, and so, presented with that choice, this coalition would, again predictably, move down at the middle node. But now consider how the coalition of shareholders and employees would choose at the left-hand node having also solved for *w* as the outcome from moving across at that node. Clearly, *x* provides for higher payoffs to both shareholders and employees than *w*, and so this coalition would move down at the left-hand node and the game would end. The result, therefore, is being stuck in social state x, a social state that has lower payoffs for *every* stakeholder than another social state that was available, social state y.

However, I have been arguing in this chapter that the backward induction argument works with too thin a conception of practical rationality, either for individuals or for groups. How, exactly, does that overly thin conception show itself here? It does so in a range of different ways, all of which are related or, I would argue, come to much the same thing. For a start, without legal enforceability, the argument effectively presumes that the prior commitments of merely implicit bargaining are always empty for individuals. They have no impact on subsequent behavior if execution of the commitment is contrary to what is dictated by reasons (or payoffs). This is no doubt a fair characterization of how individuals will behave much of the time, but it seems somewhat gratuitous to assume that it is how individuals must, as a matter of *rationality*, behave *all* of the time. Sometimes, at least, one might expect rational individuals to be implicated by the normative requirements of practical rationality as well as by reasons, something that might allow them to move across in the centipede game and, further, to be *predictable* in moving across. After all, it is the shareholders at the left-hand node who are looking forward to *their own* behavior at the right-hand node; why should they predict that, as rational individuals, they should be so unmoved by their own commitments?

But I want to suggest that the real problem of interpretation in this backward induction argument is at the group rather than the individual level. At the right-hand node the assumption is that those charged with the management of the corporation, at least in the context of a takeover, owe their fiduciary obligations, not to the corporation as a whole, but rather to some part of that whole, the shareholders. This is what allows the manager–shareholder coalition to be decisive at this node. But, as is suggested more generally by the ideas of limited liability and asset partitioning, it is the corporation that is the principal actor here rather than the shareholders. Why, at this particular moment, should those who manage the corporation choose to manage it for someone else (its shareholders) rather than for the corporation itself? This much of the question follows simply from comprehending the distinct agency of the body corporate, something that I tried to demonstrate with my example in Table 10.1. But the question can be put even more specifically. Why, at this particular moment, should the corporation, as a *rational* association, and not just a group agent or association *simpliciter*, abandon its own prior commitments at the left-hand node? A partnership, as a *non-rational* association, might be the sort of group agent that permits its members (unilaterally) to exit the (capital) commitments that they have made, particularly if there are reasons, grounded in profit maximization, to do so. But the corporation differs from the partnership in precisely that respect, a respect that gives it its own independent and coherent personality over time, the benefits for its member investors of asset partitioning (in both its defensive and affirmative forms), *and* the burden on its member investors in being unable to exit the corporation (either unilaterally with their capital stake or in combination by sale into a takeover) without giving rational consideration to those prior commitments that have been made by the corporation as a whole.[21] The fiduciary obligation of the corporate managers, properly understood, is to attend to these broader corporate commitments, the commitments that characterize the corporation as a rational association.[22]

It is tempting, of course, to think, that in a corporation organized 'for profit', the fiduciary obligations of the managers must be owed exclusively to the shareholders who enjoy those profits and who originally organized and invested in the corporation for that purpose. Drift away from the for-profit mission is likely to be construed as a drift into the pet projects of managers or stakeholders whose investments are not footing the bill. 'Let them set up their own *non*-profit corporation to pursue that mission if they want!' the shareholders' argument might go. But the takeover example as modeled in Figures 10.1 and 10.2 shows that it is a mistake to think that profits are even sensibly pursued or maximized without rational commitment. After all, without rational commitment, the shareholders, as much as any other stakeholder group, are caught in social state *x*, a social state that *loses* profits compared to social state *y* where broader corporate commitments are respected and not undermined. Of course, this *does* mean that the shareholders must restrict their pursuit of profit in social state y by *not* giving in to what is, admittedly, the (immediately) *profitable* temptation to sell into the takeover. Or they must have the management team *help* them to do that under a more rational understanding of fiduciary obligations.[23] For, given their anonymous exit from the firm, there is no long-run forward-looking argument, constructed out of reputation or further repeat play, which will otherwise save the shareholders as individuals here. There is only the backward-looking rationally grounded respect for prior corporate commitments or, equivalently, for the prior commitments that shareholders have made in their capacities as *members* of an ongoing rational association. Far from getting in the way of profit maximization, these sorts of corporate commitments, and the broader fiduciary obligations that they entail, are required for it.

5   Conclusions

I have argued elsewhere that some of the legal rules governing non-profit corporations, such as charities, can be explained as methods to control for 'ideological drift', that is, drift away from the mission or purpose that the non-profit has adopted for itself.[24] For example, a periodic disbursements obligation forces the managers of a charity to return regularly to their ideologically motivated donors and investors for further funds, something they can do comfortably and successfully only if they have been faithful to the charitable cause. Restrictions on the investments that charities can make, and on the 'unrelated business activities' in which they can engage, even if the managers promise to spend the funds thereby gained on charitable causes, can be explained the same way. The idea is not merely to subsidize just *any* charitable purpose with these funds, but rather the one that motivated the original charitable investors to invest in some particular common cause. And, of course, the concern that a charitable organization might be tempted to drift away from its mission to what higher profit might demand provides a rationale for why the charity, committed perhaps to the delivery of certain goods 'in kind' (not cash), does not organize for the delivery of these goods under the for-profit corporate form. The non-profit corporate form acts as a kind of pre-commitment device.

However, it should now be apparent that the for-profit corporation is also subject to a certain kind of ideological drift, and for much the same reasons. The corporation might be organized around the idea (or ideology) of making profits, but that *very same idea*, if pursued in too narrow a way, can lead to the corporation defecting from what is required by the maximization of profit. So the for-profit corporation, just as much as the non-profit corporation, needs to be seen as requiring a pre-commitment device against ideological drift.

When it is suggested that it is the maximization of profit that might tempt some charitable organization while it is trying to keep to its *non*-profit mission, it is not difficult to see the problem of commitment. The source of temptation at some later time is so different from the original mission that originally prompted the formation of the organization; why should we be surprised by the appearance of inconsistency between these two? But when it is the *same* reason, the maximization of profit, which is advanced as undermining an organization committed to the maximization of profit, it is much harder to fathom the source of the difficulty. It must seem that we have not been sophisticated enough in our analysis of this one reason that motivates the organization, and that if we had only looked at it in the long run or under repeat play, for example, we would be able to tame what is only an *apparent* inconsistency in how this single reason applies to this one organization over time.

However, I hope to have shown that the problem does not lie in a lack of sophistication in the application of profit maximization as a reason for the forming of a corporation. Rather, the problem is that reasons of any kind are simply inadequate, structurally, to account for all that is rational in the conduct of a corporation. The normative requirements of practical rationality, or the stuff of rational commitment *contrary to reason*, must also play a role. In being *capable* of this richer conception of rationality, and in *requiring* it if it is to maximize profits, the for-profit corporation, as a rational association, is no more, and no less, than the full person that law takes it to be. It should be no surprise, therefore, that as a legal person separate from the individual agents who are its members, and upon whom it must, of course, supervene for its agency, it ought to own its own assets, meet its own liabilities (and no others), and be managed by fiduciaries so as to fulfill its own prior commitments.

Notes

1. Kutz (2000, 236–53).
2. Hansmann and Kraakman (2000). More recently Hansmann, Kraakman, and Squire (2006) have used the terms 'owner shielding' and 'entity shielding' for defensive and affirmative asset partitioning respectively.
3. Broome (1999, 2001, 2002, 2004); Chapman (2004, 2005).
4. Blair (2003); Stout (2005).
5. Arrow (1959); Sen (1971).
6. See the references cited in note 3 above; also see Kolodny (2005).
7. Broome (2004). For some suggestion that *rational* persuasion, while strict, might be less helpful in resolving disputes than *reasoned* persuasion precisely because it has 'wide scope' and is, therefore, indeterminate as to particular resolutions of what is most at issue between the parties, see Chapman (2009).
8. I say 'at least' because it might also be that the normative requirements of practical rationality require action in accordance with a prior intention or commitment even when new and unanticipated reasons arise which argue against the action. However, my arguments do not address this possibility.
9. There is an interesting difference between the two accounts of shared agency that are offered in the philosophical literature by Bratman (1999) and Gilbert (1996) which seems to turn on whether or not there must be some sort of joint commitment (incompatible with unilateral disengagement) when two or more agents act together. Bratman's account, which denies a joint commitment requirement, might be interpreted here as coming closer to the idea of parties acting in partnership, and Gilbert's, which does require joint commitment, closer to the idea of a body corporate (her term is 'plural subject'). Neither account, of course, presumes that a joint commitment would be a legally enforceable obligation.
10. What follows is an example of what was originally called 'the doctrinal paradox' (when applied to judicial voting) and is now more generally called the 'discursive dilemma' or the 'judgement aggregation paradox'. The literature is now huge. See, e.g., Kornhauser and Sager (1986, 2004), Chapman (1998, 2002), Pettit (2001, 2003), List and Pettit (2002). For a good recent survey, see List (2006). Rock (2006) has recently sought to apply its insights to corporate law.
11. The delegation strategy is emphasized by Rock (2006) as one method by which the corporation might avoid the difficulty that is about to surface here.
12. This is the simplest version of the so-called 'Learned Hand' formula which is used to support an economic interpretation of negligence within economic analyses of law; see, for example, Posner (2002). The example in the text is close to the one offered by Pettit (2007) at p. 197.
13. Of course, the actions of the corporation (and, therefore, its responsibilities and liabilities) *supervene* on the attitudes of the individuals that make it up. There is no possibility, for example, of any (independent) change in the conduct of the corporation without some change in these underlying attitudes. In other words, the corporation does not exist (mysteriously) without its members. Nevertheless, the judgement

of corporate responsibility or liability for some outcome X that supervenes in this way on the underlying individual attitudes (e.g., individual intentions, desires or beliefs) is not reducible to, or built out of, any sensible underlying idea of individual *responsibility* and/or *liability* for outcome X. As the example is meant to show, that may be totally absent. For further discussion of group agency and the supervenience requirement, see List and Pettit (2006).

14. Pettit (2003).
15. The 'nexus of contracts' characterization of the corporation seems to have originated with Jensen and Meckling (1976). For a systematic and impressive application of this contractual approach to issues in corporate law, see Easterbrook and Fischel (1991).
16. I have used this example elsewhere to make a slightly different point about the importance of trust within a corporation; see Chapman (1993). That argument employed social choice theory to argue that Kaldor–Hicks efficient contracting within the corporation, without trust and/or loyalty, could give rise to cycling or instability inside the firm. The argument that hostile takeovers sometimes involve a breach of trust by shareholders against employees was originally advanced by Shleifer and Summers (1988).
17. See *Shamrock Holdings Inc.* v. *Polaroid Corporation* 559 A.2d 257, 275–6 (Del. Ch. 1989) where it is held that a 'shareholder-neutral' ESOP (that is, one funded through employee wage concessions rather than share dilution) is intrinsically fair and, therefore, not subject to the same degree of judicial supervision as other defensive actions undertaken by the board in the course of a takeover bid.
18. In *Revlon* v. *MacAndrews and Forbes Holding Inc.* 506 A.2d 173 (Del. 1986) the Delaware Supreme Court held that when directors decide to sell the company, their role changes from protectors of the corporate entity to 'auctioneers' whose duty is to get the best price for stockholders. Subsequently, the Court explained that a board enters the '*Revlon* mode' whenever the corporation initiates an active bidding process aimed at selling itself, seeks a transaction that will result in its break-up, or pursues a change of control; see *Paramount Communications, Inc.* v. *QVC Network Inc.*, 637 A.2d 34 (Del. 1994).
19. See n. 17.
20. The term 'centipede' derives from the appearance of the game when it is shown, as in Figure 10.2, in extensive form, that is, as a long horizontal figure with many legs. The game seems to originate with Rosenthal (1981).
21. Member investors or shareholders enjoy the free transferability of their shares in the public market outside the takeover context. But these sorts of transactions, typically smaller in size, do not threaten to have the same impact on the prior (policy) commitments of the corporation as does a takeover or other fundamental change. Thus, they do not require the same sort of attention from fiduciaries.
22. One might question whether there is much to be gained in predicating the richer notion of rational commitment of the corporation as opposed to the shareholders themselves. Is the corporation not simply *their* pre-commitment device? So, when the shareholders choose to be rationally committed, they will choose the corporate device, and when the corporation is rationally committed, the shareholders will be committed too? The problem with this reductionist account of the commitment is that it fails fully to appreciate the earlier argument that the corporation's commitments will not in general be the same as the commitments the shareholders would choose to make. The takeover scenario discussed in the text might suggest this sameness, but it is only an example, one designed to show that shareholders can *sometimes* gain by organizing within a rational association and under corporate

commitments. However, suppose in Table 10.2, for example, that shareholder B and shareholder C were other sorts of corporate stakeholders who either had voting power or to whom corporate obligations were owed. Then, while shareholder A would *not* choose to rationally commit (by voting Yes both in column 1 and in column 2) to voting Yes in column 3, the corporation would so rationally commit. So the notion of rational corporate commitment, while *sometimes* useful to shareholders, is not generally reducible to such an instrumental account.

23. As, for example, in the two Delaware Supreme court Cases *Unocal v. Mesa Petroleum* 493 A.2d 946 (Del. 1985) (predating the *Revlon* case, discussed in note 18) and *Paramount v. Time* 571 A.2d 1140 (Del. 1990) (which sought to limit the *Revlon* duty to auction the company for the exclusive benefit of shareholders, thus reinforcing the broader duties of *Unocal*).

24. Chapman (2001).

References

Arrow, K.J. (1959) 'Rational Choice Functions and Orderings', *Economica*, vol. 26(102), pp. 121–7.

Blair, M. (2003) 'Locking in Capital: What Corporate Law Achieved for Business Organizers in the Nineteenth Century', *UCLA Law Review*, vol. 51, pp. 387–455.

Broome, J. (1999) 'Normative Requirements', *Ratio*, vol. 12(4), pp. 398–419.

Broome, J. (2001) 'Normative Practical Reasoning', *Proceedings of the Aristotelian Society*, vol. 75(1), Supp., pp. 175–93.

Broome, J. (2002) 'Practical Reasoning', in J.L. Bermudez and A. Millar (eds), *Reason and Nature*. Oxford: Oxford University Press.

Broome, J. (2004) 'Reasons' in R. Wallace, P. Pettit, S. Scheffler and M. Smith (eds), *Reason and Value*. Oxford: Oxford University Press.

Bratman, M.E. (1999) *Faces of Intention*. Cambridge: Cambridge University Press.

Chapman, B. (1993) 'Trust, Economic Rationality, and the Corporate Fiduciary Obligation', *University of Toronto Law Journal*, vol. 43(3), pp. 547–88.

Chapman, B. (1998) 'More Easily Done Than Said: Rules, Reasons, and Rational Social Choice', *Oxford Journal of Legal Studies*, vol. 18(2), pp. 293–329.

Chapman, B. (2001) 'Rational Voluntarism and the Charitable Sector' in J. Phillips, B. Chapman, and D. Stevens (eds), *Between State and Market*. Montreal: McGill-Queen's University Press.

Chapman, B. (2002) 'Rational Aggregation', *Politics, Philosophy and Economics*, vol. 1(3), pp. 337–54.

Chapman, B. (2004) 'Legal Analysis of Economics: Solving the Problem of Rational Commitment', *Chicago-Kent Law Review*, vol. 79(2), pp. 471–95.

Chapman, B. (2005) 'Rational Commitment and Legal Reason', *San Diego Law Review*, vol. 42(1), pp. 91–127.

Chapman, B. (2009) 'Leading You Down the Choice Path: Towards an Economics of Rational Persuasion', *Queen's Law Journal*, vol. 35, 327–58.

Easterbrook, F. and D. Fischel (1991) *The Economic Structure of Corporate Law*. Cambridge, MA: Harvard University Press.

Gilbert, M. (1996) *Living Together*. New York: Rowman and Littlefield.

Hansmann, H. and R. Kraakman (2000) 'The Essential Role of Organizational Law', *Yale Law Journal*, vol. 110(3), pp. 387–440.

Hansmann, H., R. Kraakman and R.C. Squire (2006) 'Law and the Rise of the Firm', *Harvard Law Review*, vol. 119(5), pp. 1333–1403.

Jensen, M. and Meckling, W. (1976) 'Theory of the Firm: Managerial Behavior, Agency Costs and Ownership Structure', *Journal of Financial Economics*, vol. 3(4), pp. 305–60.

Kolodny, N. (2005) 'Why Be Rational?', *Mind*, vol. 114(455), pp. 509–63.

Kornhauser, L. and Sager, L. (1986) 'Unpacking the Court' *Yale Law Journal*, vol. 96, pp. 82–117.

Kornhauser L.A. and L.G. Sager (2004) 'The Many as One: Integrity and Group Choice in Paradoxical Cases', *Philosophy and Public Affairs*, vol. 32(3). pp. 249–76.

Kutz, C. (2000) *Complicity*. Cambridge: Cambridge University Press.

List, C. (2006) 'The Discursive Dilemma and Public Reason', *Ethics*, vol. 116(2), pp. 362–402.

List, C. and P. Pettit (2002) 'The Aggregation of Sets of Judgments: An Impossibility Result', *Economics and Philosophy*, vol. 18(1), pp. 89–110.

List, C. and P. Pettit (2006) 'Group Agency and Supervenience', *Southern Journal of Philosophy*, Spindel Supp., vol. 44, pp. 85–105.

Pettit, P. (2001) 'Deliberative Democracy and the Discursive Dilemma', *Noûs*, vol. 35(1), pp. 268–99.

Pettit, P. (2003) 'Groups with Minds of their Own', in F. Schmitt (ed.), *Socializing Metaphysics: The Nature of Social Reality*. New York: Rowman and Littlefield.

Pettit, P. (2007), 'Responsibility Incorporated', *Ethics*, vol. 117(2), pp. 171–201.

Posner, R. (2002) *Economic Analysis of Law*, 6th edn. New York: Aspen Publishers.

Rock, E. (2006) 'The Corporate Form as a Solution to a Discursive Dilemma', *Journal of Institutional and Theoretical Economics*, vol. 162(1), pp. 57–71.

Rosenthal, R. W. (1981) 'Games of Perfect Information, Predatory Pricing and the Chain Store Paradox', *Journal of Economic Theory*, vol. 25(1), pp. 92–100.

Sen, A. (1971) 'Choice Functions and Revealed Preference', *Review of Economic Studies*, vol. 38(3), pp. 307–17.

Shleifer, A. and L. Summers (1988) 'Breach of Trust in Hostile Takeovers', in A. J. Auerbach (ed.), *Corporate Takeovers: Causes and Consequences*. Chicago: University of Chicago Press.

Stout, L. (2005) 'On the Nature of Corporations', *University of Illinois Law Review*, vol. 1, pp. 253–67.

Part III

CSR, Social Standards and Multi-Stakeholder Organisations According to the Behavioral Economics Perspective

11

The Roles of Standardization, Certification, and Assurance Services in Global Commerce*

Margaret M. Blair, Cynthia A. Williams and Li-Wen Lin

1 Introduction

Two of the major problems that permeate complex modern production and distribution enterprises are coordination and enforcement. While mechanisms of coordination have been studied extensively in management science and organizational economics, issues raised by the second set of problems have been the focus of microeconomic theory, organizational economics, and law, especially property, contract and business entity law (e.g., North, 1990). At least two major mechanisms of enforcement of business and commercial understandings and agreements – legal contracts, and the organization of activities within firms – have been studied at considerable length by scholars in the law and economics tradition (e.g., Coase, 1937; Williamson, 1975). More recently, a third cluster of mechanisms, including norms and reputation, have become an object of study by economists and legal scholars (Richman, 2004; Bernstein, 1996; Bernstein, 1992; Bernstein, 2001; Grief, 1989).

Both organization within firms and organization by contract rely heavily on rule of law.

* Professor of Law at Vanderbilt University Law School, Professor of Law at the University of Illinois College of Law, and JSD candidate at the University of Illinois College of Law, respectively. The authors have had the benefit of substantial research assistance from Everett Peaden, Bixuan Wu, Rebecca Conley, Brandon Martin, Yun Chen, Joshua Rosenblatt, Tracy Dry Kane, Lily Huang and Emily Kamm. We appreciate the comments of participants in the IEA meeting in Trento, Italy on Corporate Social Responsibility and Corporate Governance in July 2006; participants at faculty workshops at the University of Georgia Law School, the University of North Carolina Law School and Vanderbilt University Law School, participants in Prof. Stephen Bainbridge's student workshop at UCLA Law School; and the participants in the University of Illinois and Sun Yat-Sen University School of Law, Guangzhou, China, conference on the Role of Law in Economic Development in March 2007. Particular thanks are owed to Ed Rock, Oliver Williamson, Mike Vandenberg, David Zaring, and John Conley for their careful attention to earlier drafts.

Hence one might expect that they would be unavailable or ineffective for businesses operating in a global environment, especially in countries that do not have an established rule of law and well-developed independent courts and legal systems. It might seem that the explosion in global communications capabilities in the past decade would counteract or offset that problem by making it easier for the third mechanism – norms and reputation – to serve as an effective way to enforce contracts and expectations in the absence of law. But while reputational enforcement mechanisms can be quite powerful in getting large, highly visible organizations to live up to contract requirements and social norms, the same communications capabilities that can make reputation important can also be used to publish misleading information, distort perceptions, free-ride on the reputations of others, conceal norm violations, and generally introduce at least as much noise as useful information into the process of determining whether legitimate expectations have been met on all sides, and economic gains have been divided up accordingly.

In this chapter we discuss the role of a fourth enforcement mechanism that we claim is rapidly becoming extremely important in global business and trade. This is the use of third-party, non-governmental standard-setting, inspection, assurance and certification services. Not only has there been an explosion in recent years in the demand for third-party assurance services, as we describe below, but there has also been a proliferation of quantifiable standards and metrics by which such services can measure and report on performance by parties to actual and potential contracts. Many of these performance metrics define standards for acceptable social and environmental behavior, as well as for such things as quality control and on-time delivery, so that third-party assurance services also appear to exercise a regulatory function, importing and enforcing norms of acceptable conduct throughout lengthening supply chains.

Probably the most familiar and well-established type of third-party standard-setting and assurance service is the body of accounting rules as applied by external auditors, who examine financial statements and the processes by which they were generated, and opine on whether the statements were produced in accordance with generally accepted accounting principles and fairly present the underlying economic reality of the firm. There is evidence that 'boards of state accountants' were used to verify state revenues and expenditures in ancient Athens, circa 500–300 BC, for example (Costouros, 1978). Financial institutions that invest in or insure business ventures have also long made use of other kinds of non-financial measures and assurance services. As maritime commerce expanded centuries ago, for example, marine insurance companies in France, Britain, the Netherlands, and Italy hired inspectors to make sure that ships being used for international commerce were sea-worthy. Indeed, several of the global assurance organizations that today certify adherence to a wide range of product specifications, or to the effectiveness of specific quality or management systems within firms, initially began as maritime inspectors.[1]

Our thesis in this chapter is that a number of factors are coming together in the global business environment to cause an explosion in the demand for management standards and third-party assurance services. In fact, we speculate that the role played by standardization and third-party assurance is rapidly becoming so important that, in some parts of the world where rule of law is weak, business norms unreliable, and the regulation of business practices erratic or non-existent, private sector players may be turning to third-party assurance services as the dominant mechanism for regulating business and enforcing contracts. We offer reasons for this development, evidence of its scope and scale, and then describe the phenomenon in more detail by examining two industries, food products and apparel, where the use of third-party standards and assurance services has expanded especially rapidly in the last decade.

We conclude with a discussion of the implications for the 'make or buy' decision at the core of the theory of the firm (Coase, 1937). In this section of the chapter we argue that as quasi-regulatory standards are developed within various industries, and as performance to those standards can be systematically evaluated using third-party inspectors and certifiers, the costs of moving production outside of vertical firm hierarchies drop. We believe this may be an important factor in accelerating the shift to outsourcing that has been observed over the last two decades.

2 The third-party standard-setting and assurance industry[2]

As mentioned above, one of the most familiar types of third-party standard-setting and assurance service is the external auditor. Independent external auditors have been critical to the development of liquid financial markets in which individuals have reasonable confidence that information provided by companies in which they invest is an accurate reflection of the condition of the underlying business.[3]

Financial institutions that invest in or insure business ventures have also long made use of other kinds of assurance services, including credit rating, title services, inspections for hazardous materials such as asbestos, and independent appraisals. But in recent years, the range of international trade matters that are the subject of standardization, inspection, verification, assurance, and certification has grown substantially.

2.1 The impact of ISO

A major example and driver of the development of global standards has been the widespread development since the mid-twentieth century of international standards and technical specifications for a vast array of products and processes by the ISO. Since its founding in 1946, the International Organization for Standardization (ISO) has promulgated tens of thousands of technical standards.[4] ISO also publishes a list of accreditation bodies that, in turn, accredit hundreds of organizations around the world that are in the business of carrying out various evaluations to determine if products or processes or management systems are in conformance with the specifications in ISO standards.

Twenty years ago, in 1987, the ISO embarked on a significant new path when it adopted the 'ISO 9000' standards of quality management.[5] These were the first sets of international standards that applied to *management systems* that firms use to meet customer and regulatory requirements, rather than to the characteristics of the products firms produce or to units and methods of measuring those characteristics (Roht-Arriaza, 1995). Since the ISO 9000 series of standards was adopted, many firms have chosen to have their systems independently audited and certified to them,[6] and certification rapidly 'became a *de facto* requirement for doing business in Europe and other parts of the world', as well as being actually required for certain products sold in Europe and the United States (Roht-Arriaza, 1995, p. 500).

The idea of creating standards for management systems embodied in ISO 9000 has greatly fuelled the development of the assurance industry (Wood, 2006). One reason is that, while buyer firms likely have the appropriate expertise and incentive to inspect *products* to be sure they meet specifications, buyer firms may not have the necessary expertise to inspect the *processes* by which the products were made. Meanwhile, supplier firms might have the necessary expertise, but are unlikely to have the necessary independence to inspect and certify the operation of their own factories. Thus when it comes to process inspection, trading partners may be more likely to agree to third-party inspection rather than first-party (supplier firm) or second-party (buyer firm) inspections. Organizations that were among the first to qualify as certifiers for ISO 9000 compliance were generally European organizations that had already been providing quality inspection services for various products; more recently, accounting and audit firms have been expanding their business services portfolios to add capability to perform ISO 9000 certifications.[7]

Data collected by ISO show that the number of firms and facilities in the world that were ISO 9000 certified grew from 27,816 in 48 countries in 1993, to 670,399 in 154 countries by 2004 (ISO Survey).[8] ISO provides no comparable data on the number of active certifying bodies, but this dramatic expansion in the number of firms and plants that have been certified could only be accomplished if the number of people and firms doing certification work had also grown dramatically.

Once the demand for management quality and process certification had developed sufficiently to support a private sector infrastructure to certify management systems, it was only a small step for business, government, non-governmental organizations ('NGOs'), and social activists to look to these same sorts of certifying organizations to provide assurance when asking companies to demonstrate that they are meeting specified criteria for social performance.[9]

In 1996, the ISO adopted the ISO 14000 series of standards for evaluating environmental management systems (Peglau, 2002). By 2004, 90,569 facilities and firms, in 127 countries, had been certified as meeting these standards.[10] And ISO is currently developing standards for social responsibility as well.[11]

2.2 An overview of assurance organizations

In the past ten to 15 years, numerous corporations, NGOs, industry groups, and other organizations have developed codes of practice for various industries. Firms that have long been in the business of inspecting the quality, quantity, and weight of traded goods – especially those that evaluate and certify conformance with ISO standards – have quickly expanded to offer their services in auditing and certifying that firm operations satisfy these new codes of practice. Firms such as SGS, Intertek, DNV (Det Norske Veritas), RINA (Registro Italiano Navale), and the TÜVs (Technischer Überwachungsverein) have all been in business as inspectors of goods and ships in international trade since before 1900. They all operate globally and have had a quasi-official status as inspectors for customs officials or government agencies regulating products moving in international markets. All have recently expanded their business to do audits and inspections to verify compliance with social responsibility standards.[12]

In addition, dozens of new firms have entered the business as certification bodies, including firms like Cal Safety Compliance Corp. (CSCC), ALGI, and the Hong Kong Quality Assurance Agency (HKQAA). CSCC, for example, is a division of Specialized Technology Resources, Inc. in Los Angeles. It was established in 1991 to provide social responsibility auditing services, initially in the garment sector and now in a broad range of industries including home furnishings, food and agriculture, cosmetics, toys, and high-tech products, and has operations in more than 110 countries. Similarly, ALGI, headquartered in Nyack, NY, was founded in 1994 by several former Department of Labor officials to carry out social accountability auditing. TransFair USA was launched in 1998 and began the 'fair trade' certification of coffee purchased from developing countries in 1999. It has since expanded to the certification of other food products. HKQA was established in 1989 by the Hong Kong government to do social compliance audits.[13]

2.3 'Professionalization' of the standard-setting and assurance industry

The assurance business is itself largely unregulated. Standards are often set in collaborative processes led by industry trade groups, NGOs, and/or government regulators. For example, a 'Voluntary Carbon Standard' (VCS) that provides 'quality assurance for certification of credible voluntary offsets' was announced recently by The Climate Group, a nonprofit formed in 2004 as a consortium of industry, nonprofit groups and emissions market specialists including the International Emissions Trading Association (IETA) and the World Business

Council for Sustainable Development.[14] But there are no well-established and accepted training procedures or professional standards for those who 'audit' non-financial performance indicators. Yet, by its nature it is a business that is rife with potential for abuse. This is because, as is true for financial audits, inspections and evaluations of systems and operating practices are usually arranged and purchased by a supplier company in order to provide assurance to a purchasing company that the supplier can meet – or has met – contract terms, or complied with certain norms and standards. And, as is true in the business of providing financial audits, individual auditors might have incentives to accept payoffs in exchange for approval by the auditors. Likewise, the client firms whose facilities are being inspected might have incentives to offer such payoffs if it is cheaper for them to make the side payments than it is to comply with the codes or standards. Indeed, factory owners in developing countries who are being asked by their developed-country customers to subject themselves to audit frequently complain that the demands for audits are a form of extortion (Roberts et al., 2006). Inspection organizations also complain of finding double books, or that workers have been instructed to answer questions in certain ways, or other deceptive practices. And factory owners complain of having to meet multiple, sometimes conflicting standards, and be subject to repetitive inspections to satisfy different customers.

Suppliers of financial auditing services long ago figured out that there are two basic mechanisms for addressing this problem: the professionalization of the providers of the service, and investments by the providers in securing reputations for independence and honesty. Professional accountants are now required to go through formal training and licensing by organizations representing accountants, and they typically organize themselves into large, high-visibility firms with substantial interests in maintaining reputations for honesty, independence, and competence. Those firms, in turn, have incentives to see to it that their auditors are competent, disciplined, and behave professionally.

These things are only beginning to happen in the non-financial assurance business. Although the leading international firms in the business have substantial reputational capital at risk, many smaller, newer assurance firms are in the business that may not yet have established reputations. Moreover, there appears to be only one significant professional organization that offers any standardization and assurance of the assurance professionals themselves.[15] This is the International Register of Certificated Auditors (IRCA), a UK organization based in London that was founded in 1984 as part of a UK government initiative to establish and certify quality management standards. IRCA certifies auditors of management systems, approves training organizations and certifies their auditor training courses. It claims to have certified more than 13,750 auditors in over 120 countries worldwide. Generally, however, there is 'very little oversight' over the assurance industry (Wood, 2006).

3   Factors causing proliferation of standards and growth in demand for assurance services

A number of different factors seem to be at work that, together, are driving the rapid proliferation of standards and associated growth in demand for assurance services, as well as in the supply of businesses that offer their services as inspectors and auditors to meet this demand.

3.1   Expanding international markets increased reliance on outsourcing, and longer supply chains

Other scholars have written at length about the growth in international commerce in the last few decades,[16] and the extent to which corporations in developed countries now contract with developing country firms for parts manufacturing, assembly, testing, and even sales (e.g., call centers) and record-keeping (Geis, 2006; Lohr, 2006). When products are made in factories owned by – and under the immediate supervision of – the managerial employees of a large firm, that firm can directly implement its own quality, timely delivery, labor, and environmental operating norms and standards. When the same firm contracts with a factory owner in Bangladesh, or Vietnam, or Costa Rica to make the products, the parties to the contract will probably need to develop detailed product specifications and alternative mechanisms, other than direct managerial control, to make certain that the products are made according to these specifications (both as to product characteristics and quality, and as to the processes used). These mechanisms may range from the hiring firm having its own inspectors in the contractor's plant at all times, to having third-party inspectors check the plant's operations from time to time, to relying solely on inspection of the final product at the time the hiring firm takes possession of it. This last mechanism may be widely used for simple commodity-type products made in uncontroversial ways. But, they are less likely to be effective where there are hidden attributes of a product, or the process by which it was made, that are important to the buying firm.

3.2   The growing complexity of products and increased division of labor

More of the products being exchanged between firms in international markets are intermediate products that must meet strict specifications as inputs or components of other products, or are made utilizing processes that are controversial (e.g., strip mining, farming with patented seeds, or fertilizers and pest control chemicals, or labor-intensive assembly potentially involving sweatshop conditions or child labor) (Arndt and Kierzkowski, 2001; Kysar, 2004). It is common, for example, for products to be designed in one country, components to be purchased from suppliers in other countries, assembly work done in yet another country, all for shipment to markets in a number of other countries.[17]

At each step of the way, the corporations that are organizing all of this productive activity need to be able to control for quality, conformance to specifications, the timely delivery of intermediate products to final assembly plants, and safety in both the manufacturing and use of the product. Throughout this process, inventories must be managed for cost-efficiency, and to provide required levels of customer service (Schary & Skjott-Larsen, 1998; Jespersen, Skjott-Larsen, 2005; and Ayers, 2001). For such products, the purchasing company may have compelling reasons to want to specify performance features and monitor steps in the production process in one way or another.

3.3   Role of international trade regulations

The growth of the third-party assurance industry based on ISO standard-setting has also been fueled by developments in the regulation of international trade. Efforts in Europe to facilitate intra-European trade by harmonizing regulatory requirements initially emphasized compliance with European technical standards as a necessary condition for selling any goods in Europe. Thus, the standards developed by the European standard-setting agency, the Comité Européen de Normalisation (CEN), were applied to any goods sold in Europe. This led non-European companies to argue that technical and other standards, such as for quality and product safety, should be developed by the international standard-setting process of the ISO, rather than through a European process. That position was persuasive to negotiators developing the General Agreement on Tariffs and Trade (GATT) 1994/World Trade Organization (WTO) Agreement on Technical Barriers to Trade, which thus provides that where international standards for technical requirements exist, member states should use those standards as the basis for their own technical requirements (Roht-Arriaza, 1995).[18] As a consequence, ISO certification became necessary for a growing number of products, and as ISO standards expanded beyond technical specifications to quality and environmental management systems, a 'huge industry of auditors, certifiers and accreditation bodies has emerged to serve these expanding certification needs' (Wood, 2006).

3.4   The growing demand for workplace safety, acceptable labor and human rights performance, and acceptable environmental standards

In the last decade, for reasons we discuss below, many global corporations have begun seeking assurance that firms they do business with can meet social and environmental standards, in addition to technical and quality standards.[19] This development is causing corporations in developing countries that are suppliers to more well-known global corporations to insist that their suppliers, in turn, also meet certain standards.

In this way, multinational firms may be drawing more small and local firms in more countries into their orbit. As this happens, we are observing a movement toward global standard setting and the associated use of third-party assurance firms to certify that standards are being met, even by supplier firms that still operate and sell primarily in their home country.[20]

3.4.1   *Recognition of the risks to global brands from problems in the supply chains*

In the past two decades global corporations have also been more inclined to insist that suppliers, as well as their own facilities, meet certain social standards because they recognize that each link in the supply chain potentially exposes the whole operation to risks associated with that link.

The experience of companies in the chemical industry (beginning with companies operating in Canada) illustrate the pattern. Canadian chemical firms recognized as long ago as 1983 that risks in the handling of hazardous wastes in foreign operations can affect reputation and profitability of their worldwide organizations. To address these risks, a group of chemical companies led by Dow Canada and the Canadian Chemical Producers Association (CCPA), with encouragement from the Canadian government, agreed to develop a set of safe operating principles (O'Conner, 2006). The 1984 explosion of a Union Carbide plant in Bhopal, India, accelerated the development and adoption of these principles, which came to be called the Responsible Care Initiative (RCI). Other chemical companies joined the initiative in an effort to improve the industry's reputation (Bélanger, 2005).

The initiative originally included six standards for safe practice in chemical production, transport and control.[21] Although the standards had been adopted by numerous chemical companies by 1988,[22] by 1993, chemical firms were learning, as Responsible Care executive Brian Wastle explained to us, that the mere fact that 'CEOs stated they had met their commitment meant nothing to an untrusting public'. So the standards were expanded to include provision for verification and ongoing improvement of performance.

Responsible Care executive Wastle reports that the standards now require that 'teams of industry experts, public advocates and local citizens' review each company every three years, and 'write a consensus report summarizing the verification process and players, opportunities for improvement, findings, required corrective action and successful practices', with verification certificates awarded once the work is completed.

Similarly, firms that use highly labor-intensive manufacturing and assembly processes, such as apparel and toy manufacturers, have responded to media attacks on firms whose products were allegedly made in 'sweatshop' conditions[23] by developing codes of practice for their own factories and for supplier factories. But these firms have also learned that announcing codes of practice is not sufficient to solve the problem[24] – they must also develop implementation strategies and arrange for inspection and certification to be sure the codes are in fact implemented.

To enhance brand protection by tackling the implementation problem in one industry, for example, a group of corporations in the apparel and 'sewn products' industries, together with industry trade associations,[25] provided seed money and technical support to form a third-party standard-setting organization called WRAP (Worldwide Responsible Apparel Production) in the late 1990s. WRAP was given the goal of establishing worker safety and human rights performance standards to be applied at the factory level, and to implement inspection and certification procedures.[26] WRAP is now formally an independent non-profit organization, governed by a board of directors of which, by the organization's bylaws, more than half must be unaffiliated with the apparel industry.[27] Factory certification by WRAP requires that the facilities meet initial standards, as certified by an approved independent monitor, and be subject to unannounced audits, and annual renewal.[28]

The awareness of supply chain risks is amplified by a recognition on the part of corporations and their investors that a large share of the economic value that firms create is tied to their 'brand value'. But, as discussed above, brand value is only as good as its weakest link because expansion in international travel and communications makes it harder for firms to hide their 'dirty laundry'. Wal-Mart, for example, has undertaken a massive public-relations campaign, including drawing attention to its new code of ethics, to attempt to respond to critics who charge that its suppliers violate international labor norms.[29] Although its code notably lacks both specifics about standards of treatment for workers, and enforcement mechanisms,[30] Wal-Mart may very well not be the worst offender among US retailers in its tolerance of labor abuses in supplier factories. But because of the high visibility of its brand, it is believed to be very influential in establishing industry norms, and hence may be targeted more intensely by NGOs and other activists than smaller, less well-known firms.

3.4.2   *The increasing sophistication of NGOs, activists, and institutional investors*

As corporations find themselves in the glare of the NGO spotlight for their social and environmental practices, a growing number of firms are looking for better ways to make sure they know what is actually happening out in their supply chains. Moreover, activists and investors are increasingly asking corporations to provide information about their social performance. Certain sectors of the investment community, such as public pension funds and the self-described 'SRI' (Socially Responsible Investment) funds in the EU, UK and US, and insurance investors in the UK, are increasingly looking at the social and environmental performance of their portfolio companies and those companies' trading partners in an attempt to identify risks associated with the portfolio firms as well as their trading partners out in the supply chain.[31] This, in turn, has created demand for services of firms that can audit the quality of the non-financial information being produced. Some major accounting firms, such as KPMG and

PricewaterhouseCoopers, have recently established global sustainability practice groups, for example, with the specialized expertise necessary to attest to environmental and social data.[32]

The activism of NGOs is accompanied by a proliferation of social and environmental responsibility standards over the past ten years. These initiatives have been developed by states, public/private partnerships, multi-stakeholder negotiation processes, industries and companies, institutional investors, functional groups such as accountancy firms and social assurance consulting groups (many of which did not exist more than about five years ago), NGOs, and non-financial ratings agencies (Conley & Williams, 2005; Williams & Conley, 2005; Williams, 2004).

One example (among many) is Social Accountability 8000 (SA 8000), a project of Social Accountability International. SA 8000 is an auditable certification standard based on international labor and human rights standards.[33] SA8000 also provides a social accountability management system to guide firms in implementing standards and to demonstrate ongoing conformance with the standards. In particular, to meet SA 8000 standards requires third-party certification of individual production facilities such as factories or farms, based upon an inspection by SAI-approved inspectors and other third party inspectors. Corporations that seek SA 8000 stamp of approval must stipulate in written purchase contracts with all suppliers that those suppliers conform to the SA 8000 standards.

In addition to apparel and chemicals, discussed above, a number of other industries have promulgated voluntary corporate social responsibility standards that incorporate third-party certification that products being sold have been produced, harvested or extracted according to the standards, such as certification of conflict-free diamonds,[34] sustainable fisheries[35] and forestry;[36] and fair-trade goods such as coffee, tea, cocoa and cotton.[37] Thousands of individual companies have also adopted voluntary codes of conduct establishing their standards for responsible business behavior, and some companies then engage third-party certifiers to ensure that their suppliers and subsidiaries are meeting those codes. The development of codes and standards and the increasing expectation that global firms take responsibility for implementing and enforcing these standards throughout their supply chains have greatly expanded the role of third-party standard-setting and assurance in global business, even though the early impetus for this expansion was driven by demand quality, speed, timely delivery and cost control.

3.5   The growing demands from investors for transparency, quality and social responsibility

Institutional investor networks are also asking for improved quality and quantity of information from their portfolio companies. Investors in the UK have been leaders in this development. In 2002, for example, the Association of British Insurers (ABI), which represents insurers that control 17 per cent of stocks listed in the UK, issued its Disclosure Guidelines on Social Responsibility.[38] In those guidelines, which it updated in 2005 and 2007, the ABI stated that it expects portfolio companies to provide information on an annual basis about how boards of directors evaluate and are addressing environmental, social, and governance risks, in the context of the entire range of risks and opportunities facing the company.[39]

Climate change has become a particularly salient environmental risk that UK investor networks target in their disclosure requests. One example is the Carbon Disclosure Project (CDP), a process by a group now comprised of 284 British, European and American institutional investors, with $41 trillion of money under management.[40] The CDP elicits information on an annual basis from companies worldwide about the financial risks to the companies from the physical effects of climate change or from regulatory efforts to mitigate those physical changes, and about company actions to manage and reduce greenhouse gas emissions. In 2007, CDP sought information from 2,400 of the world's largest quoted companies, by market capitalization, expanding its requests beyond the Global 500 to include the largest companies in various developed and rapidly developing markets, as well as the largest companies in transport and utilities. These pressures from institutional investors in the UK and Europe have been an important impetus for new requirements in those jurisdictions for companies to discuss future risks to the business from social, environmental and community matters in their Annual Reports.[41]

At the same time, firms and investors increasingly recognize that traditional financial measures fail to capture the value within companies from intangible factors such as employees' knowledge, training and development (Blair & Wallman, 2001; Lev, 2001; Eccles, 2006). The recognition that such factors are important is driving a search by corporations, consultants, auditors and institutional investors for auditable non-financial metrics that can be used to measure and report on company performance in developing and protecting important intangible assets such as employee capabilities, brand, and reputation.

The pressure on companies to collect and disclose more relevant non-financial information has been accompanied by pressure to have their approach to assembling such data subject to third-party review. In 2005, 52 per cent of Global 250 companies issued non-financial, sustainability reports, including social, environmental and economic data; of these, 30 per cent included independent, third-party assurance of the quality and accuracy of the underlying data. Major accounting firms currently dominate the non-financial assurance and attestation market, issuing attestation statements for 60 per cent of those sustainability reports that are independently verified.[42]

At least two global standards are under development for the assurance of non-financial reports. In March 2003, the UK-based AccountAbility organization issued AA 1000AS, which focuses on evaluating the materiality, completeness and responsiveness of a company's reporting to its various stakeholder groups.[43] In December 2003, the International Federation of Accountants (IFAC)'s International Auditing and Assurance Standards Board (IAASB), which is the body responsible for issuing international accounting and auditing standards, issued guidance for accounting firms to use in order to guide their assurance work for non-financial reports. This standard is applicable to any assurance work by accountants after 1 January 2005, and was needed, according to the IFAC, to meet the increasing demand for assurance reports on '[e]nvironmental, social and sustainability reports, information systems, internal control, corporate governance processes and compliance with grant conditions, contracts and regulations'.[44]

4 Third-party assurance in food products and apparel industries

Extensive use of third-party inspection, assurance, and certification services has been noted by scholars who have studied and analyzed the reorganization of specific industries in recent years to use supply chain production methods spanning multiple countries. Two prominent examples of such industries are food products and apparel. In this section we discuss the growing role of standards in production processes and of third-party inspectors to help enforce standards in these two industries.

4.1 Supply chain characteristics

The organization of production through 'chains' of firms in different countries, linked by contracts and long-term relationships in which suppliers produce goods to meet detailed specifications by buying firms, has been discussed extensively in the literature on 'supply chain management'.[45] An important recent article in this literature categorizes governance arrangements in what it calls 'global value chains' into five types, which they label 'hierarchy', 'captive', 'relational', 'modular' and 'market' (Gereffi, Humphrey & Sturgeon, 2005).

'Hierarchy' refers to production within a single, vertically integrated corporation, where that corporation can directly control the activities of the overseas subsidiaries or subunits that are designing the products, acquiring raw materials, making components, assembling them into finished products, shipping the products to market, and marketing them. Hierarchical governance, these authors argue, is most likely to be used when the production chain is especially complex, with substantial interdependencies between steps of production, and when it requires firm-specific, or relationship-specific investments and a high level of coordination between steps.

At the other end of the spectrum, 'market' governance refers to production carried out by a series of independent firms each producing generic products that are sold in arm's-length transactions, perhaps even on a 'spot' market, to the trader or broker or firm carrying out the next step or activity. Market governance is more likely to be used where products are simple, outputs of each step are commodities, and production steps are not interdependent. These two types correspond to the broad alternatives identified by Oliver Williamson in his classic work on transactions costs, and the choice between 'markets' and 'hierarchies' (Williamson, 1975). If production is governed by an internal hierarchy there is no need to rely on standardization and third-party assurance, since the firm can monitor and manage the production process directly. Likewise, production governed by markets requires no third-party inspection or assurance because the process by which products are produced is not relevant to the buyer, terms of engagement are set by competition, and the products themselves can be inspected before or at the time they are purchased.

A large proportion of goods and services that move in international commerce are not commodities, however, but involve some intermediate level of complexity, specificity, and coordination problems. The design, production, and marketing of those goods are increasingly carried out through some intermediate governance arrangement, involving a combination of contractual, network, and norm-driven relationships between firms in the chain Gereffi, Humphrey and Sturgeon (2005) classify these intermediate arrangements as 'modular', 'relational' and 'captive', according to the degree to which the 'lead firm' in the chain of producers controls the other firms.

'Captive' governance refers to 'networks of small suppliers [that] are transactionally dependent on much larger buyers' (Gereffi, Humphrey and Sturgeon, 2005, p. 84). In such arrangements the large buyer firms often have substantial market power in relation to the small firms, and exercise a large degree of control over them. This control may be exercised by having managers and inspectors from the buyer firm supervise production within the supplier firm factories. Alternatively, and with growing frequency, both buyer firms and supplier firms may prefer that contractors submit to third-party inspection, verification, and certification (Humphrey & Schmitz, 2003).

In the apparel industry, for example, if lead firms turn to contractors merely to assemble cut fabric according to detailed instructions from the lead firm in the supply chain, this relationship is considered an example of 'captive' governance. Contractors that interpret designs, convert sketches and general instructions to detailed patterns, find their own sources of fabrics and trim components, and cut the fabric as well as assemble the components, by contrast, are considered 'full package suppliers', involved in a 'relational' governance arrangement with the branded apparel firms and retailers.

'Relational' governance applies to production carried out across multiple independent firms, involving 'complex interactions between buyers and sellers', 'mutual dependence' and 'high levels of asset specificity'. Here the firms in the production chain do not control each other, but since each will have to make some investments that are specific to the relationship, each may need reassurance that the other party can and will deliver on its end of the contract. Third-party inspection and/or certification can help provide that assurance.

In 'modular' production, the product is one that can be assembled from modules or components for which the buyer's specifications, even highly sophisticated and complex ones, can be 'codified' and adequately interpreted and carried out by supplier firms that are capable of carrying out sophisticated production activities. If production activities can be separated into modules, the buying firm may need to exercise little or no control over the supplier firm and the chain of production may be governed by 'turn-key' contracts between otherwise independent firms. Third-party inspection and certification is most likely to play a role in a 'modular' type of governance at the stage when the contract is negotiated, to reassure the buying firm that the supplier firm has the capabilities required to carry out the contract.

Modular production is also facilitated by the development of product and process standards that are measurable and quantifiable and that reduce uncertainty at the interfaces between steps in the production process and misfits between components of the finished product. These standards may often be set by third parties, and in some cases may be enforced by third-party inspection regimes. The US electronics industry provides an example of supply chain production in which major activities have been 'modularized', so that 'standardized protocols for handing-off computerized design files and highly automated and standardized process technologies [make] it easy for lead firms to switch and share contractors, and [reduce] the build-up of specific assets' according to Gereffi, Humphrey and Sturgeon (2005: 95).

For a variety of reasons, pure market governance and pure hierarchical governance arrangements are becoming much less likely to be used in many industries, and intermediate governance arrangements in supply chains are becoming more common. And it is in these intermediate governance arrangements that we are most likely to find deployment and use of third-party inspection, certification, and assurance organizations in supply chains. As it happens, both the food products industry and the apparel industry are increasingly dominated by supply chain governance arrangements of these intermediate types rather than by pure markets or by vertically integrated hierarchical firms.

4.2 Food products

The supply chains that bring fresh produce and processed food to grocery store shelves[46] have become thoroughly 'globalized', in the sense that production and distribution activities are functionally integrated and coordinated across several countries (Gereffi, 1999). Until about a decade ago, however, governance arrangements were generally wholly market-oriented, with some steps of food production hierarchically controlled by branded food processing companies. Wholesale grain dealers, for example, bought grain in mostly anonymous markets, both domestic and foreign, and food product companies bought produce or corn syrup or flour or meat from first-level processors and wholesalers, and transformed them into branded products which were then sold in market transactions to grocery stores. Government agencies inspected and graded many wholesale food products, and branded food processors tested purchased products for quality (Hatanaka, Bain & Busch, 2005), but there was very little backward integration by food companies into growing or harvesting activities, and very little forward integration into retailing. Government agencies established certain safety and quality standards, graded products such as milk and meat, and inspected processing facilities. Supermarkets generally took responsibility only for how the products were handled once they hit the store warehouse.

In the last 15 to twenty years, however, consumers have begun paying much more attention to issues food safety and health, as well as to issues related to the production of food, including the use of pesticides, fertilizers, preservatives, and other chemicals, human rights and fair wages for farm workers, the clearing of rainforests, the renewability of fisheries, and the ethical treatment of animals. Indeed consumers have shown a willingness to pay higher prices for food products that satisfy these preferences. Grocery store chains and some restaurant chains have seized on the interest by consumers in these issues to find ways to differentiate their products by the process by which they reach consumers, as well as by quality (Hatanaka, Bain & Busch, 2005). As a result many retail food companies, especially high-end grocery stores and high-visibility branded restaurant chains, have moved away from pure market approaches to supply chain management. Instead, these firms have been steadily building supply chains that are more 'relational', in which they enter into long-term contracts with specialty firms that in turn work only with a select group of large farming companies that either directly operate, or oversee the operations of farms that use acceptable farming methods.

To do this, however, both the specialty wholesale firms and the retailers must have ways of assuring that the farming and/or husbandry methods used in fact meet the specifications of the retailer. The solution has been the development of a large variety of standards for agribusiness and food processing, sometimes in collaboration with industry trade groups, environmentalists, organic food advocates, and/or NGOs.[47] An important example of a food safety certification program that was developed through many iterations of private sector and government action is the Hazard Analysis and Critical Control Point (HACCP) program used to identify, prevent, and control food safety hazards.

This program was first developed in the US in the 1960s, but is now recognized and used worldwide, with various Chinese government agencies, for example, trying to implement and apply the standard for both domestic and exported food products,[48] and a new ISO food safety management system, ISO 22000, incorporating HACCP and standardizing it across countries.[49]

But while government-imposed standards have long been important in the food industry, the private sector is now taking the lead in developing, implementing, and enforcing standards in most of the developed world.[50] The proliferation of private standards for use in business-to-business transactions has extremely high transactions costs, however, and is leading, in many areas, to efforts within industries to consolidate and develop harmonized standards (Henson, 2006).

Standards are of little use unless they can be implemented and enforced, however, and this is where the role of third-party inspectors and certifiers comes in – to provide assurance to customers that the products were in fact produced and prepared in the manner the retailer claims (Hatanaka, Bain & Busch, 2005).[51] Hence both private and public standards and third-party inspection, assurance and certification have proliferated in recent years.[52]

4.3   Apparel

Apparel production is highly labor-intensive and the technology involved is relatively primitive. Thus apparel is an industry for which a developing country with an abundance of low-skilled labor might have a 'comparative advantage' (Abernathy et al., 1999; Gereffi, 1999). In the last few decades, nearly all US apparel assembly factories have been closed, and firms have moved production offshore in order to take advantage of low wages in developing countries. The move to offshore production has generally been accompanied by changes in the structure of the apparel industry that link retail, apparel production, and textile sectors tightly together in coordinated supply chains (Abernathy et al., 1999). Rather than integrating vertically by combining these activities in hierarchical firms, however, most of the large branded apparel firms (e.g., Liz Claiborne) have 'outsourced' production to contractors in developing countries, while major retailers have developed their own network of contract suppliers for store-brand products. These new supply chain arrangements typically utilize some combination of 'captured' and 'relational' supply chain governance arrangements (Gereffi, 1999; Abernathy et al., 1999).

Initially, the transnational corporations that were the 'lead firms' in these supply chains, such as Nike, The Gap, and Wal-Mart, maintained tight control of their overseas contractor firms to ensure that they could supply sufficient quantities of the desired product, at a high enough level of quality and low enough price, and in a timely manner.[53] These contractors, in turn, began to establish networks of subcontractors that carried out much of the production for the lead firm's market on demand,[54] but the overall supply chain governance model could still be characterized as 'captive'. For some products, however, Nike and the others established looser relations with garment manufacturers who all use standardized bar codes, electronic data exchange platforms, labelling, and other methods of coordination. Codification and standardization of information systems enhances coordination between supplier and retailer, while also making it possible for the manufacturers to work for a variety of apparel firms and retailers. Thus we see a shift in the apparel industry from tightly controlled 'captive' governance arrangements to looser, more flexible 'relational' governance arrangements (Gereffi, 1999). And instead of putting their own employees into contractors plants to make sure the job is done right, they are relying more heavily on 'vendor certification systems to improve performance' (Gereffi, 1999, p. 47).

In the 1990s, consumers and labor activists around the world began inquiring into the labor conditions at factories making branded apparel and footwear products. At Nike in particular, activists called attention to problems of 'underpaid workers in Indonesia, child labor in Cambodia and Pakistan, and poor working conditions in China and Vietnam' (Locke, 2002, p. 9), among other problems. At first, Nike tried to dismiss these criticisms as not their problem because the factories were owned and operated by other firms. Regardless of how much actual control Nike exerted at the factory level, however, in the 1990s Nike found that it would be held to account for working conditions not only in 'captive' manufacturing plants, but in all factories where its products were made (Locke, 2002).

Nike's experience was shared by several other high-visibility branded apparel firms, including Kathy Lee Gifford and Liz Claiborne. As a result of activism by labor and NGOs, a number of standards for labor and environmental conditions in apparel and footwear factories have been developed, and a small army of inspectors and certifiers have taken up the task of attempting to enforce these standards in factories around the world.

At least half a dozen NGOs, as well as numerous apparel firms and retailers, have now established labor standards for apparel manufacturing facilities,[55] and dozens of organizations conduct 'audits' of apparel plants around the world to promote compliance with these standards.

5 Implications for the theory of the firm

For the most part the problem of organizing complex production has been analyzed by law and economics scholars in a dichotomous way: production can be accomplished either through a series of market transactions, or under the guidance and control of a hierarchical governance structure within a firm (Coase, 1937; Williamson, 1975). A rich and well-developed literature has emerged in the last few decades analyzing these two modes, as well as 'hybrid' modes such as relational contracts, and considering why one mode might be used in some circumstances, and the other in different circumstances (Williamson, 2005; Williamson, 1975; Klein, Crawford & Alchian, 1978). And, as discussed above, a more recent, but rapidly growing literature has explored how globalization is leading to increasing levels of 'outsourcing', in which activities that were once carried on within a single firm are now being organized by contracts, across multiple firms, and often in multiple countries (Grossman & Helpman, 2005; Feenstra, 1998).

Nearly all of the economic literature on the choice of organizational form, globalization, and the 'outsourcing' phenomenon, however, implicitly assumes the existence of an institutional context in which rule of law is followed, minimum social standards and business norms are established and regulated (or are at least commonly accepted and followed within a given trade), and contracts can be enforced. We have seen, however, that production through supply chains as described above is moving into countries where rule of law is weak, property rights are uncertain, and courts cannot be depended upon to enforce contracts efficiently. This suggests a puzzle. How are firms overcoming weak rule of law to move production outside of the firm into countries with underdeveloped legal regimes, since organizing production through contracts, especially with hybrid bilateral, long-term relational contracts, depends upon clear property rights and efficient enforcement of contracts?

One mechanism is to import rule of law by, in essence, using private ordering to 'mitigate conflicts and realize mutual gains from trade' (Williamson, 2005, p. 14). Some mechanisms of private ordering, such as arbitration agreements, may be effective as a backstop to enforce global contracts between large, sophisticated parties. But the hazards of contracting seem unrelieved by an agreement to arbitrate between a small, foreign supplier and a large, branded buyer in such industries as apparel, food, flowers, commodities, electronics, and so forth, because an arbitration finding must still, somehow, be enforced. Moreover, where commercial regimes that depend on private ordering have been studied, such as ranchers' border disputes in Shasta County (Ellickson, 1991) or diamond merchants in New York (Bernstein, 1992), it has been concluded that such private ordering requires voluntary communities coherent enough to use the social sanctions of inclusion and exclusion effectively (Richman, 2004). These private ordering regimes thus pose high barriers to entry (Richman, 2004, p. 2346), and seem unlikely to provide a general, transnational solution.

In this chapter we posit that increasing standardization of products and processes, such as through ISO processes, in conjunction with third-party assurance and certification, provides an important institutional solution to the puzzle otherwise posed by moving production out of firms and into hybrids, networks, and global supply chains spanning 'lawless' environments. Standardization and certification reduce a number of the costs of contracting that Coase identified with market transactions – undertaking negotiations, writing contracts and settling disputes – and so allow moving transactions out of firms. Standardization and certification can also provide a workable substitute for management within firms in a number of different kinds of productive arrangements, such as within supply chains, in joint ventures and within regional industrial systems. This approach may reduce the costs of communication about both contracting and management, again, making it easier to move production outside of firms. Beyond that, if regulation is understood to encompass establishing standards of behavior and providing a mechanism for evaluating compliance and enforcing those standards, standardization and third-party assurance provide a workable substitute for government regulation as well, permitting companies to enter long-term supply relationships with some confidence, notwithstanding weak rule of law environments. We will briefly elaborate upon these points.

In addressing the question of why some production is organized within firms instead of across markets, given the powerful price incentives that market transactions allow, Coase recognized various costs of market transactions that can be reduced by organizing within firms (Coase, 1937, p. 38). Included within these transaction costs were the cost of discovering what prices are; and of negotiating contracts, addressing future uncertainties and resolving disputes (Coase, 1937, pp. 38–41).

A number of the transaction costs identified by Coase are clearly reduced by the use of broadly recognized standards for both products and processes. The ISO standards now cover product specifications for everything from nanotechnology to container ships, allowing suppliers to develop and market products that will be competitive across markets, and allowing buyers and suppliers to negotiate cheaply and with little ambiguity about product characteristics. Contracts can be more easily specified by reference to standards and certification processes to ensure enforcement, leaving fewer aspects incomplete.

Certifiable standards and third-party assurance have reduced the transaction costs of ensuring the quality of products produced outside the firm. The concept of the 'quality' of a product has become more complex over the past decade, incorporating aspects of product differentiation, health, safety, social and environmental implications of both products and processes, trends that would otherwise seem to require more managerial involvement and thus the movement of production into vertically integrated firms (Ponte and Gibbon, 2005, p. 3). Yet, ISO and other reliable standards have been developed that permit the standardization of these otherwise complex phenomena, including the management systems to address them, permitting clear communication to industrial buyers and consumers through third-party assurance and certification to credible quality standards. Thus, we have not seen a movement of production back into vertically integrated firms that we might otherwise expect as a consequence of the managerial challenges inherent in the increased complexity of the concept of product 'quality'.

Standardization has also reduced the transaction costs of managing the types of inter-firm relationships necessary to move supply chain production away from 'hierarchy' and toward 'markets'. Nassimbeni (1998) identifies the managerial challenge of the intermediate governance arrangements seen in supply chains ('captive', 'relational' and 'modular'), described above, as the need to strike the right balance between not managing too tightly, in which case one loses the advantages of inter-firm production (i.e., flexibility and the involvement of independent units), while still allowing enough coordination to render the activities of the independent units coherent with the overall goals of the productive project as a whole (Nassimbeni, 1998, p. 545). Nassimbeni, relying upon Mintzberg (1983), emphasizes the importance of standardization of products, skills and processes as the main management technique necessary to coordinate various inter-firm inputs effectively.

Standardization also reduces the costs of communicating within supply chains. In a study of value creation in supply chain relationships, Cannon and Homburg (2001) summarized communications research showing that face-to-face communication is better for customized communication and for immediate feedback, but that it is more expensive than written or electronic communication, which is best reserved for the communication of standardized information. Given the proliferation of standards, cheaper communications technologies can be used to manage supply chain relationships, once established, by referring to recognized standards in contractual documents that largely follow standard formats, and by using third-party assurance to determine if those standards have been met.

Third-party assurance to various standards has a particularly important role to play in permitting private ordering regimes to extend globally and beyond close-knit commercial communities. Empirical evidence has demonstrated that certification is more likely to be sought the greater the distance suppliers and buyers are from each other, the more export-oriented the industry (Chapple et al., 2001); and the more difficult the process or quality is to observe (Jiang & Bansal, 2003). Park, Reddy & Sakar (2000) summarize empirical data showing that many firms in the United States have begun using supplier certification processes to formally assess the management systems suppliers have in place, and that such supplier certification systems facilitate the move away from 'captive' supply chain management structures to 'relational' structures. These studies suggest that certification can provide a mechanism to permit the development of the trust that is necessary to sustain private ordering arrangements, notwithstanding a lack of geographical and social proximity.

6 Conclusions

We have argued in this chapter that one important contributor to globalization in recent years has been the rapid development of norms and standards for business processes (as well as products), and of third-party inspection and certification services that can provide assurance to contracting parties that acceptable processes will be followed. Following the model of financial accounting and auditing, which have been important to business activity for centuries, the idea of standardization, assurance, and certification of process and activities by third parties has spread rapidly from providing assurance that firms can meet quality standards, to assurance that social and environmental norms are being met.

As global trade has expanded, and multinational firms have extended their reach into all corners of the globe, the standardization of business norms and practices has often been led by large, high-visibility branded firms that are organizing these activities. These firms have pushed to increase the share of inputs into complex products or services that are produced or carried out in parts of the world characterized by low labor costs. Global firms have also wanted to increase their presence in and participation in the expanding markets in these same parts of the world.

But while they have wanted to participate in developing economy markets, global corporations have also wanted to avoid direct responsibility for day-to-day operations at the shopfloor level in those countries. The result has been a greater reliance by lead firms in supply chains on complex contracts to govern the relationships between the lead firms and the contractors, rather than vertical integration, or extensive direct control of the contractor by the lead firm. The standard explanation for how this has been possible is that there has been an improvement in the technologies for transportation and communications. The efficiency of transportation and communication has undoubtedly improved, but this may only explain the spread of business production and trade to new parts of the world, not the organization of this activity via contract rather than vertical integration. Complex contracts are only a viable method of organizing supply chain production if they are capable of being adequately enforced. Because a great deal of supply chain activity takes place in parts of the world where rule of law is absent or weak, and courts are likely to be absent, corrupt, or incompetent, businesses cannot necessarily rely on formal legal contract enforcement.

We suggest instead that the move towards 'relational' contracting rather than integration and direct control of contractors is a product of the development of new business institutions. We have examined two related institutions in particular – the development by business interests, NGOs, and other international organizations of clear standards for evaluating business processes, from quality management to the observance of human rights to environmental responsibility, and the simultaneous emergence of assurance services that can inspect, evaluate, assure, and certify that contractors are satisfying the required norms.

Although these business institutions emerged initially to help solve purely commercial problems, they have been enlisted by activists concerned about environmental and other social performance as a mechanism for putting pressure on global corporations to internalize the full social costs of their activities. In this way, these institutions may also serve the function of regulating global business activity, in a way that formal regulation at the state level, or formal international law, has so far not been able to accomplish.

The development of widely applicable social and environmental norms for business processes and behavior, and private enforcement by third-party inspection and supervision, is by no means a mature or efficient institution. In the current environment, corporate codes of conduct and social responsibility standards have proliferated, resulting in considerable duplication in some sectors, with factory owners complaining that they may have to have 40 or 50 inspections per year to satisfy 20 or 30 different customers, each with their own standards (Rafter, 2005). Moreover, many of the standards are vague, and clear unambiguous performance indicators have not yet been created for satisfying those standards, unlike the ISO standards for products and management processes such as ISO 9000 or ISO 14001. The assurance industry also lacks its own professional standards and norms, and is often viewed as corrupt or corruptible by business people who are pressured to meet the standards. These are significant problems, to be sure.

But we believe that these problems will be resolved over time, and that third-party assurance will mature. Moreover, because it has emerged largely as a market-based solution, based on private ordering, third-party assurance may be an enduring feature of the global business environment.

Notes

1. See discussion of the origins of the assurance service business in maritime and customs inspection at section 2.2 below.
2. Sections 2 and 3 of this chapter are largely taken from Blair, Williams and Lin (2008).
3. As an indication of the explosion in demand for audit services in developing countries as those countries begin to develop liquid financial markets, the Chinese market for accountants' services grew by 304.5 per cent over the years from 1999 to 2003. The market is predicted to expand by 149 per cent to $4,022 million by 2008. Auditing took the largest share in China in 2003, accounting for 66.2 per cent. See http://www.euromonitor.com/.
4. 'ISO', from the Greek word for 'equal', was adopted as the 'standardized' name for the organization whose English name is the International Organization for Standardization. ISO is a non-governmental organization whose member institutes are part of the governmental structure of their countries, or are mandated by their government. Typically, members have their roots in the private sector, having been set up by national partnerships of industry associations. ISO uses technical committees organized by subjects for standards development, and at this time has more than 200 such committees. Since its founding in 1947, ISO has published more than 16,000 product, technical, and performance standards for the characteristics

and quality of raw materials and other tangible production inputs, ranging from agricultural products, grades of oil and gasoline, metals, ceramics and glues to electrical parts, nanotechnology, information processing, digital equipment, and so forth. See http://www.iso.org/iso/en/aboutiso/introduction/index.html (last visited 9 March, 2007). ISO standards often form the basis for trade treaties and agreements. See also Roht-Arriaza (1995).

5. Prior to publication of ISO 9000 standards, the ISO had focused largely on developing internationally applicable technical standards for products and materials. ISO 9000 was established under the Technical Committee No. 176 (TC176).

6. The ISO Survey 2004, available at http://www.iso.org/iso/en/prods-services/otherpubs/pdf/survey2004.pdf (last visited 3 July 2006), provides data on the number of establishments that have been certified to ISO 9000 and some other standards. See also Wood (2006).

7. Organizations originally in financial auditing, such as KPMG Performance Registra Inc., a wholly owned subsidiary in Canada of KPMG, LLP, and PricewaterhouseCoopers in Canada, have extended their services to ISO certification. See http://www.kpmg. ca/en/ms/performanceregistrar/services.html and http://www.pwc.com/extweb/ service.nsf/docid/5401765577527120852570CA001771D2 (last visited 10 August 2006). However, a number of the certification bodies providing ISO9000 certification, including BVQI, UL, SGS-ICS, and the like, were already in the quality inspection services sector when the ISO 9000 standards were developed and promulgated.

8. See http://www.iso.org/iso/en/iso9000-14000/pdf/survey10thcycle.pdf; at p. 15, and http://www.iso.org/iso/en/prods-services/otherpubs/pdf/survey2004.pdf, at p. 10.

9. The American National Standards Institute (which is the US organizational representative to the ISO) notes growing pressures toward social performance certification on its website. See http://www.ansi.org/about_ansi/introduction/history. aspx?menuid=1 ('During the first years of the 21st Century, those involved in standards-setting activities clearly recognized a growing need for globally relevant standards and related conformity assessment mechanisms. "Market forces" such as global trade and competition; societal issues such as health, safety and the environment; an enhanced focus on consumer needs and involvement and increasing interaction between public-sector and private-sector interests were significantly impacting standardization and conformity assessment programs. Standards themselves had expanded well beyond documents identifying product specifications to instead focus on performance issues and to also include processes, systems and personnel.')

10. See http://www.iso.org/iso/en/prods-services/otherpubs/pdf/survey2004.pdf, at p. 20.

11. See http://isotc.iso.org/livelink/livelink/fetch/2000/2122/830949/3934883/3935096/ home.html?nodeid=4451259&vernum=0 ('The guidance standard will be published in 2008 as ISO 26000 and be voluntary to use. It will not include requirements and will thus not be a certification standard. . . . The need for organizations in both public and private sectors to behave in a socially responsible way is becoming a generalized requirement of society. It is shared by the stakeholder groups that are participating in the WG SR [Working Group on Social Responsibility] to develop ISO 26000: industry, government, labour, consumers, nongovernmental organizations and others, in addition to geographical and gender-based balance.' ISO asserts that these standards are not intended to be the basis for third-party certifications, however.

12. DNV, established in 1864, primarily focuses on risk management certification and consulting, in particular for maritime, oil and gas, process and transportation industries. See http://www.dnv.com/. Intertek can be traced to three separate companies in 1885, including Thomas Edison's Lamp Testing Bureau. It initially provided

maritime surveying and testing of electrical equipment; it now provides testing services and risk management for a wide range of businesses. See http://www.intertek. com/. RINA (Registro Italiano Navale), a company established in 1861 in Genoa, has been providing ship classification and certification services since its establishment. See http://www.rina.it/. SGS, originally founded in 1878 in Rouen as a French grain shipment inspection house and later registered in Geneva in 1919, provides inspection services of traded goods, product testing services, and certification services for products, systems or services. See www.sgs.com/.
13. See CSCC, at http://www.cscc-online.com; ALGI, at http://www.algi.net/en/company. htm; IKQAA, at http://www.hkqaa.org/index.html.
14. See 'Emissions Trading: Consortium Issues Carbon Standard to Certify Credits Earned in Voluntary Carbon Markets', *Daily Environment*, No. 223, 30 November 2007.
15. Several Chinese government agencies have taken steps in the direction of providing some sort of government regulation of the inspection and assurance business, however. In 2003, the Chinese government promulgated the Certification and Accreditation Act, under which certification institutions are required to obtain governmental approval, meet the minimum capital requirement (RMB 3 million, which is about US$407,000), and comply with conduct standards addressing potential conflicts of interest (e.g., institutions cannot accept financial contributions that would impair their independence; auditors cannot be employed by two certification institutions simultaneously). In 2004, the Chinese government passed Regulations on Auditors, Certification trainers and consultants, under which auditors, trainers and consultants are required to be registered with the government. To become registered, auditors, trainers, and consultants must meet certain eligibility requirements, take various courses, and pass a series of exams. Currently the registration process is administered by the China Certification and Accreditation Association (CCAA), a non-profit organization subject to the supervision of the Chinese government. See CCAA, http://www.ccaa.org.cn/ccaa/default.html. As of 31 December 2005, there were 55,340 registered auditors for ISO 9001 certification and 17,550 registered auditors for ISO 14001certification in China. See Certification and Accreditation Administration of the People's Republic of China, ALMANAC OF ASSURANCE SERVICES IN CHINA 499 (2006) [Zhongguo renzheng renke nian jian 2006].
16. The international trade literature in particular tracks this growth. See, e.g., International Monetary Fund and World Bank (2001) and OECD (2006).
17. Grossman and Helpman (2005) report that 30 per cent of a particular American car's value 'goes to Korea for assembly, 17.5% to Japan for components and advanced technology, 7.5% to Germany for design, 4% to Taiwan and Singapore for minor parts, 2.5% to the United Kingdom for advertising and marketing services and 1.5% to Ireland for data processing. This means that only 37% of the production value ... is generated in the United States' (p. 36)).
18. See id. at 494–5, citing the Final Act Embodying the Results of the Uruguay Round of Multilateral Trade Negotiations, Agreement on Technical Barriers to Trade, 15 April 1994, art. 2.4, reprinted in H.R. Doc. No. 316, 103d Cong., 2d Sess. 1428 (1994).
19. One indication of the new attention by business firms to social and environmental performance is the publication in early 2007 of the first edition of the CSR PROFESSIONAL SERVICES DIRECTORY, which lists 443 organizations worldwide under 49 different service categories, offering assistance in meeting so-called 'corporate social responsibility' (CSR) norms and standards. See http://www.ethicalperformance. com/csrdirectory/index.php?PHPSESSID=c78e0151641014186bd7a2fa9d305c49 (last visited Jan. 19, 2007).

20. Konzelmann et al. (2005) argue that IKEA, for example, is transferring its standards for quality, efficiency, and socially responsible behavior 'globally to the mutual benefit of all the system's stakeholder groups' by implementing its 'IKEA Way on Purchasing Home Furnishing Products (IWAY) throughout its global supply chain'. To implement its standards, 'IKEA contracts with independent auditors to inspect and monitor all suppliers with whom the company does business on an on-going basis', according to Konzelmann et al., at 19. Similarly, British Petroleum and Shell are imposing requirements on smaller companies that provide maritime services to raise their standards for health, environment and safety and to secure certification of having met those higher standards. Interview with Anne-Maree O'Connor, Core Ratings (Member of the DNV Group), London, 26 June 2006 (notes on file with authors). That supply chain pressures can affect the standards of conduct expected of companies is consistent with the legal transplant literature. See Vandenberg (2007) and Miller (2003).

21. The six categories of the original standards included: (1) Community aware-ness and emergency response; (2) Research and development; (3) Manufacturing; (4) Transportation; (5) Distribution; and (6) Hazardous waste management. See Canada's Chemical Producers: Chemistry – a part of everyday life/Responsible Care, http://www.ccpa.ca/ResponsibleCare/ (last visited 22 June, 2006).

22. Chemical companies that were part of the original Responsible Care Initiative include Dow Chemical Canada, ICI subsidiary CIL, Union Carbide Canada, Imperial Oil Chemicals, H.L. Blachford, Rhone-Poulenc Canada, Ethyl Canada, Rohm & Haas Canada, Hoescht Celanese, General Chemical, Allied Chemicals, Shell (chemical division), Cyanamide Canada, and Polysar. Email from Brian Wastle, Vice President, Responsible Care®, Canadian Chemical Producers' Association, Ottowa Ontario, 22 June, 2006.

23. The iconic examples here include the negative publicity in the late 1990s sur-rounding sweatshop working conditions in manufacturing plants making Nike products and Kathy Lee Gifford brand apparel for Wal-Mart. Williams (1999) and Schoenberger (2000).

24. Wal-Mart has posted 10 'Guiding Ethical Principles' on its website, and states that it periodically inspects its factories for implementation, and yet continues to come under fire for tolerating poor working conditions in supplier factories. Konzelmann et al., (2005); Brooksbank (2006); Greenhouse and Barbaro (2006); Ellis (2006).

25. In 1998, several prominent US apparel producers approached the American Apparel Manufacturers Association (which subsequently merged with the Footwear Industries of American and the Fashion Association to form the American Apparel and Footwear Association) to work collaboratively to develop and implement labor, health, safety and environmental standards at the factory level. See WRAP website at http://www.wrapapparel.org/ (last visited 21 June 2006).

26. The first result of the AAMA initiative was the 12 Worldwide Responsible Apparel Production Principles – standards of labor practices, factory conditions, and environ-mental and customs compliance. The AAMA Board of Directors publicly endorsed these principles in 1998. For the next two years, the Association worked with pro-ducers, public interest groups, and development agencies to 'design a process and develop an organization to monitor and certify factories for compliance – in hundreds of details – with the principles'. Statement of AAMA Board of Directors, available at http://www.wrapapparel.org/modules.php?name=Congent&pa=whowpage&pid=26 (last visited 21 June 2006). The fruit of this work was the incorporation of WRAP in 2000 as a '01 [c] 6' organization.

27. See http://www.wrapapparel.org/modules.php?name=Content&pa=showpage&pid=5. One of us (Blair) has served as an independent board member of WRAP since 2005.
28. The organization is working to obtain commitments from apparel firms and retailers that products that carry certain brands must be made in factories that are certified. O'Rourke (2005) describes and compares six major international programs that provide what he calls 'non-governmental regulation' in the apparel and sewn products industries, including WRAP, Social Accountability International (SA8000), Fair Labor Association, Ethical Trading Initiative, Fair Wear Foundation, and Worker Rights Consortium. WRAP now has three levels of certification, with level C requiring six-month renewal, level B requiring annual renewal, and level A, representing the highest level of compliance, requiring only biannual renewal.
29. Wal-Mart's website notes that its 'Global Ethics Office' was established in June 2004, and, on 4 June 2004, according to the website, 'Wal-Mart released a revised Global Statement of Ethics to communicate our ethical standards to all Wal-Mart facilities and stakeholders. The Global Ethics Office provides guidance in making ethical decisions based on the Global Statement of Ethics and a process for anonymous reporting of suspected ethics violation. . . .'.
30. 'Wal-Mart's principles are:

Follow the law at all times.

Be honest and fair

Never manipulate, misrepresent, abuse or conceal information

Avoid conflicts of interest between work and personal affairs

Never discriminate against anyone

Never act unethically – even if someone else instructs you to do so

Never ask someone to act unethically

Seek assistance if you have questions about the Statement of Ethics or if you face an ethical dilemma

Cooperate with any investigation of a possible ethics violation

Report ethics violations or suspected violations.

31. Brooksbank (2006) reports an announcement by Norwegian Government Pension Fund that it had divested its holdings in Wal-Mart on the grounds that the fund would 'incur an unacceptable risk of contributing to serious or systematic violations of human rights by maintaining its investments in the company'. Another example of investors being concerned about social compliance is the Association of British Insurers in London, which represents 94 per cent of UK insurers. Insurance companies in the UK offer savings and investment products in addition to insurance, and control 17 per cent of all UK company publicly listed equity. See http://www.abi.org.uk/BookShop/ResearchReports/Key%20facts%202005_LR.pdf (last visited 14 February 2007). These insurers ask their clients to provide information on environmental, social, and governance risks. See section 3.5 below.
32. See KPMG Sustainability Services, available at http://www.kpmg.nl/site.asp?Id=40378 (last visited 5 February 2007); Price Waterhouse/Coopers Sustainability

Practice Website, available at http://www.pwc.com/extweb/challenges.nsf/docid/ 58E92287890B5314852570980064ACC2 (last visited 5 February 2007).

33. This standard is a voluntary, universal standard for companies interested in auditing and certifying labor practices in their facilities and those of their suppliers and vendors, based on the principles of international human rights norms as described in International Labour Organisation conventions, the United Nations Convention on the Rights of the Child and the Universal Declaration of Human Rights (Overview of SA8000, available at http://www.sa-intl.org/index.cfm?fuseaction=Page. viewPage&pageId=473 (last visited 10 August 2006).)

34. The Kimberley Process, available at http://www.kimberleyprocess.com:8080. The Kimberley Process is a joint government, international diamond industry and civil society initiative to ensure that shipments of diamonds are free of 'conflict diamonds' that have been sold to support wars in such countries as Angola, Côte d'Ivoire, the Democratic Republic of Congo and Sierra Leone. All significant diamond producing and trading centers, with the exception of Liberia, are now operating within the framework of the Kimberley Process.

35. The Marine Stewardship Council certification process, *available at* http://www.msc. org. The Marine Stewardship Council is a global non-profit that has created an environmental standard for well-managed fisheries, according to which third-party certifiers can grant labels that assure that fish have been grown in well-managed fisheries, or caught according to environmentally sustainable principles. As with many of the certification schemes for products, an important part of the certification is of 'chain of custody' procedures that attempt to ensure the value of the certified label.

36. Forest Stewardship Council: Principles and Criteria for Forest Stewardship, *available at* http://www1.umn.edu/humanrts/links/fscprinciples.html. The Forest Stewardship Council (FSC) is an international body composed of industry participants, transnational environmental NGOs and social justice NGOs, strongly influenced by international standard setting processes at the ISO, and which accredits organizations to certify timber and forest products as meeting the FSC standard for sustainable forest management. Meidinger (2006).

37. See http://www.fairtrade.net/certification_mark.html for an overview of the fair trade requirements.

38. See http://www.abi.org.uk/Newsreleases/viewNewsRelease.asp?nrid=3676.

39. See http://www.politics.co.uk/press-releases/domestic-policy/environment/environment/abi-publishes-responsible-investment-disclosure-guidelines-$464874.htm (last visited 14 February 2007).

40. See Carbon Disclosure Website and Reports, available at http://www.cdproject.net.

41. As of 2005, companies in Europe are required to include 'a fair review of the development and performance of the company's business and of its position, together with a description of the principal risks and uncertainties that it faces'. In addition, 'to the extent necessary for an understanding of the company's development, performance or position, the analysis shall include both financial and where appropriate, nonfinancial key performance indicators relevant to the particular business, including information relating to environmental and employee matters'. Directive of Parliament 2003/51, art. 1, 14(a), 2003 O.J. (L 178), at 18. For a further discussion of these requirements, see Williams & Conley (2005).

42. KPMG Global Sustainability Services, *KPMG International Survey of Corporate Responsibility Reporting, 2005*(2005), available at http://www.kpmg.com/NR/ rdonlyres/66422F7F-35AD-4256-9BF8-F36FACCA9164/0/KPMGIntlCRSurvey2005. pdf (last visited 7 March 2006).

43. See http://www.accountability.org.uk/news/default.asp?id=158 for a description of AA 1000AS and related technical materials.

44. See International Standard on Assurance Engagements (ISAE) 3000: Assurance Engagements other than Audits or Reviews of Historical Financial Information *See* IFAC Press Release, *IAASB Issues a New Framework and Standard for Assurance Engagement*, 23 January 2004, available at http://www.ifac.org/News/LatestReleases. tmpl?NID=10748895832047605.

45. See, e.g., PHILIP B. SCHARY & TAGE SKJOTT-LARSEN, MANAGING THE GLOBAL SUPPLY CHAIN (Copenhagen Bus. Sch. Press 2nd edn 2001) (describing the supply chain literature); BIRGIT DAM JESPERSEN, TAGE SKJOTT-LARSEN, SUPPLY CHAIN MANAGEMENT: IN THEORY AND PRACTICE (2005) (giving a varied picture of supply chain management); JAMES B. AYERS, HANDBOOK OF SUPPLY CHAIN MANAGEMENT (2001) (presenting a broad view of the supply chain).

46. Although a growing share of food consumed in the US is restaurant food, we discuss the evolution of the industry that supplies food to grocery store. Many of the same factors are driving similar changes in the supply of food to branded restaurant chains, so we mention these factors as well.

47. Hatanaka Bain, & Busch (2005, p. 357) notes that both public and private standards now exist for 'food safety (e.g., Codex standards), food quality (private retailer or processor standards), Good Agricultural Practices, Good Manufacturing Practices and/or Good Management Practices (e.g., ISO 9000 standards), labor practices (e.g., SA 8000, ETI Baseline, and Fairtrade standards), environmental standards (e.g., ISO 14000 standards, Rainforest Alliance ECO-OK standards), and/or non-genetically modified materials'. See also Busch (2000).

48. In April 2002, the General Administration of Quality Supervision, Inspection and Quarantine of the People's Republic of China (AQSIQ) formally released the Regulation on Sanitarian Registration of Firms for Export Foods, in which it requires firms that export six kinds of foods (canned food, fish and fishery products, meat, frozen vegetables, juices, fast food containing meat or fish) to implement HACCP. See AQSIQ Order No. 20, April 19, 2002. In March 2002, the Certification and Accreditation Administration of the People's Republic of China (CNCA) promulgated regulation based on HACCP Certification. See CNCA Public Notice No. 3, 2002, at http://www.cnca.gov.cn/rjwzcfl/flfg/xzgf/644.shtml.

49. Stories concerning the safety of imported food products, especially food from China were prominent in the news at the time of writing this article. See, e.g., Weisman (2007); Barionuevo (2007); Zhang & King Jr. (2007); 'China's Food Safety', Economist. com Opinion, 12 June 2007.

50. Major food retailers in the UK, for example, have, since 1990 increasingly utilized 'private label products as a means to differentiate themselves from competitors and achieve market power through the supply chain', and have adopted 'protocols for suppliers that were enforced through second-party audits'. Henson (2006).

51. Hatanaka, Bain & Busch (2005) assert that 'one of the primary reasons given for the proliferation of TPC [third party certification] is its perceived character as independent and objective.'

52. The UN Commission on Trade and Development (UNCTAD) has estimated that as many as 400 private standards may exist for agriculture and food processing. See WTO G/SPS/GEN/746, Private Standards and the SPS Agreement, January 2007.

53. Gereffi (1999, at p. 47) quotes Jerome Chazen, one of the founders of Liz Claiborne, saying that '... we had to train and develop [overseas manufactureres] by supplying technical help, trim, findings, and virtually all components. While we counted on

them for their labor, we had to tell them exactly how to use the basic skills of their people and we had to watch them carefully, every step of the way.').

54. Locke observes, for example, that 'by guaranteeing a significant number of orders and by placing Nike employees at these new factories to help monitor product quality and production processes, Nike was able to help its lead vendors establish an extensive network of footwear factories throughout Southeast Asia'.

55. Prominent independent standard setters for apparel firms include Social Accountability International, Fair Labor Association, Worker Rights Consortium, Worldwide Responsible Apparel Production, Ethical Trading Initiative, and the Clean Clothes Campaign. See discussion above in part 3.4.1. In addition, the US Dept. of Labor has identified more than 35 US manufacturers of apparel or retailers of apparel products that have developed and subscribe to codes of conduct regarding their foreign operations. US Dept. of Labor, ILAB – II., Codes of Conduct in the US Apparel Industry, available at http://www.dol.gov/ilab/media/reports/iclp/apparel/2b.htm, last visited 28 June 2006.

References

Abernathy, F., J. Dunlop, J. Hammond, and D. Weil (1999) *A Stitch in Time, Lean Retailing and the Transformation of Manufacturing – Lessons from the Apparel and Textile Industries.* New York: Oxford University Press.

Arndt, S. and H. Kierzkowski (eds) (2001) *Fragmentation: New Production Patterns in the World Economy.* Oxford: Oxford University Press.

Ayers, J. (ed.) (2001) *Handbook of Supply Chain Management.* Boca Raton, FL: St. Lucie Press.

Barionuevo, A. (2007) 'Globalization in Every Loaf', *New York Times*, 16 June.

Bélanger, J.M. (2005) 'Responsible Care in Canada: The Evolution of an Ethic and a Commitment', *Chemistry International*, vol. 21(2), pp. 1–8.

Bernstein, L. (1992) 'Opting Out of the Legal System: Extralegal Contractual Relations in the Diamond Industry', *Journal of Legal Studies*, vol. 21(1), pp. 115–57.

Bernstein, L. (1996) 'Merchant Law in a Merchant Court: Rethinking the Codes's Search for Immanent Business Norms', *University of Pennsylvania Law Review*, vol. 144, pp. 1765–821.

Bernstein, L. (2001) 'Private Commercial Law in the Cotton Industry: Creating Cooperation through Rules, Norms and Institutions', *Michigan Law Review*, vol. 99, pp. 1724–88.

Blair, M. and S. Wallman (2001) *Unseen Wealth: Report of the Brookings Task Force on Intangibles.* Washington, DC: Brookings Institute Press.

Blair, M., C. Williams and L. Lin (2008) 'The New Role for Assurance Services in Global Commerce', *Journal of Corporation Law*, January (1) p. 325+.

Brooksbank, D. (2006) 'Norwegian Government Fund Excludes Wal-Mart,' IPE.com, 6 June.

Busch, L. (2000) 'The Moral Economy of Grades and Standards', *Journal of Rural Studies*, vol. 16(3), pp. 273–83.

Cannon, J.P. and C. Homburg (2001) 'Buyer–Supplier Relationships and Customer Firm Costs', *Journal of Marketing*, vol. 65(1), pp. 29–43.

Chapple, W., A. Cooke, V. Galt and D. Paton (2001) 'The Characteristics and Attributes of UK Firms Obtaining Accreditation to ISO 14001', *Business Strategy and the Environment*, vol. 10(4), pp. 238–44.

\ieigfiwekwgfi

Coase, R. (1937) 'The Nature of the Firm', *Economica*, vol. 4(1), pp. 386–405.

Conley, J. and C. Williams (2005) 'Engage, Embed and Embellish: The Theory and Practice of Corporate Social Responsibility', *Journal of Corporate Law*, vol. 31(1), pp. 1–38.

Costouros, G. (1978) 'Auditing in the Athenian State of the Golden Age (500–300 B.C.)', *Accounting Historian's Journal*, vol. 5(1), pp. 41–50.

Eccles, Robert G. et al. (2001) *The Value Reporting Revolution*. Hoboken, NJ: Wiley.

Eccles, Robert G. (2006) 'The Relevance of Reputational Risk', *Media Tenor Forschungsbericht*, no. 155(3), Quartal.

Ellis, K. (2006) 'House Democrats Ask Bush to Investigate Jordan Abuse', WWD. COM, 4 May.

Ellickson, R.C. (1991) *Order Without Law: How Neighbors Settle Disputes*. Cambridge, MA: Harvard University Press.

Feenstra, R.C. (1998) 'Integration of Trade and Disintegration of Production in the Global Economy', *Journal of Economic Perspectives*, vol. 12(4), pp. 31–50.

Geis, G. (2006) 'Business Outsourcing and the Agency Cost Problem'. Unpublished manuscript.

Gereffi, G. (1999) 'International Trade and Industrial Upgrading in the Apparel Commodity Chain', *Journal of International Economics*, vol. 48(1), pp. 37–70.

Gereffi, G., J. Humphrey and T. Sturgeon (2005) 'The Governance of Global Value Chains', *Review of International Political Economy*, vol. 12(1), pp. 78–104.

Greenhouse, S. and M. Barbaro (2006) 'An Ugly Side of Free Trade: Sweatshops in Jordan', *New York Times*, 3 May.

Greif, A. (1989) 'Reputation and Coalitions in Medieval Trade: Evidence on the Maghribi Traders', *Journal of Economic History*, vol. 49(4), pp. 857–82.

Grossman, G.M. and E. Helpman (2005) 'Outsourcing in a Global Economy', *Review of Economic Studies*, vol. 72(250), pp. 135–59.

Hamilton, G. and M. Petrovic (2006) *Global Retailers and Asian Manufacturers: Handbook of Asian Business*. Northampton, MA: Edward Elgar.

Hatanaka, M., C. Bain and L. Busch (2005) 'Third Party Certification in the Global Agrifoods System', *Food Policy*, vol. 30(3), pp. 354–69.

Henson, S. (2006) 'The Role of Public and Private Standards in Regulating International Food Markets', in *Food Regulation and Trade: Institutional Framework, Concepts of Analysis and Empirical Evidence*, Bonn, Germany, 28–30 May.

Humphrey, J. and H. Schmitz (2003) 'Governance in Global Value Chains', in Hubert Schmitz (ed.), *Local Enterprises in the Global Economy: Issues of Governance and Upgrading*. Northhampton, MA: Edward Elgar Publishing, pp. 95–109.

Institute of Chartered Accountants in Australia (2006) *Extended Performance Reporting: A Review of Empirical Studies*. Sydney, NSW: ICA.

International Monetary Fund and World Bank (2001) *Market Access for Developing Countries' Exports*. Washington, DC: IMF and World Bank.

Jespersen, B. and T. Skjott-Larsen (2005) *Supply Chain Management: In Theory and Practice*. Copenhagen: Copenhagen Business School Press.

Jiang, R.J. and P. Bansal (2003) 'Seeing the Need for ISO 14001', *Journal of Management Studies*, vol. 40(4), pp. 1047–67.

Klein, B., R.A. Crawford and A.A. Alchian (1978) 'Vertical Integration, Appropriable Rents, and the Competitive Contracting Process', *Journal of Law and Economics*, vol. 21(2), pp. 297–326.

Konzelmann, S., F. Wilkinson, C. Craypoand R. Aridi (2005) 'The Export of National Varieties of Capitalism: The Cases of Wal-Mart and IKEA', University of Cambridge Centre for Business Research Working Paper No. 314.

Kysar, D. (2004) 'Preferences for Processes: The Process/Product Distinction and the Regulation of Consumer Choice', *Harvard Law Review*. vol. 118(2), pp. 525–642.

Lev, B. (2001) *Intangibles: Management, Measurement, and Reporting*. Washington, DC: Brookings Institution Press.

Locke, R. (2002) 'The Promise and Perils of Globalization: The Case of Nike', Massachusetts Institute of Technology Industrial Performance Center Working Paper No. MIT-IPC-02-007.

Lohr, S. (2006) 'Outsourcing is Climbing Skills Ladder', *New York Times*, 16 February.

Meidinger, E. (2006) 'The Administrative Law of Global Private–Public Regulation: the Case of Forestry', *European Journal of International Law*, vol. 17(1), pp. 47–51.

Miller, J.M. (2003) 'A Typology of Legal Transplants: Using Sociology, Legal History and Argentine Examples to Explain the Transplant Process', *American Journal of Comparative Law*, vol. 51(4), pp. 839–85.

Mintzberg, H. (1979) *The Structuring of Organizations*. New York: Prentice-Hall.

Nassimbeni, G. (1998) 'Network Structures and Co-Ordination Mechanisms', *International Journal of Operations & Production Management*, vol. 18(6), pp. 538–54.

O'Conner, J.A. 'Responsible Care: Doing the Right Thing', *Canada's Chemical Producers*, Available from http://www.ccpa.ca/files/Library/Documents/RC/Doing_the_Right_Thing_history_of_RC.doc. Accessed 22 June 2006.

Organisation for Economic Co-operation and Development (2006) *OECD Statistics on International Trade in Services: Detailed by Partner Country 2000–2003*. Paris: OECD.

O'Rourke, D. (2005) *Global Economic Governance Programme*, Dept. of Politics and International Relations, Oxford University Working Paper No. 2005/16.

Park, H.Y., C.S. Reddy, and S. Sarkar (2000) 'Make or Buy Strategy of Firms in the U.S.', *Multinational Business Review*, vol. 8(2), pp. 89–97.

Peglau, R. (2002) 'Applauding the Success of ISO 14001 Should Not Deafen Us to the Challenges', *ISO Management Systems*, vol. 2(1), pp. 15–16.

Ponte, S. and P. Gibbon (2005) 'Quality Standards, Conventions, and the Governance of Global Value Chains', *Economy and Society*, vol. 34(1), pp. 1–31.

Rafter, M. (2005) 'Have Outsourcer Monitoring Programs Run their Course?', *Workforce Management*, vol. 84(10), pp. 62–7.

Richman, B. (2004) 'Firms, Courts, and Reputation Mechanisms: Towards a Positive Theory of Private Ordering', *Columbia Law Review*, vol. 104(8), pp. 2328–67.

Roberts, D., E. Engardio, A. Bernstein, S. Holmes and X. Ji (2006) 'Secrets, Lies, and Sweatshops', *Business Week*, 27 November.

Roht-Arriaza, N. (1995) 'Shifting the Point of Regulation: The International Organization for Standardization and Global Lawmaking on Trade and the Environment', *Ecology Law Quarterly*, vol. 22(3), pp. 479, 489–91.

Schary, P.B. and T. Skjott-Larsen (1998) *Managing the Global Supply Chain*. Copenhagen: Copenhagen Business School Press.

Schoenberger, K. (2000) *Levi's Children: Coming to Terms with Human Rights in the Global Marketplace*. New York: Grove Press.

Vandenbergh, M.P. (2007) 'The New Wal-Mart Effect: The Role of Private Contracting in Global Governance', *University of California at Los Angeles Law Review*, vol. 54, pp. 913–69.

Weisman, S.R. (2007) 'Food Safety Joins Issues at US–China Talks', *New York Times*, 23 May.

Williams, C. (1999) 'The Securities and Exchange Commission and Corporate Social Transparency', *Harvard Law Review*, vol. 112(6), pp. 1197–1311.

Williams, C. (2004) 'Civil Society Initiatives and "Soft Law" in the Oil and Gas Industry', *New York University Journal of International Law and Politics*, vol. 36, pp. 457–502.

Williams, C. and J. Conley (2005) 'An Emerging Third Way? The Erosion of the Anglo-American Shareholder Value Construct', *Cornell International Law Journal*, vol. 38(2), pp. 493–551.

Williamson, O.E. (1975) *Markets and Hierarchies: Analysis and Antitrust Implications*. New York: Free Press.

Williamson, O.E. (2005) 'The Economics of Governance', *American Economic Review*, vol. 95(2), pp. 1–18.

Wood, S. (2006) 'Voluntary Environmental Codes and Sustainability', in B. Richardson and S. Wood (eds), *Environmental Law for Sustainability*. Oxford: Hart.

Zhang, J. and N. King Jr. (2007) 'FDA Blocks Chinese Seafood on Contamination Concerns', *Wall Street Journal*, 29 June.

12
Voluntary Co-determination Produces Sustainable Competitive Advantage

Margit Osterloh, Bruno S. Frey and Hossam Zeitoun

The importance of firm-specific knowledge for a company's sustainable competitive advantage is well established in the knowledge-based theory of the firm. However, the impact of corporate governance design on firm-specific knowledge investments is underexplored. We assess existing co-determination systems in Europe and their impact on firm performance; then we discuss voluntary co-determination as a new corporate governance design that fosters firm-specific knowledge investments, intrinsic work motivation, efficient monitoring, and board diversity while lowering transaction costs. Our analysis indicates that shareholders can increase their company's value by adopting customized co-determination rules.

1 Introduction

In many European countries, co-determination laws were introduced in order to foster democracy within the economic system. After adopting and strengthening democratic mechanisms at the political level, co-determination within companies was the next step. The reasons given for co-determination were based on moral or political grounds rather than efficiency considerations (Höpner, 2004).

Today, co-determination is criticized by some practitioners. There are attempts to restrain or even to abolish existing co-determination regulations. Recent developments at the level of the European Union (EU) have led to loopholes – companies are able to evade co-determination laws – for example, by incorporating in another EU country with less co-determination requirements. In 2005, every seventh newly founded limited liability company in Germany was incorporated under the British legal form (Bundesregierung, 2006).

While *mandatory* co-determination regulation has become less important, we suggest *voluntary* introduction of customized co-determination rules as promising for the future. A company's competitive advantage is based largely on

332

firm-specific knowledge created by its employees. Investments in firm-specific knowledge can neither taken for granted nor be enforced through contracts. Employees who invest in firm-specific knowledge become vulnerable; the value of their knowledge diminishes when they work for a different employer. Therefore, employees prefer to acquire general (rather than firm-specific) knowledge unless their interests are protected. If employees refuse to make firm-specific investments, the company's competitive advantage will be easier to imitate and hence is less sustainable.

We suggest three measures to solve this problem: (1) The board should rely more on insiders. (2) The insiders should be elected by those employees of the firm who undertake firm-specific knowledge investments. (3) The board should be chaired by a neutral person.

In addition to encouraging firm-specific knowledge investments, our proposals offer further advantages: They countervail the dominance of executives, they encourage intrinsic work motivation by strengthening distributive and procedural justice, and they ensure diversity on the board while lowering transaction costs. Our proposed measures for reforming the board may help to overcome the current crisis of corporate governance. At the same time, they provide a step in the direction of a more adequate theory of the firm as a basis for corporate governance.

2   Is co-determination a phase-out model?

During the twentieth century, several European countries introduced co-determination regulations. In August 2006, Germany celebrated the thirtieth anniversary of its co-determination law. Apart from jubilee speeches, there were many critical comments. The controversial discussion on co-determination was mirrored in press reports, reflected in headlines such as 'Power Struggle on Co-determination', '30 Years of Dispute' and 'No Reason to Celebrate?'

In her speech, the German Chancellor Angela Merkel stated her opinion that co-determination is a 'big achievement' (Bundesregierung, 2006). She said: 'The German model has an exceptional position. It hasn't been adopted in this manner by any other country.' This statement, however, might be misleading. Today, co-determination regulations are a widespread phenomenon in European countries (Kluge & Stollt, 2006). Each country has developed its own model of co-determination; none of the models are identical (see Table 12.1). In some areas, there are even more comprehensive forms of co-determination than in Germany. Many co-determination laws were legislated as early as the 1970s.

Among the 25 countries belonging to the European Union (EU) in December 2006, 11 countries have relatively far-reaching co-determination laws (see Table 12.1). In seven other EU countries, there are limited co-determination

Table 12.1 European countries with far-reaching co-determination laws

Country	Criteria for board-level representation	Workers' representation	Selection of workers' representatives
Austria	Joint-stock companies Limited liability companies with more than 300 employees	33% of the supervisory board	Workers' representatives are appointed by the works council and have to be members of the works council.
Czech Republic	Joint-stock companies with more than 50 employees	33% of the supervisory board	Employees and external trade union officials are elected by employees as workers' representatives.
Denmark	> 35 employees	33% of the board of directors (at least 2 members)	Only employees can be elected as workers' representatives.
Finland	> 150 employees	Agreement between employer and personnel groups	If no agreement has been reached between the personnel groups, workers' representatives are elected by employees.
Germany	500–2,000 employees	33% of the supervisory board	Only employees can be elected as workers' representatives. Trade unions nominate candidates for the trade union seats.
	> 2,000 employees	50% of the supervisory board	There is a special regulation for the iron, coal and steel industry.
Hungary	Joint-stock companies and limited liability companies with more than 200 employees	33% of the supervisory board	Workers' representatives are appointed by the works council and have to be employees of the same company.
Luxemburg	> 1,000 employees	33% of the board of directors	Workers' representatives are appointed by the works council and have to be employees of the same company.

(Continued)

Table 12.1 (*Continued*)

Country	Criteria for board-level representation	Workers' representation	Selection of workers' representatives
Netherlands	> 100 employees Equity capital > 16 Mio. € Existence of a works council	(up to) 33% of the supervisory board	All members of the board have to be independent. Workers' representatives cannot be employees of the same company; they are nominated by the works council and appointed by the general meeting of shareholders.
Slovak Republic	Joint-stock companies with more than 50 employees	33% of the supervisory board	Only employees can be elected as workers' representatives.
Slovenia	Joint-stock companies with a supervisory board	33–50% of the supervisory board (defined in the companies' statutes)	Workers' representatives are appointed by the works council. In companies with more than 500 employees, there is an additional representative on the management board; this representative is proposed by the works council and appointed by shareholders.
Sweden	25–1,000 employees	2 members of the board of directors	Workers' representatives are appointed by trade unions that have concluded a collective labor agreement.
	> 1,000 employees	3 members of the board of directors	

Source: The information in Table 12.1 is based on Kluge and Stollt (2006).
Table 12.1 presents the most relevant regulations for companies. However, the co-determination laws regulate some exceptions and separate rules (e.g. for state-owned enterprises).

regulations (e.g. restricted to state-owned enterprises), and the remaining seven countries do not have any legislation on co-determination (Vitols, 2005; Kluge & Stollt, 2006).

Most of the co-determination laws allow the employees to take up one-third of the seats on the board of directors. The German model is unique insofar as it provides for parity co-determination for companies with more than 2,000 employees (i.e. 50 per cent of the board seats are allocated to employee representatives). However, the parity is attenuated in two respects: One employee representative is a representative of middle management. Furthermore, the chairperson of the supervisory board is chosen by shareholders. In the case of a stand-off, the chairperson can cast a double vote (Vitols, 2005).

Another important feature of co-determination is the level at which it applies. *Co-determination at the plant level* (through works councils) gives employees co-determination rights on some topics and rights to information or consultation on other topics. *Co-determination at the board level*, however, allows for co-determination on all essential decisions regarding the company. In the latter case, employee representatives bear legal obligations due to the fact that they are members of the board. The two levels of co-determination are not independent; in some countries, for example, employee representatives at the board level are nominated by the works council (Kluge & Stollt, 2006).

3   The relationship between co-determination and firm performance

A number of different performance measures have been used in empirical studies. Most performance measures can be clustered into four areas (Vitols, 2005): Labor variables (e.g. satisfaction, commitment, and employee turnover), company operations (e.g. productivity and innovation), financial performance (e.g. profitability), and stock market performance (e.g. share price increase). Furthermore, most empirical studies examine the impact of works councils (co-determination at plant level); only a few studies explore the impact of co-determination at the board level. The majority of the empirical studies (in both areas) focus on German company data.

3.1   Co-determination at the plant level

Jirjahn (2006) and Addison, Schnabel and Wagner (2004) provide a recent overview of empirical research on works councils. The main findings are summarized hereafter. Studies on productivity show uneven results unless collective labor agreements are taken into account. Several studies show that works councils increase productivity under the condition that the enterprise is bound to a collective labor agreement (Jirjahn, 2003; Wagner, 2005; Hübler, 2003). Hübler and Jirjahn (2003) suggest that Germany's system of collective labor agreements makes works councils focus more on increasing the company's surplus, since they are less involved in the conflict of the division of that surplus. In companies that are not bound to a collective labor agreement, works councils lead to a higher wage level of employees (Jirjahn & Klodt, 1999). Works councils influence not only wage levels but also wage spreads: Enterprises with a works council have a smaller wage differential between qualified and less qualified employees (Hübler & Meyer, 2001) and between men and women (Gartner & Stephan, 2004). Moreover, works councils are related to a lower rate of personnel turnover (Frick & Sadowski, 1995; Addison, Schnabel, & Wagner, 2001; Dilger, 2002) – this effect is amplified when the enterprise is bound to a collective labor agreement (Frick & Möller, 2003). On the other hand, the combination of a works council and a collective labor agreement is associated with a lower willingness to recruit elder employees, since these companies tend to accentuate internal labor markets (Heywood, Jirjahn, & Tsertsvadze, 2005). Enterprises with a works council run a higher risk of being closed – however, this effect is significantly smaller for enterprises that are bound to a collective labor agreement (Addison, Bellmann, & Kölling, 2002). Works councils are also associated with a higher probability of performance-linked payments (Heywood & Jirjahn, 2002). Enterprises with works councils offer more training to their employees, especially when new technologies and products are introduced (Hübler, 2003). The training's impact on productivity is increased through the existence of a works council (Smith, 2006; Zwick, 2004). With respect to working time models, works councils are related to a higher use of working-time accounts (Dilger, 2002; Hübler & Jirjahn, 2003; Ellguth & Promberger, 2004) and shift-work (Jirjahn, 2004). This effect may be interpreted as an enhanced willingness of the employees to cooperate. The trend towards flexible production concepts poses a challenge for works councils: Enterprises with semi-autonomous teams are less likely to have works councils (Hübler & Jirjahn, 2003). However, the existence of a works council raises the probability of introducing teams (Hübler & Jirjahn, 2002), which indicates that enterprises with works councils may be catching up. Introducing teamwork combined with the existence of a works council leads to higher enterprise performance (Zwick, 2003). Askildsen, Jirjahn, and Smith (2006) find a positive impact of works councils on environmental investment and on product innovations. According to Jirjahn and Kraft (2005), works councils have a positive effect on incremental product innovations and a neutral effect on radical product innovations.

Overall, the empirical work suggests that co-determination at the plant level has the potential to create a number of positive effects if it is embedded in an appropriate general framework. Workers appear to be more willing to cooperate (e.g. by working in shifts) when their preferences are taken into account; and a lower turnover of personnel is a good precondition for the acquisition of firm-specific knowledge (Jirjahn, 2006). However, some methodological problems need to be acknowledged. Longitudinal analysis is difficult to accomplish since very few plants introduce or abandon works councils during the observed period (Addison et al., 2004). Furthermore, almost all large-scale enterprises in the samples have works councils, which makes it difficult to distinguish specific effects of works councils for these enterprises (Höpner, 2004).

3.2   Co-determination at the board level

There has been much less research on co-determination at the board level compared to co-determination at the plant level. Most empirical studies have focused on *co-determination in Germany*, particularly on the politically imposed introduction of parity co-determination in 1976. Empirical research on co-determination at board level has shown mixed and partly contradictory results, which are summarized by Vitols (2005) and Jirjahn (2006). Svejnar (1982), Benelli, Loderer, and Lys (1987), and Baums and Frick (1998) find no significant effect of co-determination on firm performance and stock prices. Other studies show a negative effect on productivity (FitzRoy & Kraft, 1993) and stock market performance (Schmid & Seger, 1998; Gorton & Schmid, 2000). In contrast, recent studies indicate small positive effects on innovation (Kraft & Stank, 2004) and productivity (FitzRoy & Kraft, 2005). Gurdon and Rai (1990) present a positive effect on profits and a negative effect on sales. Finally, Gorton and Schmid (2004) analyze the causes of the negative impact on stock market performance; they find that parity co-determination negatively affects the relationship between shareholder value and management compensation and positively affects the relationship between employment and sales – which indicates over-employment and neglect of shareholders' interests. Gorton and Schmid (2004) point out that shareholders react to their loss of control by linking supervisory board compensation to firm performance and by increasing the firms' leverage (through borrowed capital).

Altogether, the results about co-determination in Germany hardly lead to a conclusive overall picture. Some of the studies have been criticized for methodological problems, such as simple comparisons of mean values, the use of cross-sectional data and short data series (FitzRoy & Kraft, 2005). Furthermore, the samples, time periods, and methods of estimation vary considerably from one study to another (Jirjahn, 2006).

Studies on *board co-determination outside Germany* are rare, and they tend to use the subjective evaluations of managers and workers (Vitols, 2005). For example, Levinson (2001) asks managers about how they perceive the effects of co-determination. The managers perceive the workers' representation as a resource rather than a burden, which leads to a cooperative climate and an easier implementation of difficult decisions. The workers' representatives play a rather peripheral role in board activities unless topics like personnel issues, competence development, workplace questions, or reorganizations are concerned.

Empirical research on board co-determination is inconclusive at the *company level*. But what about the observed effects at the *national level*? Are co-determination and a strong national economic performance mutually exclusive? Vitols (2005) divides the EU countries into two groups: those with far-reaching co-determination laws (see Table 12.1) and those with limited or no co-determination laws. The group of nations with far-reaching co-determination laws shows superior performance with regard to many indicators, e.g. unemployment, labor productivity, research spending, and labor peace. The strike rate is more than ten times lower in countries with far-reaching co-determination laws. To be sure, co-determination laws are not necessarily the cause for superior economic indicators. However, the results show that co-determination and a sound economic performance are not inconsistent with one another.

Finally, Höpner (2004) examines the proposition that countries with co-determination laws suffer a 'co-determination discount' at the stock market. Based on McKinsey's 'Investor Opinion Surveys', Höpner finds no significant correlation between the countries' share price discount and their scope of co-determination. However, there are significant relationships between the countries' share price discount and their systems of corporate control. For example, Germany became one of the countries with the lowest share price discount after introducing new accounting standards and a better protection of minority shareholders.

To summarize, research on co-determination (at both the plant and board levels) has provided useful insights as it has shown that co-determination in general is not a phase-out model. However, the quantitative studies have been limited by the 'dummy variable approach', which differentiates only the presence and the absence of co-determination. Future empirical research could examine different intensities of co-determination (Höpner, 2004; Zugehör, 2003) or use in-depth case studies (Addison et al., 2004).

Moreover, empirical co-determination research has two theoretical shortcomings. Firstly, it analyzes the impact of co-determination under past and present conditions. It does not take into account what today is common understanding in the strategic management literature, namely that the key task of modern corporations in the future is to generate, accumulate, transfer and protect firm-specific knowledge to create a sustaining competitive advantage (e.g. Penrose, 1959; Rumelt, 1984; Grant, 1996; Teece et al., 1997; Kogut & Zander, 1996; Spender, 1996; Foss & Foss, 2000). Secondly, so far empirical co-determination research is unconnected to modern knowledge-based theories of the firm as a theoretical basis for corporate governance (Osterloh & Zeitoun, 2006). In the following section, we therefore discuss two existing theories of the firm, which claim to give a theoretical basis for corporate governance. On that basis, we develop our own view of why a specific type of voluntary co-determination is fruitful in promoting a knowledge-based competitive advantage for firms.

4   Different theories of the firm as a basis for different corporate governance perspectives

4.1   The firm as a nexus of contracts

The dominant view of corporate governance is based on new institutional economics. The underlying theory of the firm, called the 'governance perspective' (Williamson, 1999), is an application of agency and property rights theory. It has been derived from the view of the firm as a nexus of contracts (Jensen & Meckling, 1976).

It starts with a conflict of interest between managers (agents) and shareholders (principals), caused by the separation of ownership and control in public corporations (Berle & Means, 1932). These conflicts as well as conflicts between shareholders and other stakeholders (including the employees) can be solved *ex ante* by contracts. Only shareholders carry a residual risk and should therefore have residual ownership and control.

In order to align the interests between shareholders and managers, firstly, the control of management must be transferred to an independent board of directors. Secondly, managers' and directors' pay should be tied to their performance (e.g. Jensen & Murphy, 1990; Jensen, 1993).

The wave of corporate scandals and the explosion of management compensation drew attention to flaws in the corporate governance structure according to this view. Even its proponents now admit that the explosion of executives' and directors' pay has proven to be 'pay without performance' (Bebchuk & Fried, 2004) or 'managerial and organizational heroin' (Jensen, Murphy & Wruck, 2004: 45). In order to improve corporate governance, the boards should become more responsible to their shareholders. Board members should be made more attentive to the shareholders' interests. For instance, board members should stand for annual election by the shareholders (Bebchuk & Fried, 2004).

The idea of board independence has been widely accepted but seems to contribute little to solving the problem. Most importantly, it has not led to any moderation in pay increases for chief executive officers (CEOs) and other managers. The stronger dependency of directors on shareholders might even have fueled the pay explosion, because in speculative markets it tends to align interests of CEOs to short-term share price maximization (Bolton, Scheinkman & Xiong, 2006). In addition, a meta-analysis of 54 studies on board dependence shows no statistical relationship between board independence and firm financial performance (Dalton et al., 1998).

4.2   The firm as a nexus of firm-specific investments

Blair (1995), Zingales (1998) and Blair and Stout (1999) argue that it is not in the interest of the shareholders to be the exclusive owners of residual control.

Firms exist because they produce what are commonly called quasi-rents (Klein, Crawford & Alchian, 1978) or synergies (Foss & Iversen, 1997). Quasi-rents represent the difference between what the parties inside the firm jointly generate and what each of them can obtain in the market. Quasi-rents are the outcome of mutually specialized assets of people who make firm-specific investments (Rajan & Zingales, 1998). These investments cannot, or only at high cost, be protected by contracts *ex ante* when the parties enter into a relationship. They represent transaction-specific investments that cause sunk costs once the contract has been made and are subjected to hold up. What matters is that investors' *ex post* bargaining position is weakened when the quasi-rents are divided (e.g. by discussing their wages after entering the contract). Their firm-specific investment is of little or no value outside the firm and decreases their outside opportunities during the term of the contract. It is primarily employees who are affected by such hold up. It has been shown empirically that employees who are forced to find new jobs lose, on average, 15 per cent of their wages (Osterman, 1999). If they were employed in the firm for more than 21 years, they stand to lose as much as 44 percent of their wages (Topel, 1991). As a consequence, employees have no incentive to undertake firm-specific investments if their bargaining position is not protected after they enter into the labor contract (Freeman & Lazear, 1996).

This critique of the view of the firm as a nexus of contracts leads to a view of the firm as a nexus of firm-specific investments. These firm-specific investments create room for *ex post* bargaining after the contracts have been finalized. For this reason, corporate governance can be defined as a set of constraints shaping the *ex post* bargaining over the joint output of firm-specific investments (Zingales, 1998). Blair and Stout (1999, 2001) claim that it is the board that has to take over the task of governing the firm-specific investments and mediating between possibly conflicting interests of investors in firm-specific assets that cannot be contracted *ex ante*. The board should act as a neutral third party, which is not involved in firm-specific investments. It should act as an impartial 'mediating hierarch' and therefore should consist mainly of outside directors. Voting rights are only given to shareholders, thus maintaining shareholders' supremacy.

4.3 The firm as a nexus of knowledge-specific investments

Blair and Stout's proposal is important but nevertheless neglects to address the crucial differences between firm-specific investments in *knowledge* and physical or financial capital. There are fundamental differences between firm-specific investments in knowledge and physical goods.

Firstly, as far as knowledge investments are concerned, it is not only too expensive to contract firm-specific investments *ex ante* before entering a contract, but it is simply impossible. A knowledge worker cannot contract his or her future knowledge as such due to the 'knowledge paradox' highlighted by

Arrow (1973: 171): The value of knowledge invested in the potential acquirer is not known until after the knowledge is revealed. Once revealed, the potential acquirer has no need to pay for it.

Secondly, the generation of knowledge cannot be evaluated in the same way as physical goods during the contract term. Only insiders or peers can evaluate firm-specific knowledge generation and transformation, because outsiders are rarely able to comprehend the processes involved, and are thus not able to protect knowledge investors from a deterioration of their bargaining position during the interim period when joint knowledge has not yet led to a recoverable output.

Thirdly, the information asymmetry between management and outside directors leads to the external board members being dependent on executives for information. Under present conditions, a board dominated by outside directors has to rely largely on information provided by the top executives.

These arguments link corporate governance to the 'competence perspective' of the theory of the firm (Williamson 1999), which today dominates the strategic management literature but which so far has not been considered in the literature on corporate governance. The 'competence perspective' or the knowledge-based theory of the firm suggests that firm-specific knowledge investments are crucial for a sustained competitive advantage of the firm. As a consequence, corporate governance should involve inside knowledge workers in the decision-making process of the firms' boards. There are two justifications. Firstly, according to the 'competence perspective', firm-specific knowledge, in particular of a tacit nature, is the most critical resource. Outside board members cannot understand the firm's tacit knowledge base and its strategic relevance (Coff, 1999: 126; Barney, 2005: 946). Secondly, contractual provisions such as regulating exit, the vesting of options, and repayment schemes are in most cases no valid alternatives to board representation of knowledge workers. The reason is that the underlying conflicts between shareholders and knowledge workers concerning the appropriation of the quasi-rents appear in full force only at the level of the board. In developed market economies, principal authority over corporate affairs is typically vested in a board of directors, which is formally distinct from the firm's shareholders (Hansmann & Kraakman, 2004). Conflict resolution between shareholders and knowledge workers is in the interests of the shareholders themselves as it leads to an increase in the value of the firm.

5   New corporate governance design

The distinct characteristics of firm-specific knowledge investments justify that knowledge workers are represented on the board. All other stakeholders, with the exception of shareholders, are better able to form *ex ante* contracts and therefore need not be represented on the board. Knowledge is indeed a special resource unlike any other resources, as highlighted by Arrow's (1973) knowledge paradox. All other resources can in principle be contracted, though sometimes at a high cost. This is not the case for knowledge as long as it is not encapsulated in a marketable product. Moreover, even in this case the problem of attributing the contribution of each worker to the product is unresolved. Thus, the knowledge workers and the shareholders should be involved in the residual control as they bear the brunt of the non-contractible residual risk. Contrary to what has been proposed by the dominant view of shareholders' supremacy, this leads us to propose the following board arrangements:

Firstly, the board should rely more on *insiders*. The percentage of insiders relative to outsiders should be determined by the relationship of firm-specific knowledge capital to financial capital.

Secondly, these insiders should be elected by, and responsible to, those *employees of the firm who make firm-specific knowledge investments*. The board should no longer be solely an instrument of financial investors, but also an instrument of knowledge investors, and should have the task of aligning the interests of these constituents.

Thirdly, a *neutral person* should chair the board. His or her main task is to enable the board members to engage in a productive discourse to the mutual benefit of all members of the firm. Moreover, he or she has to ensure that the conditions are such that the board members are prepared to contribute to the firm's common good and to refrain from rent seeking.

5.1 Insiders on the board

Insiders of the firm, especially those who are knowledge workers, have three major advantages over outsiders on the board. Firstly, they are better informed about the issues and problems concerning the firm's business (Baysinger & Hoskisson, 1990; Hillman & Dalziel, 2003), in particular they can better understand the firm's tacit knowledge base (Coff, 1999: 126). The more firms compete on the basis of innovation, the more this applies. In times of high uncertainty and rapid change, it is no longer possible to maintain control through targets set by hierarchical control, because targets in these cases have to be reset at regular intervals. It follows that control has to be based on a mutually agreed, ongoing revision of goals that takes into account new search procedures.

A second important advantage of having insiders on the board is that it lessens the board's dependence on CEOs for supplying information. Knowledge workers as directors are a well-informed source of inside information not filtered by the CEOs. These inside directors have superior explicit knowledge, as well as tacit knowledge, on the specific issues and problems facing the firm. Moreover, employee board representation can serve as a partial substitute for mandatory disclosure in bank-oriented financial systems (Hertig, 2006).

Thirdly, it is not in the interests of outside executive directors, who are also CEOs of other firms, to seriously challenge the policies, especially the remuneration of executives. It is well known that outside CEOs view the board through CEO eyes, i.e. through a lens that does not seriously challenge the power of the CEO. For example, a study by O'Reilly et al. (1988) found that the pay of the compensation committee members was a better predictor of CEO compensation than the actual performance of the firm. Thus, the membership of employees in the compensation committees would have a moderating effect upon the mutual hiking up of compensations by the cross-board membership of outside CEOs.

5.2   Representation of knowledge investors on the board

To solve the problem that contracts cannot be formed *ex ante* and that the insiders may be subservient to the very managers whom they are supposed to control, we propose an institutional solution: *Financial and knowledge investors should be represented on the board.* The relationship of the two groups ought to be proportional to the relation of investment in financial capital and investment in firm-specific knowledge capital. As a consequence, in a firm in which firm-specific knowledge investment is very important, the board should contain a large percentage of representatives of knowledge investors. If such employees have to leave the firm, they do not only lose their relational capital but cannot convincingly show another employer what their contribution was worth. Investing in such a way means losing bargaining power compared to investment in general marketable knowledge. In contrast, knowledge that has the same marketable value irrespective of the firm in which it is used should not be represented on the board. Examples are professionals working in consultancies, accounting firms, or legal companies, who often have closer relationships to their customers than to their firm. When they decide to work for another company, they often take their customers with them and have no sunk costs.

There are several proposals for measuring knowledge capital (e.g. Bontis, 2001; Lev, 2001; Lev & Radhakrishnan, 2003; Strassmann, 1999). To get the firm-specific investment of employees in knowledge capital, the knowledge capital must be reduced by a factor that, on the one hand, captures the average reduction in wages employees of the firm would suffer if they had to work in another firm. On the other hand, it should include the average investment the firm has made in the knowledge of its employees. This calculation requires an econometric analysis in which average wage rates in the firm are estimated, depending on a set of individual characteristics of the employees, as well as a variable that measures the time each employee spent in the firm.

As an alternative to this intricate process, a firm could voluntarily offer its employees a share of seats in the board corresponding to the attractiveness it desires to exhibit towards potential contributors to firm-specific knowledge. Such a procedure has the advantage of being future oriented.

We suggest that each employee has voting rights according to his or her firm-specific investment. It ranges from zero to one. The size of this investment is captured by the estimated individual reduction in wage an employee would sustain if he or she had to transfer to another firm. Employees who sustain no estimated loss from having invested in their firm-specific knowledge, or who gain an estimated net profit from knowledge investments by the firm, should have no vote.

5.3 Neutral chair of the board

We envisage a *neutral chair* whose task it would be to guarantee an open discussion on the board so that all aspects can be given due consideration. He or she should establish, as fully as possible, what has been called an ideal speech situation (Habermas, 1987; Steinmann, 1990). In particular, he or she has to make sure that the procedural rules are strictly observed and that all relevant arguments are heard and considered. The chair should make an effort to secure consensus on the board, especially when complicated issues are at stake. Unanimous decisions on the board should be required for constitutional issues of the firm (Buchanan & Tullock, 1962; Romme, 2004). The chair should also decide when, and when not, it would be useful to have the executives partake in the meetings of the board, thus securing the board a further measure of independence. The chair is therefore a specialist in procedures; he or she should not have any voting rights in order to remain truly independent. This can be compared to the task of a judge in relation to the jury.

The neutral chair of the board should be elected by the unanimous vote of its members. This ensures *ex ante* neutrality and grants him or her independence vis-à-vis any special faction of the board. Therefore, this person should be an outsider to the firm and should not be connected to the firm through previous employment or through any other capacity. Thus, we reject the common practice of appointing former CEOs as chairpersons of the board.

6 Advantages of our proposal

6.1 Providing incentives for knowledge investors

It is worth repeating our plan's greatest strength. Employees have a stronger incentive to become knowledge investors, i.e. to invest in firm-specific knowledge capital. This incentive is particularly important for highly educated professionals who, under the present corporate governance conditions, have little incentive to become more fully engaged with the firm they are working for. Investing in firm-specific knowledge reduces their outside options and thus their bargaining position inside and outside of the firm.

These missing incentives stand in sharp contrast to the emphasis on firm-specific knowledge as the most important source of sustained competitive advantage in the dominating strategic management literature. In contrast, our plan provides these incentives and contributes to building up firm-specific knowledge capital and therewith leads to sustainable efficiency rents for firms. Our proposal helps us to overcome one important flaw of the 'governance perspective': This theory disregards the individuals' incentives to generate and transfer knowledge (Dosi & Marengo, 2000; Osterloh, Frey & Frost, 2002). It only considers value generation and disregards the interaction between value distribution and value generation (Asher, Mahoney & Mahoney, 2005).

6.2   Countervailing the dominance of executives

Insiders who possess a great familiarity with internal processes and with internal tacit knowledge are able to monitor the executives more efficiently than outsiders, since they are less dependent on the information provided by executives. In addition, their function as representatives of the employees strengthens participation and self-governance by the corporate community as a part of corporate governance. Anyone breaking the rules is more easily identified by colleagues than by superiors and can be informally admonished. This assures that others are doing their part in contributing to the firm's common good and are refraining from rent seeking (Osterloh & Frey, 2004).

6.3   Strengthening intrinsic work motivation and loyalty

Many employees, in particular knowledge workers, are to a considerable extent intrinsically motivated. In order be creative, knowledge work needs autonomy (Amabile, 1996), which is the most important condition for becoming intrinsically motivated (Deci & Ryan, 2000; Frey, 1997; Osterloh & Frey, 2004; Osterloh, 2006). But such intrinsic motivation is undermined if individuals feel treated unfairly or exploited by conditions in which distributive justice is disregarded. At the same time, loyalty to superiors and to the firm as a whole diminishes, which has been shown by the literature on psychological contracts (Rousseau, 1995) and Organizational Citizenship Behavior (Organ & Ryan, 1995).

6.4   Ensuring diversity on the board while lowering transaction costs

The neutral chair has a second important function on the board. On the one hand, representation by shareholders and knowledge workers ensures that a multitude of different aspects are represented on the board. Such diversity is important for making wise strategic decisions (Grandori, 2005), particularly in diversified and decentralized organizational structures (Child & Rodrigues, 2003). On the other hand, diversity of interests and control rights also raises the transaction costs of the decision-making process on the board (Hansmann, 1996), a disadvantage that needs to be counterbalanced by the advantages of having diversity. The neutral chairperson, as a specialist in procedures or a 'facilitator' (Grandori, 2001), is able to find generally acceptable solutions to conflicting issues.

7 Conclusion

Mandatory co-determination regulations (both at the plant level and at the board level) have been established across Europe. Despite heavy criticism against co-determination laws, empirical research produces an uneven overall picture: Some studies show the negative effects of co-determination; however, there are many studies that exhibit neutral or positive effects of co-determination on various measures of performance. We suggest that co-determination laws might force a too rigid framework upon companies. They do not make sure that enough knowledge investors are represented on the board and thus have an incentive to invest in firm-specific instead of general knowledge.

In contrast, *voluntary co-determination rules* have a promising future. We argue that it is in the enlightened self-interest of shareholders to introduce customized co-determination rules. Our approach takes into account that a modern corporation's key task is to generate, accumulate and transfer firm-specific knowledge. Firm-specific knowledge investments are the essential basis for a sustainable competitive advantage. Financial *and* knowledge investments must be combined to produce what are commonly called synergies or quasi-rents. As a consequence, these quasi-rents need to be divided in a way perceived to be fair by the participants. In particular, knowledge investors should not feel exploited; otherwise they will refuse to make firm-specific investments and will prefer to make investments in outside options. Corporate governance must secure their ex post bargaining position, once the (necessarily incomplete) labor contracts have been fixed. It is the board that has to take over this task.

With this end in mind, this chapter advances three specific proposals:

Firstly, the board should rely more on *insiders*. The percentage of insiders relative to outsiders should be determined by the relationship of firm-specific knowledge capital to financial capital.

Secondly, these insiders should be elected by, and responsible to, those *employees of the firm who make firm-specific knowledge investments*.

Thirdly, a *neutral person* should chair the board. His or her main task is to enable the board members to engage in a productive discourse to the mutual benefit of all members of the firm. The chairperson also has to make sure that the board members are prepared to contribute to the firm's common good and refrain from rent seeking.

Our proposals have major advantages over the reforms suggested by the dominant corporate governance approach. With respect to *corporate governance design*, our proposals provide incentives for knowledge investors; they countervail the dominance of executives; they strengthen intrinsic work motivation and loyalty to the firm through distributive as well as procedural justice; and they ensure diversity on the board while lowering transaction costs.

With respect to *corporate governance theory*, our approach links corporate governance to the theory of the firm. On the one hand, we consider the 'competence perspective' or knowledge-based theory of the firm focusing on value generation and on the production of a sustained competitive advantage. On the other hand, we take account of the 'governance perspective' of the theory of the firm, based on new institutional economics, which focuses on the distribution of values. Thus, our approach overcomes the separation of theories focusing on value generation *or* value distribution by showing how value generation and value distribution interact.

References

Addison, J.T., C. Schnabel and J. Wagner (2001) 'Works Councils in Germany: Their Effects on Firm Performance', *Oxford Economic Papers*, vol. 53, pp. 659–94.

Addison, J.T., L. Bellmann and A. Kölling (2002) *Unions, Works Councils and Plant Closing in Germany*. IZA Discussion Paper No. 474.

Addison, J.T., C. Schnabel and J. Wagner (2004) 'The Course of Research into the Economic Consequences of German Works Councils', *British Journal of Industrial Relations*, vol. 42, pp. 255–81.

Amabile, T. (1996) *Creativity in Context*. Boulder, CO: Westview Press.

Arrow, K.J. (1973) *Information and Economic Behaviour*. Stockholm: Federation of Swedish Industries.

Asher, C.C., J.M. Mahoney and J.T. Mahoney (2005) 'Towards a Property Rights Foundation for a Stakeholder Theory of the Firm', *Journal of Management and Governance*, vol. 9, pp. 5–32.

Askildsen, J.E., U. Jirjahn and S.C. Smith (2006) 'Works Councils and Environmental Investment: Theory and Evidence from German Panel Data', *Journal of Economic Behavior & Organization*, vol. 60(3), pp. 346–72.

Barney, J.B. (2005) 'Should Strategic Management Research Engage Public Policy Debates?', *Academy of Management Journal*, vol. 48, pp. 945–8.

Baums, T. and B. Frick (1998) 'Co-determination in Germany: The Impact of Court Decisions on the Market Value of Firms', *Economic Analysis*, vol. 1, pp. 143–61.

Baysinger, B. and R. Hoskisson (1990) 'The Composition of Boards of Directors and Strategic Control', *Academy of Management Review*, vol. 15, pp. 72–87.

Bebchuk, L.A. and J. Fried (2004) *Pay Without Performance: The Unfulfilled Promise of Executive Compensation*. Cambridge, MA: Harvard University Press.

Benelli, G., C. Loderer and T. Lys (1987) 'Labor Participation in Corporate Policy-making Decisions: West Germany's Experience with Codetermination', *Journal of Business*, vol. 60, pp. 553–75.

Berle, A.A. and G.C. Means (1932) *The Modern Corporation and Private Property*. New York: Macmillan.

Blair, M. (1995) *Ownership and Control: Rethinking Corporate Governance for the Twenty-First Century*. Washington, DC: Brookings Institution.

Blair, M. and L.A. Stout (1999) 'A Team Production Theory of Corporate Law', *Virginia Law Review*, vol. 85(2), pp. 246–328.

Blair, M. and L.A. Stout (2001) 'Director Accountability and the Mediating Role of the Corporate Board', *Washington University Law Quarterly*, vol. 79(2), pp. 403–49.

Bolton, P., J. Scheinkman and W. Xiong (2006) 'Executive Compensation and Short-Termist Behaviour in Speculative Markets', *Review of Economic Studies*, vol. 73(3), pp. 577–610.

Bontis, N. (2001) 'Assessing Knowledge Assets: A Review of the Models Used to Measure Intellectual Capital', *International Journal of Management Reviews*, vol. 3, pp. 41–60.

Buchanan, J.M. and G. Tullock (1962) *The Calculus of Consent*. Ann Arbor, MI: University of Michigan Press.

Bundesregierung (2006) *Rede von Bundeskanzlerin Merkel anlässlich der Jubiläumsverans-taltung '30 Jahre Mitbestimmungsgesetz' der Hans-Böckler-Stiftung*, http://www.bundesregierung.de/Content/DE/Rede/2006/08/2006-08-30-bkin-jubilaeumsveranstal-tung-30-jahre-mitbestimmungsgesetz.html. Accessed 1 June 2007.

Child, J. and S.B. Rodrigues (2003) 'Corporate Governance and New Organizational Forms: Issues of Double and Multiple Agency', *Journal of Management and Governance*, vol. 7, pp. 337–60.

Coff, R.W. (1999) 'When Competitive Advantage Doesn't Lead to Performance: The Resource Based View and Stakeholder Bargaining Power', *Organization Science*, vol. 10(2), pp. 119–33.

Dalton, D.R., C.M. Daily, A.E. Ellstrand and J.L. Johnson (1998) 'Meta-Analytic Reviews of Board Composition, Leadership Structure, and Financial Performance', *Strategic Management Journal*, vol. 19, pp. 269–90.

Deci, E.L. and R.M. Ryan (2000) 'The "What" and "Why" of Goal Pursuits: Human Needs and the Self-determination of Behavior', *Psychological Inquiry*, vol. 11(4), pp. 227–68.

Dilger, A. (2002) *Ökonomik betrieblicher Mitbestimmung* (München und Mering: Rainer Hampp Verlag).

Dosi, G. and L. Marengo (2000) 'On the Tangled Discourse between Transaction Cost Economics and Competence-Based View of the Firm: Some Comments', in N. J. Foss and V. Mahnke (eds), *Competence, Governance, and Entrepreneurship: Advances in Economic Strategy Research* (Oxford: Oxford University Press), pp. 80–92.

Ellguth, P. and M. Promberger (2004) 'Arbeitszeitsituation und Betriebsrat – eine Matched-Pair-Analyse mit Daten des IAB-Betriebspanels' in L. Bellmann and C. Schnabel (eds), *Betriebliche Arbeitszeitpolitik im Wandel* (Nürnberg: BeitrAB), pp. 111–31.

FitzRoy, F.R. and K. Kraft (1993) 'Economic Effects of Codetermination', *Scandinavian Journal of Economics*, vol. 95, pp. 365–75.

FitzRoy, F.R. and K. Kraft (2005) 'Co-determination, Efficiency and Productivity', *British Journal of Industrial Relations*, vol. 43, pp. 233–47.

Foss, N.J. and M. Iversen (1997) *Promoting Synergies in Multiproduct Firms: Toward a Resource-Based View*. Copenhagen: Department of Industrial Economics and Strategy, Copenhagen Business School.

Foss, K. and N.J. Foss (2000) 'Competence and Governance Perspective: How Much Do They Differ? And How Does it Matter?', in N.J. Foss and V. Mahnke (eds), *Competence, Governance, and Entrepreneurship*. Oxford: Oxford University Press, pp. 55–79.

Freeman, R.B. and E.P. Lazear (1995) 'An Economic Analysis of Works Councils', in J. Rogers and W. Streeck (eds), *Works Councils: Consultation, Representation, and Cooperation in Industrial Relations*. Chicago: University of Chicago Press, pp. 27–52.

Frey, B. S. (1997) *Not Just for the Money: An Economic Theory of Personal Motivation*. Brookfield, VT: Edward Elgar.

Frick, B. and D. Sadowski (1995) 'Works Councils, Unions and Firm Performance – The Impact of Workers' Participation in Germany' in F. Buttler, W. Franz, R. Schettkat and D. Soskice (eds), *Institutional Frameworks and Labor Market Performance: Comparative Views on the U.S. and German Economies*. New York: Routledge, pp. 46–81.

Frick, B. and I. Möller (2003) 'Mandated Works Councils and Firm Performance: Labor Productivity and Personnel Turnover in German Establishments', *Schmollers Jahrbuch*, vol. 123, pp. 423–54.

Gartner, H. and G. Stephan (2004) *How Collective Contracts and Works Councils Reduce the Gender Wage Gap*. Nuremberg: IAB Discussion Paper No. 07.

Gorton, G. and F.A. Schmid (2000) *Class Struggle inside the Firm: A Study of German Codetermination*. The Federal Reserve Bank of Saint-Louis: Working Paper 2000-025.

Gorton, G. and F.A. Schmid (2004) 'Capital, Labor, and the Codetermined Firm: A Study of German Codetermination', *Journal of the European Economic Association*, vol. 2, pp. 863–905.

Grandori, A. (2001) 'Neither Hierarchy Nor Identity: Knowledge-Governance Mechanisms and the Theory of the Firm', *Journal of Management and Governance*, vol. 5, pp. 381–99.

Grandori, A. (2005) 'Neither Stakeholder Nor Shareholder "Theories": How Property Right and Contract Theory can Help in Getting Out of the Dilemma', *Journal of Management and Governance*, vol. 9, pp. 41–6.

Grant, R.M. (1996) 'Towards a Knowledge-Based Theory of the Firm', *Strategic Management Journal*, vol. 17, pp. 109–22.

Gurdon, M.A. and A. Rai (1990) 'Codetermination and Enterprise Performance: Empirical Evidence from West Germany', *Journal of Economics and Business*, vol. 42, pp. 289–302.

Habermas, J. (1987) *The Theory of Communicative Action*. Boston, MA: Beacon Press.

Hansmann, H. (1996) *The Ownership of Enterprise*. Cambridge, MA: Harvard University Press.

Hansmann, H. and R.H. Kraakman (2004) 'What Is Corporate Law?', in R.H. Kraakman, P. Davies, H. Hansmann, G. Hertig, K.J. Hopt, H. Kanda and E.B. Rock (eds), *The Anatomy of Corporate Law: A Comparative and Functional Approach*. Oxford: Oxford University Press, pp. 1–19.

Hertig, G. (2006) 'Codetermination as a (Partial) Substitute for Mandatory Disclosure?', *European Business Organization Law Review*, vol. 7, pp. 123–30.

Heywood, J.S. and U. Jirjahn (2002) 'Payment Schemes and Gender in Germany', *Industrial and Labor Relations Review*, vol. 56, pp. 44–64.

Heywood, J.S., U. Jirjahn and G. Tsertsvadze (2005) *Hiring Older Workers and Employing Older Workers: German Evidence*. University of Hannover: Working Paper.

Hillman, A.J. and T. Dalziel (2003) 'Boards of Directors and Firm Performance: Integrating Agency and Resource Dependence Perspectives', *Academy of Management Review*, vol. 28, pp. 383–96.

Höpner, M. (2004) *Unternehmensmitbestimmung unter Beschuss – Die Mitbestimmungsdebatte im Licht der sozialwissenschaftlichen Forschung* (Köln: MPIfG Paper 04/8, Max-Planck-Institut für Gesellschaftsforschung).

Hübler, O. and W. Meyer (2001) 'Industrial Relations and the Wage Dispersion within Firms', *Schmollers Jahrbuch*, vol. 121, pp. 285–312.

Hübler, O. and U. Jirjahn (2002) 'Arbeitsproduktivität, Reorganisationsmaßnahmen und Betriebsräte', in L. Bellmann and A. Kölling (eds), *Betrieblicher Wandel und Fachkräftebedarf*. Nürnberg: BeitrAB, pp. 1–45.

Hübler, O. (2003) 'Zum Einfluss des Betriebsrats in mittelgroßen Unternehmen auf Investitionen, Löhne, Produktivität und Renten – Empirische Befunde' in N. Goldschmidt (ed.), *Wunderbare Wirtschaftswelt – Die New Economy und ihre Herausforderungen*. Baden-Baden: Nomos, pp. 77–94.

Hübler, O. and U. Jirjahn (2003) 'Works Councils and Collective Bargaining in Germany: The Impact on Productivity and Wages', *Scottish Journal of Political Economy*, vol. 50, pp. 1–21.

Jensen, M.C. (1993) 'The Modern Industrial Revolution, Exit, and the Failure of Internal Control Systems', *Journal of Finance*, vol. 48, pp. 831–80.

Jensen, M.C. and W.H. Meckling (1976) 'Theory of the Firm. Managerial Behavior, Agency Costs and Ownership Structure', *Journal of Financial Economics*, vol. 3, pp. 305–60.

Jensen, M.C. and K.J. Murphy (1990) 'CEO Incentives – It's Not How Much You Pay, But How', *Harvard Business Review*, May–June, pp. 138–53.

Jensen, M.C., K.J. Murphy and E.G. Wruck (2004) *Remuneration: Where We've Been, How We Got to Here, What Are the Problems, and How to Fix Them*. European Corporate Governance Institute: Finance Working Paper 44/2004.

Jirjahn, U. and T. Klodt (1999) 'Lohnhöhe, industrielle Beziehungen und Produktmärkte', in L. Bellmann, S. Kohaut and M. Lahner (eds), *Zur Entwicklung von Lohn und Beschäftigung auf der Basis von Betriebs- und Unternehmensdaten* (Nürnberg: Beiträge zur Arbeitsmarkt- und Berufsforschung), pp. 27–54.

Jirjahn, U. (2003) 'Produktivitätswirkungen betrieblicher Mitbestimmung – Welchen Einfluss haben Betriebsgrösse und Tarifbindung?', *Zeitschrift für Betriebswirtschaft*, vol. 73(4), pp. 63–85.

Jirjahn, U. (2004) 'Welche Betriebe nutzen Schichtarbeit?' in L. Bellmann and C. Schnabel (eds.) *Betriebliche Arbeitszeitpolitik im Wandel*. Nürnberg: BeitrAB, pp. 67–85.

Jirjahn, U. (2006) 'Ökonomische Wirkungen der Mitbestimmung in Deutschland: Überblick über den Stand der Forschung und Perspektiven für zukünftige Studien', *Sozialer Fortschritt*, vol. 9, pp. 215–26.

Jirjahn, U. and K. Kraft (2005) *Do Spillovers Stimulate Incremental or Drastic Product Innovations? Hypotheses and Evidence from German Establishment Data*. ZEW Discussion Paper.

Klein, B., R.G. Crawford and A.A. Alchian (1978) 'Vertical Integration, Appropriable Rents, and the Competitive Contracting Process', *Journal of Law and Economics*, vol. 21, pp. 297–326.

Kluge, N. and M. Stollt (2006) 'Unternehmensmitbestimmung in den 25 EU-Mitgliedstaaten' in N. Kluge and M. Stollt (eds), *Die Europäische Aktiengesellschaft (SE) – Perspektiven für eine europäische Unternehmensmitbestimmung*. Brussels: ETUI-REHS.

Kogut, B. and U. Zander (1996) 'What Firms Do? Coordination, Identity, and Learning', *Organization Science*, vol. 7, pp. 502–18.

Kraft, K. and J. Stank (2004) 'Die Auswirkungen der gesetzlichen Mitbestimmung auf die Innovationsaktivitäten deutscher Unternehmen', *Schmollers Jahrbuch*, vol. 124, pp. 421–49.

Lev, B. (2001) *Intangibles: Management, Measuring, and Reporting*. Washington, DC: Brookings Institute.

Lev, B. and S. Radhakrishnan (2003) *The Measurement of Firm Specific Organizational Capital*. NBER Working Paper No. W958.

Levinson, K. (2001) 'Employee Representatives on Company Boards in Sweden', *Industrial Relations Journal*, vol. 32(3), pp. 264–74.

O'Reilly III, C.A., B.G. Main and G.S. Crystal (1988) 'CEO Compensation as Tournament and Social Comparison: A Tale of Two Theories', *Administrative Science Quarterly*, vol. 33, pp. 257–74.

Organ, D.W. and K. Ryan (1995) 'A Meta-Analytic Review of Attitudinal and Dispositional Predictors of Organizational Citizenship Behavior', *Personnel Psychology*, vol. 48, pp. 775–82.

Osterloh, M., B.S. Frey and J. Frost (2002) 'The Dynamics of Motivation in New Organizational Forms', *International Journal of the Economics of Business*, vol. 9, pp. 61–77.

Osterloh, M. and B.S. Frey (2004) 'Corporate Governance for Crooks. The Case for Corporate Virtue', in A. Grandori (ed.) *Corporate Governance and Firm Organization*. Oxford: Oxford University Press, pp. 191–211.

352 *Co-determination and Competitive Advantage*

33333Osterloh, M. (2006) 'Human Resources Management and Knowledge Creation', in I. Nonaka and I. Kazuo (eds), *Knowledge Creation and Management: New Challenges for Managers*. Oxford: Oxford University Press, pp. 158–75.

Osterloh, M. and H. Zeitoun (2006) 'Mitbestimmung schützt wichtiges Wissen in der Firma: Mitwirkungsregeln zur Balance der Interessen von Aktionären und "Wissensarbeitern"', *Neue Zürcher Zeitung*, 30 September.

Osterman, P. (1999) *Securing Prosperity*. Princeton, NJ: Princeton University Press.

Penrose, E.T. (1959) *The Theory of the Growth of the Firm*. Oxford: Oxford University Press.

Rajan, R.G. and L. Zingales (1998) 'Power in a Theory of the Firm', *Quarterly Journal of Economics*, vol. 113, pp. 387–432.

Romme, G.L. (2004) 'Unanimity Rule and Organizational Decision Making: A Simulation Model', *Organization Science*, vol. 15, pp. 704–18.

Rousseau, D.M. (1995) *Psychological Contracts in Organizations: Understanding Written and Unwritten Agreements*. London: Sage Publications.

Rumelt, R. (1984) 'Towards a Strategic Theory of the Firm', in R. Lamb (ed.), *Competitive Strategic Management*. Englewood Cliffs, NJ: Prentice Hall, pp. 556–70.

Schmid, F.A. and F. Seger (1998) 'Arbeitnehmermitbestimmung, Allokation von Entscheidungsrechten und Shareholder Value', *Zeitschrift für Betriebswirtschaft*, vol. 68, pp. 453–73.

Smith, S.C. (2006) 'Employee Participation Rights in Corporate Governance: An Economic Rationale, a Test of a Leading Theory, and Some Initial Policy Proposals', *Advances in the Economic Analysis of Participatory & Labor-Managed Firms*, vol. 9, pp. 105–46.

Spender, J.C. (1996) 'Making Knowledge the Basis of a Dynamic Theory of the Firm', *Strategic Management Journal*, vol. 17, pp. 45–62.

Steinmann, H. (1990) 'Corporate Governance', in E. Grochla (ed.), *Handbook of German Business Management*. Stuttgart: Poeschel, pp. 580–90.

Strassmann, P.A. (1999) 'Measuring and Managing Knowledge Capital', *Knowledge Executive Report*, June.

Svejnar, J. (1982) 'Codetermination and Productivity: Empirical Evidence from the Federal Republic of Germany', in D. Jones and J. Svejnar (eds), *Participatory and Self Managed Firms*. Lexington, MA: D.C. Heath, pp. 199–212.

Teece, D.G., G. Pisano and A. Shuen (1997) 'Dynamic Capabilities and Strategic Management', *Strategic Management Journal*, vol. 18, pp. 509–33.

Topel, R.C. (1991) 'Specific Capital, Mobility, and Wages: Wages Rise With Job Security', *Journal of Political Economy*, vol. 99, pp. 145–76.

Vitols, S. (2005) *Prospects for Trade Unions in the Evolving European System of Corporate Governance*. Brussels: ETUI-REHS.

Wagner, J. (2005) *German Works Councils and Productivity: First Evidence from a Nonparametric Test*. IZA Discussion Paper No. 1757.

Williamson, O.E. (1999) 'Strategy Research: Governance and Competence Perspectives', *Strategic Management Journal*, vol. 20(12), pp. 1087–108.

Zingales, L. (1998) 'Corporate Governance', in P. Newman (ed.), *The New Palgrave Dictionary of Economics and the Law*. London: Macmillan, pp. 497–503.

Zugehör, R. (2003) *Die Zukunft des rheinischen Kapitalismus. Unternehmen zwischen Kapitalmarkt und Mitbestimmung*. Opladen: Leske und Budrich.

Zwick, T. (2003) *Works Councils and the Productivity Impact of Direct Employee Participation*. ZEW Discussion Paper No. 03-47.

Zwick, T. (2004) 'Weiterbildungsintensität und betriebliche Produktivität', *Zeitschrift für Betriebswirtschaft*, vol. 74, pp. 651–68.

13
Corporate Trust Games in Modern Knowledge Economies

Leonardo Becchetti* and Noemi Pace

1 Introduction

Over the past decade developments in game theory and experimental games have made trust games very popular. Their success depends also on the fact that they represent an interesting benchmark for testing the anthropological restrictions that mainstream economics poses on the behaviour of economic agents. Following the well-known reference of Sen (1977), the identification of (myopic) self-interest as the unique driver of human action makes economic agents 'rational fouls' and rules out at least other two fundamental motivations of human behaviour: 'sympathy' and 'commitment'. With the former we may make choices that are not in our self-interest, but in that of individuals or groups that we care for. With the latter we perform actions that do not maximize our direct goals but that are consistent with the fulfilment of some duties based on internal acknowledged laws. Some of the mainstream theorists often think that these additional motivations of human behaviour may be easily incorporated into standard modelling with the direct inclusion into the individual's utility function or with the incorporation in some kind of ad hoc contingent goods (i.e. care for relational goods may be incorporated in a higher demand for recreational places which are more efficient in promoting interpersonal exchanges).

*Address for correspondence: Facolta' di Economia, Dipartimento di Economia e Istituzioni, Via Columbia 2, 00133 Roma. E-mail: Becchetti@economia.uniroma2.it.
CEIS Working Paper no. 233, presented at the 2006 Conference of the European Association for Research on Industrial Economics (EARIE) in Amsterdam, at the 2006 Conference of the AIEL (Italian Association of Labour Economics) in Udine, at the 2006 CORE conference organised by Fondazione 'Mattei' in Milan and at the 2006 workshop on 'CSR and Corporate Governance' of the International Economic Association. The authors thank Luciano Andreozzi, Masahiko Aoki, Avner Ben Ner, Bruce Chapman, Allen Kaufman, Bruno Frey, Lorenzo Sacconi, Margit Osterloh, Alessandro Vercelli, Oliver Williamson and all other participants to these conferences for their comments and suggestions. A special thanks to Annalisa Luporini for her precious suggestions. The usual disclaimer applies.

The solution of the problem is not so simple. We pursue relational goods not just when they are related to the consumption of marketable goods and services and, when we behave on the basis of moral commitment and our course of actions may even contradict the principle of constrained maximization. Furthermore, as in the famous 'battle of the sexes' the care for relational goods may not just be solved by slightly modifying the utility function with the inclusion of the other player's utility. Without a form of coordination such a small change may in fact lead to the paradox of altruistic utility functions creating an equilibrium in which each player chooses the favourite entertainment of the other and they paradoxically fail to go together to the same happening. Within this debate experimental trust games (along with ultimatum games) are among the most exploited theoretical framework used to demonstrate that individuals are not myopic, self-interested maximisers. In a sequential game in which a trustor gives to the trustee the possibility of choosing between the opportunity to abuse or that to cooperate, the subgame perfect equilibrium for a *homo economicus* should univocally be that of abusing, if its payoff is higher under this strategy than under all the alternative strategies. On the contrary, most trust games show that, when the trustee has a wide range of choices, whose extremes are taking the entire payoff or leaving it all to the opponent, the first solution is chosen with a probability which is far below the average. Another typical question which is never taken into account in standard economic modelling is not only that individual choices are a mix of myopic self interest, commitment and sympathy, but also that individual dispositions toward these three polar behaviours are not fixed but evolve across time according to a law of motion which is influenced by the structure of the game played and by inputs given by agencies which 'produce' values such as trust, willingness to pay for public goods (family, institutions, media governmental and non-governmental organizations).

The current contribution starts from these considerations by arguing that the evolution of the productive system, from a Tayloristic to a fully flexible system in which human capital and its creativity are crucial to the creation of new varieties of goods and services, makes the study and the analysis of the trust game essential also in production theory. In this framework it has been shown that, when we consider firm activity as a trust game, the law of motion of dispositions, such as trust and willingness to cooperate, is crucial and that a virtuous circle may exists among productivity, job satisfaction and quality of the working environment. Our final point is that the identification of these mechanisms highlights a potential virtuous circle between Corporate Social Responsibility (CSR) and corporate performance if firms are able to recognize them and invest in CSR under the form of improvement of relationships among workers.

2 Why contemporary productive environments are trust game corporations based on knowledge

The premise of our work is that, increasingly, the bulk of the economic activity of modern corporations depends upon a series of trust games played by their employees. Every activity carried on in the firm, beyond cleaning services and a few other blue-collar activities, requires the combination of no overlapping skills of several workers and possesses the intrinsic characteristics of trust games with superadditivity. The definition of a marketing strategy, the preparation of a project or the development of a new innovation necessarily involve different individuals, skills and firm divisions. In this framework team working becomes more and more important. In support of our assumption we can draw on the work of many other authors in the personnel and organizational management literature and also to recent firm practices of hiring teams rather than individuals or of placing a high priority on the social and team-working attitudes of people applying for jobs.[1] In the following sections we try to show that, if we do not conceive the most important part of productive activity as a trust game, we may struggle to understand two existing puzzles of personnel and labor economics. The first puzzle that need to be solved is why pay for performance fees (team compensation fees) are less (more) widespread than it is actually the case in modern corporations, especially when we focus on non-manual occupations (Baker, Jensen and Murphy, 1998; Baker, Gibbons and Murphy, 2002).[2] According to the standard labor economics literature workers are individual productive units driven by self-interested motivation whose performance may be enhanced by the promise of a remuneration that is proportional to the level of their efforts. Since effort is often unobservable, the monetary incentive is tied to the observable output and should in this way solve the moral hazard problem by inducing workers to exert their highest possible level of effort, even though they are not observed when doing so. One explanation for the puzzle is provided by Frey (1997) who identifies a trade-off between intrinsic motivation and monetary rewards. The trade-off is particularly binding for creative white-collar workers and much less for manual workers (who are reasonably supposed to be less intrinsically motivated at the origin). This line of reasoning has also been taken by Benabou and Tirole (2003) who acknowledge that the monetary incentive solution to the principal–agent theory (to which they greatly contributed) finds a limit in the crowding out of intrinsic motivations. Our point of view on this first puzzle is that the simple conception of corporate activity as a series of trust games provides an original line of explanation for it beyond the introduction of intrinsic motivations. In the following model we show indeed that pay for performance fees, by increasing the opportunity cost of the sharing/cooperative behaviour of the trustor, have the negative effect of making more likely the occurrence of non-cooperative solutions in trust games, thereby having a negative effect on firm productivity. Furthermore, the corporate trust game model also helps to explain a second puzzle – that is, the decision of corporations to invest in the quality of relationships among colleagues (or even, related to this, of hiring teams in order to have *ex ante* a higher relational quality among employees).[3]

Another innovative feature of our contribution is the departure from the standard economic assumption that individual dispositions are fixed and generally self-interested by assuming that our players give value to the quality of their relational goods which, in turn, is not fixed and evolves according to the success or failure of repeated interactions. To base our assumptions not just on speculation but on empirical evidence we synthetically report empirical findings from a related paper on the determinants of happiness (Becchetti et al. 2006). In this chapter we have tested whether the time spent for relationships has a positive effect on declared happiness and/or declared overall life satisfaction. The sample is taken from the World Value Survey database and includes more than 100,000 individuals from 82 countries. In the econometric analysis we introduce the time spent for different types of relational activities (friends, family, sport mates, etc.) including those with job colleagues outside the workplace. In the estimates we have controlled control for sociodemographic characteristics (age, gender, level of education, religious practice, marital status, employment status, household composition) and found robust evidence of a positive and significant effect of the time spent with job friends outside the workplace on happiness (see the Appendix at the end of the chapter).

To sum up, the two assumptions of firms conceived as trust games and of workers having preferences for the relationship with their colleagues allow us to build a model which shows that a virtuous circle among accumulation of trust, relational goods and productivity exists and help to explain why firms' policies may be oriented to investing in quality of relationship among colleagues. To relate this discussion to the technicalities of our model, by introducing these two elements we are able to show, under different versions (uniperiodal, infinitely repeated, with perfect or imperfect information) of our basic 'corporate trust game', that lower quality of relational goods, individual pay for performance schemes and (single winner) tournament incentive structures significantly widen the parametric space of 'non-cooperative'[4] equilibria which, in turn, dampen the circulation of knowledge and the cooperation of workers with different competencies, yielding suboptimal output for the firm.

The novelty of our approach with respect to the existing literature is the following. First, we introduce in the trust game model a concept of relational goods which is slightly different from the dominant one of fairness or reciprocity. As is well known, starting from the anomalies of laboratory experiments on ultimatum games in which a high share of respondents turn down low offers, or on public good experiments where people tend to contribute with non-zero amounts even when there is the possibility of free-riding, Fehr and Schmidt (1999) develop a model, consistent with these findings, by simply introducing inequality aversion arguments in their utility functions. In further extensions Fehr and Gächter (2000) show that reciprocity (or the intention to reciprocate an action which has been received) is an important determinant in the enforcement of incomplete contracts (Fehr, Gächter and Kirchsteiger, 1997; Fehr and Gächter, 2000; Bewley, 1995).[5] Our concept of relational goods is slightly different from those of inequality aversion or reciprocity. In our model we explicitly assume that players have accumulated a stock of relational goods (friendship, pleasure to spend time with people with whom they have interacted in the past) which can be implemented by further interaction or be entirely depleted in the case of abuse or the violation of friendship. In such a case the stock of relational goods becomes the opportunity cost of an opportunistic behaviour. The concept of relational goods is obviously not entirely novel in the literature where it is specified that they are local public goods (Ash, 2000; Uhlaner, 1989; Gui, 2000) which are simultaneously produced and consumed.[6] To our opinion, the main difference between relational goods and reciprocity is that, for the latter, what is just required is a general sense of duty while, in the former, reciprocity is fuelled by the quality of the relationship between the two players.

3   The basic corporate trust game

Our basic assumption is that the core of the firm's productive activity is represented by a complex task which requires the application of non-overlapping skills from different workers. To start with the simplest example, we introduce a basic case with two workers, players A and B, whose stand alone contributions to final output are, respectively, $h_a \in \Re^+$ and $h_b \in \Re^+$. As is well known, one of the main characteristics of the trust game is its non-simultaneity: in a first stage player A (the trustor) chooses between two strategies and, specifically, whether sharing or not his skills with the other player. In the following stage of the game player B (the trustee) has to choose in turn between cooperating or abusing. What we assume here by devising corporate trust games with a sequential structure is that any joint endeavour within the firm originates from a first stage in which one of the participants can share his knowledge with the other participants to the venture. It can be sending a file by e-mail or being the first to present one's own arguments in a joint meeting. It is highly unreasonable, and practically impossible, that these actions (or similar ones which are typically at the origin of a joint activity) may be done simultaneously by more than one player. Another crucial assumption of the model is that the interaction creates an externality (which we assume to be nonnegative even though the model may be reasonable and interesting to explore also under the assumption of negative externalities in case of very critical relationships between the two players). The externality is represented by the super additive component $e \in [0, \infty]$- generated by the dialogic process of jointly performing the task and by the initial sharing of knowledge (Figure 13.1).[7]

To sum up the set of available strategies, we know that player A (the trustor) may decide to share (s strategy) or not to share (ns strategy) his initial ideas with the trustee who, in turn, may decide to abuse (a strategy) or not (na strategy). If the trustee decides to abuse he will 'steal' trustor's ideas, join them with his own ones and present everything as his own work, while, if he decides to share, the two players will interact and produce a super additive component e as additional contribution to the output stemming from the integration of players perspectives and skills. We reasonably assume that, if the trustee chooses the cooperation, the final output is shared between the two players.

The set of payoffs (player A, player B and firm's output) are:

$\{(0|h_a < h_b, h_a|h_a > h_b), (0|h_a > h_b, h_b|h_a < h_b), Max(h_a, h_b)\}$ if player A does not share;

$\{0, h_a + h_b, h_a + h_b\}$ if player A shares but player B chooses to abuse;[8]

$\left\{ \dfrac{h_a + h_b + e}{2}, \dfrac{h_a + h_b + e}{2}, h_a + h_b + e \right\}$ if player A shares and player B cooperates.

The game is represented in the extensive form in Figure 13.1.

These payoffs imply several important assumptions. First, the stand alone contributions are not overlapping. Second, the trustee must have enough 'absorptive capacity' to be able to abuse of the skills of the other players. If the

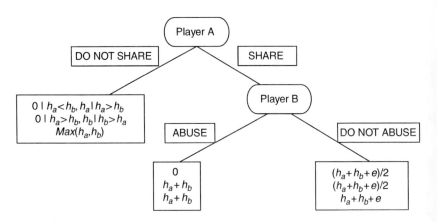

Figure 13.1   The uniperiodal full information game

fields of knowledge of the two players are too distant this assumption is unrealistic and the possibility of abusing of the contribution of the trustor is more unlikely. Third, in this simplest example in which the firm is made exclusively by the two players, we assume that the joint task is something similar to the participation to an open bid for a project, or to a patent race where some authority (external to the firm) may decide for the best project. Fourth, we do not examine cases in which players exchange, randomly or according to an a priori fixed criteria, the roles of trustor and trustee, even though this may be a nice extension of our game.

The analysis of the uniperiodal trust game shows clearly that the 'non-sharing' solution yielding a suboptimal firm output is the Symmetric Perfect Nash Equilibrium (SPNE) of the uniperiodal full information game when (i) the trustor has higher stand alone contribution to output than the trustee and (ii) the super additive component is inferior to the sum of trustee and trustor stand alone contributions. The 'non-sharing' solution is also the Self Confirming Equilibrium of the game if the trustor believes in (i) and (ii), even though these beliefs do not corresponds to reality. To demonstrate the first part of our claim consider that the crucial condition to take into account is the comparison between the trustee's payoff when he cooperates and that when he abuses (abuse condition), even though the solution of the game also depends on the comparison between the two players' stand alone contributions. Consider first the case in which the trustor has superior stand alone contribution, namely $h_a > h_b$. In this case his payoff is h_a, if he does not cooperate, and zero, if he decides to cooperate but player B abuses. As mentioned above the abuse condition tells us that player B will abuse if $h_a + h_b > \dfrac{h_a + h_b + e}{2}$ or $e < h_a + h_b$.

To sum up, if $h_a > h_b$ (superior trustor's stand alone contribution) and $e < h_a + h_b$ (super additive component lower than the sum of the two stand alone contributions) the 'non-sharing' solution is the SPNE of the uniperiodal full information game.[9]

The relevant consequence of this SPNE is that it yields a 'third-best' firm output – $Max(h_a, h_b)$ – lower than the one achievable under cooperation $h_a + h_b + e$, and even lower than the 'second-best' output obtainable under the (share, abuse) pair of strategies.

If we define the social surplus of the game as the difference between the maximum achievable output and the output arising from the solution of the game we conclude that the SPNE yields a loss of social surplus (and of firm productive potential) equal to $h_a + h_b + e - Max[h_a, h_b]$.

Let us consider now the alternative scenario in which the stand alone contribution of the trustor is inferior to that of the trustee or $h_a < h_b$. In this case, if the abuse condition is met, or $e < h_a + h_b$, the trustor becomes indifferent between sharing or not, since the payoff that he will receive is the same in both cases.

As a consequence, we have two SPN equilibria represented by the pairs of strategy (ns, .) or (s, a) yielding, respectively, a second or third best output with a consequent social loss, respectively equal to $h_a + h_b + e - Max[h_a, h_b]$ or e.[10]

To sum up, the first part of our claim demonstrates that, in the full information single-period game when the trustor has a higher stand alone contribution than the trustee, under reasonable parametric conditions on the value of the super additive component, the subgame perfect equilibrium is a non-information-sharing solution and the firm output is inferior to its maximum potential. Under the alternative assumption on the relative human capital endowments of the two players we have two possible solutions. Both of them do not imply information sharing and still yield a suboptimal firm output.

A graphic representation of the cooperation area is provided in Figure 13.2 in which the super additivity component is on the horizontal axis, the trustor stand alone contribution is on the vertical axis and the trustee stand alone contribution is fixed. The area of information sharing equilibria is the one, below the fixed level of trustee stand alone contribution, in which $e > h_a + h_b$.

With regard to the second part of our reasoning, consider that, if we take into account the concept of Self Confirming Equilibria developed by Fudenberg and Levine (1993), we additionally extend the range of solutions yielding non-cooperation and suboptimal firm's output. As is well known, in sequential games we may have Self Confirming Equilibria which are not Nash Equilibria. The difference between Self Confirming Equilibria is that players' beliefs may not be correct. Two additional basic assumptions which are commonly shared with Nash equilibrium is that players are rational (or maximize their payoff

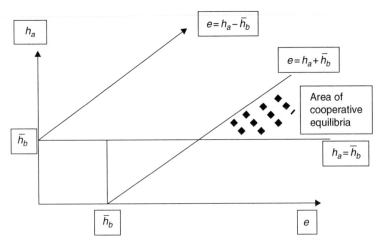

Figure 13.2 Graphic representation of players' payoffs in the uniperiodal full information game (for a given level of $\bar{h}_b$)

conditional to their beliefs over the opponent behaviour) and their beliefs cannot conflict with empirical evidence. In our sequential game the relevant situation is when the trustor believes he has the higher stand alone contribution and that the super additive component is lower than the sum of the stand alone contributions of the two players, even though it is not the case. If, however, based on his erroneous beliefs, the trustor rationally chooses not to cooperate he will never have an empirical proof of his error and the (*ns*, .) will be the self-confirming equilibrium of the game even though it is not a SPNE. Hence, the departure from the full information framework, and the admission that players' beliefs may be incorrect, enlarges the parametric area in which the solution of the game leads to lack of cooperation and suboptimal output.

Consider that the analysis of self-confirming equilibria is a departure from the perfect information framework by allowing the possibility that the two players have incorrect beliefs on the payoffs of the game. A more detailed analysis of the game under imperfect information will be developed in the following sections.

3.1 The one-period corporate trust game with relational goods

The strength of our argument on the non-cooperative inefficiencies in modern corporations based on knowledge sharing and trust games relies on the fact that the 'third-best' output result comes out by assuming standard purely self-interested player preferences. Nonetheless, in this version of the basic game, we want to see how our results change when we introduce in players' utility function the quality of relationships which we demonstrated grounded on empirical results (see Appendix). As we will show in the model, we can anticipate that the taste for personal relationships increases the propensity to be trustworthy since violation of trust involves a reduction in the quality of relationships.

In this section, without directly modelling the law of motion of the relational goods (given the one-period framework), we assume that the two players arrive at the trust game with a stock of accumulated relational goods equal to F which depends on their past friendship and, consistent with the Smithian 'fellow feeling' principle, may jointly produce a relational good f with their decision to cooperate. Under this modified framework, the solution of the uniperiodal game with relational goods is that, when $\frac{h_a + h_b - e}{2} > F$, there exists a threshold value of the relational good in the trustee utility function (f^*) which triggers the switch from the non cooperative to the cooperative (share, not abuse) equilibrium.

To show this point, consider that the new payoff set with the existence of relational goods (player A and player B payoffs and firm output) is:

$\{(F|h_a < h_b, F + h|h_a > h_b), (F|h_a > h_b, F + h_b|h_a < h_b), Max[h_a, h_b]\}$ if player A does not share;

$\{0, h_a + h_b, h_a + h_b\}$ if player A shares but player B chooses to abuse;

$\left\{\dfrac{h_a + h_b + e}{2} + F + f, \dfrac{h_a + h_b + e}{2} + F + f, h_a + h_b + e\right\}$ if player A shares and player

B does no abuse (Figure 13.3).[11]

If we consider the case in which the trustor has a higher stand alone contribution than the trustee, $h_a > h_b$, we easily find that the subgame perfect equilibrium of the full information uniperiodal game is (ns, .). The same occurs when the inequality is inverted, namely $h_b > h_a$. Again, the non-cooperative solution yields a 'third-best' firm's output, $Max[h_a, h_b]$, which is lower than $h_a + h_b + e$ (that is the firm output under the (s, na) equilibrium) and lower than that obtained under the (s, a) solution. The main difference with respect to the basic game without relational goods is that the threshold value of the super additive component which divides cooperation from abuse is now lower since the value of relational goods works as an opportunity cost for the decision to abuse. This implies that, given the new abuse condition, if $\dfrac{h_a + h_b - e}{2} > F$, we may identify a threshold (f^*) in the value of the relational goods for the trustee above which the (share, no abuse) couple of strategies becomes the SPNE of the single-period full information game. Such a threshold is equal to $f^* = Max\left\{\dfrac{h_a + h_b - e}{2} - F, \dfrac{h_a - h_b - e}{2}\right\}$.

The wider parametric space for the cooperative solutions is evident also in Figure 13.4. By interpreting this result we may conclude that the empirically grounded consideration for the preference of relational goods among workers outlines a potential virtuous circle among quality of worker relationships,

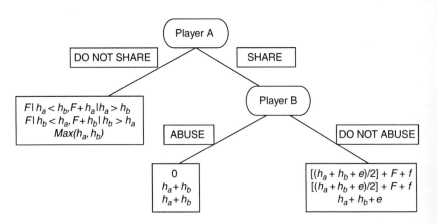

Figure 13.3 The uniperiodal full information game with relational goods

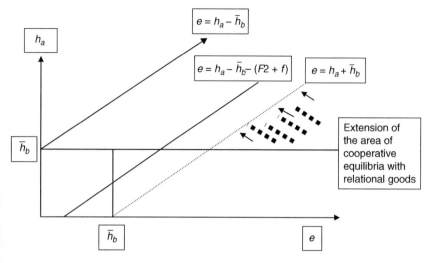

Figure 13.4   Graphic representation of players' payoff in the uniperiodal full information game with relational goods (for a given level of $\bar{h}_b$)

decision to cooperate (which further increases the quality of relationships) and firm productivity, or among relational goods, social capital (under the form of trust and trustworthiness) and firm's productivity.

3.2   The two-period full information trust game when the players own the firm

With a two-period example we want to show that solutions of the game are substantially unaltered with respect to those of the single-period game for similar parametric ranges. Let us first consider the model without relational goods. In this case, if the abuse condition is met and if the trustor has higher stand alone contribution than the trustee, the trustor anticipates that the trustee is going to abuse in both periods and therefore will choose not to share. The SPNE is therefore: (*i*) (*ns*, .) if the trustor has higher stand alone contribution and if the super additive component is not too high (or if the abuse condition holds); (*ii*) (*ns*, .) and (*s*, *a*) if the trustor has lower stand alone contribution and if the abuse condition is met.

Let us explore the possibility of more complex equilibria by examining whether the (*s*, *na*) equilibrium may be enforced when the trustor threatens a punishment to the other player in case of abuse in the first period.

A simple punishment strategy may be represented by the refusal to share in the second period game. The extensive form of the game is presented in Figure 13.5.

If player A decides not to share, the firm's payoff will be $h_a(1 + \delta)$, if $h_a > h_b$, while it will be $h_b(1 + \delta)$, if $h_a < h_b$, with δ the inverse of the subjective discount rate or the standard measure of players' 'patience'.[12]

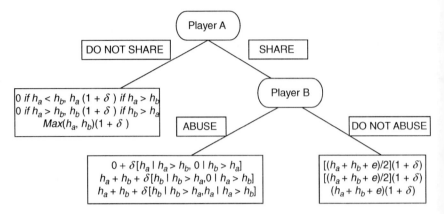

Figure 13.5   The two-period full information game

On the other hand, if player B does not abuse, the payoff of each player will be $\dfrac{h_a + h_b + e}{2}(1 + \delta)$. If player A shares and player B decides to abuse, player A payoff will h_a, if $h_a > h_b$, while player B payoff depends on the difference between the skills of two players. If $h_a > h_b$, player B payoff is the sum of the two players' stand alone contributions, $h_a + h_b$, given that there is not any added value to be discounted in the second period, (player A will decide not to share in the second stage if player B abused in the first), while, if $h_a < h_b$, we must add to $h_a + h_b$ player B stand alone contribution multiplied by the discount rate. Hence, under the $h_a > h_b$ hypothesis, the no abuse condition in the first period is $e > (h_a + h_b)\left(\dfrac{1 - \delta}{1 + \delta}\right)$, or $\delta > \dfrac{h_a + h_b - e}{h_a + h_b + e}$. The condition may be met for reasonable values of $\delta \in [0,1]$, e and players' stand alone contributions. More specifically, with minimum patience, $\delta = 0$, we get back to the no abuse condition of the uniperiodal game $e > h_a + h_b$ while, with maximum patience $\delta = 1$, the no abuse condition is much easier to be respected as it just requires a nonzero super additive component ($e > 0$). If, on the contrary, $h_a < h_b$ the no abuse condition is $e > h_b + h_a\left(\dfrac{1 - \delta}{1 + \delta}\right)$.[13]

Again, with minimum patience $\delta = 0$, we get back to the no abuse condition of the uniperiodal game $e > h_a + h_b$, while, with maximum patience $\delta = 1$, the no abuse condition reduces to $e > h_b$. In graphical terms in Figure 13.5 with trustee maximum patience $\delta = 1$ the two period game no abuse area would be represented by all the positive quadrant, under the $h_a > h_b$ hypothesis, and by the area at the right of the $e = h_b$ vertical line, under the $h_a < h_b$ hypothesis (see Figure 13.5).

Even though the no abuse condition is respected, this solution is not renegotiation proof. In fact, the punishment strategy costs in the second period to the trustor $\frac{h_a+h_b+e}{2}$, if $h_a < h_b$, and $\frac{h_a+h_b+e}{2}-h_a$, if $h_a > h_b$ (under the assumption that the trustee would cooperate in that period) but it is zero if the trustor rationally assumes that the trustee will abuse again. Hence, the trustee may propose, after abusing in the first period, a preliminary side payment – in case the trustor decides to share – of ε, when $h_a < h_b$, or $h_a + \varepsilon$, when $h_a > h_b$. The trustor should strictly prefer the new proposal.

Hence, the new no abuse condition will be $e > h_a + h_b - \frac{2\delta\varepsilon}{1+\delta}$, when $h_a < h_b$, and $e > h_a + h_b - \frac{2\delta(h_a+\varepsilon)}{1+\delta}$, when $h_a > h_b$.

Renegotiation therefore reduces significantly the parametric space of the no abuse condition.

To sum up, we have then shown that the biperiodal game yields solutions equal to those of the single-period game when we do not include punishment strategies, plus a more complex solution if the trustor defines a simple punishment strategy. The intuition is that, under the (ns, .) equilibrium, the trustor will have a zero gain if he has lower stand alone contribution than the trustee or $2h_a$ otherwise. If the trustor threatens the trustee with non-cooperation in the second period, in case he is abused in the first, he has to deal with the fact that his punishment is not at proof of renegotiation at the end of the first period in case of trustee's commitment to cooperation, but, if we consider that the trustee will continue to abuse also in the second period the punishment strategy does not cost anything to the trustor. The trustee, after having abused in the first period, may always propose a side-payment which makes it convenient for the trustor not to enact its punishment. Hence, with the introduction of a simple trustor punishment strategy we have a slightly different equilibrium in which an ε of the total output in the second period goes to the trustor.

3.3 The two-period full information trust game with relational goods when players own the firm

Following the same reasoning, without considering trustor punishment strategies the two-period game with relational goods yields the same results as the single-period one. There are two differences with the two-period game without relational goods: the abuse condition is less likely to be met (lower values of the super additive component violate it) and, when the trustor has lower stand alone contribution than the trustee we obtain a unique (ns, a) equilibrium instead of the two – (ns, .) and (s, a) – of the game without relational goods. In the two-period trust game with relational goods, the abuse strategy of player A determines the 'destruction' of the accumulated relational stock F (as in the one-period game). In such a case, player B's payoff is $h_a + h_b + \delta(h_b|h_a < h_b, 0|h_a > h_b)$ (Figure 13.6).

On the other hand, if player B does not abuse, each player obtains the following payoff $F + \left(\dfrac{h_a + h_b + e}{2} + f\right)(1 + \delta)$. Hence, the no abuse condition in the first period is $F + \left(\dfrac{h_a + h_b + e}{2} + f\right)(1 + \delta) > h_a + h_b + \delta(h_b|h_a < h_b, 0|h_a + h_b)$. If $h_a > h_b$, the no abuse condition becomes $F + \left(\dfrac{h_a + h_b + e}{2} + f\right)(1 + \delta) > h_a + h_b$ or

$$e > \left(h_a + h_b - F\right)\left(\frac{1 - \delta}{1 + \delta}\right) - 2f.$$

The presence of the relational good arguments makes the no abuse condition less stringent and widens the parametric space of cooperative equilibria. Consider now the case in which $h_a < h_b$.

The no abuse condition is $F + \left(\dfrac{h_a + h_b + e}{2} + f\right)(1 + \delta) > h_a + h_b(1 + \delta)$ or

$$e > \left(h_a + h_b - F\right)\left(\frac{1 - \delta}{1 + \delta}\right) - 2f + 2\frac{\delta}{1 + \delta}h_b.$$

In such a case it is more difficult to meet the no abuse condition, even in the presence of an inclination towards relational goods.

As in the single-period game the presence of relational goods in the two-period full information game widens the parametric space in which cooperative (no abuse) equilibria are attained. Even though the no abuse condition is respected, this solution is not renegotiation proof. In fact, the punishment strategy costs in the second period to the trustor is $f + \dfrac{h_a + h_b + e}{2}$, if $h_a < h_b$,

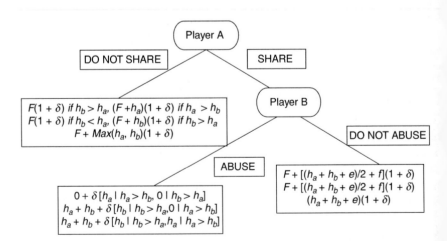

Figure 13.6   The two-period full information game with relational goods

and $f + \dfrac{h_a + h_b + e}{2} - h_a$, if $h_a > h_b$. As a consequence, the trustee may propose, after abusing in the first period, a preliminary side-payment – in case the trustor decides to share – of ε, when $h_a < h_b$, or $h_a + \varepsilon$, when $h_a > h_b$. Hence, the new no abuse condition will be $e > h_a + h_b - SF - 2f - \dfrac{2\delta\varepsilon}{1+\delta}$, when $h_a < h_b$, and $e > h_a + h_b - 2F - 2f - \dfrac{2\delta(h_a + \varepsilon)}{1+\delta}$, when $h_a > h_b$.

Once again, the renegotiation significantly reduces the parametric space of the no abuse condition. Again, even though the trustor anticipates that the trustee will find it convenient to renegotiate after abusing in the first period, the punishment strategy may be convenient since it allows him to earn an additional ε of the total output in the second period.

3.4   The infinitely repeated game

It may seem odd to discuss infinitely repeated games in the context of corporate trust games, but we have to consider that the interactions among workers are extremely frequent so that the large number of games played during a working life may be approximated by infinitely repeated games.

The analysis of the infinitely repeated version of the game without relational goods shows clearly that the (s, na) profile is the SPNE for reasonable discount rates, but it may never hold, under given parametric conditions, when the trustee has a higher stand alone contribution than the trustor. Even when the (s, na) profile is a SPNE, it is, however, based on a trustor threat which is not renegotiation proof. To demonstrate this, consider that, as is well known, the Folk Theorem applies to the infinitely repeated game if there exists a $\delta \in [0,1]$ such that the (share, not abuse) equilibrium is enforceable. By applying it to this modified version of the game we get $(1 - \tilde{\delta})(h_a + h_b) = \dfrac{h_a + h_b + e}{2}$, if $h_a > h_b$, and $(1 - \tilde{\delta})(h_a + h_b) + \tilde{\delta}h_b = \dfrac{h_a + h_b + e}{2}$, if $h_a < h_b$. If $h_a > h_b$, $\tilde{\delta} = \dfrac{1}{2} - \dfrac{e}{2(h_a + h_b)}$, which is below 1 for reasonable parametric values. On the other hand, if $h_b > h_a$,

$$\tilde{\delta} = \dfrac{\dfrac{1}{2} + \dfrac{1}{2}\left(\dfrac{h_b}{h_a}\right) - e}{2h_a}.$$

Under reasonable parametric conditions – and, more specifically, when $h_b - h_a > e$ – we get $\tilde{\delta} > 1$ and the cooperative equilibrium may not be enforced. In other words, if the trustor may commit himself to an infinite punishment strategy starting from the period following the trustee abuse, and if the discount rate of the trustee is not very high, the (s, na) profile in which the two players cooperate may be the NE of the game. However, as is well known, the hypothesis of infinite punishment is not always credible, especially when the punishment has a cost for the punisher as it is in our case. Consider that the punishment strategy costs any period to the trustor $\frac{h_a + h_b + e}{2}$, if $h_a < h_b$, and $\frac{h_a + h_b + e}{2} - h_a$ if $h_a > h_b$. Hence, the trustee may propose, after abusing in the first period, a preliminary side payment of ε, when $h_a < h_b$, or $h_a + \varepsilon$, when $h_a > h_b$, conditional to the trustor's commitment to share in the following period. The trustor should strictly prefer the new proposal which may be repeated an infinite number of times after any abuse by the trustee. Hence, we get $(1 - \tilde{\delta})(h_a + h_b) + \tilde{\delta}(h_a + h_b - \varepsilon) = \frac{h_a + h_b + e}{2}$, if $h_a < h_b$, and $(1 - \tilde{\delta})(h_a + h_b) + \tilde{\delta}(h_b - \varepsilon) = \frac{h_a + h_b + \varepsilon}{2}$, if $h_a > h_b$. It is easy to check that, in both cases, and especially when $h_a < h_b$, $\tilde{\delta} > 1$ under reasonable parametric conditions. Notice that, under the case in which the trustor has a higher stand alone contribution than the trustee, namely $h_a > h_b$, the new condition implies that the minimum trustee patience required to have a cooperation equilibrium is negatively related to the ratio between the super additive component and the sum of the two players' stand alone contributions. In other words, since the super additive component is the cost of applying the punishment strategy, the higher it is, the more the cooperative solution may be enforced, even in presence of low levels of trustee patience. When the relationship between the two stand alone contributions is reversed, namely $h_a > h_b$, the minimum trustee patience required to have a cooperation equilibrium is higher and depends positively from the trustee stand alone contribution and negatively from the super additive component and trustor stand alone contribution which are part of the punishment in case of abuse.

Consider again that milder punishment strategies may pass renegotiation demonstrability and be enforced more easily. If, for example, the trustor devises a punishment strategy lasting for N (extension of the punishment strategy for the next N periods) and the trustor commits itself to a random strategy in which he will share for x times and not share for 1-x times. It is in principle possible in this case to find a number N and a probability x such that the punishment strategy is not costly for the punisher and therefore is renegotiation proof.

4   The trust game with imperfect information

In our discussion of the Self Confirming Equilibria we showed that, when departing from the full information framework, by simply assuming that players might have incorrect beliefs over the game payoffs, we were more likely to fall into the non-cooperation equilibria of the game. We now tackle more generally the problem of imperfect information by looking at the two more general forms of imperfect information related to: (*i*) the relational attitude of the other player, that is, the presence in his utility function of a positive argument related to the cooperation with his colleague; (*ii*) the stand alone contribution to output of the other player.

Under assumption (*i*) it is clear that the two players do not know each other well and, therefore, it is reasonable to assume that $F = 0$. More specifically, if we assume that each player assigns a probability $p \in [0,1]$ to the likelihood that his counterpart gives a value f to the relational good produced by the cooperative working activity (see Figure 13.7), we may easily check that the threshold value of the relational good required to ensure the (share, not abuse) equilibrium is now higher. Hence, the effective value of relational goods in the utility function is less likely to generate equilibria of cooperation between the two workers. Consider in fact that, if each player assigns a probability p to the likelihood that his counterpart gives a value f to the relational good produced by the cooperative working activity, the no abuse condition becomes $2pf + e > h_a + h_b$. Hence, the Bayesian NE of the game is: (*i*) (*ns*, .) if $2pf + e < h_a + h_b$ and $h_a > h_b$; (*ii*) (*ns*, .) or (*s*, *a*) if $2pf + e < h_a + h_b$ and $h_a < h_b$; (*iii*) (*s*, *na*) if $2pf + e > h_a + h_b$. Hence, a 'threshold probability value' $p^{*\prime}$ exists, such that, when $p > p^{*\prime}$, the (share, not abuse) pair of strategies becomes the NE of the game. We can obtain $p^{*\prime}$ as $p^{*\prime} = \dfrac{h_a + h_b - e}{2}$. For $p^{*\prime} < 1$ we need $f^{*\prime} > \dfrac{h_a + h_b - e}{2p^{*\prime}}$. This implies a 'threshold value of the relational good under uncertainty' which is higher than its certainty correspondent (in which $p = 1$).

Let us consider now the second case of imperfect information related to the counterpart stand alone contribution. We may assume here that player A

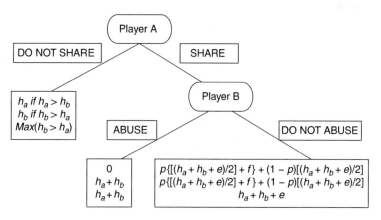

Figure 13.7   The uniperiodal game with imperfect information on trustee relational preferences

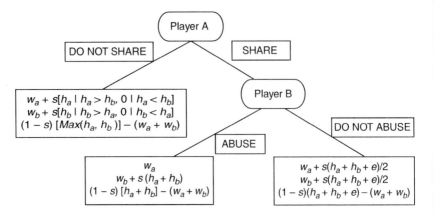

Figure 13.8   The uniperiodal full information game with pay for performance schemes

assigns a subjective probability p_1 ($p_1 \in [0,1]$) to the $h_a > h_b$ hypothesis, while
player B assigns a subjective probability p_2 ($p_2 \in [0,1]$) to the alternative $h_a < h_b$
hypothesis (see Figure 13.8). If we also assume that each player does not know
the guess of the other we easily find that the abuse condition is unaltered with
respect to the basic uniperiodal game. The intuition is obvious. The no abuse
condition compares two payoffs of two trustees (conditional to the abuse and
not abuse strategies respectively) under the assumption that the trustor has
decided to share information. In both cases the trustee payoff includes the sum
of the two players' contributions and therefore the relative superiority of one
of the two stand alone contributions does not matter. As a consequence, the
(*ns*, .) profile is the equilibrium when the super additive component is inferior
to the sum of the trustee and trustor stand alone contributions to output. An
interesting element in this new framework is that, when the trustee has higher
a stand alone contribution than the trustor, we do not have anymore two equilibria – (*s*, *na*) and (*ns*, .) – but only the (*ns*, .) equilibrium.[14]

5   Basic trust game when the players do not own the company

The more natural framework in which corporate trust games must be analyzed
consists of the interaction of employees who do not possess the firm. With the
exception of specialized professionals (such as engineers and architects), a large
firm in which wage-earning employees play many times and in many different situations corporate trust games should be our natural scenario. In such a
scenario we aim to evaluate what is the effect that traditional forms of incentives, such as individual pay for performance fees and tournament prizes, have
on workers' incentives when the sequential structure of workers' interactions,
discussed in the previous sections, is assumed.

We show that the assumption that players' interactions have the form of the corporate trust game is a sufficient condition for determining the relative inconvenience of single winner tournaments (or pay for performance schemes in the presence of worker's preference for relational goods). The novelty of our approach is that we do not need to consider crowding-out effects on intrinsic motivations to obtain this result. This is because: (*i*) when the activity of a firm is conceived as a trust game and, in presence of relational goods, a steeper pay for performance scheme increases the probability of non-cooperative equilibria for given parametric values; and (*ii*) the cooperative equilibrium can never be attained with the introduction of a single winner tournament scheme, even in the absence of relational goods. In the next two sections we show these two points.

5.1 Pay for performance schemes

Consider a standard performance-incentive structure, based on a fixed remuneration (w_a for player A, and w_b for player B), plus an additional share $s \in [0,1]$ of the employee's performance when the latter contributes to firm output. Within this framework we may easily observe that individual payments for performance schemes are neutral in corporate trust games in which players do not own the firm, as they do not help to widen the parametric space of the cooperative equilibrium. On the contrary, in presence of relational goods, a steeper pay for performance scheme may trigger the switch from a cooperative (productively optimal) to a non-cooperative (productively suboptimal) equilibrium and may therefore crowd out cooperation.

The set of payoffs is now

$$\{w_a + s(h_a|h_a > h_b, 0|h_a < h_b), w_b + s(h_b|h_a < h_b, 0|h_a > h_b), (1-s)Max[h_a, h_b] - w_a - w_b\}$$

under the (*ns*, .) pair of strategies, while it is

$$\{w_a, w_b + s(h_a + h_b), (1-s)(h_a + h_b) - w_a - w_b\} \quad \text{and}$$

$$\left\{ w_a + s\left(\frac{h_a + h_b + e}{2}\right), \; w_b + s\frac{h_a + h_b + e}{2}, \; (1-s)(h_a + h_b + e) - w_a - w_b \right\}$$

under the (*s, a*) and (*s, na*) pairs, respectively (see Figure 13.8).

Without relational goods the no abuse condition is unaltered, while, with relational goods, it becomes $e > h_a + h_b - 2\dfrac{F+f}{s}$. Hence, a steeper pay for performance fee (a higher s) raises the opportunity cost of the cooperation strategy and reduces the parametric space of the cooperation equilibria. In this sense our result provides a simple rationale to the puzzle evidenced, among others, by Baker, Jensen and Murphy (1998) on the relatively low use of individual pay for performance schemes in personnel management. We may easily observe that the negative effect of pay for performance fees on cooperative equilibria persists in the two-period games and in the infinitely repeated trust games.

In the two-period game the solution crucially depends again on the relative stand alone contributions. When we assume $h_a > h_b$ the 'no abuse' condition is $\delta > \dfrac{h_a + h_b - e}{h_a + h_b + e}$.[15]

Consider that, here again, the no abuse condition does not depend on s. The no abuse condition is $\delta > h_b + h_a\left(\dfrac{1-\delta}{1+\delta}\right)$, which may be easily satisfied under reasonable parametric assumptions.

Let us suppose now that $h_a < h_b$. In this case, the no abuse condition is $\dfrac{w_b + s(h_a + h_b + e)}{2}(1+\delta) > w_b + s(h_a + h_b) + \delta(w_b + sh_b)$ which reduces, again, to $e > h_a + h_b$, that is, the no abuse condition of single period full information game when the two players own the firm. Consider now the presence of relational goods in the two-period game (Figure 13.9).

Under $h_a > h_b$ the no abuse condition is

$$w_b + s(h_a + h_b) + \delta w_b < F + \left(\dfrac{f + w_b + s(h_a + h_b + e)}{2}\right)(1+\delta)$$

yielding

$$\delta > \dfrac{s(h_a + h_b - e) - 2F - 2f}{2f + s(h_a + h_b + e)}.$$

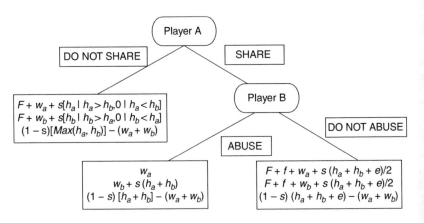

Figure 13.9 The uniperiodal full information game with relational goods and pay for performance schemes

Under $h_a < h_b$ the no abuse condition is

$$w_b + s(h_a + h_b) + \delta(w_b + sh_b) < F + \left[f + w_b + s\left(\frac{h_a + h_b + e}{2}\right)(1 + \delta)\right]$$

yielding

$$\delta > \frac{s(h_a + h_b - e) - 2F - 2f}{2f + s(h_a - h_b + e)}.$$

Hence we conclude that, even in the two-period game, steeper pay for performance schemes are neutral in the absence of relational goods, while they reduce the parametric space of cooperation in the presence of relational goods.

5.2 Firms with a vertical hierarchical structure

Promotions are another basic mechanism which increases employees' wages and create monetary rewards for their performance.[16] Let us consider in our case a basic tournament promotion system, in which the two players are at the same hierarchy level and the best performer in the corporate trust game gets the promotion. We also conveniently assume that, when the (s, na) equilibrium applies, the winner is randomly selected and each of the two players has a 50 per cent chance of getting the promotion.

It is trivial to check that, with the introduction of such a tournament promotion system in the corporate trust game, the no abuse condition never applies. If the trustor (player A) decides not to share his information, the payoff set is: $\{w_a + (PR|h_a > h_b, 0|h_a < h_b), w_b + (PR|h_a < h_b, 0|h_a > h_b), Max[h_a, h_b] - w_a - w_b - PR\}$ where PR is the promotion wage premium.

If the trustor decides to share, we have to consider the (s, a) and (s, na) pairs of strategies. In the first case, the payoff set is: $\{w_a, w_b + PR, h_a + h_b - w_a - w_b - PR\}$ while, in the second case, the payoff set is

$$\left\{w_a + \frac{PR}{2}, w_b + \frac{PR}{2}, h_a + h_b + e - w_a - w_b - PR\right\}.$$

Hence, the no abuse condition is $w_b + \dfrac{PR}{2} > w_b + PR$ and can never hold. As a consequence, when $h_a > h_b$, the $(ns, .)$ is the unique equilibrium of the game, while, when $h_a < h_b$, the trustor is indifferent between sharing or not and we have the two equilibria $(ns, .)$ and (s, a).

Quite interestingly, in this case, the presence of relational goods may partially mitigate this result. The payoff set will be (respectively for the trustor, the trustee and for the firm):

$$\{F + w_a + (PR|h_a > h_b, 0|h_b > h_a), F + w_b + (PR|h_a < h_b, 0|h_a > h_b),$$

$$Max[h_a, h_b] - w_a - w_b - PR\}.$$

If the trustor decides to share the idea, the payoff set is

$$\{w_a, w_b + PR, h_a + h_b - w_a - w_b - PR\} \text{ or}$$

$$\left\{ w_a + \frac{PR}{2} + F + f, w_b + \frac{PR}{2} + F + f, h_a + h_b - w_a - w_b - PR \right\}$$

under the (s, a) and (s, na) pairs of strategies respectively.

Hence, the no abuse condition is $F + f > \dfrac{PR}{2}$, and may now be respected in presence of a high stock or flow of relational goods.

6 Conclusions

Corporate social responsibility is not a free lunch. The debate around corporate social responsibility and corporate performance generally evidences a trade-off between on the one hand a higher degree of care for stakeholders other than shareholders and the economic performance of the firm, on the other hand the other the economic performance of the firm. In this chapter we show that this is not always the case by devising a possible virtuous circle between a specific type of corporate social responsibility (care for worker relationship) and performance. If we consider that the main feature of modern corporations is that most productive activities take the form of corporate trust games (that is, complex activities requiring the sequential interaction of workers with no overlapping skills) we find that the quality of relationships among workers may be crucial to avoid paradoxical 'third-best' outcomes and that individual pay for performance schemes or tournament structures may have counterintuitive effects. Hence, if the costs of investing in the quality of workers' relationships are lower than the output gains arising when passing from third-best to first-best productive solutions, a corporate social responsibility policy in this direction may identify a virtuous circle between social responsibility and efficiency. The assumptions and conclusions of our chapter are grounded on the observed empirical reality. The existence of relational preferences for co-workers is demonstrated by empirical evidence, while results of our model help to explain the puzzles of the lower than expected application of pay for performance schemes and the recent propensity of modern corporations to hire teams and to invest in the improvement of the working environment.

Finally, since under the different versions of the model we reasonably find that cooperative solutions become slightly easier in the case of repeated games, corporate trust games identify a novel limit for corporate turnover policies which consists of the reduction of the opportunities for developing relational goods and enforcing trust among workers.

Appendix

The relevance of relational goods in the workplace

In Becchetti et al. (2006), a sample of 82 countries from the World Value Survey has been selected and the following log it model has been estimated to evaluate the impact of different determinants of self declared happiness:[17]

$$Happy_i = \alpha_0 + \alpha_1 Eqincome + \alpha_2 Eqincome^2 + \alpha_3 Male$$
$$+ \alpha_4 Mideduc + \alpha_5 Upeduc + \alpha_6 Age + \alpha_7 Age^2$$
$$+ \alpha_8 Unempl + \alpha_9 Selfempl + \Sigma_{k=1}^{K} \vartheta_k Timeforrel_k$$
$$+ \Sigma_{j=1}^{J} \gamma Drelincome_j + \Sigma_i^I \varphi Marstatus_i$$
$$\Sigma_{l=1} \delta_l Dcountry_l$$

The dependent variable (*Happy*) is built on the answers to the following question – *All considered, you would say that you are: (i) very happy; (ii) pretty happy; (iii) not too happy; (iv) not happy at all* – by giving descending values (from 3 to zero) to answers (*i*) to (*iv*).

Eqincome is a continuous measure of (income class median) income expressed in year 2000 US dollar purchasing power parities, *Male* is a dummy which takes the value of one for men and zero otherwise. To measure the impact of education two dummies are included for individuals with high school diploma (*Mideduc*) and with university degree (*Upeduc*). *Age* is the respondent age (introduced in levels and in squares) to take into account nonlinearities in its relationship with happiness (see, among others, Alesina et al., 2001 and Frey and Stutzer, 2000). The professional status is measured by two different job condition variables, *Unempl* and *Selfempl*, recording unemployed and self-employed individuals respectively.

Timeforrel is a vector including a series of variables measuring the time spent: (*i*) with friends (*timefriends*); (*ii*) with working colleagues outside the workplace (*timejobfriends*); (*iii*) with the family (*timefamily*); (*iv*) in the worship place (parish, mosque, synagogue) with friends sharing the same religious confession (*timerelig*); (*v*) in clubs or volunteering (sport, culture, etc.) association (*timesportfriend*). For each of these questions the answers can be: (*i*) every week; (*ii*) once or twice a month; (*iii*) a few times per year; (*iv*) never. The difference among intensity modes is not continuous and we rank each of the answers on a scale with values which are increasing in the time spent for relationship (i.e., 3 if the answer is every week and 0 if it is never).[18] The relative income effect is calculated by introducing nine dummies (*Drelincome*) measuring individual position in the relevant domestic income decile. The four marital status (*Marstatus*) variables (*Single*, *Married*, *Divorced* and *Separated*) are all dummies taking the value of one if the individual has the given status and zero otherwise. Country dummies are also included.

The results (Table A13.1) show a positive and significant relationship between relational time spent with colleagues at work and individual happiness in the subsample of male, European Union and high-income OECD countries.

Table A13.1   The effect of relational time on happiness

Dependent Variable: Happiness	Male	Female	Hi-oecd	NoHi-oecd	European Union
Timefriends	0.052**	0.053**	0.162**	0.042**	0.056
	[0.023]	[0.021]	[0.048]	[0.016]	[0.113]
Timejobfriends	0.047**	–0.009	0.07**	0.013	0.169**
	[0.016]	[0.016]	[0.032]	[0.012]	[0.077]
Timefamily	0.055**	0.055	0.08**	0.051**	0.055
	[0.022]	[0.022]	[0.039]	[0.017]	[0.113]
Timerelig	0.138**	0.113**	0.155**	0.107**	0.135
	[0.017]	[0.016]	[0.031]	[0.012]	[0.078]
Timesportfriends	0.065**	0.058	0.088**	0.057**	0.14
	[0.017]	[0.019]	[0.03]	[0.014]	[0.078]

Notes

1. Thompson and Wallace (1996) conclude that team working has currently emerged as a central focus of redesigning production, due to the development of lean production and other forms of work organization under advanced manufacturing. Katz and Rosenberg (2004) emphasize that 'the productivity of an organization crucially depends on cooperation between workers' and underline the importance of altruistic and cooperative attributes in workers. This point of view is largely agreed in the organizational theory (see, among others, Smith et al. (1983), Organ (1988), Organ and Ryan (1995), McNeely and Meglino (1994), Penner et al. (1997) and Podsakoff and Mackenzie (1993).
2. Empirical evidence documents that, in 1988, 20 per cent of the US labour force (22 million employees) participated in over 400,000 workplace profit-sharing plans. Lawler (1971, p. 158) quotes six different works on the relationship between pay and performance, and finds that 'their evidence indicates that pay is not very closely related to performance in many organizations that claim to have merit increase salary systems. The studies suggest that many business organizations do not gain additional profit tying pay to performance. This conclusion is rather surprising in light of many companies' very frequent claims that their pay systems are based on merit.'
3. Regarding this point, a good example is an original initiative of one of the biggest Italian banks, Mediobanca, that finances weekend skiing holidays for its managers with the motivation that it 'makes the business more fluid'. In the US, the NRG Systems, a global manufacturer of wind measuring systems, received the 2004 Psychologically Healthy Workplace Award for small businesses from the Vermont Psychological Association (VPA) thanks to their overall workforce practices and benefits and the emphasis they have placed on creating a healthy workplace.

4. Note that in the paper we define as *cooperative solution* the equilibrium given by the share–not abuse pair of strategies (see Figure 13.1) and as *non-cooperative solutions* the two equilibria which do not imply the joint work of the two players. Hence, the term cooperative is not referred to the structure of the game (or to the coordination/non coordination of players decisions) but to the characteristics of its equilibrium.

5. The employment relationship may be characterized by complete or incomplete contracts. Under complete contracts, a cooperative job attitude would be superfluous because all relevant actions would be described and enforceable, while, under incomplete contracts, workers have a high degree of discretion over effort levels since no explicit performance incentives are defined. In this case reciprocity can be very important in the labour process since, if a substantial fraction of the work force is motivated by reciprocity considerations, employers can affect the degree of cooperation by varying the generosity of the compensation package.

6. Adam Smith (1759), in his publication 'The Theory of Moral Sentiments', may be considered one of the finest forerunners of this theory with his concept of 'fellow feelings'. His argument is that relational happiness increases in: (i) the amount of time and experiences that two individuals have lived together and have shared in the past; and (ii) their common consent, with the former significantly affecting the latter.

7. The rationales for a positive effect of the interaction are mainly two. First, part of productive skills may be acquired only by integrating experiences of different people. This is exactly the story of the wise man and the blind, where the blind asks the wise man what is an elephant. The wise man proposes them to go, touch it and report to each other. Every blind man comes back with a specific and unique knowledge of the elephant. When the different experiences are shared, the group of the blind comes up with a clearer idea of what is an elephant. The second rationale is that the super additive component may stem from the interaction, even though not directly by what learned from the other. As it is well known individuals clarify to themselves what they know about an issue in their effort of explaining it to others, often discovering and overcoming in this way inconsistencies and limits in their own concepts and reasoning.

8. The reasonable assumption is that, when the trustee abuses, he decides to do so before the cooperation between the two players starts. Therefore, $e = 0$.

9. Two intuitions stemming from this result are that: (i) non-cooperation will be more likely to occur when the trustor has higher skills; (ii) the cooperative solution is more likely to occur when the two players' stand alone contributions are small with respect to the output they can generate by dealing together with some issue (i.e. the task has complex rules that can be interpreted only by combining players' skills).

10. Note that if we would introduce some forms of inequity aversion of the type documented in experimental games and modelled by Fehr and Schmidt (1999) the trustor would strictly prefer the $(ns, .)$ solution as it would get a disutility increasing in the difference between the trustee and his output. In that case only the third best output would apply.

11. The implicit assumption here is that the trustee decision to abuse completely depletes the stock of accumulated relational goods, while the trustor decision not to share neither affects the stock nor it creates a new relational good. Under our assumptions, in presence of relational goods, the trustor will not be indifferent anymore between sharing or not when $h_a < h_b$ and the no abuse condition is not met since, by sharing, he will "induce into temptation" the counterpart with the risk of loosing the accumulated stock of relational goods. Hence, if $F > 0$ and $h_a < h_b$, the $(ns, .)$ is the only SPNE. In this case the introduction of relational goods may have negative effects since

the 'third-best' output is the only solution while, without relational goods, the two possibilities of a second best and third best output were equally available.

12. Consider that higher values of δ can also be viewed as a measure of the reduced distance between two consecutive stages of the game.

13. Remember that, also in this case, when the no abuse condition is not met, player A is still indifferent on whether to share or not and may still decide to share. We therefore have two SPNE, $(ns, .)$ and (s, a), both yielding suboptimal output for the firm. The output loss is respectively $(h_a + e)(1 + \delta)$ and $e(1 + \delta)$ under the assumption that player A reiterates the same strategy in the two periods.

14. This is because, under imperfect information on counterpart's skills, each player always attaches a non zero probability to the fact that his skills may be superior to those of the other player.

15. Note that, with $s = 1$ and $\delta = 0$, we get back to the no abuse condition of the full information single period game, while, with $s = 0$ and $\delta = 0$, to a single period fixed wage model.

16. The existing literature provides an extensive discussion of pros and cons of promotion-based incentives. Baker, Jensen and Murphy (1998) underline that promotion-based incentives: (i) do not work properly after promotion of a young employee with a long expected horizon in the job since this kind of promotions decrease the probability of future promotion and the incentive to work hard for co-workers; (ii) are reduced for employees that already obtained it; (iii) are absent for employees that fall short of the promotion standard; iv) generate problems in slowly growing or shrinking firms.

17. Reliability of self-declared happiness data is supported by Alesina et al. (2001) when they recall that psychologists extensively use these data. Alesina et al. (2001) also observe that there exists a well documented evidence of a positive correlation between self declared happiness and healthy physical reactions such as smiling attitudes (Pavot, 1991; Ekman et al., 1990), heart rate and blood pressure responses to stress (Shedler, Mayman and Manis, 1993), electroencephalogram measures of parefrontal brain activity (Sutton and Davidson, 1997) and of a negative correlation between the same variable and the attitude to commit suicide (Koivumaa-Honkanen et al., 2001).

18. By looking at the relationship between our indicator and the likely number of times per month spent in relationship which can be inferred from sample answers we figure out that our scale risks to flatten the actual frequency of the time spent in relationship. A robustness check in which we attribute an approximate per month frequency and use the value of 4, 1.5 and 0.3 for the 'every week', 'once or twice in a month' and 'a few times per year' answers respectively, shows that our findings are substantially unaltered. Results are available upon request.

References

Alesina, A., R. Di Tella and R. MacCulloch (2001) 'Inequality and Happiness: Are Europeans and Americans Different?', *NBER Working Paper* No. 8198. Cambridge, MA: NBER.

Ash, C. (2000) 'Social Self Interest', *Annals on Public and Cooperative Economics*, vol. 71(2), pp. 261–84.

Baker, G. M.C. Jensen and K.J. Murphy (1998) 'Compensation and Incentives: Practice vs. Theory', *Journal of Finance*, vol. 63(3), pp. 593–616.

Baker, G., R. Gibbons and K.J. Murphy (2002) 'Relational Contracts and the Theory of the Firm', *The Quarterly Journal of Economics*, vol. 117(1), pp. 39–84.

Becchetti, L., D.A. Londono-Bedoya and G. Trovato (2006) 'Income, Relational Goods and Happiness', CEIS Working Paper No. 227.

Benabou R. and J. Tirole (2003) 'Intrinsic and Extrinsic Motivation', *Review of Economic Studies*, vol. 70, pp. 489–520.

Bewley, T. (1995) 'A Depressed Labor Market as Explained by Participants', *American Economic Review Papers and Proceedings*, vol. 85, pp. 250–4.

Ekman, P. R. Davidson and W. Friesen (1990) 'The Duchenne Smile: Emotional Expression and Brain Physiology', *Journal of Personality and Social Psychology*, vol. 58, pp. 342–53.

Fehr, E. and K.M. Schmidt (1999) 'A Theory of Fairness, Competition and Cooperation', *Quarterly Journal of Economics*, vol. 114, pp. 817–51.

Fehr, E. and K.M. Schmidt (2005) 'The Economics of Fairness, Reciprocity and Altruism – Experimental Evidence and New Theories', *Discussion Papers in Economics* 726, University of Munich, Department of Economics.

Fehr, E. and S. Gächter (2000) 'Fairness and Retaliation: The Economics of Reciprocity', *Journal of Economic Perspectives*, vol. 14(3), pp. 159–81.

Fehr, E., S. Gächter and G. Kirchsteiger (1997) 'Reciprocity as a Contract Enforcement Device – Experimental Evidence', *Econometrica*, vol. 65, pp. 833–60.

Frey, B.S. (1997) 'On the Relationship Between Intrinsic and Extrinsic Work Motivation', *International Journal of Industrial Organization*, vol. 15, pp. 427–39.

Frey, B.S. and A. Stutzer (2000) 'Happiness, Economy and Institutions', *Economic Journal*, vol. 110, pp. 918–38.

Fudenberg, D. and D.K. Levine (1993) 'Steady State Learning and Nash Equilibrium', *Econometrica*, vol. 61, pp. 547–73.

Gui, B. (2000) 'Beyond Transactions: On the Interpersonal Dimension of Economic Reality', *Annals of Public and Cooperative Economics*, vol. 71, pp. 139–69.

Holmstrom B. and P. Milgrom (1994) 'The Firm as an Incentive System', *American Economic Review*, vol. 84(4), pp. 972–91.

Katz, E. and J. Rosenberg (2004) 'Reward Offered, No Questions Asked: An Analysis of Rewarded Theft', *Economica*, vol. 71, pp. 501–6.

Koivumaa-Honkanen, H., R. Honkanen, H. Viinamäki, K. Heikkilä, J. Kaprio and M. Koskenvuo (2001) 'Self-reported Life Satisfaction and 20-Year Mortality in Healthy Finnish Adults', *American Journal of Epidemiology*, vol. 152(10), pp. 983–91.

Kreps, D.M. (1997) 'Intrinsic Motivation and Extrinsic Incentives', *American Economic Review*, vol. 87(2), pp. 359–64.

Lawler, E.E. (1971) *Pay and Organizational Effectiveness: A Psychological View*. New York: McGraw-Hill.

Lazear, E.P. (1999) 'The Future of Personnel Economics', Working Paper presented in the IZA European Summer Symposium in Labour Economics.

McNeely, B.L. and B.M. Meglino (1994) 'The Role of Dispositional and Situational Antecedents in Prosocial Organizational Behavior: An Examination of the Intended Beneficiaries of Prosocial Behavior', *Journal of Applied Psychology*, vol. 79, pp. 836–44.

Organ, D.W. (1988) *Organizational Citizenship Behavior: The Good Soldier Syndrome*. Lexington, MA: Lexington.

Organ, D.W. and K. Ryan (1995) 'A Meta-analytic Review of Attitudinal and Dispositional Predictors of Organizational Citizenship Behavior', *Personnel Psychology*, vol. 48, pp. 775–802.

Pavot, W. (1991) 'Further Validation of the Satisfaction with Life Scale: Evidence for the Convergence of Well-being Measures', *Journal of Personality Assessment*, vol. 57, pp. 149–61.

Penner, L.A., A.R. Midili and J. Kegelmeyer (1997) 'Beyond Job Attitudes: A Personality and Social Psychology Perspective on the Causes of Organizational Citizenship Behavior', *Human Performance*, vol. 10(2), pp. 111–31.

Podsakoff, P.M. and S.B MacKenzie (1993) 'Citizenship Behavior and Fairness in Organizations: Issues and Directions for Future Research', *Employee Responsibilities and Rights Journal*, vol. 6, pp. 257–69.

Sen, A.K. (1977) 'Rational Fools: A Critique of the Behavioral Foundations of Economic Theory', *Philosophy and Public Affairs*, 6(4): 317–44.

Sen, A. (1997) 'Inequality, Unemployment and Contemporary Europe', STICERD – Development Economics Papers 07, Suntory and Toyota International Centres for Economics and Related Disciplines, LSE.

Shedler, J., M. Mayman and M. Manis (1993) 'The Illusion of Mental Health', *American Psychologist*, vol. 48, pp. 1117–31.

Smith, A. (1759) [1981] 'The Theory of Moral Sentiments', edited by D.D. Raphel and A.L. Macfie. Indianapolis: Liberty Found.

Smith, C.A., D.W. Organ and J.P. Near (1983) 'Organizational Citizenship Behavior: Its Nature and Antecedents', *Journal of Applied Psychology*, vol. 68, pp. 653–63.

Sutton, S.K. and R.J. Davidson (1997) 'Prefrontal Brain Asymmetry: A Biological Substrate of the Behavioral Approach and Inhibition Systems', *Psychological Science*, vol. 8, pp. 204–10.

Thompson, P. and T. Wallace (1996) 'Redesigning Production Through Teamwork', *International Journal of Operations and Production Management*, vol. 16, pp. 103–18.

Uhlaner, C.J. (1989) 'Relational Goods and Participation: Incorporating Sociability into a Theory of Rational Action', *Public Choice*, vol. 62, pp. 253–85.

14
Effects of Different Stakeholder Groups' Strategic Control on Organizational Effectiveness and Well-Being of Customers and Employees: An Empirical Investigation*

Avner Ben-Ner and Ting Ren

1 Introduction

The allocation of strategic decision-making authority in an organization has both efficiency and distributional effects. Effective allocation takes into account the availability of information and knowledge relevant to decision-making in different areas, and is supported by adequate incentives for decision-makers. Irrespective of how and why they obtained their decision-making roles, those with decision-making power will likely seek to affect outcomes in favor of their objectives, which includes their own well-being or that of groups or goals they favor.

This chapter examines the effects of participation in decision-making on strategic matters by different groups of stakeholders – employees, executives, community representatives, owners and customers – on organizational efficiency and the well-being of two key stakeholder groups, customers and employees. This is the first study to examine the impact of decision-making by various stakeholder groups on such outcomes. We focus on a narrowly defined industry, nursing homes for the elderly, in a single state in the US, Minnesota, in order to minimize unobserved heterogeneity in industry characteristics, legal, cultural and social influences and geographic conditions, and in order to be able to study for-profit, nonprofit and government organizations that operate side by side in the same industry and market. The nursing homes industry is particularly interesting because customers – elderly residents – are frail and

* We thank the Aspen Institute for funding this research. We are grateful to Carlo Borzaga and Ermanno Tortia for their helpful comments.

vulnerable and therefore cannot evaluate very well the care they receive and lack the strongest elements that are required for market competition, 'voice' and 'exit'. Residents cannot in general be effective advocates for their own care and are unable to shop before and after entering a home: entry to a home usually follows an incident or accident that renders a person unable to care for him or herself, and once a person is in a nursing home, he or she is substantially immobile. Family and friends are often in a fiduciary role (in the legal sense), but they are rarely present in a nursing home long enough to witness the nature and quality of care provided. In these circumstances corporate social responsibility (CSR) is a particularly powerful concept.

We analyze a cross-section of nursing homes that responded to a detailed survey instrument that was mailed to all Minnesota nursing homes, using information from the survey and additional sources. The dataset provides rich information on organizational characteristics, decision-making participation by stakeholder groups, organizational outcomes, and residents' and employees' well-being. We examine the relationship between strategic decision-making held by one or more stakeholder groups and organizational efficiency, and the well-being of employees and residents. We find that the identity of stakeholders who hold strategic control powers matters to these outcomes. Different stakeholder groups have different effects on the three sets of outcomes considered in this essay, and which groups promote CSR most depends on one's definition of CSR.

The chapter is organized as follows. In section 2 we develop a theoretical framework for understanding the role of different groups of stakeholders in generating differential outcomes. Section 3 presents the data and the variables used in the empirical analysis, which is developed in section 4. In section 5 we detail the results of the empirical analysis, and in section 6 we discuss the implications of our findings for stakeholder theory and offer some conclusions.

2   Conceptual framework

2.1   The stakeholder paradigm

For a long time now the question 'Who controls?' has exercised the minds of many researchers and practitioners in a variety of business specialisms. From Adam Smith (1776) to Berle and Means (1932) and to recent debates on corporate social responsibility, it has been argued that lack of accountability, usually meaning excessive decision-making held by executives, leads to the pursuit of the interests of empowered executives at the expense of other stakeholders: small shareholders, employees, customers, and the public at large. In recent years, there has been an increased public demand on organizations to serve broader interests and to incorporate the goals of various stakeholders other than just major shareholders and top management. There are diverse reasons for the demands for increased corporate social responsibility, from exploitation by high-level corporate executives of employees, consumers, small shareholders, regulators, and the public at large, to concerns expressed in many countries that globalization will lead to the purchase of local companies by multinational ones, resulting in corporate goals that ignore certain stakeholders such as employees, the public, and anybody else who does not have a seat at the decision-making table. The most talked-about case of Enron is an illustration of the first case of alleged corporate social irresponsibility, whereas numerous firms in every corner of the developed and underdeveloped world whose ownership changed in recent years are considered examples of the elimination of concern for stakeholders other than executives and the major shareholders.

Stakeholders are defined broadly as 'persons or groups that have, or claim, ownership, rights, or interests in a corporation and its activities, past, present, or future' (Clarkson, 1995: 106). Many who think of the concept of stakeholders restrict this definition in some dimensions by limiting the types of claims, rights, time horizon, and so forth to the effect that only shareholders, longtime workers, steady customers and suppliers, and the community in which an organization operates are considered. In a society that emphasizes the well-being of multiple stakeholders, which we may call a 'stakeholder society' (Giddens, 1998), management may be expected to maximize social welfare defined as the sum of the various stakeholders' surpluses, and not just the maximization of shareholders' profits or executives' benefits or even the standard definition of social welfare that includes profits and consumer surplus.[1] However, such demands are commonly stated in vague terms, without specifying the weight to be attached to the goals of diverse stakeholder groups or even who those stakeholders might be. The demands are anchored in the presumed fiduciary duty of management to stakeholders, the civil responsibility of organizations to avoid exploitation of negative externalities and monopoly power, and other precepts derived from various ethical and religious perspectives (see, for example, Freeman, 1999; Goodpaster, 1991; Blair, 1995; and Bowie, 1991). In some countries there is, or has been in the recent past, a cultural norm of organizations serving multiple stakeholders (for example, Aoki, 1984, reflecting Japanese practices), and in other places attempts are made to bring representatives of stakeholder groups at the national and supranational levels to discuss means to implement elements of a stakeholder society. But to achieve the goal of some sort of social welfare maximization at the firm level, a stakeholder society should have concrete mechanisms for *allocating organizational control* across various groups of stakeholders rather than expect executives to act as if they cared about diverse stakeholder groups (Tirole, 2001).

2.2 Strategic control by stakeholders

The identity of those stakeholders with strategic control in an organization is important, because control permits them to steer the organization in pursuit of their own objectives. The roles of different stakeholders may be ingrained in an organization's makeup as a result of a balance of power, although it is possible that stakeholders with ultimate control may voluntarily engage other stakeholders in strategic decision-making, either because of their specialized information and knowledge, because they want their organization to pursue also the goals of those stakeholders, or because they accede to certain social norms or political demands.

What are the goals of different stakeholders, such as owners, executives, employees, customers, boards of directors, suppliers and community? They may have different motivations, along with the pursuit of self-interest. Such divergent motivations may be present in any type of organization, although some authors ascribe them more to members of nonprofit organizations (for example, Rose-Ackerman, 1996; Grimalda & Sacconi, 2005) and perhaps of government agencies than of for-profit firms. Some shareholders, such as pension funds and trade unions, may demand that organizations in which they have substantial holdings conform to certain practices that reflect their social preferences. Social preferences are not unique. They mean generally favorable treatment of other stakeholders but no specific weights attached to the well-being of other stakeholders can be specified in general.

Which stakeholder groups are likely to exhibit greater social responsibility? Can favorable treatment be afforded simultaneously to more than one group, when there are common resource constraints that limit what an organization can do? To examine these related questions, consider the potential objectives of different stakeholder groups that may hold strategic decision-making power. By strategic decision-making power we mean the ability to make decisions that affect fundamentally the nature of an organization's current and future activities, including the nature of its product in terms of its specifications, quantity and quality and major changes in it, expansion of the productive capacity, and the hiring of executives and key employees. We focus on stakeholder groups that exist potentially in any organization; hence our analysis is not specific to nursing homes, although we will illustrate the concepts with examples from nursing homes.

The groups that often hold strategic decision-making power are top executives and owners (individually, collectively as shareholders, or as parent organizations). Groups of key employees may be accorded or may attain considerable decision-making power over strategic decisions that are beyond the scope of their daily tasks; for example, such employees include, in some organizations, faculty in a university, engineers in a software company, physicians in a medical clinic, lawyers in a law firm, and registered nurses in a nursing home. Boards of directors have formal, although not always actual, strategic decision-making power. Thus there are variations in the distribution of strategic decision-making power, which may be held exclusively by a single group or shared with other groups. For example, executives and owners often jointly hold dominant strategic positions in an organization.

Another source of variation in objectives that may be associated with the identity of strategic decision-makers is the type of organization, i.e., for-profit, nonprofit or government. The general objective of for-profit firms is profit maximization. Nonprofit organizations usually pursue the well-being of some beneficiaries, whereas government organizations often pursue redistributive goals. The difference of organizational mission may influence the distribution of decision-making power across stakeholder groups.

2.3   Theoretical framework and hypotheses

The standard *shareholder model* states that a firm's objective is to maximize shareholder value, and any concern for other stakeholders detected in a firm's behavior results from reward to inputs or similar concerns, or explicit consideration of CSR (Harrison & Freeman, 1999; Berman, Wicks, Kotha & Jones, 1999). In an alternative *stakeholder model* the firm seeks to maximize stakeholder value, which is a function that attaches varying weights to the objectives of different stakeholder groups. This weighted function is derived from the weight of strategic decision-making power held by various groups. Whereas management is just an agent in the shareholder value model, in the stakeholder-value model management is one of the groups that compete for the allocation of control on an organization's strategic decision-making. The result of the competition will impact the organization's overall performance and the well-being of each stakeholder group.

Although the allocation of strategic decision-making is driven substantially by an organization's internal forces, it is also influenced by external factors beyond the organization's control. In particular, the economic and legal systems may affect which stakeholder groups have control.

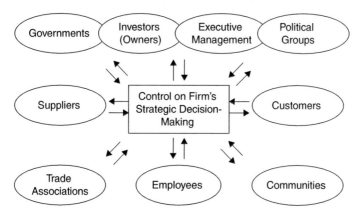

Figure 14.1   Stakeholder model of allocation of organizational strategic decision-making
Source: Adapted from Donaldson & Preston (1995)

Irrespective of their goals, all stakeholder groups have an interest in maximizing organizational efficiency because the larger the size of the pie afforded by efficiency, the greater the well-being they can derive from the organization. However, strategic control by some stakeholders may be inherently inefficient if they do not have the skill or information to exercise it efficiently. This problem can be ameliorated by joint control with another group, particularly high-level managers, with one stakeholder group advocating objectives of their liking while engaging managers to ensure efficiency. Efficiency losses may also be incurred due to struggles among stakeholder groups that may prevent the choice of best decisions (Ben-Ner, 1993). The foregoing discussion has several implications, which may be summarized as follows:

(I)   Stakeholder groups are likely to use decision-making power in favor of their own or their favored stakeholder groups' objectives; hence control by different groups will have a different impact on the well-being of customers and employees. We may surmise that: (1) executives will favor themselves, but with a strong professional ethic many will be champions of customers; (2) employees will favor themselves, and also, driven by professional norms, customers; (3) community representatives' interest in a nursing home is likely to focus on customers; (4) owners' interests depend on the form of organization, with for-profit owners caring about profit, and nonprofit and government focusing primarily on customers; and (5) customers care principally about their own well-being.

(II) Information about organizational strategic issues and ability to deal effectively with such issues is distributed asymmetrically across stakeholder groups, hence (a) the efficiency of stakeholder control is likely to vary across groups, and with it will vary organizational effectiveness, and, all things equal (b) reduced organizational efficiency will cause a reduction in the well-being of all stakeholders. We may further surmise that: (1) executives will promote efficiency effectively, although if left to make strategic decisions alone, they might be less focused on efficiency than if monitored by a strategic partner; (2) employees will promote organizational efficiency, if they have the information and incentives to do so; (3) community representatives are generally not placed very well to emphasize efficiency, if they have sole strategic control; (4) owners promote efficiency best if they have executives as their informed and capable partners; and (5) customers, whether residents or their families, are in general least well placed to run an organization efficiently, because knowledge and information about pertinent issues are not available to them in a direct manner.

(III) The interests of different stakeholder groups are often in competition with each other. In organizations that are managed efficiently, there will be a manifest trade-off among the measures of well-being of different groups but not so in inefficient organizations.

In this chapter, we examine organizational efficiency as a measure of the size of the total pie available for distribution among all the stakeholders of a nursing home, and the well-being of two key stakeholder groups: customers and employees. We investigate how these outcomes are affected by differences in the degree of strategic control, if any, held by employees, executives, community representatives, owners and customers, either alone or in combination with other groups.

3   Data and variables

The study focuses on a narrowly defined industry, nursing homes for the elderly, in a single US state, Minnesota. A nursing home is a residence for elderly people who have physical or mental problems that prevent them from living on their own. A nursing home provides residents with a room, meals and assistance with their daily activities as well as a level of medical care that is less intense than that provided in a hospital. The average nursing home in the US has about 100 beds, ranging from approximately 25 to 500 beds. Most nursing homes operate independently and separately from hospitals, but nearly one-tenth of them are affiliated with a hospital. Some nursing homes specialize in different types of care or medical conditions, but the majority of homes have residents with diverse medical conditions and ages. Nursing homes are operated as for-profit firms, nonprofit organizations and as government-owned organizations, and may be independent or part of a chain. Nursing homes are subject to state health regulations and to federal Centers for Medicare and Medicaid regulations[2] that prescribe certain minimum practices concerning care, housing, food and other aspects of nursing home living as well as collect information about residents, staff, quality of care and other matters, and perform unannounced inspections to ensure compliance with regulation.

3.1   Data

The data are drawn from three primary sources: (1) the Minnesota Nursing Homes Employer Survey – Structure and Behavior (MNHES); (2) the Online Survey, Certification, and Reporting database managed by the federal Centers for Medicare & Medicaid Services (OSCAR); and (3) the Minnesota Department of Human Services (DHS). We also obtained information about the area in which a nursing home is located from the 2000 US Census.

The survey was administered in late 2005 to all 409 nursing homes identified in the OSCAR database (follow-up surveys were mailed to non-respondents twice in the spring of 2006), with 120 homes responding, for a response rate of 29 per cent.[3] Four homes did not provide information on key variables, and one home was dropped because it had unique features, so the working sample is 115; the actual number of observations used in regression estimations is smaller due to missing observations for some variables. The survey was

Table 14.1 Description and sources of variables[1]

	Description	Mean[2] (s.d.)	Sources[3]
Dependent variables			
Resident's well-being			
1. Resident satisfaction/quality of life	Resident's rating of overall satisfaction with the quality of life in the nursing home	9.83 (0.29)	DHS
2. Quality of service	Rating of overall home quality by the state department of human services	24.75 (4.61)	DHS
3. Deficiency citations	Number of deficiency citation in the most recent nursing home inspection	13.23 (7.94)	OSCAR
4. Back pressure sores	Percentage of long-stay high-risk residents having back pressure sores	4.60 (4.96)	OSCAR
Employee's well-being			
5. Employee–management relationship	Employee–management relationship compared to other organizations (Five-point scale)	3.91 (0.81)	MNHES
6. Wage of CNAs	Hourly wage of certified nursing assistants	11.16 (1.48)	MNHES
7. Workload of CNAs	Degree of certified nursing assistant's workload (Five-point scale)	4.09 (0.74)	MNHES
Organizational effectiveness			
8. Development of new services	Performance of developing new services compared to other organizations (Five-point scale)	3.65 (0.87)	MNHES
9. Ability to retain essential employees	Performance of retaining essential employees compared to other organizations (Five-point scale)	3.84 (0.86)	MNHES
Independent variables			
Level of decision-making control by stakeholders (five-point scale)			
10. Employee	Level of employee's participation in decision-making (Average of the four strategic decision-making items)	2.31 (0.62)	MNHES

	of the four strategic decision-making items)	1.86 (0.58)	MNHES
12. Community	Level of board of directors and community representative's participation in decision-making (Average of the four strategic decision-making items)	2.20 (0.91)	MNHES
13. Owner	Level of owner's participation in decision-making (Average of the four strategic decision-making items)	3.44 (1.42)	MNHES
14. Executive	Level of executive director's participation in decision-making (Average of the three strategic decision-making items)	4.01 (1.02)	MNHES
Exclusive control (dummy variables)			
15. Owner	Whether owners have *exclusive* control	7.83	MNHES
16. Executive	Whether executive directors have *exclusive* control	14.78	MNHES
17. Community	Whether board of directors or community representatives have *exclusive* control	2.61	MNHES
Joint exclusive control (dummy variables)			
18. Employees and executives	Whether employees and executive directors have *joint exclusive* control	1.74	MNHES
19. Residents and executives	Whether residents and their families and executive directors have *joint exclusive* control	0.87	MNHES
20. Community and owners	Whether board of directors and community representatives and owners have *joint exclusive* control	0.87	MNHES
21. Community and executives	Whether board of directors and community representatives and executive directors have *joint exclusive* control	11.30	MNHES
22. Owners and executives	Whether owners and executive directors have *joint exclusive* control	26.09	MNHES
23. Employees, executives, and owners	Whether employees, owners and executive directors have *joint exclusive* control	0.87	MNHES
24. Employees, executives, and community	Whether employees, board of directors and community representatives, and executive directors have *joint exclusive* control	2.61	MNHES
25. Executives, owners and community	Whether executive directors, owners, board of directors and community representatives have *joint exclusive* control	18.26	MNHES

(Continued)

Table 14.1 (Continued)

	Description	Mean[2] (s.d.)	Sources[3]
26. Executives, owners, community and employees	Whether executive directors, owners, board of directors and community representatives, and employees have *joint exclusive* control	1.74	MNHES
27. Executives, owners, community and residents	Whether executive directors, owners, board of directors and community representatives, and residents have *joint exclusive* control	0.87	MNHES
Control variables			
28. For-profit dummy	1- for-profit 0- otherwise	21.74	OSCAR
29. Nonprofit chain dummy	1- nonprofit chain 0-otherwise	33.04	OSCAR
30. Nonprofit autonomous dummy	1- nonprofit autonomous 0-otherwise	26.96	OSCAR
31. Government dummy	1- government 0- otherwise	18.26	OSCAR
32. Employees' belief in organization mission	Level of employees' belief in organizational mission (average of an eight-item five-point scale)	3.94 (0.58)	MNHES
33. Case mix index	Level of overall resident acuity of the nursing home with a state average of 1.01	1.00 (0.09)	DHS
34. Hospital affiliation	1- if the facility reports affiliation with a hospital 0- otherwise	15.74	OSCAR
35. Percentage of Medicare residents		11.86 (13.46)	OSCAR

#	Variable	Description	Mean (SD)	Source
36.	Herfindahl–Hirschman Index in county area	The total number of residents of all the nursing homes within a county is used as the proxy of market demand in the county, and the ratio of number of residents of each nursing home to the total market demand is computed as the measure of each home's market share. Each home's HHI is calculated by using the standard formula $HHI = \sum_{i=1}^{n} S_i^2$. (Range from 0 to 10,000 with 10,000 indicating monopoly).	2467.94 (1654.26)	ZIP code
37.	Per capita income in the ZIP code area (thousands)		20.19 (6.14)	2000 Census
Variables for production function				
38.	Log of total number of residents		4.20 (0.49)	OSCAR
39.	Log of total number of licensed nursing hours per day (*RNs* and *LPNs*)		4.47 (0.50)	OSCAR
40.	Log of total number of certified nursing assistant hours per day (*CNAs*)		5.04 (0.51)	OSCAR

Notes: 1. The statistics refers to the sample of 115 nursing homes.
2. Means of dummy variables are in percentage.
3. MNHES – Minnesota Nursing Home Survey
OSCAR – **Online Survey, Certification and Reporting data of nursing facilities**, maintained by the Centers for Medicare and Medicaid Services (CMS)
DHS – Minnesota State Department of Human Services

addressed to nursing home administrators and asked for wide-ranging information concerning ownership, residents, revenues, comparison with other nursing homes, the wages of nursing staff, workload of employees, human resource practices, attitudes of nursing employees, participation in decision-making on various issues by diverse groups, and more. OSCAR data provide information about nursing home capacity, nursing inputs, violation of regulations, health condition of residents, and more. DHS data include information from a resident satisfaction survey, and indicators of service quality assessed by professional surveyors.

3.2   Variables

The variables discussed in this section are described in Table 14.1.

3.2.1   *Dependent variables*

The study is concerned with the effect of stakeholder participation in decision-making on three types of outcomes: the well-being of residents, the well-being of employees, and organizational effectiveness. In recognition of the fact that well-being and effectiveness have multiple dimensions that may compete with each other, we used multiple variables to characterize each type of outcome.

Resident well-being was measured using four variables: resident satisfaction with the quality of life in the nursing home; quality indicator of the home; deficiency citations; and the percentage of residents having back pressure sores. The *resident satisfaction rating*, obtained through interviews conducted by DHS with a sample of residents in each nursing home, was aggregated from a variety of resident satisfaction and perception of quality of life measures such as comfort, environmental adaptations, privacy, dignity, and other measures. The *quality of service indicator* is also an index composed from items evaluated by DHS concerning resident quality of life, continence problems and their treatment, infections, accidents, nutrition and more, adjusted for resident age, gender, cognitive performance, Alzheimer's disease, stroke, functional ability and more in order to control for factors that may affect residents' quality of life (Minnesota Department of Health and Human Services, 2006). The *deficiency citations* variable represents violations identified by regulators of over 150 regulatory standards that nursing homes must meet at all times, covering a wide range of aspects of resident life from standards for the safe storage and preparation of food to protection of residents from physical or mental abuse and inadequate care practices. The *proportion of residents having back pressure sores* is reported by nursing homes (and is included in OSCAR). A pressure sore is a skin wound usually caused by constant pressure on one part of the skin when residents remain in the same position in bed, chair or wheelchair for a long time, due to improper nutrition or ineffective preventive care. For reasons of data availability, we focused on high-risk long-stay residents.

Employee well-being was measured by three variables that are reported in MNHES: management–employee relations, the wages of certified nursing assistants, and the workload of these employees. Nursing homes were asked to compare their management–employee relations to other nursing homes in Minnesota over a three-year period. Use was made of a five-point scale, ranging from 1 (much worse) to 5 (much better).[4] Certified nursing assistants' workload was measured by a single item, 'How demanding is your employees' workload?' Possible responses ranged from 1 (very low) to 5 (very high) on a five-point scale.

Organizational effectiveness was measured by two variables: the organization's self-evaluation of its performance on developing new services, and of its ability to retain essential employees, as compared to other nursing homes in Minnesota over the past three years. These measures are likely to reflect on the ability of an organization to be dynamic and compete for its most important resource, employees, and as such on organizational effectiveness. However, they suffer from the bias inherent in the self-evaluation of performance, with a likely upward bias and limited variation, making it difficult to differentiate among organizations. To gain additional insight into possible differences in organizational effectiveness and indeed efficiency, we also estimate a production function.

3.2.2 Independent variables

The independent variables capture different stakeholder groups' influence over an organization's strategic decision-making. The stakeholder groups include executive director, owners/representatives of the parent organization, nursing staff, supervisors of nursing staff, residents, residents' families or other agents, board of directors, and community representatives. The nursing staff consists of registered nurses (RNs), licensed practicing nurses (LPNs) and certified nursing assistants (CNAs). We narrowed these eight stakeholder groups down to five to reflect broad types of organizational control: executive control (executive director), owner control (owners or representatives of parent organization), employee control (RNs, LPNs, CNAs or their supervisors), resident control (residents or their families/agents), and community control (board of directors or community representatives). The four items that reflect strategic decision-making are the degree to which members of a group influences the hiring of executive director, expansion of facilities, change in the services on offer, and the determination of standards for the care of residents, with possible responses ranging from 1 (not at all) to 5 (extreme). We used the average of these four items to measure the level of decision-making control by each stakeholder group, with the exception of executive control, in measuring which we used only the last three items (variables 10–14 in Table 14.1). As expected, executives' level of decision-making control is the highest among all the stakeholder groups (4.01 of the five-point scale with a standard deviation of 1.02), followed by owners (3.44), employees (2.31), community (2.20), and residents (1.86).

Next we constructed a classification of organizations according to how many groups have dominant control in an organization and the identity of those groups; we refer to this as *exclusive control*. To do this we first classified the degree of influence of each group as *dominant control* if the underlying scores were 4 (large) or 5 (extreme) on at least three of the four strategic decision-making items. For executive control we considered dominance on at least two items, excluding the hiring of executive director. Owners have exclusive control in 8 per cent of nursing homes (variable 15 in Table 14.1), executives in 15 per cent (variable 16), and community in 3 per cent (variable 17). There are no organizations in which employees or residents (or their families) have exclusive control. Executives have joint dominant control with employees in 2 per cent of homes (variable 18), with residents in 1 per cent (variable 19), with community in 11 per cent (variable 21), with owners in 26 per cent (variable 22), with employees and owners in 1 per cent (variable 23), with employees and community in 3 per cent (variable 24), with owners and community in 18 per cent (variable 25), with owners, community and employees in 2 per cent (variable 26), and with owners, community and residents in 1 per cent (variable 27), whereas community and owners have joint exclusive control in just 1 percent of homes (variable 20). All other possible combinations of joint control are absent inform our sample. No group held exclusive control in about 10 per cent of nursing homes. To account for the effect that employee or resident participation in jointly exclusive control may exert on the effectiveness of the home and the well-being of the key stakeholders, we also include a dummy variable for these nursing homes that incorporates variables 18, 19, 23, 24, 26 and 27.

3.2.3 Control variables

The control variables include a set of dummy variables for ownership status: independent nonprofit nursing home, chain-affiliated nonprofit home, for-profit home (we have too few observations on for-profit homes to make the independent–chain distinction) and government homes (we use for-profit homes as the reference group in the estimation of the full sample, and independent nonprofit homes in the estimation of the nonprofit sub-sample). In addition, we control for hospital affiliation, the percentage of Medicare patients, the case mix of residents, market competition in the county area measured by the Herfindahl–Hirschman Index, per capita income in the home's ZIP code area, and the degree to which employees share the organization's values. The values variable is the weighted (by employment share) average of the responses to survey questions asking to evaluate RNs', LPNs', CNAs' and supervisors' belief in the mission of the organization, and whether they considered working for the organization as just a job (reverse scoring).

4 Empirical strategy

We use OLS for estimations with continuous dependent variables, ordered logit (referred to as 'ologit' in tables) for variables on a five-point scale to account for the fact that the scale is ordinal, and negative binomial estimation for the deficiency citation and back pressure sores variables, which have skewed and overly dispersed distributions. For the production function we employed a Cobb–Douglas specification, with the number of residents as output and the number of working hours per day by the nursing staff (RNs and LPNs combined and of CNAs) as inputs, augmented by the decision-making and control variables that are used in all other analyses. We have no data about other (non-nursing) labor inputs, or about capital and material costs. We do have the total cost of labor and total revenue and experimented with alternative definitions of inputs; the estimates for the variables of interest are very similar to those presented in Table 14.4.

We also carry out separate analyses for nonprofit nursing homes, which account for 60 per cent of the 115 nursing homes our analyses are based on (69 homes), to investigate whether the effects of different stakeholder groups vary with the type of organization. (A detailed analysis of differences in performance across difference types of organization can be found in Ben-Ner and Ren, 2007.) For each dependent variable we use two different specifications, one employing the concept of level of decision-making control, and the other the concept of exclusive control.

5 Results

Tables 14.2, 14.3 and 14.4 present the results for resident well-being, employee well-being and organizational effectiveness, respectively.[5] Each table presents the two specifications for the entire sample (where the for-profit dummy is the excluded variable) and for nonprofit nursing homes alone.

5.1 Resident well-being

We consider first the two measures derived from survey responses and then move to the two measures obtained from external agencies. Table 14.2 indicates that resident satisfaction and quality of services are fairly well determined and similar variables explain the relatively small differences in these resident well-being measures across nursing homes. Owner control generally has negative effect on the two well-being measures (Specification I), especially owner control on quality of services ($p < 0.05$) in nonprofit homes. Community control is positively related to resident satisfaction, especially in nonprofit homes ($p < 0.05$). Employee control is positively related to the quality of services, particularly in nonprofit homes ($p < 0.05$). Resident control has no significant or

Table 14.2 Resident well-being

	Resident satisfaction (OLS)				Quality of services (OLS)			
	I		II		I		II	
	All	Nonprofit	All	Nonprofit	All	Nonprofit	All	Nonprofit
Employee control	-0.04	-0.01			0.37	2.17**		
	(0.07)	(0.08)			(1.15)	(1.06)		
Resident control	0.01	0.01			1.31	-0.50		
	(0.06)	(0.07)			(1.22)	(1.40)		
Community control	0.09	0.13**			0.20	0.10		
	(0.04)	(0.06)			(0.74)	(0.83)		
Owner control	-0.04	-0.04			-0.42	-0.77**		
	(0.02)	(0.03)			(0.39)	(0.35)		
Executive control	0.01	-0.01			0.30	0.08		
	(0.03)	(0.04)			(0.62)	(0.58)		
Community exclusive control			0.08	0.14			-1.96	-1.86
			(0.15)	(0.18)			(2.19)	(2.31)
Owner exclusive control			-0.07	0.19			-1.81	1.06
			(0.19)	(0.18)			(1.91)	(1.97)
Executive exclusive control			0.03	0.00			-0.09	0.97
			(0.18)	(0.21)			(1.64)	(2.10)
Owner and executive joint exclusive control			-0.01	0.06			-1.12	-1.34
			(0.15)	(0.17)			(1.52)	(2.12)
Community and executive joint exclusive control			0.07	0.24			0.47	1.06
			(0.16)	(0.15)			(1.51)	(2.04)

Executive, owner and community joint exclusive control			0.06	0.17			-0.55	-0.36
			(0.15)	(0.18)			(1.83)	(2.44)
Employee or resident participation in joint exclusive control			0.03	0.06			1.30	0.55
			(0.16)	(0.19)			(1.74)	(2.17)
Control variables	Yes	Yes	Yes	Yes	Yes	Yes	Yes	Yes
N	94	58	94	58	94	58	94	58
F	2.81	2.94	1.12	1.55	1.61	2.65	1.30	1.29
Prob > F	0.00	0.01	0.36	0.14	0.10	0.01	0.22	0.25
R-squared	0.20	0.27	0.14	0.24	0.16	0.28	0.14	0.25

Notes: 1. Numbers in parentheses are robust standard errors. *, ** and *** indicate significance at the 10%, 5%, and 1% levels, respectively.

2. We control for hospital affiliation, proportion of Medicare residents, Herfindahl–Hirschman Index in the county area, per capita income in the ZIP code area, and employees' belief in organization mission. We also control for organization's ownership type (when estimating the full sample we include nonprofit chain, nonprofit autonomous and government, with for-profit as the reference group; in the nonprofit sub-sample we include nonprofit chain, with nonprofit autonomous as the reference group).

398

Table 14.2 (Continued)

	Back pressure sores (negative binomial)				Deficiency citations (negative binomial)			
	I		II		I		II	
	All	Nonprofit	All	Nonprofit	All	Nonprofit	All	Nonprofit
Employee control	-0.27	-0.17			-0.27**	-0.25		
	(0.29)	(0.35)			(0.11)	(0.18)		
Resident control	0.28	0.21			0.15	0.30		
	(0.29)	(0.42)			(0.10)	(0.19)		
Community control	-0.00	0.08			-0.03	-0.17		
	(0.19)	(0.27)			(0.07)	(0.13)		
Owner control	-0.06	-0.00			0.09**	0.04		
	(0.10)	(0.10)			(0.04)	(0.05)		
Executive control	-0.01	-0.26			-0.04	-0.01		
	(0.15)	(0.17)			(0.06)	(0.08)		
Community exclusive control			0.21	-0.02			0.30	0.20
			(0.48)	(0.40)			(0.32)	(0.36)
Owner exclusive control			-0.12	0.26			-0.03	-0.20
			(0.56)	(0.45)			(0.27)	(0.29)
Executive exclusive control			0.16	-0.33			-0.09	-0.18
			(0.51)	(0.42)			(0.29)	(0.35)
Owner and executive joint exclusive control			-0.25	-0.34			0.03	-0.00
			(0.47)	(0.43)			(0.27)	(0.34)
Community and executive joint exclusive control			-0.16	-0.22			-0.19	-0.19
			(0.55)	(0.46)			(0.27)	(0.30)

Executive, owner and community joint exclusive control			-0.42	-0.71			0.05	-0.16
			(0.54)	(0.57)			(0.30)	(0.36)
Employee or resident participation in joint exclusive control			-2.08**	-16.46***			-0.34	-0.18
			(0.89)	(0.59)			(0.35)	(0.43)
Control variables	Yes	Yes	Yes	Yes	Yes	Yes	Yes	Yes
N	94	58	94	58	94	58	94	58
Log pseudolikelihood	-244.62	-158.12	-239.95	-148.53	-314.86	-196.66	-315.92	-197.63
Wald chi-squared	13.17	12.06	26.73	1268.63	11.25	14.10	12.59	15.95
Prob > chi-squared	0.51	0.44	0.04	0.00	0.67	0.29	0.70	0.32

Notes: 1. Numbers in parentheses are robust standard errors. *, ** and *** indicate significance at the 10%, 5%, and 1% levels, respectively.

2. We control for hospital affiliation, proportion of Medicare residents, Herfindahl–Hirschman Index in the county area, per capita income in the ZIP code area, employees' belief in organization mission, and resident case mix. We also control for organization's ownership type (when estimating the full sample we include non-profit chain, nonprofit autonomous and government, with for-profit as the reference group; in the non-profit sub-sample we include nonprofit chain, with non-profit autonomous as the reference group).

Table 14.3 Employee well-being

	Employee-management relationship (ologit)				Log of wage of certified nursing assistants (OLS)				Workload of certified nursing assistants (ologit)			
	I		II		I		II		I		II	
	All	Nonprofit	All	Nonprofit	All	Nonprofit	All	Nonprofit	All	Nonprofit	All	Nonprofit
Employee control	0.18	0.84			-0.03	-0.01			-1.41**	-2.39**		
	(0.48)	(0.71)			(0.03)	(0.04)			(0.63)	(1.19)		
Resident control	-0.32	-0.63			0.01	-0.01			0.90*	2.16**		
	(0.56)	(0.77)			(0.02)	(0.03)			(0.49)	(0.99)		
Community control	0.31	0.16			-0.01	-0.02			0.28	-0.47		
	(0.33)	(0.53)			(0.02)	(0.02)			(0.36)	(0.67)		
Owner control	0.08	-0.08			0.00	0.00			0.17	0.00		
	(0.19)	(0.27)			(0.01)	(0.02)			(0.17)	(0.25)		
Executive control	-0.05	-0.17			-0.01	-0.01			-0.08	0.12		
	(0.35)	(0.36)			(0.01)	(0.02)			(0.27)	(0.30)		
Community exclusive control			-5.88***	-3.27			-0.07	-0.10*			0.68	0.91
			(1.95)	(2.35)			(0.05)	(0.05)			(1.20)	(1.41)
Owner exclusive control			-0.22	0.84			0.11**	0.12			-0.68	-0.81
			(1.42)	(1.95)			(0.05)	(0.07)			(0.86)	(1.31)
Executive exclusive control			-0.45	-0.51			0.06	0.03			-0.92	-0.64
			(1.10)	(1.04)			(0.04)	(0.05)			(0.91)	(1.17)
Owner and executive joint exclusive control			-0.57	-0.56			0.04	0.01			-0.23	-0.64
			(0.89)	(0.86)			(0.04)	(0.06)			(0.84)	(0.92)

… and executive joint exclusive control			-0.33 (1.13)	-0.31 (1.25)			0.03 (0.05)	0.04 (0.06)			0.12 (0.82)	0.76 (0.97)
Executive, owner and community joint exclusive control			-0.08 (1.06)	-0.52 (1.02)			0.00 (0.04)	-0.05 (0.06)			0.18 (0.90)	-0.52 (0.91)
Employee or resident participation in joint exclusive control			-0.25 (1.13)	-0.37 (1.28)			-0.04 (0.05)	-0.09 (0.07)			-0.03 (1.01)	-0.63 (1.34)
Control variables	Yes	Yes	Yes	Yes	Yes	Yes	Yes	Yes	Yes	Yes	Yes	Yes
N	89	55	89	55	89	55	89	55	89	55	89	55
Wald chi-squared	16.52	16.55	24.88	59* 11.00					21.53	21.70	13.06	10.92
Prob > chi-squared	0.28	0.17	0.07	0.61					0.09	0.04	0.67	0.69
Pseudo R2	0.06	0.10	0.10	0.09					0.09	0.16	0.07	0.09
F					3.45	2.71	8.66	9.11				
Prob > F					0.00	0.01	0.00	0.00				
R-squared					0.47	0.46	0.53	0.58				

Notes: 1. Numbers in parentheses are robust standard errors. *, ** and *** indicate significance at the 10%, 5%, and 1% levels, respectively.

2. We control for hospital affiliation, proportion of Medicare residents, Herfindahl–Hirschman Index in the county area, per capita income in the ZIP code area, employees' belief in organization mission, and resident case mix. We also control for organization's ownership type (when estimating the full sample we include nonprofit chain, nonprofit autonomous and government, with for-profit as the reference group; in the nonprofit sub-sample we include nonprofit chain, with nonprofit autonomous as the reference group).

* Maximum likelihood estimation can not converge using only the 55 observations as in other regressions.

Table 14.4 Organizational effectiveness

| | Development of new services (ologit) | | | | Ability to retain essential employees (ologit) | | | | Log of number of residents (OLS)* | | | |
| | I | | II | | I | | II | | I | | II | |
	All	Nonprofit	All	Nonprofit	All	Nonprofit	All	Nonprofit	All	Nonprofit	All	Nonprofit
Employee control	-0.91** (0.41)	-1.59* (0.82)			-0.02 (0.45)	1.08* (0.64)			0.03 (0.03)	0.06 (0.05)		
Resident control	0.96** (0.48)	1.42* (0.84)			0.45 (0.51)	-0.61 (0.66)			-0.00 (0.03)	-0.05 (0.05)		
Community control	-0.33 (0.30)	-0.51 (0.52)			-0.06 (0.28)	-0.07 (0.36)			-0.01 (0.02)	0.01 (0.04)		
Owner control	-0.09 (0.20)	-0.32 (0.26)			-0.18 (0.19)	-0.36 (0.24)			-0.01 (0.01)	-0.02 (0.01)		
Executive control	-0.19 (0.31)	-0.05 (0.41)			-0.22 (0.28)	-0.23 (0.33)			-0.01 (0.01)	-0.01 (0.02)		
Community exclusive control			-0.33 (1.09)	-0.94 (1.52)			0.37 (0.89)	0.19 (0.76)			-0.01 (0.06)	-0.04 (0.07)
Owner exclusive control			-0.18 (1.26)	-0.38 (1.71)			2.49** (1.19)	1.39 (1.18)			0.08* (0.05)	0.07 (0.06)
Executive exclusive control			0.21 (0.64)	0.22 (0.98)			2.65** (1.11)	2.43** (0.96)			-0.00 (0.08)	0.00 (0.09)
Owner and executive joint exclusive control			-1.03 (0.65)	-1.51 (1.00)			0.50 (0.98)	0.45 (0.93)			0.02 (0.05)	-0.04 (0.07)

executive joint exclusive control	(0.80)	(1.33)					(1.24)	(1.22)			(0.05)	(0.07)
Executive, owner and community joint exclusive control	-1.50*	-3.35**					0.54	-0.72			-0.03	-0.06
	(0.83)	(1.54)					(0.98)	(0.89)			(0.05)	(0.06)
Employee or resident participation in joint exclusive control	-1.78***	-2.76**					2.35**	2.12**			-0.02	-0.08
	(0.66)	(1.20)					(1.00)	(1.04)			(0.06)	(0.11)
Control variables	Yes	Yes	Yes	Yes	Yes	Yes	Yes	Yes	Yes	Yes	Yes	Yes
N	88	56	88	56	88	56	88	56	88	56	88	56
Wald chi-squared	20.68	25.05	29.05	37.94	22.73	18.08	32.43	11.78				
Prob > chi-squared	0.11	0.01	0.02	0.00	0.06	0.11	0.01	0.62				
Pseudo R2	0.08	0.22	0.09	0.27	0.09	0.10	0.16	0.16				
F									101.57	66.51	91.44	47.73
Prob > F									0.00	0.00	0.00	0.00
R-squared									0.93	0.92	0.93	0.92

Notes: 1. Numbers in parentheses are robust standard errors. *, ** and *** indicate significance at the 10%, 5%, and 1% levels, respectively.

2. We control for hospital affiliation, proportion of Medicare residents, Herfindahl–Hirschman Index in the county area, per capita income in the ZIP code area, employees' belief in organization mission, and resident case mix. We also control for organization's ownership type (when estimating the full sample we include nonprofit chain, nonprofit autonomous and government, with for-profit as the reference group; in the nonprofit sub-sample we include nonprofit chain, with nonprofit autonomous as the reference group).

* We include nursing hours (registered and licensed practical nurses, and certified nursing assistants, respectively) as input for the estimation of the production function.

consistent association tends with satisfaction and quality of services; the same holds for executive control.

Exclusive control by any group tends to be associated with lower service quality (Specification II), whereas joint control of two or more stakeholder groups as weak favorable impact, especially when employees or residents are involved; however, none of the effects are statistically significant.

Turning to the measures obtained from external agencies (thus avoiding the 'common method bias' with the independent variables), we find in Specification I that employee control is generally associated with lower undesirable outcomes, either back pressure sores or deficiency citations. Resident control is weakly associated with *more* undesirable outcomes, whereas other groups' control is not substantially or significantly associated with these outcomes, with the exception of an increase in the incidence of deficiency citations associated with great owner control (but not in nonprofit homes).

In Specification II there are mixed and weak tendencies; the strongest finding the lower incidence of back pressure sores when either employees or residents participate in joint exclusive control ($p < 0.05$ for the entire sample and $p < 0.01$ for the nonprofit sub-sample).

5.2   Employee well-being

Table 14.3 indicates the effects on employee well-being, focusing on employee–management relations, and the wages and workload of certified nursing assistants, with only a few relationships being strong and signficant.[6] Consider first Specification I; employee control is associated negatively with the workload of certified nursing assistants ($p < 0.05$ in both the full sample and non-profit sub-sample), in contrast with resident control ($p < 0.10$ in the full sample and $p < 0.05$ in the non-profit subsample). In specification II, community exclusive control shows negative association with employee well-being, particularly with employee–management relationship in the full sample ($p < 0.01$) and wages of certified nursing assistants ($p < 0.10$ in the non-profit organizations sample), in contrast with the effects of owner exclusive control.

5.3   Organizational effectiveness

Table 14.4 shows results concerning three measures of organizational effectiveness. Two results stand out in specification I. First, employee control is adverse to the development of new services ($p < 0.05$ in the full sample, and $p < 0.10$ in the nonprofit sub-sample), but advantageous to the retention of essential employees in the nonprofit sub-sample ($p < 0.10$), and has no statistically significant effect on productivity. Second, resident control is associated positively with the development of new services ($p < 0.05$ in the full sample, and $p < 0.10$ in the nonprofit sub-sample). Other types of control have smaller and generally negative effects on the three outcomes and are discussed in connection with specification II.

Joint exclusive control, especially involving residents and employees, is generally associated with less development of new services but better retention of employees and no significant effect on productivity. Exclusive control by owners contributes to both retention and productivity, and executive control supports retention (with both dependent and independent variables reported by executives) but not productivity (independently measured).

The production function is well determined. In specification II, owner exclusive control has positive impact on the efficiency measure in the full sample ($p < 0.10$), but not found in the nonprofit subsample. This suggests that the effect may be driven by the motive of maximizing profit in for-profit organizations, which is acted upon most successfully when owners have full strategic control in their organizations. Other strategic control variables do not show a statistically significant association with productivity, suggesting that the identity of the stakeholders who control strategic decisions has little impact on this important efficiency measure.

5.4 Trade-offs among the well-being of different stakeholder groups

Correlations among the well-being measures of residents and employees as well as among the different measures for each group indicate the presence of very small trade-offs (to economize on space, we do not report the correlation table). Most of the correlations between the two sets of well-being suggest that the measures are complementary. Better employee–management relationships have a statistically significant correlation with higher levels of resident satisfaction ($p < 0.05$), fewer deficiency citations ($p < 0.10$), better ability to develop new services ($p < 0.01$), and better ability to retain essential employees ($p < 0.01$). Ability to retain essential employees is positively correlated with resident satisfaction and quality of services ($p < 0.01$ and $p < 0.10$, respectively). A positive correlation is also found between a nursing home's ability to develop new services and the quality of its services ($p < 0.01$). On the other hand, wages of certified nursing assistants are positively correlated with the prevalence of back pressure sores ($p < 0.01$).

6 Discussion and implications

The behavior of an organization is directed by whoever has control of it, and it is for this reason that strategic control is contested and usually rests in the hands of owners or their agents, board of directors and executives, who rarely share it with other stakeholders. Any influence that other stakeholders – consumers, employees, community – may have is exercised typically through markets or political channels. The well-being of these stakeholders is likewise determined by factors associated with these markets. It is therefore interesting to investigate what happens if, for whatever reasons, various stakeholder groups that are ordinarily shut out from control gain some measure of it.

To explore this question we studied nursing homes, which provide a personal service to vulnerable individuals, are relatively small establishments and many are owned by nonprofit and government organizations. These features are probably responsible for the apparent role diverse stakeholder groups play in them.

In our sample, executives have important strategic control in most, but not all organizations. Owners also have an important role. However, in most homes these groups share control jointly with other groups. Executives and owners have exclusive control (either each group by itself or the two together) in less than half of nursing homes; in about 40 per cent of homes they share strategic control with other groups (in about 10 per cent of homes there is no group with dominant control). Despite the fact that residents and their families have access to formal representation through resident and family councils established in almost all nursing homes, their role in strategic control is marginal, and they have exclusive control in only less than 2 per cent of the sample, which they share with others. This is likely the case because residents are weak and vulnerable, their families live in different locations, and they do not expect to have continued association with the particular home. Community representation in strategic control is much more substantial, and is exercised through a variety of channels, including locally constituted boards of directors or trustees.

We advanced several hypotheses regarding the effects of strategic control wielded by different stakeholder groups, suggesting that most of them will focus first on their own well-being or that of those they represent (residents in the case of community), although they will also of course follow professional norms and organizational requirement. We also predicted that organizational effectiveness will be promoted with differential success by the various stakeholder groups. We find only limited support for the idea that residents and their family are focused more on resident well-being than on employee well-being, and that their limited information and knowledge have adverse effects on organizational effectiveness. Community representatives may have an important role in advancing resident interests that might otherwise not be as strongly defended as they should be in the absence of strong market mechanisms, as is the case with nursing homes. Our analysis detects such an effect, but only weakly: community control is generally associated with positive effects on resident well-being, negative effects on employee well-being, and no discernible effect on effectiveness. Employees' exercise of strategic control is generally consistent in accord with the interests of residents, but has no consistent or significant effect on their own well-being. In terms of effectiveness, employee control seems to be adverse to the development of new services but favorable to retention of employees, and of no significant effect on productivity. Executives, the key strategic decision-makers in most nursing homes in the sample, do not seem to have a discernible differential effect on any of the outcomes we consider (we do not include executive well-being). This may be so because the responding executives in the one-fifth of the nursing homes reporting executive control in strategic decision-making below the level we deemed dominant just *feel* that they do not have enough control – indeed, in many of these organizations nobody is reported to have much control. Hence this non-effect may just be a reflection of absence of variation in the role of executives in our sample. Owner control, whether in the full sample or just the nonprofit sub-sample, seems to be exercised in favor of greater productivity even at the expense of quality.

Joint control by two or three stakeholder groups is the norm in our sample. An important question is whether the number of groups sharing dominant control affects outcomes in a particular manner; a particular concern is the possibility of delays in decision-making and strife that may harm organizational efficiency. However, we do not find strong evidence to show joint control of multiple stakeholder groups is inferior to executive exclusive control in determining organizational efficiency. The picture is not much different with respect to employee well-being.

Very few trade-offs are detected between the well-being of the two stakeholder groups. In fact, the relationship among these outcomes is generally complementary. This finding has possibly two implications. First, the interests of employees and residents may not be in competition with each other in the nursing home setting. Second, nursing homes in our sample may operate suboptimally so that the well-being of both groups can be advance simultaneously; however, we did not find that control by any particular group of stakeholders is associated with lower productivity.

This study uses a small sample and on these grounds alone its results can only be regarded as exploratory. Furthermore, the nature of the service provided by nursing homes is rather special and the findings of this study may not be easily applicable to other industries. We considered only a narrow range of outcomes and ignored any possible costs of stakeholder participation in control. It is therefore necessary to conduct more research on both the determinants and the consequences of stakeholder involvement in strategic decision-making and control before a sound conclusion can be drawn about the advantages and disadvantages of stakeholder participation in respect of corporate social responsibility.

Notes

1. An informal discussion of the conditions under which profit maximization does and does not coincide with social welfare maximization, see Ben-Ner (2006).
2. Practically all nursing homes have residents who benefit from the federal Medicare and Medicaid programs (benefiting the elderly and the poor, respectively); hence they are all subject to these regulations.

3. The survey is at http://webpages.csom.umn.edu/hrir/abenner/web/papers/work-surv/Nursing-homes-survey.pdf.
4. This item was taken from Price (1997), who reports that the items correlate well with objective measures.
5. We have also experimented with seemingly unrelated regression estimation of each group of dependent variables, and obtained similar results to those presented in Tables 14.2–14.4.
6. We are presenting an analysis of wages and workload of only CNAs, who are the largest group of employees in nursing homes. Analyses of wages and workload of RNs and LPNs generate substantively similar results and are available upon request.

References

Aoki, M. (1984) *The Cooperative Game Theory of the Firm*. London: Oxford University Press.
Ben-Ner, A. (1993) 'Cooperation, Conflict, and Control in Organizations', in S. Bowles, H. Gintis and B. Gustafsson (eds), *Markets and Democracy: Participation, Accountability and Efficiency*. Cambridge, UK: Cambridge University Press.
Ben-Ner, A. (2006) 'For-Profit, State and Non-Profit: How to Cut the Pie among the Three Sectors', in J.P. Touffut (ed.), *Advancing Public Goods*. Cheltenham, UK, and Northampton, MA: Edward Elgar.
Ben-Ner, A., and T. Ren (2007) 'A Comparative Study of Structure and Performance in For Profit, Nonprofit and Government Organizations,' Working Paper, Industrial Relations Center, University of Minnesota.
Berle, A., and G. Means (1932) *The Modern Corporation and Private Property*. New York: Harcourt, Brace & World.
Berman, S.L., A.C. Wicks, S. Kotha, and T.M. Jones (1999) 'Does Stakeholder Orientation Matter? The Relationship between Stakeholder Management Models and Firm Financial Performance', *Academy of Management Journal*, vol. 42(5), pp. 488–506.
Blair, M.M. (1995) *Ownership and Control: Rethinking Corporate Governance for the Twenty-First Century*. Washington, DC: Brookings Institute.
Bowie, N. (1991) 'New Directions in Corporate Social Responsibility', *Business Horizons*, vol. 34(4), pp. 56–65.
Clarkson, M.B.E. (1995) 'A Stakeholder Framework for Analyzing and Evaluating Corporate Social Performance,' *Academy of Management Review*, vol. 20(1), pp. 92–117.
Donaldson, T. and L.E. Preston (1995) 'The Stakeholder Theory of the Corporation: Concepts, Evidence, and Implications', *Academy of Management Review*, vol. 20(1), pp. 65–91.
Freeman, R.E. (1999) 'Response: Divergent Stakeholder Theory', *Academy of Management Review*, vol. 24(2), pp. 233–6.
Giddens, A. (1998) *The Third Way*. Cambridge, UK: Polity Press.
Goodpaster, K.E. (1991) 'Business Ethics and Stakeholder Analysis', *Business Ethics Quarterly*, vol. 1(1), pp. 53–72.
Grimalda, G., and L. Sacconi (2005) 'The Constitution of the Not-For-Profit Organization: Reciprocal Conformity to Morality', *Constitutional Political Economy*, vol. 16(3), pp. 249–76.
Harrison, J.S. and R.E. Freeman (1999) 'Stakeholders, Social Responsibility, and Performance: Empirical Evidence and Theoretical Perspectives', *Academy of Management Journal*, vol. 42(5), pp. 479–85.

Minnesota Department of Health and Human Services (2006) *Technical User Guide: Minnesota Nursing Facility Report Card.*
Price, J. (1997) 'Handbook of Organizational Measurement', *International Journal of Manpower*, vol. 18(4/5/6), pp. 305–558.
Rose-Ackerman, S. (1996) 'Altruism, Nonprofits, and Economic Theory', *Journal of Economic Literature*, vol. 34(2), pp. 701–28.
Smith, A. (1776) *The Wealth of Nations*. Reprinted by New York: Knopf, 1991.
Tirole, J. (2001) 'Corporate Governance', *Econometrica*, vol. 69(1), pp. 1–35.

15
Trusting, Trustworthiness, and CSR: Some Experiments and Implications*

Avner Ben-Ner and Louis Putterman

1 Introduction

Corporate social responsibility (CSR) has been the subject of much discussion in recent years, and it is hard to find any sizeable company that does not try to present its employment practices, environmental behavior, and involvement with the communities in which it operates in a favorable light. Yet the concept of CSR remains problematic for economic theory.

In his book *Capitalism and Freedom*, Milton Friedman (1982) called the notion that businesses have responsibilities other than to make profits a 'fundamentally subversive doctrine' and stated that 'there is one and only one social responsibility of business – to use its resources and engage in activities designed to increase its profits so long as it stays within the rules of the game, which is to say, engages in open and free competition without deception or fraud'.[1]

Friedman (1970) noted that 'it may well be in the long run interest of a corporation that is a major employer in a small community to devote resources to providing amenities to that community or to improving its government. That may make it easier to attract desirable employees, it may reduce the wage bill or lessen losses from pilferage and sabotage or have other worthwhile effects.' In such cases,

> there is a strong temptation to rationalize these actions as an exercise of 'social responsibility.' In the present climate of opinion ... this is one way for a corporation to generate goodwill as a by-product of expenditures that are entirely justified in its own self-interest. ... If our institutions, and the attitudes of the public make it in their self-interest to cloak their actions

* We thank the Russell Sage Foundation for support of this research. We wish to thank Ting Ren for critical research assistance including data management and analysis. We are grateful to Freyr Halldorsson and Ting Ren for their help in planning and carrying out the experiments.

in this way, I cannot summon much indignation to denounce them. At the same time, I can express admiration for those individual proprietors or owners of closely held corporations or stockholders of more broadly held corporations who disdain such tactics as approaching fraud.

Whatever one makes of the philosophical position staked out by Friedman, it seems undeniable that in a textbook world in which consumers care only about obtaining products at the lowest price, workers care only about achieving maximum pay for their effort, and firms care only about maximizing profits, the socially responsible corporation would be a non-starter. Of course, conventional price theory implies that in the absence of externalities and other problems, what is profitable to business increases social welfare since it implies using resources for purposes most valued by consumers and producing each product or service using the minimum quantity of scarce resources. Governmental regulation – for instance, levying fines for the release of toxic substances – can also help to align profitability with social welfare. But there remain other respects in which social responsibility and profit maximization may not coincide.

In this chapter, we argue that in a world of social human beings who tend to relate to companies as if they were social and moral agents in their own rights, there are pressures on even profit-maximizing companies to project favorable social personae. In a classic example, Akerlof (1982) suggested that companies that pay their employees more than the opportunity cost of their labor are rewarded with higher effort due to normal human reciprocity, and that in response to this, a profit-maximizing company should calculate the optimal employment rent to offer its workers.[2] Branded sneaker and clothing manufacturers who can create a warm glow that translates into more sales at higher prices by conducting and advertising higher employment standards in poor countries would be remiss to their shareholders were they to abstain from such a strategy. If a 'clean energy' image translates into sufficient additional visits to the pump, it pays for an oil company to invest in an environmentally progressive image. Prominently displaying energy-saving light bulbs in its stores might improve Wal-Mart's sales of more than just bulbs, in some regions. And coffee produced by cooperatives of small growers may lure enough customers willing to pay sufficiently more into the store, so selling 'fairly traded' coffee might require no special conscience on the seller's part.

The efforts made by many companies in these directions, in recent years, are in themselves prima facie evidence that their managements believe that projecting a socially responsible image is profitable. More systematic evidence that 'socially responsible' companies are in fact rewarded by their customers might be obtained by careful market studies. In this chapter, we report on a study of social preferences based on person-to-person, rather than person-to-company, interactions. We use experimental methods to add to evidence that the human propensity to reciprocate generous behavior is a strong one. More specifically, we show that trusting and trustworthiness are supported by social motivations to reciprocate trust and to avoid harming by misleading. The fact that laboratory manipulations that make an interaction partner more real and that allow him to project a favorable image lead to more trust and to the conduct of more business (sending, trusting) suggests that companies too may benefit from investing in benevolent personae.

2   Social preferences and trust

During most of the last century, economic analysis, including those parts which used game theory, operated under the standard '*homo economicus*' assumption according to which individuals' only objectives are to obtain income or wealth and to avoid effort. As Francis Edgeworth (1881) put it: 'The first principle of Economics is that every agent is actuated only by self-interest'. But this situation has begun to change. In Ben-Ner and Putterman (2000), we suggested that the consistency of many experimental economics findings with behavioral approaches, progress in evolutionary modeling, and the accumulating scientific evidence of an evolved human social nature, have encouraged more economists to recognize that humans are social animals and that prediction and explanation of their behaviors sometimes calls for recognition of other predispositions and preferences.

A central human predisposition identified by behaviorists is the tendency to reciprocate kindness with kindness and unkindness with punishment. Reciprocity offers a potential explanation for rejections of 'unfair' offers in ultimatum games, for the tendency of voluntary contributions to move in the direction of others' average contribution, for subjects to punish free riders in voluntary contribution experiments, and for trustees to return money in trust games.[3] Expectations regarding the probability that one's partner is a reciprocator can accordingly explain otherwise anomalous behaviors by subjects seeking to maximize their own payoffs – i.e., the tendency to make 'fair' offers in ultimatum games, the tendency to contribute to a public good when others have the power to punish, and the tendency to trust in trust games.

In the trust game (Berg, Dickhaut and McCabe, 1995, hereafter BDM), two subjects, usually anonymous to one another and unable to communicate, are each given an endowment (typically $10). Subject A, called the trustor, can give any of her $10 to B, with the experimenter tripling the amount sent. Then B, called the trustee, can send any of the money received back to A, and the interaction ends. Both subjects can be better off if A is trusting and B trustworthy; for instance, A can send $10, B receives $30, and B can return between $11 and $29, giving both final earnings above their original $10. If A knows B

to be rational and payoff-maximizing, A will send nothing, since B will return none of what he receives (unless the game is repeated or future partners are to be informed of B's actions). But if A believes there to be a sufficient probability that B will reciprocate her trust, she may send a positive amount out of self-interest, sending more the greater the probability she assigns to B's reciprocity and the less her risk aversion. A's may also be influenced by other preferences, for example some will send less due to regret avoidance, and some will send more due to altruism toward B (their utility is increasing in B's earnings).

In Ben-Ner and Putterman (2001), we discussed the roles of both self-interested and social preferences in determining trusting and trustworthiness in the trust game. In a one-shot game, returning money received is never rational for a trustee who cares about payoffs alone, whereas sending money can be rational for a self-interested trustor depending on her priors about the trustee. This gives the trustee an incentive to create an impression of trustworthiness if opportunities to do so are present. In our experiment, such opportunities come in the form of chances to send pre-play messages. If trustors' preferences extend beyond payoff maximization, they may also look for clues of general worthiness or need on the part of the trustee. Symmetrically, trustors too have incentives to convey impressions of niceness or worthiness, so that their counterparts might be inclined to return more. Interestingly, trusting and trustworthiness could be enhanced by communication simply because these human propensities are activated by impressions of the realness or similarity of the counterpart. This point seems pertinent to CSR because a customer or potential employee's orientation with respect to a company, hence their desire to do business with, seek employment with, or provide consummate effort to the company, may be influenced by the company's projection of personality, trustworthiness, and moral worthiness to those constituencies.

It's worth pointing out that although we use our recent experiments with the trust game to illustrate the role of 'sociality', as opposed to simply payoff maximization, in economic interactions, an 'extended preference' or behavioral point of view regarding human nature, preferences, and predispositions is likely to have many other implications for CSR. Profit-maximizing companies may adopt pro-social employment policies, rules on product procurement, concerns for environmental impact, and so forth, because while the company itself is not a human being with an evolved social nature, its managers, other employees, customers, and even the politicians who determine relevant regulations and their constituents, are. It may pay to be 'nice' if this attracts better employees and managers and elicits greater loyalty and effort from them, if it attracts and keeps customers, and if it reduces demands for intrusive regulations. We view indications of sociality in the determinants of trusting and trustworthiness in our experiments not only as indicators of reciprocity itself, but as one example, among many, of the significance of human sociality.

3   Trust, contracts and communication

In everyday usage, to say that *A* trusts *B* is to make a statement about *A*'s favorable mental disposition towards *B*. However, the idea of trust is usually applied in economics with a more specific meaning. How much, if at all, *A* trusts *B* is in principle measurable by the degree to which *A* displays a willingness to engage with *B* in an interaction that has the potential to benefit both *A* and *B*, but that would end up harming *A* were *B* to respond in a purely self-regarding fashion. *A* manifests trust by making herself vulnerable to *B*'s response in the hope or expectation that *B* will act at least in part with *A*'s interest in mind.[4]

Consider the interaction between a car buyer and an auto dealer. Usually, the buyer must make full payment before driving the car from the lot, although she may be able to do a short test drive to see that there are no obvious defects. The money received by the dealer is of known value, but should the car prove to be defective after a few hundred miles of driving, the owner has a 'lemon' on her hands, with its well-known consequences (Akerlof, 1970). To increase its trustworthiness, the auto company typically warrantees certain parts for a period of time, but there are annoyance costs to the customer that the company cannot make good, so a general reputation for quality and service remains of value to it in attracting customers and a good price on their vehicles. There may even by a tie-in to CSR: some customers' views of the company, and thus their inclination to trust it, might be influenced by attributes other than those of the product itself, such as whether the company is known to be showing leadership in developing environmentally friendly models, or whether it has created or sustained employment in their community.

Communication

In laboratory experiments, face-to-face communication has been found to be one of the most powerful ways of increasing trust and cooperation. Isaac and Walker (1988) found that pre-play communication led their experimental subjects to contribute considerably more to a public good. Their study is one of 37 that report 130 different experimental treatments whose results Sally (1995) entered in multivariate regressions to study which treatment variables best account for differing levels of cooperation and free riding in public goods games. Sally concluded that face-to-face communication was the most influential of the treatment variables studied. Ostrom, Walker and Gardner (1992) found that the combination of communication and the ability to sanction other group members led to significantly higher efficiencies in their common pool resource experiment.

There have been fewer experiments with pre-play communication in trust games, and none in which both parties could exchange proposals or verbal messages. Malhotra and Murnighan (2002) had a computer program posing as trustee sometimes propose a non-binding contract for mutual cooperation, and found that trustors who agreed to such a contract sent more to their 'counterpart'. Buchan, Croson and Johnson (2006) allowed subjects to engage in communication before playing trust games, but theirs was a manipulation of social distance prior to informing subjects of their decision task, so there was no task-relevant communication. Fehr and Rockenbach (2003), Houser, Xiao, McCabe and Smith (2008) and Rigdon (2005) conducted games in which trustors could suggest amounts to be returned by their trustee counterparts and in some conditions threaten punishment should they not do so. Rigdon's subjects could reject or accept proposals. In none of their treatments is communication fully two-sided, and their papers focus principally on the effects of threatening or not threatening punishment, rather than on the effects of differing proposal terms. Charness and Dufwenberg (2006) permit either trustor or trustee, but not both, to send a single message in a binary trust game. They find that the amounts of both trusting and trustworthiness increase significantly when trustees can send messages, but are not influenced by letting trustors send them.

In a trust game, we conjecture that communication may increase trusting and trustworthiness by: (i) permitting subjects to signal their characters; (ii) attaching 'realness' to the other, thus triggering responses of human sociality; and (iii) permitting trustees to self-commit, which could generate internal psychic penalties for non-fulfillment. But a problem with interpreting the impact of face-to-face communication is that it adds a number of potentially separable elements to treatments involving subject anonymity and absence of communication, making it difficult to know what accounts for its influence. When subjects communicate face to face, anonymity is lost, which introduces the possible influence of identity (one learns the counterpart's gender, race, height, etc.). Concerns about possible post-interaction reward or punishment arise. Psychological costs may also be altered: a subject may feel greater obligation to trust, or to be trustworthy towards, a concrete other. Face-to-face meetings also make possible verbal communication, in which promises can be delivered. Commitment, sympathy, and other emotions can also be conveyed by vocal intonation, facial expression, and body language. Interpersonal attraction, aversion, or bonding may result from physical proximity.

To understand better what lies behind the effects of face-to-face communication, Brosig, Ockenfels and Weimann (2003) and Bochet, Page and Putterman (2006) conducted VCM experiments in which other forms of communication were substituted for face-to-face discussion. Brosig et al.'s comparison treatments included a no-communication baseline, a treatment with audio and visual communication from separated compartments, a treatment with only audio communication from separated compartments, and a treatment in which subjects could view one another on video terminals but could not communicate, prior to making their decisions. Bochet et al.'s alternative treatments included a no-communication baseline, but in addition, a treatment in which subjects could communicate text messages in a chat room, and one in which subjects could relay non-binding possible choices in numerical form, with time for iterative reactions before each binding decision stage. Bochet et al.'s chat room treatment resembles Frohlich and Oppenheimer's (1998) VCM in which group members could communicate with e-mail messages, while their non-binding numerical communication treatment, which they labeled 'numerical cheap talk', resembles the numerical pre-announcement treatment of Wilson and Sell (1997), except that subjects in Bochet et al. could react to one another's announcements with new non-binding announcements for a period of a minute or longer before making binding decisions, whereas Wilson and Sell's subjects could send only one announcement before each binding decision.[5]

The results of these various treatments can be summarized by saying that (a) one treatment – Brosig et al.'s audio + video treatment – achieved levels of cooperation statistically indistinguishable from those achieved through face-to-face meetings; (b) three treatments – Bochet et al.'s chat room treatment, Brosig et al.'s audio-only treatment and Frohlich and Oppenheimer's e-mail treatment – generated more cooperation than the no-communication baseline, but less than face-to-face communication; and (c) the remaining treatments – Brosig et al.'s video only, Bochet et al. and Wilson and Sell's numerical communication treatments – led to no greater cooperation than in no-communication conditions. Taken together, these results suggest that tone of voice, body language, and physical proximity are not crucial to increasing cooperation, but the ability to exchange verbal and not merely numerical messages may well be critical. The difference between the Frohlich–Oppenheimer e-mail and the Bochet et al. chat room results suggest that having visible confirmation that one's partners are actual individuals – as opposed, for instance, to robotic agents programmed by the experimenter – may also be important.[6]

We asked our subjects to play trust games with forms of numerical announcements that resemble those in Wilson and Sell and in Bochet et al.'s 'numerical cheap talk' treatment, and with text communication resembling that in Frohlich and Oppenheimer and in Bochet et al.'s chat room treatment. Comparing trust game play without prior announcements to that with numerical announcements should help us to see whether announcements help the partners to coordinate or to achieve trust, while comparing treatments with text messages and studying the content of those messages will provide indications of when and how the exchange of verbal messages can increase trust.

Contracting

Entering into a contract can be a substitute for trust. Whereas it is in *B*'s material interest to act in an untrustworthy fashion towards *A* when *A* takes trusting actions in a one-shot interaction, a contract with sufficiently sure and costly penalties for non-fulfillment can transform the interaction into one that is both mutually beneficial and that both have material incentives to execute. As a simple example, consider the same trust game as above and suppose, for the sake of simplicity, that a contract can be written and enforced for a cost C, shared equally between A and B, under which any violator will be fined the amount that brings his or her overall earnings to zero. Let A and B agree that A will send B $10 and be given back $20. Then if, as in BDM, B also has an initial endowment of $10, earnings will be ($20 – ½C, $20 – ½C) if the contract is carried out, and if either party violates the contract, that person will earn 0. Then as long as C < $20, the parties value earnings, and there are no conflicting emotional or other considerations, the contract can be expected to be fulfilled even in the complete absence of trust. Of course, both would prefer earnings of ($20, $20), but both prefer ($20 – ½C, $20 – ½C) to ($10, $10), and ($20, $20) is unachievable without trust.

Sometimes trusting is the only way to achieve the potential gains from an interaction. At other times, costly contracts are available but are of questionable desirability because of their cost. Suppose, in the above example, that C = $18, so that net earnings after carrying out the contract would be $11 for each party, a gain of $1 for each over the no-trade situation. Then if they are sufficiently confident that the agreement will be adhered to even without a contract, A and B will prefer to rely exclusively on trust. Suppose, for instance, that each of the two believes the chances are 80 per cent that his or her counterpart will adhere to an agreement that A send B $10 and B return to A $20, that the only alternatives to which probabilities are attached are that A sends nothing or B returns nothing, and that each plans to fulfill his own part (in B's case, provisional upon A doing so). In this case, A's expected earnings from the interaction without contract are $16 (= 0.2*0 + 0.8*$20) and B's expected earnings are $8 (= 0.2*0 + 0.8*10) from the interaction plus his endowment of $10. Since each expects total earnings of $11 with a contract, they will not wish to enter into a contract unless they are very risk averse. Only if subjective probabilities of the agreement being fulfilled are much lower will they turn to so costly a contract; and as the example shows, there will be circumstances in which recourse to a contract the costs of which are shared equally raises the expected earnings of A but not those of B. If we assume other-regarding concerns to be absent, then we can make inferences about the probabilities each attaches to fulfillment of the agreement by the other by examining their choices of whether to enter into a contract or not to do so.

There are some instances in which either the reliability of contract enforcement or the penalties associated with noncompliance are too low to make a contract self-enforcing solely in terms of material incentives. For instance, the penalty bringing earnings to zero might be brought to bear with only 50 per cent probability, or a penalty may be imposed with certainty but may take away only 50 per cent of the violator's pre-penalty earnings. Nevertheless, the parties may still wish to enter into a contract as a way to formalize their agreement, and this may be the case even in the limiting condition in which there is no possibility of monetary penalties for non-fulfillment. Sally (1995) found that more cooperation was achieved in social dilemma experiments in which experimenters suggested to subjects, prior to communication, that they could exchange promises. Bochet and Putterman (2009) found that giving subjects the opportunity to select a statement promising to contribute to a public good led to higher average contributions, in a condition in which group members also had the ability to sanction others using costly material punishments. In our experiment, we infer the value subjects attach to contracts independent of their material impact on payoffs by making contracts without penalties available but costly to enter into.

4 Experimental design and predictions

We conducted a series of one-shot trust game experiments in each of which a subject designated A interacted by computer link with a new counterpart designated B seated in a different room. Each had no information about the other's identity and knew they would remain anonymous to one another and play only once. Each subject was given ten dollars of laboratory money (denoted E\$) for each interaction, with the pre-announced conversion rate to real money being calibrated to yield expected payouts of about \$26 for a one-hour session consisting of either 7 or 10 interactions, plus a nearly one-hour pre-session survey (completed on-line days before at the subject's convenience).

All games had the same underlying structure as in BDM. Subject A was asked to choose a whole number of experiment dollars, $E\$X_a \in (0,1,...,10)$, to send to subject B on the understanding that B would receive triple the amount sent and could send back any or no part of that as B wished. Thus, A would earn with certainty any part of the E\$10 she kept and could additionally earn an amount between 0 and E\$30, depending on B's choice, while B would earn between E\$10 and $E\$(10 + 3X_a - X_b)$, where $X_b \leq 3X_a$ is the amount B sends to A.

We restricted the amount sent by B to sixths of the amount received to facilitate communication of proposals and counterproposals. For this purpose, subjects were shown an interaction table (Figure 15.1), in which each row heading lists an amount that could be sent by A and each of the seven column headings to the right lists a proportion of the amount received that could be sent by B. In the **simple trust game (S)** condition involving neither numerical nor verbal preplay communication, subjects registered their choices by A clicking first on a row heading followed by B (seeing A's choice highlighted on his screen) clicking on a column heading, causing the associated row and column to become highlighted

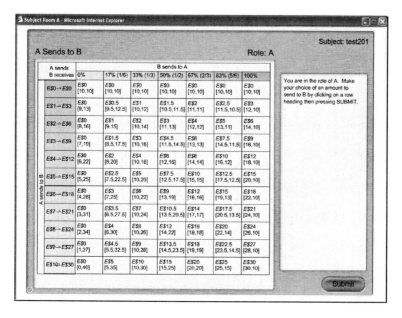

Figure 15.1   Interaction table

on both of their screens. In games with numerical communication, rows and columns that were clicked on became highlighted as a way of communicating proposals, with *A* first proposing both a row and a column, then *B* proposing a row and column. Decisions were framed as '*A* sends *B* a number of experiment dollars' (e.g., '*A* sends *B* E$3') and '*B* sends *A* a fraction of the amount received' (e.g., '*B* sends 50 per cent'). To make sure that subjects understood the implications of their choices for the payout of their interaction, the table's cells list both the experiment dollar amount that *B* is sending *A* and (below and in brackets) the implied payouts to *A* and *B*, including *B*'s endowment (which *B* always retains). We suspected that inclusion of final payouts might induce more equal splits. That is, while it would be easy for a subject *B* to believe using casual reasoning that sending half of her receipts back to *A* is equitable, the table makes it clear that *B* must return 2/3 of her receipts to put their actual earnings at parity.

In addition to the simple interaction condition, with no communication, the experiments include three communication conditions. In **single proposal (SP)** interactions, *A* clicked on and highlighted both a row and a column of the table as a form of proposal, then *B* clicked on and highlighted a row and column, which might be the same or different. **Multiple proposal (MP)** interactions were the same, except that each party could make up to three proposals and counterproposals until either identical proposals were made consecutively or all six opportunities were used up. The single and multiple proposal conditions resemble Bochet et al.'s 'numerical cheap talk' in that no verbal or text messages are exchanged, so subjects cannot issue promises, express commitment, etc. Finally, in **chat + single proposal (CSP)** interactions, *A* and *B* could exchange a series of text messages in a private on-line chat room, then proceeded directly to the same process as in **single proposal**.

We consider two sets of treatments: Experiment 1, in which subjects who concurred on the same proposal were offered the chance to enter into a contract; and Experiment 2, in which they were not. In Experiment 1, any *A*, *B* pair who agreed on terms were asked to choose (simultaneously and without communication) between a contract and no contract, with at least a contract without penalties being entered into if both said yes, and no contract if either or both said no. If both subjects said yes to the first question, they were asked if they wanted a contract with penalties. If both said yes, they entered into such a contract; if either or both said no, they remained with a contract without penalties. Once the question of contracts was concluded, they proceeded to their binding choices – i.e., *A* clicking on a row heading, highlighting the row, and then *B* clicking on a column heading, highlighting the column.

A contract without penalties cost each party *E*$1 or *E*$2, depending upon the experiment session, while one with penalties cost each twice that amount (hence, either *E*$2 or *E*$4), regardless of whether penalties needed to be imposed. The penalty rate was 110 per cent of whatever stipulated amount was not sent. For example, if *A* agreed to send *E*$10 but actually sent *E*$9, *E*$1.10 was deducted from *A*'s earnings for the interaction. If *B* received *E*$20, had agreed to return 50 per cent, but actually sent *E*$5, *E*$5.50 (= ([.5 × *E*$20] – *E*$5) × 1.10) was deducted from *B*'s earnings. Note that if a contract was agreed upon and *A* sent a positive amount to *B*, *B* was obligated to return *the proportion* agreed to even if the amount sent by *A* fell short of that stipulated.

Table 15.1 summarizes the sequences of interaction conditions in the two experiments. Experiment 1 included seven trust game interactions, of which we discuss only the first four, which were always conducted in the same order.[7] Experiment 2 included ten interactions consisting of five of one condition followed by five of another condition, every interaction being with a different anonymous and unseen counterpart. In experiment 2, orders of interactions were switched in the first two pairs of treatments to make possible tests of order effects.[8]

Predictions and hypotheses

The predictions of neoclassical theory under the assumptions that subjects: (i) are concerned only with their own payoffs; (ii) are not guided by values and ethical concerns; (iii) are rational in the sense that they can foresee their counterpart's reaction to their own actions; and (iv) assume that their counterparts

Table 15.1 Summary of experimental conditions and treatment orders

Experiment 1 (Contract Possibilities)	Experiment 2 (without Contract Possibilities) Treatments				
Interactions	# 1 Interactions	# 2 Interactions	# 3 Interactions	# 4 Interactions	# 5 Interactions
1 S 1 SP	5 S interactions	5 SP interactions	5 S interactions	5 CSP interactions	5 SP interactions
1 MP 1 CSP 3 other interactions	5 SP interactions	5 S interactions	5 CSP interactions	5 S interactions	5 CSP interactions

Key:
S = simple trust game
SP = single proposal trust game
MP = multiple (three) proposals trust game
CSP = chat + single proposal trust game

in the experiment are like them in these respects, serve as a useful analytical benchmark. Under these assumptions (and assuming further that reputation has no role[9]) *B* should send no money to *A*, regardless of how much he receives and (understanding this) *A* will therefore send nothing to *B*. *A* and *B* thus each keep their initial endowments and earn *E*$10 from their interaction.

Based on such reasoning, standard theory would predict that nothing would be sent in the simple interactions and in the interactions without the possibility of contract (Experiment 2), and that in the remaining interactions, money would be sent by *A* to *B* and by *B* to *A* only in those cases in which contracts with costly penalties were agreed to. Specifically, *A* should propose and *B*, having no better alternative, should agree to a transaction in which *A* sends *E*$10, *B* returns *E*$25, giving final earnings of *E*$25 and *E*$15 minus contract cost (*E*$1 or *E*$2 depending on the session).[10] Contracts without penalties should have no effect and, being costly, should never be chosen by rational subjects. Messages sent in chat rooms should likewise have no effect; they will be pure 'cheap talk' because the logic that *B* earns more by returning nothing, hence *A* should also send nothing, remains unchanged by anything that may be said.

An alternative framework to standard economic theory is provided by behavioral economics. Although neither theoretical nor experimental behavioral economics provide a set of tight and specific assumptions, they do supply a set of four observations that permit the characterization of trusting and trustworthiness: (a) people often display trust and trustworthiness in real-life interactions resembling trust games, and large numbers have done so as well in past experimental trust games; (b) communication is helpful in engendering trust; (c) reciprocity is often observed (that is, many people act as if obligated to return kindness to someone who acts in a kind or trusting fashion toward them);[11] and (d) many people have a preference for keeping their word if the gains from breaking their word are not very great. Another key observation, supported by our experimental investigations, is that there exist individual differences (associated with personality, cognitive ability, life experiences, and more) that generate a distribution of types in terms of proclivity for trusting and trustworthiness and associated traits and preferences. We can thus posit that individuals, whose own preferences vary from strict money maximization to ones inclusive of various values, norms of behavior, and other-regarding preferences, know there to be some proportion of others with relevant preferences, and choose their actions to maximize utility subject to beliefs about partners' types, which may be influenced by information about partner characteristics or past actions. We expect that:

- as in past trust game experiments, there will be considerable amounts of sending and returning even in interactions without pre-play communication;
- the amounts sent and returned will be greater the greater the amount of communication between partners, not only because of the way in which this aids coordination, signaling and screening of types, but also because with text messages especially, individuals can sometimes build a sense of trust in and responsibility to their partners, and because the exchange of promises will make many feel bound to keep their word;
- trustors (*A*) will send more when trustees (*B*) have concurred on a proposal;
- subjects will show particular interest in proposals that achieve both efficiency and equity, thus gravitating towards the proposal that *A* send *E*$10 and *B* return two-thirds of the amount received, for payoffs (*E*$20,*E*$20)

The hypotheses generated by standard and behavioral economics thus disagree on most predictions. In particular, whereas standard theory predicts uniform reliance on contracts with penalties when contract costs are less than the surplus that can be appropriated with certainty, and absence of exchange in all other cases, behavioral economics suggests that the prevalence of trusting and trustworthiness (whatever their sources) will induce some proportion of pairs to dispense with costly contracts and to interact even when contracts are not a possibility. Whereas contracts favoring the first mover, *A*, are predicted by standard theory, behavioral theory sees a greater likelihood of fair divisions.

5   Results

Table 15.2 summarizes behaviors and payoffs in each of the four interactions of Experiment 1. It shows that cooperation between *A*'s and *B*'s was on average

Table 15.2 Average outcomes by interaction, Experiment 1

Interaction Type	A sends E$ (1)	A's payoff[2] E$ (2)	B sends[3] % (3)	B sends[3] E$[4] (4)	B's payoff[2,5] E$ (5)
Simple (1)	5.47 (3.16)[1]	11.52 (5.71)	0.42 (0.26)	7.45 (6.86)	19.42 (7.97)
One proposal (2)	7.69 (3.42)	13.89 (6.44)	0.49 (0.26)	12.70 (8.15)	20.86 (7.64)
≤ Three proposals (3)	8.06 (3.28)	13.18 (7.41)	0.46 (0.28)	12.60 (8.57)	22.37 (8.68)
Chat + one proposal (4)	9.20 (2.47)	16.63 (6.26)	0.59 (0.22)	17.18 (6.77)	20.96 (6.65)

Notes:
1 Numbers in parentheses are standard deviations.
2 Earnings after deduction of contract costs, where applicable.
3 Refers to cases in which A sends positive amount.
4 After tripling A's sending.
5 Includes cases in which A sends zero.

smallest in the first interaction; that cooperation was higher in the two interactions allowing proposals but not verbal messages; and that cooperation was highest in the interaction with chat. Behavior by B's does not seem to differ as much across the first three interactions, with the proportion returned being around 46 per cent, but B's average return proportion jumps to 59 per cent after chat. We find that 12.6 per cent of interactions 2–4 were without agreement, 71.8 per cent with agreement but no contract, 9.5 percent with a non-binding contract, and 6.1 per cent with a binding contract. The prediction that all would select binding contracts when available is clearly contradicted.[12]

In Table 15.3 we investigate the statistical significance of the methods of communicating using GLS regressions (including individual fixed effects).[13] We also examine the impact of reaching agreement, taking possible endogeneity into account by controlling for proposal terms. The first two regressions show that A's both sent and earned significantly more in interactions with chat and when their counterpart agreed to their proposal.[14,15] The last two regressions suggest that B's sent more and thus earned less when they agreed to A's proposal and when they engaged in chat with their counterpart, while multiple proposals had the opposite effect on proportion returned. In sum, many B's act as if committed to their agreements, especially if they have chatted.[16] Further analysis of the data shows that A's who sent more earned significantly more (trust paid off), that A's sent and B's returned more with non-binding contracts than with agreement but no contract, and that chat significantly increased sending and returning conditional on agreement and controlling for choice of contract.[17]

Table 15.3   Effects of agreement, communication type, and proposals, Experiment 1

	Dependent Variable			
	A sends E$	A's payoff E$	B sends %	B's payoff E$
	(1)	(2)	(3)	(4)
Sending by A			−0.011	1.639***
			(0.068)	(0.316)
Agreement dummy	3.161***	4.370***	1.051**	−3.804*
	(0.606)	(1.621)	(0.428)	(1.993)
A's row proposal⁺	0.221*	−0.063	−0.033	0.180
	(0.117)	(0312)	(0.084)	(−.389)
A's column proposal⁺	0.702***	0.985	0.417**	−1.516*
	(0.258)	(0.690)	(0.195)	(0.909)
Interaction 3 dummy	−0.302	−1.473	−0.353*	1.543
(multiple proposals)	(0.343)	(0.918)	(0.218)	(1.015)
Interaction 4 dummy	0.812**	2.171**	0.382*	−1.807*
(chat + proposal)	(0.812)	(0.925)	(0.225)	(1.047)
# obs.	294	294	275	275
Wald χ^2	352.61	180.33	166.63	176.27
Prob. > χ^2	<0.001	<0.001	<0.001	<0.001

Notes: GLS regressions. Numbers in parentheses are standard errors. All estimates include individual fixed effects. *, ** and *** indicate significance at the 1%, 5%, and 10% levels, respectively. B's sending and payoff are contingent on A's sending more than 0. + In multiple-proposal interactions, A's final proposals.

Contrary to the prediction that A's would propose and B's accept exchanges giving a disproportionate share of the total returns to A, in actuality A's first proposal was the 'fair and efficient' exchange in which A and B split equally the maximum earnings 79.6 per cent of the time, and such proposals were agreed to 96.2 per cent of the times when they were made, versus 53.3 per cent of the time on average for other proposals.[18] Sending by A and returning by B equaled or exceeded the proposed levels 66.24 per cent of the time when they were fair and efficient, versus 41.67 per cent of the time when they were not.

Experiment 2 allows us to check whether the apparent impact of communication on trusting and trustworthiness is due to the order in which the conditions occur and whether, despite the fact that most subjects in Experiment 1 ended up interacting without contracts, the presence of the contract option in that experiment was critical to the outcomes. Table 15.4 permits a brief overview of the results. In general, they support the qualitative findings from Experiment 1 in that subjects are more trusting and more trustworthy when there is pre-play communication, and especially so when there is pre-play chat. The order in which the conditions are experienced has an effect in that subjects who have engaged in interactions with pre-play communication in earlier

Table 15.4 Summary of sending and returning, Experiment 2

Design	Amount sent (A)		Proportion returned (B)*	
	Interactions of First Condition	Interactions of Second Condition	Interactions of First Condition	Interactions of Second Condition
S-SP	Mean = 7.67 Median = 10 St. Dev. = 3.46 # 0 = 5.13% (6/117)	Mean = 7.76 Median = 10 St. Dev. = 3.55 # 0 = 11.30% (13/115)	Mean = 39.43% Median = 50% St. Dev. = 26.19% # 0 = 19.82% (22/111)	Mean = 47.70% Median = 50% St. Dev. = 24.18% # 0 = 14.71% (15/102)
SP-S	Mean = 7.03 Median = 10 St. Dev. = 3.80 # 0 = 8.13% (10/123)	Mean = 7.86 Median = 10 St. Dev. = 3.21 # 0 = 5.08% (6/118)	Mean = 49.72% Median = 67% St. Dev. = 25.43% # 0 = 12.39% (14/113)	Mean = 47.61% Median = 50% St. Dev. = 26.09% # 0 = 14.29% (16/112)
S-CSP	Mean = 7.20 Median = 8 St. Dev. = 2.95 # 0 = 4.43% (7/158)	Mean = 9.87 Median = 10 St. Dev. = 0.67 # 0 = 0% (0/151)	Mean = 46.34% Median = 50% St. Dev. = 23.01% # 0 = 11.26% (17/151)	Mean = 58.99% Median = 67% St. Dev. = 20.64% # 0 = 9.93% (15/151)
CSP-S	Mean = 8.65 Median = 10 St. Dev. = 3.01 # 0 = 6.47% (11/170)	Mean = 8.09 Median = 10 St. Dev. = 3.51 # 0 = 9.09% (15/165)	Mean = 57.36% Median = 67% St. Dev. = 22.32% # 0 = 10.69% (17/159)	Mean = 49.27% Median = 67% St. Dev. = 26.09% # 0 = 18% (27/150)
SP-CSP	Mean = 8.61 Median = 10 St. Dev. = 2.61 # 0 = 2.35% (2/85)	Mean = 9.14 Median = 10 St. Dev. = 2.42 # 0 = 5.26% (4/76)	Mean = 50.36% Median = 67% St. Dev. = 28.91% # 0 = 20.48% (17/83)	Mean = 51.86% Median = 67% St. Dev. = 28.12% # 0 = 20.83% (15/72)

*Excluding the cases when A sent zero.

periods tend to send and return more in the **simple** condition than those who have not. For example, sending averages 7.7 and 7.2 in interactions **S** of the **S-SP** and **S-CSP** treatments, respectively, versus 7.9 and 8.1 in interactions **S** that follow interactions with communication, in **SP-S** and **CSP-S**. Likewise, the proportion returned, among those *B*'s who receive positive amounts, averages 39.4 per cent and 46.3 per cent, respectively, in simple interactions of the **S-SP** and **S-CSP** treatments, versus 49.7 per cent and 57.4 per cent in simple interactions of the **SP-S** and **CSP-S** treatments. This order effect does not contradict the conclusion, from Experiment 1, that communication increases trusting and trustworthiness. Rather, it suggests that once communication opportunities have encouraged subjects to risk trusting and have spurred the inclination to reciprocate such trust, *A*'s and *B*'s both show some tendency to persist in those behaviors. Sending is nevertheless lower without than with communication in **S** interactions that succeed **CSP** ones (**CSP-S** treatment), and the proportion returned is lower without than with communication when **S** interactions succeed **SP** or **CSP** (**SP-S** and **CSP-S** treatments).

Finally, the tendency to choose interactions leading to equal earnings of *E*$20 and *E*$20, rather than the neoclassically predicted *E*$25 and *E*$15, is also strongly manifested in Experiment 2. When agreements are reached in pre-play communication, 86.2 per cent of these are to (*E*$20,*E*$20) interactions, only 0.75 per cent on (*E*$25,*E*$15). 76.52 per cent of the (*E*$20,*E*$20) agreements are implemented by both sides, versus 25 per cent of the (*E*$25,*E*$15) ones and 72.6 per cent of agreements other than (*E*$20,*E*$20), overall. Even when there is no pre-play communication, a (*E*$20,*E*$20) outcome obtains in 31.9 per cent of interactions. Thus, a fair and efficient exchange is clearly far more common than the exchange that maximizes the earnings of the first-mover.[19]

6   Conclusions

We conducted a series of one-shot trust interactions with anonymous partners in some of which subjects sent non-binding pre-play proposals and counter-proposals, sometimes with prior exchange of chat messages. Pre-play communication was accompanied, in some treatments, by the opportunity to enter either a binding or a non-binding formal contract if agreement was reached on a course of action.

In our experiments, trusting and trustworthiness were significantly increased by opportunities to exchange proposals and counterproposals, and further increased when verbal messages could also be sent. Most agreements reached by the simple exchange of proposals were adhered to, with a still higher rate of follow-through when the subjects had also 'chatted' and/or when the agreement had the characteristic of being efficient and 'fair'. Trust 'paid off' under all conditions in our experiment, with more trusting seeming to engender more trustworthiness. The modal agreement was to the most equitable of the efficient sets of actions, and such agreements were carried out by both parties significantly more often than were other agreements.

We provided a laboratory illustration of the familiar proposition that the presence of trust can save on transactions costs: a great deal of mutually profitable trusting and trustworthiness took place in interactions even though the alternative of costly contracts was available, and those who transacted under costly contracts earned less after taking into account the contract costs. In other words, many individuals were able to commit themselves – credibly, in the eyes of their partners – to courses of action that were not *ex post* materially profitable, contrary to the assumption of the standard neoclassical model.

The large majority of instances of trusting and trustworthiness in those interactions in which contracts could be opted for took place without contracts. Out of all interactions in our experiment in which agreements and contracts were possible, agreements (concurrence on the same proposal by *A* and *B*) occurred in 87.4 per cent of cases, contracts without penalties were adopted in 9.5 per cent of cases, and contracts with penalties were adopted in 6.1 per cent of cases. Of the cases in which *A* exhibited trust by sending a positive amount to *B*, only a small minority were ones in which a contract with penalties was in force. The fact that the vast majority of sending took place without a binding contract, even though such a contract was available and led to the highest outcome considered feasible under the assumptions of standard game theory, is noteworthy.[20]

Our findings, like those of many other experiments, suggest that major revisions are required in economic theory for it to be predictive of behavior in situations where cooperation and trust might play important roles. Although the amounts of money at stake were relatively small, it must be emphasized that the vast majority of our subjects went to the trouble of reporting to the lab mainly because they were interested in earning some extra money, as their chat room statements frequently attest. Each time a trustee sent E$20 to their counterpart, rather than keep it, he or she was giving up $2.80 in potential take-home earnings, in Experiment 1, $2.00 in Experiment 2. And many subjects did this several times, giving up a considerable proportion of potential earnings of potential earnings. That so many refrained from behaving opportunistically towards anonymous partners is a strong indication of the impact of social norms on interactions of the kind that make up so much of the everyday life of organizations. And the observed powerful effects of communication suggest that the more 'real' those whom an individual interacts with become to him or her, the more likely it is that these norms will be triggered.

Corporations are not individuals, and market forces may press corporations more than most other actors to pursue profit maximization to the exclusion of other goals. But because they interact with individuals in labor, product, and

428 Trusting, Trustworthiness and CSR

other markets, earning individuals' trust and a favorable image in their eyes may be important for corporations to do even in terms of the calculus of profits. Like the individuals in our experiment, companies might elicit more trust from their customers and employees by projecting a human face and by communicating and adhering to commitments that are consonant with prevailing standards of fairness. Although the pre-play communication of our experiments may have no exact counterpart when businesses deal with workers and customers, there are many analogues, such as advertising, announcement of policies, employee relations, union–management bargaining, and the conduct of communications with shareholders and of shareholder meetings.

Pre-play communication in our experiments may enhance trusting partly because it increases the degree to which the interacting parties come to view each other as real individuals. Although a company is not an individual, the human psyche tends to treat it as if it were one, ascribing identity and moral qualities to it. By helping to project a more likeable or worthy persona, publicized socially responsible actions may help corporations to acquire customer loyalty and to elicit greater effort from employees. Even the extra few cents that a customer is willing to pay for a brand name as opposed to a generic product may in part reflect the associations she has with the known, personified producer. Conversely, a brand name associated with factory closures, employee exploitation, and negative environmental impacts may turn customers away.

Notes

1. Quoted in Friedman (1970).
2. In a series of decision-making experiments, Ernst Fehr and co-authors have found support for Akerlof's proposition in the laboratory. See, for example, Fehr, Gächter and Kirchsteiger (1997).
3. For an experimental demonstration of an inclination to reciprocate even in a zero-sum situation, see Ben-Ner, Putterman, Kong and Magan (2004).
4. 'To say "A trusts B" means that A expects B will not exploit a vulnerability A has created for himself by taking the action' (James, 2002). If A entered the relationship with the sole aim of aiding B, A's act would be one of altruism, not trust. If A 'trusts' B because A knows that B has (selfish) incentives to do what is in the interest of A, this also fails to satisfy our definition. For similar definitions, see Bohnet and Zeckhauser, 2004, Eckel and Wilson, 2004, and Ben-Ner and Putterman, 2001.
5. Bochet et al. also included comparison treatments in which group members could impose costly monetary punishment on one another, as in Fehr and Gächter (2000a). We ignore these in our discussion.
6. Bochet et al.'s subjects were seated in the same room with all potential group-mates, although they could not tell who was in their group. Frohlich and Oppenheimer's subjects, by contract, had no possibility of seeing one another. Sally (1995) finds that the ability to see one's prospective partners appears to have a positive and statistically significant effect on cooperation.

7 The other three conditions involved providing the subjects with information about characteristics of their counterparts, such as gender, or about their counterparts' past choices, or both. These interactions always came later and thus had no bearing on the ones we discuss here. In addition, the fact that information about past behavior would later be revealed was not pre-announced and therefore the subjects knew of no potential benefit from a 'good reputation'.

8. The experiment instructions are available from the authors.

9. In the last conditions of Experiment 1, not discussed here, some information about subjects' decisions in earlier conditions was revealed to their counterparts. In order not to overtly mislead our subjects, we said nothing about whether information from past encounters would be conveyed to future interaction partners, in the Design I sessions. Because subjects were told that each future partner would be a new individual, because nothing was said about the matter, and because no such information was in fact conveyed until the sixth interaction – near the end of the session – we think it safe to assume that most subjects did not expect such information to be conveyed.

10. Even when up to three proposals each are possible, B has the last opportunity to accept or reject a proposal, so if A continues to propose the send 10, return 25 interaction, B will have no better choice than to accept.

11. References to the literature on reciprocity include Hoffman, McCabe and Smith (1998), Fehr and Gächter (2000b), Ben-Ner and Putterman (2000) and Gintis, Bowles, Boyd and Fehr (eds) (2005), among many other contributions.

12. Binding contracts ended up being observed in all cases. In the case of contracts without penalties, the rate of adherence to their terms was no greater than for agreements without contracts. There are indications that this is due to the presence of some adverse selection: less trusting A's who actually wanted a binding contract, and a few opportunistic B's who didn't want a binding contract but believed a contract without penalties might reassure and thus entrap their partner, may have been disproportionately present among those interacting with such contracts. We discuss this and other issues further in Ben-Ner and Putterman (2009).

13. Tobit results are similar but the tobit version of column 1 has low χ^2 due to non-normality of errors and the high proportion of A's who sent the maximum of 10 – over 75 per cent in rounds 2 and 3 and over 92 per cent in round 4.

14. The effect of chat is understated because chat also increased the likelihood of agreement.

15. Because the four conditions occur in one order only in Experiment 1, disentangling treatment effects and order effects is difficult. However, the Experiment 2 sessions in which five simple interactions preceded five interactions with exchange of proposals or chat and exchange of proposals allow us to check whether increases in trust and trustworthiness could reflect experience alone. While sending did in fact increase over time in the first four simple interactions of the S-SP and S-CSP treatments, the rate of increase is substantially smaller, differing significantly at the 0.1% level in a one-tailed Mann–Whitney test.

16. Multiple proposals may have undermined good faith because they encouraged haggling.

17. Contract choice is not included in Table 3 due to its endogeneity. To check that the effect of agreement in this table is not due to inclusion of interactions under contract, all regressions were also run excluding cases that led to contracts, with qualitatively the same results.

18. The difference is significant at the 0.1 per cent level in a two-tailed Mann–Whitney test.

19. For further discussion of this experiment, see Ben-Ner, Putterman and Ren, forthcoming.
20. Note, however, that the low incidence of contracts may give an exaggerated sense of subjects' disinterest in having contracts. In particular, many *A*'s requested but failed to get a contract because their counterpart didn't request one.

References

Akerlof, G. (1970) 'The Market for Lemons: Quality Uncertainty and the Market Mechanism', *Quarterly Journal of Economics*, vol. 84(3), pp. 488–500.

Akerlof, G. (1982) 'Labor Contracts as Partial Gift Exchange', *Quarterly Journal of Economics*, vol. 97(4), pp. 543–69.

Ben-Ner, A. and L. Putterman (2000) 'On Some Implications of Evolutionary Psychology for the Study of Preferences and Institutions', *Journal of Economic Behavior and Organization*, vol. 43(1), pp. 91–9.

Ben-Ner, A. and L. Putterman (2001) 'Trusting and Trustworthiness', *Boston University Law Review*, vol. 81(3), pp. 523–51.

Ben-Ner, A. and L. Putterman (2009) 'Trust, Communication and Contracts: An Experiment', *Journal of Economic Behavior and Organization*, vol. 70: 106–21.

Ben-Ner, A. and L. Putterman, F. Kong and D. Magan (2004) 'Reciprocity in a Two Part Dictator Game', *Journal of Economic Behavior and Organization*, vol. 53(3), pp. 333–52.

Ben-Ner, A., L. Putterman and T. Ren, forthcoming, "Lavish Returns on Cheap Talk: Two-Way Communication in Trust Games," *Journal of Socio-Economics* (in press).

Berg, J., J. Dickhaut, and K. McCabe (1995) 'Trust, Reciprocity and Social History', *Games and Economic Behavior*, vol. 10(1), pp. 122–42.

Bochet, O., T. Page and L. Putterman (2006) 'Communication and Punishment in Voluntary Contribution Experiments', *Journal of Economic Behavior and Organization*, vol. 60(1), pp. 11–26.

Bochet, O. and L. Putterman (2009) 'Not Just Babble: Opening the Black Box of Communication in a Voluntary Contribution Experiment', *European Economic Review* 53: 309–26.

Bohnet, I. and R. Zeckhauser (2004) 'Trust, Risk and Betrayal', *Journal of Economic Behavior and Organization*, vol. 55(4), pp. 467–84.

Brosig, J., A. Ockenfels, and J. Weimann (2003) 'The Effect of Communication Media on Cooperation', *German Economic Review*, vol. 4(2), pp. 217–42.

Buchan, N., R. Croson, and E. Johnson (2006) 'Let's Get Personal: An International Examination of the Influence of Communication, Culture and Social Distance on Other Regarding Preferences', *Journal of Economic Behavior and Organization*, vol. 60(3), pp. 373–98.

Charness, G. and M. Dufwenberg (2006) 'Promises and Partnerships', *Econometrica*, vol. 74(6), pp. 1579–601.

Eckel, C. and R. Wilson (2004) 'Is Trust a Risky Decision?', *Journal of Economic Behavior and Organization*, vol. 55(4), pp. 447–65.

Edgeworth, Francis Y. (1881) *Mathematical psychics; an essay on the application of mathematics to the moral sciences*. London: C. K. Paul.

Fehr, E. and S. Gächter (2000a) 'Cooperation and Punishment in Public Goods Experiments', *American Economic Review*, vol. 90(4), pp. 980–94.

Fehr, E. and S. Gächter (2000b) 'Fairness and Retaliation: The Economics of Reciprocity', *Journal of Economic Perspectives*, vol. 14(3), pp. 159–81.

Fehr, E., S. Gächter and G. Kirchsteiger (1997) 'Reciprocity as a Contract Enforcement Device: Experimental Evidence', *Econometrica*, vol. 65(4), pp. 833–60.

Fehr, E. and B. Rockenbach (2003) 'Detrimental Effects of Sanctions on Human Altruism', *Nature*, vol. 422(13), pp. 137–40.

Friedman, M. (1970) 'The Social Responsibility of Business is to Increase its Profits', *The New York Times Magazine*, 13 September.

Friedman, M. (1982) *Capitalism and Freedom*. Chicago: University of Chicago Press.

Frohlich, N. and J. Oppenheimer (1998) 'Some Consequences of E-mail vs. Face-to-Face Communication in Experiment', *Journal of Economic Behavior and Organization*, vol. 35(3), pp. 389–403.

Gintis, H., S. Bowles, R. Boyd and E. Fehr (eds) (2005) *Moral Sentiments and Material Interests: The Foundations of Cooperation in Economic Life*. Cambridge, MA: MIT Press.

Hoffman, E., K. McCabe and V. Smith (1998) 'Behavioral Foundations of Reciprocity: Experimental Economics and Evolutionary Psychology', *Economic Inquiry*, vol. 36(3), pp. 335–52.

Houser, D., E. Xiao, K. McCabe and V. Smith (2008) 'When Punishment Fails: Research on Sanctions, Intentions and Non-Cooperation', *Games and Economic Behavior*, vol. 62(2), 509–32.

Isaac, R. Mark and James M. Walker (1988) 'Communication and Free-Riding Behavior: The Voluntary Contributions Mechanism', *Economic Inquiry*, vol. 26(4), pp. 585–608.

James, Harvey S. (2002) 'The Trust Paradox: a Survey of Economic Inquiries into the Nature of Trust and Trustworthiness', *Journal of Economic Behavior and Organization*, vol. 47(3), pp. 291–307.

Malhotra, D. and J. K. Murnighan (2002) 'The Effects of Contracts on Interpersonal Trust', *Administrative Science Quarterly*, vol. 47(3), pp. 534–59.

Ostrom, E., J. Walker and R. Gardner (1992) 'Covenants With and Without a Sword: Self Governance is Possible', *American Political Science Review*, vol. 86(2), pp. 404–16.

Rigdon, M. (2005) 'Trust and Reciprocity in Incentive Contracting', University of Michigan. Online at http://mpra.ub.uni-muenchen.de/2007/ – MPRA Paper No. 2007, November 2007.

Sally, D. (1995) 'Conversation and Cooperation in Social Dilemmas: A Meta-Analysis of Experiments from 1958 to 1992', *Rationality and Society*, vol. 7(1), pp. 58–92.

Wilson, R. and J. Sell (1997) '"Liar, Liar...": Cheap Talk and Reputation in Repeated Public Goods Settings', *Journal of Conflict Resolution*, vol. 41(5), pp. 695–717.

Index

motivation   76, 77, 221–2, 237, 282–3,
  357, 386
  intrinsic   347–8, 357, 373
motivational role   180
multi-stakeholder model   155–91
multiple proposal interactions   421, 426,
  431
multiplicity (multiple equilibrium)   184
mutual gains   5, 81–2, 130

Nardelli, Robert   29
Nash bargaining solutions   xix, 203, 206,
  216
Nash equilibrium   xix, xxxi, 81, 157,
  170, 264
  subgame perfect   256, 259, 356, 362,
    364
  symmetric perfect   361
natural selection   11
neoclassical economics   76
new institutional economics   155, 160,
  164, 194, 244, 341, 349
nexus of contracts   165, 291, 341
Nguyen-Dang, Bang   24
non-conformity   169
non-cooperative games   212, 358
non-cooperative solutions   379
non-governmental organizations   300,
  306–7
non-human assets   36, 37
non-profit corporations   387
non-profit organizations   387
norm   172, 298
  cognitive function   183
  contractarian   174
  ethical   76, 90, 159, 162
normative individualism   130
normative model   xxix, 172–3, 194–208
normative requirements of practical
  rationality   281
normative role   180
numerical communication   418, 421
nursing homes   383–410

obligations   159, 167, 173, 186
  contractual   104, 106, 139, 140, 287,
    290
  corporate   273, 292
  fiduciary   84, 87, 180, 285, 288
  legal   34, 89, 101, 337
  moral   222
one-period trust game   363–5

open question argument   53
opportunism   6, 54–5, 60, 162
organization theory   xxii
organizational architecture (OA)   34–5,
  40, 44
organizational conditions   22–3
organizational effectiveness   395, 404–5,
  406–7
Osterloh, M.   xxxiv–xxxv, **332–52**
outsourcing   303, 315
owner shielding   290
ownership   106, 111, 242, 365–7
  and control   242–3
ownership team   21

Pace, N.   xxxv, **353–80**
Pagano, Marco   28
paradigms   100
Paramount v. *Time*   292
Pareto dominance   228, 233, 259
Pareto efficiency   xxv, 194
Pareto optimality   205, 236
Parmar, Bidhan   xxiii–xxv, **52–72**, 73–4,
  90
partnership   271–2
partnership law   108
pay for performance   373–5
payoffs   360–1
  one-period trust game   364–5
  two-period trust game   365–6
payoff space   195, 199–200, 205, 214,
  229
payoff-maximizing   415
pernicious benevolence   xi
personnel management   373
physical assets   33, 87, 163, 165, 177,
  217
political state   44
power   14, 22–3, 28, 57, 60, 104–6, 124,
  208, 255, 345, 385–6
  bargaining   79–80, 193
practical rationality   274–8
  normative requirements   281
pre-play communication   415, 416, 424,
  426, 428, 430
prescription   26, 172
principal–agent model   xxvi, 34, 99–101,
  102–9, 357
private sector   8, 85, 299, 300, 312, 313,
  319, 320
professionalization   301–2
profit maximization   104, 273, 413